Basic Types of Pastoral Care & Counseling

Resources for the Ministry of Healing and Growth

Howard Clinebell
Updated and Revised by
Bridget Clare McKeever, SSL

Abingdon Press

Nashville

Library of Congress Cataloging-in-Publication Data

Clinebell, Howard John, 1922-
  Basic types of pastoral care & counseling : resources for the ministry of healing and growth / Howard Clinebell. — Updated and rev. / Bridget Clare McKeever.
     p. cm.
  Includes bibliographical references and index.
  ISBN 978-0-687-66380-4 (trade pbk. : alk. paper)
  1. Pastoral counseling. 2. Pastoral care. I. McKeever, Bridget Clare. II. Title. III. Title: Basic types of pastoral care and counseling.
  BV4012.2.C528 2011
  253.5—dc23

2011020286

Originally published as *Basic Types of Pastoral Counseling: New Resources for the Troubled*. ISBN 0-687-02491-9, cloth, and ISBN 0-687-02490-0, paper.

CONTENTS

PREFACE

Howard would be extraordinarily pleased to know that *Basic Types* continues to be an important text for pastoral counseling students nearly fifty years after it was first written. The present revision and updating, which Howard was drafting when he became ill and which Bridget Clare McKeever has so successfully completed, make it even more relevant—relevant to the discipline as well as to the life of our explosively changing world. She has managed to capture the spirit of his vision and to distill the flow of his ideas and words into a manuscript that speaks to current needs and issues and to those who focus on them.

Bridget Clare has done a remarkable job of revising and updating Howard's work. Thanks also to Christie Neuger for her contributions to the project. Profound gratitude goes to Abingdon editor Kathryn Armistead for her guidance and dedication in making this edition of *Basic Types* possible. Without her, it would not now be a reality.

In the first publication of *Basic Types* in 1966, Howard observed that the field of pastoral counseling was "at a crossroads" and needed to "turn a corner." For that need he developed a "revised model" of pastoral counseling for use as a resource in what he described as the "contemporary renaissance" in pastoral care and counseling at that time. In the first revision in 1984 he listed, among other characteristics, "a more holistic and explicitly liberation-growth paradigm." In addition to the ongoing development of pastoral counseling, the current revision emphasizes the continuous expansion of the pastoral counselor's horizons in a plethora of personal issues and social needs everywhere on our shrinking globe.

There's a story early in the current revision, of a time early in Howard's parish ministry. He remembers standing in the pulpit looking out over the congregation and seeing the varied and overwhelming pain in so many people's lives. Such early and ongoing awareness meant that he realized that he needed knowledge and training. Thus he explored and mastered the secular schools of psychology and the therapeutic disciplines and worked with the pioneers in pastoral counseling. He became more and more certain that pastoral counseling needed a major change in order to remain relevant and to become the powerful influence it has become. *Basic Types* has been influential in implementing that change.

Had Howard been alive to complete the current revision that he began some years ago, I believe that he would now put significantly more emphasis on the pastoral counselor taking care of herself or himself and of her or his significant relationships. There is indeed in this revision more emphasis on the counselor's needs. He would now say even more about the importance to both counselor and counselee of cultivating one's important relationships.

Howard's family—John, Donald, Susan, and Charlotte (his spouse of sixty years)—hopes that you will think of him as you read and that you will also think about the remarkable growth of the pastoral counseling discipline to which he devoted his career.

Charlotte Ellen, PhD
March 2011

CHAPTER 1

PASTORAL CARE AND COUNSELING: CHALLENGES AND OPPORTUNITIES

On a dangerous seacoast where shipwrecks often occur there was once a little lifesaving station. The building was just a hut and there was only one boat, but the few devoted members kept a constant watch over the sea, and with no thought of themselves went out day and night tirelessly searching for the lost. Many lives were saved by this wonderful little station, so that it became famous. Some of those who were saved, and various others in the surrounding area, wanted to become associated with the station and gave their time and money and effort for the support of its work. New boats were bought and new crews trained. The little lifesaving station grew.

Some of the members of the lifesaving station were unhappy that the building was so crude and poorly equipped. They felt that a more comfortable place should be provided as the first refuge of those saved from the sea. So they replaced the emergency cots with beds and put better furniture in the enlarged building. Now the lifesaving station became a popular gathering place for its members, and they decorated it beautifully and furnished it exquisitely, because they used it as a sort of club. Fewer members were now interested in going to sea on lifesaving missions, so they hired lifeboat crews to do this work. The lifesaving motif still prevailed in the club's decoration, and there was a liturgical lifeboat in the room where the club initiations were held. About this time a large ship was wrecked off the coast, and the hired crew brought in the boatloads of cold, wet, and half-drowned people. They were dirty and sick and some of them had black skins and some had yellow skins. The beautiful new club was in chaos. So the property committee immediately had a shower house built outside the club where the victims of shipwreck could be cleaned up before coming inside.

At the next meeting, there was a split in the club membership. Most of the members wanted to stop the club's lifesaving activities as being unpleasant and a hindrance to the normal social life of the club. Some members insisted upon lifesaving as their primary purpose and pointed out that they were still called a lifesaving station. But they were finally voted down and told that if they wanted to save the lives of all the various kinds of people who were shipwrecked in those waters, they could begin their own lifesaving station down the coast. They did. As the years went by, the new station experienced the same changes that had occurred in the old. It evolved into a club, and yet another lifesaving station was founded. History continued to repeat itself, and if you visit that seacoast today, you will find a number of exclusive clubs along the shore. Shipwrecks are frequent in those waters, but most of the people drown.[1]

This powerful parable by Theodore Wedel depicts vividly a danger confronting many congregations today—loss of commitment to their lifesaving and healing mission in the stormy seas of a turbulent world. When this loss occurs, churches become increasingly irrelevant to the brokenness of individuals, families, and communities. Relevance means presence to where persons hurt and hope, curse and pray, hunger for meaning, and thirst for significant relationships. It also means helping to heal the wounds of injustice in society and the wounding of the earth's biosphere upon which all life ultimately depends.

Holistic caregiving is an important way by which religious leaders can transform this irrelevance into direct engagement in healing the many forms of brokenness that are pandemic today. In fact, pastoral care and counseling are among the most effective instruments by which churches stay relevant to changing human needs in our rapidly changing society and churches. Caregiving can help save those areas of people's lives that are shipwrecked in the storms of daily living, broken on the hidden reefs of evil and tragedy, injustice and despair. The caregiving arts enable a congregation to translate the good news of the gospel into a down-to-earth language that brings healing and wholeness to people in everyday life crises and opportunities. With this language clergy and laypersons in ministry can communicate the good news to countless wounded persons who cannot hear it if it is spoken only in "religious" language. Thus pastoral care and counseling are valuable tools with which a church can function as a lifesaving station and not a social club, a healing place rather than a museum where old beliefs and practices are enshrined. An effective caring and counseling program in which clergy and trained laypeople minister in partnership can transform the interpersonal climate of a faith community. It can make congregations life-transforming places where wholeness is nurtured in persons throughout their life journeys. And significantly such giving and receiving care helps inspire and equip members to express their own God-given vocations in healing outreach beyond their congregations.

Enlarging the Horizons of Healing and Circles of Caring

Today's world challenges pastoral caregivers to continue enlarging their horizons of healing and circles of caring to make their ministries more inclusive. To guide this crucial process, new images must be added to that of the rescue station. What follows is one way to imagine the life-station parable as increasingly relevant to today's church and world.

The membership discussed various options and affirmed a broader plan. Fierce storms continued to result in shipwrecks. The vital lifesaving work could continue with better rescue boats and training. However, the station also needed to collaborate with other groups and public officials to get buoys installed to mark more clearly the hidden rocks that caused shipwrecks. Preventive measures began. A brighter light and a more penetrating foghorn were installed in the lighthouse that marked the entrance to the safe harbor nearby. To further reduce shipwrecks, the station planned to offer training in sailing and marine safety to all interested persons in the area.

As the members implemented their preventive plans, they were energized and challenged as the vision of their mission enlarged. They welcomed with open arms the rescued people as full partners in the station's exciting work. Survivors were encouraged to receive the swimming instructions that the station offered if they lacked this essential survival skill. They were also encouraged to enhance their knowledge of how to sail safely. In these ways survivors began to feel empowered as their nearly tragic experiences became an opportunity to grow new skills and understandings. These practices proved valuable in both the rescuing and the preventive programs.

As these preventive measures were being taken, developments moved in unexpected directions. Members elected a task group charged with continuing evaluation and re-visioning of all programs so as to respond quickly to emerging needs. This group looked beyond the still-needed rescuing and preventive programs to raise questions about the overall well-being of their members and also the surrounding community. As they did, they were struck by several pressing needs. Two of these were related to food. What could be done about the health problems caused by the unhealthy nutritional patterns of many members? And very important, what could be done to assist the poor, hungry people in their station and community? Another task group brainstormed these issues. They started a community garden in which people learned how to grow healthy organic food. Some of this produce provided temporary food for poor families who were invited to join in the gardening to learn how to grow healthy food. Many of those who gardened enjoyed the emotional satisfaction of working together as a team on this worthwhile project. Some also found that reflecting on what they called "the miracle of gardening" increased their general concern about developing more earth-respecting, earth-caring lifestyles for themselves and for their community.

Several gardeners said that they were enjoying two added health benefits: exercising outdoors vigorously and eating fresh, healthier fruits and vegetables. Eventually the gardening project sparked an eating-for-health educational program open to the whole community. Over several years this nutritional emphasis gradually broadened so that the station developed a wellness training and resource program. Both members and people attracted from the surrounding community learned new methods of caring for themselves and others. All the programs emphasized enabling people to cultivate the spiritual roots as well as the spiritual fruits of their lives. Thus what had begun as a one-purpose rescue station gradually reinvented itself to become a multipurpose healing, growth, and wellness training center. There people could nurture their own wellness and reach out to touch the wider community with healing hands.

As this story illustrates, pastoral caregivers need to add two mission-widening images that complement the crucial rescuing and healing images. The gardening image suggests cultivating spiritually centered wholeness throughout people's lives. This image helps our society recover an ancient, life-nurturing awareness that bonding with nature connects us intimately with the healing energies of God's wonder-filled creation. This awareness is particularly necessary in the current global ecological-justice crisis.

Pastoral psychotherapist Margaret Zipse Kornfeld elaborates on a gardening image with the sensitivities of an experienced growth-enabler. She urges the caregiver to "Be a Gardener!" and then declares:

> Counselors in [the religious] community assist God's children as they grow in the natural cycle of life. A gardener must observe Nature to find how plants grow and develop. The counselor, too, must learn how God's children grow to become themselves—to thrive, blossom, die, and be transformed. This knowledge helps the counselor know how *to support the natural process* in our many beginnings. Counselors in community do not make these new beginnings—birth, maturation, independence, falling in love, new families, vision quests, meaning making—happen. Like the gardener, they are present at these times of beginnings and are in awe.[2]

Beyond the images of rescuing and gardening, it is crucial to add the image of caregivers as coaches who equip care receivers to nurture spiritually empowered wellness in others. As faith communities function as wellness training centers, people are inspired and equipped to be instruments, however imperfect, of God's healing, redemptive love in the lives of people, society, and nature. In short, all the working theories and methods in this volume are tools for clergy and lay caregivers to enable faith communities to engage in the wholeness missions of rescuing and healing stations, gardens cultivating lifelong growth, and training-for-wholeness centers.

Enlarging the horizons of healing involves mending the torn fabric of human lives and relationships as well as the wider systems that affect troubled people's lives. Caregivers are called to facilitate healing of brokenness, not only with those who are like themselves, but also with marginalized persons and groups who unfortunately are usually seen as "other" or "alien." The mission is to be innovative and proactive in helping mend the shattered sense of community in the neighborhoods and society around them. They are called to work with other people of goodwill in all faith traditions in God's world. But first they must find healing for the brokenness in themselves and then reach out as healing catalysts in their own families, congregations, and wider community. This is the path to continuing rebirth in caregiving congregations that serve as redemptive social organisms. By becoming healing environments, faith communities can enable people to experience mutual nurture in all its dimensions in their lives. In this way they respond to God's call to be abundant life training centers that inspire and equip people for their caring ministries of outreach to the pain and brokenness all around them.

Truly holistic caregivers must resist the temptation to succumb to the privatized healing and health seeking that are so widespread in our individualistic culture. As a corrective to the spiritual myopia of this view, remember that Jesus went far beyond his healing ministry with sick and troubled individuals. He also inspired and taught people how to grow in complete wholeness. By his teachings and prophetic actions, he challenged the unjust religious, social, and economic structures at the roots of human brokenness and oppression. From his courageous example, it is clear that love, power, and justice are essential ingredients in healing, growth, and salvation.

Walking in the footsteps of the great prophets of his spiritual heritage, Jesus challenged the religious establishment with disturbing good news that laid the foundation for a justice-and-love-based approach to caregiving ministry. But it is wise not to forget that Jesus' prophetic ministry was also costly. Widening the circles of healing and wholeness to challenge and help heal injustices often arouses vigorous opposition. In these times of shaking transitions, powerful forces resist creative change vigorously, often violently. Bringing together loving caregiving with the honest, caring confrontation of injustice is threatening, even to marriages. It is difficult to relate to individuals, groups, and institutions with tough-minded, caring love rooted in justice. But only caring relationships that challenge inequities can enable caregivers to respond to both the great peril and the great promise of our world.

How Important Are Caregiving Skills?

Let me share a vivid experience that etched in my mind an awareness of the importance of pastoral caregiving. I was struck one Sunday morning, during the years when I was a parish pastor, by the individual and collective pain of the people I saw as I looked over the congregation. I saw a man who had admitted his wife to a state mental hospital the week before, a young wife deeply depressed by the sudden death of her husband, and a couple who recently had learned that their child had leukemia. Also present were an alcoholic who I knew was struggling with his addiction, a high school youth who recently had discovered that his girlfriend was pregnant, and the wife of a couple I knew was agonizing over marital alienation. I was aware of a man facing surgery for a condition he feared was malignant and an older man confronting retirement with mounting anxiety and feelings of emptiness. I'm also sure that others were carrying hidden loads of which I was not aware. Whenever you look at any group of people, remember that many of them have heavy hearts and that they are walking through shadowed valleys, even if their outward appearance doesn't reveal their pain.

Such burdened people often trust the entire fabric of their lives to the caregiving skills of religious leaders. Frequently these are the first persons outside of family that these burdened people allow to enter their private hells. Driven by desperate needs and hope for help, they open their hearts to pastors, whether or not they merit that trust. With wisdom derived from long, creative pioneering in the pastoral care field, my friend the late

Wayne Oates pointed out that pastors, whatever their training, do not enjoy the privilege of deciding whether to counsel with people. Their "choice is not between counseling and not counseling, but between counseling in a disciplined and skilled way and counseling in an undisciplined and unskilled way."[3] Countless wounded persons, including many not active in any congregation, seek help from clergy because they see them as competent professionals whom they trust to walk beside them through long-shadowed valleys. If these religious caregivers lack basic skills, such hurting persons often receive a stone when they are starving for bread.

Persons suffering from socially stigmatized problems often avoid seeking pastoral help because they fear rejection. Many persons who do come to clergy are the lonely, extremely dependent, and alienated in our society. They are persons without homes, spiritually and psychologically if not literally, whose need for care-in-community is acute. No less painful, though often hidden and therefore ignored, are those once described by pastoral care pioneer Paul Johnson as "lost within themselves in our own congregations." Thus a congregation's ministry of care and counseling includes an *inreaching* and an *outreaching* mission, wherever people are wounded. Because of the pandemic of personal crises and violent social disorganization in our society, the need for caregiving has never been greater. The deepening chasms in public services that unfortunately exist in our society mean that human services by religious institutions, including counseling, constitute at least a partial safety net for countless troubled people. Given all this, in the years ahead pastoral caregivers can expect even more requests from persons in their congregations and communities.

There is no doubt that clergy caregivers are on the front lines in helping people struggle through all kinds of crises, losses, and other high-stress situations. A series of national surveys, during the second half of the twentieth century, discovered empirical evidence that a high percentage of Americans who seek counseling choose to see clergy. In an early study 10 percent of Americans reported that they had talked to clergy about personal problems at one time or another. Various subsequent surveys revealed that from 39 to 57 percent of help seekers turned first to clergy. One Gallup survey showed that clergy were judged, by around 65 percent of respondents, to be more trustworthy than mental health professionals. Surveys also confirmed that recipients of clergy caregiving reported generally high levels of helpfulness (an exception being domestic violence crises). In short, a higher percentage of Americans seek help from clergy than from any other counseling professionals.[4] An expanded national survey in 2000 revealed that 75 percent of respondents said that it is important to see a professional counselor who integrates their values and beliefs into the counseling process. Eighty-five percent feel that their spiritual faith and religious beliefs are closely linked to their mental and emotional health. More people said they prefer pastoral counselors and others with religious training than any other category of counseling professionals.[5]

Our society has enormous unmet needs for healing and wholeness. In responding to these needs it is clear that religion, religious leaders, and religious organizations are now playing significant roles and will do even more in the future. Beyond what is now occurring, there is no doubt that a tremendous amount of additional healing and wholeness can occur as religious leaders and organizations become more involved and effective in responding to unmet needs for care.[6] In this response, a wealth of teachable lay caregivers can play a major role as they join hands with clergy in meeting more of the pressing needs of many persons.

Renewal through Caregiving

A holistic approach can be a catalyst for individual and congregational healing. These caring arts can also contribute to the continuing revitalization of a congregation's spiritual aliveness by providing multileveled spiritual healing and renewal in individuals, families, and groups, among its members and in its wider community. By strengthening the ability of people to give and receive love in community, caregivers can help church people *be* the church, a community where God's love and justice are experienced realities bringing healing, enlivening, and growth.

Healing and renewal occur when bridges are built that span people's multiple chasms of estrangement. These alienations are from themselves, friends, and families; from "outsiders" who are "different"; from the enlivening energy of God's natural world; and basic to all of other alienations, from a growing relationship with God. Renewal occurs when people learn how to love unconditionally. This process begins when they learn to love themselves—body, mind, spirit, and relationships.

Pastoral caregiving can cultivate healing and growth by enabling people to develop what is increasingly difficult in our depersonalizing times—depth relationships of mutual love and integrity. Many people, including religious leaders, can identify with the loneliness of the pastor who said to his psychotherapist, "My life is characterized by a plethora of contacts and a poverty of deep relationships!" This is a widespread blight that diminishes spiritually centered well-being in our high-tech, touch-and-run society, that breeds interpersonal superficiality, manipulation, and terrible loneliness.

A closely related blight feeds the one just described. It is our human self-absorption and narcissism that cause us to sit as bystanders when others suffer from agonizing personal problems, including those stemming from the systemic evils that our society breeds. Culturally reinforced self-absorption impoverishes us by breeding a lack of awareness of how profoundly we are interrelated with one another. This blindness to relationality lets us avoid the truth that evil done to anyone—through violence, marginalization, or neglect—is evil done to all of us. All this prevents people of goodwill from living out the divine intention to become channels through whose lives God's justice-based, healing love can flow. Furthermore, it prevents the church from being the lifesaving station that rescues struggling persons from society's countless forms of brokenness, and a spiritually empowering garden where people's gifts can be cultivated in a community of mutual caring and growth.

Understanding Basic Terms

Holistic pastoral care involves the use of religious resources for the purpose of empowering people, families, and congregations to heal their brokenness and to grow toward wholeness in their lives. Healing is a journey that transcends curing, to include the transformation of circumstances by awakening the spiritual perspectives of people in crises. The ongoing journey of spiritually centered wholeness involves cultivating people's abilities to balance and enhance the health of all dimensions of their lives and integrate this process around healthy spiritual and ethical living. To be truly holistic, pastoral care and counseling also employ caregiving tools to equip people with the understanding and skills they need to be instruments of healing and wholeness in the lives of other burdened people. A part of this outreach is being agents of constructive change and wholeness in their community, society, and natural environment.

Pastoral caregiving is used in this book as an overall term to include the three main ways by which those in ministry provide help for persons in periods of physical, mental, spiritual, and relational crises, losses, dilemmas, and stresses. These three equally significant channels of ministry are *pastoral care*, *pastoral counseling*, and *pastoral psychotherapy*. Competency in each requires differing but overlapping training. Which form of caregiving should be made available depends on the unique needs, resources, and desires of each individual or family. The word *pastoral* refers to both ordained clergy and laity who understand caregiving to be their ministry. In light of the nurturing-for-wholeness function of caregiving, it is noteworthy that the term is derived from the Latin *pascere*, meaning simply "to feed."

Pastoral care is the broad ministry that includes the many ways that spiritually energized care is given to people in faith communities for the basic purpose of enabling them to live life with the maximum possible wholeness in all their dark valleys, sunlit peaks, and everyday plateaus. This means living constructively with personal meanings and larger purposes beyond themselves that motivate them to reach out to respond to the needs of others. Holistic pastoral caregiving starts with the care of individuals, their families, and other close relationships. It also involves enabling people to create caregiving community in their congregations. But to become fully holistic, pastoral care involves practicing and promoting peace and justice as the only firm foundation for wellness in relationships and communities. To reach out even more holistically, pastoral caregiving also involves caring about and for God's wounded natural world. Because social and natural environments have an impact on the sickness and health of everyone continually, care for these is essential to caring for ourselves and others most fully. Living in this spiritual caring way means embracing the good, resisting evil, following one's unique vocation and finding God's imminent and transcendent spirit of love and justice in the good, the bad, and the ordinary times of life. Pastoral care responds in an ongoing way to the deep and continuing need in all of us for loving support and nurture of our well-being. This need is heightened during times of personal crises and losses, including social chaos and natural disasters. Pastoral care involves helping people learn continuing self-care that will enable them to cultivate wellness in all dimensions of their lives while also reaching out in healing ways to respond to others. The broad ministry of mutual caregiving occurs within faith communities and, through them, reaches out to persons in the wider community and society. In contrast to pastoral counseling, pastoral care often takes place informally and spontaneously within congregations guided by this holistic vision.

Pastoral care is a shared ministry of clergy and laypersons, including those who receive training for this special ministry, and the countless people who engage spontaneously in caregiving within the many relationships and groups that constitute the living fabric of a faith community. This ongoing shared ministry can and should happen anywhere—for example, on the steps of the church, in an educational setting, from the pulpit, in the pastor's office, in a hospital room, in a home visit, or even in a chance encounter on a street or in an airplane.

Pastoral care is the appropriate function of parish clergy, institutional chaplains, and well-trained laity who understand it as their ministry. Minimal competence in pastoral care requires basic self-understanding and self-care as well as basic knowledge from theological disciplines and the human (psychosocial) sciences. It also requires extensive hands-on coaching in the art and science of effective, growth-oriented listening to and caring for hurting people. Academic courses and in-depth reading, however valuable, usually are not adequate preparation unless these are undergirded by opportunities to practice those skills with competent supervision. This supervision may occur in a classroom, in ongoing consultation groups, or through a unit of clinical pastoral education (CPE).

Pastoral counseling, as understood in these pages, is a focused form of pastoral care geared toward enabling individuals, couples, and families to cope more constructively with crises, losses, difficult decisions, and other anxiety-laden experiences. In congregational and chaplaincy settings it is usually relatively brief, consisting of only one or two—and generally less than six—sessions. Pastoral counseling, in contrast to pastoral care, involves the explicit desire of recipients to receive help from the counselor. It also involves a mutual understanding of the goals, probable length of the helping process, and responsibilities of both the helper and the person(s) seeking help. It often involves enabling burdened people to learn how to wrestle constructively with crisis-induced psychological, physical, spiritual, and/or relational problems. It aims at enabling troubled people to make constructive choices and changes as well as to learn new skills that will improve the quality of their lifestyles, strengthen their relationships, and help them handle stressful situations more effectively. It is usually time-limited and relatively brief, often with an initial agreement negotiated between the counselor and the counselee to work together for a certain time to address particular life problems. This agreement can be renegotiated and extended or shortened.

Pastoral counseling should be a function of parish clergy, chaplains, and religiously oriented lay counselors, who are well trained in its theory and methods. This training should go well beyond academic counseling courses in seminary or postseminary degrees to include extensive coaching, by competent supervisors, of the actual practice of individual, couple, and group counseling. This learning process should develop understanding of how one's personality affects all caregiving relationships and some awareness of transference and countertransference dynamics. It should also entail learning how to integrate healthy theological resources and values in the helping process.

Skilled counselors use a variety of short-term therapeutic methods to help people learn how to handle their problems more constructively. They seek to enable people to help themselves by learning how to mobilize their strengths and make changes that will improve the quality of their personal lives and relationships. Unlike the umbrella of ongoing pastoral care, pastoral counseling should be a time-limited and relatively brief process that focuses on solving concrete problems. In contrast, pastoral care, as John Patton points out, is "care of the whole person in relationship, not the treatment of a specific dysfunction."[7]

Pastoral counseling begins when a counselor and a counselee agree to work together to develop more effective ways to cope with particular life choices, dilemmas, and problems. People benefit from pastoral care at times of crises and stress-overload throughout their lives. They need pastoral counseling when a severe problem strikes and previously learned coping skills do not suffice or when their behavior becomes self-defeating. Pastoral counseling often begins as a repair or guidance function and unfortunately often ends prematurely when the crises seem resolved. Ideally it should continue long enough to enable people to use their problems and crises as opportunities for psychological, spiritual, and coping growth.

Pastoral psychotherapy (also called "pastoral therapy") is usually a more extended form of pastoral counseling that involves exploring complex emotional and relationship issues. Those whose brokenness is pronounced and whose growth is deeply or chronically blocked often benefit from reconstructive therapeutic methods. The brokenness can result from severe need deprivation in early life relationships or from devastating and often multiple crises in adult life. The therapeutic goal is to facilitate reconstructive healing and growth that make the very foundations of people's lives stronger, more satisfying, and more productive. The process is usually longer than pastoral counseling because persons seeking help deal with their deeper conflicts and problems, including those that may have been out of their awareness.

Because of its complex and time-extended nature, pastoral psychotherapy should be done by specialists who have had rigorous academic and clinically supervised training far beyond their seminary education in pastoral psychology and counseling. Given the intricacies of human personalities and relationships, this advanced training is essential. Even if clergy in parish and other generalist ministries, such as chaplains, have the necessary training, most do not have the time in their busy professional lives to do longer-term psychotherapy. Furthermore, psychotherapy often awakens powerful, archaic feelings that are transferred onto the therapist. Special therapeutic skills are required to resolve these constructively. The multiple roles of clergy generalists make it very problematic for them to attempt to do pastoral psychotherapy. The qualifications and basic theories of pastoral psychotherapy will be summarized briefly in chapter 16 to provide generalists in ministry with adequate understanding to make appropriate referrals when needed.[8]

Having reviewed the working definitions used in this book, we turn to the cultural dynamics in these definitions. All such definitions, as well as the understanding of what constitutes wholeness or well-being inherent in the definitions, are profoundly influenced by the attitudes, practices, and what are accepted as "truths" in the culture that generates them. These dynamic forces empower those with privilege in the society and disempower those who are poor, undereducated, and culturally impoverished. As our society becomes increasingly multicultural, basic defining concepts will change to include fresh understandings from widening cultural perspectives. Fortunately the shaping forces in our society are beginning to include more perspectives on the caregiving process from women (and/or those who are not privileged) from other cultures. The insights and perspectives of persons from many cultures will cause our understandings of the nature and processes of caregiving to become increasingly diverse and effective.

The Continuing Pastoral Care Renaissance

For more than twenty centuries, in each new historical period, the church has developed fresh ways of meeting the needs of troubled as well as troubling persons. In today's fast-changing world, religious caregivers must continue this tradition by developing new channels for the church's wholeness ministry of caring, healing, and growth nurturing. Only thus can they remain relevant to the changing needs of persons in our society.

To respond to the challenge, caregivers have more effective resources today than ever before in the long distinguished history of pastoral caregiving. They can draw valuable insights from four streams—the two wide streams of innovative developments in both pastoral theology and pastoral psychology, on the one hand, and the equally wide streams of the psychosocial sciences and psychotherapeutic disciplines, on the other. When these four streams converge in caregiving ministries, an Amazon-like river of healing and wholeness is released in and through a church that continues to flow into its wider community and world. To become a small channel for the life-transforming spirit of God can be one of the most fulfilling expressions of ministry. The hope and the expectation in these pages are that the conceptual maps and practical methods from these four streams will prove to be valuable resources for participating in this renaissance.

Many signs of growing vitality in pastoral care and counseling today will be explored in the following chapters. Some of these include

- burgeoning theory-strengthening literature in the field (reflected in the "Recommended Reading" sections concluding most chapters in this book);
- increasing commitment to recovering the theological and ethical heart of this pastoral art;
- the increasing number of women and men, across all continents and from ethnic minorities, in the field of pastoral care and counseling who are making significant contributions to reshaping pastoral caregiving in more diverse ways;
- the flowering of intercultural and global cross-fertilization, as reflected in the quadrennial International Congresses on Pastoral Care and Counseling over more than three decades;
- growing commitment to contextual issues of justice, peacemaking, and healing God's wounded creation, reflected in the literature, in International Congresses, and in the International Pastoral Care Network for Social Responsibility;
- innovative approaches to clinical pastoral education and strengthening of seminary education and graduate programs in pastoral theology and pastoral care and counseling;
- maturing of pastoral counseling as a rigorously trained specialty within the ministry, the proliferation of accredited church-related counseling programs, the theory-generating programs of the Society for Pastoral Theology (SPT), and the strengthening of standard-setting guilds such as the Association of

Clinical Pastoral Education (ACPE) and the American Association of
Pastoral Counselors (AAPC);

- denominational counseling services for the many burdened clergy and their
families;
- widespread programs to train laypersons for their vital caring ministries.

All these developments are hope awakening because they indicate that we indeed are
in an accelerating renaissance in the church's ancient ministry of spiritually centered
healing and growth cultivation. These dynamic developments strengthen the healing
hands and hearts that are sorely needed by the countless people lying beside our modern
Jericho roads, robbed of their self-esteem and beaten by the crises and tragedies of life.
In short, a fresh creative chapter in the church's caregiving ministry, without equal in
the long history of faith-based caregiving, is now occurring.

What is the challenge in all this to you as a caregiver? It is to become a skilled par-
ticipant-contributor to help pastoral caregiving become the growing force it has the
potential to be, in and beyond the church. To do this, we need to strengthen our self-
identity by deepening our theological roots, learn to use our rich heritage of ethical and
spiritual resources more effectively, fine-tune our methodologies to make them more
short term and goal directed, become more holistic, and develop our distinctive individual contributions to enable troubled human beings to develop liberating wholeness.

In our increasingly diverse and conflicted society, many traditional approaches to caregiving, shaped mainly by the old ways, are no longer adequate. To be more holistic and
effective, caregivers must become increasingly multicultural in their awareness, working
theories, and methods. They must give more attention to the impact on healing and
wholeness of power differentials between individuals, cultures, and classes. In addition,
with escalating violence and injustice, caregivers need increased understanding of the
complex causes and skills needed to help heal multifaceted violence and oppression.[9]

In this period of multiple transitions, it is essential that caring and counseling continue to be enriched by drawing on innovative therapies and theological insights. In
their classic volume *Pastoral Care in Historical Perspective*, church historian William A.
Clebsch and pastoral care specialist Charles R. Jaekle address the criticisms that are
sometimes made that pastoral care latches on to current psychologies and therapies:

> The lesson to be learned in this connection from the history of pastoral care is simply that open-
> ness to new psychological theories and notions in fact represents and continues a powerful trend
> found in every epoch of pastoring. The great tradition of pastoral care stands constantly ready to
> receive its ideas and its vocabulary both from psychological theoreticians and from popular lan-
> guage about the soul. The normative feature of pastoral care in historical perspective is neither a
> uniquely Christian psychology nor a particular language in which human troubles are described.[10]

In light of pastoral care's heritage, the authors recommend that we remain open to the insights of various and even conflicting psychological theories. This is essential because the human capacities for inflicting suffering and sabotaging wholeness are intricate and inventive. This heritage-informed guidance is sound. We need to maintain alertness to fresh theological and psychological understandings of the brokenness, healing, and wholeness while also being critical of the implicit theological assumptions in different psychologies and counseling theories. Time undoubtedly will prove that some innovative insights and methods are of little or no usefulness for religious caregivers. The road to better counseling skills has always included dead ends and detours. But the only alternative is not to travel in new directions at all. Experimenting with new approaches in counseling and in pastoral theology can enable pastoral counselors to generate the changes needed to stay relevant.

Valuing Theological and Spiritual Resources for Caregiving

The ability of pastors to help troubled people is enhanced when they value and learn how to use more fully their unique resources as caregivers. This understanding also increases their effectiveness in collaborating with other therapeutic professionals. The keys to clergy's uniqueness and special expertise as caregivers are their theological heritage and training, their pastoral identity and relationship with God, and the religious setting in which they serve. Because the church authorizes their work, caregiving is an expression of their ministry in whatever setting it occurs. Their awareness of the ever-present spirit of God, the wellspring of all healing and wholeness, will influence their caregiving profoundly, wherever it occurs. This spiritual frame of reference empowers their special expertise.

Dietrich Bonhoeffer's insightful observation that "God is the 'beyond' in the midst of our life" highlights the unique perspective of all truly pastoral care.[11] Wayne Oates called this awareness "the God-in-Relation-to-Persons-Consciousness."[12] This consciousness helps clergy recognize the image of God in all persons with whom they work, however hidden this image or difficult this recognition. Their awareness lets them see God's active presence in the midst of every problem, however messy it may be. It lets them sense the power of God's grace, justice, and love in all life experiences, including the most difficult to understand. The awareness energizes their caregiving spiritually by opening them to sense God's continuing lure toward increasing wholeness.

Speaking to a conference of CPE supervisors, theologian Paul Tillich once aptly described pastoral care as a "helping encounter in the dimension of ultimate concern."[13] The special caregiving insights and skills of clergy are learned during their dual education—in biblical, theological, historical, and ethical wisdom, on the one hand, and in the psychosocial sciences and psychotherapeutic disciplines, on the other.[14] If they acquire adequate understanding of both theological and psychological healing wisdom, they are equipped to be uniquely helpful to troubled persons. This dual understanding is particularly helpful when counseling careseekers whose crises, problems, and growth struggles focus on ethical dilemmas, religious conflicts, value distortions, or the ultimate concern of finding meaning and constructive ways to cope with crises and death. Because clergy are widely perceived as representatives of the value and belief systems of their religious traditions, many counselees feel free to bring up troubling ethical and faith issues with them for exploration and possible resolution. If clergy have integrated their theological and psychological learnings, they are prepared to be helpful in the *ministry of meanings* for which our society yearns.

Both the *professional setting* and the *context* of parish-based caregiving provide invaluable assets to pastors. The setting is the life of a gathered community of faith in which mutual caregiving occurs regularly among many members. Pastors offer care within a complex network of relationships where people are regularly together, know one another well, and see their pastor in a variety of situations. Ongoing, day-to-day relationships with people of all ages, in sunlight and shadows, provide religious leaders with innumerable caregiving opportunities.

Wholeness-nurturing congregations have an abundance of caring and growth-nurturing resources not available in other settings. This lively network of small and large groups, if they are healthy and growth nurturing, can complement, undergird, facilitate, and enrich caregiving with individuals and families. No other helping profession has a comparable supportive community of caring people available week in, week out, year after year. In such a community of mutual care, many lonely persons in our depersonalizing society discover the interpersonal and spiritual home for which they long. The many ministry functions of parish clergy constitute a professional context within which caregiving can nurture spiritual growth and wholeness.

An advantage of parish counseling is that troubled persons usually can see a pastor without appointment and without having to wait several days, as is true of many mental health professionals. This is an obvious advantage with persons requiring emergency care.[15] The fact that parish clergy usually do not charge for this professional service allows them to see persons, including the very poor, entirely on the basis of their need. But the downside is that counselees may lack the motivation that paying can supply. For this and other reasons, pastors need to protect themselves from those who may want to use a lot of their time in unproductive ways.

The relatively easy accessibility of clergy allows some people who are too embarrassed to make appointments for counseling to get help by "dropping by" for nonthreatening reasons. Others may not be familiar with the notion of structured counseling sessions. For example, for persons from other than middle-class backgrounds, structured counseling interviews often are foreign to their lifestyle or cultural expectations. Hence, in contrast to other counseling professionals, the availability of pastors for informal conversations in a variety of settings is a distinct advantage for them.

An invaluable professional advantage of parish pastors is that they can take the initiative in reaching out to those who need care but do not seek it. By reaching out, pastors model caring behavior for potential counselees and also strengthen a relationship bridge, which counselees may cross to seek help long before they might otherwise do. Pastoral conversations in people's homes, workplaces, or community settings are expressions of ministerial initiative that may begin a process of healing and wholeness.

Transcending the Limitations of Pastors as Caregivers

While using their advantages as caregivers, pastors also need to make peace with their limitations, remembering that their professional assets far outweigh their liabilities. Caregiving is only one of their numerous demanding and vital tasks. Therefore, they must devise creative ways to do caregiving that respects this multiplicity of ministerial functions. Constructive coping involves four strategies that will be explored later in this volume:

1. using short-term methods that can enable many troubled people to mobilize their inherent coping resources and learn to cope with their problems more effectively in a few contacts;
2. making effective referrals to competent, caring therapists and community agencies, while understanding referral as a vital caregiving function;
3. using brief crisis counseling joined with the mutual learning and caregiving that occur in a variety of small classes and support groups; and
4. training and coaching lay caregivers, including leaders of church classes and groups, to enhance the quality of the informal caregiving that occurs spontaneously throughout a congregation.

Another limitation of pastors as counselors is that they usually depend on their congregations to pay their salaries. This is a limitation if it conflicts with their objectivity and inhibits them in doing the caring confrontation that may be needed in caregiving. The need to not disappoint or alienate care receivers and their families by being candid about their problems can inhibit such constructive confrontation.[16] But if brief, solution-focused methods are used in counseling and referrals are made when these do not suffice, these dangers are greatly reduced.

Parishioners burdened with an exaggerated need to "look good" in the eyes of their pastor and other congregants, and those who project onto pastors an exaggerated transference image of supergood or godly persons, may avoid discussing embarrassing personal problems with them. Because parishioners encounter their pastors in a variety of priestly and pastoral roles, some are reluctant to take embarrassing problems to them. As one man put it, "I like and respect my pastor, so I'd rather not have him know about my affair." Some such congregants respond by seeking counseling from secular therapists, from pastors in other congregations, or in neutral settings such as chaplaincies.

Some people perceive clergy as defenders and not just representatives of the beliefs and values of their religious traditions and of God. This poses a problem for some people burdened by guilt, shame, or low self-esteem. They avoid seeking help from clergy because they fear and expect to be judged. Of course, those who *have* been treated judgmentally by churches are understandably reluctant to seek help from clergy.

These factors prevent some potential care receivers from seeking help in early stages of their crises, particularly if they have a socially stigmatized problem such as extramarital affairs, HIV/AIDs, incest, domestic violence, or suicide. If they do seek counseling, feelings of shame may limit their willingness to share candidly the information that is essential for the counselor to know in order to be helpful. Or after they reveal such facts in counseling, they may terminate their relationships with their pastor and congregation, or they may act out by withholding their money or sabotaging the pastor or other church ministries.

Furthermore, some guilt-burdened people project judgmental images onto all clergy, even those who are actually nonjudgmental, accepting human beings. Fortunately pastors who are aware of their own weaknesses and need for forgiveness, and have experienced the healing of forgiveness, become genuinely self-accepting, grace-full people. This enables them to be genuinely accepting of other people whatever their sins, weaknesses, and failures. Such pastoral caregivers communicate acceptance through the quality of their relationships and thus become psychologically accessible to those who otherwise would avoid seeking their care.

The Continental Plates Are Shifting and Shaking[17]

The San Andreas earth fault runs through several hundred miles of California. It passes only a few hundred feet from the cabin at the six-thousand-foot level of the mountains where I enjoyed going to rest, reflect, recreate, and write for many years. When I jogged across this fault zone, it boggled my mind to remember that this is where the huge Pacific plate meets the continental plate that undergirds North America. The shifting of vast continental plates around the planet produces earthquakes and volcanoes, and creates new mountain ranges that continue to change the earth's face in profound, unpredictable ways.

This is an illuminating image for our world of kaleidoscopic change in this new century. Reflecting on the current pastoral care situation, from the perspective of the movement's modern history, Rodney J. Hunter and John Patton are on target in declaring that "the movement today is being powerfully challenged and changed by issues of social conflict." They continue, "A great ferment is occurring in the pastoral care field that involves its deepest historical convictions and value commitments."[18]

Huge cultural earthquakes produced by multiple positive and negative social revolutions, are taking place around the planet. These revolutions challenge pastoral caregivers to enlarge their working concepts and methods to respond to the needs of countless people suffering an incredible variety of brokenness. They are producing negative and positive challenges to caregivers:

- soaring cycles of violence, suffering, collective evil, and the collective anxiety and grief triggered by terrorist attacks and genocidal violence among ethnic and religious groups;
- pervasive violence against women rooted in the destructive realities of patriarchy in societies around the globe;
- the growing complexity of understanding "truth" in any field with the blossoming of systemic understandings in many fields of knowledge, showing that all knowledge and life are interconnected and that the well-being of all people is deeply interdependent;
- global cybernetic communication networking through the Internet, Facebook, Twitter, and so on, connecting more of humankind faster than ever before; this amazing development continues to transform human life in profound ways, offering unprecedented ethical problems and constructive resources for innovative, imaginative caregiving;[19]
- scientific research and technology generating amazing breakthroughs that are opening doors to lifestyle transformations in many fundamental areas of human life, including communication, energy, transportation, and work;
- health-care breakthroughs, including mind-brain research and mapping the human genome, the blueprint of life, which offers potential blessings for the prevention and cure of devastating diseases but also raises unprecedented ethical issues about genetic manipulation;

- chaos and creativity in intimate relationships, with women's empowerment affecting family life as well as women's, men's, and same-gender relationships;
- profound transformations in global demographics generated by steadily lengthening longevity (projected far beyond the present 76.5 years in the United States) and a proliferating world population, resulting in increasing and devastating crowding, hunger, sickness, and damage to the health of the biosphere on which all life depends;
- increasing globalization, including global economic interdependence with the increasing power of transnational corporations, resulting in growing obsolescence of nation-states as well as an increasingly gaping chasm between have and have-not countries;
- the "greening" of industry, governments, education, and religion, with rising urgency for international responses to the global ecojustice crisis;
- challenges to autocratic organizations, governments, and power hierarchies, with growing demands for full liberation, democratization, and egalitarian social structures in family, community, national, and global arenas;
- the mapping of galaxies at the extreme reaches of the universe by the Hubble and other superpowerful telescopes, confronting humankind with new perspectives and questions about our real place in a universe of which our planet and humankind are infinitely small but interconnected parts.

These profound changes challenge many of our aspirations and beliefs, together with the values, philosophies, and guiding images of the human family. They create enormous pressures on persons, including those who are unaware of the changes. Much of the violence, turmoil, conflict, meaninglessness, value confusion, and spiritual vacuums that increase the need for skilled caregiving is rooted in this radical shaking of society's foundational beliefs, values, and structures.

Christie Neuger highlights the spiritual hungers and vacuum in our world that make spiritually empowering caregiving so crucial:

> In this largely post-modern world of many layers, we create ourselves, our truths and one another, often without frameworks to make sense of these shifts in perspective. We are aware of diversity, of power structures, of oppressive discourse, and of relativized truth claims, but we often don't know how to reconcile these with our need for anchors of certainty and belonging. We need the language and the framework to make sense of these realities.
>
> We live in a world hungry for accessible spirituality. Even as there is ongoing distrust of religious institutions, there is longing for ways to understand and believe in that which is greater than ourselves, the God beyond our gods. There is a spiritual longing, pining for new ways to find meaning in life, to resist evil, to embrace Good, and to live with Hope.[20]

To respond to these unprecedented challenges and opportunities in our *broken* but *rebirthing* world, the next chapter describes a working model reflecting the guiding images described above. The model is designed to guide you in using the various types of pastoral care and counseling to develop your unique differential approaches as you respond. In short, this paradigm can help you facilitate the everyday miracles that can occur in effective, spiritually empowered caregiving.

CHAPTER 2

A MODEL FOR SPIRITUALLY CENTERED HOLISTIC PASTORAL CAREGIVING

The model that guides one's caregiving ministry is crucial to its effectiveness, serving like a compass on a sea voyage. Any such model must be grounded firmly in present realities; but it must also be open to respond to God's call to a new, more whole future. Pastoral caregiving is guided by a vision that evolves as the growing edges of the world and the pastoral care field change in unexpected ways. To respond effectively, spiritually centered caregivers must have three basic resources: (1) a comprehensive, systemic, holistic guiding model; (2) a current understanding of the varied dynamics of problems and contexts; and (3) competence in fundamental caregiving skills. This chapter describes a model for pastoral caregivers and counselors designed to enable them to respond to the healing and growth needs of individuals, families, and congregations in our constantly and radically changing society. The other two foundational resources will be addressed in other chapters.

The Model's Defining Objectives

The unifying, overarching objective of spiritually centered holistic pastoral care and counseling is to enable people to experience healing and growth in all the dimensions and stages of their lives. *Holistic* means the unity of all dimensions of our complex selves.[1] The mission of pastoral caregivers in the twenty-first century is to empower care receivers to discover and develop God's gifts by becoming lifelong learners, Spirit-empowered caregivers, and responsible world citizens. Spiritually centered wholeness is a contemporary synonym for what the Fourth Gospel calls "life...in all its fullness" (John 10:10 NEB) or "the abundant life" (KJV). Thus congregations and other faith-based institutions are called by God to be abundant life centers. Caregivers and educators in such spiritually enlivening communities are partners in cultivating life in all its fullness through programs, activities, and worship experiences. This holistic ministry of mutual caregiving involves nurturing wholeness in individuals and their relationships, in a congregation's overall life as a social system, and also in the groups and institutions that continually have an impact on people's lives in their community and society. An essential aspect of enabling people to develop life in all its fullness is to help them learn how to resist and overcome evil and oppression that diminish wholeness for themselves and countless others.

The training of pastors, in contrast to that of most secular counselors, shapes them professionally as generalists.[2] Because of this and the whole-person orientation of the Christian message, clergy tend to be holistic and multidimensional in their understanding of people's problems. The relevance of this orientation will increase as holistic, systemic understandings of human personality, relationships, healing, and health grow more pervasive.

Hope and Growth—Key Metaphors for Pastoral Caregiving

The path of healing and growth is a spiraling process rather than a linear one. Caregiving with people who have suffered shattering crises begins with explicitly healing methods. But these methods are growth directed because their aim is to heal the brokenness that blocks or retards growth in care receivers. As healing of brokenness occurs, more explicitly educative or guiding counseling methods are used, aimed at enabling care receivers to develop more of their God-given possibilities. In the spiral of healing and growth, as people become healthier they may become aware of new or continuing woundedness that needs healing. Even people suffering from severe brokenness have areas of strength and health in their lives, however difficult these may be for them or others to see. These healthy areas provide essential resources for them to use in their healing and growth.

Growth and hope-oriented pastoral caregiving is based on the conviction that most people possess a variety of undiscovered and therefore underdeveloped strengths, assets, and possibilities in their mental, spiritual, and relational lives. Most people use only a fraction of their latent creativity, intelligence, and capacity to respond with informed caring to the needs of others and society. Awareness of this potential makes the model's understanding of people both hope and growth oriented. Furthermore, seeing care receivers in this positive, hopeful way actually encourages them to discover and use more of their latent gifts.

Transformational Caregiving

The model in this book is centered in a positive, transformational approach to caregiving that takes as fundamental the multiple dimensions of people and their contexts. This approach involves moving beyond the traditional counseling approaches focused mainly on understanding and fixing people's problems, even though doing that is vitally important. To be wholeness cultivating, a transformational perspective must be added to a repair perspective.

An inspiring example of the effectiveness of positive transformational approaches to human problems is found in the health-care philosophy of Jonas Salk, the medical pioneer who developed the first lifesaving polio vaccine. He had a hope-awakening approach to problems that included concern for future generations. When people asked about medical problems, he would respond with questions aimed at broadening their horizons of concern beyond diagnosis and treatment to a positive health-care perspective. For example, he would say, "Tell me your story. What maintains your health? What lessons would you like to teach your children and grandchildren about maintaining health? What must we do to create a healthier world for those children and their future?"[3]

In this spirit, holistic pastoral caregivers today have an unprecedented opportunity to help grow a forest of spiritually empowered wholeness.[4] To cultivate such a forest, caregivers must move beyond focusing primarily on people's problems, pathology, and dysfunction to a balancing focus on their strengths, assets, hopes, and life goals. Even painfully wounded people can be coached to use these resources for stimulating their healing, creative coping, and enhancing the overall quality of their lives.

It must be noted, as a word of caution, that emphasizing human possibilities and growth without also acknowledging the limitations and brokenness in people's lives can create serious problems. This is particularly true when people confront crises and losses.

The Importance of Story in a Transformational Model of Pastoral Caregiving

As a wise storyteller in a science fiction narrative, Ursula K. Le Guin declares, "Story is our only boat for sailing on the river of time, but in the great rapids and the winding shallows, no boat is safe."[5] In our world of lightning-fast change, old stories are being challenged and rejected by many people in their struggles to find new stories to give their lives meaning and hope. Holistic caregivers have many opportunities to help people who are caught in obsolete or destructive cultural stories to deconstruct those discourses and develop more constructive stories that can help restore life-enhancing meaning.

Cognitive-behavioral theory has been an important source of insights about the power of story. Most psychotherapies have underemphasized the role of concepts and beliefs in producing emotional distress and distorted behavior. They have held that concepts and beliefs can become more constructive only after positive changes have occurred in persons' feelings and perceptions. In contrast, the cognitive-behavioral therapies hold that disturbances in our perceptions, feelings, and actions stem from irrational thoughts and invalid beliefs.[6] One such cognitive-behavioral therapy developed by psychologist Albert Ellis is called Rational-Emotive Therapy (RET). He holds that our irrational beliefs are the source of the negative, self-depreciating messages we repetitiously say to ourselves and with which we continue to chastise ourselves.

Narrative counseling theory, which provides a constructive critique to cognitive-behavioral theory, suggests that many of these negative belief systems are grounded in the dominant, power-organizing discourses of our culture. Narrative counseling is an approach developed in recent years by Michael White, David Epston, and others.

Narrative theory emphasizes two things. First, our lives and meanings are constructed in a world organized through cultural discourses of power. As Stephen Madigan, drawing on Michel Foucault, points out, cultural discourses are the structures that determine what story is told, who can tell it, and what it means. Narrative theory offers a way to help people notice, or make transparent, the cultural power dynamics that are often at the heart of people's problems. These discourses include racism, sexism, heterosexism, classism, ageism, ableism, and so on. By the kinds of questions that narrative counselors ask, people able to get some distance from the problem discourse in such a way that they are able to see how their value and meaning have been constituted by how they fit in the social structure of the culture. This deconstructive function of narrative counseling is an important resource for a transformational model of pastoral care that seeks to address issues of injustice and disempowerment in people's lives. A second emphasis of narrative counseling theory is its awareness that people should not be defined by their problems. The kinds of questions asked by narrative counselors help separate people from their problems in such a way that they can explore those problems and the support systems that keep the problems in place. As Jill Freedman and Gene Coombs suggest, narrative counseling theory starts with the premise that we listen to people's stories with a particular intention and that intention guides the way we listen, what we listen for, and what we do with what we hear. If we listen with the intention of helping this person solve his or her problem, we will listen for the problem in the midst of the story, work to help the person get more precise about the problem, and set a counseling goal around helping to alleviate or solve the problem. This would be a problem-focused approach, as much counseling theory suggests. However, if we listen to the story with the intention of trying to separate the person from the problem story so that a new story can be developed less around the problem and more around living a satisfying life, we will listen to the problem but find ways to externalize it, look for exceptions to it, and strengthen alternative, invisible stories.[7]

When one is working from a narrative perspective, there are certain philosophical and psychological assumptions in mind. In fact, the assumptions in which the counselor is grounded guide the questions and the intentions for listening. Narrative theory assumes that people have many experiences in their lives that would challenge or redirect their problem narrative toward new interpretations and meanings but these don't get storied because they are in conflict with the dominant narrative. As Freedman and Coombs describe, "People who come to therapy can be viewed as living in stories where choice is restricted and available options are painful and unfulfilling. Counseling involves facilitating experience of new stories—life narratives that are more empowering, more satisfying, and give hope for better futures."[8] This notion of deconstructing personal and cultural problem narratives and restorying existing but invisible stories of hope and possibility is at the postmodern heart of narrative counseling theory.

These postmodern ideas are a significant departure from many ideas found in much counseling theory and provide important resources for a transformational holistic model of pastoral caregiving.[9] Today's global crises of injustice and environmental degradation require this shift in order to empower better narratives of social justice. We will explore these ideas further in later chapters.

Importance of Community and Collaboration in a Transformational Model of Pastoral Caregiving

Spiritually centered, holistic caregivers understand that healing and growth are nurtured most effectively in religious communities in which caregivers and care receivers relate as partners with shared openness to receive God's gifts of healing and wholeness. The caring community of a spiritually energized congregation is the growth-nurturing environment of pastoral care and the supportive context for the healing ministry of pastoral counseling. This view reflects the New Testament understanding of caregiving as the task of Spirit-empowered faith communities functioning as loving, healing, honest, growth-cultivating environments of mutual ministries. Such contexts provide supportive networks that are especially crucial for people struggling with crises and losses. Being undergirded by such a mutually caring community can soften the pain of crises and prevent them from escalating. This context energizes the healing and growth-cultivating ministry of all caregivers within such a congregation.

Holistic caregiving in faith communities is most effective when it is done as a working partnership of ordained clergy and laypersons, all of whom are "in ministry." Ordained clergy are called to serve like skilled guides on mountainous trails. Or to use another image, clergy are called to be player-coaches. Their training, expertise, leadership role, and pastoral identity equip them to coach the mutual ministry of laypersons while also providing their own valuable care and counseling. Their dual task uses the rich resources of their professional background to provide care directly to burdened people, and also to inspire, train, and coach laypersons in their vital caregiving ministry.

Holistic growth counseling and coaching have similarities in their philosophy, goals, and methodologies and also in their wholeness and systems orientation. In contrast to the goal of classical psychotherapy—treating significant dysfunctions—both aim at enabling relatively healthy, functional people to develop more of their latent strengths in order to fulfill more of their hopes, dreams, and potentialities. Both do this by empowering people to learn how to develop and implement intentional growth plans based on evaluating their assets and life goals. However, growth counseling goes beyond coaching to help people learn how to grow through the way they cope with their times of crises, distress, and dysfunction. Educative counseling or coaching provide useful tools in many types of holistic caregiving. These include caregiving for spiritual and ethical growth, community building in groups, growing through crises and grief, enhancing intimate relationships, and handling life transitions and changing stages, as well as coaching laypersons to do caregiving.[10]

The images of guide, player-coach, and nonhierarchical partner illuminate optimal wholeness-nurturing relationships between caregivers and care receivers in general. To maximize the cultivation of life in all its fullness, the power distribution between the two needs to be much more egalitarian than in authority-centered approaches. Experience shows that in such collaborative relationships, care receivers tend to bring more of their own resources to the mutual process. They also provide opportunities for caregivers to learn and grow with care receivers. Of course, it's important to acknowledge unavoidable power differences and the need for appropriate professional boundaries. We will explore these throughout the book.

The Importance of Liberation and Justice Making in a Transformational Model of Caregiving

A crucial focus of this model is its emphasis on liberating and prophetic caregiving. In this context, liberation means maximizing people's opportunities to discover and use more of their latent gifts in ways that increase their overall well-being and that of other individuals and of society. It also means that we work to identify the structures of injustice in our culture and their role in the problems people, families, and communities experience. Engaging in pastoral caregiving means working against dominant cultural discourses that support unjust power arrangements in our world. This commitment to justice making is an expression of the central motif shared by many diverse liberation movements—namely, the insistence that the injustices preventing millions of people from developing their gifts must be healed by justice-making actions. Such prophetic actions are one expression of the persistent liberation theme in both the Jewish and the Christian traditions. The exodus motif in Hebrew Scripture reflects the key personal needs and hopes of individual care receivers trapped in painful problems. In its biblical and counseling contexts, this story points to God's call to respond to community oppression. Participating in the liberation and empowerment of exodus involves moving "out of oppression into a new sense of community and a new accountability." A new accountability today means "that we do not take part in or allow oppression and injustice without resistance. This is the work of ongoing cultural transformation."[11]

In the Christian context, "freedom in Christ" (John 8:36; Rom. 8:2) suggests that the gospel is experienced as good news when it frees, equips, and empowers people to grow in living out God's intention that they develop life in its fullness. Holistic pastoral care and counseling are powerful instruments for use in this wholeness-liberating ministry. When it is appropriate, caregivers should encourage care receivers to become aware of the social and ecological issues that are among the root causes of their problems in living. It may be appropriate to coach some care receivers in doing whatever they can to help lower the barriers to injustices and oppression. Such prophetic action increases wholeness in themselves and others. It also enhances their freedom to grow toward the fullness of life that is God's dream for all of us. The process of liberation by means of caregiving involves three interdependent subgoals: liberation *to*, liberation *for*, and liberation *from*. Liberation is *to* life in all its fullness, meaning the fullest possible developments of people's gifts and potentialities. Liberation is *for* enabling people to grow in their own wholeness but also become facilitators of wholeness in widening circles of outreach in a society suffering from multiple oppressions producing pandemic brokenness. Liberation is *from* the many forces in individuals, relationships, groups, and social institutions that foster brokenness and diminished wholeness for countless people. It includes liberation from the severe deprivation of trust-generating love in early life and other emotional wounding that has produced inner conflicts, anxieties, and depleted self-esteem. Liberation is also from mutually damaging toxic relationships as well as traumatic crises such as tragic losses, accidents, unemployment, illnesses, disabilities, natural disasters, and human violence. Furthermore, caregivers guided by a holistic vision help liberate careseekers from social, economic, political, and ecological injustices. These societal pathologies produce widespread brokenness and drastically diminish the opportunities of oppressed people to grow in wholeness. Thus holistic caregiving may involve facilitating healing and growth on interdependent levels in individuals, families, churches, and workplaces, and in both the social and the natural environments.

There are painful illustrations of the need for multileveled liberating caregiving in the practices created by patriarchal values and beliefs in our society and churches. As we have said elsewhere, "The pastoral counselor needs to be informed about, sensitive to, and resistant to the overwhelming realities of patriarchy and how they affect women (and men) at every level of their lives. Every woman lives in a world that devalues her because of her sex."[12] The same statement can be made about how the power structures of our culture affect people of color; people of diverse sexual orientations; people who are not in the dominant social classes, ages, ethnicities, and so on. These systems of oppression influence and are influenced by economics and employment, dynamics of systematic violence and abuse, media and advertising. The wholeness-diminishing effect of this reality must be addressed by caregiving on several levels. These include caregiving aimed at liberating empowerment of individual women and men, of family dynamics, and of local and national structures of oppression.

Traditional pastoral care theories and practices have focused mainly on individual and family healing. The holistic model encourages caregivers to go beyond this starting point in our caring ministry with burdened people. Because personal and societal liberation are deeply interdependent, liberation and justice making are essential parts of holistic pastoral care. Neither individual nor social liberation can be accomplished fully without the other also occurring. People are liberated within their unique contexts. This enables them to move away from being bystanders in a society that does collective harm to countless people, to become motivated and equipped to help liberate wholeness in all the interdependent dimensions of their personal and social lives. When people join hands in the liberation of others, their lives often tend to be liberated and enlivened more deeply.

The communal orientation of this model is expressed in its focus on caregiving both to and through communities, groups, and institutions. From this perspective, the book offers (in the chapters on crisis and grief caregiving) insights for understanding the unique dynamics and methods of caregiving in collective crises and grief such as the unprecedented terrorist disaster of September 11, 2001. Genocidal killings in many other countries make clear the global scope of this need.

The Importance of Inclusivity and Diversity in a Transformational Model of Pastoral Caregiving

The increasing diversity of careseekers is a major challenge facing caregivers in the twenty-first century. This diversity brings complex multicultural issues into the practice of Spirit-empowered caregiving. In this context, pastoral caregivers are challenged to become more multicultural in their awarenesses and methodologies. They are confronted by the need to cultivate understanding of the very diverse worlds in which the identities of persons are shaped. These worlds include gender differences; diverse ethnic, racial, and language groups; and a wide diversity of social class and faith traditions. In the pluralistic world of our times, it is fortunate that a growing proportion of clergy and pastoral counseling specialists are women and persons from nonmiddle-class, nonwhite, and non-Western backgrounds. Caregivers from increasingly multicultural backgrounds bring new, invigorating strengths from their diverse roots.[13]

In light of the needs posed by increasing diversity, the caregiving model in these pages begins by encouraging persons to develop their own unique personhood using the resources of their social, cultural, racial, ethnic, and religious traditions. To balance this, it also emphasizes openness to learning from one another's traditions. Because extending their circles of healing and building multicultural bridges of care across chasms of diversity are so crucial for caregiving, this topic will be discussed more fully in chapter 17.

The Importance of Outreach in a Transformational Model of Pastoral Caregiving

One guiding principle of this wholeness model is that reaching out to others who are in need of care can be a vital part of care receivers' continuing healing and growth. Equipping and motivating people to help themselves by helping others are healing objectives in caregiving. Given the theological roots of this concept in the biblical heritage, it is surprising that it has not been emphasized more prominently in the literature of pastoral caregiving. Using this outreach principle in counseling parallels the healing wisdom of 12-step work in Alcoholics Anonymous. Reaching out to share one's recovery story and learnings with another addicted person can strengthen one's hold on sobriety.

During difficult times, many people concentrate mainly on their own problems. But the terrorist attack of September 11, 2001, produced countless stories of people reaching out in caring, self-giving ways to the victims as a way of coping with their own shattered feelings. Several university studies have discovered that volunteering for community service may actually prolong life. A Harvard study found that older people with productive activities, including volunteering, improved their chances of living long lives as much as those who engaged in physical fitness activities.[14]

The Importance of Flexibility in a Transformational Model of Pastoral Caregiving

The structure of pastoral care and counseling in this model is much broader and more flexible than formal interviews in a pastor's office. In congregations many fruitful opportunities for caregiving occur in informal settings. These may include a parishioner's home or office; after a worship service, committee meeting, or social event; in a hospital waiting room; or during chance encounters. The usual structure of formal pastoral counseling includes appointments, a definite time and place, a private meeting place, an agreed upon counseling "contract," perhaps a fee, and the label *counseling*. Often these are not needed, appropriate, or possible for helpful caregiving to occur. To give empowering help to the maximum number of hurting persons, pastors need to apply their caregiving sensitivities and skills in a host of informal, often unexpected encounters with persons struggling with complex decisions and burdens. The congregational setting and resources enable the use, as appropriate, of informal caregiving conversations, formal counseling, small growth-nurturing and healing groups, and personally focused coaching or educative counseling.

Cultivating Wholeness in Seven Dimensions of People's Lives[15]

The most fundamental way that the horizons of pastoral caregiving are extended in this model is by seeing seven dimensions of people's lives as relevant to their fullest healing and growth. This broader focus is in contrast to most traditional pastoral caregiving that has focused mainly on the spiritual, psychological, and relational dimensions of people's lives. Yet it is evident that each of the seven dimensions influences all the others. Furthermore, each can be a vital arena for whole-person ministries of care, counseling, healing, and education.

I am indebted to the late Nelle Morton, pioneer feminist theologian, innovative Christian educator, and friend, for suggesting a diagram. She drew it to resemble the heart of an atom as depicted in physics textbooks. Nelle's comments about the diagram reflect her wise woman insights as a caregiving person. She said, "Wholeness is never static but always in ferment and growth. Since we live in a global community and are rapidly emerging into a cosmic mind, could we not think of spirit as that flow of energy that brings us and the other six aspects of wholeness into dynamic relationship with one another and the whole—ever in movement, in tension, interactive, interconnected and interdependent, yet powerfully present?"[16] The following diagram depicts the seven dimensions:

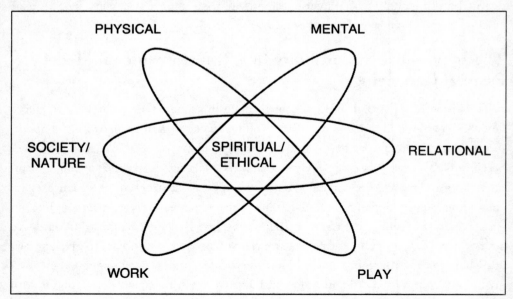

A surprising but very welcome discovery is that this seven-dimensional model of caregiving has proved to be useful in a variety of non-Western countries where I have lectured or where my writings have been translated and published. Feedback from pastoral caregivers in Asian, African, Latin American, and South Pacific countries has brought this word. To share a vivid illustration, Cecilia O. Lioanag, a caregiver-educator in the Philippines, e-mailed me saying that the holistic growth program she leads has "made your seven dimensions of life part of our psycho-social-spiritual approach to human rights education." She reported that a friend of hers who is a human rights education expert "tried it with Burmese refugees in Thailand and got positive feedback. They liked the seven-dimensions framework."[17]

Because the seven-dimensions perspective is so useful in holistic healing and growth ministries, an overview of all seven follows. The spiritual, ethical, and relational dimensions of people's lives are explored in some depth in later chapters so they will be briefer than the other four dimensions: physical, work, play, and society/nature.

I. Healing and Wholeness in Spirit and Ethics

Spiritual and ethical wholeness is located at the center of Morton's diagram to suggest that this dimension of life is not just one among seven. Rather, it is the heart of wholeness, the unifying, integrating core around which all the other dimensions interact. It is the axle of the wheel of people's lives on which all their other dimensions—mind, body, physical and mental relationships, work, play, and society/nature—turn, more or less effectively. The strength, integrity, and wholeness of this axle profoundly influence people's overall well-being and how well they function in the other important dimensions of their lives. The spiritual key to whole-person wellness is a trustful, nourishing, growing relationship with the divine Spirit—the ultimate source of all life. The degree of health in this crucial area has a profound influence on the health of the other six dimensions.

The spiritual-ethical center influences, to some degree, all the issues and crises, problems and possibilities, fears and hopes that people bring to pastoral caregivers. Fortunately, well-trained clergy are equipped with expertise in cultivating healing and wholeness in this pivotal spiritual-ethical arena. Pastoral caregivers use their skills to heal spiritual-ethical brokenness and nurture healthy spirituality in all dimensions of human life and relationships. Methods of counseling with persons who are struggling with spiritual issues and who are hungry for spiritual growth will be explored, and counseling on ethical problems and nurturing ethical growth will be covered, later in this book.

II. Wholeness in the Mind and Personality

Caregiving in this dimension involves two continually interacting functions, intellectual and emotional. Nurturing these is essential to the growth and wholeness of human personality. Mental well-being is the ability of people to exercise reason, wrestle effectively with intellectual issues, make constructive decisions, and develop their creativity. Emotional well-being involves experiencing feelings appropriate to changing relationships and reality, controlling impulses and negative emotions, and having life-enhancing feelings of self-worth, agency, hope, empathy, love, and trust.

Serious deficits of self-esteem and agency, and a weak sense of identity, breed destructive problems in many areas of people's lives. *Genuine self-esteem* is the inner conviction that one is a person of inherent value. All of us need some affirmation from others, but persons suffering from weak self-esteem are largely dependent on seeking a sense of worth from others. This need makes them vulnerable to wholeness-damaging perfectionism, people pleasing, and compulsive work patterns in an endless effort to feel worthwhile. *Agency* means the strength that comes from the inner awareness that one can achieve self-chosen, worthwhile goals and make some difference in life that matters to oneself and others. To the degree that people have this sense of inner strength and confidence, they do not need to seek power by domination, control, or violence toward others. Instead of power over or against, they find satisfaction in power with others. *Clear identity* means a robust sense of who one is as a person, a sense not derived mainly from social roles or relationships with dominant people in one's life, although identity is always a relational reality.

A vital healing and growth function of pastoral caregiving is to help strengthen these core attributes to some degree. This occurs as caregivers respect and relate to care receivers as unique, autonomous persons of inherent worth and help them learn how to develop their strengths, gifts, and capacities for living responsible, productive, and fulfilling lives.

Related to the importance of these core attributes of self-esteem, agency, and identity is the concept of emotional intelligence. Psychologist Daniel Goleman illuminates the vital intellectual resources of the nonanalytic right-brain capacities of human minds. He gives evidence demonstrating that emotional intelligence (EQ) can be more important than the intellectual capacities measured by IQ tests, so far as constructive relationships, vocational success, life satisfactions, and mental well-being are concerned. EQ includes the basic human capacities needed for our society to thrive. The strengths associated with EQ include empathy, relationship skills, impulse control, zest and self-motivation, character, self-discipline, altruism, and compassion.[18] EQ can be enhanced by constructive parenting, creative mentors, healthy friendships, reaching out to others, and growth experiences in churches, as well as by psychotherapy that produces emotional relearning.

Holistic caregiving aims at enabling care receivers to enliven their minds and personalities by removing impediments and cultivating continuous lifelong learning. This process enables people to discover and develop more of their resources for thinking, feeling, creating, and imagining, all of which can enhance living and coping with crises, grief, and problematic decisions. Holistic caregivers encourage the use of these growing mental resources to reach out, responding to the needs of persons, institutions, and our wounded earth. The unused mental and emotional capacities of most people parallel and are interdependent with their unused spiritual resources. Educative caregiving, aimed at these issues, includes empowering people to enrich their consciousness, enhance their self-esteem and creativity, increase their caring empathy, expand their intellectual and artistic horizons, learn to distinguish wisdom from information, and nurture their capacity to love and serve others.

The methods in this book aim at increasing the constructiveness of feelings, attitudes, beliefs, and cognitive maps, on the one hand, and behavior and relationships, on the other. Traditional pastoral care theory has often mirrored insight-oriented psychotherapy by holding that before changes in behavior can occur, inner changes through insight must take place. There may be some truth in this, but the converse is also true. Constructive changes in behavior and relationships often produce significant improvement in self-identity and feelings. Pastoral caregiving should aim at facilitating both types of interdependent changes.

III. Healing and Wholeness in the Body

Body self-care has not been discussed adequately in mainstream pastoral counseling and education literature. This deficit must be corrected. We human beings are embodied selves. The wellness and sickness of our bodies are inextricably intertwined and interdependent with all other dimensions of our lives. And we experience our world through our bodies. They are the essential context of our lives. If caregiving is truly holistic, it often must include empowering care receivers to learn to do what is needed for the healing, strengthening, and enlivening of their bodies in five areas: nutrition, sleep, exercise, stress reduction, and toxin reduction (for example, eliminating or reducing the intake of such things as nicotine, junk foods, alcohol, caffeine, and other problematic chemicals).

Caregiving in this physical dimension also may include helping people to

- do whatever is necessary to obtain effective treatment for physical problems;
- learn to prevent illnesses and maximize wellness by using mental imagery, exercise, and healthy diet to enhance immune systems;
- increase the fitness of their bodies to become more effective in handling the physical demands of daily living and the crises and rigors of aging;

- learn to enjoy their God-given body pleasures more fully and constructively, including sensuality and sexuality;
- learn to make some peace with physical problems that cannot be healed;
- learn to use the interdependence of body, mind, and spirit to increase wellness;
- overcome body alienation so that they can love their embodied selves more, despite physical limitations, imperfections, or disabilities.

People are most often motivated to seek counseling because of pain from emotional, spiritual, or relational crises. Asking them about their physical problems and self-care often broadens the horizons of their concern and that of the caregivers. Those who are suffering from self-care neglect should be coached in educative counseling to develop doable health-care plans. People who show evidence of neglecting physical illnesses should be urged to consult competent health-care professionals for the diagnosis and treatment they need. Coaching people to improve their body self-care often brings surprising benefits, not only to their physical well-being, but also to the quality of their mental, spiritual, and relational lives.

Many women and men suffer from body shame and alienation, causing them to reject their body images and body care. In our youth-worshiping, women-objectifying, sexist society, many women reject their bodies (and have their bodies rejected) because they don't measure up to media and advertising images of beauty. Many men reject their bodies because they don't measure up to macho, superathletic images that the culture tells men they should have. Some take dangerous body-building steroids in order to achieve the cultural ideal of the male body. Whole-person caregiving aims at helping care receivers deconstruct such damaging cultural images and discourses and reclaim and reconcile with their bodies. Helping people make peace with their bodily limitations, large or small, can be facilitated by helping them reframe the meaning of their embodied self-identity.

IV. Healing and Wholeness in Relationships

In an oft-quoted insight, Martin Buber declared, "All real living is meeting."[19] From a psychological perspective this means that our human identity and personality are formed, deformed, and if we're fortunate, healed and transformed in crucial relationships. For this reason, the holistic model of caregiving in these pages is essentially relational. The health of people's most important relationships influences deeply their physical as well as their mental and spiritual healing and health. Therefore, whole-person healing and growth frequently depend on nurturing intimate relationships. For many people, the crucial task in helping them enhance their overall wellness is enabling them to learn how to repair and enrich their caring circle of relationships. This is the network of mutually accepting, supportive, loving relationships that all people need to sustain them in coping with life. We humans can live holistic lives only to the degree that we participate in covenants of mutual wholeness nurturing. Because relational caregiving skills are so central in wholeness ministries, two chapters are devoted to nurturing love—in intimate couple relationships and in families, broadly defined.

V. *Healing and Wholeness in Work*

In light of the proliferating workplace pressures and frustrations in our society, holistic caregiving often involves work-related problems. Work satisfaction is highly correlated with general well-being, especially for middle-class people. Let yourself imagine the impact on overall wellness of forcing oneself to keep doing work one finds boring, unfulfilling, distasteful, or ethically problematic for forty or more hours a week, forty-eight or more weeks a year, for forty years. Unfortunately work-related caregiving has not received the attention it merits in most pastoral care literature and training. This gap must be filled because today's world of work is changing with unprecedented speed, causing it to be chaotic, stressful, and diminishing for millions of people. Many forces are shaking workplaces today. These include the transition to the postindustrial information age in the global economy, the increasingly high-tech stress of the computer and Internet revolution, company downsizing and outsourcing and the trauma of subsequent unemployment and underemployment, and the enormous pressures on single-parent and many two-career families. Many people find their work lives to be filled with frustration and hopelessness.

In our society's epidemic of workplace brokenness, vocational guidance is increasingly important. Such educative counseling should focus on growing through job crises and job opportunities. As professionals with special training and expertise in addressing ethics, religious leaders can help youth and adults wrestle with work-related choices. However, it is crucial to be aware that effective vocational guidance and planning must be correlated with intentional life guidance and planning. Providing this dual guidance is a challenging pastoral opportunity in which laypersons with varied job experience and awareness of the complex ethical issues in all vocations can serve as valuable resource persons and coach-mentors. They usually find sharing their experiences and insights very fulfilling. Support groups for people who are unemployed or underemployed or facing job stresses can also be a very effective means of pastoral care.

The primary goal of workplace caregiving is to enable care receivers to cope constructively with their job crises and burnout and, in the process, grow in this crucial area of their lives. Beyond this, the ideal objective is increasing their work wellness by developing more purpose, creativity, zest, and sense of calling in their work life. Because vocational caregiving should be an integral part of congregational educative ministries, it will be discussed later in this book.

VI. Healing and Wholeness through Laughter and Playfulness

The crucial role of laughter, playfulness, and recreation in nurturing, healing, and health merits far more recognition than it has received in the past. The healing, health-enhancing impact of humor is affirmed by intuitive wisdom through the ages and confirmed by scientific research findings. In short, it is healthy to laugh at oneself and with others. Humor is a God-given survival resource and a source of healthy cultural resistance that contributes to physical, mental, spiritual, and relational health.

Balancing work with healthy recreation (that is really re-creating) makes work more satisfying as well as more productive. Unfortunately much so-called recreation should be described as "wreck-creation" because it militates against overall wellness. Playful attitudes and practices can help people in high-pressure workplaces prevent burnout by reducing their stress levels. All this underlines the importance of helping people learn to play in health-nurturing ways and laugh in the midst of their tears and frustrations. Religious caregivers can create opportunities to use humor creatively in healing ways in their marriage and family caregiving and educative counseling, although it should always be appropriate to the feelings and topics of the moment.

VII. Healing and Wholeness in Society and Nature

To be both holistic and effective today, caregiving must often include coaching care receivers to offer care to their community and to the earth around them. For them to do so increases the probability, to some small degree, that all children of the human family and all other species will inherit a healthy planet on which they have the best opportunities to live healthy lives. By encouraging care for these interdependent social and natural environments, caregiving becomes more scripturally faithful as well as more holistic.

Society

The societal side of the seventh dimension aims at healing and enhancing the growthfulness of institutions and social systems. In the twentieth century, individualistic pastoral caregiving often focused primarily on privatized healing reinforced by privatized salvation seeking. This tended to ignore the pervasive ways that the intertwining oppressions of racism, sexism, homophobia, violence, ageism, classism, speciesism, nationalism, militarism, political oppression, economic exploitation and poverty, and other injustices diminish human wholeness in widespread ways in our society and across the globe. As we have said elsewhere, "The reality is that women and men still live out their lives in a world that is profoundly sexist, racist, ageist, classist, and heterosexist and that these harmful dynamics are at the heart of much of the distress and 'pathology' that is brought to the pastoral counselor."[20]

Richard Voss, an astute pastoral psychotherapist and clinical social worker, is on target in declaring that pastoral counselors need to be aware that "a 'therapy' that does not confront and challenge violence, exploitation, or otherwise abusive behavior, may tacitly reinforce it and actually be counter-therapeutic."[21] To correct this caregiving myopia, pastoral care of, to, and through social groups and institutions must be practiced whenever possible as an essential part of truly holistic healing. When this occurs, Christians are responding to Jesus' call to become the salt of the earth and light for the world.

Prophetic pastoral caregiving of oppressed individuals and families often includes the consciousness-raising. This means helping them become aware of the social roots of their pain, brokenness, and truncated lives so that they stop blaming themselves inappropriately for causes over which they have had little or no control. It may also mean cultivating prophetic healing and growth that enable people to generate action resources within themselves and in groups of oppressed people and faith communities. The overall aim is to free, motivate, and equip people to join hands with others to make the families, congregations, communities, and significant institutions in their lives places where wholeness is cultivated more effectively and mutually in everyone.

Prophetic caregiving aims at empowerment. Rather than seeking to enable care receivers to adjust to the procrustean beds of sick institutions, it coaches them in developing strengths that they can use to enable these institutions to become less oppressive. As people deal with their personal problems, they gain strength that can be used in challenging and changing oppressive situations. As care receivers develop inner strengths, some choose to work with others in changing the oppressive collective causes of their individual problems. Their social advocacy and activism become a vital aspect of holistic caregiving, aimed at the intertwining well-being of individuals, institutions, churches, and cultures. The inner soul journey of individual pastoral caregiving and this outer, justice-based caregiving are mutually reinforcing.

The key to prophetic living and caregiving can be described as the Gandhi-Day-King-Lee principle. What did these persons have in common: Mahatma Gandhi, nonviolent freedom crusader in India; Dorothy Day, courageous leader of the Catholic Worker ministry to the oppressed; Martin Luther King Jr., Nobel laureate and civil rights prophet; and Tai-Young Lee, lawyer crusader for women's and human rights in South Korea?[22] In radically different spiritual and cultural contexts, their inspired and inspiring lives embodied an empowering passion for personal and spiritual growth with courageous, passionate justice that helped transform social malignancies. Following their example can help correct the weakness of privatized pastoral caregiving by integrating personal healing and growth with the confrontation of injustices. To do so is difficult but possible and rewarding.

Nature

The other major expression of the prophetic dimension of holistic caregiving is interdependent with and as crucial with the first. It is ecotherapeutic caregiving. This involves enabling care receivers to experience the healing energies of the earth regularly and deeply and then to respond by helping heal God's wounded world. These practices embody the spirit of Albert Schweitzer's wise observation: "As we know life in ourselves, we want to understand life in the universe, in order to enter into harmony with it."[23] In our machine-dominated society of megacities, countless people suffer some degree of what has been termed *ecological autism*.[24] That is, their sensual awareness and nurturing interaction with the living planet are blunted. Such earth alienation has two aspects. People are alienated from the earth in their inner feelings and also in their outer relationship with the natural world.

Caregivers and care receivers should work to enhance their own health and that of those they love by caring for the living earth around them. Through many eons, people have experienced the wisdom of opening themselves fully to the wholeness-nurturing energies in God's wonder-filled continuous creating. Now, physicians specializing in environmental medicine have discovered convincing evidence that higher levels of wellness for everyone are ultimately dependent on living in a healthy natural environment. Religious caregivers should give themselves the gift of frequent nurturing interaction with nature and encourage care receivers and students to do the same. People are often surprised when they experience nature's good gifts of increased energy and aliveness—physically, mentally, spiritually, and relationally. As they enjoy being nurtured by nature, intimately and intentionally, they often experience God's living presence there. Their love for the earth tends to increase spontaneously, motivating them to join likeminded people in helping to heal the environmental brokenness around, and also within, them. The reciprocal healing of ourselves and the earth is another demonstration of the circular wisdom and enlightened self-interest of prophetic caregiving.

This caregiving innovation could not be more timely. Around the planet, increasing urbanization, industrialization, toxic chemical production, deforestation, overpopulation, and overconsumption feed widespread alienation from an enlivening relationship with nature. In the brief span of one century (the twentieth) the global population more than tripled and world economies together increased some nineteenfold twenty-eight times.[25] As a result of these runaway forces, our species exhausted almost a third of the planet's limited natural resources by shortsighted unsustainable living. At the same time, the virtual realities of the world of television, computers, and the Internet cause many people, especially young people, to distance themselves from life-energizing relationships with nature, as well as from mutually nurturing human relationships.

Religious leaders and caregivers in all faith traditions have indispensable roles in helping to heal God's wounded earth and the social pathology of injustices because the deepest causes of the global ecojustice crisis are spiritual and ethical, a key domain for religious leaders. In this unprecedented time of crisis around the planet, leaders in all the healing, teaching, and religious professions are challenged to make their unique contributions to helping save the earth, the only home where all the children of the human family and God's other living creatures can live healthy lives through all future generations. The wisdom of the Hebrew Scriptures makes clear that social injustices are at the roots of environmental destruction. Learning and using the skills of prophetic caregiving on this challenging frontier of our field should be a motivating passion for holistic caregivers. We will explore this challenge further in the next chapter.

The two-part seventh dimension of prophetic caregiving should influence the ways all the basic types of care and counseling are done. It includes making a commitment to two interdependent subgoals. The first is to motivate and train ourselves and our congregations to do everything possible to make institutions in our society more just, caring, and growth nurturing. The second is to do everything possible to protect and enhance the health of our natural environment. The good news is that people are often motivated to make their lifestyles more earth caring and justice cultivating when they discover that doing so is a path to whole-person health for themselves and their children. Seeing that the social and natural worlds right around them have an impact on wellness or sickness in all seven dimensions of their own and their children's lives is like turning on a light in a dark room. It is clear that prophetic caregiving can contribute significantly to the health of individuals and their world. Clearly, this prophetic outreach expression of pastoral care is innovative, crucial, and challenging.[26]

Using the Seven-Dimensions Model in Caregiving

Having now looked briefly at each of the seven dimensions of holistic caregiving, it is well to reemphasize that these are different dimensions of everyone's life. People's degrees of wholeness or brokenness are influenced continually by interacting among these dimensions and with other individuals, groups, and natural systems. Increasing wellness in any of the seven dimensions tends to nurture growth-in-wholeness in the other areas.

But is this multidimensional model really useful in light of the fact that most congregations are relatively small, served by one clergyperson whose caregiving must, consequently, be somewhat limited? Is this model of the basic dimensions of human brokenness, healing, and growth relevant in such contexts, or does it simply complicate caregivers' tasks? The answer to these questions is illuminated by seeing the model simply as a flexible perspective, a set of glasses with which to see people and their problems holistically. It provides a cognitive map that helps caregivers become aware of important dimensions of people's lives hidden behind the problems that motivated them to seek help. It also reminds one to look beyond the three dimensions on which traditional pastoral caregiving has focused—spiritual, psychological, and relational—and to consider exploring one or more of the other four where hidden resources or problems may exist. Subsequent chapters in this book will from, time to time, illustrate ways in which these seven dimensions can be woven into pastoral counseling interviews as well as educational counseling and everyday pastoral caregiving.

Enlarging Classical Pastoral Care Functions

In their overview of evolving pastoral caregiving during the first twenty centuries of the Christian story, church historian William A. Clebsch and pastoral care specialist Charles R. Jaekle lifted up the four classical pastoral caregiving functions:[27]

- Healing care—"a pastoral function that aims to overcome some impairment by restoring the person to wholeness and by leading him [or her] to advance beyond his [or her] previous condition."
- Sustaining care—"helping a hurting person to endure and to transcend a circumstance in which restoration to his [or her] malady is either impossible or so remote as to seem improbable."
- Guiding care—"assisting perplexed persons to make confident choices between alternative courses of thought and action, when such choices are viewed as affecting the present and future state of the soul."
- Reconciling care—"seeks to re-establish broken relationships between [person] and fellow [person] and between [humanity] and God." Historically reconciling has employed two modes—forgiveness and discipline.

In today's world, two other vital pastoral care functions have strategic importance. These intertwine with the traditional four and, like them, are deeply rooted in the long history of caregiving ministries:

- Nurturing care—this caregiving process seeks to enable persons to discover their unique gifts and graces and to find the resources to develop these, throughout their lives. In traditional theological language, this ongoing growth process has been called "sanctification"—a response to God's great gift of wholeness. Although nurturing occurs frequently in the other four functions as well as in religious education, it also is a distinct and crucial pastoral care function. Nurturing and guiding are the caregiving functions in which education and counseling are most intertwined.

- Prophetic care—the aim of this function is to give care to and through the social systems that profoundly influence people's lives, their hurting and healing, and the degree of well-being they develop in all seven dimensions of wholeness. The ultimate aim of prophetic caregiving is to motivate and equip care recipients to be agents of constructive change in the wider social and natural pathologies that are among the causes and contexts of their need for care.

Caregiving, as understood in this model, is effective to the degree that it nurtures healing and wholeness in care receivers and, through them, in the persons, institutions, and natural systems that their lives touch. As this occurs, people become better able to handle constructively the losses, demands, and responsibilities in their lives. The model emphasizes enabling care receivers to continue developing their unique personal resources at each life stage centered in meaningful life-guiding values and a growing relationship with God. In these ways, care receivers increase their ability to be agents of reconciliation, healing, and wholeness in their families, communities, and churches.

Recommended Reading

Dinkins, Burrell David. *Narrative Pastoral Counseling*. Longwood, Fla.: Xulon Press, 2005.

Eisland, Nancy. *The Disabled God*. Nashville: Abingdon Press, 1997.

Lartey, Emmanuel. *In Living Color: An Intercultural Approach to Pastoral Care and Counseling*. 2nd ed. London: Jessica Kingsley Publishers, 2003.

Purnell, Douglas. *Conversation as Ministry: Stories and Strategies for Confident Caregiving*. Cleveland: Pilgrim Press, 2003.

Ramsay, Nancy, ed. *Pastoral Care and Counseling: Redefining the Paradigms*. Nashville: Abingdon Press, 2004.

Stone, Howard. *Strategies for Brief Pastoral Counseling*. Minneapolis: Augsburg Fortress Press, 2001.

CHAPTER 3

THE HISTORY, MISSION, AND THEOLOGICAL-BIBLICAL FOUNDATIONS OF PASTORAL CAREGIVING

Pastoral caregiving is a sturdy plant with deep roots in time-tested wisdom from the past enhanced by contemporary psychosocial knowledge and healing methods. The current flowering of pastoral caregiving should not cause us to ignore our precious heritage. It is crucial that pastoral caregivers let their identity be shaped and enriched by seeing themselves as rooted in a long, rich heritage. Attempting to give viable care in the present and plan for an emerging future without some sense of the past is like trying to plant cut flowers.[1] Knowing that we are walking in the footsteps of a long line of dedicated caregivers stretching back over at least three millennia can impart a sense of strong identity when we do caring counseling with troubled people. We walk, however falteringly, in the footsteps of a young Jewish carpenter whose words and touch brought about wholeness in persons with many kinds of problems in the first century, Jesus walked in the footsteps of "wise guides" and the courageous prophetic caregivers of his Hebrew tradition.

The counseling ministry of clergy and lay caregivers acquires a depth dimension if they sense that they are part of a heritage that includes such great pastors as John Chrysostom (347–407), Ambrose of Milan (340–397), Martin Luther (1483–1546), Hildegard of Bingen (1098–1179), Richard Baxter (1615–1691), Horace Bushnell (1802–1876), Washington Gladden (1836–1918), and Harry Emerson Fosdick (1878–1969).

Religious caregivers today can draw inspiration and energy from knowing that they are part of humankind's most ancient caring and healing heritage that combined the roles of religious leader and physician-healers; but caregivers also should learn all that they can from contemporary theological, sociological, and psychological sources. In addition, their self-identity as counselors should be shaped as much by the time-validated wisdom of caregivers as by recent psychotherapies. Their use of relevant therapeutic resources should be guided by theological critiques of the philosophical assumptions implicit in all such healing modalities.

Looking back over the years since the early twentieth century, we can see that the convergence of four streams has fed the flourishing of the modern pastoral care and counseling movement: (1) the deepening understanding of human dynamics from the social, psychological, and biomedical sciences; (2) the transforming revolution sparked by the clinical pastoral education movement; (3) creative psychotherapeutic theories and practices beginning with Freud; and (4) the new insights from creative pastoral theologies of ministry. These streams continue to flow together, enhancing the century-spanning stream of pastoral caregiving. The ancient plant of pastoral caregiving has been watered abundantly from this river, producing new growth. It is hoped that this flowering will continue, offering the promise that it will continue to increase.[2]

The modern pastoral care movement had its early roots in the application of the new science of psychology to ministry during the early decades of the twentieth century. It gained a major impetus in the mid-1920s with the pioneering contributions of Anton Boisen, Richard Cabot, Philip Guiles, and Russell Dicks, who began the clinical pastoral education (CPE) movement. Out of their own illnesses—Boisen's psychotic episodes and Dicks's tuberculosis of the bone—these two chaplains began to train seminary students and pastors in mental and general hospitals.[3] The students cared for persons in severe crises and learned through in-depth mentoring by trained chaplain supervisors. This approach fueled a reform movement in ministry that moved away from moralizing theologies and superficial advice giving and toward more psychologically informed theories and practice. It transformed pastoral theology from being a mainly theoretical discipline to one that was clinically informed and strengthened.

The focus on counseling surged with the strong wave of interest in psychology and psychotherapy after World War II. The pathology orientation of early psychoanalysis and the treatment settings within which most CPE occurred caused pastoral counseling to be heavily pathology oriented during its early years. However, the influence of Carl Rogers during this period gave it some balance through an emphasis on growth centeredness. Both the psychoanalytic and Rogerian influences tended to make the formal psychotherapeutic interview with intrapsychic insight the dominant goal normative in the early years of pastoral counseling.

The "revised model" in the first (1966) edition of this book aimed at enlarging this guiding image of pastoral counseling by adding more relational, active, behavioral, and pastoral emphases. The second revision (1984) continued this process as it also sought greater inclusivity. In keeping with these emphases, this latest revision offers an evolving guiding image that is more multidimensional, holistic, growth centered, systemic, multicultural, and liberation oriented, reflecting insights of nondominant groups such as women and racial/ethnic minority caregivers. It draws on the systematic critiques and multicultural analysis of contemporary pastoral theologians; nevertheless, this model remains deeply rooted in our spiritual heritage and pastoral identity.[4]

Doing Theology in Pastoral Care and Counseling

Christie C. Neuger identified three primary functions of pastoral theology in caregiving: (1) as a source of commitment in one's operational theology and spiritual practice that guide one's pastoral attitudes and actions; (2) as an assessment lens for the caregiver, guiding the kinds of questions asked and the perspective on situations that help reveal the spiritual dimensions of people's counseling issues; and (3) as that which generates resources such as scriptural stories, meaningful rituals, sacramental ministry, and prayer.[5]

The interaction between the practice of pastoral caregiving and our theological-biblical heritage should be a two-way interchange. Insights from the heritage illuminate, inform, correct, and guide the practice of the caregiving art, while this practice brings to life basic biblical truths as they become incarnate in caregiving relationships. The truths are illuminated by being applied and tested in the arena of human struggles and losses and that of growth, wholeness, and transformation. Furthermore, traditions are challenged and reinterpreted as they encounter a widening variety of human experiences with many unique particularities. New understandings of healing and brokenness, growth and wholeness, continue to inform and reshape the visions guiding caregiving practice.

In pastoral care and counseling relationships, caregivers struggle as partners with care receivers while engaging in the dialogue between traditions and contemporary culture on a practical and deeply personal level. This practice occurs whether or not theological or biblical words are used to describe the issues. In our secular-minded society, religious issues are not always so identified, but nonetheless they are hidden in the heart of all spiritually aware caring and counseling. Sin and salvation, alienation and communion, shame and reconciliation, guilt and forgiveness, judgment and grace, spiritual death and rebirth, despair and joy-bringing hope—all these are interwoven into the fabric of the healing-growthing interaction of caregivers and care receivers. It is in these ways that pastoral care and counseling are methods of doing theology experientially.

It should not be surprising that truths from the Hebrew and Christian Scriptures and stories can come alive in the living experiences of pastoral caregiving. To the degree that people find release, through counseling or psychotherapy, from the captivity of their inner conflicts and self-idolatry, they can then build bridges over chasms of alienation from others, increase their ability to give as well as receive love, seek justice and wholeness in the world, and learn to live the joys and sorrows of life in all its fullness—to that extent the caregiving relationship has embodied the theological wisdom that helps struggling human beings move toward healing and wholeness. Thus an effective caring/counseling relationship brings alive the mystery of the continuing incarnation of the spirit of the creating God in the lives of hurting but hoping people.

Biblical Roots and Resources for Holistic Caregiving

This chapter aims at providing a biblically grounded theology as a foundation of the operational model described in the previous chapter. It does this by shedding light on these key questions:

1. What are the biblical images, insights, and narratives that provide foundations for a theological understanding of wholeness-oriented caring and counseling?
2. What biblical insights can come alive for caregivers and care receivers in their dialogue?
3. With what theological themes can caregivers stay in dialogue to illuminate and energize this ministry?

There are several reasons to integrate biblically grounded theological insights with the practice of holistic ministry. First, both the Hebrew Scriptures and the New Testament are primary wellsprings of our Western spiritual traditions. Staying connected with biblical truths understood from the perspective of critical biblical scholarship, as one creates one's working pastoral theology, can keep it firmly rooted. Second, a biblically based theology provides a focus of commitment and authority for the caregiver. Third, being in ongoing dialogue with biblical insights can generate attitudes and awareness in the caring person that facilitate healing and growth in wholeness. Fourth, in working with persons who have even limited biblical literacy, caregivers can use the archetypal images and truths of the Bible as resources for creative change. These truth encounters can provide sustaining power, particularly for socially disempowered people who love the Bible. Fifth, biblical wisdom about wholeness is needed to critique, correct, complement, and enrich contemporary understandings of wholeness in our psychologized culture.[6]

****

What follow are biblical themes and commentary that together constitute a working theology of caregiving.

1. *Jesus the Christ, as understood by mainstream Christians, is a paradigm of spiritually empowered wholeness.* Beyond seeing him as a gifted teacher of liberating truths and an empowering healer, they regard him as actually living life in all its fullness. In this he

demonstrated concretely the full possibilities of humans empowered by God. In him one meets a liberated, fully alive, love-filled, God-centered, growing person who makes visible God's dream of unfolding healing and wholeness for the whole human family. The divine purpose is embodied so that the Spirit of the universe is no longer distanced from our human situation.

When people touched Jesus' life, they experienced in him the healing power that comes from openness to oneself, others, God, and God's whole creation. They encountered a person whose life was a deepening channel through whom the creative spirit of God's love and justice, the wellspring of all healing and wholeness, flowed freely and fully. What do people experience when they touch our lives? Asking this troubling question today usually challenges us caregivers. Perhaps the noisy static of our overstretched lives in harried times obscures Jesus' transforming aliveness that for many Christians somehow transcends the centuries. I remember Paul Tillich referring to this wholeness-nurturing reality as the "new being." Experiencing this new being cultivates growth into "the full stature of Christ" (Eph. 4:13 NEB) by developing our unique expression of life in all its fullness.

2. *Holistic healing is a fundamental dimension of religion.* Biblical wisdom affirms the whole-person understanding of healing and the good life. Healing of many forms of human brokenness (including sickness and grief) is a persistent motif in the Bible. Nearly one-fifth of the four Gospels deals with stories of Jesus' healings. Because of his healing presence and ministry, Jesus was known in New Testament times and throughout much of church history as "the great physician" (Matt. 9:12; Mark 2:17). His healing ministry was grounded in the Jewish holistic tradition as shown by the fact that he healed persons with all types of illnesses and disabilities—physical, psychological, emotional, psychosomatic, relational, and spiritual. He restored the sight of both the physically and the spiritually blinded, quieted people's fears and anxieties, and with great courage, stood up for justice. Jesus' strong commitment to healing is reflected in the imagery of his response to the religious leaders who criticized him for eating with the despised tax collectors and other sinners: "Those who are well have no need of a physician, but those who are sick" (Mark 2:17). The importance that Jesus attached to responding to the needs of each individual is highlighted in his teaching story of the shepherd who left ninety-nine sheep in order to look for the lost one.

In various ways, Jesus revealed that healing and wholeness are the divine purpose and the birthright of all of God's children. His attitude underlines the importance of recovering today the oft-neglected ministry of healing by using a whole-person-in-community approach. Certainly holistic pastoral care and counseling are effective ways to participate in this vital recovery.

3. *Healing and salvation are interdependent and complementary.* Salvation and healing are often intertwined in the Bible, both being understood as gifts of a just and loving God. Daniel Day Williams makes it clear that the language of salvation and the language of healing are interlaced throughout the Bible, though the two are not identical.[7] Williams defines salvation as fulfillment for a person "in a new relationship to God and neighbor in which the threats of death, of meaninglessness, of unrelieved guilt, are overcome. To be saved is to know that one's life belongs with God and has a fulfillment in him for eternity."[8] Salvation is understood in the New Testament as a kind of ultimate healing that takes place in the transforming age of wholeness (the kingdom of God), which is already dawning within and among us. Spirit-centered caregiving seeks to cultivate this healing.

4. *We humans possess rich, God-given capacities for living life in all its fullness, and we have a spiritual responsibility to discover and develop these gifts.* The biblical record affirms repeatedly the remarkable gifts human beings possess. The psalmist describes humans as created "a little lower than God" (Ps. 8:5). The first of the two creation stories in Genesis asserts that we are made in the image or likeness of God (Gen. 1:27). This statement is a ringing affirmation of humankind's creative, loving, self-transcending spiritual potential. A primary goal of Christian living is to grow our personhood in the likeness of the divine by developing more of the remarkable gifts and graces we possess as members of a blessed species. Facilitating this development is the ultimate purpose of all ministry, including pastoral care and counseling.

Careseekers who have suffered social oppression face special challenges in moving toward this goal. We experience and interpret our relationship with God primarily through the images of God we carry. When the possibilities for those images are limited, especially by what the culture values in terms of maleness, power, and whiteness, we are limited in being able to experience God's unlimited abundance. This has been a particular problem for women. Although it is not necessary here to reiterate all of the insights that feminist theology has provided regarding the problems we have as a culture with dominant imagery for God, it is enough to say that the images we carry about God are critical not only to experiencing the divine presence but also to understanding ourselves, our place in creation, and God's ongoing intentions for our world.[9] The good news according to John describes Jesus' purpose in coming in these hope-generating terms— to enable people to have "life . . . in all its fullness" (John 10:10 NEB).

Jesus' parable of the talents (Matt. 25:14-30) is a dramatic statement of the importance of developing God's gifts wisely and fully and in socially responsible ways. That story also highlights the cost of neglecting to develop and grow our many gifts. In his second letter to Timothy, Paul identifies the transcendent source as well as the transfornational goal of the wholeness process. He challenges Timothy, a younger leader in the early church, "to stir into flame the gift of God which is within [him]. . . . For the spirit that God gave us is . . . one to inspire strength, love, and self-discipline" (2 Tim. 1:6-7 NEB).

An important caution is needed at this point. Psychologist Rollo May identified a problem raised by emphasizing or prescribing self-actualization in counseling and therapy. He observed that saying to people that their possibilities are unlimited can be de-energizing, even frightening: "It is like putting someone into a canoe and pushing him into the Atlantic toward England with the cheery comment, 'The sky's the limit.' The canoer is only too aware of the fact that an inescapably real limit is also the bottom of the ocean."[10]

Holding in mind that our wholeness is limited by our finitude and by the unchangeable, frustrating "givens" of our lives can help us keep a healthy awareness of our ultimate vulnerability. These givens include our genetic assets and liabilities; our familial, sociocultural, and historical contexts; and our physical limitations and disabilities. Surrendering denials of our finitude involves letting go of grandiose illusions of invulnerability. But this surrender brings the reward of relief from the colossal responsibility that invulnerability imposes.

5. *Cultivating healing and wholeness effectively requires enabling people to deal with their violence, brokenness, destructiveness, and sinfulness.* To minister in healing ways to the multiple forms of human brokenness encountered in pastoral care and counseling today, caregivers need to have a tough, realistic understanding of this potentially destructive side of human beings and their social institutions. In today's violence-addicted world, pastoral caregivers must have effective strategies for dealing with the potentially destructive capacities of human beings. We humans hunger to develop the spiritual capacities of our souls as well as remarkable capacities to develop spiritual gifts that give us something of the divine likeness. But biblical stories make it crystal clear that we are not God. In fact, we often misuse our creative intelligence and ingenuity to sabotage our growth and that of countless others. Powerful conflicts in our deeper minds can block our conscious healthy intentions. Paul reflected this conflict in his candid confession to the little band of Christians in first-century Rome: "I do not understand my own actions. . . . For I do not do the good I want, but the evil I do not want is what I do" (Rom. 7:15, 19).

Biblical writers were keenly aware of the destructiveness of stymied growth that makes many people caricatures of the creative selves they have the potential to be. Mental illnesses were understood to be caused by the invasion of evil spirits. But while rejecting this prescientific "demonic" destructiveness of severe mental, spiritual, ethical, and relationship illnesses, it is also important to recognize the demonic destructiveness in the social insanity of institutionalized racism, sexism, and militarism, as well as the wounding of the health of the entire global environment by massive pollution, over-population, and economic injustice. In understanding the depths of the human mind, it is vital to be aware of the creative energies and resources in the hidden self that is the unconscious mind. Getting acquainted with (or befriending) both the potentially destructive and the creative sides of our deeper selves and integrating their resources with each other and with our conscious resources can enhance our total minds and diminish our inner sources of destructiveness.

The biblical view of human evil offers a healthy corrective to the superficial optimism that sometimes appears in humanistic psychologies. The Bible reflects awareness that our estrangement from ourselves, others, and nature is somehow rooted in our estrange-ment from God's life-giving love and justice. Freud called the ingenious ways humans block their own healing and growth "resistance." Carl Jung labeled the unattractive, rejected side of people's selves our "shadow" side. But whatever it is called, dealing with this recalcitrant reality is crucial in all effective pastoral care and counseling.

The story of the "fall" from the innocence of the Garden of Eden (Gen. 3) is a mythic way of communicating the fact that we are alienated from the divine and, therefore, from the spiritual source of our potential wholeness. To paraphrase Tillich's insight: humans are estranged from the ground of their being, from other beings, and from them-selves.[11] *Sin* is the traditional religious word for this spiritual alienation and the result-ant proclivity to inflict violence on ourselves, other people, society, and nature.

One of several interpretations of the fall in classical theology is that it refers to a deep, inborn, irreparable flaw in our humanity that tends to sabotage our strivings toward wholeness. This interpretation is deeply problematic from a pastoral psychology perspective. Clinical evidence shows that when the deep roots of evil behavior are healed, or the social environment that bred evil becomes more constructive, perpetra-tors are often freed to live more constructive lives. It *is* meaningful, however, to under-stand the fall as a powerful metaphor pointing to the fact that all humans and their contexts suffer from some degree of personal, interpersonal, and societal brokenness and alienation.

I remember the sickening shock of standing in the crematorium at Buchenwald in what was then East Germany. That was the region from which my maternal ancestors probably migrated to become farmers in southern Illinois. That ghastly death camp and the homes of Goethe, Luther, and Bach, not far away, symbolize the psychological prox-imity of the diabolical destructiveness and the potential grandeur of which we humans are capable. If we make the mistake of underestimating the power of human evil, alienation, and destructiveness in ourselves and others, our effectiveness will be diminished as agents of reconciliation and healing through caregiving and education.

Although our caregiving sometimes nurtures surprising healing and growth, this wholeness is at best only partial. Our best efforts are too often ineffective. At worst, they can, against our good intentions, be harmful. Counseling, therapy, and teaching are imperfect arts, used by us imperfect human beings, who live in an imperfect society and work in imperfect faith communities. Furthermore, many careseekers suffer from psychological, interpersonal, and spiritual damage so deep and prolonged that resistances to healing and growth are extremely powerful. However caring, creative, and competent we may be as caregivers, what is the best that can be hoped for? It is that deeply wounded people may gain enough strength and serenity to accept and live more constructively with whatever cannot be changed in their lives.

Yet it is crucial always to remember that the powerful *resistances* to growth, as understood in the biblical heritage, are seen in the context of the more powerful *resources* for growth. Sin is viewed in the wider context of salvation, despair in the context of hope, dying in the context of resurrection, and judgment in the context of grace.

6. *Struggle, intentionality, disciplined hard work, and sacrifice are often required in order to actualize God's gift of growing in wholeness.* Because of resistances, counselees often learn that healing brokenness and moving toward wholeness take more disciplined efforts than they could have imagined when they began the process. It usually takes strenuous effort to actualize God's grace. Christianity is not just a set of beliefs; it is a constructive direction for traveling on one's life journey. Jesus' statements to individuals were full of action imperatives. The New Testament affirmation that salvation is by grace through faith (Rom. 3:25) is a liberating truth. It is especially so for those of us who are trapped on the works-righteousness treadmill, feverishly seeking to earn a sense of worth by collecting achievements. The message of grace is also freeing when we have struggled to change our lives but failed miserably. The awareness that we can "accept ourselves as being accepted by God" (Tillich) awakens hope and liberates energy for creative change. This experience of grace *with responsibility*, in contrast to cheap grace, can produce inner transformation, enhancing self-esteem and a sense of aliveness. Behavior generated by grace stands in sharp contrast to behavior changed by a guilt-driven conscience that produces controlling moralism and rigid oughts and shoulds. The recognition that the capacity, energy, and inherent élan for growth are gifts from God can help save healing and wholeness nurturers from believing that any growth entirely depends on them.

The rich New Testament image of resurrection is a joyful affirmation of the powerful possibilities of new and fulfilling living. But the process of growth toward this enlivened quality of life often feels like a series of painful deaths and rebirthing struggles. The

Easter experience of rebirth to greater aliveness and larger dimensions of liberating truth seems possible only after the death of some of our narcissism and defenses against the risk of coming alive more fully. The struggle and eventual joy of the process of human transformation are communicated in this moving image attributed to Jesus: "You will be sorrowful, but your sorrow will turn into joy. When a woman is in travail she has sorrow, . . . but when she is delivered of the child, she no longer remembers the anguish, for joy that a child is born into the world" (John 16:20-21 RSV).

7. *Wholeness is a lifelong growth journey.* It is a process of healing, learning, moving ahead, and slipping back. The psalmist used a growth image to liken a good person to "a tree planted by streams of water, that yields its fruit in its season" (Ps. 1:3 RSV). The growth parables of Jesus elaborate on his understanding of this theme—the woman putting yeast in bread dough (Matt. 13:33), the farmer sowing seeds (Matt. 13:3-8), and the tiny mustard seed's remarkable growth (Matt. 13:31-32). The farming image sheds hope on both the possibilities and the resistances to growth in counseling and education. Some of the seeds we plant will fall on unreceptive soil or be crowded out by weeds in the lives and social environment of people's lives. But the seeds that fall in fertile, receptive soil will produce abundant food for nourishing recipients' healing and wholeness.

8. *Healing and wholeness are cultivated best in the soil of relationships where healing affirmation and caring confrontation are experienced together.* Pastoral caregivers need to put on the bifocal glasses of growth that enable them to see the hidden problems and the possibilities in persons whose unique wholeness they seek to nurture. Creative change occurs in relationships in which recipients experience unearned love and accountability for the ways they are hurting themselves and others. The Apostle Paul highlights this experience in his invitation to the first-century Christians in Ephesus: "Let us speak the truth in love; so shall we fully grow up into Christ" (Eph. 4:15 NEB). This love is essential in all pastoral care and counseling if they are to result in healing and growth in wholeness.

Caregivers should never use confrontation to impose their opinions on others. But it is constructive when used to lift up honestly the people-hurting attitudes and actions of care receivers. Jesus' relationships embodied this mode. He cared deeply but with confronting honesty for all kinds of men and women, including society's powerless outcasts, the mentally and spiritually ill, the sick and sinners, and the marginalized poor. He related to people in terms of what they could become as well as what they were. It is no wonder that ordinary people welcomed his message and responded to him in extraordinary, growthful ways.

9. *Cultivating healing and growth involves giving back.* Jesus articulated the principle of growth through reaching out in these words to the learners who sought his wisdom: "For

those who want to save their life will lose it, and those who lose their life for my sake will find it. For what will it profit them if they gain the whole world but forfeit their life?" (Matt. 16:25-26). Translated into contemporary terms, if people narcissistically hoard whatever wholeness they have developed, it will atrophy. In contrast, if they use the healing and growth they experience to reach out to share these gifts, they may contribute something to the healing and growth of others. In so doing, they will open the door to experience profound spiritual satisfaction and even personal growth. This is the surprising gift of becoming small channels for carrying God's healing, transforming power into the lives of other hurting humans.

10. *All of us are to participate in discerning and living out God's call to greater wholeness.* The New Testament understanding sees healing in the context of a new age developing from wholeness-generating relationships with God. In the hierarchical language of the biblical culture, this new age is called the "kingdom of God." This vision of the new age is one of caring, conscience, and community in which equality, justice, and wholeness flourish. In our day the theme of nonhierarchical, redemptive community is better expressed by the "kin-dom of God."[12] The vision goes far beyond personal healing and wholeness to include social well-being: a vision of whole persons, in loving and just communities; in a healthy, peaceful society; on a healthy planet.

Wholeness-oriented pastoral caregiving should include opportunities to learn how to become active participants in the already dawning age of wholeness. A vision of a transformed future is important in counseling with both troubled and growth-hungering individuals because it stimulates constructive action energized by reality-based hope. When faith communities share such a vision, it can and should motivate prophetic caregiving and other creative action by its members.

Biblical-Theological Foundations of the Seven Dimensions

The model of wholeness proposed in this text locates itself in the seven dimensions of life named in chapter 2. It's helpful to spend a few pages looking at theological and biblical themes that address those multiple dimensions.

1. The Spiritual and Ethical

These, the primary and integrating dimension of caregiving, are at the very core of the biblical understanding of the nature of life in all its fullness. Wholeness, like life, is a gift of the creating Spirit of the universe. The power of the universe energizes and supports the fulfillment of our God-given potentiality. The growth élan in every acorn makes it strive to become an oak tree. In every person it provides the longing to become more alive and well. It is as though the gravitational pull of the spiritual universe is drawing us toward becoming what we have the possibility to become. Biblical scholar J. B. Phillips paraphrases Romans 8:19 this way: "The whole creation is on tiptoe to see the wonderful sight of the sons [and daughters] of God coming into their own." When we seek to nurture wholeness in ourselves and others, we partner with the divine intention as we seek to enable God's gifts to flower in all dimensions of persons' lives.

We can be thankful that we need not and, in fact, cannot create either the potential for growth or the élan within people that makes them strive to grow. Both are there as gifts from God. As wholeness-oriented counselors, we work to help people respond to the hunger for wholeness that is available to them. Paul's words can be reassuring as well as humbling to us as counselors and educators: "I planted, Apollos watered, but God gave the growth" (1 Cor. 3:6). By aligning our best efforts with the creating Spirit, we become cocreators of wholeness. Healing, caring relationships become channels for the grace of God, the transforming love that is the source of all salvation and all wholeness (Gal. 2:8; Rom. 3:23-31). The ultimate source of wholeness is identified clearly in Paul's letter in this wonderful statement to the church at Ephesus: "May your roots go down deep into the soil of God's marvelous love" (Eph. 3:17 TLB). Caregivers' or teachers' awareness that growth toward wholeness is a gift can free them from the inappropriate notion that effectiveness or failure in their ministry is entirely the result of their own efforts.

2. Mental Healing and Wholeness Foundations

The second dimension of life in all its fullness is undergirded by the biblical injunction quoted by Jesus from his Hebrew Scriptures—to love God with "all your heart, and with all your soul, and with all your mind, and with all your strength" (Mark 12:30). Loving God with one's total personality highlights the importance of the intellectual as well as the emotional and spiritual. Loving God with one's mind involves the continuing unfolding of one's mental and emotional potentialities through lifelong learning and using this to reach out in service to a world starving for truth. In caregiving, all around the healing-growth spiral, the challenge is to keep the educative counseling, learning and relearning ingredient focused and strong.

3. Physical Healing and Wholeness Foundations

The physical dimension, as understood in the Hebrew perspective, regards persons in nondualistic, social systemic terms. Wholeness involves the unity of whole persons— bodies, minds, and spirits—in their communities. New Testament images depict the body of believers as "a temple of the Holy Spirit within you, which you have from God." Paul extrapolates from this view to challenge the Christians in Corinth to "glorify God in [their bodies]" (1 Cor. 6:19-20). These texts reflect a high view of the physical body that undergirds nurturing physical wholeness.

But the Bible is also clear that the body's health is not essential for either mental or spiritual wholeness, though it is valuable for both. A remarkable fact about humans is that most persons with major, even multiple, disabilities have the capacity to integrate their physical limitations and develop their potentialities for intellectual acumen, creative productivity, and spiritual maturity.

4. Foundations for Healing and Wholeness of Relationships

Relationality is a strong motif in both testaments. Wholeness is seen as nurtured in honest, caring, loving relationships. The second Great Commandment quoted by Jesus demonstrates the relational nature of the Christian way: "You shall love your neighbor as yourself" (Mark 12:31 from Lev. 19:18, 34). Jesus chooses a despised Samaritan as the hero of the parable to redefine in a more inclusive way who one's neighbor is.

The characteristics of wholeness-cultivating love are also described in one of the most loved biblical passages—the great hymn to love in 1 Corinthians 13, often read during wedding celebrations. The ringing refrain in the last verse—"the greatest of these is love"—expresses a profound truth that experienced counselors know by heart. They know from repeated caregiving encounters that when healthy love is missing or in short supply, the mutual growth-nurturing that is the hallmark of genuine love is diminished.

Relational wholeness is affirmed for Christians in Jesus' commandment: "Love one another as I have loved you" (John 15:12). The self-giving quality of this love is expressed in these words in John's first letter (paraphrased here to make them inclusive): If persons know that the world's good and their brothers or sisters are in need, yet close their hearts against them, how does God's love abide in them (1 John 3:17)? Beloved, let us love one another, for love is of God, and those who love are born of God and know God. Those who do not love do not know God, for God is love (1 John 4:7-8).

In the biblical view, wholeness grows best in relationships in Spirit-energized caring communities where God's justice-based love comes alive in caring group commitments. In modern terms, social systems such as families and congregations can either facilitate or deplete their members by their psychological and spiritual climates. Those who work therapeutically with family systems observe that successive generations often pass on patterns of health and dysfunction. This insight was anticipated in the biblical awareness that the impact of the "iniquity of the parents upon the children" (Exod. 34:7) is an ongoing factor in diminishing the well-being of their children and grandchildren. In a similar way, wholeness-nurturing patterns of relating in family systems can be transmitted through multiple generations.

The view that relationships with a therapeutic quality provide a wholeness-growing environment is implicit in the rich Hebrew word *shalom* and its equivalent Arabic word *salaam*. These words, most frequently translated "peace," also mean sound, healthy, or wholeness. *Shalom* or *salaam* is cultivated in Spirit-empowered communities where the quality of relationships provides a nurturing environment. In fact, in the New Testament Greek, *koinonia* is used to describe the church as a healing, transforming community enlivened by God's spirit. The image of the church as the body of Christ with many members communicates this social-systems understanding of mutually nurturing relationships within a unifying religious commitment (Rom. 12:5).

5. Foundations of Healing and Wholeness in and through Work

The importance of work in people's lives has strong scriptural foundations. The Wisdom literature of the Hebrew Scriptures communicates the understanding that using God's gifts in worthwhile work is a calling, a vocation. Here is the invitation in the wisdom of Proverbs: "Commit your work to the LORD, / and your plans will be established. / The LORD has made everything for its purpose." After affirming God's stake in constructive work, the passage continues, "Better is a little with righteousness than large income with injustice." Then with concrete practicality, "Honest balances and scales are the LORD's" (Prov. 16:3-4, 8, 11). The book of James recognizes the importance of implementing our beliefs and values in constructive action. The author declares, "If [faith] does not lead to action, it is in itself a lifeless thing" (James 2:17 NEB). The biblical view sees all worthwhile work as worthy of respect, as indicated by the diverse lifetime occupations of many religious leaders, including Jesus as a carpenter and Paul as a tentmaker like Aquila with whom he stayed in Corinth.

6. Foundations of Healing and Wholeness through Playfulness and Laughter

Playfulness has fewer obvious biblical antecedents than the other dimensions, but its strong roots are there nonetheless. The poet-lyricist creator of the Psalms describes God as laughing at the kings of the earth who conspire against God's justice (Ps. 2:2-5). The word *joy* is used more than sixty times in the Hebrew Scriptures and a little less than fifty in the New Testament. The Wisdom literature in Proverbs declares, "A cheerful heart is good medicine, but a downcast spirit dries up the bones" (17:22). Modern research on the therapeutic effects of laughter confirms this ancient insight. What is the New Testament story that most clearly reflects Jesus' celebration of life and love and liberation? It is the account of his choosing to use his miraculous powers first at a wedding party to replenish the refreshment by making good wine in large quantities (John 2:1-11). In the table talk at his last supper with his inner circle, Jesus spoke of joy several times. He must have surprised his disciples when he identified the purpose of his sharing: "These things I have spoken to you, that my joy may be in you, and that your joy may be full" (John 15:11 RSV). Later he said, "These things I speak in the world, that they may have my joy fulfilled in themselves" (John 17:13 RSV). Among God's countless precious gifts to our species, laughter and playfulness serve wholeness by lightening the loads of crises and adding a spiritual dynamic to our joy. They also balance and energize God's other good gifts including work, responsibility, commitment, self-discipline, and self-sacrifice.

7A. *Foundations of Healing and Wholeness in and through Society's Institutions*

This part of the seventh dimension of wholeness is an inspiring motif throughout the Hebrew Scriptures. Passionate opposition to the dehumanizing impact of injustice and oppression is central in the prophetic tradition. Today's awareness that social institutions collectively stimulate or stymie life in all its fullness was anticipated in eighth-century BCE biblical wisdom. Jesus clearly identified his ministry with this prophetic heritage when he visited his hometown synagogue and chose to read from the scroll of the prophet Isaiah:

> The Spirit of the Lord is upon me,
>   because he has anointed me to bring good news to the poor.
> He has sent me to proclaim release to the captives
>   and recovery of sight to the blind,
>   to let the oppressed go free,
> to proclaim the year of the Lord's favor. (Luke 4:18-19)

This passage highlights the interdependence of love and justice, and therefore of personal and social liberation, healing, and salvation. The prophetic tradition underscores God's intention that society and its institutions be liberated so that they will nurture rather than negate human wholeness. By living out God's love and justice, Jesus identified his ministry with the impoverished, oppressed, and rejected people in his society. He acted on this principle when he threw the greedy money changers out of the temple because they were cheating worshipers by charging exorbitant prices for sacrificial animals required for their rituals.

To implement the prophetic dimension of ministry, caregivers can draw illuminating insights from liberation theologies with roots in Latin American, Asian, African, African American, and feminist perspectives. These theologies understand God as liberator and see the divine promise of liberation as fulfilled to the degree that the social, economic, political, and religious structures of society are transformed by justice making.

The theology of caregivers can be empowered by the thought of Martin Luther King

Jr., who made it clear that we cannot understand God's love separated from God's justice. In an insightful application of King's views to pastoral caregiving with the oppressed, Donald M. Chinula, a teacher from Malawi, declares, "It is not sufficient that we heal suffering persons; we must also be concerned about healing the suffering communities such persons come from and return to. The goal of pastoral caregiving must include a vision of the optimal functional society whose evocative symbol provides quintessential norms for intervention."[13] The theology of justice-based caregiving should motivate us to develop innovative methods of prophetic caregiving. By using these, caregivers and care receivers can learn to live the prophetic call of Hebrew Scriptures in which *shalom* was understood as involving *justice in community*. (See Isa. 11:6-9; 24:4-5; Hos. 2:18; 4:3; Luke 4:18-19.) Thus they can join hands with persons of goodwill in many traditions in helping to heal injustices, oppression, poverty, and environmental destruction on a massive scale.

7B. Foundations of Healing and Wholeness through Enhancing Ecological Well-being

This other, complementary part of the prophetic dimension of wholeness also has deep biblical roots. The poetic images of the two Genesis creation stories communicate respectful and caring stewardship of all of God's wonder-filled creation. In the first narrative, this earth-respecting attitude is expressed in the refrains after each of the great epochs (called days) of creation and the ringing refrain after the last one: "And God saw everything that he had made, and behold, it was very good" (Gen. 1:31 RSV). In the biblical view, we humans do not own the planet but have it as a trust from God. This truth is further expressed in Exodus 9:29: "The earth is the LORD's." The intimate bonding of Jesus with nature is evident in his persistent use of earthy images and stories to communicate the spiritual truths he was teaching. Birds, flowers, a shepherd tending sheep, a farmer planting seeds, and a woman making bread are among many examples. Jesus did most of his preaching and teaching in the outdoors, surrounded by the natural world. Where did he go to wrestle with difficult decisions or to find renewal when ministering to many sick and needy people had exhausted him? He chose to go to a wilderness area to be alone with himself and God.

Persons committed to religious lifestyles have crucial roles in saving God's creation as a healthy place for all future generations. Their obligation comes from the fact that the deepest causes of humankind's destructive treatment of the biosphere, at the roots of the complex economic, social, and justice causes, are spiritual problems. These are the collective psychological-spiritual idolatries and moral pathologies of the human family culture that justify exploiting nature along with women and poor persons. These spiritual-ethical sicknesses produce lifestyles that are harmful to the health of individuals and social institutions and the life-sustaining vitality of nature.

A hopeful development is that a growing interfaith movement called "The United Religions Initiative" (URI) has generated such a peacemaking, earth-saving, global ethical consensus. Persons from many of the world's religions are joining hands across national and faith boundaries to work together for the "peace and healing among religions, peoples and nations, and for the wholeness of the earth." All who are a part of URI, this multifaith network, commit themselves to using their "combined resources in [their] whole-hearted efforts to manifest divine love among all life on earth."[14]

Eight centuries before Jesus lived, a wise Hebrew prophet used these earthy poetic images to picture the rejoicing of the whole earth when it is treated with loving respect and spiritual care: "The mountains and the hills before you shall burst into song, / and all the trees of the field shall clap their hands" (Isa. 55:12). Spiritually aware caregivers should aim at enabling care receivers to open themselves to the sacredness of God's continuing creation and to its healing, enlivening energies. They can join in the celebration by engaging in the mutuality of being nurtured by nature and, in response, nurturing nature with loving care. The earth's woundedness calls religious people of all faiths to reject exploitation of nature and to go beyond stewardship of nature to partnership with nature![15]

Biblical Images of Nurturing Congregations

The New Testament sees the church as (1) the people of God, a mutually caring community united by a sacred covenant with God (2 Cor. 6:16); (2) the body of Christ, an organic unity in which each member, as parts of a living body, has her or his unique gifts and ministry (Rom. 12:4-5; 1 Cor. 10:17); and (3) the community of the Holy Spirit, a redemptive, spiritually empowered community within which the living Spirit can work to bring healing to a needy, broken world (Acts 10:44-47).

Many people feel deeply that God is irrelevant to their real lives as the central source of meaning and wholeness. They are, therefore, unable to hear the good news. Caring and counseling can be methods for communicating the gospel by helping them open themselves to healing relationships. Until they have experienced accepting, unearned love in a human relationship, grace cannot come alive for most of them. They must be grasped by caring acceptance—the very limited human counterpart of God's grace—in a life-to-life encounter. The good news of the Christian message cannot become a liberating reality for them until this happens. Caregiving relationships, lay and professional, are strategic places where this limited, fragmentary but transforming incarnation of grace can occur.

For a variety of personal and contextual reasons, not all church members can contribute to the establishment of a Spirit-centered relational climate in a congregation. Their presence may be divisive rather than uniting and healing. Care and counseling can help such persons experience healing love and thus become participants in the life of a congregation as a healing community, for itself and for the wider community.[16]

Implementing the Wholeness Triad in Caregiving

As a practical expression of their holistic, Spirit-empowered objectives, pastoral caregivers should nurture the three things that Paul identifies as the key dynamics in living healthy lifestyles. The ringing refrain of the great hymn to love in 1 Corinthians 13:13 highlights the transformation that comes by experiencing faith, hope, and most important of the three, love. Enabling care receivers to experience these in their everyday lives can be called using the "healing-wholeness triad." All members of our species have profound heart hungers for these essential psychological-spiritual foods.

Using this biblical wisdom in caregiving involves intentionally teaching care receivers how to awaken *healing faith*, meaning wholeness-enhancing beliefs, religious experiences, and ethical practices; *healing hope*, meaning reality-based expectations of a more whole future; and *healing love*, meaning self-transcending caring that nurtures wholeness in individuals, their relationships, and through them, out in widening circles to include their congregations, communities, and God's earth.

Faith That Heals

We humans live and die in our meanings. Our level of health is continually influenced by how effective we are in generating viable meanings and purposes to give our lives direction, motivation, vision, and uplift. The vast majority of human beings use some form of religious or philosophical beliefs and ethical guidelines to generate meaning in their lives. For this reason the quality of our spiritual and ethical lives determines, to a considerable extent, the degree of our overall wellness.

Hope That Heals

As we saw earlier, awakening reality-based hope is a key dynamic in cultivating whole-person healing and wholeness because positive expectations about the future influence very powerfully the quality of life in the present. Believing that a more hopeful future is possible and visualizing it can provide motivating energy to make constructive but difficult changes. Having the lure of even a *slightly* more hopeful future for oneself, other people, and society is as important for motivation as the push of hoping to lessen the pain of living, especially during crises, losses, and other times of stress. The hope-sustaining role of the biblical vision of a new age discussed above is an expression of this principle.

Love That Heals

We humans have a profound, inescapable need to give as well as to receive love. Counselors and other healers often neglect to enable care recipients to discover that giving love opens the door to receiving it and that giving love is as vital to their wellness as receiving it. Teaching care receivers how to use the outreach principle discussed above can be a path to this energizing discovery. However, some people, especially women, have been taught to give themselves away repeatedly in loving relationships. Their task is to learn to hold onto enough love for themselves to engender their own strength and self-esteem.

Awakening Faith, Hope, and Love in Care and Counseling

How can healthy faith, hope, and love be awakened in care and counseling? Caregivers should communicate these precious gifts by embodying them in clear, well-established boundaries as much as they can. They should also communicate them explicitly in words and in loving, accepting behavior whenever it is appropriate. Meaningful faith is often awakened when a caring person reframes a problem from a faith perspective. Hope is stimulated when a caregiver believes in persons' realistic potentials more than they do, tells them so, and helps them learn ways to sustain hope by making constructive changes. Health-giving love is stimulated when someone communicates loving acceptance that flows from that person's self-acceptance. From a spiritual perspective this love-awakening process is rooted in what Tillich once described as "accepting oneself as being accepted" by God.

Caregivers should gently support care recipients' reality-based faith, hope, and love whenever these are expressed, however tentatively, in attitudes, feelings, or actions. Research on the process by which people learn and grow shows that low-key affirmation of small changes increases the likelihood that persons will continue growing in these constructive directions.

The implicit premise of this chapter is that to the degree that faith, hope, and love theology comes alive in persons, the more they will awaken health and recognize remarkable opportunities. The next chapter will build on the foundation provided by this chapter and the previous two by reviewing the essential skills needed in all types of effective holistic caregiving.

Biblical Awareness Imaging Exercise

Quieting your busy stream of consciousness for a few minutes by going to your inner "serenity zone" can help you become renewed and reenergized. Doing this enables you to be more present with yourself and therefore with others. This is particularly important for you as a caregiver when you are feeling "beside yourself" or inwardly fragmented by stress overload. Focusing on a lively religious image while in this quiet inner space can be particularly enlivening and spiritually nurturing.

Here is a simple meditation-imaging exercise designed for spiritual self-renewal, energizing, and healing. The exercise can generate a sense of spiritual aliveness in those who feel a need for spiritual renewing. You can teach it to care receivers in a few minutes by leading them through it as you also do it. I recommend that you pause for a few minutes and give yourself a renewal break by trying it now:

1. Using whatever methods work for you, prepare yourself by causing your mind-body-spirit organism to become very relaxed while at the same time it is very alert.

2. When you are prepared, recall a vivid peak experience, an energized spiritual experience that gave you some gifts of uplift, renewal, or healing. (If your spiritual life has been flat for a while, go back as long as necessary to recall a spiritual experience that energized and healed you in some way.)

3. Now, in your imagination, return to and be in that time and place, and let yourself relive that experience as fully and vividly as possible for a few minutes. Enjoy letting your spirit be nurtured and renewed by experiencing that spiritual uplift and inner peace and purpose. Savor again the warm inner glow of spiritual serenity and well-being.

4. As you continue the exercise, see what biblical images or stories emerge in your mind and heart associated with reliving this uplifting experience. Picture these, and see how they touch your mind, heart, and spirit.

5. When you finish the exercise, be aware of how you feel in your whole mind-body-spirit organism.

6. Take a few minutes to jot down learnings you wish to remember and perhaps implement.

7. If this exercise has been meaningful, decide to repeat it whenever your spirit needs a renewal lift.

Recommended Reading

Gerkin, Charles V. *An Introduction to Pastoral Care*. Nashville: Abingdon Press, 1997.

Holifield, E. Brooks. *A History of Pastoral Care in America: From Salvation to Self-Realization*. Nashville: Abingdon Press, 1983.

Lester, Andrew. *Hope in Pastoral Care and Counseling*. Louisville: Westminster John Knox Press, 1995.

Neuger, Christie Cozad. *Counseling Women: A Narrative, Pastoral Approach.* Minneapolis: Fortress Press, 2001.

Patton, John. *Pastoral Care: An Essential Guide.* Nashville: Abingdon Press, 2005.

Stevenson-Moessner, Jeanne, ed. *In Her Own Time: Women and Developmental Issues in Pastoral Care.* Minneapolis: Fortress Press, 2000.

CHAPTER 4

FOUNDATIONAL SKILLS FOR MOST TYPES OF CARING AND COUNSELING

I don't care how much you know—until I know how much you care!
—Insightful bumper sticker

Just as carpenters need a variety of tools to build an attractive house or a piece of fine furniture, counselors require a variety of methods to help people rebuild tragedy-shattered lives, dysfunctional relationships, or destructive religious beliefs and values. The wide range of caregiving opportunities that pastors confront requires them to have both flexibility and ingenuity. They sometimes must go beyond everything they know about healing, growth, and transformation to learn new insights from their efforts to help those with unfamiliar problems. What their own healing and growth struggles have taught them—including the lessons they really didn't want to learn—can be very valuable. These personal learnings will influence everything they do in caregiving, but never are they adequate substitutes for clear understanding of counseling principles and knowledge of counseling skills.

In the process of responding to the diverse needs of people who seek pastoral care and counseling, caregivers often must shift gears. They must choose to use the particular methods that are called for by the unique problems, limitations, strengths, and latent resources of each care receiver. Different methods are frequently used during the same session and certainly at various stages of caregiving relationships. This chapter begins the process of introducing important attitudes and skills for basic pastoral care. The primary focus will be on active listening. A second focus is on the basic frameworks undergirding the practice of pastoral care. These attitudes, skills, and strategies will be revisited throughout this text.

Using Basic Caregiving Responses and Skills

Psychologist Robert R. Carkhuff and his associates have developed a widely used system for teaching and learning these core skills in sequence.[1] Here is my summary of essential skills, paraphrased in part from Carkhuff's formulation:

1. Exhibiting attending and caring behavior, including making frequent eye contact (depending on the cultural context) and expressing interest and hospitality by one's facial expressions and posture; for example, leaning toward the person rather than away.

2. Inviting the person to talk about significant issues by reflective responses, open-ended questions, and brief comments or gestures.

3. Listening carefully, and observing nonverbal messages.

4. Following the person's lead by staying with the here-and-now flow of the dialogue instead of switching topics.

5. Responding and clarifying empathetically by summarizing in paraphrased form the high points that have been communicated, thus checking out the counselor's perception of their meanings for the person.

6. Exploring potentially significant areas that the person has not discussed by asking focusing questions while giving primary respect to the person's timing and preferences for the direction of the conversation.

7. Helping the person notice when the problem isn't in charge so that he or she can see strengths and agency for the life he or she prefers to lead.

8. Confronting or challenging the person, as needed, balanced with genuine affirmations, while also recognizing that the right to confront has to be earned through persistent active listening and trusting the inner wisdom of the care receiver.

9. Inviting the person to think about and take next steps based on the person's understanding of her or his future story—its meaning, its potential, and the things that may be getting in the way of living the way the person is called to live.

It can be helpful to understand basic caregiving skills in terms of how various responses reflect differing attitudes and intentions on the part of caregivers. This awareness can enable counselors-in-training to identify, evaluate, and correct their responses. Below is a list of eight types of counselor responses, beginning with five responses initially proposed by psychologist Elias H. Porter Jr. To these I have added three more:

E—*Evaluative:* responses expressing counselors' judgment concerning the relative constructiveness, validity, values, or effectiveness of clients' feelings or behavior. Such responses can be used constructively in caregiving guidance on complex ethical issues. Yet it's important to use evaluative comments sparingly since they emphasize the authority of the caregiver rather than the wisdom of the care receiver.

I—*Interpretive:* responses by which counselors seek to shed helpful light on the *whys* of persons' feelings and behavior. In moderation, such responses can be useful to those who are searching for understanding of the roots of their baffling beliefs or behavior.

S—*Supportive:* responses by which counselors seek to reassure, reduce intense feelings, or give needed emotional undergirding to persons immobilized by overwhelming feelings or circumstances.

P—*Probing:* responses by which counselors pose questions in order to seek further information or encourage further discussion along certain lines. Such responses imply that the person might profitably develop or discuss a point further. Probing responses are of two types: *PF, probing for feelings,* and *PI, probing for factual information.* It's easy for caregivers to ask too many questions based on their curiosity or interest and not on the real needs of care receivers. Probing responses are more suitable for counseling than for pastoral care. Good reflective listening can invite care receivers to expand on their feelings or experience without the risk of pursuing a direction that is not of primary interest to care receivers.

U—*Understanding:* responses by which a caregiver seeks to communicate understanding and empathy while checking whether he or she understands accurately the feelings, attitudes, and actions being communicated. This is a key function of active listening.

A—*Advising:* responses by which counselors seek to teach useful information and recommend that people consider certain actions, beliefs, or attitudes. These responses can be very valuable in educative counseling, usually called "pastoral guidance." However, they tend to be overused. Most advice is more beneficial to the one giving it than to the one receiving it.

C—*Clarifying:* responses by which counselors seek to enable counselees to organize and find patterns and meanings in what they are expressing in confused, chaotic ways. This is often called "advanced or secondary active listening."

EM—*Empowering:* responses by which counselors aim at enabling clients to gain a sense of their own inner strengths and worth and, when appropriate, to use this empowering in constructive action, including seeking greater justice for themselves and their communities. Obviously this is different from positive evaluation. Rather, it is an attitude that looks for and helps care receivers look for their own strength and, more important, their own agency. It may also involve helping care receivers identify and deconstruct cultural discourses (like sexism and racism) that are often at the heart of their pain.

This typology has proved useful in helping seminarians and clergy become aware of and correct gaps and lopsidedness in their patterns of responses. Each of these responses can be used constructively but selectively in different types and stages of pastoral care and counseling. Several responses tend to be overused or used inappropriately by inexperienced caregivers. In fact, caregiving by some clergy consists mainly of P (probing), S (supportive), and A (advising) responses. Those with strong moralistic orientations tend to overuse E (evaluative) as well as A (advising). Students recently exposed to abnormal psychology theories often misuse I (interpretive) responses in unhelpful ways, giving people speculative theories about why they feel and act as they do. The style of caregivers with little or no training is weakest in the paucity of U (understanding) and EM (empowering) responses. Most effective caregiving makes frequent use of U (understanding) responses.

The aim should be to use all these responses with appropriate selectivity, reflecting the healing and growth needs of particular care receivers and the stage of helping relationships. In the early, rapport-building phase of caregiving, it is essential to use U (understanding) responses primarily, with a few PF and PI (probing for feelings and information) responses as needed. In all stages and types of caregiving relationships, U (understanding), C (clarifying), and EM (empowering) responses are key. In crisis counseling, S (supportive), C (clarifying), and EM (empowering) responses often are essential, as are P (probing) strategies in situations like suicide assessment. In counseling on value and meaning-of-life issues, E (evaluative) and occasional A (advising by personalized teaching) responses can be helpful *if they are used in a caring, nonjudgmental way as recommendations for counselees to consider.* In short-term educative counseling (premarital or preretirement, for example), A (advising), PI (probing for information), and S (supportive) responses usually are useful.

To practice using these different responses, see if you can identify the responses listed after this statement by a counselee. Put the initials of your choice—including PF (probing for feelings) and PI (probing for information)—in the blank before each response. You'll find the key for this exercise is in note.[2]

****

Martha, an agitated eighteen-year-old, declares with intense feelings: "I tell you I hate my father! I hate him! I hate him! And there's no reason for it. He is a minister—a good person. He has never laid a hand on me—but I have this terrific feeling against him and it makes me feel awful because there is no reason for it. It's a sin to hate your father—especially if you don't have any reason for it. It really worries me."

_____ (1) How did you feel about your father as you were growing up?

_____ (2) I sense that you feel guilty about hating him because you were taught in your religious life that it's sinful to feel this way toward you father. But I think you'll find that underneath it all you have some love for him, and this plays a part in your feelings of guilt.

_____ (3) When did you begin to feel this way?

_____ (4) This is certainly something you'll want to get cleared up. Good relationships with parents are very important. You wouldn't want to jeopardize what a happy relationship with your father can mean to you.

_____ (5) Everyone at some time or another goes through a period when they hate one or both of their parents. It's really not at all uncommon. Most people find they can work out some way of getting along until things settle down.

_____ (6) It really weighs on you that you hate your father without any apparent reason.

_____ (7) What gave you the courage and strength to face your painful feelings and decide to come for help?

_____ (8) It seems that your conflicted feelings are baffling you—feeling confused about why you hate your father, and feeling guilty because it seems sinful to you, especially since your hatred seems unfair to him.

_____ (9) Let me recommend that you try talking with your father about your feelings—level with him and see if this helps.[3]

****

This system is useful for analyzing written verbatim reports as well as audio or video recordings of caregiving contact because it can help identify blind spots in caregivers' responses. In reality practice sessions, the supervisor or observer-coach can keep track of different types of responses, thus helping those practicing as "counselor" recognize lopsidedness in their patterns of responding. Of course, the typology can be a mechanical gimmick of little value. But it also can be illuminating when used as an awareness-enhancement device by persons learning caregiving and their mentors. Another useful tool for learning basic counseling skills systematically is Gerard Egan's *The Skilled Helper*.[4] This approach is based on the findings of several decades of research regarding which professional counseling skills are effective in facilitating constructive changes in both attitudes and behaviors.

Developing Healing, Empowering Relationships

By using the skills just described, caregivers aim at establishing a special quality of relationships described as *therapeutic* (meaning healing) and *maieutic*[5] (meaning midwifing or facilitating birth). Such relationships provide the interpersonal environment in which the supportive caregiving and the problem solving of crisis counseling can best take place. The effectiveness of the various types of caring and counseling depends, to a considerable degree, on developing and sustaining such a solid foundation. Generating such an interpersonal relationship is the starting point in most pastoral caregiving. Furthermore, experiencing this quality of relating can be healing and growth stimulating in itself.

What skills are required to develop healing relationships? They grow as caregivers listen actively and respond with caring empathy, thus focusing on really being *with* burdened care receivers. This relationship-building skill is important throughout the caregiving process, but in the beginning phase it is the primary means of establishing a trustful relationship within which healing dialogue can occur. Instead of worrying about what one is going to say or do next, as inexperienced caregivers tend to do, it is important to focus energy on being with the person and as aware as possible in this unique human relationship. You undoubtedly have known the empty, depersonalized feelings resulting from being with a person who is not really present. Experiencing a person who is really present is required to produce healing, growth-stimulating relationships in counseling and other pastoral roles as well as in family and friendship relationships. And knowing that the respectful attentiveness of the caregiving relationship is safe and well boundaried will assist the care receiver to explore his or her experiences without worrying about their effect on the caregiver or the therapeutic relationship. We will explore the important topic of boundaries in a later chapter.

These healing and wholeness-cultivating relationships tend to grow as caregivers achieve some significant degree of what Carl Rogers called "empathic understanding" of persons' often chaotic perceptions, thoughts, feelings, and actions. Empathy means seeking, as much as one can, to understand careseekers' stories from within their perspective. This is very different from sympathy, which literally means "suffering with." Sympathy by itself tends to give caregivers distorted views of care receivers' inner worlds because it causes them to use their own subjective feelings and life experiences as the primary lens for understanding the other. Empathy is a disciplined exercise requiring that we try to understand the other person's experience through his or her lenses. It requires both cognitive and affective attention to really try to grasp not only the other person's experience, but also the meaning the person gives to that experience.

Active Listening and Responding

Active listening and responding with empathy enable care receivers to know that caregivers are trying to understand their inner world. Significant research done by R. D. Quinn revealed that the counselor's *desire to understand* communicates caring acceptance to care receivers.[6] If a careseeker is convinced that a caregiver is genuinely trying to listen deeply and be *with* him or her in caring ways, attempts to understand issues and reflect feelings may miss the mark without loss of connection and trust. A fragile nexus, as delicate as a spiderweb, begins to connect the two in a growing therapeutic relationship. This bond is the first, vital strand of what will become a sturdy bridge of rapport connecting the separate islands of experience of two human beings.

The art of *active empathic listening* involves listening to ideas and feelings. It also involves listening to feelings too painful to trust to words, feelings expressed between the lines or in body language. Furthermore, it involves listening to meanings in the silences between words as well as to the mixed or conflicted messages reflected in lack of congruence between content and feelings expressed in voice tones or body language.

Skilled listening enables caregivers to respond in ways that are at least somewhat relevant to how people really understand and feel about their situation. I shall always be thankful to an older woman patient in a Long Island, New York, mental hospital where I was doing a unit of clinical pastoral education. This woman unwittingly gave me a very precious gift without knowing it as she was about to die. It was the gift of helping a young pastor learn the vital importance of listening carefully before talking at length in caregiving. The nurses called me to her bedside because the doctors believed she was close to death. The woman had been in that crowded hospital for more than two decades, during the years before major tranquilizers were available to treat mental illnesses. She had been in and out of awareness of external reality, but just before she died, her mind was clear. I introduced myself, and her immediate response surprised and shook me: "Chaplain, I'm dying!" Before I tried to comfort her with the religious assurances and scripture I had planned to use, something told me to ask her how she felt about dying. Her honest reply made what I was planning to say absurdly irrelevant. She responded with intense feeling, "Chaplain, I'll be so glad to get out of this damned place!" I responded by reflecting that feeling, and she expressed more longing for the blessed release of death. I had come perilously close to making the mistake of assuming that I knew how people feel about dying. The reason that would have been terribly wrong was that there is no such thing as the way people in general feel about dying—or for that matter, any other major experience on their life journeys.

Pastoral caregivers aim at listening in as much depth as possible to careseekers' multiple levels of verbal and nonverbal communication. In a powerful earth poem, William Stafford describes in-depth listening: "Within people's voices, under their words or woven into the pauses, I hear a hidden sound."[7] Periodically caregivers reflect back, with warmth and empathy, brief paraphrased summaries of the major information and dominant feelings around which the most confusion and pain seem to be attached. They also may begin to awaken hopes by brief summaries of the meanings, hopes, resources, and strengths that they have perceived. By summarizing significant points and occasionally asking brief clarifying questions or offering inviting reflections, caregivers help persons begin to organize their inner world and perhaps gradually understand their problems more clearly.

In contrast to unfocused, casual listening, responsive listening is disciplined and focused. It seeks to enable people to focus on what they regard as their significant issues.

This process may enable caregivers to identify important patterns in what care receivers are saying. Caregivers thus gain a tentative understanding of careseekers' inner worlds, an understanding that is essential to making their skills and knowledge useful. More important, it allows the care receiver to hear her or his own story and inner wisdom and resources as the caregiver reflects them to the care receiver. All this stimulates the flow of therapeutic dialogue and the process of enabling the care receiver to find resources to cope more constructively and to begin to live a more abundant and faithful life.

Active Listening Is Liberating and Empowering

The healing power of empathic listening was recognized clearly by pioneering feminist educator Nelle Morton, who coined the apt phrase "hearing into speech." She coined this memorable phrase when she reflected on the process of mutual empowerment of women who are oppressed and silenced in male-dominated societies and churches. She recognized that they could hear one another into speech and with speech power, by deep, mutual listening and honest sharing of their common sense of being treated as "other" and "lesser than." She wrote of her moment of discovery when a distressed woman spoke openly and in depth in a women's small sharing group about her painful experiences:

> I knew I had been experiencing something I had never experienced before. A complete reversal of the going logic in which someone speaks precisely so that more accurate hearing may take place. This woman was saying, and I had experienced, a depth hearing...a hearing that is far more than accurate listening. A hearing engaged in by the whole body that evokes speech—a new speech— a new creation. The woman had been heard to her own speech.

Nelle continued,

> While I experience this kind of hearing through women, I am convinced it is one of those essential dimensions of the full human experience long programmed out of our culture and our religious tradition. In time I came to understand the wider implications of this reversal as revolutionary and profoundly theological. Hearing of this sort is equivalent to empowerment.[8]

Having often listened to and learned from Nelle, I believe she would agree that caregivers have a crucial task beyond listening in depth and hearing women into speech. They also are called to hear into speech and empower men oppressed by intrapsychic, family, churchly, economic, and societal forces that constrict their growth in spiritually centered wholeness.

Overcoming Barriers to Active Listening

Theologian Dietrich Bonhoeffer, the courageous hero of the resistance to the Nazi Holocaust, once said,

Many people are looking for an ear that will listen. They do not find it among Christians, because Christians are talking when they should be listening. He [or she] who no longer listens to his [or her] brother [or sister] will soon no longer be listening to God either. One who cannot listen long and patiently will presently be talking beside the point and never really be speaking to others, albeit he [or she] be not conscious of it.[9]

In a similar vein, a character in one of Shakespeare's plays describes the problem of unawareness, the cause of many failures in caregiving relationships: "It is the disease of not listening, the malady of not marking, that I am troubled withal."[10]

The good news is that caregivers can increase their ability to really hear and respond with caring empathy to careseekers' issues, attitudes, and feelings because these are teachable-learnable skills. Practice, perhaps accompanied by competent coaching, can enable the overcoming of the following inner barriers and thus increase this fundamental skill in caregivers.

Here are some barriers to good listening:

1. Blind spots that hide one's own feelings, issues, and inner conflicts are one barrier. This is particularly crucial when caregivers try to help counselees resolve feelings similar to their own unfaced feelings. Such out-of-awareness feelings produce anxieties that generate emotional deafness. A perceptive theological student in a reality practice session articulated his discovery well: "Counselors who cannot feel their own feelings (particularly anger and grief) because of inner blocks are seriously handicapped. They are limited in their ability to experience 'resonance,' the responsive chord between two persons that makes possible relating in depth, including therapeutic relating."

2. Overinvestment in one's own feelings and ideas is another barrier. Active empathic listening demands an emotional investment in the other person's world. Although this requires awareness of one's own feelings and problems, it does not mean being absorbed in them. Listening to oneself *is* a prerequisite to listening to others and to God. But if the volume of inner noise from caregivers' distress and self-absorption is too loud, it blocks depth listening. This deafness often has psychological and spiritual roots and consequences. It makes persons unable to hear messages from their deeper selves and hear God's spirit at work within them and in their world.

3. Overconcern with counseling theories and techniques—a problem of many beginning caregivers—can diminish accurate listening and responding. The bumper sticker cited at the beginning of this chapter can remind caregivers that their effectiveness depends much less on using certain techniques than on the quality of their healing, growth-nurturing relationships.

4. The need to prove one's counseling competence by solving people's problems quickly with wise advice is still another barrier. Instead of concentrating on solutions, caregivers should focus on understanding and being *with* people. The dialogue resulting from this quality of active presence tends to increase the most crucial understanding generated in caregiving—the *care receivers' self-understanding*. It also increases the probability that solutions will be developed collaboratively and will be implemented because the care receivers have ownership of the action plan. Because listening is so crucial in supportive caregiving, the exploration of active listening will be continued in the next chapter.

Facilitating Expression of Feelings

Although the expression of feelings is not the only, or even primary, goal of pastoral caregiving, it is an important dimension. Care receivers often have a variety of strong feelings when they are under stress or experience a trauma. They may also experience a great deal of relief in being able to articulate and share those feelings with a trusted listener. To help persons in distress to express themselves in a meaningful way, caregivers may use some of the actions suggested below:

1. Permit the dialogical process to be led mainly by the care receiver. Focus of the caregiving process should be on whatever feelings and meanings the person communicates spontaneously, verbally or nonverbally. Just listen attentively, avoiding more than occasional nods, brief information-seeking queries, and reflective summaries. Remember that reflective listening invites people to clarify and expand their stories according to their needs. Such listening usually does this much better than asking an abundance of questions.

2. Occasionally paraphrase in your own words what you have heard to check out the accuracy of your understanding. If encouraging further expression and exploration of thoughts and feelings seems safe and useful, use feeling-full words and voice tones in your responses. A query such as this often encourages further expression and exploration: "Let's see if I understand how this crisis is hitting you. . . ." or "If I'm getting what you're saying . . ." Many people don't have an adequate feeling vocabulary and thus have trouble articulating what they are feeling. One way that caregivers can be helpful is to tentatively offer feeling words in their reflections to see if those words help the person speak his or her feelings. However, do not finish sentences or thoughts for the other person; rather, offer the feeling word as part of the active listening process. To do this well, caregivers need to have a full vocabulary of feeling words.

3. Be especially responsive to so-called negative feelings and attitudes. These may

include anger, rage, guilt, shame, despair, fear, unforgiveness, self-rejection, spiritual emptiness, hopelessness, and helplessness. Such painful emotions usually dominate the chaotic world of people caught in crises and are the main forces that motivate them to seek help. These feelings frequently are hidden or repressed, and they need to be brought into the healing sunlight of a caring, nonjudgmental relationship. They are also important because they may be acted out in ways that hurt the troubled people and/or those around them. They need to be talked through so that they can be defused and resolved enough that the energy invested in them is rechanneled in more constructive feelings, attitudes, and behaviors.

It usually is more effective for caregivers to understate rather than overstate feelings. Such responses, spoken in an understated, questioning tone, usually encourage further expression of painful feelings: "When the chairperson ignored you, it sounds like you felt angry and even invisible?" Or in another situation, "You feel distressed about what happened and also worried about what you think may happen soon?" or "It hurts when you think about what could have been and you feel sad?"

4. Watch for *emotional doorways* that may lead to meaning-filled levels of communication. Such doors include expressing emotions in words, voice, face, or posture; protesting too much; making self-contradictions (probably indicating inner confusion and conflicts); and speaking with some heat about relationships loaded with emotions (often with parents, spouses, children, enemies, or authority figures). Responding to what seem to be doorways that are even a little ajar may lead the caregiving dialogue through the opening to deeper levels of expression and exploration.

5. Avoid premature interpretations concerning why people function or feel certain ways, and avoid premature advice giving. These are tempting traps because they offer ways for caregivers to feel useful and in control, particularly in areas where they feel insecure and anxious. Interpretations are usually speculative and, like advice giving, tend to block the needed flow of both feelings and essential facts. Advice and interpretation do not cultivate self-understanding, self-empowerment, or more constructive actions. These changes are most likely to occur when people mobilize their own problem-solving resources and gain a small amount of self-confidence as well as some understanding of their problems and possible solutions. Generally speaking, both interpretation and advice giving are among the least useful responses for careseekers. A related guideline can be stated simply: do not do for care receivers what they can do for themselves if they have to, except when people are in severe crises and need short-term support.

6. Recognize and affirm when people express positive feelings and attitudes or take constructive actions. Problem stories in people's lives tend to become totally defining of them and their experience. Notice times and events when the problem feelings haven't

had control of the persons and more of their "real selves" are able to be experienced. When people can remember that they are not defined by the problem or crisis they are experiencing, they can find greater strength, agency, and hope. This can help empower people to engage their problems differently, with greater confidence in a positive future.[11]

7. Reinforce what seem like constructive feelings and changes only after care recipients have discussed and explored the ambivalence that often is hidden behind such positive expressions. An older woman in a nursing home talks with the chaplain:

Older woman: My grandson I haven't seen in six years is coming to visit tomorrow.
Chaplain: That's wonderful! You must be really excited.

This might have shut the door on the woman's expression of how she really felt. Fortunately she had the strength to level with the chaplain in her next response.

Older woman: Well, I would rather he didn't come. He was so cruel to my son before he died that I really don't want anything to do with him.

Premature theological affirmations also can slam doors that might otherwise lead to healing dialogue concerning dysfunctional religious and ethical beliefs. A hospitalized man talks with his pastor:

Man: God is punishing me with this illness.
Pastor: Oh, no! God isn't punishing you. The God I know is a God of love, not punishment.

This response blocks the patient's exploration of his self-punitive belief as well as his need to talk through his neurotic guilt feelings so as to experience God's unconditional love. In contrast, a response like the following would probably have led to exploratory dialogue and perhaps spiritual healing:

Pastor: I'm not sure I understand what you mean when you say God is punishing you with your illness.

8. In the same vein, avoid what has been called "the catch in praise." Recipients know, on some level of their minds, that when caregivers express praise, they may also evaluate them critically if they do not measure up. In a similar way, it is unwise to try to

cheer up people struggling with sadness or depression by offering optimistic affirmations or religious platitudes. Such efforts often increase their sense of hopelessness and isolation.

9. Remember that sometimes people who have shared deeply may have some embarrassment. Their response may be to avoid the caregiver and/or the congregation. If caregivers sense that this may happen, they should mention it (or even predict that it might happen) and discuss it openly.

Exploring Essential Beliefs

Highly verbal or anxious caregivers often ask too many informational questions that unwittingly pull people away from what probably will be most helpful to them—telling their own stories and expressing their painful feelings. Initial questions usually should follow the agenda of the care receiver rather than that of the caregiver and emerge from the flow of the dialogue. Questions should be limited to those aimed at learning essential facts not adequately disclosed during the initial exploratory phase of counseling.

There are exceptions to this general guideline, however. One is when counseling time is short and learning essential information must be done quickly. Another is when working with persons in severe crises and gaining vital information quickly is needed in order to decide on interventions that may help prevent harm to themselves or others. If needed information to evaluate the crisis is not given spontaneously, asking a few door-opening questions, while rapport is being established, usually suffices. Such questions can invite care receivers to focus attention on what may be important issues in addition to those they discussed A question like this can open a productive door for those having trouble expressing painful feelings about messy issues: "What's happening with you and your family since the crisis [or loss] happened?" Questions such as these may open doors through which care receivers walk to look at unexamined areas or view their problems from new perspectives: "What would you like the outcome to be from this crisis? What do you have going *for* you as you try to cope with this miserable situation? How's your health care been since all this hit you? Has your spiritual life been of any help to you in these dark days?" Later in counseling, this type of query can invite people to become aware of how they have grown unexpectedly by coping with their crises: "Has anything constructive emerged from all your uphill struggles?" or "Have you learned anything worthwhile during this mess?"

Exploring Motivation

A bottom-line reality to keep in mind is that counseling that produces any healing and growth is possible only when potential counselees have two prerequisites. First, they must be aware, however vaguely or clearly, of problems with which they desire help. Second, they must have some desire, however ambivalent, to receive help from the particular counselors who are available to them. These two are the *sine qua non* that makes counseling possible. Inexperienced counselors sometimes go through the motions of counseling for a considerable time without significant healing and growth occurring because the requisite preconditions are not present in people's motivation even to a limited degree.

Early in counseling, explore as much as people will reveal about their motivation for seeking help. Human motivation to do anything difficult, including seeking counseling, is often complex and ambivalent. The frustrations, anxieties, and distress from people's problems are the major motivators that *push* them into counseling or provide whatever openness to help they have when clergy take the initiative in offering them help. But the hope of finding increased satisfaction in their lives also *pulls* some people toward getting help. Most people become open to help only when the pain of their situation outweighs the fear of change and whatever satisfactions they derive from their problematic behavior. Some burdened people refuse to ask for or accept help because the pain of their problems is far outweighed by fears of admitting they need help and by resistance to revealing their weaknesses and vulnerability to caregivers. Hidden resistances to or resources for seeking or accepting help may be uncovered by asking questions such as: "How did you make the decision to seek help? What made you decide to come here for counseling? What does it say about you that you have chosen to come for help?"

When persons come for help on their own initiative, caregivers can ask questions such as these to discover crucial facts and feelings, "Why now? Why to me? Why here?"

Pastor: As I recall, you've had some health problems for quite a while. I'm wondering, was there something that made you decide to ask for help *now?*
Male parishioner (quiet voice tone): Yes. I've had this nagging pain for a couple of months, but about a week ago my doctor pushed me to have a biopsy. I finally got the bad news yesterday. It feels like a death sentence—from God, I guess.

If careseekers are strangers, another type of question may reveal useful information.

Pastor: Why did you decide to come to me for help rather than someone else?
Stranger: I thought maybe, as a minister, you'd be able to help me find the help from God I need and sure as hell can't find.

Responses like these two point to a person's need for caregiving dialogue aimed at spiritual growth.

Deeply concerned or frustrated family members, friends, or professionals frequently pressure troubled people who are also troubling to see clergy "to get straightened out." If people come mainly because they are nagged or dragged (external motivation), they may be angry and resentful toward the pushers and the caregiver. Their negative feelings may also block them from being open and honest in counseling. When the fact that people have been coerced is discovered or even suspected, ask questions aimed at bringing their motivation and the resulting negative feelings out to be dealt with early in the initial session. Questions such as these may open doors to honest dialogue: "I get the feeling that you may have come for counseling mainly because you were pushed. Is this correct?" or "Did you decide to come because you thought I might help you get out of this jam?" External motivation, like ambivalence, should be discussed fully, if possible, so that the resistant feelings are defused by being expressed honestly and accepted by the counselor. Otherwise the odds are low that any genuine healing or constructive changes and growth will occur.

Caregiver responses like these may be effective in defusing blocked feelings so that honest communication with troubled persons becomes possible: "How do you feel about being pushed to see me?" or "It must bug you to be pressured to see a counselor," or "I would think that you'd be upset with your spouse for twisting your arm by threatening divorce if you didn't come for counseling." Counselees often deny having such feelings initially because they have not yet developed trust in the counselor. Even so, it is reassuring to them to know that the counselor has some understanding of their feelings and is not siding with whomever is the external motivator. An approach like that of the pastor in the following vignette can be effective in motivating persons who are coerced and therefore resistant:

Teenage girl: My mom thought I needed to have you talk to me. She has this thing about the friends I'm hanging out with. Sometimes she gets a little weird—thinking we're doing drugs.

Pastor: It sounds as though your mother has been putting pressure on you to quit hanging out with friends she doesn't approve of. I would think this might bug you and that being pushed into my office must give you some resentment. [Later, to discover if she has any motivation of her own]: Are any of your school relationships a problem for you?

In contrast to most secular counselors, clergy often have pastoral responsibility for the whole family system. It's well to remember that there frequently are two-sided relationship problems between family members applying pressure and those who come because of it. It is crucial for the girl in the above vignette to discover that the pastor is not on the mother's side against her, but is on the side of what's best for her and other members of that family system, including her mother. If she understands this, she may have sufficient trust to make counseling possible. By his responses, the pastor helps create an opportunity to learn more about the teenager and the quality of her relationship with the mother and perhaps her peers in school. The pastor may then decide if and when it might be therapeutically useful to invite the mother and daughter to come together for a conjoint session to discuss their conflicts and perhaps move toward reconciliation.

Careseekers and counselors often bring radically different expectations to their relationships. Because what people expect often is related to what motivated them to seek help, it is important to discover why they sought counseling. Some come to clergy counselors, for example, expecting a quick fix, a prayer pill, or some other unrealistic solutions not involving much on their part. As conflicting or unrealistic expectations emerge, they should be discussed openly so that there will be some agreement concerning what kinds of help may occur during the caregiving process. Having such an understanding enables counseling to go ahead as a collaborative partnership process. Queries such as these often elicit what people want and expect: "What is the issue with which you want my help? How do you hope counseling will help? How can I [or our congregation or God] be helpful in your situation? What have you tried before that has or hasn't worked?"

Cautions Regarding Listening

A robust emphasis on listening should not be understood to mean passive caregiving. Responsive listening involves caregivers in active dialogical interaction with care receivers. Although silence can heal, it also can wound when something needs to be said. Pastoral caregiving, through active listening, is not value free. We, as religious caregivers, take a stand against cultural discourses, like sexism and racism, that do harm to people. We need to take a stand on behalf of people being able to recognize and stand against the realities that seek to disempower them, and we need to stand with them in that resistance.[12]

Maxine Glaz reminds caregivers, "Real empathy consists of the comprehension of the other person's experience, not simply in the explosive acknowledgment of emotion."[13] An important caution related to this is to avoid protracted, empathetic listening to agonizing feelings and stories that causes emotionally disturbed care receivers to open up deep emotional wounds. This caution is crucial when there is any evidence of severe emotional wounds such as those resulting from childhood physical, emotional, or sexual abuse and other shattering trauma. Dealing therapeutically with the powerful feelings and complex problems, often with deep roots, requires the expertise developed during extensive clinical and academic psychotherapeutic training. Clergy in pastoral ministries do not need such training and, even if they have it, seldom can invest the time required to do this kind of healing work. To avoid hurting care receivers by opening old, deep wounds, caregivers should not focus long on care receivers' feelings, but instead coach them actively in planning how to cope constructively with their present life situation and take small action steps in that direction. As the old Norwegian proverb says, "Don't open a wound you can't heal." Pastoral caregivers have traditionally been better at opening wounds than providing contexts in which they can heal. Caregivers are to take seriously the importance of feeling and listening boundaries in pastoral care work with traumatized people. The focus should always be on helping care receivers see their story as larger than the problem story and remember their strength and their ability to exercise agency on their own behalf.

Collaborative Evaluation, Strategizing, and Contracting

How can caregivers decide which type of help to offer or recommend to individuals or families so that they receive the help they are most likely to find useful? The assessment of the help needed should take into account these questions: (1) What kind of help do careseekers request? (2) What are the nature and urgency of their particular crises or problems, and do they appear to result from recent life pressures or are they ongoing and chronic? (3) What are the relevant social context dynamics including cultural, ethnic, and gender backgrounds as these influence the issues? (4) What are their latent strengths, hopes, spiritual resources, positive goals, and access to supportive relationships? (5) Do they need short-term crisis or decision-making counseling, longer-term supportive care, or more specialized psychotherapy?[14]

The process of pastoral evaluation, sometimes called "pastoral diagnosis," begins early in the relationship when help is requested. In contrast to the classical focus primarily on careseekers' problems and dysfunction, pastoral evaluation should balance this by also evaluating their strengths and resources. In contrast to one-directional diagnosis in which physicians use their expertise to identify pathologies and choose treatment methods, pastoral diagnosis ideally should be as collaborative a process as possible. In this evaluative process, caregivers and care receivers together gain understanding of the issues as well as of the strengths, resources, hopes, and potentialities of care receivers. Using the counselor's expertise and knowledge of therapeutic options, the two decide collaboratively on the most promising approach to enabling the care receiver to cope more constructively using her or his latent strengths and moving toward her or his hopes. Pastoral theologian and counseling teacher Nancy J. Ramsay provides a theologically based understanding of pastoral evaluation. In her book *Pastoral Diagnosis: A Resource for Ministries of Care and Counseling*, she declares, "Pastoral diagnosis is an exercise in practical theological reflection with a praxis orientation. It begins with experience and draws on theological and other disciplines in order to mediate more effectively the transformative, redemptive love of God so as to empower for discipleship."[15] Drawing on Ramsey's perception of the mediative power of theological as well as other disciplinary understandings of experience, it seems likely that the pastoral counselor's facility in using both categories increases the possibility of the counselee's narrative, and eventually life, transformation.

The starting point for collaborative evaluation is whatever careseekers request. Is this an individual or family asking for short-term supportive care to get through a tough time or for ongoing support to cope with a chronic crisis in which little improvement can be expected? Or are they requesting help in coping with acute crises or making perplexing decisions? Or are they asking for more investigative help in dealing with troubling and conflicting emotions, shaky self-esteem, or general lifestyle patterns that they find troubling? For the latter type of help, referral to a caring, competent pastoral psychotherapist or other mental health therapist is probably appropriate. How should counselors respond when careseekers are not sure what they need or want? Are they asking for assistance that in all probability will not be helpful or will be injurious to them? Caregivers should level with them about the strengths and limitations of other live options so they can make an informed decision.

There are important exceptions to the use of a collaborative approach to evaluation and decision making. In these situations people clearly need firm explanatory advice and urging to move toward appropriate help. One such exception is when people are so overwhelmed by traumatic crises that their ability to participate effectively in making decisions is drastically reduced. Another is when an acute and dangerous crisis, such as the threat of physical or emotional violence, creates an urgent need for firm guidance on what they need to do immediately in order to protect themselves or others from physical or psychological harm. The ability of severely traumatized and dysfunctional persons to participate in the process of evaluation and decision making is often limited to some degree by their woundedness, but they should be involved as much as possible.

After a tentative evaluation is formed by collaborative dialogue undergirded by the counselor's expertise, caregivers should ask themselves: Is this person (couple or family) likely to benefit from the kind of help that my time, training, skills, and pastoral roles enable me to provide? Or is there some agency, therapist, or self-help group in our community that can better provide the specialized help that this person (couple or family) needs? On the basis of such considerations, pastors form tentative decisions concerning whether to offer general pastoral care or short-term crisis counseling or to suggest a referral and help the person (couple or family) make effective transitions to specialized help.

If the evaluation process points to short-term counseling and the care receiver agrees to try this, the caregiver and the care receiver should discuss and come to a tentative agreement concerning the objectives, probable length, and roles of both counselor and counselee. (This mutual agreement is called the "counseling contract.") Failure to develop such a joint agreement near the beginning of counseling usually results in frustration on both sides of the relationship. It also may lead to premature termination before counselees discover whether the process might be helpful to them. It will also be useful to talk about the unique nature of a counseling relationship, that is, the boundaries and short-term length. At the end of a pastoral counseling relationship, pastors should clearly bring closure so that the more ongoing (and less intense) pastor-parishioner relationship may comfortably resume if possible. Many problems (including dependencies and other boundary issues) could be avoided if this kind of intentional closure were a part of every pastoral counseling relationship.

In evaluation and planning approaches to caregiving, caregivers should be aware of the wider circles in which people live. Attending to the sociocultural context of careseekers is useful in all caregiving, but it is especially so with people affected by cultural oppression. Mainstream psychological diagnostic systems tend to underestimate or ignore the complex sociocultural dynamics that cause or at least complicate personality and relationship problems in oppressed people. For example, women's problems often are understood as pathological rather than recognized as adaptive survival responses to sexist oppression.[16]

One way to implement a positive, transformational approach in evaluating and helping counselees is to move beyond thinking of them or describing them using sickness-oriented diagnostic language. We tend to see what we look for. If we look or listen for problems, that is what we will find. If we look and listen for strength, resiliency, and agency, we will tend to find those. Careseekers often have forgotten their own strengths, so caregivers should avoid colluding with that forgetfulness in their pastoral evaluations. Looking for strength, resiliency, and agency also communicates respect for care receivers.

Respecting Pastoral Confidentiality

In most counseling relationships confidentiality should be discussed and clarified during the initial contact. Doing this increases the likelihood that the counselees will reveal painful facts honestly. It also respects the precious time-tested clergy tradition of privileged communication, rooted in the inviolability of the priestly confessional and the biblical idea of sanctuary. Secular therapists and health professionals are required by professional ethics and state laws to respect confidentiality, except when patients reveal a crime, or suicidal intent or the counselor believes suicide to be likely. Society has generally honored the clergy tradition by giving them more legal latitude regarding reporting to authorities. But state laws vary on this issue, and clergy should check the laws of their state about circumstances under which they are required to break confidentiality.

Most theological ethicists would agree that pastoral counselors are morally, if not legally, obligated to report statements from counselees that reveal danger to children or vulnerable adults. If there is substantial reason to believe that there is a threat to human life or that there is potential or actual harm being done to those unable to protect themselves, clergy need to report that to the appropriate authorities (for example, child protective services). Moreover, there are also mandatory reporting laws for clergy. And all counselors must break confidentiality if they are served with a court order to testify in cases of violent crimes. Protecting confidentiality is a sacred duty, as is speaking out when harm to the vulnerable is happening. This can be a difficult line to walk, and it is wise to have an appropriate consultant who will help when difficult decisions must be made.

Mechanics of Counseling—Setting, Record Keeping

It is much easier to do effective counseling in a quiet place free from interruptions. If one lacks a secretary who can ensure privacy during counseling, put a "Pastor in Conference" sign on the study door, and use a phone with an answering machine and a ringer that will turn off during counseling conversations. Schedule formal counseling sessions with definite beginning and ending times, and stick to that schedule. When crisis counseling opportunities emerge unexpectedly, say at the outset something like, "I have about thirty minutes for us to talk now. If that isn't enough time, we can schedule additional time to meet later." This alerts care receivers to the time available and encourages them to use that time productively.

Keeping careful written records can be an essential part of a safe and disciplined approach to pastoral counseling. This is especially true if one counsels with numerous persons because sometimes memory alone is not adequate. Some pastors develop haphazard record-keeping habits because they are "too busy" or because they underestimate the importance of the records. But clergy should be no less disciplined in ministering to people's psychological and spiritual healing than physicians are in ministering to our bodies.

Written records can serve several valuable purposes in addition to being a way of checking and supplementing one's memory, especially if one has occasional "senior moments." They encourage reflection and planning between sessions, with relevant reading or consultation in some cases, regarding how best to approach any subsequent sessions. They also encourage reflecting on and learning from one's mistakes as well as one's unexpected successes. They can be very useful in making informed referrals.

Keeping them for future reference when people return for counseling after extended absences is useful. If one has several sessions with people having complicated problems and relationships, records can help one become aware of significant patterns.

Counseling records should be kept in a locked file to protect confidentiality. Keeping records on a computer carries with it the risk of having someone break into one's computer files and gain access. A card or manila folder may be maintained for each counselee, couple, or family. Information recorded should include a coded number to protect confidentiality in case anyone else gains access. Notes about address, phone, age, interpersonal resources (family members and others), presenting problems, plans for helping, and physicians' or other helping professionals' names are often invaluable. After each counseling contact, a brief summary of significant developments may be added to the record in a few minutes.

Most counselors find that they can remember and jot down the vital aspects of an interview if they do so soon after it ends. If one takes notes during sessions, it should be done without sacrificing presence and frequent eye contact. Jotting down a few key words or dates can be done unobtrusively to provide a framework for recall during post-session recording of interview highlights. Before taking notes, it is well to say in a matter-of-fact tone, "I want to jot down a few notes so that I can keep the whole picture in mind. They will be treated confidentially, of course."[17] Notes should always be respectful toward the counselee. It may well be a helpful practice to avoid putting into notes what one wouldn't say (or hasn't said) directly to the counselee. This avoids an "expert" hierarchical mind-set and reminds the pastoral counselor of the I-Thou nature of the counseling relationship.

Increasing Caregiving Opportunities

Pastors' network of meaningful relationships usually broadens and deepens as they serve a faith community over time, and caregiving opportunities tend to increase. However, another crucial factor influences the frequency of caregiving opportunities more; that is, how hurting people experience clergy in noncounseling relationships. This can either open or close doors through which they feel free to seek help. If pastors are seen as cold, aloof, and judgmental, wounded people, as someone has said, "stay away in droves." Conversely, wounded people are much more likely to consult pastoral caregivers who relate with warmth, acceptance, openness, and a soft smile.

Of course, some people are not aware that many pastors today have training in counseling. And many who do know are reluctant to take the pastor's time to discuss their problems. Therefore, pastors may wish to let their congregations know that providing help with personal and relationship problems and injustices is one of the normal functions of pastors. A brief statement like the following in church bulletins or newsletters can open doors to help seekers:

> The Strength to Seek Pastoral Help
>
> All of us occasionally have problems in dealing with the pressures and perplexities of daily life. These are times when we can benefit from talking with a person who is trained in the skills of counseling. Our pastor [priest or rabbi] is trained in counseling and spiritual guidance, and this service is available to both our members and others in the community. Your pastor will talk confidentially with those facing personal or family problems, difficult decisions, spiritual perplexities, or the need to find competent specialized professional help. It's a sign of strength to face and seek professional guidance with such issues. Please feel free to call your pastor at the church to schedule an appointment at a mutually convenient time.

Using Electronic Technologies in Caregiving

The electronic communications revolution continues to produce amazing technologies that are transforming our world in profound, interconnected, and unprecedented ways. Telephones, radio, films, television, audio and video recordings, computers, e-mail, and the Internet are much more than communication channels. They have produced the new local and global environment in which we live, a pervasive context that shapes our lives in countless ways. This mind-boggling technology is a major dynamic in creating the wave of a new future, as shown by the fact that many children and youth have more expertise using this technology than do their parents.

All of today's electronic marvels can enhance pastoral caregiving in an increasing variety of ways, provided they are used imaginatively and with awareness of their limitations as well as their advantages.

As many innovative clergy and congregations are demonstrating, communicating through electronic channels can complement and enhance the traditional channels of caregiving communication—face-to-face contacts and the printed word. Face-to-face contacts will remain the heart of caregiving ministries because of the many unique values of communicating as embodied human beings. But as we become more accustomed to electronic communication, heart-to-heart communication will also be experienced via these channels. It behooves pastoral caregivers to celebrate the electronic revolution and use it fully and wisely.

Telephones, together with all their innovative adaptations such as answering machines, voice mail, and picture phones, are invaluable time- and travel-saving instruments in many pastoral care relationships, including precounseling and informal and crisis counseling. The familiar slogan of telephone crisis help lines—"Help is as near as your telephone!"[18]—can remind pastoral caregivers to save time and energy by using the phone more. Doing this allows clergy and lay caregivers to reach out more frequently to persons struggling through agonizing grief and chronic crises. Brief caring conversations by phone can complement time-demanding, face-to-face pastoral contacts with sick persons as well as older or homebound people and those living too far away for more than very occasional visits. Phoning or e-mailing parishioners on special occasions such as birthdays, graduations, retirements, and joyful and painful anniversaries is a valuable, thoughtful, and efficient means of reaching out to people on milestone occasions in their lives. Phoning and e-mailing (but also using social networking sites) provide time-efficient channels for being available to trained lay caring team members to offer support and coaching when they encounter baffling situations. In emergencies such as threatened suicide or domestic violence, where face-to-face communication is either not possible or not safe for caregivers, supportive, stopgap crisis counseling can best be done by phone. In crisis counseling and supportive caregiving, the phone can increase the frequency of supportive and growth-nurturing contacts as well as reinforce more constructive behaviors that people are anxious about trying.

These are exciting, challenging times, as the Internet has affected human communication more profoundly than the invention of the printing press. E-caregiving offers incredible opportunities to use this technology in ways that increase the spiritual-centered well-being of countless hurting people, touching their lives with healing empathy and resources to live their lives in greater fullness. Using e-mail, creating congregational chat rooms, and helping congregants access needed resources through technology can be important parts of pastoral care in the twenty-first century.

Awareness of Nonverbal Communication[19]

The marvelous new technologies of instant communication and the global communication revolution in our culture also threaten to drown us with information (much of it trivial) along with a plethora of visual and auditory images. In our word-saturated world it is easy to forget that we humans communicate our underlying feelings, attitudes, hopes, self-images, and problems very powerfully via a wide variety of nonverbal images and languages. Like all languages, these can be used in both healing and destructive ways.

Caregivers need keen awareness and skills in nonverbal communication, including insights about what they may communicate nonverbally. They need nonverbal awareness of care receivers, who often communicate more through nonverbal channels, which may hide instead of reveal, than through words. Burdened people sometimes communicate nonverbally their conscious and unconscious feelings as well as the hidden dynamics of their problems, particularly issues that feel messy and shame laden to them. Caregivers unwittingly often strengthen or weaken the healing dialogue more by nonverbal messages than by what they articulate verbally. The degree of congruence between counselors' verbal and nonverbal messages is a major factor in clients' trust development. Care receivers tend to believe the spoken words only to the degree that these messages are in harmony with what their five senses and their emotional antennae pick up nonverbally. In fact, tone of voice and facial/body language tend to have much more authority for people than what is spoken out loud.

All this points to the importance of caregivers' awareness of the different channels of nonverbal communication. Each channel has its own language and messages that often are in conflict among themselves and with verbal messages. Fortunately caregivers' awareness of nonverbal dynamics can enhance their ability to change nontherapeutic, nonverbal messages. What are the major channels of nonverbal communicating of which caregivers need to become aware in order to maximize their effectiveness?

1. *Kinetic communication refers to the nonverbal messages expressed by body positions, postures, and hand and whole-body gestures from either side of a caregiving relationship.*

2. *Eyes and different types of eye contact express a variety of feelings.* For example, very different emotional messages are transmitted by angry stares, loving eye caresses, and dominating power stare-downs. Low self-esteem, shame, and depression often are communicated by avoiding eye contact or focusing on the floor. As in verbal and nonverbal languages generally, a wide variety of cultural patterns and norms influence meanings. In many cultures, direct eye contact is considered aggressive or nonrespectful. In some cultures the appropriateness of eye contact varies depending on the social context of each party. We need to be careful not to assume meaning without attending to the cultural dynamics of the care receiver.

3. *Facial expressions communicate a wide variety of feelings and attitudes to those who are aware.* Our species is capable of scores of different facial messages. The meaning of these may be as obvious as a genuine smile, raised eyebrows, a tense forehead, downturned mouth, or an angry frown, while others are more subtle or confusing.

4. *Voice tone, volume, and silences constitute another complex nonverbal language.* How persons talk—loudly or quietly, rapidly or slowly—communicates much about their feelings and attitudes. To experience the messages communicated by facial expressions and hand gestures, simply turn off the sound on your TV and watch a campaigning politician, TV evangelist, or advertising pitch-person. Once when I was teaching through a translator at a theological school in Germany, a woman who was blind gave me a very generous gift after my lecture. She said that she couldn't see me or understand much of my American English, but my voice tone caused her to feel that she could trust what I had written in the German translation of one of my books and what I was saying as a teacher.

5. *Special distance from others often is a significant indicator of emotional distance and feelings of territoriality.* Again, major individual, family, and cultural differences must be taken into account in understanding such nonverbal messages. What distances feel com-

fortable depends on the nature of relationships as well as cultural and class variables. Meaningful distinctions can be made between the differing distances that feel appropriate in intimate, social, and public relationships. Standing relatively close when talking may be comfortable or uncomfortable, depending on the context in which people were educated and socially programmed as children.

6. *Physical appearances carry multiple messages, many of which are influenced by societal traditions, fads, and stereotypes.* In Western cultures, there are huge generational differences in the meaning communicated by how people dress and wear their hair. But care receivers' appearances often give revealing clues regarding their emotional condition and self-concept. Appearance clues may be explored productively in the context of other clues, so long as the caregiver doesn't make assumptions or draw stereotypical conclusions about people based on their appearance.

7. *Attitudes toward time communicate a variety of feelings and attitudes toward life and lifestyles.* In some cultures there are jokes about differences between "tourist's time" and the more relaxed indigenous sense of time. Cultures in which after-lunch siestas are regarded as normative illustrate the connection between stress levels and attitudes as well as practices regarding time. The pattern of when people arrive or start to leave counseling appointments—on time, early, or late—may communicate their attitudes toward time and/or toward being in counseling. Time boundaries for caregiving need to be negotiated overtly to avoid misunderstandings, for example, "I have about forty-five minutes now. Does this amount of time work for you?"

8. *Persistent patterns in verbal communication often are meaningful.* Pioneer family therapist Virginia Satir emphasized that in counseling with couples or families, the tone and patterns of communication offer the fastest and most effective way to sense the dynamics of those relationships. Watching who constantly interrupts or speaks for others, or allows others to speak for him or her, for example, often reveals the power dynamics and pecking order within that interpersonal system.

Becoming more aware of nonverbal signals can give caregivers significant clues about what to explore with care receivers. This awareness can bring important benefits about how to enhance the healing impact of their nonverbal messages. The starting point is to review clues they may have concerning what they are communicating through each of the channels just overviewed. Watching videotapes of themselves doing actual caregiving or reality practicing can bring clues. Or they may seek candid feedback from observant colleagues regarding what they are communicating nonverbally.

This chapter has focused on the central skills and attitudes for pastoral care and counseling. The following exercise may be helpful in identifying and improving these fundamental practices necessary for effective pastoral care.

Using Reality Practice to Enhance Caregiving Skills

Most learners feel some initial anxiety when they begin using this experiential modality of learning caregiving skills. The fear that they will look foolish or inept as counselors often creates understandable resistance to beginning. This resistance sometimes takes the form of dismissing role-playing as being contrived or artificial. But if anxious learners overcome their resistance and get involved, they usually discover that the feelings and ways of relating expressed in reality practice sessions actually are very real. (This is why it is called "reality practice.") As trust gradually develops within the group, fears of being vulnerable gradually diminish and participants usually begin to enjoy their sessions. They discover that satisfying learning of useful skills increases as they continue the sessions and/or use verbatims. Verbatims are valuable learning tools in both individual and small-group supervision. Here are guidelines for taking part in reality practice learning labs:

Reality practice. If only two persons are available, they should alternate as pastor and care receiver. If three are involved, learning may be increased by rotating as observer-coach (OC). A particular problem on which to focus the session is selected to be that of the care receiver. This can be one of the cases described at the end of most chapters or a situation that one of the learners knows well, having talked with that person and perhaps written a verbatim report of their conversation. Getting inside that individual's unique frame of reference in playing out this role provides valuable practice in empathetic understanding. Another person is the caregiver or pastor. Unlike what takes place in conventional role-playing, this person functions as herself or himself. (This is another reason "reality practice" is an appropriate label.) After ten or fifteen minutes in the session, or whenever the counselor hits a block and doesn't know how to proceed, participants stop to debrief. The one who had the care receiver's role shares his or her observations and feelings; then the caregiver does the same. The primary focus of the debriefing is on all parties evaluating both the strengths and the weaknesses of the caregiving skills that were demonstrated. In this dual evaluation, persons who are learning or improving counseling skills are affirmed in their strengths and challenged in the weaknesses of their approach. Alternative approaches to the helping approaches first used should be tried. Because the skill-learning opportunities are different in each of the three reality practice roles, participants should rotate among these often enough to give each person an opportunity to practice each of the three roles during a given session.

How does an *observer-coach* (OC) enhance the learning that occurs in reality practice sessions? This person observes things of which the active participants may be unaware because of their involvement in their roles. The OC's regular feedback about both the strengths and weaknesses of the "pastor's" responses tends to increase the awareness level of the session. For example, an OC might say, "You were both really into your roles, but I got the feeling that you were involved in a verbal power struggle. I wonder if this was the case." Or (to the "pastor"), "You were responding to the troubled person's feelings well, but at times you seemed to be trying to solve the problem before you had heard much about what the parishioner was feeling and facing."

Learning in reality practice sessions or in supervision after pastoral conversations can be increased significantly by taping them with an audio tape recorder or, better still, a video recorder.[20] If this is done, during the debriefing of taped sessions, it is useful for the caregivers to select for playback key interchanges that were either problematic or productive. Counselors who hear and see themselves in action are usually as astonished as persons who hear their own voices for the first time.

In the debriefing of a skill practice session all three participants should have opportunities to share their observations, feelings, and insights. To use the wholeness formula, begin with feedback on the strengths demonstrated by the "pastor" as a caregiver before focusing on weaknesses shown. The "pastor" should have an opportunity to reflect on a few of these questions: What did I do most effectively? What skills do I need to improve? What were the client's presenting problems and dominant feelings? Did deeper problems emerge? What skills was I practicing? What was the client feeling and thinking at the end of the interview? What do I now regard as the next steps in the helping process? Persons being the "client" and the "observer-coach" should give critical feedback and respond to some of these questions from their perspectives.

Recommended Reading

Augsburger, David. *Caring Enough to Confront*. Glendale, Calif.: GL Regal Books, 1974.

Couture, Pam, and Rod Hunter, eds. *Pastoral Care and Social Conflict*. Nashville: Abingdon Press, 1995.

Culbertson, Philip. *Caring for God's People*. Minneapolis: Fortress Press, 2000.

Dayringer, Richard. *The Heart of Pastoral Counseling: Healing through Relationship*. Rev. ed. Binghamton, N.Y.: Haworth Press, 1998.

Gerkin, Charles. *An Introduction to Pastoral Care*. Nashville: Abingdon Press, 1997.

Kornfeld, Margaret. *Cultivating Wholeness: A Guide to Care and Counseling in Faith Communities*. New York: Continuum International Publishing Group, 1998.

Lester, Andy. *Hope in Pastoral Care and Counseling*. Louisville: Westminster John Knox Press, 1995.

Miller, William, and Kathleen Jackson. *Practical Psychology for Pastors*. 2nd ed. Englewood Cliffs, N.J.: Prentice Hall, 1997.

Monk, Gerald, John Winslade, Kathie Crocket, and David Epston, eds. *Narrative Therapy in Practice: The Archaeology of Hope*. San Francisco: Jossey-Bass, 1997.

Ramsay, Nancy. *Pastoral Diagnosis*. Minneapolis: Augsburg Fortress Press, 1998.

———, ed. *Pastoral Care and Counseling: Redefining the Paradigms*. Nashville: Abingdon Press, 2005.

CHAPTER 5

METHODS OF HOLISTIC SUPPORTIVE CAREGIVING

He comforts us in all our troubles, so that we in turn may be able to comfort others in any trouble of theirs.
—2 Corinthians 1:4 NEB

Bear one another's burdens, and in this way you will fulfill the law of Christ.
—Galatians 6:2

Among the major approaches to "schools" of psychotherapy, three are the most relevant to pastoral care and counseling. Each of these has certain distinctive objectives and methods, even though there is overlapping among the three. One approach, *supportive therapy*, provides valuable tools for most types of pastoral caregiving. This is the focus of the present chapter. *Crisis intervention* provides widely used concepts and methods for caregiving in faith communities. It will be explored fully in the next chapter. The third approach, *focused counseling* or psychotherapy, aims at facilitating major constructive changes in persons' inner life, behaviors, and relationships. It is a primary tool used by pastoral counseling specialists in doing longer-term work with burdened people.

Skill in supportive pastoral care is another essential tool in care and counseling. It is particularly crucial in all types of crises and grief caregiving. In chronic crises, as distinguished from shorter-term acute crises, ongoing supportive care is the heart of what these burdened people most need.

Supportive Caregiving: Strategic Pastoral Opportunity

There are tragedies, failures, disappointments, and agonizing losses in the lives of most people, even though many keep their pain carefully hidden. Sooner or later, even the most fortunate among us suffer loss. For some people life is extremely cruel and unjust. The author of the book of Job declared wisely that we humans are born to trouble as the sparks fly upward from a campfire. In light of this universal reality, skill in supportive caregiving, together with crisis intervention and grief-healing methods, is a godsend for countless people inside congregations and in their wider communities. The ubiquitous nature of human suffering makes it clear why most people are most attracted to churches that care for their hurts and losses, their frustrations, disappointments, and crushing defeats. They look for a spiritual home where they can find some hope and healing, some comfort, peace, esteem, and joy, cultivated in a spiritual climate of family-like acceptance and belonging. These considerations are far more important to most people than denominational labels or creeds.

Church historian William A. Clebsch and pastoral care specialist Charles R. Jaekle, in their historically grounded perspective on pastoral caregiving, point to the important place of sustaining or supporting methods today:

> The sustaining function of the cure of souls in our day continues to be a crucially important helping ministry....Everywhere today busy pastors are called upon to sustain troubled persons in, through, and beyond a plethora of hurts that brook no direct restoration.... Tightly knit communities once furnished friends and neighbors who could stand by in moments of shock, whereas in a society on wheels the tasks of providing such sustenance to urban and suburban people fall heavily upon the clergy.[1]

Clergy, lay caregivers, and congregations are in strategic positions to provide the family-like caring support on a continuing basis for which increasing multitudes of people long. As the population ages and older adults rapidly increase in numbers, the hunger for caregiving will continue to proliferate. More and more individuals and families will struggle under a cloud of chronic problems with little hope for cures or even major remediation. These include persons affected by HIV/AIDS; children and adults with major and often multiple irreversible physical and mental disabilities; people suffering from the living death of Alzheimer's disease; people experiencing the trauma of autism; and those carrying the load of caring for aging, increasingly dependent parents and grandparents. While all members of the family system in which a person suffers such severe chronic problems carry heavy loads, the relatives who provide the primary care have the heaviest burdens. They need regular respites of self-care, which can help them avoid caregivers' burnout by letting them recharge their physical, emotional, and spiritual batteries. People in chronic or ongoing stress can benefit from supportive caregiving, but almost all people go through stress and struggles at times in their lives that call out for supportive care by their pastors and congregations.

What institutions in our society can best provide effective support and care with such individuals and families? When compared with other public and private providers of care, holistic congregations led by clergy with counseling and coaching skills have more key resources to assist those with chronic problems than any other institution. They often have caring people with healthy spiritual motivation and a commitment to serve others. Pastoral caregivers, then, have the resources of a spiritually nurturing faith community available to offer spiritual nutrition to themselves and care receivers. For all these reasons, understanding the working principles and learning the basic methods of supportive caregiving are essential for church-based caregivers. Furthermore, in no area of whole-congregation care is the ministry of trained lay caregivers more essential. By implementing innovative programs of supportive care, clergy and other church caregivers can provide healing, hope, and wholeness for the well-being of countless burdened individuals and families.

How does supportive caregiving relate to general pastoral care and counseling? Supportive relationships are integral to the entire fabric of a congregation's pastoral care ministry. Much of the supportive work is done spontaneously by the network of sustaining, nurturing relationships that pastors and lay caregivers already have within congregations. Caregiving relationships move into supportive counseling when counseling methods are employed to help individuals, couples, or families cope with particular problems, crises, or decisions. Like the reinforcing steel in concrete, these methods are used at stress points to strengthen and enhance the helpfulness of ongoing supportive care.

Guiding Goals and Principles of Supportive Caregiving

In supportive care and counseling, pastors use methods that *stabilize, undergird, nurture, and guide* persons experiencing troubles, enabling them to handle their problems and relationships more constructively within the context of their unique limits and possibilities. The objectives and methods of supportive care and counseling become clear when contrasted with the more change-oriented approaches of pastoral counseling and psychotherapy. The latter often seek to help clients uncover the unconscious dynamics and early life experiences that continue to influence current feelings, relationships, self-identity, and overall well-being.

In contrast, supportive care and counseling methods are not oriented toward insight, behavioral, or relational changes. Instead, their goal is to help persons gain the strength and perspective to use their psychological, spiritual, and interpersonal resources more effectively in coping as constructively as possible with difficult life situations. The aim is to help people avoid self-hurting or other-hurting behaviors and enhance their vital relationships. Personality growth often occurs gradually in supportive care and counseling as a result of persons' increased effectiveness in handling their problems and improving their relationships.

All caregiving approaches depend on healthy, nurturing pastor-parishioner relationships characterized by trust, integrity, and caring. In supportive care and counseling, the therapeutic relationship per se is the primary instrument of support. Sustaining this relationship is the heart of the process. By relating trustfully to pastors and their faith community's strength and health, persons have their inner strength and wholeness reinforced by association. This enhances their ability to handle their difficult situations more constructively.

In actual practice, the distinction between counseling, psychotherapeutic, and supportive approaches is usually a matter of emphasis and choice of primary goals. The goals and needs are set by careseekers. They determine whether they have a supportive need or a counseling need. As indicated above, most approaches to counseling and therapy have strong supportive dimensions. In primarily supportive caregiving, this aspect is central. But some increased self-awareness and self-insight as well as behavioral changes often result from using effective supportive methods. In general, supportive methods use primarily listening, empowering, and sustaining methods, helping the careseekers give voice to the struggles they are experiencing and their feelings in that struggle and assisting the care seekers to identify potential resources and directions that will improve their situations. Supportive caregiving tends to make more use of consistent reflective listening, occasional coaching or guidance, sharing relevant information, offering reassurance or inspiration, planning, asking carefully selected questions, and encouraging or discouraging certain forms of behavior.

The ultimate goal of supportive caregiving is to enhance burdened people's overall well-being as much as possible within their limitations. It seeks to avoid carrying them longer than is absolutely necessary by coaching them in coping better with their continuing burdens and empowering more of their own resources for doing so. Many individuals and families who suffer from incurable diseases, irreversible disabilities, and severe, chronic problems may require ongoing caring support in carrying their enormous loads.

Using Supportive Caregiving in Life's Seven Dimensions

To highlight the wide usefulness of supportive caregiving, let us look again at the seven dimensions of pastoral care and counseling in terms of the need for support and the supportive resources available in these basic arenas of people's lives.

People have a great need for *physical supportive care* when they are in high-stress situations. For example, when they are overloaded by heavy losses, their embodied selves need the support of increased physical self-care and physical care from loved ones by appropriate, caring hugs and gifts of healthful food.

During times of mental and emotional trials, people need the *mental supportive care* from a caring person or persons who can mentor them wisely. Experienced friends or family members can coach them and support their reality-based hopes and dreams concerning how to move toward better tomorrows. They also need enhanced mental self-care and self-nurture; for example, by listening to refreshing music or reading something that gives them a brief mental vacation.

Spiritual supportive caregiving is a vital life jacket when people are struggling in deep water. This support can come from a variety of sources—for example, from a pastor and/or spiritual guide, or from a spiritually growing friend or family member. It can come by the spiritual self-care of intentionally opening themselves more often to experience God's healing, renewing spirit. And it can come from a small sharing and caring group in a congregation, house church, or recovery program. Whatever the sources, spiritual support can be crucial in enabling the renewal of purpose, direction, and a robust sense of mission. It can also help people find deeper meaning in the struggles in which they are engaging.

Because we humans are inherently relational beings, *relationship supportive caregiving* is a potential wellspring of loving support. It is the primary channel that can carry this life-giving water into the places parched by stress and grief in all dimensions of people's lives. People in persistent stress or grief tend to withdraw from their supportive relationships for various reasons, so it is important that caregivers and friends take the initiative to stay connected during difficult times.

Vocational supportive caregiving can help workplace burnout candidates cope with frustrations and stresses and also join hands with work partners in changing unjust situations. Having even one or two workplace colleagues who will share honestly with mutual empathy and caring can make the emotional climate of that setting more wholesome. Coaching support can also ignite sparks of courage to leave debilitating workplaces that cannot be changed.

Supportive caregiving with a playful spirit can bring the healing energy of laughing at ourselves, with one another, and at the absurdities of life into many other aspects of living. These include maintaining well-being during crises and losses, in mental or physical work, and in relationships. Playful support is a vital gift that we humans can give one another in all the ups and downs of life. It is surprising how often healing laughter finds its way into moments of stress or grief (this shouldn't be initiated by the caregiver), allowing glimpses of hope that the pain will eventually lessen.

Supportive caregiving is essential in helping to heal the woundedness of the interdependent social and natural environments. Having the mutual support of a small team of caring persons committed to this dual prophetic caregiving can spell the difference between success and failure in these uphill ministries. It is also the key to preventing prophetic burnout.

Supportive Caregiving or Counseling?

It might be useful here to remind ourselves of the differences between pastoral care and pastoral counseling. Pastoral care is about empowering people to live life abundantly;

embracing the good and resisting evil; following vocations; and finding God, transcendent and imminent, in the good times, the bad times, and the ordinary times of life. It involves the care of persons, relationships, institutions, and a culture. In addition, as we have said, pastoral care is an ongoing ministry activity—it can happen on the steps of the church, in an education class, from the pulpit, in the pastor's office, in a hospital room, or in a home visit. It is about supporting folk through the ups and downs of their lives and helping them live as fully as possible in community. It also involves helping members of the congregation learn how to offer this kind of care and support to one another. Pastoral care, in its very essence, is supportive care.

Pastoral counseling is a focused form of pastoral care that is primarily geared toward caring for individuals, couples, and families who are experiencing particular personal, behavioral, or relational problems, which they wish to change. It is not about trying to sustain oneself or one's relationships through difficult times. It is time limited and oriented toward helping people make choices or changes that will improve the quality of their lives and relationships. Pastoral counseling or psychotherapy is different from pastoral care because it tends to have a clear and negotiated beginning and ending. Pastoral counseling consists of an agreement between the counselor and the counselee to work together for a limited period of time in order to address particular life problems. Something unique to both pastoral counseling and pastoral care is their openness to the religious dimension of a person's life.

Given this, how can pastoral caregivers decide whether a particular person is more likely to be helped by primarily supportive pastoral care or more focused pastoral counseling methods? What are some key signals suggesting that individuals or families need brief crisis counseling, longer-term therapy of some type, or supportive care? The answers to these questions make possible informed decisions concerning appropriate counseling approaches or effective referrals, which will be discussed at length in a later chapter.

The most useful criterion for guiding such decisions is, first, the request made by the careseekers. Are these persons or families asking for supportive care to get through a difficult time or situation, or are they asking for a focused, more investigative, therapeutic relationship to help them make changes or choices that apply to the way they live their lives in general? The first guiding principle in distinguishing between supportive care and pastoral counseling is the request by the care seekers.

However, there are times when persons or families are not sure what they are asking for or needing. At that point, they may well ask the pastoral caregiver for assistance in determining their needs. The assessment about what is needed should take into consideration three things: (1) the kinds of problems or issues with which the careseekers are struggling; (2) the context of those problems (Are they the result of a unique or recent life circumstance or stress, or are they more ongoing and related to people's more general lack of access to personal and/or communal resources?); and (3) the caregiver's training, skills, role-strain, conflicts of interest, and access to outside referral resources.

There are problems for which pastoral care alone would clearly be insufficient. Among these are alcohol or drug abuse, domestic violence, post-traumatic stress disorder, sexual abuse (either recipient or perpetrator), elder abuse, chronic depression and/or suicidal ideation, chronic anxiety, debilitating phobias, severe identity crisis such as that involving sexual orientation or sexual identity, attention deficit disorder in either adults or children, family problems involving serious child or adolescent acting out, and marital problems that threaten the stability of the marriage.

Another factor to be considered when assessing the severity of a problem is the context in which it has occurred. For example, grief following the loss of a loved one, which gradually diminishes over a period of time (at most a year), is normal and can be helped by supportive care. Grief that has not been addressed over a period of years is more complex and requires in-depth investigation and ongoing pastoral counseling or therapy. In general the issue is whether the person's reaction is normal given the circumstances or is seemingly out of proportion (either in time or in intensity) to the triggering event.

Finally, there is the issue of whether the pastoral caregiver has the training and the time to devote to pastoral care or therapy, or whether she or he has been commissioned by the employing religious body to practice counseling and therapy. A qualified pastoral counselor will have a minimum of a master's degree in pastoral counseling, which included a supervised practicum. Ideally the person will belong to the American Association of Pastoral Counselors (AAPC) and be up-to-date in counseling methodology. Even if the counselor is well qualified, there are situations, such as the relationship between supervisor and supervised, employer and employee, teacher and student, or blood and marriage relatives, that constitute conflict of interest and exclude a counseling relationship.

Whenever it is deemed necessary to refer someone for counseling or therapy, caregivers should follow up on the referral and maintain supportive care for the duration of the counseling or therapy. Life changes are stressful, even painful. The recipient of counseling or therapy will sometimes become discouraged, even frightened, during this experience. The encouraging presence of a caregiver can help the person stay the course when times become difficult and the troubled person is tempted to give up.

Basic Methods of Supportive Caregiving

Here are eight overlapping methods of supportive pastoral caregiving. The first five are modified and extended from psychiatrist Franz Alexander's classic description of basic procedures used in supportive psychotherapy. The others are added to reflect a wider pastoral perspective. Caregivers can use several of these with given individuals.[2]

1. *Offering emotional and physical support.* During times of crisis, few people function at their best. This is a time when empathic caring and understanding are fundamental. The caregiver can be relied on to offer assistance in a way that allows the person to be temporarily dependent without diminishing his or her sense of ultimate competence. The support giver is one on whom the troubled parishioner can lean for a time. Among the numerous ways of meeting people's needs are loving, comforting, feeding (emotionally or physically), inspiring, guiding, protecting, coaching, and mentoring them. Setting wise ethical limits to encourage them to avoid self-hurting or other-damaging behaviors is a healthy ingredient in supportive caregiving.

2. *Empathetic listening.* As psychologist Carl Rogers emphasized, the acceptance of a person's burdensome feelings is one of the most supportive things a counselor can do.[3] Telling one's story in an understanding relationship drains the poison from the wounds of the spirit. It also helps reduce the paralyzing anxieties that inhibit the use of judgment and rational problem-solving abilities. To sense that another person knows and cares about their inner pain gives troubled persons supportive strength. Giving voice to one's thoughts and feelings helps one to see experiences in a new way. This new perspective may undergird a new and more effective way of dealing with problems.

3. *Helping persons become less identified with their problems.* Problems are something we have, not who we are. However, when we are overwhelmed by a situation, we tend to lose the ability to experience ourselves as separate from them. Narrative therapy can be helpful in this regard because it helps people gain distance from painful events by placing them outside the self. Because stories have a beginning and an ending, the narrator can be helped to envision an alternative ending. Help in seeing one's problems as having a beginning and envisioning a possibly better ending assists sufferers to regain a sense of control. Even a small degree of control may enable them to begin to look at their situation from new angles or perspectives. They may then be encouraged to take steps to respond differently and more constructively to it and (after the worst is past) to identify any small positive benefits accruing from their burdens or tragedies.[4]

4. *Aiding the ego defenses of troubled persons.* This supportive method is the opposite of using uncovering, confronting, or probing methods. Here is an illustration of how this can be done. A middle-aged salesman was at the wheel of the car when an accident resulted in the death of his wife. In ministering to him during his protracted bereavement, the pastor listened as the man repeated the grim events of the accident. The pastor noted that he minimized his responsibility by ignoring the excessive speed at which

he was traveling and blamed the driver of the slow-moving truck that his car struck from the rear. The pastor respected the man's present need for the ego defenses of *repression* (of the memory of his speeding) and *projection* (of blame). The appropriate guilt that awareness of his responsibility in the accident would have brought could have overwhelmed the man or precipitated self-destructive behavior in an attempt to atone. As the acute pain of the crisis gradually diminished, the man's defenses relaxed, and slowly he was able to face his responsibility and guilt. With the pastor's grief counseling help with his infected grief wound, the man worked through these feelings enough to gradually accept healing forgiveness—his own and God's.

5. *Encouraging changing life situations and taking appropriate action*. Caregivers help care receivers make constructive changes or, if this is not possible, arrange, with their permission, to have changes made in the physical, economic, or interpersonal circumstances that are feeding the debilitating disturbances in their lives. To illustrate, a pastor assisted a distressed family in finding an adequate nursing home for an older, senile father. She also helped them face their sadness and resolve their inappropriate guilt feelings regarding this necessary action. There is strong, down-to-earth support in the practical help that caregivers give by doing things such as helping disabled persons find jobs or arranging for a volunteer to drive them to a rehabilitation center.

When persons are stunned or paralyzed by feelings of anxiety, defeat, failure, tragic loss, or damaged self-esteem, it is often helpful for clergy to urge them to do particular activities that will keep them functioning and in touch with people. Doing this diminishes the tendency to retreat into depression and to withdraw from relationships at the very time when they need people the most. Constructive activity can provide temporary structure to the person's chaotic world. It may even provide ways of beginning to change painful situations.

6. *Helping generate whatever hope is reality based*. When burdened people learn how to develop realistic hopes for an improved future, they feel supported psychologically. If these hopes are grounded in their faith, they also feel supported spiritually. The hopes need not be big hopes for major improvements. What often suffice, as a person who was terminally ill with cancer put it, are "one or two small hopes today or tomorrow."

7. *Using religious resources appropriately*. Carefully worded prayer and carefully chosen scripture and devotional literature, sacraments, and healing rituals constitute valuable supportive resources that pastoral caregivers are trained to use or not use, as appropriate. When employed skillfully, they often enable care receivers to discover renewed awareness that their lives have meaning that transcends the pain and tragedies they are experiencing. Equally important, in moments of spiritual openness, elicited by the meaningful use of spiritual resources, both caregivers and receivers can become aware of

the supportive power of God's love that is available to both of them in, through, and beyond the external circumstances and the caregiving relationship.

8. *Mobilizing networks of support.* Both pastoral experience and psychosocial research confirm that for most burdened people, the major source of supportive power is people power. Congregations have a wealth of this power available in the networks of mutually sustaining, nurturing relationships among individuals, families, and small groups. When traumatized persons lack such needed human support, caregivers should take the initiative, in collaboration with them, to develop a small caring community to undergird their lives. Caring communities distribute by involving many others in this vital ministry, thereby enabling them to experience the spiritual satisfaction and personal growth that can accrue from being open channels of God's healing love.

Four types of supportive care and counseling often overlap in caregiving relationships: *stopgap, sustaining, crisis,* and *growth. Stopgap supportive caregiving* consists of time-limited use of supportive methods with severely troubled persons until they can be referred to a pastoral counseling specialist or a mental health professional or center. *Supportive crisis counseling* constitutes a major challenge and opportunity for parish clergy and lay caregivers. (It will be discussed in chapter 6.) We will take a closer look now at the other two types—using supportive methods in *sustaining caregiving* and *supportive growth counseling.*

Understanding Sustaining Supportive Caregiving

The primary mission of pastoral caregivers is to be channels of God's healing and wholeness whenever and to whatever degree possible in particular situations. But the reality that must be faced is that countless individuals and families carry the continuing burden of chronic disabilities and crises that cannot be cured. Many such problems cannot even be ameliorated substantially, given the current limitations of all healing methodologies. This is the arena where the distinction between care and cure becomes most essential. Giving loving care is invaluable when cure is impossible. This is also an arena where caregivers skilled in providing continuing support are the most needed.

Sustaining caregiving involves the use of various supportive methods to provide ongoing care with persons suffering from chronic illness, emotional roundedness, or severe physical disabilities for which current therapies and rehabilitation methods can, at best, promise only minimal benefits. It is also helpful when persons are the objects of cultural ills such as racial prejudice, homophobia, or poverty. The goal of this ongoing support is to help such persons experience the highest possible quality of life and function at their optimal level, however limited this may be in their basically unchangeable life situations. Many severely limited persons are able to remain functional in large part because of the ongoing support they receive from clergy and lay caregivers, and from being involved in the supportive network of community in a caring congregation.

The heart of this approach is the ongoing supportive relationship that clergy, lay caregivers, and congregations maintain with these persons. Year after year this network of meaningful, sustaining relationships undergirds their lives. Within this context, *occasional brief counseling contacts* using supportive growth methods can have a helping effect far outweighing the limited amount of personal contact time invested. With many such persons, little can be done by anyone to change their life situations. But the fact that they can occasionally express their pain and frustrations with someone who listens with a sensitive ear, a caring spirit, and a warm heart enhances their strength to bear loads that would otherwise be crushing. Periodically the pastor or lay caregiver may check with such persons by phone or face-to-face to be brought up-to-date on their situations and to let them reexperience concern for them on an individual basis. These informal brief chats can be far more helpful to them than a formal session with another counselor outside the context of their caring community.

In supportive caregiving of this and other types, helping people reframe their problems is often the key to helping them cope. This frequently involves enabling them to achieve some acceptance of the unchangeable aspects of their lives. When acceptance replaces brooding bitterness or deenergizing self-pity, remarkable changes occur in persons' ability to live constructively within the frustrating givenness of their situation. The psychic energy that had been invested in depression, resentment, or self-pity becomes available to them for use in carrying their load.

An Example of Sustaining Care: HIV/AIDS Patients and Their Families

The global health crisis caused by the pandemic of HIV virus infections continues to make the need for caring and counseling with victims a certainty. To illustrate the complexity of supportive caregiving for multifaceted and stigmatized problems, here are some guidelines for constructive pastoral care approaches with these patients and their families.

AIDS, a stigmatized, incurable illness, is the terminal stage of HIV infection by the HIV virus for all but a tiny percentage of people who contract this deadly virus. When individuals discover that they test positive for the HIV virus, they tend to go into hiding at the very point that they desperately need caring support and perhaps guidance. Their caregiving is complicated by the social contexts of these crises—a society widely infected by judgmental attitudes toward those who engage in sexual or drug-taking behaviors that are among the transmission paths for this infection. Because the illness is so widely stigmatized and associated, in error, primarily with gay males, the victims often hide it from their families until the illness develops into full-blown AIDS and the symptoms can no longer be hidden. When AIDS patients and their families learn the grim truth, it hits them as a death sentence that throws them into an agonizing crisis. In desperation some eventually reveal the secret to their pastors. If these persons are fortunate, their caregivers will know current information about the illness, including its stages, treatments, and prognosis. Even more important, they will be nonjudgmental, accepting, empathetic, and caring because they have dealt with their own ambivalent conflicts about the illness.

What do caregivers need to make available to them? If persons suspect that they might have been exposed to the virus but have not yet been tested, it is urgent to help them find testing immediately. If the findings reveal that they are carrying HIV antibodies, indicating that their bodies are responding to the infection, they need to know this at the earliest possible moment. The earlier multidrug treatment is begun, the better their chances that they will live longer with a better quality of life. If infected individuals have not informed their significant others, they may need careful coaching concerning when and how to communicate this fact. If they are sexually active, confronting what is responsible behavior in that area is urgently needed. Clergy need to know where and how to make pastoral referrals to health professionals or programs where HIV/AIDS testing and treatment are readily available. Testing can be done anonymously at many public health centers. This anonymity enables infected persons to avoid discrimination by employers and landlords, and rejection by friends and congregations.

Support groups for AIDS patients and their families and friends can give invaluable mutual help. Such groups sponsored by enlightened caregivers within congregations provide opportunities and resources to deal with crucial and complex spiritual and ethical issues. Pastoral caregivers should be equipped to respond to the multitude of theological and ethical dilemmas and conflicts with which HIV-AIDS confronts people. Their pressing needs often include learning how to make the best use of their drastically shortened lives and finding some small reasons for reality-based hope as well as spiritual and interpersonal resources for living with dying.

In addition to informed, compassionate caregiving, the health education programs of congregations have a strategic potential role in preventive education concerning HIV/AIDS. Both mentors and caregivers should stay updated with emerging knowledge in this rapidly changing field.

Caregivers and religious health educators need to know that the HIV virus can survive only very briefly outside the human body. Therefore, fear that one will catch it from casual, nonsexual contact with AIDS patients is inappropriate, and discrimination justified by irrational fears is totally unjustified. Like diabetes, this illness, although incurable, is increasingly treatable. Multidrug treatments have increased the average length and quality of life substantially in affluent countries where the new drugs are available. Pastoral counselors need to know, however, that the suicide rate among HIV-positive persons is estimated to be three times that of uninfected persons in their age group. Skills in recognizing high suicide risks and in helping high-vulnerability people find needed referrals to medical or psychiatric facilities can be lifesaving.

In terms of preventive education, it is well to know that the vast majority of AIDS patients now acquire the infection through having sex in heterosexual relationships. Much smaller percentages acquire it through having homosexual sexual encounters or by sharing needles to inject street drugs. Only a small percentage of babies born from HIV-positive mothers contract the virus, especially if the mothers are having multidrug treatment. Persons addicted to drugs, including alcohol, have elevated rates of HIV infection if they use sex to obtain funds for their chemical self-medication or engage in compulsive promiscuity associated with sexual addictions. Fortunately many government and university research programs are awakening hope by increasing knowledge. But at this stage, HIV infections eventually progress to full-blown AIDS for all except a minority of patients (estimated at 3 percent).[5] They may have some unidentified genetic protection. When a preventive vaccine or cure will be discovered is uncertain at this point in time. But rejoicing certainly will be worldwide when it occurs.

Supportive Growth Counseling

One objective of holistic caregiving is to inspire and coach those in crises or suffering loss to enable them to learn how to grow in spiritual health and coping skills. The spiritual heart of this challenge was expressed clearly in Paul's testimony in his letter to the first-century Christian church in Rome: "We rejoice in our sufferings, knowing that suffering produces endurance, and endurance produces character, and character produces hope, and hope does not disappoint us, because God's love has been poured into our hearts" (Rom. 5:3-5 RSV).

Supportive growth counseling is a strategic opportunity in pastoral caregiving. Many people can use supportive relationships not just to continue functioning but as the psychospiritual nurturing environment in which gradual personal growth occurs. The growth takes place in their ability to handle life situations more constructively by making better use of their personal resources and relationships. Short-term supportive relationships enable some people to discover how to use their strength and assets more effectively.

An Example of Supportive Growth Counseling

The recovery of alcoholics in Alcoholics Anonymous (AA) and those in comparable 12-step programs for other addictions provides clear and inspiring examples of a supportive growth process undergirded by a spiritual foundation. As long as alcoholics and drug-dependent persons are drinking and using, their inner resources are largely immobilized. They are like an auto that has its engine racing but is out of gear. Their resources are unavailable for constructively handling such adult roles as marriage, parenthood, employment, and coping with crises. AA provides sponsors, members who have achieved more extended sobriety during which they have grown by using the 12-step program. Newcomers often establish crucial supportive relationships with their sponsors. Building on this, a small network of supportive relationships gradually develops around the person in the recovery group. The sponsor functions in a special supportive coaching role. Sponsors, backed by the group's support, help new persons interrupt the self-perpetuating vicious cycle of compulsive-addictive drinking and/or using to overcome the effects of previous excessive drinking and/or using.

This recovery process is empowered spiritually by what AA calls its "spiritual angle," in which recovering persons gradually establish spiritually meaningful relationships with their Higher Power. The permissive growth theology of recovery groups wisely encourages spiritual growth to begin at the only place it can for anyone—with God as the individual understands God. My research shows that relationships with their Higher Power by those who stay sober (meaning abstinent) tend to grow gradually toward more meaningful and spiritually energizing relationships.

Thus without focusing directly on the underlying psychological, cultural, or biochemical causes of addictions, 12-step groups provide supportive, accepting relationships that become spiritual growth environments. Within these relationships, the floundering egos of struggling persons gradually regain strength and the ability to function constructively. By this supportive growth process, AA enables alcoholics to learn from and acquire strength by identifying with and seeking advice from their sponsors and other stable members. They begin to substitute person-centered for alcohol-and-other-drugs-centered ways of dealing with problems. They discover that they *can* face their fears, shame, and guilt feelings. They gradually heal these burdensome feelings by using the moral inventory steps so that their emotional load lessens and their inner strength increases. Being accepted by the group, getting and holding a job, making workable plans, forming friendships, and growing spiritually strengthen their self-esteem and their coping abilities. Their previously weakened or paralyzed egos gradually recover the ability to cope with adult responsibilities and relationships. Without any reconstructive therapy in most cases, their personalities and lifestyles grow in this mutually caring supportive growth environment of spirit-energized acceptance. This process is reinforced by considerable informal supportive growth counseling in which more experienced members respond to the requests of newer members for coaching based on their own recovery journeys. However, after achieving stable sobriety and delocalization in their recovery groups, some recovering alcoholics seek counseling and psychotherapy because they are uncomfortable or dissatisfied with their growth and want more help with underlying personality conflicts. "Dual diagnosis" addicted persons usually do not achieve sobriety through 12-step programs alone because they suffer from other problems that require medical and psychiatric help.

Avoiding Twin Dangers in Supportive Caregiving

A supportive caregiving relationship is like an orthopedic device that has two valid uses—as temporary support while a broken bone heals and as a brace to help permanently disabled persons function in ways that maximize the quality of their lives. An inherent danger in supportive caregiving is that supportive relationships may be used as a crutch, thinking of the negative connotations of the word. If extended dependency blocks people's growth of inner strength and self-direction, it obviously is counterproductive. This is analogous to a person who continues to rely on an orthopedic device rather than do the difficult exercises that would render the device unnecessary.

A danger on the other side of the relationship is that caregivers can become dependent on the needs of dependent people. This often is an unwitting attempt to support their own shaky sense of inner strength and esteem. The need to be needed is an unconscious dynamic that produces dependencies in care receivers that are unhealthy for both helpers and those seeking help. Caregivers who like to give advice and to be very active in solving careseekers' problems are at high risk for creating dependencies.

Highly dependent people are often attracted to churches where they attach themselves to available parent figures, including warm, caring clergy. Caregivers can become less vulnerable to this hazard in three ways: (1) they become aware of and resistant to any tendency they may have to "collect" dependent relationships; (2) they learn how to say no clearly and firmly whenever this is necessary and appropriate for them to honor the important things to which they need to say yes, including self-care; and (3) they distribute and thus share overdependent people's consuming needs for support with trained lay caring team members and also church groups, whenever feasible.

Reality Practice Skill Development Session

Parishioner's role: You are Martha, an eighty-one-year-old widow. You have been chronically disabled and bedfast for several years as the result of a disastrous fall that caused multiple fractures. You live with your son and his wife. Your faith has been severely tested by your accident. You cannot understand why "God seems so far away." Many of your friends have died, and you feel extremely lonesome. You don't expect to live much longer. You feel like a burden to your son, and there is tension between your daughter-in-law and you. (Lie down as you do this role.)

Pastor's role: You are Martha's pastor. She is the oldest member of your church. You have a strong pastoral relationship with her, but prior to this visit, she has never shared her deeper feelings with you. As she talks, you sense an opportunity to do supportive caregiving in your ministry with her. Be as empathetic of her despairing feelings as you can, without spiraling down into them. By periodically reflecting briefly what you think she is feeling, let her know that you are seeking to understand these feelings. Experiment with any supportive methods described above that seem appropriate. And be sure to respond to the faith issues with which Martha is struggling. Monitor any tendency you may have to take on Martha's problems and feelings as something for you to "fix."

Observer-coach's role: Your function is to help the pastor increase his or her awareness of the emotional tone of the caregiving relationship with Martha and what is occurring between them. It is also to help the caregiver learn more effective reflective listening. Feel free to interrupt the caregiving occasionally to make suggestions concerning how it might become more helpful. Be supportive of the pastor but also candid. As an observer, you may well perceive important things of which all of you need to be aware.

Experiment with an audio tape recorder or, better still, a video recorder. Play back segments of this reality practice session. It will probably amaze you what you all learn by using this technology.

Subsequent session: Rotate roles and choose one of your skill-building team to take the role of Martha's son, Bob. Ask the pastor to do a supportive growth care session with him as he expresses his ambivalent feelings about the continuing presence of his bedfast mother and articulates his feelings about the tensions between himself and his wife, as well as between his wife and his mother.

Recommended Reading

Anderson, Herbert, and Edward Foley. *Mighty Stories, Dangerous Rituals*. San Francisco: Jossey-Bass, 1998.

Doehring, Carrie. *The Practice of Pastoral Care: A Postmodern Approach*. Louisville: Westminster John Knox Press, 2006.

Dykstra, Robert C. *Images of Pastoral Care*. St. Louis: Chalice Press, 2005.

Gorsuch, Nancy. *Pastoral Visitation*. Minneapolis: Fortress Press, 2000.

Haugk, Kenneth. *Christian Caregiving: A Way of Life*. Minneapolis: Augsburg Fortress, 1984.

Miller, William, and Kathleen Jackson. *Practical Psychology for Pastors*. 2nd ed. Englewood Cliffs, N.J.: Prentice Hall, 1997.

Patton, John. *Pastoral Care: An Essential Guide*. Nashville: Abingdon Press, 2005.

CHAPTER 6

SHORT-TERM PASTORAL COUNSELING IN CRISES

Even though I walk through the darkest valley,
I fear no evil;
for you are with me.
—Psalm 23:4

You who live in the shelter of the Most High,
who abide in the shadow of the Almighty,
will say to the LORD, "My refuge and my fortress."
—Psalm 91:1-2

Several years ago, a news story captured the imagination of millions of people in far-flung places. Jessica McClure, an eighteen-month-old toddler in Midland, Texas, had gone out to play in the family's backyard. When her mother called to check on Jessica, she was devastated to hear her faint voice coming from far down an abandoned well into which she had fallen. The desperate mother called the emergency number for help. The word got out quickly around the community. Soon several hundred people came to watch and support those trying to save the trapped little girl. There was widespread rejoicing when the rescue of Jessica was at last accomplished. This story can also make us think of the crucial nature of caregiving with people trapped in the dark, dangerous places who need short-term help.

Crucial Caregiving Skills

In times like ours—of proliferating personal and social chaos—religious leaders have frequent opportunities to give care to people struggling with crises, losses, difficult decisions, and what Herman Melville described as the "damp, drizzly November in [the] soul."[1] Today the skills used in supportive care, crisis, and grief counseling are the most frequently required caregiving tools of parish pastors and chaplains.

In short-term care, caregivers should understand the interrelationship of crises and grief. The two are not identical, but they frequently intertwine and overlap to some degree. The core triggering experience for both is the loss, or the fear or threat of a loss, of someone or something that people value in their lives. Without actual or feared losses, crises do not occur. Feelings of grief are generated, to some degree, by all crises as well as all major life changes and transitions, and because these two experiences are so interconnected, they will be discussed sequentially.

It is important to distinguish crisis and grief care from crisis and grief counseling, even though the two frequently overlap in practice. Everyone needs increased loving care when going through trying times. A considerable percentage of such burdened people can benefit from short-term informal crisis counseling, and a much smaller percentage need longer-term reparative psychotherapy for the wounding resulting from terrible crises and losses.

Brief Counseling Can Give Significant Help

Most troubled people who seek help from faith-based counselors come for only one or two sessions, seldom more than four or five.[2] It is clear, therefore, that pastors need to develop the sensitivity and skills required to give significant help in relatively brief contacts. However, even though most of their counseling is short term, it is erroneous to assume that they need relatively little training. In fact, it often requires considerable expertise to move quickly and effectively in sizing up problems, recognizing key issues, and knowing how to help people deal with them.

The brief nature of most counseling done by pastors also does not mean that the help given is necessarily superficial. Pastoral psychologist Howard Stone reports outcomes of research revealing that short-term methods for most counselees in parishes "are not only as good as longer methods but are actually better because they take less time and are equally effective. This fact alone suggests that short-term methods should be the approach of first choice for clergy in congregational settings."[3]

Most clients who seek help from mental health therapists, including pastoral counseling specialists, also come only briefly and report that this was useful to them. Clinical psychologist Moshe Talmon reported the effectiveness of brief therapy in a book that is relevant to pastoral caregivers on single-session therapy.[4] His studies revealed that many clients come to mental health facilities for only one session and often report that this experience was remarkably helpful to them. He concludes that the advantage of short-term counseling and therapy is that clients "can move quickly back to the business of life and they are more likely to own their solutions and changes without getting stuck in a long process of 'patienthood,' where naturally more dependency is likely to develop." The challenge for therapists is to be aware of this common pattern, plan carefully for it, and learn to maximize its considerable potential.[5] Short-term counseling can frequently be of major help to persons simply by steering them away from maladaptive responses and toward constructively facing their crises.

There are several reasons even very short-term counseling can often produce significant help. One is that many people have a variety of latent coping resources that they can learn to make operational during brief counseling with skilled counselors. A second reason is that many people come for such help with either specific decisions or concrete problems. When these are solved, or are discovered to be insolvable, they often have no further need or desire for counseling. Furthermore, some counselees can "turn the corner" in a few sessions, to use Seward Hiltner's apt phrase:

> Turning the corner means that the direction has been changed. Many of the problems that come to the pastor's attention are life-situation problems . . . made worse because the point of view, which the person assumes is the only one he can take toward the situation, is narrow and inadequate. . . . Even brief counseling can often do just enough to bring a slightly new perspective, hence altering the approach to the situation and giving a chance for spontaneous successful handling of it by the parishioner.[6]

Turning the corner is called "reframing a problem" today.

A further reason very brief counseling is often helpful is that dynamic forces are frequently teetering in balance within persons experiencing crises, losses, and forks in their life roads that require decisions. Because their inner dynamics are teetering back and forth, a relatively brief constructive contact with a trusted caregiver can motivate them to move in constructive directions. Some who are coping with a crises and losses in unhealthy ways can be coached quickly to face and cope in healthier ways.

Short-term counseling, both informal and formal, is likely to be helpful with persons who can mobilize their coping resources relatively quickly with only minimal help. For such persons brief assistance is enough to sort out and plan more effective approaches to whatever demanding challenges are created by their problematic life situations. In contrast, those who are so traumatized by overwhelming or multiple stresses that they are unable to mobilize quickly their coping resources often need to be referred for longer-term therapeutic help.

How can counselors decide whether short-term counseling is appropriate for certain careseekers? Experience has confirmed a simple answer to this query. It has shown that the quickest way to discover how effective short-term counseling will be is to try using these methods for a few sessions. People in crisis counseling who are regressing or are not beginning to take steps toward more effective coping usually need referral to an appropriate therapist or helping agency. Many people who do not make any changes for the better in brief counseling have intractable problems that call for specialized therapies, or they suffer from chronic problems and need long-term supportive care to enable them to live with the highest possible quality of life, given their problems.

Types of Brief Counseling

Short-term counseling methods are useful in helping people struggling in a wide variety of high-stress life situations. Pastoral caregivers need to understand the five types of crises, each of which offer opportunity for pastoral care and counseling. Of these, four types often respond to relatively brief care and counseling—*acute, developmental, collective (or community)*, and *fork-in-the road crises*. Caregiving with those in *chronic crises*, the fifth type, is discussed elsewhere in this book, where the appropriate response—sustaining support—is explored.

Acute Crises (Also Called Accidental Crises)

These can occur at any age and are precipitated by unexpected losses of whoever or whatever individuals value and regard as significant sources of satisfaction for their needs or wants. Precipitating experiences can include any significant life change, including loss of status, respect, or power; a serious accident or surgical operation; the onset or worsening of a mental illness or addiction such as alcoholism; the diagnosis or worsening of physical or mental disabilities; an unwanted pregnancy or inability to begin a desired pregnancy; a natural disaster such as the loss of one's house in a fire, hurricane, or flood; or a vocational calamity such as the loss of a valued job that had given numerous rewards including economic security and often a sense of identity, esteem, and purpose. Crises can also be triggered by seemingly positive changes such as a job promotion or graduation from academic or vocational training programs.

Short-term crisis counseling is sometimes needed during the acute phase of bereavement immediately following painful losses. In the long process of recovery from normal or uncomplicated bereavement, the first, most agonizing period of grief gradually diminishes. As this happens, needs shift gradually from crisis intervention techniques to a need for longer-term grief-healing methods. This phase of recovery may continue for several years, during which occasional crisis counseling may be needed.

Developmental Crises

These involve people's struggles to cope successfully with the series of crises that occur at each major transition on the human life journey. As psychologists who have studied human development have shown, personality change and growth through life occur through a series of stages. Each has its own losses, new challenges, and learning needs, as well as its new possibilities and strengths. Each builds on the accomplishment of the tasks in earlier phases. Transitions between stages frequently are periods of heightened anxiety, crisis, and grief. They also are times of increased ambivalence as persons are pushed forward by inner maturational forces and pulled backward by the security of the familiar stage. During these transitions, some people experience a need for crisis counseling, often without being aware of this need.

Developmental crises are normal in the sense that they are integral and necessary aspects of human growth and development. Their form and intensity are largely shaped by family, cultural, and gender differences. These stressful passages are occasions of crises for persons to the extent that they pose problems for which their previously learned coping abilities are inadequate. Among the developmental crises in Western cultures are birth; weaning; toilet training; resolving dependence/autonomy conflicts; going to school; adolescence; leaving home; completing school; choosing, preparing for, and beginning one's vocation; courting and then adjusting to marriage or singlehood; pregnancy; parenthood; the middle-age crisis; loss of parents; menopause; retirement; death of spouse; death of friends; and eventually dealing with one's own dying. The order of several of these developmental events is often different in different cultures.

Each developmental crisis is the occasion for a variety of caring and counseling opportunities. Such caregiving involves personalized coaching aimed at enabling people to learn how to do their grief work and thus let go of the past and take advantage of the growth opportunities of the new life period that is opening up for them. Coaching can cultivate renewal in each life stage as people learn how to deal with personal turbulence and grief with hopeful optimism.[7] As in all crises, caregivers and counselors function as player-coaches who teach by modeling as well as by their cognitive guidance. A collaborative alliance is used to facilitate change and empowerment by assessing strengths, energizing life goals, and becoming stronger by intentional planning and acting to move toward these goals and, thereby, develop more meaningful and productive lives. Because developmental caregiving is one expression of what is called "educative counseling," the growth opportunities will be discussed fully in another chapter.

Collective Crises and Grief

These are group responses to traumas that have an impact on groups of people, ranging from family systems, communities, and congregations, to individual nations and even the entire global community. The wide scope of collective crises is highlighted by tragic genocides in many countries and cultures, often with roots in religious hatred and religiously motivated violence. Recent examples in the United States of collective crises and grief are the tragic bombing of the Murrah Federal Building in Oklahoma City; the school shootings by peers at Columbine High School in Littleton, Colorado, and other schools; and most traumatic of all, the unprecedented terrorist disaster of September 11, 2001, in New York City, Washington, D.C., and Pennsylvania. The latter generated a national and global epidemic of traumatic feelings and behavioral responses fed by non-stop, live news coverage around the globe.

The collective nature of these tragedies points to the need for crisis and grief healing, as it did earlier because of the murder of passionately admired national heroes including President John F. Kennedy and Martin Luther King Jr., and the deaths of Princess Diana and Mother Teresa. A longer perspective produces awareness of the continuing impact and ongoing need for healing of the collective, historical tragedies at the roots of our country. These include the tragic legacy of slavery, the cultural degradation and genocide of Native Americans, the oppression of each wave of new immigrants, and the century-spanning degradation of and violence against women.

Massive collective crises and grief are caused by social catastrophes and intergroup violence resulting from cultural pathologies. Collective crises and grief also are triggered by natural disasters such as floods, tornadoes, earthquakes, and both human- and natural-caused fires. These tragedies highlight the need for innovative caregiving to help heal collective crises and the anxiety, rage, grief, and identity shattering that usually accompany them.

Caregivers around the planet need the cognitive tools of increased understanding of the unique dynamics and methods of facilitating recovery from collective trauma. Unfortunately, when compared with individual and family crises and grief, collective traumas have received relatively little attention from social scientists and healers, including pastoral counselors.

Fork-in-the-road Crises

These crises provide many opportunities to help people by using short-term counseling methods. The aim is to coach people in making wise decisions among their live options—options that often are competing fiercely in their minds. When the options are nearly equally promising or complicated and confusing, persons struggling to make wise decisions frequently experience high levels of inner turmoil and stress. Although these pressures may not be as severe as those of people caught in acute crises, people often are still motivated to seek counseling. The pressure increases if they sense that what they decide will have long-term consequences, negative or positive. They go back and forth in their minds weighing various options. Because the future is always clothed in some mystery, making any difficult decision invariably involves a scary leap of faith into the unknown. If the issues are emotionally charged, as decisions involving families frequently are, decision-making struggles and conflict increase. After decisions have been made, people often continue to worry and wonder about what poet Robert Frost called "the road not taken." For some people the stress from the conflict between the need and the difficulty of making a decision produces deep ambivalence and even inner paralysis. When this occurs, people are in acute crises. They usually hunger for help in breaking through the logjam to make wise decisions.

Fork-of-the-road counseling is often both short-term and fruitful, as illustrated by this case vignette. As a result of brief vocational guidance by his pastor, Pedro, a bright nineteen-year-old, decided to attend college, despite the indifference of his parents and extended family. The pastor helped Pedro describe and reflect on a passionate dream he had for his life, a dream that he had assumed was out of reach for him. The dream was to become a high school teacher, like one of his admired mentors who believed in his intellectual potential far more than he did and had told him so. The pastor encouraged Pedro to talk about the steps he might take to make his "impossible dream" become possible. As his need for a college education and a teaching credential became clear to him, he asked the pastor to meet with him and his family to explain how his decision could be implemented. The pastor also talked with the school guidance counselor about Pedro's aptitudes and how he might get a scholarship at various colleges in the area. Thus, by helping Pedro choose a path that eventually led to the fulfillment of more of his potentialities, the pastor, in only a few sessions, had a long-range constructive influence on the young man's life.

Understanding the Dynamics of Crises and Losses

Gerald Caplan, a pioneer in preventive psychiatry, has provided a classic description of the nature and dynamics of crises that is still relevant today.[8] He pointed out that everyone is constantly faced with situations demanding problem-solving activity. Ordinarily the disequilibrium and stress caused by problems are reduced quickly through the use of familiar skills. A crisis occurs *within persons* when their usual problem-solving activities are ineffective, allowing the stress of unmet needs to rise unabated. The stress stems from deprivation of fundamental physical or psychological needs. Caplan delineated four characteristic phases in the development of personal crises:

1. The problem (stimulus) causes tension in the organism that quickly mobilizes the person's habitual problem-solving responses.

2. Failure of these responses and the continuing unmet needs produce inner disturbances including feelings of anxiety, confusion, guilt, ineffectuality, and some degree of disorganization of functioning.

3. When the tension of the seemingly insoluble problem passes a certain threshold, it becomes a powerful stimulus to the mobilization of additional crisis-meeting resources. Individuals call on their reserves of strength and of emergency problem-solving mechanisms. They try novel methods to attack the problem and may gradually define the

problem in a new way so that it comes within the range of previous experiences. They may become aware of aspects of the problem that had been neglected, with the consequent linking with capacities and accessory problem-solving techniques that were previously neglected as irrelevant. There may be active resignation and giving up of certain aspects of goals as unattainable. They may explore by trial and error, either in action or in abstract thought, which avenues are open and which are closed.[9] In these ways the problem may be solved or avoided by resignation. Crisis counseling aims at helping persons in this third stage by encouraging them to mobilize their latent coping resources, such as thinking in new ways about solutions.

4. If the problem is not resolved, the inner stress of unmet needs mounts until it reaches another threshold. This is the breaking point where major personality disorganization and psychological, psychosomatic, interpersonal, or spiritual illness may occur.

Two other insights about the dynamics of crises merit elaboration. Experience has shown that developing awareness of two issues can point care receivers in the direction of making constructive changes that will improve their situation. One is the recognition that the nature and duration of crises are determined by people's degree of vulnerability and their ability to handle stresses constructively, as well as the intensity of the stresses. The other is the recognition that crises happen *in* people rather than *to* them. Taken together, these mean that when and how people experience crises are determined to a considerable degree by how they respond to the high-stress situations that occur frequently in most people's lives. Extremely traumatic events (such as 9/11) are so emotionally hazardous that they trigger some intensity in almost everyone they impact. But as care receivers are helped to recognize gradually that they have at least limited choices about how they respond to emotionally hazardous events, they tend to move in constructive directions: from the paralysis of feeling that they are helpless victims to a growing sense of the power to make decisions and take actions aimed at coping more constructively. However devastating external happenings are, many people discover constructive ways they can respond by changing their attitudes and/or actions.

Another dynamic factor is that constructive change usually occurs in such counseling not by first achieving insights and then acting differently, but in the opposite direction. Howard Stone states this dynamic succinctly: "In brief counseling, change normally occurs by acting and believing one's way into it. Insight happens after behavioral or cognitive change already has started, the result of change rather than a necessary step to change. Some persons change without insight."[10]

Another crucial dynamic in understanding crises, grief, and other high-stress events is that the impact of two or more is cumulative. The particular problem that motivates persons to seek pastoral help often is only the most recent in a series of stressful events.

Several heavy crises, losses, or major life changes, within a limited time period, have a cumulative effect in which one plus one stressful experience produces not two, but more units of stress in those involved. For this reason, a series of difficult life events intensifies greatly the need for pastoral support and congregational care and, in some cases, crisis counseling.

Some years ago two professors of psychiatry at the University of Washington, Thomas H. Holmes and R. H. Rahe, developed a valuable stress scale of common life experiences. They assigned the death of a spouse a stress score of 100; then they measured the relative stress caused by other changes and losses in the lives of the people they studied. You will find my modified and updated version of their scale in this note.[11]

Awareness of the cumulative nature of stressful events has these practical implications for caregivers. The first is the importance of looking for other stress events hidden behind whatever motivates people to seek help. The second is to be aware of the effects of cumulative stress. Third, the greater the stress from one or more events, the greater the probability that some physical, emotional, relational, or spiritual illness will result unless people get caring support or learn new ways of coping.

Pastor Elizabeth asks Karla, a young adult parishioner floundering in depression, these questions: "What other significant things have happened in your life during recent years? What other life changes, transitions, or losses have you experienced?" Karla's response made it clear to both women that the recent job loss that triggered Karla's depression was only "the tip of the iceberg." In the previous two years Karla had been devastated by the rejection of an unwanted divorce, her much-loved cat had been killed by a car, and her mother had died after a long battle with cancer. When asked how she felt about things in the society, beyond her personal trauma, Karla described being deeply shaken by the terrorist attack of 9/11 and the threat of bioterrorist attacks using anthrax or smallpox virus. The pastor sensed that Karla's depression was the result of this avalanche of grief-laden crises and that much more was needed than brief crisis counseling. So she referred Karla to a pastoral psychotherapy center nearby where she received help from a clergywoman colleague who had the training and time for the longer-term grief therapy Karla needed.

Pastoral Advantages in Crisis and Grief Caregiving

Pastors have numerous natural advantages in doing crisis and grief caregiving that can be used as resources to strengthen their effectiveness in this vital ministry. These advantages include

- the inherent advantages of their position and role;
- their growing network of ongoing relationships with people in all the ages, and all the ups and downs of their lives;
- their natural entrée to many family systems where people cope with crises and losses and may experience growth in the process;
- the trust that many people have in them as clergy because a pastor's image and identity have a supportive and nurturing meaning for them;
- their ready accessibility and their presence during many of the developmental and "accidental" or unexpected crises in people's lives, including illness, death, and bereavement;
- the meaning-giving rituals with which most religious heritages surround the major human crises of birth and growth, living and dying.

As professionals who symbolize the dimension of ultimate meanings and are the spiritual leaders of religious communities with rich spiritual traditions, clergy have valuable resources for responding to the spiritual needs awakened by crises and losses. In these experiences people often confront their spiritual hungers, the emptiness of their lives, and the poverty of their values and relationships. Reflecting on his experiences in Nazi death camps, psychiatrist Viktor Frankl declared, "Woe to him who saw no more sense in his life, no aim, no purpose.... He was soon lost."[12] In crisis and grief ministries, the role of pastors as *awakeners of meaning and realistic hope* is crucially important. The unique function of clergy as spiritual growth enablers is to help crisis-stricken people recover or perhaps discover in new ways the ultimate meaningfulness of life lived in relationship with God, whose steadfast love is always available, even in the midst of terrible tragedies.

Cultivating Wholeness in Pastoral Caregiving

Pastoral caregivers need to keep short-term counseling holistic and growth oriented. It is clear that many crises, losses, stressful transitions, and forks-in-the road can have possibilities that transcend the initial objectives of finding healing and learning how to cope. As mentioned earlier, they often offer opportunities for growth in wholeness, including spiritual growth. Margaret Kornfeld identifies one reason this is true: "These crises arise at points of change when decisions must be made. They cause upsets that allow unfinished business from the past to emerge. They provide another chance for growth and integration."[13] Helping people grow in their crises and grief involves enabling them to acquire new resources for coping with future difficulties. Such help may also give them the understanding and life skills that prevent some future crises and losses from occurring.

The challenge facing caregivers is to maximize their effectiveness as agents of spiritually empowered transformation in the lives of individuals, families, and faith communities and in the larger world. They have the twofold task of supporting people through their struggles and inviting them to grow beyond simply coping, to creating a new hope in which to invest themselves. Jonas Salk, the creator of the polio vaccine, was a man of many dreams, some of which came to fruition (the polio vaccine), some of which did not (a vaccine for AIDS). Carved on a memorial at The Salk Institute, which he founded in La Jolla, California, is a sentence which seem to express his vision, "Hope lies in dreams, in imagination and in the courage of those who dare to make dreams into reality."[14] This motto could well be a guiding principle for caregivers as well as for those whom they seek to help through and beyond crisis and grief.

When the timing is right, pastoral caregivers can ask hope-awakening, growth-inviting questions. Correct timing means after empathy is well established by caring, responsive listening, and after care receivers have been helped to reduce the intense pressure of painful feelings by expressing them fully. At that point, a question or two like these can be empowering and hope-awakening: "What strengths do you have that you might use in this situation? What are your hopes and dreams in the midst of this crisis?" After people have made significant progress in coping with their painful crises and losses, it can be helpful to raise questions like these: "What would you like to learn from coping effectively with this miserable situation? What would you like your children [or family] to learn from your handling of this crisis? How can you use the resources at the spiritual center of your life and perhaps help them grow stronger in this situation?"

After counselees have mobilized their resources and are coping better with their problems, asking questions such as the following tends to stimulate their continuing growth, including reaching out to other suffering people for mutual support and learning: "What have you learned by handling this crisis that you want to remember? Have your spiritual life and psychological life grown stronger and more helpful? How do you think you might use or share things you have learned with your family? In your work? In your congregation? In your community?"

Asking questions like the following during the brief evaluations near the end of counseling sessions can help you become a more effective counselor: "As you look back, what did you find helpful today (or during our sessions)? What could I have said or done to be more helpful?" Responses to such questions can elicit disturbing but also valuable insights about correcting weaknesses in your counseling. They also communicate respect and caring to counselees by affirming their feelings and insights. In addition, they defuse feelings of disappointment and anger that otherwise may cause counselees to terminate counseling prematurely.

Coaching Constructive Responses

Here is a summary of constructive responses to crises, losses, and complex decision making that tend to lead to strengthening people's resources for coping constructively with both present and future crises (brackets indicate nonconstructive responses that often lead into emotional tailspins and increase vulnerability to future failure and personality problems):

- Facing and dealing with problems, however painful. [Denial that problems exist or evasion of them via compulsive working or use of alcohol or other drugs.]
- Reaching out for competent help. [Refusal to seek or accept help.]
- Expressing and working through negative feelings such as resentment, anger, anxiety, guilt, and shame. [Remaining bogged down in feelings of self-pity, helplessness, and hopelessness.]
- Accepting appropriate responsibility for causing the problem and for dealing with it constructively. [Projection of major responsibility onto others for causing and/or curing the crisis.]
- Reaching out to supportive, helpful people such as family members, friends, counselors, and clergypersons. [Turning away from supportive, helpful persons in lonely self-isolation and self-pity, or grandiose, unrealistic expectations of solving the problems alone.]
- Making determined efforts to understand the problem and explore the live options for coping constructively with it. [Failure to explore the nature of the crisis and alternative solutions.]
- Separating the changeable from the unchangeable in their situation, and focusing problem-solving energy on efforts to make constructive changes. [Failure to distinguish changeable from unchangeable, and wasting problem-solving energy trying to change the latter.]
- Developing a concrete action plan designed to lead them in constructive directions. [Failure to do tough-minded planning of possible solutions.]
- Deciding to take concrete actions, however small, to implement a plan to handle their problems more constructively. [Remaining paralyzed in inaction.]

The crisis counselor should be alert to the presence of self-defeating responses in order to help the person move away from them and toward healthier ways of coping.

Guidelines for Short-term Counseling[15]

Almost all caregiving, including brief counseling, begins by establishing a supportive therapeutic relationship with careseekers by using dialogical listening. This encourages burdened people to express and talk through their feelings and share salient facts about their situation. Doing so is not only healing in itself, but it also tends to reduce the pressure of intense, pent-up feelings that may block clear thinking and effective problem solving. The pressure of time in short-term counseling tempts counselors to spend too little time listening. If they yield to this temptation, they deprive persons of the salutary effects of dialogical listening and deprive themselves of an essential understanding of persons' internal world. In most one-interview counseling, the pastor should spend at least half the session listening.

Early in counseling relationships discover whether seekers are disturbed psychologically or for other reasons are in need of psychotherapeutic, medical, psychiatric, or help from a specialized agency. If this appears to be the case, begin immediately the process of making an effective referral.

Interrupt panic reactions by enabling counselees to begin facing and dealing constructively with their pressing here-and-now problems and make necessary decisions responsibly.

Avoid long-term dependency while stimulating self-reliance and functional competence by offering only very few sessions. If there is a need to extend counseling by a few more sessions, that can be arranged. Assigning between-sessions "homework" that may contribute to their cope-ability tends to shorten counseling and stimulate self-empowerment.

Keep all seven dimensions of wholeness in the back of your consciousness to remind you to focus on whichever ones seem to be clinically relevant to understanding and helping particular counselees.

While focusing on the painful problems, needs, and dysfunction (that bring most people to counseling), also look for their hidden strengths, assets, hopes, life goals, and other latent resources. Affirm these valuable resources, and encourage counselees to begin using them to cope with problems more creatively and enhance the overall quality of their lives.

When persons are stunned or paralyzed by feelings of anxiety, guilt, tragic loss, or crushed self-esteem, it is often helpful to urge them to do whatever constructive activities they can do to keep themselves functioning and in touch with other people. This diminishes the tendency to retreat into depression and to withdraw from relationships at the very time when they most need people.[16] Such activities provide temporary structure to the suffering people's chaotic world and also may provide ways of beginning to change painful situations for the better.

Increasing awareness of troubled people's positive resources requires what was described earlier as "putting on the glasses of growth." This perspective will enable you to see some of the hidden potentialities in persons disabled by crises. Seeing them from this perspective may help them gradually view themselves in new ways and thus recover hope as they begin to grow again.

Concentrate on helping counselees learn what makes their behavior more constructive and on diminishing any feelings that are inhibiting their action in this direction. Focus on the past only if it haunts and limits constructive change in the present or is a source of information about earlier successes in coping.

Coach counselees in reframing their problems by developing more constructive perspectives on them. Do this by guiding them to see possibilities for more hopeful outcomes and useful learning.

After helping them explore their options, coach them in choosing the most promising ones. Collaborate with them in developing an action plan to deal with the problem selected, and then immediately take steps toward implementing that plan. This movement helps them begin the recovery process of mobilizing and using their latent problem-solving and coping resources more quickly.

Relate to counselees in terms of their families and other interpersonal networks as well as the wider societal context of their problems. These play a significant role in both the causes and the treatment of their problems in living. Even when help seekers come alone, they bring with them all those with whom they have significant relationships as integral parts of their identity. This systemic understanding sees persons in their meaningful relationships as the irreducible focus of counseling.

Balance caring and confrontation throughout counseling. Any confrontation should be very gentle in the early stages of counseling. After counselees become aware of the counselor's acceptance and caring concern, firm, caring confrontation is more likely to be accepted.

Keep aware throughout counseling of relevant spiritual and value issues, and do what is needed to help counselees grow in this pivotal arena of their lives.

Before closing counseling relationships, make sure you have an accepting relationship that will make it easy for persons to return for additional counseling if the need arises later. Wayne Oates says this well: "The door of the relationship should always be left ajar so persons can feel free to come back again if they choose to do so."[17]

By following these guidelines, you may discover unexpected learning opportunities hidden in painful experiences of many types.

ABCDE: An Operational Model for Short-term Counseling

Here is a model that has proved to be of great value to many pastoral caregivers. It is an easily learned, action-oriented, solution-aimed approach to doing brief counseling with people in many types of crises, losses, and troubling perplexities. It aims at practical solutions to immediate problems and thus is similar to some of the insights of solution-oriented therapies.[18] Many counselees can learn to use all five steps in a few sessions to cope with their problems more constructively. I have used the model profitably as a tool for introducing pastors, seminarians, and trainees for lay caring teams to the basic process of helping people efficiently and expeditiously.[19] It can be adapted for use in short-term counseling and coaching with couples, families, and other small groups.

Using the model involves coaching counselees to take the five overlapping steps designated by ABCDE. The sequence of steps delineates the basic process followed in using the model. Listed after each of the steps below are suggested methods that often assist counselees in taking that step. As is true of using any caregiving model, it should be applied flexibly using only the procedures that seem relevant to the flow of helping relationships with particular counselees.

Two recommendations: first, to gain an overview of the model, glance ahead and note the five numbered steps carefully before you read the entire lists of recommended methods. Second, to deepen your understanding of how to use the model, invest a few minutes after you finish reading the five steps, and select an issue in your life and try walking this self-help walk.

Step One: (A) Achieve a Therapeutic Relationship of Trust and Caring by Using Empathetic, Dialogical Listening and Responding

If you already are acquainted with persons seeking help, as pastors often are, your task is to intensify and deepen the relationship for purposes of counseling. Here are the basic methods for implementing this step:

Let people know how much time you have to talk, thus expressing respect for your limits and boundaries.

Listen carefully and without judgment to what the individual, couple, or family is communicating, verbally and nonverbally. Periodically respond very briefly by paraphrasing what you understand them to be saying and feeling.

See them as precious, unique individuals who, like all of us human beings, have unique problems and weaknesses but also have special strengths and potentials. Be aware that they can learn to develop their potentials so as to handle their problems more constructively and grow in their general well-being. As it seems appropriate, let them catch your hope for them by sharing that you perceive them in this positive way.

During the dialogue, ask for any important information that seems to be missing from what they are saying; for example, their feelings about needing to ask for help and what they expect or want from you, or when problems started, how they developed, their probable causes, and what the individuals have done or have considered doing about them.

Keep the main focus on current problems. Gently but firmly resist excursions they make into past problems unless they seem directly relevant to dealing with their current situation.

Affirm them whenever you can do so genuinely and it feels appropriate. You might say, "I want you to know that I'm aware that it takes real strength and courage to face painful problems like yours honestly and ask for professional help."

If you decide that short-term counseling is likely to be helpful, say to counselees, "In light of what you have shared with me, I think that you may find it helpful for us to work together a few times. The purpose would be to develop practical ways for you to handle your problems more effectively. If you'd like to try this, I'm willing." If they decide to accept your offer, ask, "What would you like the outcome of counseling to be for you?" Or ask, "What would you like to learn from dealing with the problem more effectively?"

Step Two: (B) Boil Down the Problems

This step means working with counselees collaboratively to divide confusing and complex issues into more understandable and manageable parts. (This second step usually begins during the first step as the healing relationship is being strengthened.)

If counselees describe several current problems, coach them to prioritize them in terms of urgency and importance, and then to choose which one they will work on first. Sorting out and prioritizing the parts of given problems reduce counselees' sense of helplessness and prepares them to use their coping abilities in a focused and efficient way. Prioritizing them may also help you and counselees see how the parts are interrelated.

Use questions carefully to focus on conflict areas rapidly (P responses). After giving persons an initial opportunity to describe their problems, asking a few key questions can fill in the major gaps in essential information by exploring neglected dimensions of problems and looking for solutions. Mrs. D., a woman in her midforties, consulted her pastor for help in deciding whether to leave her alcoholic husband. Through disciplined listening, the pastor began to grasp the broad outlines of the situation—many years of the husband's excessive drinking, a series of job losses, and repeated broken promises to stop drinking excessively. To be of help as a pastoral guide, the pastor had to know whether the man had any awareness of his need for help, the nature of the marital interaction, and the dynamic role of other family members. The most efficient way to acquire this knowledge was to ask the woman and eventually to ask her husband.

As you coach counselees in sorting out the parts of their problems, encourage them to distinguish the parts that they may be able to do something about from those about which little or nothing can be done. It may be well to remind them of what is obvious—but that they may be overlooking in their burdened minds—by saying, "I think you'll agree that there's no use wasting your coping energies on the latter."

Help persons review the total problem. This enables them to gain a clearer perspective and helps prepare them to make wise decisions. It also helps them mobilize their inner and outer resources. Mrs. D. had become so obsessed with her husband's drinking that she had neglected her friendships in the church, which she needed desperately. As a result of her pastor's guidance, she began to rebuild this support system.

Provide useful information. By explaining certain well-established facts about the nature and treatment of alcoholism, the pastor helped Mrs. D. abandon her futile attempts to shame her husband into controlled drinking. Such educative elements in brief counseling can provide persons with information and ideas they can use to improve their situation during and after counseling.

Remember that offering people in crises accurate information that they lack can help awaken hope in them by enabling them to understand their problems more clearly and see them as potentially solvable. Providing clear information that illuminates problems is very different from superficial advice-giving that is usually worthless.

Focus on the person's major conflicts, problems, and decisions with the aim of clarifying the viable alternatives. The pastor asked Mrs. D., "What do you see (perceive) as the real options that are open to you now?" He then helped her explore the consequences of each alternative. If she left her husband, he might intensify his drinking or even commit suicide. Could she face these possibilities? Conversely, the shock of her leaving might confront him with the painful consequences of his drinking, which could open him to help. What would be the probable destructive effects on the children if she didn't leave and he continued drinking? Without leaving, could she release him emotionally in order to insulate herself and the children from the full impact of his destructive behavior? Before counseling she had, in her words, "muddled around in the problem," never really thinking clearly about the probable consequences of her options.

Provide practical guidance when it is needed. The pastor urged Mrs. D. to do several things, including attending the local Al-Anon group regularly and obtaining psychotherapy for their disturbed adolescent son. The pastor made his recommendations in a form that would allow her to reject them without rejecting him. He respected Mrs. D.'s right not to implement them and encouraged her to express her reactions to them. All this is radically different from dispensing facile, off-the-cuff advice. Implicit in the careful use of suggestions is the view that the role of the counseling pastor is modeled more on the image of the guide and the coach than on the long-term psychotherapist. The use of the pastor's knowledge and authority is often essential in brief counseling.

Give the person emotional support and inspiration. The familiar line, "Walk softly, for every person you meet is carrying a cross," is poignantly and repeatedly illustrated in a counselor's experience. Many crosses are hidden. If persons come for counseling, it is safe to assume that (from their perspective) their cross is a heavy one. They need someone to walk with them and temporarily put a shoulder under their load. The most vital support offered in counseling is the relationship, per se. But within the relationship, it is often appropriate to give persons verbal affirmation; for example, for their courage in carrying their burden and in making efforts and achieving successes in developing better ways to cope. The careful use of religious instruments—prayer, scripture, sacraments—can deepen brief crisis counseling by strengthening contact with divine resources beyond human relationships. Pastoral counselors *confront*, but they also *comfort*! They *challenge*, but they also *care*. The bringing together of these two paradoxical dimensions (judgment and grace) produces growth in counseling.

Be aware of the spiritual and ethical beliefs and commitments implicit in what care receivers are saying, noting those that they may need to revise to cope constructively with their problems and grow toward greater wholeness.

Step Three: (C) Challenge Care Receivers to Focus on Taking Constructive Action as Quickly as Possible

Help the persons decide on the first step and then take it. Getting persons to act constructively, even if decisions and actions are on minor matters, helps break the paralysis of chronic indecision. In Mrs. D.'s case, the pastor helped her plan the steps she would take *the next day* to discover job possibilities and sources of temporary financial support. She needed to do this before she could make her larger decision.

Help them understand that taking even small steps will tend to enhance their problem-solving abilities. It also will lift their spirits by increasing their hope and energy for healing and coping. This is especially true for careseekers who have been like the sick man in John's Gospel who had been lying beside the pool called Bethesda for thirty-eight years. His healing began when he finally took action in response to Jesus' confrontation.

Help them move ahead by discussing and affirming "the things you have going for you." This will sharpen their awareness of the resources they have or can develop to use in coping with their problems. Included may be their inner strength and vision, friends, family, spiritual resources, support and help from their congregation or community, and the coaching available from you, the counselor.

Step Four: (D) Develop Concrete Growth-Action Plans Collaboratively

Coach careseekers in developing practical plans to take action on the part or parts of the problem they have chosen. They will be more motivated to do the hard work involved in planning if they feel they are about to move ahead toward changes they strongly desire to make. The plan should focus initially on parts of their problems that they have decided can be solved or at least improved. The plan should be achievable and grounded in the strengths and limitations of their unique situations.

In the planning collaboration they should be encouraged to think of new or previously successful solutions and avoid the failed ones they have already tried. After they have described action options they think of, feel free to suggest other solutions for them to consider.

Help them evaluate each option being considered in terms of probable long-range consequences as well as effectiveness: "If you take this action, what are the odds that this will work? Where is it likely to lead? Is this outcome one that you see as constructive and desirable for yourself, others, and our society?"

Encourage them to build a definite, realistic timeline in their plan by asking, "When do you plan to begin taking this action?" The timeline should include when they will begin implementing the chosen part of their plan, the steps in this process, and when they aim at completing the action.

Make sure they build accountability into their action plans. Ask questions such as, "How do you plan to measure success in making progress toward this goal you have chosen? To whom will you report regularly on your progress to help yourself keep moving as you implement your plan?"

Help counselees examine and test the accuracy of their perceptions as well as the wisdom of remedial actions they plan.

Urge them to spell out meaningful rewards they will give themselves when they take planned action or make progress toward goals, or rewards they will withhold if they don't do what they had planned. By giving or withholding rewards, they will reinforce momentum as they move toward coping more effectively.

Encourage them to name in their plan the resource people whose partnering assistance they probably will need. Include as allies supportive friends and family members as well as congregational and professional caregivers. The plan also should spell out how they will stay open to spiritual friends, the religious resources they find meaningful, and God as they relate to their problems in living.

The plan should include strategies for overcoming inner resistances and outer obstacles to taking effective actions. Encourage this by asking, "What are the barriers you think you will hit in moving toward coping more effectively? What will you do to transcend these barriers?"

Encourage counselees to plan clear backup strategies to use when moving toward certain objectives proves utterly impossible. Say, in effect, "If your plans on this issue prove to be unworkable, it's important to move to more feasible options. Let's talk about what you see as options."

Help persons decide which option in the plan they want to try first, and encourage them to commit themselves to doing this soon.

Refer counselees for longer-term counseling or psychotherapy if brief counseling does not prove adequate.

Step Five: (E) Empower Effective Coping by Implementing the Action Plans Incrementally

Encourage counselees to begin by taking planned actions on which their chances of succeeding are high. Initial successes will increase hope, energy, and momentum for keeping on. If they resist acting on planned parts of their problem, help them explore and resolve their resistances.

Share this useful image: "By taking constructive action, your coping skills will respond like muscles. They'll grow stronger as they are exercised, just as they would lose strength if they stayed dormant." To honor this principle, as well as to protect yourself from caregiver overload, follow this guideline: do not do for counselees what they could do for themselves and thus become healthier and more empowered.

Assure them that the more they struggle to cope constructively, the easier it probably will become because their coping muscles will grow stronger and more effective as they exercise them. Their hope will probably get the needed boost as they take small but important steps to implement their change plans, and they will know that they are moving ahead toward hurting less and enjoying life a little more.

Caution them not to obsess in self-blame when they don't take steps to which they have committed themselves. Say something like: "If you blow it by not doing something you had planned, it's smart not to beat yourself up with guilt. It's much better to reinvest your mental energy quickly in alternative action that seems more attractive and doable to you."

Recommend a similar approach to them when their actions fail to produce the results for which they had hoped. It can be productive to analyze such failures briefly to learn how not to repeat ineffective action plans. But rather than spend much valuable time and energy in that direction, it's better to begin implementing another option chosen from their backup strategies.

As they implement their plans, ask them to phone you once between face-to-face contacts to let you know how the action plan is working. This is a particularly helpful request for counselees who seem to be wavering in their courage and intention to take difficult steps toward responsible change.

Mrs. D. reported that she had succeeded in obtaining a job in a grocery store during the time her children were in school. She had also begun attending Al-Anon, was making new friends, and finding out that some of her responses to her husband's drinking (such as nagging him) were only aggravating the problem. She admitted that she had, nevertheless, reverted to nagging on a couple of occasions. The counselor complimented her on the two steps she had taken successfully and encouraged her to focus on times she had resisted the temptation to nag. The counselor encouraged her to consider choosing a sponsor from among her Al-Anon friends.

Keep affirming their efforts to deal with their problems incrementally, expressing low-key appreciation for any steps they take to handle their issues more constructively and responsibly. Commend them and say, "I recommend that you reward yourself by having a little celebration or doing something you will enjoy." Mini-celebrations of coping successes reinforce and thus increase the likelihood that the new actions and changes will continue.

Assure them that you will be available as they struggle to implement their plan if they feel any need for your coaching feedback or continuing support.

During a few brief subsequent contacts, after they have updated you on how things are going, coach them in deciding which parts of their problems they will focus on next and either create or revise action plans to deal with those. In most cases, these follow-up conversations can be increasingly brief, decreasingly frequent, and by phone.

In the short-term process of caregiving dialogue, you may discover if and what religious resources are meaningful to counselees. As appropriate to given individuals, support them spiritually perhaps by using brief spoken prayers and biblical insights. In such expressions you might give thanks for the many ways that God's love is undergirding their healing and growth. And perhaps ask that God's love will strengthen their struggles to cope more effectively and responsibly with their difficult problems.

Develop your own ways to surround them regularly with God's healing presence, whether or not verbal and spoken prayers are meaningful to particular counselees. A simple way to do this is one form of intercessory prayer. It is to hold their images in your imagination briefly, one by one, seeing them enveloped in the healing light of God's love. If you decide that it may be appropriate to tell particular clients you are doing this, ask them for their feedback about how they feel about this.

If and when you sense that it might be helpful, encourage care receivers to reach out to help and be helped by others. They may also learn from others going through similar crises, perhaps by joining a supportive mutual-help group such as a grief-healing group, a prayer support group, or a 12-step recovery group.

After the intense heat of severe problems diminishes significantly, it often is helpful to encourage people to reflect on and thus learn from their struggles. Thinking about their crises, losses, or stressful transitions in the context of their particular religious beliefs and values is one way to encourage this reflection. However, depending on the nature of the crises or losses, it may be years, if ever, before they are able to look at these as opportunities to learn and grow, spiritually or otherwise.

As you close short-term counseling relationships, encourage counselees to continue using the ABCDE model they have learned as an ongoing strategy for coping constructively with unfinished or new problems as they arise. If they do this, they have acquired a valuable self-help and self-care tool for use on a continuing basis.

Confrontation, Accountability, and Reframing

Responsible and caring acceptance of persons with behavior patterns that are destructive to themselves, others, society, or nature must include *caring confrontation*. The confrontation is concerned with their need to do all that they can to heal the wounds their behavior, mistakes, and sins have caused others as well as themselves by changing their behavior and making constructive amends whenever possible. Working with a child abuser or a spouse batterer is an example of the necessity to emphasize accountability and behavior change early on in counseling. Constructive methods of confrontation are discussed in relation to ethical issues later in this book.

When the safety and well-being of others are not directly involved, the ultimate goal of confrontation is self-confrontation. Healing is cultivated best in such persons when caregivers respect distortions in their stories until they are ready to correct these themselves. A middle-aged salesman was driving the car when an accident resulted in the death of his wife, who was his passenger. During the man's protracted recovery from grief, the pastor listened as the man went over and over the grim events of the accident, noting that he was minimizing his own responsibility. He was doing this by ignoring the excessive speed at which he was driving and blaming the driver of the slow-moving truck that his car rear-ended. The pastor respected the man's need to repress the memory of his speeding and to project blame for the accident. The appropriate guilt that awareness of his responsibility in the accident would have brought could have overwhelmed the man or precipitated self-destructive behavior in an attempt to atone. As the acute pain of the crisis gradually diminished, the man's defenses relaxed. Slowly he became able to face his responsibility and guilt. The pastor's grief counseling skills helped the man find healing of his infected grief wound as he gradually worked through these feelings enough to accept healing forgiveness—from himself as well as from God.

Caregivers walk beside many troubled persons who are focusing obsessively and exclusively with one-track minds on their pain and problems. Active coaching of such individuals should include guiding them in reviewing their problems more objectively and, in this process, perhaps reframing those problems. Reframing means looking at issues through more effective lenses or seeing them from clearer perspectives. As counselees enlarge their horizons of self-understanding, energy becomes available for them in exploring more constructive options and making wiser decisions concerning what they can, should, and will do. Such reframing often helps people move beyond energy-wasting self-pity, bitterness, and brooding about their misfortunes and the unchangeable "givens" of their lives.

From a narrative therapy perspective, reframing involves people's rewriting their identity-shaping stories—the ones they tell themselves obsessively in their thoughts and thus continue to reinforce. These stories shape profoundly how people respond to everything in their lives, including their crises and grief. Consider, for example, Steve, a depressed young adult counselee with a physical disability. During a counseling session, Mark, his pastor, asked, "Are there thoughts that keep going through your mind about your frustrating problem?" Steve replied, "I keep thinking that I'm the miserable victim of God's judgment—or maybe something else like terrible luck, bad genes, or fate—and there's not a damn thing I can do about it except suffer like hell!" This response alerted Mark to Steve's need to reframe radically this inner message to himself that reflected his dominant life story. Mark sensed that this long-held repetitive message was shaping not only Steve's picture of himself but also his behavior as a helpless victim. Mark explored his message about God's judgment and found that it was long held and probably rooted in Steve's irrational guilt feeling about his rage toward God for "giving me this curse." Knowing that reframing such deep programming probably would require considerable time, Mark counseled with him for two more sessions, focusing on the process of referral to a pastoral psychotherapist who was skilled in helping persons with theological components in their problems.

In a pastoral conversation two months later Steve shared with Mark how the therapist helped him face and resolve the guilt feelings in which his self-defeating feelings about God's judgment were rooted. He said that the therapist had encouraged him to explore a variety of constructive things he could do within the realistic limitations of his disability. As a result, he had become involved in a small mutual-support group made up of others who also knew the frustrations of major disabilities from inside their own experience. Steve continued to reframe his inner story as he learned from other group members some constructive attitudes he could adopt and actions he could take to cope more effectively. Mark knew that a major reframing had been taken when Steve declared, "Sure, I'm the victim of this miserable disability, but I'm anything but a helpless victim."

What Mark did first in helping Steve reframe his attitudes about his disability was to invite him to tell what narrative therapists would call his "invisible story." These stories are saturated with negative energy and often are expressed as guilt or remorse about feelings that are unacceptable to the counselees or about what they could or should have done. In contrast, hopeful, healthful stories often are hidden in the accounts by people in acute earlier crises, however rare, when people remember coping more constructively. Such hopeful stories may be elicited by asking, "Have you ever felt better about the way you handled a crisis that was in some ways like this one?" If people tell more hopeful stories, caregivers should ask, "Do you think that the way you responded to that crisis might point to some strengths in you that you can use in your present situation?" When people have emerged from acute crises, it often helps them reframe dismal situations positively to inquire, "Has weathering this tragedy taught you anything useful or perhaps brought you any unexpected benefits?" Such a query should only be asked well after people have moved beyond the first awful days of an acute crisis.

Another reframing method, also used by narrative therapists, is to enable burdened people to *separate who they are from their painful problems*. To illustrate, perceiving and talking with counselees as "depressed or disturbed people" risk causing them to internalize this sickness label in their self-identity. In contrast, it can be liberating for them to sense that their caregiver is thinking about them and relating to them as persons struggling with depression or other disturbing problems rather than thinking of them as pathological labels. When care receivers separate their self-identity from their problems, they often find energy to become more active in resolving or transcending their problems rather than staying "stuck" as powerless victims.

Using Imaging and Storytelling in Reframing

Another reframing method involves coaching people to change their inner dialogues with themselves, including the images and stories that accompany them. The aim is to enable them to change these dynamic forces so as to make these enhance rather than deplete people's sense of hope, worth, and strength to cope constructively. This is the basic methodology of cognitive-behavioral therapy, a useful approach for enabling people to change their spiritual beliefs and values to make them more wholeness nurturing.

Applying the Seven Dimensions in Brief Counseling

Perhaps you're wondering, "How can any counselor focus on all seven dimensions of a whole-person/whole-earth working model in short-term or even longer counseling?" Here is the answer to this dilemma: understand that this multidimensional model is a flexible tool, a set of glasses with which to see people and their life problems more holistically. Seldom, if ever, does one need to deal with all seven dimensions in counseling relationships. The focus instead should be on spiritual-ethical issues and on only the other dimensions that are relevant to the healing and growth needs of the unique individuals, couples, or families involved. Until attention has been paid to the dimensions involved in counselees' presenting problems, or others that are obvious or urgent, it is inappropriate to initiate exploration of other dimensions. However, while listening and gaining a tentative sense of the nature and dynamics of crises, counselors should hold the seven dimensions in the backs of their minds. This often enables them to gain diagnostic impressions concerning which others of the seven dimensions may be in need of healing, self-care, and growth. It also may provide clues concerning coaching more holistic action plans.

Reality Practice Skill Development Session

Parishioner's role: Recall a significant crisis in your life and let yourself relive that now. Seek the pastor's help in dealing with your unfinished feelings, making the decisions and taking the action needed to resolve this crisis fully. Or role-play someone you know well who is going through a painful crisis. Get inside that person's situation and feelings so that you can be that person as empathically as possible. You may find it helpful to role-play someone you have been attempting to help with less than overwhelming success.

Pastor's role: Use the ABCDE approach to crisis help as you are doing short-term counseling with this person. Be aware of the ways in which your experiences of crises and losses influence your counseling, positively or negatively.

Observer-coach's role: Be aware and comment on how the pastor is moving the parishioner through the first three steps of the ABCDE process.

Recommended Reading

Floyd, Scott. *Crisis Counseling*. Grand Rapids: Kregel Publications, 2008.

Gerkin, Charles V. *Crisis Experience in Modern Life: Theory and Theology for Pastoral Care*. Nashville: Abingdon Press, 1989.

Hudson, Frederic M. *The Handbook of Coaching: A Comprehensive Resource Guide for Managers, Executives, Consultants, and Human Resource Professionals*. San Francisco: Jossey-Bass, 1999.

Stone, Howard. *Crisis Counseling*. Minneapolis: Augsburg Fortress Press, 1993.

Wright, H. Norman. *Crisis Counseling: What to Do and Say during the First 72 Hours: A Practical Guide for Pastors, Counselors and Friends*. Ventura, Calif.: Regal Books, 1993.

CHAPTER 7

HOLISTIC CAREGIVING IN
CHALLENGING CRISES

> *God is our refuge and strength,*
> *a very present help in trouble.*
> *Therefore we will not fear, though the earth should change.*
> —Psalm 46:1-2

In these turbulent times of proliferating personal and social crises, clergy are on the front lines of caregiving for millions of burdened people struggling with many types of crises, losses, and traumas. These demanding caregiving challenges include individual and family crises such as disrupting conflicts, illnesses, and death; societal crises such as wars, terrorist attacks, school violence, poverty, and ethnic and racial oppression; natural disasters such as earthquakes, floods, forest fires, and hurricanes; and global crises such as ecological disasters.

It is fortunate for people struck by crises that pastors are natural crisis counselors because of the inherent advantages of their position and role and their network of ongoing relationships in their congregations. Their other advantages include being in traditionally trusted positions and having ready entrée and accessibility to family systems, which includes their presence during many of the developmental and accidental crises in people's lives, and the rituals with which religious traditions support people in the major human crises of birth and growth, living and dying. Pastors have reason to be thankful for all these natural advantages.

Building on the insights and methods already described, this chapter presents an overview of crises that are especially challenging or frequently encountered by faith-based caregivers. Pastoral caregivers must be prepared to respond to these by understanding their nature, by providing essential knowledge as well as concrete strategies for coping, and by giving information about appropriate therapists and community resources. Having this knowledge and understanding tends to lower caregivers' anxiety when they are contacted unexpectedly by persons with complex or life-threatening crises. The chapter focuses first on caregiving in collective crises that have an impact on countless people in our society. This section is followed by an exploration of the crises of suicide. Then there are brief discussions of caregiving in crises such as sudden mental and physical illnesses (including terminal illness), and rape and domestic violence. Crises in relationships, including the process of separating and divorce, will be discussed later in the book. Here then is an overview of recommended ways to respond to some of these common individual, family, and collective emergencies.[1]

Caregiving in Collective Crises and Grief

On September 11, 2001, people in the United States either making their way to work (in the East) or drinking their morning cup of coffee (in the West) were startled, then horrified, at the news of the destruction of the Twin Towers in Manhattan and of part of the Pentagon in Washington, D.C. As was the case with similar moments in history (the bombing of Pearl Harbor and the assassinations of John F. Kennedy and Martin Luther King Jr.), people will remember forever where they were when the news struck. Though the previous catastrophic events were occasions of universal grief and mourning, they did not alert pastoral caregivers to the need for specific collective care. However, the disaster to be known as 9/11, with its physical, emotional, intellectual, ecological, social, and spiritual/ethical aftermath, has become a wake-up call to the reality of collective crises and the need for a many-faceted pastoral response.

A collective crisis like 9/11 produces a wide variety of individual, family, and community problems that call for pastoral caregiving. Holistic counselors should be prepared to respond to collective crises on interrelated levels; for example, individual, family, group, and community. They should enable healing of the wounds and grief experienced by individuals and families and, as an essential part of this process, also help create group-oriented healing modalities. The latter should include the healing that comes from engaging in group actions aimed at dealing constructively with the systemic causes of the crises. The need for healing is most obvious in acute collective traumas like terrorist attacks and natural disasters. But the need is also produced by the wounding that comes from the less dramatic and continuing impact of social injustices and oppression.

These are losses stemming from pervasive social, economic, political, and interreligious violence, oppression, and injustice—much of which results from profound, superfast, disorienting social change. The background pressures of collective crises and grief contribute in major ways to human suffering and diminished wellness. They add to the weight of individual and family problems and increase the difficulties of their full healing. The impact of these collective crises obviously affects victims of social injustices the most. But these crises also wound other people who care about societal as well as individual problems. Being aware of this ubiquitous grief and responding prophetically to its painful symptoms and its underlying social causes are essential aims of truly holistic caregiving.

The symptoms include

1. the shattering of a group's collective identity, producing ubiquitous anxiety;
2. instant, intense bonding of victims as they are collectively threatened by loyal members of the in-group;
3. instant collective support and overdependence on political leaders who become anxiety-reducing glorified transference figures to the loyal members;
4. individual and family grief reinforced by the collective grief, creating a negative synergy in which both need healing;
5. overwhelming stress and chronic depletion of creative energy throughout the affected social systems;
6. increased inappropriate individual and group frustration and rage, producing escalating interpersonal and intergroup conflict and violence;
7. fragmented or shattered sense of the persecuted group's collective identity, beliefs, purpose, and hope;
8. futile longing and glorification (worship) of what is dead and gone, producing paralysis of the group's (victims and perpetrators) ability to move ahead in more constructive directions;
9. spiritual deadness and depression, which replace spiritual vitality and aliveness in collective identity; and
10. protracted recovery for many people and post-traumatic stress disorder (PTSD) proliferation.

Understanding the Dynamics of Collective Crises

Understanding the dynamics of collective crises and grief is essential to effective caregiving. To make these dynamics concrete, here is an analysis of the most devastating of these collective traumas in the United States. The dynamics of this unprecedented tragedy, often referred to simply as "9/11," had much in common with those of earlier national and international tragedies. But this one is likely to be seen in retrospect as surpassing the others in the intensity and scope of the trauma, the depth of responses, and the time required for the process of individual and systemic recovery. Returning to the pre-9/11 level of national consciousness and security will be impossible because the oftheard description of 9/11 as "the day that changed the world—forever" is on target. Like the collective trauma of the Pearl Harbor tragedy, and in contrast to natural disasters,

9/11 dynamics were profoundly shaped by the fact that the perpetrators were enemies from outside this country. Here then is a summary of prominent dynamics:

The most destructive attack ever on the American homeland had an incredibly shattering and continuing impact radiating far beyond the targeted reinforced concrete and steel buildings. The interdependent psychological, cultural, political, economic, and spiritual impacts radiated out via CNN television and the Internet in a few moments. Tidal waves of collective feelings swept the country and resonated internationally with many millions experiencing shock, confusion, disbelief, depression, fear, helplessness, grief, rage, and impulses to retaliate. The collective impact struck the lives of millions of people around the planet.

This transforming national crisis from outside the country shattered the collective identity of millions of Americans, including their shared security-giving belief that the most powerful nation on the planet was basically a safe place, invulnerable to attack. This belief died a sudden death in a few devastating instants. This identity shattering was at the root of all the other dynamic symptoms of the event.

The targets cleverly chosen by the bombers were prime symbols of American power, wealth, and prestige—the World Trade Center in lower Manhattan and the Pentagon in Washington, D.C. The terrorists deliberately piloted three hijacked commercial airliners loaded with aviation fuel into these symbolic buildings. The Twin Towers of the World Trade Center imploded and collapsed in huge piles of rubble. One-fourth of the heavily fortified Pentagon was destroyed. More than two thousand innocent people died almost instantly, and countless others were wounded. Live pictures of this disaster and its grizzly aftermath were shown twenty-four hours a day, seven days each week on television and the Internet around the world, fanning the flames of a global response.

Many of us watched in shock, obsessed with what resembled a videoed nightmare. By devising this novel, low-tech method of attack, the terrorists achieved their probable objective of generating maximum collective fear, dread, and insecurity. The collective shattering of the dominant security-giving self-image of Americans by 9/11 was described by astute observers as "the death of the American dream." This dream of Americans' invulnerability was revealed to have been a comfortable, cherished national illusion. Observers in friendly countries reported similar widespread anxieties and disillusionment. This was particularly true among those who had felt secure under the protective umbrella of the only surviving superpower after the cold war thawed.

In the weeks and months after 9/11, tidal waves of collective shock, grief, and stress hit countless people, not only in New York and D.C., but across the country. Healthcare providers, including chaplains and pastoral psychotherapists, reported sharp increases in depression, disorientation, anxiety disorders, chronic fatigue syndrome, and

PTSD among counselees and patients. These responses were understandably most pronounced among those directly involved as victims, families of victims, and rescuers. But the responses also were widely prevalent among the general American population and the populations of many other countries.

An immense outpouring of collective concern for the victims and their families was expressed by countless volunteers who contributed large sums of money, gave an oversupply of blood, and joined in the frantic efforts to rescue living victims and recover the bodies of the vast majority of those who died. An appropriate hero status was bestowed spontaneously on the police, fire personnel, paramedics, and other rescuers, and on those who died and those who joined in the frantic recovery efforts. The esprit de corps of battlefields developed as many survivors among these heroes worked hour after hour, day after day in almost nonstop efforts to try to rescue or find the shattered remains of fallen comrades.

The threat of a mysterious, largely hidden enemy quickly caused many politically and culturally diverse individuals, groups, and nations to unite behind political and military leaders. The public images of key politicians were transformed overnight by the unconscious psychological process called "transference." Many frightened, traumatized people perceived them as powerful, protective parent figures rather than very imperfect leaders. Healthy dissent in the media was seen by some as dangerous for a while, and polls showed that many Americans were willing to give up some of their civil liberties in exchange for increased security.

Astute analysts of the social dynamics of these widespread responses pointed out that they could be understood less by an objective evaluation of the actual quality of presidential decisions and leadership and more by the transference needs of the majority of Americans to see the president as a strong, protective father figure. As is often true when social systems feel threatened by external forces, there was an intense in-group response of patriotism expressed in flag-waving and repetitive singing of "God Bless America." It also produced uncritical support by the vast majority of Americans of the massive military violence aimed at those believed to be perpetrators or supporters of the terrorist disaster. Congress granted the administration homeland security powers that many defenders of civil liberties saw as compromising those liberties.

Amid the defensive national bonding, criticisms of the undeclared war in a poverty-ravaged, drought-stricken country came only from a small minority of commentators and a few prophetic church leaders and peacemaking organizations. The crucial question in preventing future terrorist attacks, namely, *What are the root causes of the widespread hatred of America?* was asked very infrequently and answered even less frequently in public discourse.

Another prominent dynamic of 9/11 was a sharp increase in fear-driven individual and group frustration expressed in anger and, in some cases, rage. This produced increased interpersonal and intergroup conflicts, violence, and the threat of retaliation against individuals and groups seen by some as representing the Islamic terrorists who had perpetrated the disaster. There was a rise in hate crimes against persons so perceived. Fortunately there was a healthy response by the national government, as well as by many church leaders and individuals, aimed at preventing this irrational retaliation and increasing interfaith understanding. One positive result of the terrible 9/11 disaster was increased interest in understanding the Muslim faith, in Christian-Muslim dialogues, and in interfaith religious services of reconciliation across the land.

Another anxiety-driven response to this collective crisis was a short-term surge in religious practices, often mixed with expressions of patriotism, as people sought to cope with their sense of heightened vulnerability. This was a living out of the psychology of "there are no atheists in foxholes," as many people sensed that terrorism puts everyone in foxholes. But it also reflected the search for more adequate spiritual resources to undergird their lives and personal sense of identity. The instant deaths of three thousand innocent human beings going about their everyday lives turned up the volume of people's existential anxiety, that is, their awareness of their mortality. Thoughts like the following were voiced by some parents, grandparents, and teachers, and undoubtedly were in the minds of many others: "My children live in a very dangerous world. Life will never be the same again for loved ones!" One constructive effect of this awareness was to push some people to critique their priorities and elevate their family and friends on their scale of values. Spontaneously people reached out to their family and loved ones to make sure they were OK and to give loving support to one another. These positive responses are striking examples of the remarkable human capacity to grow through grief, even catastrophic collective grief. All in all, it is clear that the oft-heard description of September 11, 2001, as "the day that changed the world" was no exaggeration.

Methods for Healing Collective Crises and Grief

In a different type of collective crisis, a California congregation had been collectively traumatized by the sexual boundary violations of their otherwise effective pastor—a man who had been loved and trusted by most members. Fortunately the interim pastor, who followed him for about a year, had received in-depth training in the Interim Pastors Training Network[2] and knew how to help the congregation do its collective grief-healing work. This focused on bringing the congregation's dark secret out of the collective closet to be faced and resolved so that the congregation could return to its mission. A small representative task group of trusted church leaders was recruited to collaborate with the interim pastor in planning a collective crisis healing program. The intentional healing program they implemented used small grief-healing groups led by the interim pastor and a clinically trained chaplain. In these, hurting people, beginning with key lay leaders, were encouraged to share and talk through their intense feelings of anger, betrayal, and loss toward the perpetrating pastor. Using a transformational approach, the facilitators also encouraged group participants to reflect together on how they could help their congregation return to its Christian mission after the acute phase of the crisis had been healed. A congregational service of reconciliation, rededication, and thanksgiving was held after the grief-healing groups had done their essential work.

The overall goals of the collective healing actions, like those used in this faith community, are to encourage, support, and train crisis-wounded people to move ahead on their journeys of coping and recovering. Ideally the recovery should include learning and growing together in collective crises. It is well to remember that different individuals and groups respond in an endless diversity of ways to the same shared crises and grief experiences. Which of the following caregiving actions will be helpful depends on their idiosyncratic modes of responding.

Help people gradually overcome the collective shock, denial, and nightmarish sense of unreality by repeatedly expressing and talking through their memories and feelings about the trauma in families and other groups as long as needed in the context of mutually supportive, honest relationships. Immediately after a huge crisis, some degree of denial can be a temporary defense used to avoid emotional overload. But if it persists, it will block full recovery. As is true in individual and family grief-producing crises, a key to recovery from collective trauma is experiencing and expressing all the agonizing and conflicted feelings repeatedly until these memories and feelings are talked through and gradually released. Doing this enables the energy consumed by them gradually to be withdrawn and made available for use in coping. Denial blocks awareness of all deep feelings. The sufferer's hope—*ignore my awful feelings and they will go away*—is simply not true. Instead they will go underground where they will continue to depress people's energy and sabotage their creativity as long as they are repressed.

After a severe collective trauma, it can be healing to encourage children, youth, and adults to share their memories, fears, and fantasies as others really listen. This is a vital way for parents and teachers to help children cope constructively. Their ability to learn as well as cope will be constricted until they talk their feelings out or play them out in do-it-yourself play therapy with a caring, aware adult. Comparable approaches with youth and adults, after communal tragedies and losses, can well be used at congregational and community meetings of many kinds. Providing a limited time, initially for them to express their feelings, can help participants process painful feelings with supportive friends and other congregants. Doing this, even briefly, can enable group members to concentrate and do so more efficiently. The exception is with persons who are phobic about expressing personal feelings in public or whose feelings are so suppressed it is like opening an emotional can of worms when they do. Structuring the opening period for this group-connecting to only a limited time is prudent because this will tend to limit the feelings people share to those that are less threatening to them. It will also enable the group to move toward its primary goals.

Turn toward loved ones for the mutual comfort, reassurance, and compassion that can be shared among caring friends and family. The first responses of most people after being shocked by photos of hijacked planes shattering the World Trade Center was to try to phone their spouses and children to hear their voices saying that they were alive and safe. Among the most heart-rending images are those of doomed persons on the hijacked planes whispering on their cell phones "I love you" and "Good-bye" to spouses. One husband, knowing he might soon die, said to his wife, "Remember that whatever you do, I will be supporting you." What a tribute to his and others' inspiring spirits that they chose to say such things under the circumstances!

Use religious resources carefully after collective crises. Carefully crafted prayers, well-chosen scripture readings, and confident words from respected religious leaders tend to allay people's runaway anxieties and also provide a doorway for sharing painful feelings. Equally important, religious resources can help religious people keep their responses to the crisis connected with the healing resources of their faith tradition.

Walter Brueggemann is a Hebrew Scripture scholar who frequently offers caregiving wisdom to clergy from a biblical perspective. He did this insightfully in a talk at his theological seminary on September 12. He began by affirming the crucial importance of active, prolonged grieving after this disaster:

> My expectation is that pastors, liturgically and pastorally, most need to provide opportunities for lament and complaint and grief for a long time.... The first word to be spoken in and by the church of course concerns grief and comfort over the insane loss of life.... The grief is about loss, more so about meaningless, violent loss, and it must be uttered deep and loud and long, and not quenched soon.

He recommended that the psalms of lament be used as powerful caregiving resources that could enable people to find voice for expressing their painful feelings surrounding the personal dimension of the loss.[3]

Brueggemann's insights transcended those of most grief specialists in recognizing collective crises and grief when he said that "the public dimension of grief is deep underneath personal loss, and for the most part, not easily articulated among us. But grief will not be worked well or adequately until attention goes underneath the personal to the public and communal." About the nature of the public dimensions of loss, he continued, "The loss, beyond the personal, is a systemic shattering, a new public sense of vulnerability and outrage, an abrupt subverting of our shared sense that we in the US are somehow immune from the rage of the world."

Open to the spiritual resources that are meaningful and security-giving in a community of shared faith. Brueggemann emphasized the ultimate spiritual source of human comfort in these words: "Eventually we must speak about the God of all comfort beyond our feeble but indispensable personal offer of comfort.... For it is the comfort out beyond our management, the reality of God, that makes grief without protective denial possible." Based on his study of the Psalms and Jeremiah, he declared, "I have no doubt that the community of faith in the Bible knew how to engage in systemic grief."[4] He recommended the communal laments (such as Pss. 44; 74; 79; 137) as valuable caregiving resources for expressing the community dimension of grieving.[5] He said that these "bespeak the shattering of the most elemental public symbols of coherence and meaning, in the Old Testament embodied in the Jerusalem Temple." It is worth noting that what were embodied and attacked on September 11 were not prominent symbols of spiritual power and well-being, but of dominant commercial and military ascendancy in the only surviving "superpower."

After the September 11 events, millions of people spontaneously sought spiritual comfort that would help allay their collective grief and anxiety. They did this in countless informal as well as formal memorial services and prayer vigils for the victims and their families. Rituals of candle lighting and other collective healing were part of most of these religious activities. Many of them were interfaith and colored with passionate patriotism and assurances from both religious and political leaders about eventual "victory in our war" with terrorism. Much of the religious and ideological diversity, as well as many conflicts inside the country, was set aside for a time. Intense bonding across wide gulfs of differences brought at least short-term national unity against the new enemy, terrorism. Attendance soared at religious services of all faiths, as did the sale of Bibles and other religious books. As frequently happens in severe individual losses, huge communal losses often shake and shatter many people's works-righteousness beliefs. This creates opportunities for growth toward a more reality-based, less magical faith.

Be aware of the ethical issues and implications in the tragic precipitating event and in what is and should happen in responding to it. The timing of going public with any critical insights about the complicity of victim groups (including nations) in the collective tragedy is crucial. When groups of people are bonding in terror and defending themselves against death and anxiety by upsurges of group glorification and passionate, unreflective religious expressions, they react with defensive rage against any person or group that raises even gentle questions about the group complicity in the tragedy. Dissent becomes extremely unpopular because it threatens the defenses. Ethical over-simplification is rampant as the in-group sees itself as reflecting only the good and the enemy as utterly evil. Blind righteous indignation justifies demonizing the enemy and may motivate and justify raw vengeance against a targeted group or nation. If this happens, the self-defined "good side" usually sabotages itself and its causes. The September 11 disaster offered the opportunity for ethically aware people in affluent, overconsuming countries like the United States to reflect on and change the social patterns of collective narcissism that were so prominent before this wake-up crisis.

Reach out actively with helping hands and hearts to victims of communal crises as part of constructive coping and recovery. That humans have an intuitive awareness of this movement was clear after the September 11 disaster when millions of people did so spontaneously. The first thing that many people felt an urgent need to do, as the first devastating photographs of airplanes crashing into the World Trade Center were shown on TV news, was to phone their family and friends to bond with them and check to see if they were safe.

Reaching out quickly with care to persons most victimized by the collective tragedy was obviously helpful to many people. Two of many such spontaneous expressions were the very long lines at blood donation places and huge, multimillion dollars in contributions of funds to help the victims and their families. The rewards of such altruistic behavior include the feeling that one's need to actually "do something" receives some satisfaction. Because the grief is communal, doing something constructive, as families or in groups, can be especially helpful. Reaching out to others going through many of the same experiences and feelings can be helpful to those on both sides of relationships.

Some people need crisis counseling as they struggle to make some sense of the violence and evil involved in communal crises. The theodicy issue with which the biblical story of Job wrestles is that of finding meaningful answers to why good, innocent people suffer and die. This is always a baffling philosophical-theological challenge in collective grief. In the ghastly violence of terrorists' attacks, ethnic cleansings, and wars, this difficult issue is not confronted as long as victims understand there to be an "evil enemy who must be punished for the crime so that justice can be done." Natural disasters and horrific accidents involving no human culpability confront thoughtful people with this dilemma. When natural disasters are understood as "acts of God," however theologically problematic this belief is, theodicy rears its head in the minds and hearts of many. The central question—Why do good people suffer?—storied in the book of Job often arises as people struggle in collective crises and losses.

In his September 12, 2001, statement, Brueggemann reminded caregiving pastors of the necessity of enabling people to deal with the reality of evil as an essential part of experiencing healing after violent trauma. He asked the question that occupies the minds of countless parents, "So what shall we tell our children?" Because most children in affluent countries like ours are privileged and protected, the shock of the massive evil of violence, seen and reinforced endlessly on news channels, is great, perhaps even over-whelming. Parents who have dealt with their own shock at suffering and death eventu-ally can guide children to grow stronger by using the teachable moments, the windows so rudely opened by the shock. Children can learn that violence and evil are part of the fabric of life. They can learn how to cope with this reality by emulating the example of their parents, teachers, grandparents, and other adult role models. The hope articulated by Brueggemann is that Christian Americans have "learned enough from the Jewish Holocaust to refrain from any glib triumphalism."

Be aware that an active program of innovative caregiving tailored to recovery from particu-lar collective crises and grief is needed in congregations and probably will continue to be needed for a long time afterward. This program should include repeated, structured opportunities for people to write down and share their responses and also to talk and listen to one another's experiences. The programs should include innovative group rituals that give groups permission to express their feelings in the context of religious rituals that make them feel safer and less threatened. The passionate nationwide and worldwide rituals of remembering on the first anniversary of 9/11 are vivid examples of how social systems use group ceremonies to cope with collective tragedies. The intermingling of patriotic and religious symbols voiced by key national leaders was a prominent aspect of these events. Also prominent was the celebration of the heroism and compassionate actions elicited by 9/11 and the call to move ahead in fighting terrorism and building a stronger and better society.

Growing through Collective Crises

Pulitzer Prize–winning journalist Haynes Johnson offered wise observations concern-ing the tragedy of 9/11.[6] He pointed out that the tragedy complicates things, but it also refocuses the American psyche in multiple and profound ways: "In the rubble of the World Trade Center Americans have a sliver of opportunity: the chance to become a more mature nation." The mature society that he hoped would develop from this col-lective crisis would be realistic but full of energy, better educated, wise, and prudent, a society coming together in solving the difficult issues of the rapidly emerging future, such as how society can afford to respond to the rapidly increasing life expectancy of its people—in short, a wise society that invests in its future.

A challenge like 9/11 is immense and multifaceted for pastoral caregivers. Let's hope that we who are trained to think in disciplined ways about cultivating spiritually centered, holistic healing will use such challenges as windows of opportunity to make innovative discoveries of healing modalities for countless wounded persons and families, and also for our wounded nation and global community. Let's hope and pray that we can use our expertise to help our beloved country stop contributing to the widespread causes of terrorism in poor countries and thus grow into an even more mature and ethical member of the family of nations!

Caregiving in Suicidal Crises

After several decades, I still have painful memories of two suicidal tragedies in congregations I pastored in my early ministry. One victim was a youth whose depression went unrecognized by all of us until he hanged himself with a belt in his bedroom. His death produced collective shock, guilt, and fear in the youth group in which he had participated. These feelings radiated through the congregation, the junior high school, and the wider community. The other suicide was by an apparently successful stockbroker whose family members were on the fringes of that congregation. He shot himself in the head while his wife was away. He had hidden his serious financial crisis and health problems from nearly everyone.

Those two traumas, which were etched in my consciousness as a young pastor, created an indelible awareness that suicidal crisis calls for the special knowledge, sensitivity, and caregiving skills that I lacked then. In fact, suicidal thinking, impulses, threats, and behavior create urgent emergencies calling for immediate proactive responses by clergy, working collaboratively with family members, physicians, and mental health professionals trained in suicide prevention. Suicidal persons are more likely to turn to clergy than to any other professionals except physicians.

Recognizing High Lethality Risks

Pastors need to know how to prevent suicide and to have enough information to make quick evaluations of the likelihood that people in different categories—age, gender, suicidal thinking, life crises, or levels of depression—will act on their suicidal threats or impulses. Self-inflicted deaths are more prevalent than homicides in the United States. More women than men threaten and attempt suicide, but far more men succeed because they more often use guns rather than pills to kill themselves. Depressed older males are particularly at risk, as are severely addicted persons and those suffering traumatic losses or threatened losses, illnesses, shame, and meaning vacuums. In this country, suicide is ranked eighth among all causes of death, second among persons between ages fifteen and twenty-four (exceeded only by auto crash fatalities), and thirteenth among those over sixty-five.[7] Nearly 20 percent of high school students report that they have seriously considered or attempted suicide at least once. In a recent year, more teenagers and young adults ended their own lives than died from cancer, heart disease, AIDS, birth defects, stroke, and chronic lung disease combined.[8]

Suicide among teens is especially tragic because the cause is often an event such as the breakup of a romantic relationship or friendship, something adults in their lives may not consider particularly serious. Bullying, a despicable practice that has now spread into cyberspace, may also precipitate suicide in a victim, especially if it is prolonged and vicious.

Suicide is seldom a sudden, unpremeditated act. Before attempting suicide, most people send out cries for help. These distress signals are often disguised and therefore missed by those around them. It is important for caregivers to know how to evaluate suicidal lethality, meaning how likely persons who make threats are to implement them. The warning cries include the following:

Obvious suicidal threats. The old belief that "people who talk about suicide don't kill themselves" dies much more slowly than the countless people who demonstrate its falsity. The only safe axiom to follow when people make suicide threats is simple: *all* suicidal threats must be taken very seriously, even if the ones who make threats are only trying to manipulate others and have no intention of carrying out the threats. The fact that they use such a deadly threat indicates that they and their relationships are profoundly disturbed.

Covert suicidal threats. People who articulate feelings that life is empty and meaningless, who believe they are no longer valued or needed by others, who wish they could go to sleep and not wake up, or who feel trapped and powerless in a no-exit situation often are expressing presuicidal feelings.

Depression. Psychiatrist Karl A. Menninger once declared, "All deeply depressed people are potential suicides!"[9] The only safe approach is to regard all seriously depressed persons as potential suicide risks until it is determined that they are not.[10] Other warning signs include *crushing losses, pathological grief,* and *shattering blows to self-esteem.* Acute losses may produce suicidal thoughts and behavior during the reactive depression that follows—the greater the anger and frustrated dependency, the more likely a suicidal response.

Psychological disturbances and chronic illnesses. Some mentally ill persons are suicidal, but most suicidal persons are not mentally ill in the sense of being out of touch with reality. They are experiencing agonizing inner disturbances and conflicts, however. Anyone in a disorganized, chaotic mental state, who feels rejected and/or hopeless, should be regarded as a suicidal risk. Those in chronic pain and/or suffering from incurable illnesses may become suicidal, especially if they have intense fears of dependency, helplessness, or the financial disaster that often results from protracted illnesses.

Guidelines for Caregiving with Suicidal Persons

Pastoral caregivers should make determined efforts to refer those threatening suicide, and their families, to the nearest suicide prevention center. There the trained staff is equipped to assess quickly the probable lethality risk in such threats and take needed actions. Whether such a center is available or if a referral cannot be made, clergy often have to be actively involved in short-term responses to meet the immediate needs of the individual or family.

Caregivers often learn about suicidal crises by phone calls from persons threatening suicide or from worried family members. If the callers are strangers, it is essential before conversations end to get information that will enable one to take urgent action. Included should be the caller's name, phone number, and address, together with the names of key family members and the family doctor.

If suicidal strangers call and the lethality risk seems high but they refuse to reveal the needed information, keep the person talking so that a 911 call can be made on another phone line. This will initiate the process of tracing the call so that emergency intervention can take place. In talking with persons who are known or suspected to be suicidal, it is crucial to ask about suicidal impulses, fantasies, or intentions. Inexperienced counselors often avoid asking directly if depressed people are thinking about self-hurting behavior, because of unfounded fears of planting this idea in their minds. In fact, asking direct questions, after some trust is established, often brings suicidal feelings, thinking, and planning into open dialogue, lessening the likelihood that suicide attempts will be tried. During this dialogue, counselors who know the indicators of the probable lethality of suicidal threats can evaluate the danger and, if needed, take responsible actions. Toward the conclusion of a caregiving dialogue with persons discovered to be actively suicidal, it is good to ask them if they are still planning to kill themselves. If they give equivocal or half-hearted negative responses to the question, it is good to ask, "Why not?" Vague responses to this query may reveal that they really mean "yes" or "maybe." Those who pose little or no threat to themselves usually can give clear rational reasons for their "no."[11]

During the first conversation with suicidal persons, obtain the names and phone numbers of close relatives, friends, and their physician. Explain why it is necessary to let these people know that they need extra emotional support during their crisis. The family should be told not to leave persons alone during their acutely suicidal phase. Involving the family physician as soon as possible is also important in case antidepressant medication or temporary hospitalization is needed. An evaluation, by mental health or suicide prevention professionals, of persons making suicidal threats can ascertain whether hospitalization and psychiatric treatment are needed. The methods of crisis counseling described earlier are relevant in working with suicidal people.

The Los Angeles Suicide Prevention Center, where I had brief supervised training, gives these instructions to its counselors:

> Your own openness and willingness to confront the patient directly with the problem of suicide is very helpful in reducing the patient's anxiety. Inquire about the suicidal aspects of the behavior matter-of-factly. Ask about prior attempts and when they occurred; whether he is presently planning an attempt, and, if so, specifically what his plans are; and whether he has the means available to carry out his plans.[12]

The higher lethality probability, the greater the need for caregivers to use whatever approach is necessary to prevent suicidal action. In a caring, accepting, but very firm manner, pastoral counselors should use persuasion, offer theological arguments, stay with the person, drive her or him to a physician or hospital emergency room, or—if all else fails—phone 911 and use physical restraint. An appeal to at least postpone suicide is sometimes effective:

Pastor: Killing yourself may seem to you, in your present despair, to be the only way out. But I'm sure we can find a better way. If you end your life, you'll deprive yourself of any possibilities of our finding a better solution to your situation. At least wait until we've tried!

Most suicidal persons need three forms of help once they are beyond the acute suicidal crisis: (1) ongoing, supportive pastoral care; (2) psychotherapy and/or family counseling to resolve the underlying intrapsychic problems and the interpersonal pathology that fed the suicidal behavior; and (3) help with the spiritual and value problems at the root of their feelings of meaninglessness and despair. At its deepest level, the suicidal person's problem is a theological problem. As professionals with some expertise in spiritual diagnosis and growth, clergy have a unique and indispensable contribution to make to the longer-term healing of suicidal persons and their families.

Counseling with suicidal persons is threatening as well as demanding. It confronts us with the ultimate issues of life, death, and finitude. It may also confront us with our own hidden or suppressed suicidal impulses and behavior, including protracted suicide by chronic overwork, overstressing, and poor self-care. Our effectiveness in helping persons who are struggling with such thoughts and/or behavior will be enhanced by our developing some awareness of these inner dynamics. The hope or hopelessness flowing from existential, spiritual meaning issues with which suicidal persons often are struggling depends on how we are dealing with these issues. If we have found meaning in our lives that enables us to transcend and transform, to some degree, the pain and tragedies of our human existence, we will be better equipped to help them.

Some suicides in Western cultures, probably a minority, can be described as rational suicides. These are people who decide to end their lives for reasons that seem to them and many others to be both rational and valid. Many church leaders were shocked when a retired president of Union Theological Seminary and his wife chose to end their lives together rather than die slowly and at great financial cost from their illnesses. The widespread debate surrounding doctor-assisted suicides involves the issues of determining when requests for such assistance are really rational. Protections against abuse include establishing criteria for a panel of physicians to use in establishing whether those requesting this help are really terminally ill, their pain cannot be controlled by the use of medication, and their desire to die is not motivated by severe depression or other psychological disturbance.

Suicidal-homicidal bombers, as well as some persons whose deaths are identified as rational suicides, illustrate the diverse motivations that lead to different types of suicides. A Palestinian psychiatrist, who has studied suicidal violence in his oppressed culture, labels as "positive suicides" the self-chosen deaths of the many young men who voluntarily die for what they mistakenly believe to be the liberation and common good of their oppressed people by violent attacks on the Jewish "occupiers" of their sacred Palestine. When they are killed, they are honored as heroes by their families and community, who believe that they have died for a sacred cause and therefore will be welcomed immediately into the afterlife. They become role models who are emulated by other young volunteers.[13]

In working with suicidal persons, it is anxiety reducing to remember that only a small portion of those who threaten suicide actually attempt it and, of those, only a fraction actually kill themselves. It is also important to remember that the ultimate decision and responsibility for suicide remain with the person. If people have decided *unequivocally* to end their lives (which only a very small percentage of suicidal persons actually have decided), they will probably do so eventually, no matter how competent the persons who attempt to prevent it.

Here is an overview of the role of holistic pastoral caregivers in suicidal crises:

1. recognizing those who are suicidal and responding so as to prevent their acting on their suicidal thoughts and depression;
2. providing stopgap emergency help until referral to an appropriate suicide prevention center or mental health professional can be made;
3. making such a referral, often with the help of a physician;
4. mobilizing caring support within the faith community;

5. giving referral, if appropriate, for ongoing psychotherapy of the person and the family to address underlying causes of the suicidal behavior within the individual and in the family dynamics;
6. helping family and friends, including those in the congregation, deal constructively with the harmful consequences of either incomplete or completed suicides; and
7. educating the congregation about preventing suicides and dealing with them constructively when they occur.

One reason for asking questions is to get information to evaluate the degree of danger involved in suicide threats. The presence of any of the following factors increases the statistical probability that persons will actually destroy themselves:

- male—men attempt suicide less frequently but succeed more often than women
- older age—older persons who threaten suicide are more apt to attempt it than younger persons (however, suicide is the second highest cause of death among teenagers)
- a specific suicide plan with the means necessary to implement the plan (for example, a gun or sleeping pills)
- prior suicidal behavior
- recent severe losses or medical problems
- depression
- alcoholism
- lack of a strong support system
- mental illness
- poor communication with significant people
- defensive reactions to family members

Family Issues

Threatened, attempted, and completed suicides, like many other personal problems, are also painful family problems. They produce severe crises in family and friend circles as well as in faith communities. The collective grief wounds that result usually are deeply infected by feelings such as shame, bitterness, guilt, anger, and a profound sense of betrayal by the one who committed suicide. Being deeply infected, the wounds heal slowly, if at all. Few losses isolate and stigmatize family members so severely.

Because suicide is deeply stigmatized in our culture, the families and suicide survivors usually receive much less social support than they need and less than other grieving people. Often their shame and feelings of stigma drive them into protective self-isolation at precisely the time when they most need caring support from others. Many suffer alone in awful silence. Furthermore, family interpersonal dynamics are among the multiple causes of some threatened, attempted, and completed suicides. For example, bitter family members who feel neglected, ignored, or deeply hurt sometimes try to manipulate those around them by arousing their fears and guilt feelings or by acting out festering anger with threats of suicide or actual attempts. The use of such dire manipulation to gain sorely needed attention and control or to express unresolved rage is symptomatic of painful dysfunction in the family system. Although a referral to a trained family therapist is needed, making such referrals often is impossible because of the resistance, denial, and hiding by family members. The same tends to be true of involving family members in grief groups or even postsuicide support groups. However, such group support can be invaluable for those walking the long road following a family member's suicide. Initially one-on-one or single-family counseling is the only effective option that they will accept. The hope is that the help they receive may enable them to release enough of their feelings of shame to agree to participate in a small caring group.

Though it may seem obvious that the families of persons who commit suicide are in need of pastoral care, it may not be so apparent that congregations, schools, and other groups in which the suicide was a member are also severely affected by the tragic event. Pastors and other caregivers need to provide time for sharing, mourning rituals for such groups. Schools from which a student has taken her or his life are particularly in need of such ministry. It is well known that in such schools there are often subsequent suicides among the students, as though the tragedy had a contagious element. It may be helpful to provide a structure in which friends and companion students give time to considering the finality of death and its effect on others, particularly loved ones. They should also receive instruction on signs of suicidal intent or impulses in others and what to do about reporting such signs.

Holistic Caregiving in Crises of Violence against Persons

Crises of violence include rape, homicide, hate crimes, child and elder abuse, and domestic partners' battering. In our violence-saturated, gun-loving society, pastoral caregivers are often confronted with the need to respond in crises involving domestic violence or its threat. Interrupting combative confrontations and attacks before they degenerate into mental or physical violence is difficult and often very risky for caregivers. Doing so face-to-face should be avoided in most cases because it is unproductive, if not personally dangerous, unless both sides invite and at least are accepting of the pastoral intervention. Preventing or reducing the likelihood of violence requires skilled coaching of those who indulge in heated family fights and other altercations in how to resolve their conflicts nonviolently using the skills of negotiation and compromise. Valuable developing resources in resolving family conflict are the training and the services of mediators with skills to help couples and families torn by continuing conflict move toward nonviolent mediated solutions.

Helping adult survivors of childhood violence is vital for their well-being and for the prevention of their acting out unresolved residual pain through violent behavior.

Caregiving to Prevent Child Abuse

Child abuse and neglect constitute a widespread global tragedy. Nearly three-quarters of Americans report that they have witnessed abuse or neglect of children. A national program called Prevent Child Abuse America has a public service advertising campaign that recommends these ways of preventing child abuse:

> Reach out and support parents and kids. Anything you can do, from babysitting to running errands, can reduce stress that often leads to abuse. Raise the issue by educating yourself and others in your community. Remember the risk factors, such as economic hardship, isolation or substance abuse problems. Recognize the warning signs in children; these may include nervousness around adults, aggression or low self-esteem. Report suspected abuse or neglect.

Here is a website to find out more: www.preventchildabuse.org; or call 800-244-5373.

When dealing with child abuse, clergy must know the legal limits of confidentiality—when, what, and to whom to report suspected and known child abuse.

Elder Abuse: A Growing Problem

The aging of the populations has created a variety of major challenges in many countries. Elder abuse is not a new problem, but today's demographics make it a growing issue. This is true in some long-term care facilities and for some of the increasing numbers of older people who are being cared for in their own homes where limited financial resources and overstressed caretakers are producing inadequate care. Here is a legal description of the problem:

> Abuse is the infliction of injury, intimidation, cruel punishment, or other treatment with the resulting physical harm of pain or mental suffering, or the deprivation by a caretaker of goods or services which are necessary to avoid physical harm or suffering.... Abuse and/or neglect may be intentional, or due to the caretaker's lack of knowledge or capacity to care for the older (or dependent) person.

Included are physical, mental, and financial abuse plus neglect, abandonment, self-neglect, and isolation by cutting off mail and phone contacts or using physical restraints.

The vast majority of abused elders are women over age seventy-five, who often are frail, dependent, depressed, and compliant as well as loyal to the abuser with whom they often live. Many abusers are older, socially isolated male relatives with alcohol problems and poor impulse control. The multiple causes of elder abuse include severe physical or mental impairment, financial problems, and learned patterns of violence as acceptable responses to family stress. Other prominent causes include caregivers' physical or mental problems (including alcohol and drug dependency) and a feeling of being overwhelmed by the heavy stress of their burdensome, often involuntary responsibilities.

Pastors should be on the lookout for symptoms of elder abuse and know how to respond immediately and effectively. Here again, when dealing with elder abuse, clergy must know the legal limits of confidentiality—when, what, and to whom to report both suspected and known elder abuse.

Nursing homes, for example, that smell like urinals, probably provide inferior care of residents. Responding includes informing the social services agencies serving older persons, which are staffed by professionals who are trained to investigate and then to take appropriate legal or remedial action. These services should include providing a twenty-four-hour help line, emergency help, housing, homemakers, respite care, safety devices, police protection, friendly visitors, telephone and other social support, and mental and physical health care. Such services often are life enhancing and sometimes lifesaving for abused elder and other very dependent persons.[14]

Caregiving in Sexual Violence

Worldwide estimates report that at least one woman in every three has been beaten, coerced to have sex, or abused in other ways. Most frequently the abuser is a member of the woman's family. Rape and other sexual assaults have reached epidemic levels in the United States. The prevalence is very difficult to determine because more than six out of ten victims do not report these violent crimes to police. Fortunately the percentage of women victims reporting has risen significantly in recent years. The Department of Justice estimates are that 91 percent of victims are female and 9 percent are male. Per capita victim rates are highest among those ages sixteen to nineteen and persons of low income. People with annual household incomes under $7,500 are twice as likely as the general population to be victims of sexual assaults. There are no significant differences of rates among different racial groups.

Female victims of abuse and violence are deeply wounded by these traumas. Women who have the highest rates of rape are those who were sexually and physically abused as children. Rape, childhood sexual abuse, and domestic violence are among the most common causes of PTSD in women. A study of more than three thousand women at thirty-two colleges and universities in the United States found that 30 percent of those who were victims of rape by dates or acquaintances contemplated suicide after the attack; 31

percent sought psychotherapy; 22 percent took self-defense courses; and 82 percent said they had been permanently changed by the trauma.

Women victims of childhood abuse—physical, sexual, emotional, or neglect—have significantly poorer health than their peers. Women rape victims have much higher rates of alcohol abuse and eating disorders than nonvictimized women. Unfortunately some theologies that proclaim the superiority of male over female and promote the subjection of women in the family system are used to validate the abuse of women by those who have vowed to love and cherish them.

Caregivers' Response to Sexual Offenses

Illegal sexual offenses involving minors, women, and people with disabilities occur very frequently in our society.[15] To respond effectively, caregivers need to be informed about the nature of these crimes. Here are the major types of illegal sexual behavior: rape, pedophilia, incest, exhibitionism, voyeurism, obscene phone calls, public masturbation, and bestiality (sex with animals). More than 90 percent of victims are females, including many teenagers and younger girls. More than 85 percent of the offenders are males, most of whom do so repeatedly. Half of them have alcohol and/or other drug problems. They tend to have male chauvinist beliefs accompanied by low self-esteem and high anxiety. Many have rage toward women and grossly distorted thinking about women and/or children. Sexualizing and objectifying women and children are among the societal causes of sex crimes, and there is evidence that pornography, including compulsive Internet viewing of pornography, contributes to many sexual offenses. Victims of domestic violence in childhood have a high rate of sexual offenses in adulthood.

In the past twenty years sexual crimes against children (mainly boys) perpetrated by pastors in the Catholic Church in the United States and elsewhere have come to light. Unfortunately, breaches of boundaries and even downright sexual abuse of minors have been found to be more widespread than initially discovered and/or revealed. Added to the many instances of abuse, there has been evidence that when such violations were made known to clergypersons in positions of authority, they were either denied or not taken seriously. The perpetrators were often reassigned (sometimes after, and sometimes without, treatment). Even when such reactions were the result of insufficient understanding of the nature of pedophilia, they spawned widespread distrust of religious authorities and systems. There is a growing belief that shielding the reputation of the religious institution was deemed more important than the safety of children and other vulnerable persons.

Pastors and pastoral caregivers must be alert to the possibility of abuse perpetrated by colleagues, and they must be careful to report it to the appropriate authorities. They also need to be zealous in implementing the various safeguards that churches have set up for the protection of minors. Only through meticulous adherence to these guidelines can children be protected and trust in clergypersons restored.

The mandatory rehabilitative treatment that has proved to be most effective uses cognitive-behavioral methods, but it is very difficult, costly, and long term. The goal is to get perpetrators to accept some responsibility for their sexual acting out. The hope for successful outcomes is limited because of denial and rationalization by the offenders and the compulsivity of their behavior. Narcissistically, many believe they are entitled to their illegal sexual gratification. Pedophiles rationalize their behavior by believing that it does not harm the children "because I was gentle and loving" or "because she was seductive and wanted sex." In trials against them some feign religious transformation or say, "I'm glad I was caught because I got treatment and now I'm cured."

When pastoral caregivers learn about or suspect that sexual crimes have occurred, their first response must be to report what they believe has happened or is happening to the appropriate social agency with staff trained to investigate the allegations and take appropriate legal and/or therapeutic action. Caregivers should not try to counsel perpetrators. That should be left to those with the special training needed to intervene therapeutically. Pastoral support of victims should be accompanied by also referring them to agencies with staff trained to deal with persons suffering from this trauma.

Caregiving with Violent Teens

Violent behavior by emotionally disturbed teenagers is widespread. Tragic school shootings in recent years, highlighted by the Columbine, Colorado, high school tragedy, have etched this problem in public consciousness and parental anxieties. In most such tragedies, violence is a surface expression of a variety of sometimes hidden causes. These include one or more of the following: family violence; clinical depression; sexual and/or physical abuse as children; painful emotional disturbance in their family systems; vacuous self-esteem and peer rejection; copy-cat violence imitating other teens; and identification with the pervasive social violence in the youth culture and on TV, computer games, and the Internet. Therefore, having accurate information concerning prevention and treatment programs in one's community is invaluable.

Bullying, both verbal and physical, is another form of violence that has resulted in tragic suicides of victims. Pastors are in a position to exhort parents to check with their children to find out if they are either victims or perpetrators of this cowardly behavior. They can also become collaborators with teachers and parents to diminish and even eliminate this often hidden form of violence.

Holistic Caregiving in Financial and Vocational Crises

Even in times of general prosperity, people need money for various reasons. However, in times of economic recession, job loss and severe financial crisis can become epidemic. Without income, people become unable to pay their home mortgage or rent, and the number of homeless increases drastically. Overcome with concern, caregivers may be tempted to give money to alleviate distress. However, it is usually a therapeutic mistake to give money from personal or congregational sources to persons in fiscal crises. It is wiser to refer those with emergency needs to the religious or civic agencies that have social workers trained to evaluate such urgent requests and then offer whole-person assistance if this is appropriate. This help often includes crisis counseling and physical-mental-spiritual rehabilitation as well as short-term provision of food, shelter, and clothing. I can remember too many times when sad consequences resulted from attempting to respond to urgent appeals for money that proved to be clever manipulations by addicts and others who were skilled at manipulating clergy, who are what they call "do-gooders."

Caregiving in the Crisis of Job Loss

"Sorry, but we're going to have to let you go." These are words of rejection from a boss that, like a pink slip in one's pay envelope, send most people into a crisis. The nature and severity of the crisis depend on many things, including how important the job was to one's self-esteem and financial well-being, and whether the prospect of finding another satisfactory job looks easy, difficult, or impossible. Many laid-off workers experience an emotional roller coaster that includes panic, paralysis, grief, anger (or rage), depression, self-recrimination, and hopelessness. In many ways recovery is like that after a death. But most people can't take time to do their grief work because they must start almost immediately pounding the pavement searching for a new job.

Beyond losing essential income, job loss usually involves numerous other losses. These may include loss of status, friendship circle, security, feelings of self-worth, and the structure of one's days, weeks, and life. Recovery usually involves finding a new job that replaces some of these losses. But it also involves working through the negative feelings and channeling the energy of these feelings into action that will revive some hope for the future.

These steps have proved to be helpful in coaching people in job-loss crises:

- Encourage them to talk through their negative feelings and destructive fantasies (such as injuring the boss or supervisor), and urge them to avoid acting out their anger violently or in any other ways that will be counterproductive to their vocational and general well-being. Talking with other victims of job loss who have coped successfully can be helpful and hope awakening.

Working through feelings is a process with ups and downs, requiring an extended period of counseling or coaching.

- Coach persons in putting together a step-by-step plan for handling the crisis as effectively as possible, including finding a new job. Then urge them to implement the first steps of their plans immediately, before they have resolved their intense feelings. Depression often occurs right after the job loss, but it may reoccur or intensify after people are turned down for one or more job prospects. Remember that job hunting usually involves weathering frequent rejections and going on in spite of the temptation to give up. One career counselor advises reframing the rejections by telling job seekers, "The sooner you get through the nos, the faster you'll get to the yes." Encourage panicked job loss sufferers to avoid taking the first job that is offered for fear it is their only possibility. Such decisions frequently are regretted later with a thought like, *I can't believe I took this miserable job.* Persons in dire need may be encouraged to take a lesser job temporarily just to keep bread on the table or a roof over their family's heads.

- Encourage people to take at least a few weeks to take careful stock of their lives and careers—if this is possible—and then use their crisis as an opportunity to move in new directions that have the promise of being more fulfilling and health sustaining. This may include seeking the guidance of a professional career counselor, updating their skills, and then launching on a whole new life-career pathway. This is an example of using crises as growth opportunities.

Pastoral counselors should be aware that in times of prolonged economic recession, persons who have lost life savings or find themselves deeply in debt may be tempted to end their lives. These people need help and support to put their losses into perspective and to regain hope. Others, even ordinarily honest people, may be sufficiently desperate to engage in criminal activities, such a selling drugs or robbing homes or banks. Caregivers should not hesitate to bring up the possibility of such temptations when appropriate and call attention to the moral and legal consequences of such supposed moneymaking remedies.

Caregiving in the Crisis of Sudden Illness

Sudden illness can strike anyone at any time. It may come in the form of an accident or violence; it may be the result of an epidemic; or it may be caused by a hitherto undetected health problem. When sudden illness or death strikes, both the individual and the family are affected. At this time pastoral care is particularly important because neither the person nor the family is prepared to cope with changed circumstances or with the strong emotions evoked. In the case of the individual and her or his loved ones the caregiver can provide support in working through the Kübler-Ross steps in grieving: listening carefully and empathetically to the feelings expressed, gently encouraging them to break through denial either of the illness or its seriousness, and helping them move out of depression by expressing feelings such as fear, anger, sadness, hopelessness, and so on. The person may need a degree of denial at first until gradually it is possible for him or her to accept the difficult reality. Sudden shattering of denial before shock has diminished may expose the sufferer to unbearable emotional pain.

When someone else is responsible for serious injury (as in the event of an accident), the victim and her or his loved ones need to express, in a safe environment, their anger toward the person responsible for it. The caregiver may facilitate this venting of anger so that the victim or victims may move gradually toward forgiveness and the spiritual freedom it entails. In the event of sudden illness, not only are the individuals involved in need of care, but the family as a whole needs help to cope with the vacuum created by the person's illness, especially if that person is a parent or major breadwinner. The caregiver can assist the family in finding financial help and child care when necessary.

Often illness, which seems a short-term crisis in the beginning, can become a longer-term or terminal illness or a chronic disability. Caregiving in these situations will be addressed in the following chapter.

Recommended Reading

Dass-Brailsford, Priscilla. *Crisis and Disaster Counseling: Lessons Learned from Hurricane Katrina and Other Disasters*. Thousand Oaks, Calif.: Sage, 2009.

Davis, Patricia H. *Counseling Adolescent Girls*. Minneapolis: Augsburg Fortress, 1996.

Roberts, Stephen B., and Willard W. C. Ashley. *Disaster Spiritual Care: Practical Clergy Responses to Community, Regional and National Tragedy*. Woodstock, Vt.: SkyLight Paths, 2008.

Shelton, Charles M. *Pastoral Counseling with Adolescents and Young Adults*. New York: Crossroads, 1995.

Townsend, Loren L. *Suicide: Pastoral Responses*. Nashville: Abingdon Press, 2006.

Weaver, Andrew J. *Counseling Survivors of Traumatic Events: A Handbook for Those Counseling in Disaster and Crisis*. Nashville: Abingdon Press, 2008.

CHAPTER 8

CAREGIVING IN CHRONIC AND LONG-TERM ILLNESS

Historical Roots of Religious Healing

Religious caregiving with persons suffering from many types of illnesses has deep roots in a centuries-long tradition of holistic healing. This heritage undergirds the contemporary surge of interest in holistic healing and wellness that is occurring among both health professionals and religious leaders.[1] The English words *health, heal, hale, whole,* and *holy* are derived from the same or closely related Old English root words. In the New Testament, the search for salvation is intertwined with the search for healing. In Jesus' Great Commission he sent his followers to heal as well as to baptize and preach the good news (Mark 16:15-18). Jesus has been called the "great physician" since the early centuries of the Christian era. The writings of the early church include specific instruction(s) for healing of the sick (James 5:13-16). A strong emphasis on the spiritual healing of physical illness continued through medieval times. Unfortunately this aspect of ministry has been ignored in recent centuries in many mainstream churches, and in some church circles it has an unsavory reputation. The enthusiastic focus on the findings of the psychological sciences and psychotherapeutic methodologies has been a major source of the modern pastoral counseling movement's surging vitality. But it also has contributed to the neglect of the church's heritage of spiritual healing. An exciting challenge in caregivers' future is to recover the riches of this heritage and integrate them with the abundant resources of contemporary counseling, psychotherapy, spiritual direction, and holistic health.

Here are some guidelines for effective caregiving with persons and their families in crises of sickness:

There is truth in the joke "The definition of a minor operation is one that happens to someone else." The dependence associated with many sicknesses tends to awaken in adults latent childhood emotions and responses. Even relatively minor health problems can trigger high levels of fear, anxiety, anger, guilt, shame, and stress. These emotions and the untreated pain can immobilize rational thought and inhibit constructive coping. Empathetic listening, understanding, acceptance, and warm support are the most appropriate caregiving responses.

Remember that individuals' stress levels are affected by many factors, including the diagnosis and prognosis of the illness; pain levels, medication, and the frustrations of treatment; the competence, bedside manner, and relationships among the health professionals involved; the ambiance of the treatment setting; their frustration tolerance and coping resources; the images in their minds and the meanings they have developed as they struggle to understand the problem; the strength of their circle of mutual support and caring; and the vitality of their faith and its ability to find meaningful answers to basic theodicy issues of why good people suffer.

Be aware of their need for extra caregiving at critical points in the sicknesses and treatments. These may include waiting for the results of the findings of diagnostic tests, disclosure of unfavorable diagnoses (particularly the "Big C"), and poor prognoses (especially untreatable or terminal illnesses).

During caregiving with persons suffering from physical or mental illnesses, it is wise to be alert to the possibility of the misuse and overuse of prescribed medications. In our society this is a widespread problem that is fueled by the aggressive multibillion-dollar advertising campaigns of pharmaceutical companies. Consequently many desperate people search frantically for the drugs they have been led to believe are the magical solutions to their problems. Many billions of dollars are spent treating adverse drug reactions, and nearly a quarter of a million deaths result from drug misuse, including overuse.[2] Studies have found that many people are taking several prescribed drugs simultaneously, creating a problem called "polypharmacy." When several drugs are involved, there is a quantum leap of adverse effects that might be fatal.

Pain and Suffering

Severe pain is an all-consuming experience. It colors the entire inner landscape of sufferers in dark, despairing hues as it has an impact on all seven dimensions of their lives. Unrelenting pain can interfere with needed sleep, retard healing, diminish work effectiveness, strain personal relationships, and cause persons to feel hopelessly depressed and angry. Major advances in the field of pain management have occurred in recent years, including more effective use of less addictive medications and technological devices such as spinal stimulators for some patients whose pain is not reduced by other means. Pastoral caregivers should make sure that suffering persons receive help from an interdisciplinary health-care team trained in state-of-the-art pain management. This team should include anesthesiologist physicians; nurses; clinical psychologists; clinically trained chaplains; and as, needed, professionals specializing in biofeedback, physical therapy, and nutritional, educational, rehabilitation, and social services.

Chaplains need expertise in using religious resources to bring some comfort to people in pain. They also need skill in diagnosing and treating pathogenic religious beliefs that may be adding painful feelings to the burden of physical pain. In ministering with those in pain, heed the warning implicit in the old saying, "It's easy to be philosophical about a toothache—providing it is someone else's!" Your empathy for those in pain can be enhanced by letting yourself relive the last time you had a toothache or even a very sore toe.

Caregiving in Mental Illnesses

Responding to the needs of mentally ill persons is one of the most difficult challenges confronting pastoral caregivers. In his prophetic book on caregiving with people suffering from mental health problems, John Swinton declares that "effective care for persons with enduring mental health problems is not an option for the Church, but is in fact a fundamental mark of its identity and a vital indication of its continuing faithfulness."[3] If the church is to regain its healing ministry with the sick, the poor, and the oppressed, the church must liberate itself from the fear and stigma of mental health problems. It must also help liberate patients from diagnostic labels that often hide their humanity and distort their self-identity. Swinton develops a therapeutic model that goes beyond caring for individuals and their families by adding care for the mental health institutions and systems.

Depression and schizophrenia are the two most common forms of mental illness.[4] Depression is a mood disorder characterized by variety of symptoms, some or all of which may be present. These symptoms include marked retardation in speaking and moving; severe agitation; irritability; severe feelings of hopelessness and worthlessness; chronic insomnia; loss of appetite or overeating; loss of interest in other previously enjoyed activities; crying for no apparent reason; difficulty making decisions; difficulty concentrating; severe apathy and chronic exhaustion; and frequent minor physical illnesses such as colds, suggesting that some forms of depression are *biochemical*. In addition, some studies seem to show that depression may run in families; in other words, it may have a *genetic* cause. There is also a common belief that depression can be caused by or aggravated by experiences such as loss of loved ones or possessions, physical or sexual abuse, drug or alcohol abuse, or repressed feelings such as anger that the person turns inward on herself or himself. This latter type of depression is *situational*.

A way to differentiate types of depression is to categorize them as dysthymic disorder, minor depression, major depression, bipolar disorder, or hormonal depression. *Dysthymic* disorder is chronic depression with several of the characteristics of depression listed above. This is not, however, nearly as debilitating as major depression. Persons who have dysthymic disorder can function reasonably well but have low energy and persistent emotional distress. To further differentiate it, we will refer to this short-term low-grade depression, usually arising from stress, as *minor depression*. Persons suffering from *major depression* have, in a severe form, many characteristics of depression. They also have great difficulty functioning in everyday life, and may have a history of several hospitalizations. *Bipolar disorder* is characterized by mood swings from extreme depression to extreme euphoria, with intervals of normal mood levels between. Depression that occurs in some women during a time of hormonal change, such as puberty, menopause, or postpartum, or in conjunction with the menstrual cycle, has been dubbed *hormonal*.[5] This term creates problems for women because it places normal feminine processes in a negative light.

Failing a solidly based verification of genetic, biochemical, and/or hormonal causes of depression, this author will assume that the common denominator of all forms of depression is that they are situational. Other factors such as hormones, genetics, or biochemistry may heighten the vulnerability of persons to chronic or acute situational stress.

Depression is one of the most serious disorders in the United States. It is estimated that 18.8 million American adults (9.5 percent) suffer from depression, and it is predicted that by 2020 it will be the second largest killer after heart disease. Moreover, it is likely that everyone will at some time in life be affected by depression—either one's own or someone else's. Depression-caused absenteeism costs employers more than $51 billion each year. The cost to families and friends of depressed persons is inestimable.[6] Society itself is deprived of the contributions of so many people whose gifts are rendered inoperable by depression.

Based on these statistics alone, pastors and pastoral caregivers are likely to meet several depressed persons in the course of a day. For this reason it is imperative that they know how to offer pastoral care to these suffering people. The pastoral caregiver can initially be helpful to them in several ways. He or she can help them recognize their depression. (Some, especially chronically depressed people, may not realize that their experience is not the same as everyone else's.) Supportive counseling breaks the isolation in which the person is liable to be trapped; it alleviates some of the pain by assuring the person that she or he is not to blame for the depression; and it generates hope by providing information about the nature of the disorder and treatments that have had relative success. The caregiver can offer understanding, help, support to establish trust, especially in those who have become isolated, helping them reconnect with individuals or groups. He or she may also find out if the persons are suicidal and take action as described in chapter 7. The pastoral caregiver, who as noted earlier often has access to families, may help the family understand and respond compassionately to the depressed member. While continuing to give support, the caregiver may make appropriate referral to more qualified helpers such as primary doctors, pastoral therapists, and psychiatrists.

Regardless of the cause of depression, it is safe to say that it always involves a distorted perception of some aspects of reality. Whether as proponents of a biochemical theory might say, depression causes the distortion, or as proponents of situational theory hold, the distortion causes the depression, this disorder is always attended by some distortion or other. Cognitive therapists believe that cognitive and behavioral experiences are so related to each other that they must be studied, changed, or eliminated together.

Here is a list of cognitive factors involved in depression, drawn up by the Mayo Clinic staff:

1. Evaluation of life experiences. Depressed people tend to focus on the negative aspects of an experience to the detriment of the positive. For example, if nine out of ten evaluations of a project they have done give them a high rating, they will remember only the tenth that gave them a low evaluation. As a result, their memories are unusually negative. They tend to evaluate themselves against an unattainable goal.

2. Self-talk. Self-talk is the inner stream of consciousness that goes on constantly within us. The self-talk of depressed persons is mostly or all negative. When faced with problems, they tell themselves, "I can't do this; I will fail again."

3. Automatic thoughts. Automatic thoughts are repetitive automatic self-statements that result not from analysis of the situation but from a knee-jerk reaction. They control our reactions to people and events. For example, when depressed persons meet someone, they always presume that the person does not like them. Even if the person says complimentary things, they assume that she or he is being insincere. Many things in life are ambiguous; it all depends on how we interpret them. Depressed people interpret them negatively.

4. Irrational beliefs. Albert Ellis believes that the core of all psychological problems is irrational beliefs, such as "I cannot be happy unless everyone likes me," and "If I work hard, I will be successful." On the contrary, our happiness does not depend on being liked by everyone, and it is possible to work hard and yet fail.

5. Catastrophizing. Catastrophizing is negative generalization. If a friend hurts you once, he or she hates you, or you are incapable of keeping a friend. You try to repair a flat tire. It goes flat again after you have driven a few miles. You conclude that you are not good at anything.

6. Pessimistic thinking. If you tend to view life pessimistically, you are in danger of becoming depressed. You tend to think that things will not work out

well, that life will deal you a bad hand. Such thinking feeds into negative self-talk and cognitive distortions.[7]

Cognitive psychotherapists help depressed persons identify and understand how cognitive distortions affect their lives. They help them change these cognitions so that they can develop a more optimistic but realistic view of themselves and their lives. With this view they are better able to differentiate between major and minor problems and to develop positive and attainable goals. The counselor can then coach them to take steps to reach these goals.

Using Cognitive-Behavioral Counseling to Help Persons Suffering from Depression

Mild to moderate depression and even some major depression responds well to cognitive-behavioral counseling methods. A guide to this healing process by psychiatrist David D. Burns is *Feeling Good: The New Mood Therapy*.[8] It is a clinically based self-help approach for interrupting hopelessness and depression by intentionally changing one's perception and thinking. This approach can be used by clinically trained clergy. Here is an exercise from Albert Ellis's Rational-Emotive Therapy (RET), one form of cognitive-behavioral therapy. I suggest you try it now to prepare to help counselees move from depression to self-esteem:

Step one. Recall an event that left you feeling depressed with your self-esteem diminished; for example, a time when you failed miserably at something that was important to you or when someone criticized you unfairly. / [The slash mark means interrupt your reading while you do what has been suggested.]

Step two. Let yourself relive that event, reexperiencing the painful feelings that still are triggered by that memory. These may include feelings of regret, guilt, shame, remorse, anger, rage or agonizing self-rejection, self-doubt, and low self-worth. /

Step three. Become aware of the obsolete, exaggerated, depressing beliefs that these feelings trigger—beliefs that are expressed in statements you spontaneously repeat to yourself in your head. Such esteem-diminishing statements may be like these: *I am a bad person!* or *Why do I always spoil things like this?* or *I am a miserable failure!* or *I have to be perfect and succeed in everything to be accepted—and I can never do that!* /

Step four. Become aware of the person from whom you first heard statements like these before you internalized them so that you now believe and repeat them in your head to yourself. Usually these are the judgmental voices of perceived authority figures from early life—people like parents, teachers, preachers, or even school bullies.

Step five. In order to interrupt these self-talk voices and the negative beliefs from which they flow, you must challenge them and gradually transform them. You do this by seeing them as destructive and relevant to the problematic beliefs, deciding on more reasonable and affirming statements, and then intentionally substituting these to transform them as you relive the old memory. For example: *I don't have to listen to these old voices in my head that I know are voices from someone in my early life whom I can now choose to ignore!* or *Certainly I sometimes do bad or stupid things like this, but this does not make me a bad or stupid person—just a very human one!* or *I can't and don't have to be perfect or be liked by everyone! My self-acceptance is as a good and imperfect human being!*

Step six. It will probably be necessary to repeat this exercise several times in order to put the negative experience into perspective and to disempower it.

Step seven. Decide on behavior in opposition to the demeaning self-message. For example, if the message is, *You will never amount to anything,* decide to take on a project that has a reasonable chance for success: enrolling in a college course, learning to play a musical instrument, or working on a project to help those less fortunate than yourself. Plot out the steps you will take and when you will take them. Ask for help from a trusted friend, and commit yourself to report your progress in order to keep yourself accountable and to receive encouragement.

Referring Depressed Persons

If the depressed person is in a severe crisis, extremely incapacitated, or in danger of suicide, refer her or him to a psychiatrist (or failing that, the person's primary doctor) to be evaluated and, if necessary, to be prescribed an antidepressant. The pastoral caregiver should keep in touch with the person during the course of drug therapy for the following reasons:

1. The prescribed drug may not work in the first week, and the person may stop taking it without consulting the prescriber.
2. The person may need a short-acting drug temporarily to help her or him through the intervening time until the antidepressant kicks in.
3. Several antidepressants may need to be tried before an effective one is found.

4. Even if the drug therapy is effective in alleviating the depression at first, it may, over time, become less effective or ineffective.
5. The person will still need help to cope with life problems and may, if the drug therapy is somewhat effective, be better able to avail of cognitive-behavioral therapy.
6. Spiritual issues such as guilt (*I am being punished by God for my sins*), a feeling of worthlessness (*I have failed everyone*), and hopelessness often accompany depression. The pastoral caregiver has the background to help the depressed person deal with these painful experiences.

Bipolar Depression

As indicated earlier in this chapter, bipolar depression is characterized by swings of mood from depression to extreme euphoria. Persons who suffer from it often sleep excessively and experience daytime fatigue. In contrast, people with depression tend to wake up often throughout the night or may awaken early in the morning and be unable to return to sleep. Persons who have bipolar depression are likely to show symptoms of anxiety, obsessive-compulsive behavior, panic, or social anxiety disorder. At times some may exhibit psychotic symptoms. During the so-called manic phase, though some may be highly creative and productive, others may exercise poor judgment, make rash decisions, and spend large amounts of money, which they cannot afford. They need help to assess their grandiose inclinations as part of disordered thinking and to enlist their more rational capabilities in resisting them. Carefully monitored drug therapy may be of help; however, finding a dosage that balances both ends of the depression-manic pole is extremely difficult. Persons suffering from this disorder tend to stop taking their medication during a euphoric stage and plummet rapidly into depression. The pastoral caregiver can be of help in exhorting the person to continue taking the medication and, when necessary, to have it reassessed by the prescribing physician.

Depression and Women

According to government statistics, twice as many women (one in three) as men (one in six) suffer from depression. It is unclear whether the higher rate is because of the fact that more women than men seek treatment or whether it does point to an actual higher prevalence of depression in women. Be that as it may, it is clear that situational conditions make women more vulnerable to depression:

1. One in three women will be abused during her lifetime.
2. In spite of the efforts of the women's movement, many women have been reared to feel responsible for maintaining relationships, and the prevailing

culture still promotes this belief, hence the tendency to remain in abusive situations.

3. Fleeing an abusive relationship is known to be dangerous because the partner or spouse may take revenge. Many women choose to remain with an abuser because of fear of retaliation or because they see no other way to provide for their children if they leave.
4. Some women, who internalize negative cultural stereotypes, develop low self-esteem with accompanying depression.
5. Women are sometimes harassed in the workplace.
6. Women who work outside the home often have a second job of rearing children and maintaining the home. This is particularly true of single mothers. Without time for self-care they are liable to become depressed.

Given all or even some of the above conditions, it is likely that many women who seek help because of depression are not so much the victims of "old tapes" as of current home or work conditions. Their immediate need is help to become empowered to take steps to change or escape the oppressive situation. Unfortunately, women who tell their primary doctors about their depression are liable to be prescribed an antidepressant rather than be asked about their living situation.

If a depression is mainly or totally situational, the use of an antidepressant is likely to mask the real problem, leaving it unaddressed. It is not unusual for women to be prescribed sedatives after the death of a loved one or after a miscarriage. This author (Bridget McKeever) met a woman who ten years after the death of her husband had never grieved and who was so sedated at the time that she could not remember his funeral. She was eventually hospitalized after she overdosed on tranquilizers.

Pastoral caregivers, who are not beholden to drug companies, are in a position to offer more effective care to depressed women by inquiring about their home and work conditions and by helping them take steps to protect themselves and to demand justice.

There is evidence that some women do suffer from depression during times of hormonal change (puberty, menopause, postpartum). These are times of normal change in a woman's body. It may be that some female bodies have more difficulty adjusting during this time of physiological change. However, it is also true that there are psychosocial changes to be negotiated during the transition from girlhood to womanhood, after the birth of a child, and during midlife. The informed pastoral caregiver who is at hand during these times can help families and individuals negotiate them in a more positive manner. Rite-of-passage rituals as well as the support of women friends can be particularly helpful.

Depressed Children and Teens

Children and teens can be moody from time to time, so it is difficult to determine when they actually suffer from depression. Until the 1980s many psychologists believed that children did not suffer from depression. Some believed children could be depressed, but would most likely express their depression indirectly through behavior problems. Research in the past thirty years has dispelled these myths. Today, we know that children experience and manifest depression in ways similar to adults, albeit with some symptoms unique to their developmental age.

Children can experience depression at any age, even shortly after birth. In very young children, depression can manifest in a number of ways, including failure to thrive, disrupted attachments to others, developmental delays, social withdrawal, separation anxiety, and excessive sleeping and eating. Depressed teens may manifest depression through symptoms similar to those seen in depressed children. In addition, some may act out their frustration through bouts of anger, even rage, and through violence.[9]

Children and the Risk of Suicide

In general, depression affects a person's physical, cognitive, emotional/affective, and motivational well-being, no matter the age. For example, a child with depression problems and dangerous behaviors, between the ages of six and twelve, may exhibit fatigue, difficulty with schoolwork, apathy, and/or a lack of motivation. An adolescent or teen may oversleep, be socially isolated, act out in self-destructive ways, and/or have a sense of hopelessness.

Prevalence and Risk Factors

Although only 2 percent of preteen school-age children and 3 to 5 percent of teenagers have clinical depression, it is the most common diagnosis of children in a clinical setting (40 to 50 percent of diagnoses). The lifetime risk of depression in females is 10 to 25 percent and in males, 5 to 12 percent.

Children and teens who are considered at high risk for depression disorders include

- children referred to a mental health provider for school problems;
- children with medical problems;
- gay and lesbian adolescents;
- rural versus urban adolescents;
- incarcerated adolescents;
- pregnant adolescents;

- children with a family history of depression; and
- children who have been or are being abused physically or sexually.[10]

Several signs, however, differentiate this disorder from normal mood swings. A child or teen may be depressed if he or she

1. is sad or bored most of the time or no longer enjoys things she or he used to enjoy;
2. stops normal eating or overeats for a period of time;
3. sleeps too much or too little over a period of time;
4. expresses feelings of hopelessness or inappropriate guilt;
5. is withdrawn or preoccupied with death or suicide;
6. exhibits physical symptoms such as headaches or stomachaches, has difficulty sleeping, or hallucinates or has delusions.[11]

Often children or teens may become depressed after a parental divorce or the death of a friend or family member, if they are being bullied, or if they are experimenting with drugs or alcohol. Depressed children can be helped with play therapy; adolescents, with cognitive-behavioral therapy. If the depression is severe and/or does not diffuse with therapy, drug treatment may be tried.

Hazards of Drug Treatment for Children and Teens

Suicidality and Antidepressant Drugs

Compared to placebos, antidepressants increase the risk of suicidal thinking and behavior in children, teens, and young adults. Depression and certain other psychiatric disorders are associated with increases in the risk of suicide. Patients of all ages who are started on antidepressant therapy should be monitored appropriately and observed closely for clinical worsening, suicidal ideation, attempted suicide, or other unusual changes in behavior.

When an antidepressant is started or when the dose is changed, persons should be watched for agitation, irritability, hostility, aggressiveness, impulsiveness, or restlessness. These symptoms should be reported to the person's health-care professional right away.

It is well documented that depressed persons who receive antidepressant medication and do not feel better in the first week often stop taking their pills or give up and plunge deeper into depression. This makes it important for them to have a physician prescribe one of the newer, fast-acting antidepressants.[12]

Caregiving with Persons Suffering from Schizophrenia

Schizophrenia is believed to be a psychophysical disorder that distorts the way a person experiences the world and, as a result, causes her or him to think and act in an extremely unrealistic manner. People with schizophrenia may hear voices that tell them to act in a particular manner (sometimes with danger to self and others), or they may see things that do not exist in reality (hallucinations). Their speech is often obscure and highly metaphorical to the point that they cannot be understood. Others may be unable to speak at all (*alogia*) or may remain immobile for long periods (*catatonia*). Some may believe that others are out to do them harm (*paranoia*) or that they are privy to communication from another world. Because of the nature of their illness, it is very difficult for them to relate to others, and they often withdraw from social contact.

Schizophrenia afflicts approximately 1 percent of the American population (approximately 2.5 million) in all segments of society. Its direct costs are estimated at approximately $20 billion every year. Among lifetime sufferers, 20.4 percent are in mental hospitals, whereas 6.7 percent are in prisons and 3.8 percent in nursing homes. Because of the acute shortage of outpatient treatment services, thousands wander the streets among the homeless and receive little or no regular drugs to help control their symptoms. Four out of ten are unemployed. Nevertheless, despite the serious nature of this illness, it is possible for some sufferers to be helped through drug therapy and psychotherapy and to live productive and satisfying lives.[13]

How can caregivers and families locate help? Several national organizations are sources of reliable information, including referral resources. The American Psychiatric Association provides referrals to psychiatrists around the country (call 888-357-7924, or log on to www.psych.org). The National Alliance for the Mentally Ill has a help line (call 1-800-950-6264, or go online to www.nami.org). The National Mental Health Association lobbies state and federal governments on mental health issues (call 1-800-969-6642). The National Schizophrenia Foundation provides information about the illness and about support groups (call 1-800-482-9534, or log on to sanonymous.org).

Sufferers of this serious mental illness need long-term psychotherapy as well as drug therapy, so it is necessary for the pastoral caregiver to refer them to psychiatrists and pastoral psychotherapists. However, the pastoral caregiver can help the families of sufferers through support counseling and pastoral care. When and if the person's symptoms are under control, a pastoral caregiver can be of great assistance in helping the person adjust to the work and social world and continue to take prescribed medication. When appropriate, he or she can provide spiritual support to persons in recovery and their families.

Holistic Caregiving in Physical Illness

During the time I served as a hospital chaplain, I frequently felt frustrated by the limited way some health professionals misperceived my role. They saw my job as chaplain as exclusively that of bringing traditional religious resources, anxiety reduction, and comfort to patients, especially when medical treatment had done all it could and had failed. Although I regarded those traditional functions as valuable, I sensed that a pastor's role with sick people also had another vital dimension—to contribute significantly to the healing process. The growing interest in holistic[14] healing and wellness in recent decades has increased awareness of the unique and significant roles of congregations, clergy, and pastoral caregivers in particular as cultivators of healthy spirituality that contributes to whole-person treatment and prevention of many types of health problems. These developments have increased the recognition of pastoral caregivers' vital roles as essential members of health-care teams.

Here is a useful way for pastoral caregivers to understand their special contribution to holistic healing. The skillful use of caring and counseling methods can enable many ill persons to become more open to the God-given healing resources within their bodies, minds, spirits, and relationships. When counseling skills are encompassed in this spiritual dimension and religious resources are used appropriately, caregivers can enable many ill people to open their bodies, minds, and spirits to the inflowing of the ultimate source of *all* healing—the empowering energies of the ever-present love of God.

The holistic health movement, a flourishing development that is influencing more and more health professionals today, throws light on the nature and importance of the roles of clergy as an essential part of any whole-person approach to healing. This movement has the potential of accelerating the process of recovering and enlarging the vision of the Christian heritage of healing.

Four key truths are foundational in holistic health thinking and practice:

1. *Health is much more than the absence of illness; it is the presence of high-level wellness,* a concept akin to the New Testament term "life . . . in all its fullness" (John 10:10 NEB). There are as many degrees of wellness as there are of sickness.
2. *High-level wellness involves nurturing wholeness in all seven interdependent dimensions of persons' lives*—body, mind, spirit, relationships, work, play, and the world (including society and the natural environment).
3. *The major determinants of levels of wellness or sickness* are genetics, lifestyle, chronic stress levels, general levels of happiness, and job satisfaction (or, for retired persons, life activity satisfaction).

4. *The keys to moving toward higher levels of wellness are wellness awareness and understanding* achieved through wellness education; self-responsibility for self-care (accepting primary responsibility for living in ways that enhance wellness); and learning to use one's mind and spirit to enhance the effectiveness of one's immune system.

Using Stories and Imaging for Healing

Mind-body physician Howard Brody holds to the clinically based view that people can learn self-help strategies to send healing messages to themselves:

> One strategy is to examine the stories we tell ourselves (and others) about our illnesses. Stories are powerful tools, for when we create a narrative about something; we feel we have explained it. In states of sickness, we tend to focus on what might go wrong and how little we can do for it ourselves. Such stories actually worsen the illness. But they're not the only scenarios we can construct.[15]

Brody tells of a patient suffering from frequent, severe migraines. When he was between jobs, he sought medical treatment, during which he looked at his "headache story." He found that it was dominated by fear that his headaches would render him unemployable. At the first painful twinge he constructed a disaster scenario in which he became totally incapacitated—a story that made his migraines worse. But when he learned to reassure himself that he could handle his headaches, they improved markedly. During the first year after he started a new job, he lost only one workday as a result of a migraine.[16]

Brody has shown in his practice of holistic medicine how people can use their minds to stimulate the production of many biochemical substances that strengthen their immune systems and help heal a wide variety of physical illnesses. He calls this "releasing the body's inner pharmacy for better health."[17] Telling stories, he holds, is the most basic method we humans use to give meaning to puzzling or threatening events. Our expectations, our previous conditioning, and the meanings we use to make sense of events in our lives (including illnesses and other crises) release or block the release of these healing hormones in our bodies. Changing the stories we tell ourselves is the key to releasing these biochemical facilitators of wellness.

Research in mind-body medicine has shown that when people make one or both of two changes, the wellness-enhancing biochemicals in their body-mind organisms tend to increase. The first change is to increase the meaning-giving beliefs in their lives, including the meanings about their illnesses. The second is to increase their hopes or positive expectations for their futures. When these changes happen, people tend, as the man did in the vignette described above, to move from being passive victims of their illnesses to being active, intentional participants in their treatment and their lives. Brody coaches patients as they learn to do what he calls their "story work" about their lives and health problems.

Brody's approach to helping people heal their health problems can readily be adapted to coach people caught in crises, losses, and confusing decisions. It can guide them in learning to generate self-empowering, self-healing changes using what he calls the "meaning model of story work."[18]

Here are the steps he recommends taking:

1. *Story making.* Tell yourself the full story of your illness and its probable causes in the context of your life story or autobiography.
2. *Story telling.* Share your illness story, embedded in your life story, to someone who will really listen, for example, a skilled pastoral caregiver.
3. *Rewrite your illness story.* Revise it so that it has a better, more hopeful ending.
4. *Retell your revised story to yourself and to a willing listener.* This process makes you the author of this new chapter in your life story—your new wellness story. This puts you more in charge of your life, increases your positive meanings and expectations for the future, and activates your inner biochemical (and psychological) pharmacy.
5. *Decide what you need to do to make the positive outcome of this new story a reality and then do these things.* The healing, empowering results of this storying process can be as impressive in counseling with persons in crises and grief as with those coping with illnesses.

Brody's conclusion is this: "Clearly the mind can heal the body when bolstered by hope and expectation. . . . Virtually anything that sends a patient one of four messages— someone is listening to me; other people care about me; my symptoms are explainable; my symptoms are controllable—can bring measurable improvement in health." He reports that the healing effects of listening were confirmed by a Canadian researcher who followed people who had recently discussed their headaches with family physicians. Those who said that their doctors had listened carefully to them reported receiving more headache relief than a matching control group, and the effect could still be measured a year after their visits.[19]

Holistic Caregiving in Substance Abuse and Addictions[20]

In our addictive society, addictions are pandemic, affecting millions of individuals and families. Many addiction-prone people suffer simultaneously from several of these obsessive-compulsive destructive illnesses. Included are addiction to alcohol (the West's favorite domesticated drug)and many other drugs: prescribed, over-the-counter, and illegal street drugs. The pandemic also includes behavioral addictions that afflict countless people, trapping them in compulsive gambling; destructive sexuality; excessive TV viewing; rigid, sickness-spawning religions; and the addictive uses of computers and the Internet. Food addictions are both substance and behavioral addictions resulting in anorexia (self-starvation) or obesity.

Among the treatment resources that are increasingly available, the most effective and accessible are the scores of small-group 12-step recovery programs modeled on AA. These now offer worldwide, free, spiritually empowered hope and help to those suffering from scores of different substance and behavioral addictions. For substance abusers, medical treatment and, in some cases, short-term hospitalization can improve their odds for recovery and even save their lives.

Clergy most frequently are contacted first not by addicted persons but by distraught family members and friends in the circles of tragedy (averaging at least half a dozen people) that usually surround victims of these obsessive-compulsive illnesses. In such cases, caregivers should concentrate first on the needs of these suffering persons.

Effective counseling with them includes focused listening with occasional door-opening questions such as:

- "What led you to decide that your family member needed help?" (Checking the evidence.)
- "Does the person want help?" or "Would he [or she] be open to an offer of help?" (Is the person still trapped in denial?)
- "Is it possible that your frustrated and frustrating efforts to enable your family member to change behavior or to accept help actually could be hurting you and your children, as well as not accomplishing what seems to you to be needed?"

Asking whether the addicted persons are in denial or are becoming aware of a need for help is especially important. This is particularly true because addicted persons can change their responses to addictive behavior so as to protect their own well-being. If they do this, they may also interrupt responses that may unwittingly be contributing to the addictive-compulsive family interaction. The working concept that is most important for them to understand and implement is "releasing" the addicted family member. First, this means letting go of vain, obsessive attempts to cause the addicted persons to stop their destructive behavior. Second, it means confronting the addicted persons with what they will actually do if this behavior and their refusal to accept treatment continue.

Third, it means letting go of the assumption that their own self-care must be postponed until the addicted ones recover and, instead, doing self-care for themselves, including attending mutual-support groups.

Prophetic Caregiving in Collective Addictions

These addictions are easy to ignore simply because our society regards them not only as normal but also as desirable achievements. Spiritually centered caregivers have special resources for understanding and treating social addictions because their roots are in the widespread spiritual and ethical pathologies in our society.

What are these collective addictions, and how can they be diminished in individuals, families, congregations, and communities? *Hyperindividualism*, the product of the Enlightenment, Western cultures, self-centered capitalism, and the decline of the extended family, is a pervasive social addiction that contributes to and exacerbates human problems and reduces the quality of people's well-being. The positive social value that becomes caricatured in this addiction is the Christian recognition of the inherent value of each individual person as a child of God. But when individual success is defined as separate from community well-being, self-actualizing persons feel isolated, lonely, and supervulnerable. Only as individuals' wholeness is defined as inseparable from the well-being of others, and self-actualization is understood as impossible, can people move to valuing individuals in community.

Another wholeness-diminishing collective addiction is *exclusivism* or *superiority feelings*. This is expressed in a diversity of often interrelated *isms* including *sexism, racism, classism, culturism, nationalism, speciesism,* and *religious exclusivism reinforced by one's in-group*. In ways comparable to hyperindividualism, this addiction isolates and alienates individuals and groups of people from other groups by defining them as inherently inferior and "other." These others are perceived as potential enemies who must be treated with suspicion and fear. This behavior makes the belief system self-fulfilling and tends to elicit mutual distrust, fears, and antagonisms. The healing of these addictions involves balancing the need for in-group security and esteem with valuing the potential mutual life enhancement of the wonderful webs of diversity among people, cultures, religions, and natural ecosystems. The natural world with its amazing symbiosis and mutually sustaining interdependencies can be a natural model for healthy intergroup relationships among humans. Healing this social addiction will be explored briefly in the chapter on making caregiving more inclusive.

Controlism is another individual and social addiction, often interrelated with ethnocentrism. It involves seeking to gain a sense of security in a world where the only certainty is uncertainty by controlling objects (through technology), other people (through personal, political, religious, or economic domination), or nature (through technology, property insurance, and engineering). Controlism blossoms in our times because many security-giving social institutions are weakened or in shambles and many people are disconnected from those that could still provide some sense of genuine security. People most addicted to controlism feel lacking in inner controls or social power. Like all addictions, this one fails to provide the security and power that motivated the attempts to control people and things. Healing this addiction involves enabling people to learn how to find the security and empowerment that they were seeking without success in their addictions. Power manipulation and its twin, controlism, are used by many insecure people in troubled marriages and families.

Consumerism is another powerful societal addiction that rapidly diminishes the health of individuals, families, communities, congregations, and the natural world. Addicts are trapped on the success-earning-spending-wasting treadmill. Getting off, even for occasional minivacations, is very difficult because our culture rewards many of the illusory benefits of such lifestyles. When an illness forces people to reevaluate their lives, it is no wonder that many who question their previous value become spiritual seekers.

Holistic Caregiving in Crises of Disabilities

Having lived with an incurable but very treatable disability (diabetes) for much of my adult life, I have intimate awareness of the inner struggles of those of us who euphemistically are labeled "challenged" in our society. (The evolving euphemisms point to the negative connotations that continue to make words like *handicapped* and *disabled* hurtful to those directly involved.) I still struggle with intense feelings engendered by the conflict between denial and acceptance of the reality of my limitations. It helps to take an occasional brief retrospective look at the four decades since my problem was diagnosed and hit me out of the blue. This glance back makes me aware of several unexpected gifts that my disability continues to give me. These are gifts that came in disguise—gifts that often don't feel like the gifts they really are. My problem has forced me not to take my body as much for granted but to do a better job of self-care by healthier diet, exercise, and rest. It has given me increased empathy for the forty million "otherwise-abled" persons in my country. It has confronted me with an awareness that most nondisabled people do not have. This is an easily forgotten awareness that every day of being alive is a precious gift, as are all the people with whom I share caring and love.

My disability makes this gift particularly poignant. It happens that in the year of my birth, a Canadian research physician and a medical student first learned how to extract insulin from animal pancreases and inject it in humans with diabetes, enabling them to control the levels of glucose in their bloodstream. If it were not for this lifesaving discovery, I undoubtedly would have died more than three decades ago. All the things I have enjoyed and done in these years could not have occurred. This knowledge helps me remember to celebrate the gift of each day. It also gives me the gift of gratitude for the marvels of modern medicine. And it ignites my passionate hope for the expected break-throughs in clinical research that promise far more effective treatments and even pre-vention of the problem.

The issue of what has been called "ableism" consists of the widespread discrimination, prejudice, and stereotyping of people with disabilities. The unfortunate attitudes that fuel this social violence against the millions of us who have significant disabilities die very hard. Only in the last few decades, since the Americans with Disabilities Act was passed by Congress, has our society had to confront this myopic perspective and the esteem-damaging practices that flow from it. These practices limit unfairly the abilities of the millions of people with disabilities to fully use their God-given capacities, strengths, and potentialities. Pastoral caregivers often encounter people who have been constricted and hurt by this social evil. Here are some guidelines for ministering to their woundedness and for preventing such wounding:

A friend of mine is a physician who has surmounted her disability and established a pioneering program that enables disabled persons to become doctors in the medical school where she teaches. In January 2001, she sent me an inspiring report on the ded-ication of a statue of President Franklin Delano Roosevelt in a wheelchair at the memo-rial honoring him near the Potomac River in Washington, D.C. On the back of that bronze statue, there is a quotation from his wife, Eleanor Roosevelt. She pointed out that before he was disabled by polio, a condition that could have ended his political career, he had never been forced to develop the habits of infinite patience and persistence that were essential in his becoming an outstanding political leader who guided the country through the Great Depression and World War II.

In the summer of 1944, FDR visited a naval hospital in Hawaii that treated persons who had suffered severe battle wounds, including many who had lost limbs in the tragedy of war. He insisted on wheeling himself into their wards because he wanted to show them that he, the president of the United States, could not walk any better than they could, but he could still show courage, inner strength, and hope.

At the dedication of the statue, then U.S. President Bill Clinton reflected on FDR's life and Eleanor's statement: "And so we celebrate freedom and dignity for incredibly brave people, whose lives were all embodied by that incredibly brave man, whose dis-ability made him more free for his spirit to soar and his nation to survive and prosper."[21]

CHAPTER 9

BEREAVEMENT CAREGIVING: BEFORE, DURING, AND AFTER LOSSES

Rejoice with those who rejoice, [and] weep with those who weep.
—Romans 12:15

Blessed are those who mourn, for they will be comforted.
—Matthew 5:4

Bereavement is a universal human crisis that strikes everyone sooner or later. In terms of human wholeness there is no aspect of pastoral care ministry in which the stakes are higher. The fact that clergy have automatic entrée to the agonizing world of most sorrowing people gives them unparalleled opportunity as well as responsibility. They are the only professional persons with substantial training in grief caregiving. They are called to be effective guides and companions of the bereaved as they walk through the shadowed valleys of life's multiple losses. Obviously it behooves pastors to develop a high degree of competence in bereavement care and counseling.

Insightful Studies of Grief and Crisis Healing

Contemporary approaches to both crisis intervention and grief caregiving have their roots in the pioneering research of a young Boston area psychiatrist named Erich Lindemann. In 1942 there was a tragic fire in which several hundred people died at the Cocoanut Grove nightclub in Boston. Lindemann decided to study the varied responses among survivors and close relatives of those who died, focusing on the consequences for their health or illness of how they handled their profound individual and family grief.[1] His most significant finding was that those who did what he called their "grief work" well recovered much faster than those who repressed their sorrow. He later summarized his findings, which have been confirmed by other research:

> Studies show that many people become sick following the death of a loved person. A great many more hospital patients have had recent bereavement than people in the general population. And in psychiatric hospitals, about six times as many are recently bereaved than in the general population. . . . Furthermore, in a great many conditions, both physical and psychological, the mechanics of grieving play a significant role.[2]

Lindemann and countless other grief researchers have shed light on the dynamics of the healing process. These dynamics have many similarities with those of any severe crisis. But the loss of someone or something that has been a significant part of a person's world of meanings and satisfactions is a psychological and spiritual amputation. How traumatic it is depends on the nature and importance in their lives of what they lose, and also on the development of their coping skills. The responses employed in coping with new losses are the same ones they have learned in coping with previous deprivations, frustrations, and losses, large or small. These coping skills, learned from their culture, are filtered through their parents' responses to losses. If individuals have learned constructive, reality-oriented coping skills, they will follow a somewhat predictable process of working through the mixture of powerful feelings resulting from the bereavement and making the adjustments required to live without what has been lost. This work (called "grief work") must be done by grieving persons themselves, hopefully with strong support from family, close friends, caregivers, and their faith community.

In the decades since Lindemann's pioneering research, crisis intervention and grief-healing methods have been studied extensively, refined, and greatly improved. Caregivers today have more understanding and better methods available for making this vital healing ministry effective than ever before in the century-spanning history of care with persons suffering from life's many-faceted problems.

Grief: A Strand in Life's Multicolored Fabric

As we have seen, some feelings of grief result from all significant crises, losses, life transitions, and changes, not just in the deaths of loved persons. Every life event on the Holmes-Rahe stress scale involves some losses and therefore grieving. The price people pay in health problems for unresolved grief is extremely high, and there is evidence that many psychosomatic illnesses are related to unhealed grief. The same is often true of alcoholism and other drug and behavioral addictive illnesses, including compulsive sexuality, gambling, and religiosity.[3]

Some years ago, the staff of the pastoral counseling and growth center with which I was associated[4] decided to ask all of the people who came for help if they had experienced major changes or losses within the preceding two years. More than one-third of our clients could identify a painful loss or a cluster of several losses, often correlated with the onset or dramatic worsening of the pain that had brought them for help. These counselees suffered from a wide range of presenting problems, including marriage and family crises, sexual dysfunction, depression, job difficulties, substance abuse, psychophysiological illnesses, and religious and ethical problems. Many reported general psychological-spiritual malaise and depression.[5]

Caregivers should know that grief experiences triggered by different types of crises typically have distinctive differences as well as similarities. They all bring some degree of sadness and longing for what was lost. The grief in *developmental crises* involves sadness and longing for the lost satisfactions of earlier life stages. Grief in *chronic crises*, as the husband of a woman with Alzheimer's put it, "hangs over me like a dark cloud that keeps blocking the sunlight and refuses to go away!" Grief feelings in collective or *community crises* are shared by most members of the large or small affected group in varying degrees and expressions. Grief feelings in *acute crises* have special poignancy resulting from the terrible sense of being hit out of the blue without any time to prepare to cope with the trauma. For this reason, the grief impact may cut deeper and be more devastating initially. Grief in long-term or chronic crises includes many opportunities to do what is described as "anticipatory grief work." If survivors have done this before their loved ones die, they still feel some pangs of loss, but the grief usually is much less protracted than in acute crises triggered by unexpected losses.

Factors that Complicate Crisis and Grief Recovery

The way people respond to losses varies tremendously depending on their culture; their resources; the quality and length of relationships; the timeliness of the loss; and, in cases of death, whether it was expected and its nature. The more dependent, conflicted, or ambivalent relationships were, the longer and more complicated the recovery process tends to be. Grieving following the deaths of children or adolescents probably produces the most agonizing and protracted recovery process. Sudden, unexpected, or violent deaths usually are followed by more extended and difficult grief work with more shock and anger than slow, expected deaths. There are more unfinished aspects of the relationship, which produces greater guilt. The vacant social roles such as companion in attending church or in recreational travel that had been filled by the deceased have not been gradually refilled.

When the bodies are not found or are terribly mutilated (so that the casket is left closed) or when the body is cremated immediately after death, recovery may be protracted because the grieving persons are not able to accept the reality of the loss by dealing with the image of the dead person's body. Since our own identity and that of others are integrally related to body image, having an opportunity to deal with feelings about the body is often necessary for the grief wound to heal as fully as possible. The traditional wake or visitation time before the funeral, when the body is visible, can be a grief-enabling experience for many mourners.

Caregivers also need to be aware of numerous societal factors today that often cause recovery from crises and grief to be very difficult, protracted, or blocked. They include the following:

1. The weakening, or rejection by many people, of traditional religious beliefs that were comforting, and the failure to develop more viable beliefs to replace them.

2. The fact that most pastoral caregiving of bereaved persons extends only a week or so beyond the funeral or memorial service, whereas the journey of recovery often extends over two years or more.

3. The fact that much, if not most, of the caring for terminally ill persons is done by impersonal medical and nursing home staff members rather than the family.

4. Our death-denying culture that programs us to deny feelings about our mortality and dying or escape from them in a variety of ways.

5. Geographical distances and interpersonal alienations deprive many friends and family members of opportunities to say "Good-bye," or "I love you!" or "Please forgive me," or simply "Thank you!" to dying people.

6. Not having opportunities to view and perhaps touch the body so that friends and family can say good-bye to the dead person's physical presence.

7. The ways that interpersonal conflicts are stirred up in broken and blended families when death occurs and wills are implemented.

8. Social stigmas that unfortunately are often attached to certain deaths, including those from suicide and AIDS.

9. The many ways that people suffering from poverty and discrimination carry a multiple load—their economic problems and one-down social esteem added to their painful losses.

10. The fact that women raised in traditional families often derive their feelings of self-worth mainly from their caretaking roles makes the deaths of persons for whom they were primary caretakers deeply disruptive to their sense of meaning and value.

To the extent that one or more of these individual or social complications apply to care receivers or caregivers, it is important to treat them and to encourage them to treat themselves with extra caring and compassion over what is usually a longer time.

Dying Persons Can Be Our Teachers

Sooner or later, crises and losses teach everyone agonizing lessons. These lessons come as unwelcome intruders and as rude confrontations with painful truths that understandably are resisted tenaciously. But as suggested earlier, they can offer unexpected opportunities to learn valuable lessons that can contribute to personal growth that enhances overall well-being and preparation for coping constructively with future crises and losses.

Let me illustrate this personally. In recent decades life has taught me much more than I wanted to learn about the process of dying. In this respect my experiences are comparable to those of many people in the last third of life expectancy. In addition to awareness brought by several near-death experiences, my main teachers have been several terminally ill persons. They include both of my parents, my spouse's parents, and two valued mentors. Also included have been a number of friends around my age and several former students whose deaths were particularly shocking because they were much younger than I. I remember each person with gentle sadness, mixed with gratitude for the precious gifts I received from many of them.

Some of my most valuable learnings came from Lois, a nurse and close friend of my spouse and me. She died in her late forties after a protracted and debilitating struggle with cancer. Shortly before her death, I asked her if she would talk with me about her experience of dying so that I could learn from her and share her insights with others (as I am doing here). In her usual generous spirit, she replied that she was glad to do so.[6] In what for me was a deeply moving conversation, she shared her intense feelings and needs. One particularly strong need was to have people *really* listen to her swirling, changing, and conflicted feelings as her malignancy gradually spread. She described how terribly let down she felt when some of her friends and one of her several physicians changed the subject or tried to give her superficial reassurances. Although she knew that they did this because of their own discomfort with the grim facts and her intense feelings, it hurt anyway. Having read Elisabeth Kübler-Ross's book *On Death and Dying*,[7] she said that the many feelings she had experienced included the five described in that book (denial, anger, bargaining, depression, and acceptance). But she added that her feelings would come and go, never following a particular sequence.[8]

Lois told of experiencing waves of fresh anger at each new stage of her progressive illness. One of her many friends was especially helpful when Lois told her that the oncologist had just informed her that the malignancy had spread to her vital organs. The friend hugged her warmly and shared her intense disappointment and anger.

After Lois shared the details of her struggles with fear and grief, I expressed my warm affirmation of the ways in recent months she had become even more vital and alive than she had been before. She responded, "When you know your future here probably will be short, it makes the present more important." As we concluded our conversation, I was pleased when she said that it had been very meaningful and helpful to talk about her experiences so fully. I expressed my deep appreciation and told her how profoundly I had been touched by all that she had shared. Lois helped me see more clearly that the process of dying can be an important stage of continuing spiritual growth for some people, even as they struggle to cope with the multiple losses of dying.

Using Losses as Growth Opportunities

Insightful novelist Alice Miller once declared, "The human soul is virtually indestructible, and its ability to rise from the ashes remains as long as the body draws breath."[9] Eleanor Roosevelt was such a person. Throughout her life, she used a series of severe crises and losses as opportunities to learn and grow, and heighten awareness and empathy for other suffering people. Eleanor's mother rejected her for "not being a beautiful child" and then died when Eleanor was only eight. One bright spot in her young life was her adoration of her father (Theodore Roosevelt's brother), who adored her in return. But his chronic alcoholism interfered with his ability to give the dependable, loving attention she desperately desired. He died from his addiction when Eleanor was only ten, just two years after Eleanor's mother died. As a young adult, she married FDR, who went on to become a four-term president during the Great Depression and the first years of World War II. During her years as First Lady, her deep empathy for the pain of the countless victims of social, economic, and civil rights oppression had a profound influence on the development of FDR's policies. Behind the scenes she helped shape the national safety net that helped millions of impoverished people (including my childhood family) during the shattering economic tragedy and collective grief of the devastating depression. After FDR's death, her courageous, prophetic outreach became overt. Her influence continued to expand through her caring service to the oppressed in her own country and the wider world.

For caregivers, it is crucial to know that wounded people usually only in retrospect make the discovery that growth has occurred through their crises or losses, after they have coped with the worst of their traumas. At that point it is appropriate to ask a door-opening question such as: "As you look back now on your terrible loss, are you aware of anything useful that you have learned as you struggled to cope?" To raise the possibility of growth before this point ignores people's intense pain, causing them to feel misunderstood and resentful. It also sets them up to feel they are failures if they do not experience some growth. It is well to remember that huge losses like the deaths of children are so utterly devastating to most parents, siblings, and grandparents that deriving any sense of having grown usually is impossible except perhaps in very long retrospect.

Opportunities for spiritual and ethical growth occur frequently in crises and grief because they often shatter false gods, such as achieving power and wealth, that many people worship in our society. Crises and losses often confront people with the need to rethink and possibly revise their spiritual beliefs and guiding values. The hope is that they will do this in directions that bring more spiritual vitality and deeper meaning to their lives.

Making Grief and Crisis Caregiving Holistic

As a caregiver, keeping the seven dimensions of wholeness in the back of your mind as you offer crisis and grief care can help you see and respond to opportunities to make your healing ministry more holistic. Severe traumas often create wounding that needs healing in many dimensions of sufferers' lives. To illustrate, basic physical self-care is usually diminished in the days and weeks following a major grief, at precisely the time when stress overload makes self-care even more important than usual.

Pastor Marjorie was on target when she paid a pastoral visit to Larry, a man in his mid-fifties. She had conducted the funeral for Larry's wife, Betty, who had died three weeks earlier. After a brief exchange of relatively superficial comments, the pastor intentionally invited Larry to move their pastoral conversation to a deeper level by asking him: "How are you doing, Larry, in handling your loss just a short time after Betty's funeral?" "OK, I guess" was his response. Marjorie then pressed him directly, "Are you taking care of your health, Larry? I mean by getting enough rest, good food, and some fast walking or other exercise on most days?" Larry said, "The trouble is I really don't have time or energy to do such things for myself right now. It makes me forget what I'm feeling when I start digging myself out from under the pile of work that I'm way behind on." The pastor responded, "I understand that you don't feel like it or have enough time given those heavy demands. But as you probably are aware, your body is under extra heavy pressures these days. To handle this load of stress and keep from getting sick, you need adequate self-care now even more than usual. So I wonder, doesn't it make sense to make time to do these things for a while, even though you don't feel like it?" Larry agreed and said he would try to talk better care of himself. Pastor Marjorie affirmed this intention and then helped him decide on a realistic plan for improving his self-care. Pastor Marjorie focused holistically on Larry's physical and mental self-care and the wellness of his vocational life as she helped him do his unfinished grief work.

Six Tasks of Coping and Growing through Grief

A transformational approach to caregiving with those suffering many types of normal grief involves going beyond the first essential goal of helping them survive, cope, and recover from their losses as fully as possible. The goal that transcends this is to help them learn how to use their grief as an opportunity to grow at least a little as whole persons by the ways they handle their grief. When grieving persons accomplish this goal, they discover a hidden possibility expressed symbolically by Albert Camus: "In the midst of winter, I finally learned that there was in me an invincible spring."[10]

The movement from the initial shock of new loss to the ultimate experience of new life involves six tasks with which the companionship of a pastoral caregiver can be very helpful.

Task One: Dealing with Numbness and Shock

When death or other severe losses strike, the usual response is feelings of psychological numbness and shock mixed with a sense of unreality. The mind cannot yet accept the overwhelming pain of facing the reality that someone or something that was loved is really gone. But gradual acceptance of the grim reality of the loss must eventually occur or the healing process will be blocked and incomplete. Full acceptance usually occurs over a period of several months or even years.

In the first hours and days after severe losses people often feel that their agony and depression will never diminish. Only as their grief work progresses with the passage of time will they discover that they can walk through the dark valley of death and eventually emerge to a brighter day. The psalmist clearly expressed this awareness: "Weeping may linger for the night, but joy comes with the morning" (Ps. 30:5).

The role of caregivers in facilitating normal grief is to cooperate with the psyche's inner process of recovery. During this shock phase, effective caring includes using supportive care methods as previously discussed in this book. These often include gratifying dependency needs. Severe losses activate grievers' "inner child," often bringing painful feelings of anxiety, deprivation, and abandonment. The need to be comforted is intense.

On a personal level, I remember nothing the pastor said at my mother's funeral, but I recall how much I appreciated his comforting touch on my shoulder as he left the funeral parlor after the service. Acts of spiritual ministry during task one, such as familiar scripture, prayers, hymns, and rituals, can bring comfort and hope to bereaved individuals and families who are religious. Taking gifts of food and offering help with practical needs, such as providing transportation, are symbolic, nonverbal ways of communicating nurturing care. A congregation's lay caring or grief recovery team should surround the grieving individual and family with the supportive care they need. Providing a meal after a funeral or memorial service is a way of providing physical nurture and affirming the ongoingness of life despite the loss. It also is a way of saying, "We can, must, and will walk on into the new, unknown future—together!"

Task Two: Expressing and Talking through Feelings as They Are Gradually Released

After the 1942 Cocoanut Grove nightclub fire, Lindemann made a most illuminating discovery. He learned that *experiencing and expressing agonizing grief feelings are indispen-*

sable to the healing process. In fact, blocked feelings result in the healing process being delayed or blocked long term, whereas facing the painful feelings is the path to eventual healing.

To help grieving people do their grief work, caregivers must go against the cultural tendency to avoid painful feelings. This is why grieving persons often need help in expressing fully and talking through the variety of powerful emotions the loss has triggered in them. This is encouraged by responsive, dialogical counseling with occasional focused questions aimed at enabling the persons to get in touch with their feelings and express them fully. Often these feelings are ambivalent and conflicted. They range from total despair to relief and joy (about which most people feel some guilt). Task two begins and continues intermittently as persons' denial gradually diminishes and they allow the stark reality of the loss to enter their awareness. By experiencing and verbalizing the feelings repeatedly, they gradually transform the raw agony of loss into gentle sadness and a renewed gratitude and love for the lost person. But grief feelings often return unexpectedly for a long time after a major loss. Grieving is unpredictable.

One primary goal of grief work following deaths is to make the relationship that has been lost in external reality strongly and vividly internal in survivors' minds and hearts. Repetitive reminiscing and storytelling help them accomplish this. Thus the relationship is not completely lost because memories and images of the deceased become more vivid and alive. Those who have internalized the lost relationship often say something like, "I feel that she is still alive, supporting and giving me strength." This can enable grief-stricken people to find comfort and solace, especially if relationships have been relatively healthy. But in toxic or dependent relationships, the negative side of this internalizing process is seen. It may be expressed in statements of feeling controlled, such as, "I feel that he is still here watching to make sure I shape up like he wanted." People who continue to feel oppression and/or protracted depression after family members die need to be helped to exorcise these mental ghosts. Doing this will help free them from being trapped in the past and enable them to get on with living in the new present and emerging future that the death has made potentially available to them. The cognitive-behavioral methods described earlier provide effective approaches to enabling this self-liberation.

The key feelings that most often infect grief wounds are unresolved *guilt* (with remorse and often shame), *anger* (with resentment and rage), and *fear* (of death and punishment among some persons with traditional religious beliefs). To encourage awareness and expression of these feelings, counselors may ask one or two opening-up questions such as: "Are you having feelings that are really disturbing? If you had your relationship to live over, what would you do differently? Have you been able to express these feelings or talk about them?" Such questions should be asked only when caregivers have the time and skills to help the person express, talk through, and begin to release and resolve the intense feelings he or she may elicit. It's also wise to balance such questions with one like, "What kind of warm, positive feelings have been occupying your mind?" or "What about the person and your relationship do you most enjoy remembering?"

Some persons can be helped on their grief work journey by being encouraged to jot down notes to themselves about their feelings and thoughts day by day. Keeping an informal grief healing journal can be of special help to many men and some women who have difficulty getting in touch with and expressing their feelings. Writing a personal letter to the loved person, expressing what they wish they had said before that person died, can also awaken suppressed feelings. Writing or verbalizing answers to self-queries such as the following often enable grieving persons to become aware of more of their feelings:[11]

- What things will I miss receiving from the lost person?
- What are the things I am sorry I did or didn't do before the loss?
- What are the things for which I am most thankful about the lost person?

In major losses, or those around which there are conflicted feelings, the working through of feelings occurs on many levels and usually takes two years or longer. Feelings of gentle sadness often linger as an ongoing legacy of the loss. Severe grief such as that triggered by the death of a passionately cherished dream, a loved spouse or child, or a parent on whom grieving persons are still dependent usually takes several years to be resolved. After many major losses, flashbacks of sad feelings may be triggered unexpectedly for many years when something associated with whomever or whatever was lost awakens forgotten memories.[12]

Tasks Three and Four: Coping and Then Rebuilding

The grief recovery work of coping with the difficult changes following losses immediately (task three) and the rebuilding of one's life without whatever one has lost (task four) is a continuing process. Coping is often highly stressful and filled with demanding challenges, especially following severe, multiple, or unexpected crises and grief. For traumatized persons to stay as fit as possible it is essential for them to increase their self-care and their receptivity to the care of others. Therefore, caregivers should encourage persons weathering crises and grief to be very kind and gentle with themselves and also to let those in their circle of mutual care know that they need extra support and loving.

The process of coping and rebuilding involves unlearning countless habitual responses and learning new behavior to meet personal needs formerly met by whomever or whatever is no longer available to them. It also involves making countless decisions about how to cope with the many new problems the loss has brought. Caring persons in their faith community, including lay caring team members, should be guided in functioning as a substitute extended family for those who lack such a family-and-friends support system. They can do this by offering whatever practical help and emotional support are needed. This support can take many forms. For example, a widow who has never handled her finances, or a widower who has never cooked for himself, needs help in learning these skills. Emotional support as well as reality testing may be needed as bereaved persons make decisions and begin to venture out into new relationships and experiences, such as going to social gatherings without the deceased and reinvesting some of that energy in other relationships.

Emotional and spiritual wounds caused by grief cannot heal fully until bereaved persons have moved ahead to accept the reality of their losses, surrendered their emotional ties to what is no longer available, and formed other relationships to provide new sources of interpersonal need-satisfaction. Psychiatrist Gerald Caplan described insightfully the importance of letting go of what is gone:

> In the crisis of bereavement the sufferer must actively resign himself to the impossibility of ever again satisfying his needs through interaction with the deceased. He must psychologically "bury the dead"; only after this has been done will he be free to seek gratification of these needs from alternative persons. Those who cope maladaptively with bereavement may pretend that the loved one is not dead, or they may magically introject his image by taking his characteristics into their own personality, and they will thus evade the painful act of resignation. This is likely to result in their energies remaining bound up with the deceased, so that they are not free to love others.[13]

The unhealthy consequence of attempting to hold on to whatever or whomever is no longer here is clear. Persons are unable to move ahead by learning new ways to help create a new future with new possibilities and gains, as well as new problems and pain.

Caregivers can encourage progress in doing tasks three and four by encouraging care receivers to respond to door-opening queries such as these:

- What will I do to improve my self-care so as to sustain my health during this time when heavy stress increases my vulnerability to illness? How will I go about developing and implementing the self-care action plans I need to do now? How will I motivate myself to take good care of my physical, mental, and spiritual wholeness even when I don't feel like doing it?
- From whom do I need and want to seek temporary help? What kinds of help do I need from them, and how will I request this help?

- What do I need to do to help fill the aching void I feel so that I can get on with living my life? When and how will I begin taking these actions?
- When will I take steps to develop a grief-healing action plan for myself?
- What cherished plans or dreams must I let go of now in order to move ahead on this new phase of my life journey?

Task Five: Enhancing Spiritual and Ethical Wholeness

Religious resources have much more than supportive and comforting functions in bereavement. The death of another person confronts us with our own mortality. Existential anxiety can be handled constructively only within the context of a vital, living faith. The symbols and affirmations of one's religious tradition can touch deep levels of the psyche, gradually renewing the feelings of basic trust in life and the universe that alone can enable persons to handle existential anxiety creatively. Therefore, the pastor's teaching and priestly roles are important in helping the bereaved put their loss in the context of faith. A pastor's skills in facilitating spiritual growth may help grieving people enlarge their faith and revitalize their relationship with God.

In crisis and bereavement counseling, the original root of the word *religion—religio* (to bind together)—has dynamic significance. When shattering loss fragments one's life, vital religion may help bind it together, restoring some sense of coherence and meaning. The crisis of death confronts some people with the poverty, obsolescence, or irrelevance of their beliefs and values. This awareness can open them to the growth process of revising and renewing their spiritual lives and their priorities. A renewed faith usually develops only after people have finished much of the most painful phases of grief work and are able to reflect on and learn from their losses.

Progress in spiritual and ethical growth can be aided by encouraging care receivers to list their answers to questions such as these:

- What beliefs and values of my loved one do I want to honor by the ways I now choose to respond to my grief and live my life?
- Do I need to seek guidance from a trained counselor, spiritual guide, or mentor, and if so, from whom?
- Which of my religious beliefs and values can be sources of spiritual recovery and renewal now? Which of my beliefs do I need to drop because they are obsolete?

Task Six: Reaching Out for Mutual Support and Care

A story about a family I know well illustrates the healing that can occur when grief-wounded people reach out to others who are also walking through shadowed valleys.

The infant daughter of a midwestern couple was desperately ill. She was called "Little Ruth" by her devoted parents, Clem Lucille and Doc, and her older siblings, Miriam and Junior. In spite of treatments by the physicians with the best medicines then available, she was growing steadily worse. She cried almost nonstop as her frantic parents took turns holding her tenderly and rocking her gently as they walked the floor day and night. All their efforts to comfort her pain proved futile. Finally, after several awful days, Ruth died on her first birthday.[14]

As usually is true in such family-shattering tragedies, Ruth's family and their relatives were devastated. Her totally exhausted parents were in shock, as were Ruth's six-year-old sister and her almost four-year-old brother. The family's pastor conducted the funeral in the family's rented home with Ruth's tiny body on the couch surrounded by flowers from their own and some neighbors' gardens. The little group of relatives and close friends present was submerged in what felt like bottomless grief. For the first time ever Miriam and Junior saw their stoic father weep. At the end of the brief service, Junior kissed Ruth good-bye on her cold forehead. Her body was buried in a tiny coffin under a large oak tree in the local cemetery just a short way from Abraham Lincoln's memorial and grave.

In dismal days and weeks of family depression after Ruth's death, Clem Lucille struggled to avoid being crushed by the enormous loss of her dear daughter. Her deep faith helped some. But she sensed intuitively that she must *do* more to help keep her sanity, cope with the tragedy, and go on with her life. Eventually she decided on the action she would take. Every morning she read the local newspaper, looking for reports about the deaths of children in that community. When she found such sad stories, she looked in the phone directory to try to find the parents' addresses. If she located their addresses, she penned them a brief note simply saying that she was very sorry about their huge loss and that she had them in her thoughts and prayers. She added that she knew something about the dark valley through which they were walking because she, too, had lost a dear child.

Clem Lucille continued to do this for several years, feeling that she was responding to God's intention for her life during the years of gradually softening pain in her slow recovery. She never talked about the responses she must have received from some of the grieving parents who were helped by her little notes. But one thing was clear to her husband Doc. He could tell that she was finding important help by reaching out to other grieving parents. On a personal level I am profoundly grateful for what Junior learned from Clem Lucille Clinebell, my mother, when I was a very young Howard Jr. By reaching out with healing love during our family's darkest time, she taught me a precious lesson about the key role of such outreach in self-healing and resolving grief.

Outreach by grief-suffering persons for mutual healing is an important aspect of the New Testament's understanding of grief healing. The Apostle Paul wrote in his second letter to the Christians in Corinth: "He comforts us in all our troubles, so that we in turn may be able to comfort others in any trouble of theirs" (2 Cor. 1:4 NEB). To the Christians in Rome, he enjoined: "Rejoice with those who rejoice, [and] weep with those who weep" (Rom. 12:15).

How can caregivers plant the seeds of mutual healing in the minds and hearts of those in crises and grief? One approach to encourage this outreach is to ask questions such as these when the timing is right in caregiving relationships, hoping that suffering persons will move toward action answers to self-queries:

- How can I best reach out to others and perhaps move beyond the awful loneliness of my personal grief?
- What are the mutual support and sharing groups in which I might be able to get but also give others some help?
- In which group or groups will I try for a while to discover whether they are helpful to me?

Caregiving with Those Whose Grief Wounds Do Not Heal

Grief is not per se an illness. Rather, it is a universal human crisis that wounds people in their minds, hearts, and spirits. This wounding makes them more vulnerable to developing physical, psychological, and spiritual problems. Fortunately the vast majority of grievers have adequate personal, social, and spiritual resources to heal their grief wounds without professional assistance. However, as pointed out earlier, numerous factors in our culture make healing more difficult and cause the grief wounds of many people to become infected. When grief wounds are deeply infected, they necessitate longer-term counseling or psychotherapy.

If grief-burdened people are recovering from crises and losses in normal, healthy ways, they accomplish the six tasks described above gradually over time. In contrast, some people continue overidealizing the deceased to defend themselves against facing the threatening negative side of their ambivalence. They use two ego defenses—denial and repression—that diminish their overall well-being. These defenses enable them to avoid experiencing the agonizing depth of their grief feelings and thereby prevent the healing of their grief wounds. Their wounds are infected and cannot heal until they face and deal with the out-of-awareness, threatening feelings.

Blocked or frozen grief takes a heavy toll on the well-being of sufferers, robbing them of creativity and aliveness so that they live with little or no zest for life. The longer grief work is delayed, the more costly it becomes to people's mental, physical, spiritual, and interpersonal health, and the more psychotherapeutic help is usually required for healing to occur. Another look at the death of my baby sister, described earlier, will illustrate the high cost of blocked grief. That tragedy cast the dark shadow of death over our whole family system. On a personal level, the shadow of death had a deep impact on my development in my troubled childhood and adolescence. More than thirty years of reduced aliveness, chronic "drivenness," and periodic depression even stretched into my adult life. In my midyears, a skilled psychotherapist effectively enabled me to uncover and lance my long-buried wound. This drained off the emotional infection so that very belated healing finally could occur.

My passionate convictions about the importance of clergy's learning basic skills in grief counseling come from asking myself some searching "what if" questions: What if our pastor had known how to help our whole family express and work through our devastating feelings of loss and guilt during the months or longer following Ruth's death? What if he had known enough about children's grief to help my parents learn how to help Miriam and me? What if he had been able to recognize the symptoms of infected grief wounds in children and had recommended that we be given help by a play therapy therapist? I know that basic training in pastoral caregiving, including grief counseling, was not available many years ago when that pastor received his training. In any case, the answer to my questions is crystal clear: if our pastor had had these basic insights and skills, all of my childhood family could have been spared years of needless suffering and diminished wholeness.[15]

Here are some danger signs that point to complicated grief, *if they persist undiminished in intensity long after a trauma:*

- continuing withdrawal from normal relationships and activities;
- undiminished mourning or the inappropriate absence of mourning;
- acute depression that does not lift and may be suicidal in intensity;
- severe and often multiple psychosomatic illnesses;
- disorientation or severe personality changes;
- severe, undiminishing guilt, shame, anger, fears, or loss of interest in life;
- continuing escape via prescribed or street drugs or alcohol;
- severe depression marked by feelings of inner deadness.

Caregivers usually encounter persons with infected grief wounds that cannot heal after suicides, homicides, conflicted divorces, and the deaths of children and youth. When they encounter what appear to be complicated grief responses, they should encourage the persons to express the full spectrum of their feelings about whom or what they have lost. By responding acceptingly to tentative expressions of mixed, conflicted, or negative feelings, further catharsis of feelings is encouraged. This process should be continued until these feelings are faced and talked through so that grieving people make some peace with themselves and their losses. Along with resentment (and/or anger toward the deceased, relatives, physicians, God, and so on), there often is a load of guilt about those feelings that must also be talked through until it is resolved.

Grief wounds must heal from the inside and in ways that reflect the uniqueness of each person. Healing cannot be forced, but the caregiving relationship can encourage and expedite the process. If inappropriate grief symptoms persist after several months in spite of caregiving efforts, it is crucial that grieving people be referred to a competent pastoral psychotherapist who is skilled in helping people with blocked grief work.

Needed: Innovative Congregational Crisis and Grief Programs

Over the years, I have asked participants in many lay and professional workshops in a variety of cultures, "How many of you have had painful changes or losses within the last few years?" Depending on the ages of those involved, 35 to 60 percent raise their hands. Because the frequency of losses accelerates with the passing years and more things are lost that cannot be replaced, learning to handle losses without being disabled or embittered becomes increasingly essential for creative aging.

In every congregation, as in our general society, there are numerous people of all ages who are the "walking wounded." They appear to be normal in their surface behavior, but at deeper, hidden levels of their lives they suffer from unhealed grief wounds. These diminish drastically their aliveness, spiritual vitality, creativity, and joy in living. Obviously, new strategies and programs are needed to help these and countless other grieving people find healing. Congregations and their leaders must have *the* central role in devising and implementing such innovative approaches. One of the most effective things faith communities can do to enhance the overall wholeness of those whose lives they touch is to create such programs to minister effectively with wounded people before, during, and after significant losses and other painful crises. The most effective existing programs are multifaceted with the following six parts:

Part One: Education to Help People Prepare to Deal Constructively with Crises, Losses, and Painful Transitions

The goal of such preventive education is to enable members of faith communities to learn about the importance and process of grief work and how they can cultivate this healing in themselves, their families, and their friendship circles. Knowledge of the six basic tasks of grief work can provide cognitive maps that learners can use to guide themselves when crises and losses strike. Sermons, one-on-one caregiving conversations, and educational programs on all age levels can be effective channels for congregation-wide learning.

End-of-life caring education, using an educative counseling or coaching approach, is an essential part of constructive grieving programs in congregations and hospitals. In spite of greater openness than in the past to talk openly about dying, our culture unfortunately is still largely death denying. In this social context, the goal of death education is to help congregants face and learn how to deal constructively with their mortality. A vital resource for use in such a program is Bill Moyers's PBS series *On Our Own Terms: Bill Moyers on Dying*. (This four-part video can be ordered from 800-PLAY-PBS.) Many other resources are available from the end-of-life care movement that has been growing in recent years. It received a major boost when former First Lady Rosalynn Carter experienced the pain of caring for her terminally ill mother. This motivated her to join with others in forming the Last Acts Coalition, which works to improve end-of-life care (their website is lastacts.org).

Crisis and grief education should include coaching people to take two essential actions that help them prepare to die well. The first is preparing a living will (also known as an advanced directive to physicians). This gives instructions to one's primary care physician about what one wants done or not done after one is no longer able to express one's desires. (Usually this includes "no heroic measures after all hope for recovery evaporates.") A second action is signing a legal document giving what is called "durable power of attorney" to a trusted, responsible family member or other such person. This empowers the person to make crucial decisions for you if and when you are no longer able to make these for yourself. Different states in the United States have somewhat varying requirements for these documents, so it is important to check with your primary care physician or the state medical association to discover what is required.

Another important objective of holistic death and grief education is to help participants increase death awareness and learn how to make some peace with this reality. Confronting death and one's feelings about it can be life enhancing if done in the contexts of a supportive, caring community with a growing, reality-based faith. Issues about death should be raised gently in the context of living life in all its fullness. When this is done effectively, many people spontaneously consider revising their short-sighted or misguided values or life plans and priorities in light of their awareness of their mortality.

It is fortunate in recent years that issues related to death and dying have been brought out of the closet to be discussed openly in many circles. But most people in

Western cultures still ignore, deny, repress, or run from their feelings about their eventual death. There is abundant evidence that it may be spiritually helpful for some people in the prime of life to develop an ongoing awareness of these anxieties. Letting themselves experience, express, and talk through these feelings, individually or in a group, with an empathetic listener can produce diminished fear of death and other life-enriching benefits. These may include a greater sense of aliveness and the preciousness of life, enhanced creativity, openness to greater intimacy, and increased empathy and compassion. Even decreased vulnerability to addictions and increased caring for and about future generations and the biosphere may result from confronting and accepting the reality of death long before it becomes imminent.

In grief caregiving, it is crucial to wait to raise issues with the bereaved about their dying until they have experienced significant healing of their initial pain and loss. This means after they are well along in doing whichever of the six tasks of the grief recovery and healing they need to do and seem open to a question such as, "What have you learned from this painful loss?"

Here are some guidelines that have proved useful in leading life-enhancing death awareness conversations and learning events:

- Raise issues of confronting death in the context of a caring relationship or caregiving community or group.
- Limit such queries to people who are mentally and emotionally stable.
- Confront feelings about death in the context of a growing, reality-based faith that includes dealing with death.
- Encourage reflection on the hidden possibilities for valuable learning and growth in learning from their painful losses.
- Help people learn to celebrate the now rather than live in the past or future.
- Raise questions about death feelings gently so that people will feel little pressure to deal with them until they are ready.
- Encourage people to revise their values, plans, and priorities in light of their awareness of their shrinking futures, and reinforce life-enhancing revisions by affirming them.

Part Two: Caregiving with Dying Persons and Their Families

Each person's dying is as unique as his or her living. We all tend to die much as we have lived, but dying always is an interpersonal event. In our lonely society, the relative richness of people's interpersonal caring networks makes a tremendous difference in the quality of their dying. The terminality and eventual death of one member usually brings grief to the whole family system. On the positive side, deaths can awaken awareness in friends and family of how precious their relationships with one another really are. In a moving story of his grief, Mitch Albom reminds readers of an easily forgotten truth about grief and relationships: "Love is how you stay alive even after you are gone."[16]

For many church families the presence of a trusted pastor during all or even part of what is often a long, lonely watch is a precious supportive and caring gift. This is primarily a ministry of presence highlighted by brief prayers, scripture, and religious rites that bring comfort and communicate personal messages, such as "Thank you," "I am very sorry," "I love you!" and "May God be with you on your journey." When dying persons or their families want their pastor to be present, their wishes should be honored if possible.

Pastoral experiences with terminally ill persons suggest that several resources that caregivers and family members can help provide often help dying persons. The resources include the following: (1) *Being nurtured by a small caring community* of one person—or, better, a few persons—who will listen with empathy and give loving support and gentle physical and spiritual care until persons die. (2) *Completing as many of the unfinished things in their lives as possible.* Tying up loose ends in their lives, especially issues in close relationships such as expressing love or thanks, or asking for forgiveness or giving it. (3) *Doing the challenging anticipatory grief work that often is needed as people try to cope with the multiple losses of dying.* Knowledge of Elisabeth Kübler-Ross's five stages of dying is useful in facilitating this process,[17] as is knowledge of the six tasks of growing through grief discussed above. (4) *Having meaningful religious or spiritual beliefs, or a personal philosophy of life that provides some sense of trust and at-homeness in the universe,* as well as some meanings that transcend the huge losses of one's own dying. (5) *Having a setting where one can die with dignity without terrible pain, surrounded by caring family and friends.* Substantial evidence suggests that people are much more afraid of the pain and indignity that often accompany dying than they are of death itself. Fortunately, medical and pharmacological science continues to make major advances in pain management. Caregivers can play significant roles in collaboration with patients, their families, hospice workers, and primary care physicians to ensure that health-care professionals with current knowledge and clinical skills do everything possible to reduce suffering to a minimum. (6) *Reviewing the good things and significant people that give their lives meaning, joy, and purpose.* (7) *Knowing that their loved ones are also receiving much-needed care.* Dying is a very private and an intensely interpersonal experience. Pastoral caregivers, like hospice workers, often spend more time serving burdened family members than they do serving the terminally ill persons. In any case, caregiving with family members gives indirect but important care to the ill persons.

When visiting terminally ill persons, it is wise to follow the insightful approach of a hospice social worker with two decades of experiences in this vital service.[18] She states,

> When I am serving the dying, I remember that I'm there to serve the living. The dying will take care of itself. Dying folks are very resilient! Until the moment of death they have strengths. When you ask them, "How are you doing?" they usually answer, "I'm doing fine." This usually isn't denial but an indication of their continuing strength in spite of the decline of their physical body.

Her approach to dialoguing with these patients is especially insightful and worth emulating:

> I dialogue with them, not about their death, but about their life. I ask a series of gentle, socially acceptable questions, like, "How long have you lived in this community? How long have you been married? How many children do you have? What was your work? How did you stay married so long? How did you make it through those difficult years?" I listen carefully for patterns in their responses because these begin to paint a picture. It's a picture of their priorities, of what gives their life meaning and purpose, who and what they value, and what they have learned about life. As I listen I mirror back to them all the things that were strong and good about their lives and all the things I admire about them and their life stories. This helps them die with meaning at peace with themselves and their lives.

The affirming dialogical process she describes is called "therapeutic reminiscences." This dialogical interaction can be very therapeutic with many healthy older people as well as terminally ill people.

Dying persons frequently ask nonmedical caregivers about the prognosis of their illness. The appropriate response is to say in effect, "I suggest that you ask your doctor, who has the knowledge to answer you accurately." On the issue of family members withholding the truth from patients, be aware that many dying persons really know the truth on some level of their minds. Furthermore, if they are not consciously aware of their terminality or are surrounded by a conspiracy of silence, they may be deprived of opportunities to complete unfinished issues in their lives as well as enjoy recalling the things that have given their lives meaning and perhaps zest.

Our identity as humans is shaped in and by our early and continuing close interpersonal relationships, primarily in our families. We incorporate those persons in our sense of identity, thus making them a significant aspect of who we are. Facilitating grief healing in family systems of dying persons, therefore, requires some understanding of how it feels to have a part of oneself and one's world torn away. This makes family grief experiences so profoundly disturbing, whatever the quality of those relationships. The more crucial to one's identity a dead person was, the deeper the sense of agonizing amputation and emptiness that follow the death. And the more painful or conflicted the relationship was, the more infected the grief wound and the longer healing will probably take. Because they were a major part of parents' identity as well as the collective identity of the family system, the process of adjusting to irreparably changed identity is particularly difficult and protracted when children die. The death of a sibling is also difficult because this robs brothers and sisters, as well as parents and others in the family system, of essential parts of their identity. The deaths of parents rob children of any age of relationships around which the family identity was formed.

Survivors of family deaths respond in a wide variety of ways. A dear friend was the full-time caretaker for his wife through a long, debilitating illness ending in her painful release in death. He reports that as he looks back, the wedding vow "in sickness and in health" took on added significance for him. He added that the words of 1 John came alive in a new way: "Beloved, let us love one another, for love is from God: everyone who loves is born of God and knows God." He then quoted Martin Luther's observation: "We are to love our neighbor just as we love ourselves, and our wife is our closest neighbor."[19]

The responses of primary family caregivers, in contrast to this friend's response, are usually ambivalent. Feelings of love, genuine caring, and longing for the dead person are in conflict with anger and often resentment toward the care receivers, who often become unreasonable and demanding as their health deteriorates. The negative emotions usually result in self-punishing guilt as caregivers say to themselves, *I shouldn't feel like this with a person in this sad condition.* Helping family members experience, express repeatedly, and talk through these negative feelings is often crucial to their healing.

Part Three: Healing Funerals, Memorial Services, Family and Congregational Rituals

During the first twenty-four hours after a death, unless preplanning has been done by the deceased, more than fifty decisions must be made, usually by family members. It can be difficult, if not impossible, for them to make rational decisions about funeral arrangements in the midst of their sorrow. Decisions made under such extreme emotional stress can be costly and later regretted. Funerals are often very expensive.[20] Preplanning can reduce this cost substantially, and membership in a low-cost funeral cooperative can result in even greater savings. A valuable resource for preplanning is *Let the Choice Be Mine: A Personal Guide and Workbook for Planning Your Own Funeral* by Barbara Hilton. When pastors sense that certain families seem particularly vulnerable to making decisions they will later regret, it is appropriate to ask them if they would like a member of the lay caregiving team to accompany and support then when they are making decisions about how much to spend on the funeral.

During the pastoral visit soon after a death, as the funeral or memorial service is being planned, the pastor should encourage the bereaved family to talk together about the circumstances of the death, how they found out about it, and their feelings. They should also be asked about the memories they cherish and the things they most valued in the person who has died. (With the family's permission, it is often meaningful to incorporate some of these valued memories and attributes in the meditation and memorial message during the funeral.)

An important purpose of funeral and memorial services is to facilitate the emotional release of grief feelings so that healing may occur. What is said during the service should be straight and clear about the painful reality of the loss and the appropriateness of mourning. Healing can be blocked in survivors if anything is said implying that stoicism in the face of grief is a sign of real strength or Christian virtue, or that one whose faith is strong and vital will not experience agonizing grief. The funeral should include familiar hymns, prayers, and scripture that bring comfort and that also help release dammed-up feelings. The funeral is also a service of thanksgiving for the deceased person, a service of mutual support of the bereaved by the Christian community, and an affirmation of the beliefs of this community that helps the bereaved put the loss in the larger context of a life-affirming faith. A pastor can help the family and friends mourn by expressing her or his feelings of grief and loss and by creating appropriate rituals of participation, such as inviting everyone to put a flower on the casket before leaving the gravesite.

Caring support of survivors needs to continue during the weeks and months following the funeral. Pouring out and eventual resolution of often mixed feelings can be encouraged by asking questions such as these during postfuneral visits with the family: "Would you tell me more about the way he [or she] died? What has your grieving experience been like since the funeral? What sorts of things seem to occupy your thoughts or feelings or dreams? What do you miss most? What seems to help you most?" After asking only one or two questions, it's wise to stay out of the griever's way by keeping quiet and simply being a listening presence.

A pastor should encourage and coach families in devising ways to celebrate the lives of family members who have died. One way of doing this that many find meaningful is to collaborate in creating loving family rituals or memorials. These can highlight the things about the person that they remember with gratitude. Some families find it helpful to designate "remembrance places" in their homes. What they decide to have there often include favorite photos of the dead person with other family members and items belonging to the person that symbolize what they wish to remember. When children die, parents often place their favorite toys on such a memorial. Informal family rituals of remembrance on important dates associated with the missing person—for example, birthdays, anniversaries, and favorite holidays—can help them transform the heightened sadness they feel on those days. Families who are members in congregations can be encouraged to find or help create healing opportunities such as grief-healing groups there.

Ritual meals can bring many people comfort and healing. An insightful writer on food describes the emotional nurturing that eating can bring: "It seems to me that our three basic needs, for food and security and love, are so entwined that we cannot think of one without the other." When the underpinnings of people's psychological world are shattered and their comfortable assumptions about the permanence of their lives are undermined by painful trauma, they often crave comforting foods. Often they crave foods that have body-mind association with their childhoods.[21] The custom in many cultures of having meals after funerals, either at churches or in homes, can be a valuable healing ritual.

Part Four: Setting Up and Leading Crisis-Coping / Grief-Healing Groups

Another essential part of a strategy for helping the bereaved is for the pastor to set up and lead or, better, to colead a crisis or grief-healing group. Such groups are efficient ways of deepening the grief ministry of a congregation and a means of beginning the training of a lay crisis and grief team. Participating in such a group can help people finish their own grief work and learn how to help other grieving persons. Using crises and losses in this way requires three things: being in mutual caring relationships, finding spiritual meaning, and generating reality-based hope during the recovery journey. Crisis and grief-healing groups offer small interpersonal communities within which these three transformational experiences often occur. Such groups are relatively easy to set up and lead. How to do so will be described in chapter 15 on group caregiving.

Part Five: Collaborating with Hospice Programs

In responding in therapeutic ways to the needs of terminally ill persons, the hospice movement is the most humanizing development in modern times. A Christian physician, Cicely Sanders, who started the first modern hospice at Saint Christopher's Hospice in a suburb of London in 1967, states, "A modern hospice, whether it is a separate unit or a ward, or home care or hospital team, aims to enable a patient to live to the limit of his potential in physical strength, mental and emotional capacity and social relationships."[22] Hospice programs enable many terminally ill people to have the blessing of dying in their homes surrounded by family members rather than in the impersonal atmosphere typical of many hospitals or nursing homes. The hospice does this by attending carefully to the control of pain and by arranging frequent visits by a trained volunteer to give the dying and their family support and care. Hospice residential facilities enable persons in the final phase of terminal illnesses to die in a humanizing environment where alternative therapies such as massage and harp music are often available. The volunteer continues to stay in touch with the family as they do their grief work after the death.

Pastoral caregivers should learn from and cooperate fully with hospice programs in their communities. If none exists, they can work with community health-care services to launch such a program locally. Clergy should encourage members of their congregation to take hospice training and volunteer in its program. Remember that the people close to dying persons are simultaneously struggling with severe anticipatory grief and with carrying the enormous load of caring for very sick family members or friends. They need the caring expertise of their pastor but also regular support from a lay caring team and/or from a community hospice program.

Part Six: Training and Coaching a Team of Lay Caregivers

Another essential part of a congregational grief-healing program is to train a carefully selected lay caring team to help carry the considerable load of supportive care of persons with normal grief feelings in congregations. Two factors make this essential. There are too many hurting persons experiencing disturbing crises, losses, perplexing decisions, and life transitions in even small congregations for a pastor working alone to respond effectively to these multiple pastoral care needs. Furthermore, the process of recovery usually is too extended—at least a year and often much more—for any one person to provide the needed ongoing care. Caregiving is ultimately the responsibility of the whole faith community, with selected members of that community leading by receiving special training for this shared ministry of healing and wholeness.

Dealing with Perplexing Theodicy Questions

A World War II tombstone at the site of the Normandy beach invasion expresses the painful hope of countless grief-shattered human beings: "Maybe someday God will tell us why he broke our hearts." When tragedy strikes good people who believe that God is both loving and just, their religious faith is often deeply shaken or shattered. The father of a six-year-old girl who had just died from cancer expressed his agonizing grief, asking his pastor, "How can a loving heavenly Father take the life of an innocent child like my dear daughter?" Caregivers must deal with the fact that the theodicy question is the jagged rock on which the ship of many people's faith crashes in their storms of crises and grief.

When religious people ask this question or express the anger toward God that often accompanies the question, pastoral caregivers should welcome their openness in expressing this anger. Such questions may open a door of opportunity for listening and accepting the person's doubts and suffering. It is usually a mistake to attempt to answer theodicy questions because there are no easy or fully satisfying answers, and most people do not expect an answer. What they most need is an empathetic listener who does not try to defend God, but supports them with caring understanding of their theological struggles. After the process of grief healing has moved far beyond the first awful agony, some bereaved people may be helped by mentioning the classical theological answers. Depending on people's beliefs, these may include pointing to the unfinishedness and imperfection of the universe, and God's respect for human freedom. Or they may be helped by looking at their suffering in the context of the mystery of Jesus' suffering and death.

Drawing on the Grief-healing Energy of Nature

In no area of caregiving is the healing energy of God's living creation more useful than in ministering with bereaved people. A major reason people find nature healing was expressed well by Henry David Thoreau. While he lived in a small self-constructed hut near Walden Pond, he wrote, "I went to the woods because I wished to live deliberately, to front only the essential facts of life, and see if I could not learn what it had to teach, and not, when I came to die, discover that I had not lived."[23] When people come alive in their awareness of the wonder and mystery of the miracle of being alive, they can transcend their haunting awareness of their mortality.

Finding Healing Resources in the Arts

Because of the universality, existential anxiety, and profound mystery most people experience during crises, disasters, and severe losses, such tragedies call out for many expressive voices. Through the centuries, music, poetry, prose, drama, and visual arts have had a place in enabling people to cope with life's many painful traumas. These media provide the symbols and images that articulate to some extent the dual mystery of living and dying in which we are involved.

Because of the multifaceted nature of grief and the great variations in ways that grief healing occurs in different people and cultures, facilitating the healing process often involves flexibility and imagination in the responses of caregivers and counselors. Music therapy has been used widely and effectively to help patients in various types of institutions, including mental hospitals. The insights and methods from that therapeutic specialty can be adapted and used by clergy in facilitating grief healing. The approach involves a complementary partnership between music and verbal interaction. The music is chosen because it has some association with a lost relationship or with painful or positive feelings associated with whomever or whatever has been lost. It may include familiar songs, loved hymns, or improvised or composed music by the counselor and/or the bereaved person. The music can be associated with a relationship that "never was." For example, an Australian music therapist describes working with a woman suffering from protracted grief following a stillbirth. The therapist asked what music she would have liked to have sung to the dead baby if it had lived. When they sang that lullaby together, the grieving woman poured out her sadness, remorse, and anger. Her feelings thus became accessible for healing dialogue and resolution.

Some grieving people, including those with no musical training, find it helpful to accept the suggestion that they create their own words and melodies to express their feelings about their loss. What they create is then played or sung, perhaps to the lost person or activity. Following a stroke, an older man found it helped heal his grief to hear a tape recording of some of his favorite music to which he had enjoyed dancing with his wife before his stroke. Therapists who do palliative care with patients in the final stages of their lives have found that music can be a healing resource for them and their relatives during these trying times.[24] If people want to plan their funeral or memorial services, choosing the music is a major feature of this process.[25]

Music has the power to awaken suppressed grief feelings that need to be experienced, expressed, and gradually worked through. This makes the process of choosing the hymns or other music for funerals or memorial services a caregiving opportunity. Active involvement of close family members in this choosing is a part of a collaborative, partnering approach to grief caregiving.

Learning from Your Own Crises and Losses—Don't Waste Your Pain

The crises, grief, sins, mistakes, and failures in your life probably have taught you some unexpected but valuable insights about handling such problems.[26] By looking back on your life, you may be surprised by the growth you have experienced during painful crises and losses. If so, it's important not to waste these fragments of pain-derived wisdom. Such difficult and costly learnings are new assets that you can use in helping other wounded people find healing. In fact, your brokenness will be either a bridge or a barrier to others who have been broken by crises and grief. If you attempt to hide your brokenness and pretend that everything in your life is healthy and whole, suffering people will sense that something in you is not authentic. But if you own your brokenness and learn from it, it becomes a bridge of empathy and acceptance, as well as a spring of healing for the brokenness of others. You can continue your healing by being a wounded healer to others. Here is an awareness exercise aimed at enabling you to reexperience how you have grown in your crises and grief. Remember that slash marks [/] mean pause, and close your eyes while you do what has been described.

Learning Exercise. To prepare yourself to be receptive to the learnings that are available in this exercise, do what is needed to let your body-mind-spirit organism become keenly alert but also very relaxed. / Go back in memory and recall a painful personal loss of someone or something you felt you couldn't live without. (Or as an alternative, recall a disturbing crisis when you felt as if the rug had been pulled out from under your life.) / Now, take a few minutes to relive that painful experience in detail, letting yourself experience again the full range of thoughts and feelings you had when it first happened. Be particularly alert for feelings of weakness and vulnerability, of desperately needing and being dependent on others for help. / As you let yourself relive that trauma, try to discover if the pain and struggle taught you anything that has proved to be useful in your caregiving or your personal life. Perhaps they brought you some new insights and skills that you have found useful in coping more effectively with later crises. Or perhaps they made you a little stronger, more empathic and caring, or changed your spirituality and ethical priorities for the better. / If you just discovered that you did grow, even a little, think about who or what enabled you to transform painful negative circumstances into a positive learning experience. / Now, with your eyes closed to focus your thoughts, reflect on what you have just relived, becoming aware of any unfinished feeling associated with that experience. / Recall what or who you found helpful in coping and how it was helpful. / Become aware of what that experience taught you about yourself and about how to cope with future crises or losses in your life. / Now, reflect on how that crisis or loss influenced your relationship with God and your real faith—meaning what you really believe. / Think about how learnings during one of the many unwelcome detours on your life journey have influenced your caregiving. And think about how you can use what you learned to help recipients of your caring skills to experience some growth during their crises and grief. / Jot down notes about what you want to remember and use in helping those who seek your care. If you have learned and grown through any of your crises and losses, Henri Nouwen's apt phrase "the wounded healer" will acquire fresh meaning for you.

In this spirit, here is a prayer-poem that came to my mind and heart unexpectedly as I struggled to make peace with two huge personal losses—the death of my father and, before that grief was fully resolved, the death of my mother:

> For my pain, O God—which I did not choose, and do not like, and would let go of if I could—
> Give me the wisdom to treat it as a bridge,
> A crossing to another's pain—to that person's private hell.
> Grant me the courage not to live alone
> Behind my shell of hiding,
> My make-believe side which tries to always seem "on top,"
> in control, adequate for any crunch, not really needing others.
> Let me own my hidden pain so that it will open me
> To those I meet,
> To their pain and caring—
> That in our shared humanity,
> We may know that we are one—in You.

Making Music with Whatever You Have Left

On November 18, 1995, Itzhak Perlman, widely recognized as one of the world's greatest violinists, gave a concert at Lincoln Center in New York City. Having been stricken with polio as a child, he walks with great difficulty, aided by braces on both legs and two crutches. When he reached his chair, he sat down slowly, put his crutches on the floor, and released the braces. Then he picked up his violin, tucked it under his chin, nodded to the orchestra conductor, and began to play.

As he finished the first few bars of the music, there was a loud snap, letting everyone in the hall know that one of the violin's strings had broken. Everyone expected that he would struggle off the stage to find a string or another violin. They knew that it is impossible to play a symphonic work with only three strings. But to everyone's surprise, he refused to believe this. He paused a few moments, closed his eyes, and then signaled to the conductor to begin again. His music was filled with more power, passion, and purity than people had heard from him before as he changed and recomposed the piece in his head. When he finished, there was awesome silence before the audience stood as they clapped, cheered, and shouted their appreciation. He smiled, wiped sweat from his forehead, and raised his bow to quiet the crowd. Then he said, in a quiet, pensive tone, "You know, sometimes it is the artist's task to find out how much music you can still make with what you have left."

Isn't this the challenge facing us when painful losses or disabilities hit us? We grow through our crises and grief when, in spite of them, we decide to make whatever music we can with what we have left. That music often is amazingly powerful!

Reality Practice Skill Development Session

Parishioner's role: If you have had a painful loss in your life that you would like to discuss—perhaps the one you relived above—go to the pastor seeking help. Or as an alternative, role-play Jane Carey, a woman in her midforties whose husband, Dick, died unexpectedly two months ago from a heart attack. You feel the loss intensely and find it almost impossible to go into social situations, especially to the church where you were active as a couple. You feel very depressed and would like to hide from people.

Pastor's role: Use what you have learned from this chapter about facilitating grief work as you counsel with one of these parishioners. Be aware of the person's need for help with particular grief work tasks as these are discussed above.

Observer-coach's role: Be aware of the interaction between the parishioner and the pastor. Interrupt periodically to ask how the parishioner is feeling and to give the pastor feedback on her or his effectiveness in facilitating the grief work process, especially task two—the pouring out of unfinished feelings.

Recommended Reading

Albom, Mitch. *Tuesdays with Morrie*. New York: Doubleday, 1997.

DeSpelder, Lynne Ann, and Albert Lee Strickland. *The Last Dance: Encountering Death and Dying*. 5th ed. Mountain View, Calif.: Mayfield Publishing, 1996.

Doka, Kenneth J., and Terry L. Martin. *Men Don't Cry . . . Women Do: Transcending Gender Stereotypes of Grief*. Philadelphia: Taylor & Francis, 2000.

Dotterweich, Kass. *Grieving as a Woman: Moving through Life's Many Losses*. St. Meinrad, Ind.: Abbey Press, 1998.

Gilbert Richard. *Finding Your Way after Your Parent Dies: Hope for Grieving Adults*. South Bend, Ind.: Ave Maria Press, 1999.

————, ed. *Healthcare and Spirituality: Listening, Assessing, Caring*. Amityville, N.Y.: Baywood, 2000.

James, John W., and Russell Friedman. *The Grief Recovery Handbook: The Action Program for Moving Beyond Death, Divorce, and Other Losses*. Rev. ed. New York: Harper Perennial, 1998.

Lund, Dale A., ed. *Men Coping with Grief*. Amityville, N.Y.: Baywood, 2000.

Meyer, Charles. *Surviving Death: A Practical Guide to Caring for the Dying and Bereaved*. Mystic, Conn.: Twenty-Third Publications, 1997.

Rando, Therese A. *Treatment of Complicated Mourning*. Champaign, Ill.: Research Press, 1993.

Reed, Kenneth. *Healing through Grieving: Learning to Live Again*. Indianapolis: Grief Healing, 2002.

CHAPTER 10

HEALING SPIRITUAL BROKENNESS AND CULTIVATING SPIRITUAL WHOLENESS IN PASTORAL CARE AND COUNSELING

The overall, unifying objective of pastoral caregiving is to heal spiritual and ethical brokenness and to nurture growth in spiritual and ethical wholeness. This overall objective should be the goal, even if spiritual issues are not the presenting problem and even if religious and value issues are never discussed explicitly in particular caregiving sessions or relationships. If a person's spiritual life is a primary source of conflict, guilt, anxiety, or truncated growth, it should become an explicit focus in pastoral care. But many people with no obvious spiritual or ethical problems continue to have areas of immaturity and distortion in these dimensions of their lives, long after they have outgrown them in other areas. For this reason, help is often needed to nurture spiritual and ethical healing and maturing.

The centrality of the spiritual in the human person underlines the vital importance of training clergy as enablers of spiritual and ethical healing and growth. To use this training effectively, caregivers must integrate insights from psychological, sociological, and theological sources. Nurturing spiritual and ethical healing is done explicitly with those suffering from obvious brokenness in these vital life areas. It is done indirectly with many persons in whom such problems are hidden below other problems, as well as in those who respond negatively to explicit "religious" language.

Fortunately, well-trained theological caregivers have unique resources and skills to bring to the challenges of empowering and caring for troubled people. To integrate the wisdom from their theological traditions with resources from the psychosocial sciences and the psychotherapeutic disciplines, pastoral caregivers must know their own heritages well. In our increasingly pluralistic society, caregivers also need accurate knowledge of other major faith traditions. Furthermore, they need to be open to learning from care receivers about their traditions.

Many of the valuable resources of clergy for spiritual and ethical caregiving are inherent in their social and symbolic roles. They are persons who are seen as representing the beliefs and values of a faith community that brings Christian meanings to bear on human problems. Careseekers' perception of clergy's symbolic identity influences care-giving relationships in subtle but significant ways, for better or for worse. Many people perceive clergy as religious authority figures and as religious figures who "stand in" for God. Such perceptions trigger a variety of early life memories and feelings, positive and negative; for example, about God, parents, good and evil, heaven and hell, sex, Sunday school, funerals, religious fears, and magical beliefs. Pastoral counselors who are aware of these unfinished psychological and spiritual issues from people's past may respond to opportunities to help them correct old distortions and thus develop more constructive attitudes toward all things religious.

Caregiving for ethical wholeness should help people enhance their well-being by fac-ing and dealing constructively with their personal sins as well as their complicity in the social sins of oppression and injustices in a society that denies wholeness to countless people. Beyond this focus on the brokenness and alienation caused by sin, caregivers should devote their skills to fostering positive values that contribute to the wholeness of individuals, families, society, and God's whole creation.

This chapter describes methods by which clergy and other religiously oriented care-givers can offer troubled individuals and families help with countless types of spiritual and ethical dilemmas and crises. Because spiritual and ethical beliefs are often deeply intertwined, one useful way to evaluate the health of particular belief systems is the health of the ethical beliefs and practices that they tend to generate. This chapter will provide methods of evaluating both spiritual and ethical health and then describe ways of facilitating healing of spiritual brokenness and enabling spiritual wholeness to blos-som. The next chapter will describe parallel methods for healing ethical brokenness and cultivating ethical wholeness.

Caregiving in a Time of Spiritual and Ethical Crises

Caregivers need keen awareness that the world in which they do their vital ministries is rocked by radical spiritual and ethical crises. The impact of these crises draws many people to seek help from counseling pastors as well as specialists in pastoral psychother-apy. This social context shapes the spiritual and ethical problems that careseekers bring and the kinds of solutions to which they are open.

In this crisis the shifting of humankind's spiritual foundations is shaking our meta-physical substructure. Taken-for-granted certainties of generations past are widely ques-tioned and openly rejected by many spiritually hungry people today. The unprecedented speed of social change has produced a massive collapse of traditional systems of religious beliefs, symbols, meanings, and values for millions. Traditional authority-centered ways of handling existential anxiety and satisfying spiritual needs are no longer acceptable or meaningful to them, but new, more creative ways have not yet become widely available.

In this time of spiritual transition, caregivers should be aware that countless people are questioning or rejecting the traditional biblical cosmology. They are searching for meaning in many new directions. Some baby boomers, for example, are creating their own belief systems that they feel meet their spiritual needs. These are more likely to be spiritual rather than formal religious beliefs.[1]

The relational, spiritual, and value vacuums suffered by millions of people provide fertile soil for the seeds of personality dysfunction, relationship pathology and toxicity, and psychospiritual-physiological illnesses to flourish. Among the many factors producing these crises are the far-reaching paradigm shifts with profound religious implications that affect humankind's understandings of the good life and of the universe. The dominant new forces in this postmodern world include transnationalism and the global economy, mind-boggling technology and the digital and cyberspace revolutions, and global telecommunications. These planetwide forces have an impact on people's spiritual and ethical lives in subtle but discernable ways:

> We live in a world hungry for accessible spirituality. Even as there is ongoing distrust of religious institutions, there is longing for ways to understand and believe in that which is greater than ourselves, the God beyond our gods. There is a spiritual longing, pining for new ways to find meaning in life, to resist evil, to embrace good, and to live with hope.[2]

As a result of these widespread spiritual and ethical crises, the lives of countless people are saturated by existential anxiety. Many flee from this anxiety by adopting authoritarian, oversimplified, fundamentalist "solutions" often espoused by charismatic pseudo-messiahs. They engage in what Erich Fromm described as "escaping from freedom," referring to the attraction of many people to the Nazi ideology. Today, those who sacrifice their freedom of thought by accepting a closed religious ideology do so to reduce the anxiety aroused by our planet's spiritual and ethical crises. The high price they pay for whatever increased sense of security they derive is abandoning their freedom to challenge simplistic traditional beliefs and exercise their intellectual and spiritual creativity by developing more liberating, empowering religious beliefs and practices.

When viewed from a transformational perspective, the spiritual and ethical crises can bring positive change. When people let go of comfortable answers that no longer make sense or satisfy, they are confronted by a need that is also an opportunity—to work out their own salvation with fear and trembling, to paraphrase Philippians 2:12. Those who risk questioning traditional authority-validated beliefs and values are confronted by a need and opportunity to discover beliefs and values that are meaningful to them because they contribute more to a healthy, peaceful, and just world. Although the process of letting go of childish but comfortable beliefs (as described in 1 Cor. 13:11) is painful, doing so is an essential part of the process of growing up spiritually and ethically. There is no doubt that spiritually centered pastoral caregivers can provide valuable help to people in their search for spiritual and value wholeness in the midst of society's chaos in these areas.

Understanding the Universality of Religious and Ethical Systems

Numerous studies of diverse cultures around the world reveal that, as one anthropologist put it, "human beings are incurably religious." What produces this universal need for some form of spirituality and for ethical codes in the hearts and minds of our species? Why are spiritual and value issues inherent at some level in all human problems? There are two basic reasons for the universality of religion. One was articulated theologically by Saint Augustine in this oft-quoted declaration addressed to God: "You have made us for yourself O Lord, and our hearts are restless until they rest in you."[3] The basic meaning of his statement could be expressed psychologically as follows: we humans have a profound need at the very center of our being for an intimate, ongoing connection with the wider spiritual universe. In religious terms this could be described as a relationship with God, the transcending Spirit of life, love, and liberty. This same truth was expressed lyrically in the words of Hildegard of Bingen, the creation-loving mystical genius and Renaissance woman who lived some eight hundred years ago in what is now Germany:

> The soul is kissed by God, in its innermost regions.
> With interior yearning, grace and blessing are bestowed.
> And so, humankind full of all creative possibilities is God's work.
> Humankind, alone, is called to assist God.
> Humankind is called to co-create.
> —Hildegard of Bingen, *Meditations*[4]

Simply put, *we humans are a species who know that we will die*—probably at an unknown place and time in the near or distant future. This awareness probably makes us unique among all species. The prophet Isaiah described this existential reality confronting our species in these images:

> A voice says, "Cry!"
>   And I said, "What shall I cry?"
> All flesh is grass,
>   and all its beauty is like the flower of the field.
> The grass withers, the flower fades
>   when the breath of the LORD blows on it;
>   surely the people are grass.
> The grass withers, the flower fades,
>   but the word of our God will stand forever. (Isa. 40:6-8 ESV)

How do we defend ourselves against the knowledge that we are living dying creatures? We usually do this by keeping it out of full awareness in our unconscious minds most of the time. But in spite of this defense, our existential awareness influences our total lives and well-being profoundly and constantly. It pushes us toward a variety of denial mechanisms and also toward religious or other meaning-of-life belief systems by which we seek to cope with this existential reality. As existential philosopher Martin Heidegger observed, our knowledge that we must die is the background music that plays faintly in the distance during our lives so that we usually do not hear it. He declared, "At times we may blot it out, but there are other times when it swells in volume and tempo, and we cannot be unaware of it."[5]

***

At a meeting of pastoral care specialists, Paul Tillich summarized his understanding of the impact of existential anxiety, pointing to the only effective way to handle it. He said that "anxiety is the awareness of finitude. Humans...always live in the conscious or unconscious anxiety of having to die. Non-being is present in every moment of their being." Tillich pointed out that the existential anxiety generated by the "threat of non-being" has three disturbing expressions—the fear of fate and death, emptiness and loss of meaning, and feelings of guilt and condemnation. This anxiety permeates our whole being.[6] It is a part of our "heritage of finitude," the dark shadow touching all our lives. Existential anxiety probably is the raw material, the prototype, and the wellspring of all other anxieties. It gives neurotic anxieties their energy and power.

As Tillich made clear, we humans confront profound existential tensions. One is the painful tension between *aloneness* and *relatedness* in which we long for relatedness, yet are aware that we ultimately live and die alone. Another is the tension between *meaning* and *meaninglessness* in which we long for our lives to have some meaning, yet know that life often seems to have no ultimate or lasting meaning. A third challenge is the tension between *freedom* and *unfreedom* in which we long to be free and utterly self-determining, yet are reminded constantly of how we are greatly limited by the heredity, biology, social and historical situations, and other givens in our lives. The fourth challenge is the tension between *life* and *death* in which we long to continue living indefinitely, yet have the growing awareness that each day we are one day closer to death. This fourth tension motivates the will to believe some variation on the theme of personal survival after death.

The vital importance of spiritual caregiving is highlighted by the fact that there are no psychological or psychotherapeutic answers to existential anxiety but, as Tillich suggested, only religious ones. This anxiety is normal, inherent, and inescapable in our very existence as self-aware creatures. But *its impact on individuals and groups can be either creative or destructive*, depending on how it is handled. In a psychological sense, whatever people use to cope with existential anxiety *is* their religion.

The deep human hunger to connect intimately with a transcending Reality and to cope with the awareness of finitude create a powerful need to have what psychoanalyst-philosopher Erich Fromm called "a framework of reference and an object of devotion." People who do not find salvific objects of devotion are, by their spiritual hungers, made vulnerable to worshiping lesser objects of devotion as their deities, eventually making lesser concerns objects of ultimate concern. These lesser gods then can become addictive and all-consuming. Overinvesting in these gods eventually leads to betrayal by them.

Neurotic anxiety and existential anxiety usually have reciprocal effects, each tending to reinforce the other. Tillich observed that a high degree of neurotic anxiety renders one vulnerable to the threat of nonbeing and that conversely, "those who are empty of meaning are easy victims of neurotic anxiety."[7] Furthermore, neurotic problems can be understood as defenses against nonbeing: attempts to avoid existential anxiety. Ironically, the use of these defenses inevitably produces precisely what is feared.[8] In the same vein, Tillich viewed neurotic anxiety as a way of avoiding the threat of nonbeing by avoiding being fully alive.

Psychiatrist Karen Horney saw neurotic anxiety as an attempt to defend oneself against fear of death by lessening the threat, by keeping oneself feeling already half dead. In a similar vein, feminist philosopher Mary Daly declared, "People attempt to overcome the threat of nonbeing by denying the self. The outcome of this is ironic: that which is dreaded triumphs, for we are caught in the self-contradictory bind of shrinking our being to avoid nonbeing. The only alternative is self-actualization in spite of the ever-present nothingness."[9]

If people try to cope with existential anxiety by idolatrous or neurotic means, the price they pay is diminished creativity, awareness, and aliveness. The only means of constructively handling existential anxiety is a vital religious life that energizes the fullest possible development of God's many gifts—that is "life in all its fullness." In what probably is the most quoted passage from Carl Jung's writings, he says, "Among all my patients in the second half of life—that is to say, over thirty-five—there has not been one whose problem in the last resort was not that of finding a religious outlook on life."[10]

Wholeness-enhancing religion enables persons to confront rather than evade their existential anxiety. As Tillich made clear, the "power of the divine" is that within which "nonbeing is eternally conquered." Only as existential anxiety and the fear of death is confronted and taken into people's self-identity can it enhance instead of disable life.

The father of existentialism, Søren Kierkegaard, suggested that in the very experience of facing this anxiety, an individual develops the inner certitude of faith. This anxiety is the teacher that searches one's life thoroughly and roots out the trivial.[11]

The Interaction of Spiritual and Psychological Dynamics in Caregiving

Facilitating spiritual wholeness in pastoral caregiving begins with seeking to understand the particular spiritual issues with which careseekers are dealing. In understanding such problems, caregivers need to remember that psychological and religious dynamics often overlap and interact. Theological, religious, and ethical problems at times are surface manifestations of deeper psychological, emotional, or relationship difficulties in living. The onset of episodes of mental illness is sometimes marked by a sudden obsessive interest in religious issues. These religious expressions are surface symptoms of serious psychological problems, not of pathogenic religion.

In any case, when spiritual or ethical issues are raised by care receivers, it is appropriate to deal with them as problems in their own right while being alert to the possibility that psychological or relationship problems may be lurking in the shadows. After a worship service, Larry, a junior-high teacher who was active in that congregation, paused to ask his pastor, Carl, "to recommend a good book on how to pray." Carl responded that he would be "glad to recommend such a book." But sensing that there might be a problem behind the request, he suggested that they go to his study nearby to chat for a few minutes about it. After showing him two books on prayer from his shelves, Carl asked a door-opening question, "Is there some special reason why you want to read a book on prayer now?" Larry's voice tone changed, reflecting increased stress as he described the loss of spiritual vitality in what had been a meaningful prayer life. As he put it sadly, "Prayer has gone dead for me." To invite him to explore his spiritual problem, the pastor asked two other door-opening questions: "Larry, when did prayer go dead for you?" Larry replied, "It began out of the blue about three months ago." The pastor responded, "Anything special happening in your life around that time?" This query opened the door for Larry to describe the tragic suicide of his uncle, with whom he had had a kind of son-father relationship. The pastor recognized Larry's unhealed grief wound and listened with caring responses as Larry detailed the tragedy, expressing his agonizing but unreasonable sense of responsibility for not preventing the uncle's death. He also expressed the grief in losing a sense of God's presence. Near the close of their brief pastoral conversation, Larry surprised Carl by nodding yes when asked if he would like to pray. Carl's prayer included these words: "God, you sometimes seem deaf or absent when we try to communicate. May Larry remember times when you were there for him and he felt some healing by opening himself to your caring spirit." Larry accepted Carl's suggestion that they meet two or three more times to continue their conversation and see if it might help him reconnect with God. A short series of grief-healing conversations (in person and by phone) followed. The frozen guilt that had blocked Larry's awareness of God's nurturing presence gradually melted. In the process he became able to accept in his heart what he knew in his head—that he could not have prevented and in no way was responsible for the tragic suicide. The fact that healing of his infected grief wound had occurred was clear when he arrived in the pastor's office smiling, with welcome news. With marked relief in his voice, he declared, "Prayer has come alive for me again." His religious problem had been an expression of his infected grief wounds.

Some psychologists with secular orientations believe that *all* spiritual problems are merely symptoms of deeper psychological problems. But convincing clinical evidence from pastoral psychologists over numerous decades shows that this generalization is a half-truth. Although religious and ethical problems sometimes hide psychological, physical, and relationship problems, the reverse is also true.[12] In my experience, spiritual and value conflicts and emptiness are significant factors at the roots of many human problems. Pastoral counseling pioneer Seward Hiltner once observed, "People may get sick emotionally not only because of immediate frustrations but also because they are troubled about their own meaning and destiny."[13]

Psychiatrist Viktor Frankl learned this truth in the ghastly trauma of Nazi death camps. He coined the apt phrase "value vacuum" to describe the existential emptiness and meaninglessness that make many people vulnerable to many types of psychological, physiological, and relationship dysfunctions. Frankl discovered that fellow prisoners who suffered value vacuums were much more likely to die and do so quickly than those who, like him, were able to generate some meaning in that awful environment of human evil.

Recognizing Hidden Spiritual Problems

In our secular society, spiritual problems are frequently described in nonreligious language. Often the messages are disguised and therefore difficult to recognize for what they are—quiet cries for spiritual help. When counselees talk about their aging and death, the meaning or meaninglessness of their lives, or their responses to sickness and crises, they usually point to spiritual issues. At times spiritual problems hide behind symptoms such as a sense of purposelessness, empty longing, chronic boredom, or lack of zest and inner joy in living.

It is easy to miss the hidden spiritual-ethical roots of the complex problems often present in help seekers. If caregivers are tuned mainly to the wavelength of the psychosocial aspects of people's issues, they tend not to hear the profound spiritual longings and existential anxieties that often are there in disguise. Such spiritual hearing loss is a significant disability that prevents holistic responses to the existential issues that are present to some degree in most, if not all, human problems at some level. At the other extreme, caregivers who focus mainly on the spiritual and ethical dimension of people's problems tend to diminish awareness of the complex psychosocial factors that are always interwoven with these issues. American pastoral caregivers have properly stressed the dangers of religious reductionism in viewing human problems, but in so doing they have sometimes fallen into psychological reductionism. To be effective as a pastoral counselor, one must be tuned simultaneously to the psychosocial and the spiritual dynamics that operate in every human life and problem.

When help seekers seem to have significant hidden spiritual and value issues, caregivers should seek to enable them to deal with these underlying issues at the roots of their painful dilemmas in living. There are usually two levels in this counseling process. The first is helping persons cope with their immediate, often pressing, problems or crises. The crucial second-level task involves encouraging them to face and deal constructively with underlying spiritual or value issues of which their current problems are painful surface symptoms. This task often involves confronting issues of inadequate meanings and distorted or destructive values and lifestyles that are hidden sources of their problems in living.

Pastors should not be timid about raising diagnostic questions regarding spiritual and ethical issues and the need for growth in these crucial areas. Door-opening questions like these can be used to invite people to explore such issues:

- "How do you understand this decision in light of what's most important in your life?"
- "How does this problem with which you're struggling relate to your personal religious faith?"
- "What have you learned from this miserable crisis? Has it changed your faith?"

Queries of this type should be asked only after a trustful relationship is established and the pressure of coping with the acute phase of a crisis is reduced. So timed, they may open doors for constructive dialogue about underlying spiritual issues such as unresolved guilt feelings and magical beliefs that persons need to replace with a more reality-respecting faith. Such dialogue can help people find meaningful answers to some of life's big questions: What does my life mean? What is the quality of my relationship with God? Is my lifestyle (and the values it reflects) destroying what's precious to me, including my health? A counselee who had suffered a severe health crisis declared, during a discussion of value and lifestyle issues, "As long as nobody asks the big questions, you can ignore them and let them be. But once they're asked, you can't put them down until you find some kind of answer." People are more likely to find meaningful answers and to grow spiritually if they have the help of a spiritual guide as they wrestle with such difficult faith issues.

In our society some people use street language to talk about their spiritual problems and to describe how they really feel about themselves and their world. It is crucial for caregivers to be as shockproof as possible as they struggle to understand the worldviews behind such street language. One young adult client kept expressing his feelings about the world as being "crappy" and "screwed up." It became clear to his pastoral counselor that he was describing both the way he saw the society and the way he felt about himself and his personal life. Asked if he had ever felt any different, he responded, "Yeah. It all started when my best friend got shot in a street fight."

Obvious and explicit theological issues such as problems of beliefs, doubts, doctrines, understanding biblical passages, and methods of prayer are "presenting problems" brought by only a minority of help seekers in most pastoral settings. In the secular climate of our society and times, spiritual problems, though epidemic, often fail to be understood or described in religious terms. When clergy encounter explicit spiritual problems, they spontaneously draw on their theological training, religious tradition, and personal religious life in responding. In so doing they should use the general methods of all effective caregiving and educative counseling, discussed later in this book.

How Faith and Values Relate to Overall Health

Among the hopeful developments in the health-care field are signs of promising new convergences between faith and health. Studies are exploring how spirituality affects individual health in coping with illnesses and preventing them. These studies point to the directions in which faith-based organizations need to move in order to have increased political and systemic influence in enhancing the overall well-being in our society and world.[14]

Several extensive studies conclude that regular participation in organized religion tends to enhance health. For example, one national study focusing on church attendance and longevity was conducted by sociologists at the Population Research Center at the University of Texas. It found that people who attend church worship once a week live an average of seven years longer than those who never attend. The researchers who analyzed the findings said that some of the difference may be because of churches' role in discouraging unhealthy behavior such as smoking and drinking, as well as giving social support that helps monitor the health of members. In commenting on the study, sociologist Kenneth Pargament declared that the "data underscores the power of religion, not only for psychological well-being but physical well-being." This positive link between religion and both physical and mental health had been revealed in several earlier studies.[15]

An example of the needed collaboration between religion and medicine is the work of Larry Dossey, MD, a leading advocate for recognizing the role of mind in health and the role of spirituality in health care. He points to the striking fact that nearly half the American population has turned to some form of alternative medical treatment usually in conjunction with conventional medicine.[16] Deeply immersed in scientific medicine, Dossey notes that "the value of beingness and spirituality is returning big time to modern medicine." Eighty percent of American medical schools now have a course in spirituality issues in medical practice, and numerous national studies have shown that people who have some kind of spiritual practice live longer and have fewer diseases than those who do not.

Studies such as the one conducted at the University of Texas focus on comparing the health of people who are religious in their beliefs and behaviors and those who are not. They do not, however, shed light on another distinction that is crucial for the effectiveness of spiritually oriented caregivers. This is the distinction between religious beliefs, values, and practices that tend to enhance people's overall health, including their spiritual health, and those that tend to deplete or damage these.

Distinguishing Salugenic and Pathogenic Religion and Ethics

The most crucial initial resources that caregivers need in order to deal effectively with spiritual and ethical issues are those that enable them to help care receivers distinguish the health-cultivating and health-diminishing elements in religions and values. The widespread assumption that "whatever religion people have is basically good for them" is a fallacy. In fact, the impact of diverse religions and ethics on people's overall wholeness is mixed, to say the least.

The disciplines of psychology and sociology of religion use the insights and methods of psychology and sociology to understand individual and group religious behaviors and experiences. There is a long, productive history of illuminating the distinction between healthful and unhealthful faith and values. William James, the philosopher-psychologist who did much of the pioneering theory-generating in these fields, wrote the classic volume *Varieties of Religious Experience*, published near the beginning of the twentieth century. It explores insightfully the crucial distinction between the "religion of the healthy minded" and "the religion of the sick soul."[17] Other scholars have examined the distinctions further.

Psychologist Gordon Allport distinguished religious beliefs that are *intrinsic* (heartfelt and valued for their own sake) and *extrinsic* (aimed at some nonreligious external objective such as conforming, pleasing, or manipulating others).[18] Much of the theory-generating done by Sigmund Freud was focused on understanding and exposing belief systems that diminish people's mental health. Many secular psychotherapists today, like Freud in his times, have a plethora of experiences with clients whose spiritual and ethical life is harmful to their overall health, but little experience with spirituality and values that can enhance people's health. Consequently they have little or no awareness or appreciation of the wholeness-generating potentiality of healthy beliefs and values.

Experience in doing spiritually centered counseling and therapy through several decades suggests that people's spirituality and values actually can serve one or more of three functions in relationship to their overall well-being. They can be negative or destructive forces that contribute to people's shame, guilt, anxiety, distrust, self-rejection, and blocked growth. I call this "pathogenic" religion and ethics. At the other extreme, religious beliefs and values can be positive, constructive forces contributing to people's ability to be loving, trusting, productive, creative, joyful, and growing. I call these beliefs and values "salugenic." In our society many people's beliefs and values can also be largely irrelevant to their deep needs, problems, hungers, and growth strivings. Having the insights and skills to identify salugenic, pathogenic, and irrelevant aspects of careseekers' religious and ethical lives is essential to the task of cultivating healing and growth in these crucial areas. But as a caution, it is well to remember that most of us humans have some elements of our faith and values that are salugenic and others that are pathogenic or irrelevant. The same is true of religious institutions. All individuals, congregations, and faith groups have need for spiritual and ethical healing as well as some room to continue growing to make their faith and values increasingly life giving.

One of the many striking but painful lessons to be learned from the terrorist tragedy of September 11, 2001, is a sharply increased awareness of the destructiveness inherent in religious fanaticism. Just a month after that terrorist tragedy, the U.S. Permanent Representative to the United Nations, Ambassador John D. Negroponte, spoke at a vesper service honoring the dedicated UN personnel who had been killed as they risked their lives offering lifesaving humanitarian help in many countries. He stated, "I would propose to you that faith surely is what gives such heroes the strength to save so many from certain disaster. But I would also propose to you that faith must follow its own path in every soul. We cannot dictate what another individual should believe about the larger purposes of human destiny.[19] The events of 9/11 highlighted the wide diversity of religious beliefs in the world and the necessity of maintaining a robust sense of connectedness and community within all the diversity.

An essential initial step in the process of facilitating spiritual and ethical healing and growth is to enable care recipients to evaluate the health of these vital interconnected areas of their lives. This involves helping people identify their areas of spiritual and ethical strength and health and their weak areas where growth work is needed. Because healing religious brokenness and pathogenic spirituality and cultivating healthy religion are the prime objective of pastoral caregiving, approaches to this dual task will be discussed in detail.

What Constitutes Healthy Spirituality and Values?

For about a decade, my life was enhanced by a friendship with Erma, a wise long-retired woman. We were drawn to become friends by our shared interest in religion and mental health. On one occasion we were discussing issues of healthy and unhealthy religion as these affect congregations. Erma shared these unforgettable images as her description of the contrasting impact of people's religious life on their sickness and health: "Religion can be either a lead weight around our neck or a set of wings with which our spirits can fly." She knew that religion can generate terrible depression or be a remarkable means by which we humans can transcend and transform our finitude in our sometimes tragic, two-dimensional lives.[20]

I often recall Erma's striking images when I reflect on the overarching goal of spiritually centered pastoral care and counseling. It is to nurture care receivers' and congregations' growth toward increasingly healthy faith and values that will enable people's spirits to fly in shadows as well as sunlight. Frequently this involves helping people learn how to increase the depth, vitality, relevance, inclusiveness, and outreach of their spiritual and ethical lives. This growth occurs as they learn to deepen their relationships with the divine Spirit of the universe (God), all God's children, God's world (both the cosmos and society), and their own spiritual center (soul). As this occurs, health-nurturing spirituality and values increasingly infiltrate and empower all seven dimensions of their lives.

An effective way to ascertain the relative health-enhancing or heath-diminishing impact of people's faith and values is to examine how healthy their ways of satisfying their basic spiritual and ethical needs are. These needs are not religious in some "churchy" sense. Rather, they are universal, inescapable human needs that are present in varied forms in all persons, even those most secularized and most alienated from institutionalized religions. Pathogenic religion and ethics result when people attempt to satisfy their spiritual needs in rigid, authoritarian, reality-denying, or idolatrous ways. Fortunately many other people have learned to satisfy their basic spiritual needs in relatively salugenic, constructive ways that nurture their healing and wholeness.

Here are twelve criteria for evaluating religious beliefs, practices, and values in terms of their impact on individual and societal health and well-being. The criteria seek to discover how well particular belief and value systems contribute to well-being by fulfilling people's basic spiritual and ethical needs. Using these criteria can help to identify quickly the ways in which one's spirituality and values are relatively healthy and those in which they are relatively toxic or weak so that constructive changes are needed:

How fully do my spiritual and ethical beliefs and practices fulfill my basic spiritual need to develop

1. a growing relationship with a God of love and justice that empowers and inspires all dimensions of my life;
2. human relationships in which I give as well as receive much-needed acceptance, caring love, and trust;
3. meaningful beliefs or a philosophy of life that provides stability, strength, serenity, and purpose to my life in the "dark nights of my soul" as well as in times of joy and celebration;
4. individual and social values that guide my overall lifestyle in directions that are constructive and responsible in terms of the well-being of myself, others, society, and nature;
5. awareness of my transpersonal, spiritual self (or soul) that helps me make it the empowering, unifying, purposeful center of my life and lifestyle;
6. regular renewal of my sense of basic trust (Erik Erikson)—trust in myself, other people, and God that enables me to maintain or recover some reality-based hopes in the midst of crises, losses, and tragedies;
7. effective ways to move from the alienation of resentment and guilt to the healing reconciliation of forgiveness of myself and others;
8. ways to undergird my self-esteem with awareness of being deeply loved and esteemed by God and thereby reduce my alienating narcissism;
9. regular moments of transcendence, wonder-filled "peak experiences" during which I connect with the eternal amid my two-dimensional space-time existence;
10. a sense of deep, organic unity with my unconscious self, with other people in the human family, and with the planet's interdependent network of living things on which human well-being ultimately depends;
11. inspiration, motivation, and training to reach out effectively with caring, justice-based love in practical ways to empower those in need;
12. a caring, supportive spiritual community (for example, a congregation, house church, or 12-step recovery group) that nurtures and sustains constructive individual and social values and supports constructive coping and continuing growth in spiritual well-being?

These criteria can be useful for counselees who need to question the health of the beliefs and ethical priorities that are guiding their current lifestyles, and those who are wrestling with troubling spiritual issues or ethical decisions. Reflecting on the relevant criteria can help them effectively evaluate and enhance their values and beliefs. It can also be helpful for counselors and educators to hold these criteria in the backs of their minds when seeking to coach clients or students concerned about evaluating and then enhancing their spiritual and ethical well-being.

Recognizing Wholeness—Cultivating Religious Beliefs and Values

Understanding the characteristics of healthy beliefs and ethical priorities that nurture wholeness can be an invaluable asset for caregivers in coaching those who seek their insights on these all-important matters. Although several of these defining characteristics are implicit in the above criteria, to spell out the characteristics more fully and explicitly, here are some significant marks of wholeness-generating religions and ethics:

Wholeness-nurturing faith and values involve developing a growing friendship with a Higher Power (called God in religious circles). This means letting one's heart resonate to the love and justice at the heart of the divine Spirit of the universe. Spiritual growth and healing can be nurtured best in the context of such a relationship. Holistic pastoral caregivers seek to help people develop and enjoy such an open, growing relationship with God, a relationship that enables them to live growthfully amid the losses, conflicts, and tragedies of life. This caregiving helps them become aware of the exciting fact that they are called to be active partners—cocreators with the Spirit of the universe in helping to transform the world. Pastoral counseling for spiritual growth seeks to help persons renew their sense of basic trust by being in touch with the Spirit of love present in this moment and to find healing for those aspects of their brokenness that can be healed only in relationship to this divine Reality.

Wholeness-nurturing faith and values are inclusive rather than exclusive. They give people an interfaith, multicultural perspective and openness to respect and learn from those from diverse religious, racial, ethnic, gender, and cultural backgrounds. Persons with salugenic faith and values are committed to building bridges of collaboration and community over the many chasms of diversity that breed conflict and violence between individuals and among different groups. (The three Western religions—Judaism, Christianity, and Islam—are particularly vulnerable to exclusiveness.) Widespread national and global violence rooted in religious conflicts demonstrates the tragic dangers of exclusive, fundamentalistic belief systems. The dynamics and healing of religious violence will be explored in chapter 17 on inclusive caregiving.[21]

Healthful, wholeness-nurturing faith and ethical values take human sin, evil, violence, and brokenness very seriously and provide guidance in preventing and healing them. This requires a tough-minded understanding of the destructive side of human behavior.

Healthful, wholeness-nurturing faith and values encourage people to grow spiritually by providing freedom to explore new understandings of religion and new approaches to ethical living. Narrow, constricting belief systems that require believers to turn off their critical faculties in church stifle spiritual and ethical creativity, innovations, and health.

Wholeness-nurturing faith and values are prophetic in the sense of having the horizons of healing and the limits of liberation extended to all those in the human family whose wholeness is limited by poverty, injustices, and oppression.

Healthful, wholeness-nurturing faith and values motivate people to become more earth friendly, earth literate, and earth caring. They are motivated to appreciate and protect the beauty and wonder of God's continuing, evolving creation of the earth and the whole universe. Salugenic faith and values sharpen awareness that the health and well-being of the children of all species, including our own, ultimately depend on their inheriting a healthy planet.

Wholeness-nurturing faith and values encourage believers to balance playfulness with their work, including their healing outreach to those in need.

Wholeness-nurturing faith and values continue to change and grow through all the ups and downs of the life journey. Salugenic spirituality encourages people to continually enlarge their horizons of understanding the purposes of God and their spiritual vocation in light of these purposes. It helps caregivers facilitate this lifelong maturing process to be acquainted with various models of the changing stages of ethical and faith development.

Wholeness-cultivating faith and values provide a sense of being deeply connected with other persons in relationships that nurture mutual wholeness, justice, and loving care, all of which are enlivened by a sense of deep connection with a Higher Power.

Wholeness-nurturing faith and values enable people to find some meaning in the midst of the profound mysteries, ambiguities, and tragedies of their life journeys. Despite all that humankind knows, life is saturated with mystery. Willingness to live with some big unanswered questions is an expression of spiritual and ethical wholeness.

Wholeness-nurturing spirituality and values help people learn how to experience wonder, awe, and transcendence. In what psychologist Abraham Maslow called "peak experiences," people become aware of their oneness with the whole living universe, including humankind, the biosphere, and the divine Spirit. Biblical scholar William A. Beardslee describes a Christian's peak experience: "Though God is constantly active in our lives, God's presence is, in each moment, a stunning surprise. That we should be given ways of opening ourselves to God of the all; that we should be able to receive

God's presence into our lives and be transformed by that presence; this is an unspeakable wonder."[22]

Wholeness-generating faith and values enable people to discover and develop their spiritual self (or soul), making it the integrating, empowering center of their lives. This involves developing spiritual capacities that are their transpersonal essence, the divine image toward which they grow. (See Gen. 1:26.)

As people mature spiritually, they overcome their most basic alienation as human beings—from the transcendent self at their spiritual center. In what is the key task of spiritual growth work, they discover and develop the divine image within them in very down-to-earth ways.

Wholeness-nurturing faith and ethical values are science friendly, meaning open to God's continuing revelations through the findings of scientific research. Religious beliefs continue to be challenged, corrected, enlarged, and enriched by spiritually and ethically relevant scientific discoveries. Many of these continuing discoveries can challenge, change, and stretch enormously the beliefs and values of care receivers and caregivers. All this reflects the spirit in Albert Einstein's declaration: "I maintain that the cosmic religious feeling is the strongest and noblest motive for scientific research."[23] For example, the "Genesis versus geology" controversy, also known as the "creationism versus evolution" debate, is based on a false assumption. It results from a failure to understand that the biblical messages were not written to provide insights about scientific truth but to illuminate vital issues of faith and the good life focusing on human-divine relationship. Healthy religion and ethics must be built on a foundation belief in a God who is big enough to take into account the findings of contemporary sciences.

Wholeness-cultivating spirituality and values help people befriend their bodies, including their sexuality, so that they care for their bodies' needs constructively like loving parents to themselves. The long story of our species is filled with tragic examples of how our animal drives and superior human brain capacities have been misused in ways that are far more violent and cruel than the behavior of other animals. Only by taking our generic animal roots seriously can our ethical capacities be used to guide behavior constructively.

Creating Sacred Space for Yourself and around Care Receivers

A simple healing way to enable spirituality to come alive in any relationship is to intentionally create sacred space in and between persons in that relationship. Sacred space is a place of both intrapersonal and interpersonal safety, empathy, caring, and compassion in which persons are empowered as the unique, precious individuals they really are. Doing this enables caregivers to be more present with themselves and therefore with the other person seeking care. And of central importance, it also helps them increase awareness of God's loving spirit in themselves and in others. Sacred space tends to generate what Martin Buber called an I-Thou quality in relationships, a quality that is sometimes called "soul."[24]

Creating sacred space is an uncomplicated, teachable process that can occur quickly and intentionally. In caregiving, sacred space is created by using the trust-building and relationship-deepening skills described earlier. Here is a spiritual enrichment exercise, one of whose benefits is generating sacred space.

Awareness exercise. Do whatever is necessary to become very relaxed at the same time you are very alert in your body, mind, and spirit. The aim is to enter your "serenity zone," below whatever turbulence is in your inner life, by connecting with your spiritual center and calming your whole being by methods such as relaxed breathing, peaceful imaging, or prayerful meditating.

As soon as you are thus prepared inwardly, repeat several times silently to yourself your intention of seeing yourself as a sacred person, a precious child of the loving Spirit.

Now form a vivid moving picture in your mind of yourself near a counselee or someone else about whom you have caring concern. Visualize both of you as loved children of God.

See the two of you and the space between you bathed by a warm, healing light empowering the two of you and your relationship.

Hold this image for a short time while you visualize the two of you experiencing the spiritual energy that enables each of you to function more effectively in your own ways.

Be aware of the feeling of being in a shared sacred space.

Both during and between sessions, it can be helpful to picture troubled counselees and yourself briefly in this healing Light. This is a form of visual intercessory prayer that reminds me of the old Quaker saying, "I'll hold you in the light!"

****

In their hectic lives, some people help themselves find inner peace and renewal by creating in their homes literal sacred spaces devoted to meditation, prayer, inspirational reading, quiet reflection, and thoughtful journaling. Such sacred spaces can be small or large, inside or out. In these spaces they respond to their inner need to reconnect regularly with their serenity zone—the tranquil inner place, below the surface storms, where they can go to find rejuvenation and renewal. They often create a little altar where they place one or more things that have some spiritual meaning or memories for them, reminding them of the most important people and values in their cluttered lives. Such objects may include photographs, drawings, books, religious symbols, or objects from nature.[25]

Asking Dialogue-opening Questions Can Help Cultivate Spiritual and Ethical Wholeness

As suggested earlier, pastoral caregivers can use well-timed, leading questions to invite care receivers to engage in creative dialogue that may help them grow spiritually and ethically. Following crises and grief, queries such as these may open dialogue doors: "How helpful was your faith in coping with this difficult problem? Has your faith or priorities changed as a result of the crisis you have been weathering?"

Christie Neuger suggests that asking theological dialogue-opening questions like these can be useful in assessing where people are spiritually and in helping them move toward spiritual empowerment: "What's at stake for you in this? What's your image of God, and how does God perceive or see you? [This may get to the core images and feelings that keep persons locked in destructive beliefs and values.] How do you experience God's grace and judgment?" Questions about the helpfulness of their faith community and family can illuminate their interpersonal sources of spiritual support. Neuger comments,

> These questions represent one way to do a primary theological framing of the counseling task. Their theological priorities address the key elements of wholeness for people—their sense of self in relationship to God, the quality of their relationship with their primary communities, and their sense of purpose, vocation, or direction.[26]

Using Personal Retreats for Spiritual and Ethical Renewal

Retreats are a time-tested method of spiritual and ethical self-care and renewal for spiritually depleted individuals as well as an effective method of renewing the spiritual aliveness of a congregation. In her illuminating book *Be Still: Designing and Leading Contemplative Retreats*, Jane Vennard describes how retreats can nurture and restore the soul of a congregation.[27] She quotes Richard Foster, an authority on retreats, describing how they bring spiritual revitalization:

> A retreat places God and the things of God in the foreground of our attention. A retreat opens the time and space so that we may hear God's still small voice. A retreat is about listening and waiting, receiving and being. A retreat is not about getting anything done.... A retreat gives us opportunity to practice "the steady gaze of the soul upon the God who loves us."[28]

Caregivers can help care receivers as well as themselves recharge their spiritual batteries by giving themselves the gift of regular times of spiritual renewal. These times can be during formal organized retreats or as informal occasions of personal rest, renewal, and recreation away from the preoccupations and pressures of their daily lives.

The importance of this self-renewal is highlighted when we consider the epidemic of sabbath-breaking in our high-pressure society. Sabbath-breaking, as used here, does not call for reintroducing archaic blue laws in a futile never-on-Sunday (or Saturday) campaign. Rather, it focuses on a major health issue with important ethical implications. What can be called the "sabbath principle" is crucial for sustaining wellness. It is becoming clear that people who, for whatever reasons, are driven to work excessively do so usually at the expense of their family relationships and their self-care and renewal times. Such persons are cases of burnout waiting to happen. Many clergy as well as congregants are wounded by work addictions and the "running to stand still or catch up" syndrome. The needed help is learning how to keep regular private sabbaths devoted to enhanced self-care, enjoyment, and nurturing relationships. In our sleep-deprived society, this usually includes getting more rest. Henri Nouwen might have been speaking to counselors when he said, "We need to have time to get to know ourselves so we can be present to others." It is akin to what he meant by "being at home with ourselves so we can invite others in."[29]

Using Religious Resources in Wholeness-generating Ways

Counseling pastors are unique among healing professionals in that they are expected and trained to use spiritual resources in working with burdened people. If this is done in a disciplined and appropriate manner, these resources can be invaluable in several types of counseling: supportive, crisis, bereavement, ethical, existential-religious counseling, and also spiritual direction. In addition to resources such as scripture, sacraments, rituals, and prayer, the time-tested wisdom of the Christian year can be a useful framework for pastoral caregiving.

Because spiritual growth is the ultimate aim of pastoral care and counseling, pastors should use with precision and care theological words, images, concepts, stories, and the religious resources of prayer, scripture, and sacraments. Such symbols and practices mean many things to many people, but for some they carry heavy, negative, emotional freight. They can be used in rigid, legalistic ways that arouse inappropriate guilt feelings and block creative dialogue and spiritual growth in counseling. The late William Hulme commented on the destructive uses of these resources when he said that rather than deal directly with a counselee's resistance, pastors may seek to suppress it by taking on the authority role in religion. Retreating to the protected sphere, they use "God talk"— religiously oriented words associated with the profession—as an attempt to maintain control of the situation. Genuine dialogue, however, requires the relinquishment of this control and risks an unpredictable outcome in each encounter.[30]

Carefully worded prayers and carefully selected scripture and devotional literature or sacraments such as Communion can be comforting and supportive. Pastoral caregivers should be trained to use or not use these as appropriate. In crisis and grief caregiving, helping people develop personal healing rituals can be supportive.[31] Life passage rituals can be helpful to people struggling in developmental transitions.

When religious resources are used appropriately, they can be powerful instruments for nurturing spiritual wholeness. Here are general guidelines for using religious resources creatively in pastoral caregiving:

1. *Use religious words and resources only after one has some awareness of care receivers' problems as well as their background, their feelings, and their attitudes about religion.* Otherwise, one is likely to pray or read the Bible in ways that produce irreligious consequences, alienating persons further from a healing relationship with a loving, living God.

2. *Ask the person if it would be meaningful before using resources such as prayer or scripture in care or counseling.* Doing this shows respect for people's feelings and beliefs. In some situations, it may open doors for potentially healing discussions of spiritual conflicts and blocks, including anger toward God.

3. *After using a traditional religious resource, give receivers opportunities to explore and understand the thoughts, feelings, and fantasies they had during the experience.* A focusing question often triggers unexpected and much-needed reflection and discussion of religious issues, hang-ups, confusion, and perplexities.

Pastor: I'm wondering what was going through your mind while I was praying.
Parishioner: I had trouble listening after you mentioned my mother. I felt a wave of sadness and wished things had been different.

4. *Use religious resources more frequently in supportive crisis and bereavement counseling and less frequently in pastoral psychotherapy.*

5. *Use these resources in ways that do not diminish a sense of initiative, strength, and responsibility in care receivers,* especially if they are highly dependent people.

6. *Use prayer and biblical material in ways that facilitate rather than block the owning and catharsis of negative feelings by arousing guilt about them.* Paraphrasing a care receiver's prominent feelings in prayer (including those that are angry, bitter, or fearful) indicates to the person that God accepts these very human feelings.

7. *Use religious resources with religious people to deepen, enrich, and strengthen their relationships by giving their relationships a vertical dimension, (but) never as a substitute for relating.*

8. *Never feel that one has to use religious words or resources.* God is continually active in all relationships, whether or not formal religious words or practices are used.

9. *Invite people during times of caregiving to pray (if this is meaningful to them).* Doing that may help them in a way different from when the counselor prays. Teaching them

methods of prayer and meditation can sometimes be helpful. It also can be a means of awakening awareness of unresolved spiritual issues that can then be discussed and perhaps resolved.

At the close of a meaningful counseling session or a series of sessions, a prayer of thanksgiving can be a fitting way to express gratitude for the healing and growth that have occurred. It is helpful to some people to see that the issues with which they are struggling in counseling—alienation, guilt, anxiety, reconciliation, rebirth, the search for wholeness—are essentially theological issues. People from religious backgrounds find it meaningful for the caregiver to state the goals of counseling in theological-biblical language as well as psychological terms. Skillfully employed biblical language may express the sense of the ineffable and the deep mystery of the transformation that can occur in counseling.

Using the Bible to Heal Brokenness and Nurture Spiritual Wholeness

There are a variety of valuable ways to use the Bible in pastoral care and counseling. The first is *to allow biblical wisdom to inform the process, spirit, and goals of caring/counseling relationships*. I suggest that pastoral counselors need to stay in continuing dialogue with biblical images and insights. My friend and former colleague John B. Cobb Jr. says, "Pastoral counselors could experience their counseling not simply as in continuity with Christianity in its ultimate purposes but as informed by the Christian heritage in both form and substance."[32]

A second and very valuable use of the Bible in pastoral care and counseling is *to comfort and strengthen people in crises*. Having a sense of the sustaining presence of God, as communicated, for example, in the familiar words of the Twenty-third or the Ninetieth Psalm, can be a source of strength for some people in handling shattering losses.

A third use of the Bible in counseling relationships is *to illuminate the spiritual dynamics and problems of counselees*. In discussing pastoral diagnosis, psychologist Paul W. Pruyser recommends that basic theological/biblical themes such as providence, repentance, faith, grace, vocation, communion, and awareness of the holy be held in a pastor's mind as unique guideposts for understanding counseling issues theologically.[33]

A biblical method that I have found useful in understanding the psychological, interpersonal, and spiritual growth issues of religious counselees and growth group members is to invite them to tell the Bible story they most like and the one they most dislike. A woman who had struggled for years with feelings of being inwardly trapped told the exodus story as her favorite, adding, "I feel like I've been trying to escape from my own Egypt, and when I do, I end up wandering in the wilderness. It's the hope of finding the freedom of the promised land that keeps me going, I guess." The inner conflicts of church people may be expressed in the biblical characters with whom they identify. For example, some women feel inwardly torn between the submissive, serving-others Martha side of themselves and the more empowered Mary side that wants to participate fully as an equal in what have traditionally been considered activities limited to men.

A fourth use of the Bible in pastoral care and counseling is *to help heal spiritual pathology by changing unhealthy beliefs.* When caregivers sense that the Bible is being misused to suppress anger, grief, guilt, or despair, a direct approach to correcting this distorted understanding of the Bible is needed. In seeking to help persons who are suppressing anger because of guilt feelings about expressing negative feelings, caregivers can say, "My understanding is that anger is a gift of God to be valued and used constructively. Jesus seems to have gotten very angry on occasion. It's storing up anger—allowing the sun to go down on anger, as the Bible puts it—that makes anger harmful to ourselves and others." When people repress their grief, caregivers can respond, "The New Testament says that it's a good thing—a blessed thing—to express one's sorrow and loss. The story of Jesus' weeping when his friend died speaks to me when I try to avoid expressing the pain of a personal loss." The hope is that such statements by a trusted caregiver will challenge the unhealthy beliefs of these persons. The cognitive dissonance that results may encourage them to adopt healthier ways of understanding the biblical teachings about emotions.

In counseling, when people ask questions about what the Bible says, particularly about emotionally loaded issues such as divorce, homosexuality, or abortion, it is important to resist the temptation to give an answer immediately. The appropriate response is to ask, "Why do you ask?" As David K. Switzer points out, this query often "will open the floodgates of a story that . . . will pour out, accompanied by a variety of emotions. Then we may move very quickly into the same type of pastoral conversation or even counseling that would have been initiated if the person had come and simply laid out a clearly delineated problem before us."[34] In such counseling, clergy's scholarly knowledge of the Bible can often be useful in correcting many people's wholeness-damaging misunderstandings of biblical texts.

A fifth use of biblical wisdom is *to be a key resource in the teaching and growth-cultivating dimensions of caregiving.* For example, the Bible can increase awareness of the Christian vision of life as a gift from God, a calling to serve those in need, and a mission to cultivate justice-based love in relationships and society.[35]

It obviously is crucial, in both caregiving and teaching, to avoid misusing the Bible in ways that inhibit growth or diminish wholeness. An example of such use is clergy's quoting of scripture in moralizing, legalistic ways to buttress their sagging authority or manipulate counselees to conform to rigid moral standards. Another example is to use the Bible to justify life-constricting attitudes toward issues such as sex, anger, divorce, and homosexuality.

An extreme example of such misuse of the Bible in pastoral counseling is the approach of Jay Adams. He begins with moralistic reductionism by saying that the cause of all psychological problems is sin and irresponsible living, thus ignoring the many other factors at their roots.[36] He rejects all psychological understandings of the human situation and all psychotherapeutic methods as "humanistic" and "nonbiblical." He claims that is the Bible is all a counselor needs to be "more competent than a psychiatrist." He recommends confronting counselees with their sins (defined moralistically), followed by quoting scripture understood legalistically and literally, to make them conform.

There are three basic flaws in this approach. It is poor counseling because it does not integrate the riches of biblical wisdom with the riches of contemporary wisdom from the human sciences and psychotherapeutic disciplines. It encourages authoritarian advice-giving, reinforced by the authority of religious leaders. This tends to increase counselees' unhealthy dependency, which blocks spiritual maturing. In addition, the rigid biblicism of this approach tends to prevent people from discovering the *living* word of the divine Spirit—wise insights that can speak in life-transforming ways to their unique problems in living.

Using Prayer and Meditation to Nurture Spiritual and Ethical Wholeness

Prayer, meditation, and imaging are right-brain, experiential methods for cultivating spiritual aliveness, creativity, and growth.[37] Other valuable right-brain resources for enhancing one's spiritual life include music, poetry, art, drama, dance, humor, and storytelling. The increased use of these resources in pastoral care and counseling can help free the intuitive, imaginative, metaphoric powers of the right hemisphere of the brain, in both the counselor and the counselee.

These spiritual disciplines have at least three uses in pastoral care and counseling: (1) they are important resources for the pastor's spiritual preparation for facilitating spiritual growth in counseling; (2) they can be used by the counselor on behalf of the counselee; and (3) they are skills that the counselee can be taught for use in spiritual self-care and self-healing.

Unfortunately for many people in our hectic, secularized culture, prayer has little or no meaning. Even when they go through the motions of praying, it does not empower them. The inner channels of their spirits are blocked by logjams of guilt, grief, and anger (including anger toward God) that prevent them from experiencing the enlivening flow of God's love, forgiveness, and justice. Caregivers should help such persons in counseling to work through their emotional logjams and then help them learn effective ways to meditate and pray. This can enable them to experience new spiritual aliveness.

There are, of course, many forms of prayer. One type that is useful to teach in pastoral care and counseling is contemplative prayer. The goal is to develop a heightened awareness of the way God is present and communicating in all experiences, including the most mundane. Caregivers can apply the approach to teaching this discipline that is used by some spiritual directors. They first help directees discover something outside themselves that allows them to move beyond the limits of self-absorption. They then are coached to engage in this activity contemplatively, meaning being aware and open to letting God become real in everyday experiences, such as looking at the beauty of nature, reading the Bible, listening to music, talking with friends, or walking city streets. Looking, listening, and attending to what occurs within oneself when one contemplates in this way are discussed with the director. A spiritual lift of a sunset, for example, if followed contemplatively, can be the beginning of a deeper relationship with the inner Spirit.

Pastoral caregivers need to stay open to the energy of God's transforming presence during their dialogical conversations with care receivers. The New Testament phrase to "pray without ceasing" (1 Thess. 5:17) can be understood to mean seeking to maintain a continuing awareness, in the background of one's consciousness, of the here-and-now presence of the Spirit of love, liberation, and justice. This means keeping oneself open to the flow of the inner Light of the divine presence. It is "practicing the presence of God," as Brother Lawrence, the humble medieval mystic, put it. Or as a young child is said to have written to God, "Dear God, I think about you sometimes even when I'm not praying."

Meditation is any method of quieting and centering one's consciousness and thereby moving into a clear, serene, uncluttered inner space psychologically. Letting one's mental motor idle for even ten minutes each day can quiet one's consciousness, increase awareness of one's body, and put one in touch with one's spiritual center. Scientific studies of various meditative and relaxation methods from both the East and the West have discovered that they all tend to produce physiological as well as psychological and spiritual benefits. Meditation is an integral part of Christian and Jewish heritages. Coaching counselees in meditative methods should be a frequently used method of helping those on the brink of burnout.

Mental imaging while in a meditative state of mind has great potential for use in healing and growth work. For reasons that are not fully understood, forming certain pictures within one's mind can activate the immune system biochemically, thus stimulating healing and also preventing some illnesses.

Teaching people in counseling and spiritual growth groups to meditate and use active imaging can help them enliven their experiences of prayer. It can also provide valuable tools for spiritual self-healing and growth between sessions. Caregivers can use these methods to deepen and enrich their own inner lives, thus enhancing the spiritual quality of their relationships with care receivers and others.

Using Women's Spiritual Wisdom to Make Caregiving More Healing and Whole

The spiritual emptiness and malaise of both men and women in our society are fed by the deep sexism of our religious institutions and the spiritual images they reinforce. As suggested earlier, both women and men need female and male images of divinity if they are to develop their full spiritual gifts and potentials. Many women have been conditioned to depend on the males in their lives for their sense of worth, identity, and power. In the church this is often reinforced by the patriarchal ethos of much of the Bible, by hymns and rituals dominated by male imagery and words for deity, and by the fact that the majority of clergy are men. Sadly the self-concept of many women in churches is so male identified that they are unaware of the profound ways in which these influences diminish their spiritual wholeness. The maleness of most of our religious images and institutions also contributes to the spiritual impoverishment of men. It helps alienate us from the female side of our spirits and from that side of deity. It also helps us justify our one-up power position in most of our culture's institutions, including churches.

In the significant paper "Why Women Need the Goddess," Carol P. Christ shows how male-oriented religion with a Father God militates against the self-esteem and personal empowerment of women.[38] She holds that as a symbol for the female in divinity, the "Goddess" helps women acknowledge the legitimacy of their female power, affirms the female will and body (both denigrated in our society), and validates bonds among women. The use of images for divinity that include rather than exclude the female experience is often resisted by male-identified women and by men whose patriarchal power is threatened. But such use can open healing dialogue about issues that are preventing women and men from making their spiritual search more wholeness generating and fulfilling.

To be liberating and empowering when counseling on spiritual as well as other matters, male and female caregivers need to have keen awareness and caring about these issues. Reading and inviting counselees to read books by feminist theologians, therapists, and pastoral counselors can help raise both consciousness and caring. Furthermore, such reading can open up exciting vistas that are being illuminated by feminist thinkers and healers exploring new dimensions of women's spirituality. In pastoral care and counseling with women and men, it is important to use words and images that communicate our awareness of and appreciation for the neglected "female" in divinity rather than the patriarchal words and images that dominate our religious traditions. An illustration of the sexist uses of the Bible relates to the symbolism of the second creation story in Hebrew Scripture (see Gen. 2). It pictures Eve, the primal woman, as being a derivative creation from the primal man, Adam's rib. This is often interpreted that the woman was created simply to keep Adam company and to serve him. Such biblical images have been used to "keep women in their (inferior) place," thereby disabling their wholeness. Such patriarchal biblical images and male-created theologies are tragic illustrations of the central thesis of liberation theology—that theological images and interpretations tend to maintain the power and privileges of the elite groups who create the theologies.

Caregivers should affirm all people's need for female images and symbols of divinity—for example, Spirit, goddess, wind and fire (as at Pentecost), rebirth—as resources for the growth of full self-esteem and spiritual wholeness. Not only women but also men need these to balance and correct the impact of the dominant male hierarchical images, such as Lord, King, and master, on their self-image. Fortunately, precious remnants of the earlier heritage of women's spirituality survived in the Bible. These include the Wisdom literature of Proverbs and so on, the growth images used by Jesus, and the strong women in the Old and New Testaments.

Pastoral caregivers should emulate the liberated wholeness of Jesus' personhood demonstrated by his relations with women and his attitudes. In his identity, he integrated the qualities that our male-oriented society identifies most often with men—courage, strength, leadership, and concern for justice—with ones most often identified with women—caring, compassion, tenderness, and responsiveness to the needs of others. Thus he demonstrated that both sets of qualities are neither masculine nor feminine but *human* capacities, all of which need to be developed by whole persons of either gender. He called God "Father," but many of the attributes of deity in his teachings are those associated most closely, in his culture and ours, with mothers—mercy, compassion, nurture, and tender love. Jesus refused to follow the dictates of his culture by restricting women to gender roles as servants of men. A vivid illustration is the story of Mary and Martha (Luke 10:38-42). In a society that considered it improper to teach women sacred truths, Jesus treated women with the same respect as he did men, sharing his brilliant new understandings of spiritual reality freely with them. In short, Jesus was a remarkably liberated, whole person who was countercultural in his inclusive, egalitarian treatment of women and others regarded as inferior in his society (for example, Samaritans and tax collectors). It behooves us pastoral caregivers to be inspired to follow him in this.

Gender studies and feminist methods of deconstruction, reclaiming, and reconstruction have produced a revolution in knowledge and knowing that have major implications for pastoral caregiving.

The Pastor's Spiritual Resources

When pastors counsel in the areas of spiritual crises and confusion, their *living* theology—the way they handle their own existential anxiety—will influence their effectiveness far more than their head-level theology. Their basic trust by which they cope with the "ego chill" (Erik Erikson's term for existential anxiety) and their real faith from which they derive courage to look into the abyss of nonbeing will be tested repeatedly; for example, in relating to a woman dying of cancer or an alcoholic teetering on the brink of meaninglessness and suicide. Their real feelings about their own lives and deaths, and the lives and deaths of those they cherish most, will influence all their counseling, especially that centering in existential issues.

Therefore, our continuing spiritual growth is essential to our effectiveness as pastoral counselors. Practicing spiritual disciplines needed to nurture this growth is not easy in the midst of demanding schedules. Fortunately our effectiveness as spiritual enablers is not entirely dependent on our degree of spiritual maturation. As representative Christian persons, we can draw on and share the resources of a rich spiritual tradition—wisdom about life and death—time-tested by many centuries of human struggle. Even at best we are very imperfect transmitters of the wisdom of this heritage. But surprisingly God can often use us with all our limitations to carry the spiritual bread of our heritage to feed the deep spiritual hungers of human hearts.

In this innovative century, with its multiple revolutions, caregivers must encourage themselves and their care receivers to be spiritually innovative and adventuresome. When traditional paths to meaningful spirituality and values are no longer effective in enabling people to blossom spiritually, it is important for them to take what Robert Frost called "the road less traveled."

Guided Meditation for Spiritual Self-care, Renewal, and Nurture

I invite you to pause now and experience an imaging meditation that has been spiritually energizing for me and others in recent years.

Begin by preparing your mind-body-spirit to be as receptive to healing and growth as possible by relaxing your whole organism intentionally but also making it as relaxed and alert as possible.

Using your creative ability, form a moving picture in your imagination of a little stream of water flowing like a small irrigation channel only a foot or two wide.

Become aware that although it is small with very limited capacity, it carries a steady stream of clear, clean, cool water.

Now follow the little stream until you see that it is flowing from an artesian spring that comes from an underground river of unlimited volume. This little channel, perhaps to your amazement, is often able to carry water that lets some of the parched places in you, others, and society flower.

Now, notice that sluice gates are near you in the inner channel. You can open and close them to block or change the directions of flow of the much-needed water. Even though the Source of the flow comes from far beyond you, you have the opportunity and responsibility to decide to whom you will cause the life-giving water to flow.

Reality Practice Skill Development Session

Parishioner's role: Become aware of an area of religious conflict, doubt, or confusion within yourself about which you would welcome help. Let yourself experience this area of your life, including the feelings associated with it. Talk with the pastor about this.

Alternative role 1, to be taken by a woman: You are becoming increasingly frustrated by the constant use of male pronouns and names for God and the generic *man* by your male pastor in his sermons and newsletter statements. Last Sunday the congregation sang "Rise Up, O Men of God" at the close of the service. You like your pastor, but you find that his sexism and the sexism of the worship service are interfering with your finding spiritual nourishment in your church. Talk with him about your concern.

Alternative role 2, to be taken by a man: You are a middle-class man, married, with two teenage daughters. You are a loyal church member, but major health problems that hit you in the past year have shaken your faith. You feel that you are a good person, and God has let you down. Your wife is critical of you for your faltering faith. Both of you are worried about the heavy medical expenses and your reduced ability to work. Things look very dark. You are in the hospital bed recovering from your last surgery when your pastor calls. (Lie down during this reality practice session.)

Pastor's role: Counsel with one of the above persons using insights you have gained from this and earlier chapters. Be particularly aware of the interconnections of the psychological, spiritual, and interpersonal dimensions of the problems brought to you. Try to sustain faith and awaken reality-based hope in the person seeking your help.

Observer-coach's role: Give feedback on the pastor's effectiveness in encouraging the expression of hopes and painful feelings and avoiding a defense of God, or an intellectualized discussion of theology.

Recommended Reading

Fowler, James W. *Stages of Faith: The Psychology of Human Development and the Quest for Meaning.* San Francisco: Harper & Row, 1981.

Kelsey, Morton T. *Prophetic Ministry: The Psychology and Spirituality of Pastoral Care*. New York: Crossroads, 1986.

Lesser, Elizabeth. *Broken Open: How Difficult Times Can Help Us Grow*. New York: Villard Books, 2005.

Lester, Andrew D. *Hope in Pastoral Care and Counseling*. Louisville: Westminster John Knox Press, 1995.

Moore, Thomas. *Care of the Soul: A Guide for Cultivating Depth and Sacredness in Everyday Life*. New York: HarperCollins, 1992.

Taylor, Charles W. *The Skilled Pastor: Counseling as the Practice of Theology*. Minneapolis: Fortress Press, 1991.

Walsh, Roger. *Essential Spirituality: The 7 Central Practices to Awaken Heart and Mind*. San Francisco: John Wiley & Sons, 2000.

Wright, Keith. *Religious Abuse: A Pastor Explores the Many Ways Religion Can Hurt as Well as Heal*. Kelowna, British Columbia, Canada: Northstone Publishing, 2001.

CHAPTER 11

ETHICAL, MEANING, AND VALUE ISSUES IN PASTORAL CARE AND COUNSELING

Deliver us, O God, from politics without principles, from wealth without work, from pleasure without conscience, from knowledge without character, from commerce without morality, from worship without sacrifice, and from science without humanity.
—"Unity of Life," anonymous in India

The Crucial Role of Ethical Values in Human Wholeness

Just as we need good nutrition for our physical health, we humans need meaning-giving, life-guiding values, ethical priorities, and commitments for our overall well-being. Growing in Spirit-centered wholeness must include growth in life-enhancing values. Because clergy's roles include coaching people to find constructive directions in ethical dilemmas, these issues are much more than the "moral context" of pastoral care, as they are sometimes described; they are at the very heart of all caregiving that is really pastoral. These issues are involved at some level, directly or indirectly, in all human dilemmas and problems. For these reasons, having the skill to guide care receivers to follow more constructive values is essential in wholeness-oriented pastoral caregiving.

There are numerous ways to describe the essential goals of ethical caregiving from a holistic, spiritual perspective. The positive aim is to enable people to increase the use of their potential strengths, assets, and wisdom in ways that will benefit their own well-being as well as that of other people and of their community and society. This is the ethics of living life in all its fullness. This perspective is expressed well in this statement attributed to Henry van Dyke: "Use what talents you possess; the woods would be very silent if no birds sang there except those that sang best."[1]

Caregiving for ethical wholeness should help people enhance their well-being by facing and dealing constructively with their personal failures and sins as well as their easily ignored complicity in the social sins of injustices that deny wholeness to countless people. The therapeutic dialogue should help equip care receivers with the motivation and skills to do what they can, working with others, to overcome these social evils, recognizing that to ignore them actually reinforces them.[2] Beyond this focus on the brokenness and alienation caused by sin, caregivers should devote their skills to fostering in care receivers positive values that contribute to the wholeness of individuals, families, society, and God's whole creation.

The enormous potential of our human species for collective and individual cruelty, destructiveness, and evil is well documented. This fact makes it essential for reality-based counseling on ethical issues to focus attention not just on individual problems, but also on wider social evils. The dark side of humankind is distressingly evident in the many large-scale atrocities and genocides of recent times. They demonstrate what ordinary people have the capacity to do to or at least to condone the actions against, those whom their group chooses to see as "other" and inferior. In American history, the inherently evil institution of slavery is a prime example, as is the abysmal treatments of Native Americans and women.

Christie Cozad Neuger illuminates the appropriate prophetic responses of holistic caregivers who understand the systemic nature of much human suffering and evil:

> When evil and sin are understood as systemic wickedness in terms of structures of oppression and acts that sustain those structures, we are able to understand violence in such a way that we see our task not just as stopping one perpetrator, but also as working to dismantle systems of oppression that make intimate violence (and indeed other kinds of violence) more likely to occur.[3]

Ethical Caregiving and the Church's Mission

As Don Browning made clear in his now classic book, the church is called to be a community of moral inquiry, guidance, and formation. The role of clergy and other caregivers is to facilitate this process and to help "create, maintain and revise the normative value symbols of their society."[4] This crucial task, done within the moral context of the Judeo-Christian heritage, characterizes all truly pastoral care and counseling. Biblical wisdom about ethical values and moral health is an invaluable resource for caregivers to offer care receivers for their use in ethical decision making.

If we pastoral caregivers are to recover the much-needed ministry of reconciliation in these times of multiple violence-breeding alienations, we must use a more muscular approach to this ethical ministry. Reflecting on the basic functions of caregiving in the context of pastoral care's history, William Clebsch and Charles Jaekle point to the most egregious lack in contemporary pastoral care: "There are many indications that the function of reconciling as a creative and meaningful part of Christian pastoral care has fallen upon evil days. Perhaps more than the other three functions of the cure of souls, reconciling has suffered from misunderstanding and erosion." They go on to show that in the Christian heritage, the ministry of reconciling has enabled persons to renew a right relationship with God and with neighbor by using two interdependent modes of caregiving: *discipline* (a word that historically has meant correction by pastoral admonition or church discipline) integrated with *forgiveness* (through confession, penance, and absolution). In mainstream Protestant denominations, these authors hold, this ministry has been underemphasized as clergy have overreacted to sterile, punitive moralizing in caregiving. This neglect has been reinforced by permissive counseling theories. As a result, a considerable segment of the overall Christian church has been virtually deprived of a ministry of pastoral reconciliation "at a time when alienation is at the root of much human woe and anxiety." It is sad but true that "there is no place in the structure and rhythm of the life of modern congregations where a serious discussion concerning the state of one's soul is expected."[5] A revival of pastoral effectiveness in reconciling is a paramount need in contemporary pastoral counseling.

In support of the important principle of not projecting their values onto clients, many psychotherapists and counselors have been trained to aim at being ethically neutral in therapeutic encounters. Many of us who honor the principle of respecting care receivers' values by not imposing our own on them have discovered that complete ethical neutrality is not a therapeutic goal and is impossible to achieve. No matter how hard we may try to be neutral our implicit values about important issues inevitably will be reflected in our caregiving responses, for better or for worse. In radical contrast to ethical neutrality, holistic pastoral caregivers must respond to the urgent need for counselors and therapists, along with other teachers, to increase ethical guidelines for living healthier lifestyles in a violent, broken society.

Though humans are finite, we enjoy a measure of freedom; some degree of freedom to choose among ethical options is in the makeup even of those in whom this freedom has been limited by adverse circumstances and destructive choices. It is also true that values like cooperation, group bonding, and altruism have survival value and therefore are in our hereditary programming. In today's global village, the need to cooperate has been extended to include the whole human family, whose survival probably depends on our learning how to collaborate to save a viable planet.

Ethical Guidance: A Pressing Need in Our Times

Many things about our society's dominant value priorities militate against people's general and ethical wellness. Society pushes people toward values and goals that, in the long run, are unhealthy for them and for their families, community, and world. Countless advertising pitches hit them each day, equating health and happiness with acquiring more and more things. Pursuing this goal day by day fails to yield lasting satisfaction or enhanced well-being. To cultivate health-enhancing values effectively, caregivers must risk being ethically countercultural when appropriate. This stance is necessary because many of the dominant ethical criteria and ideals that guide our culture do not lead to individual, family, and societal well-being. Instead they motivate individual and organizational practices that cause massive brokenness, suffering, sickness, and evils on all levels of society. Holistic prophetic caregivers must challenge many of these values, including materialism that breeds consumerism, and success understood as winning by dominating or putting others down. In this vital aspect of their ministries, prophetic holistic caregivers risk challenging many of the ethical sacred cows of economic, political, and religious systems in our greedy culture. Obviously this situation often makes prophetic caregiving stressful and sometimes hazardous to caregivers. When this happens, it is well to remember some words of Martin Luther King Jr. that suggest there is a time when even silence is betrayal.

Though there is an epidemic of widespread individual and collective moral confusion, value distortions, and injustice in our society, people are also searching for healthy ethical principles to guide them during times of crucial decision making. The collapse of old authority-centered and institutionally validated value systems, and the resulting moral and ethical confusion is the seedbed where many of the psychological, interpersonal, and spiritual problems and hopes that bring people to counseling are bred. Moral and ethical concern is one of the most needed and most often neglected in our era of ethical complexities like those created by cloning and the uses of biotech research findings.

Geoffrey Peterson is on target when he declares,

> Our culture's moral confusion, conflicts, and pluralism all contribute to the complex conscience problems that pastoral counselors often encounter. In counseling on value problems, it is important to be aware of the ways in which the contemporary crisis in values makes it difficult for many people to find a viable philosophy in life. Millions are uprooted from a sense of community within which sound values flourish and existential anxiety can be handled constructively.[6]

They suffer from a social climate of normlessness.

Peterson continues to describe a constructive response in this situation: "We pastoral counselors cannot attempt to give authoritative answers to all the value problems brought to us. What we can do—and this is more helpful—is to provide a caring and supportive environment in which values may be clarified and strengthened and, when necessary, revised so as to reflect more faithfully the values of Christ."[7]

Using Reality Therapy in Ethical Caregiving

As persons relate more responsibly and responsively (to others), new sources of need satisfaction are open to them. William Glasser declares, "As important as confronting reality is, it is only part of the therapy. The patient must learn to fulfill his needs in the real world [of relationship]...and we must teach him how whenever we can."[8] Confrontational counseling aims at facilitating counselees' firsthand encounter with the part of reality that they have defied or ignored and helping them make the changes in their behavior that will enable them to live more constructively.

Pastoral counselor Philip Anderson describes his counseling with a recovered alcoholic, Bill, who said he was "just plain not happy":

> My response to this was to say that when I was not happy about myself it usually involved a rather simple mechanism, namely, I had done something which I was not very proud of or happy about or I had not done something I should have done. I went on to illustrate my point by citing a personal experience....When I had not adequately prepared a sermon, I was most unhappy on Sunday morning. So I was prompted to ask Bill what he had been doing lately.

The counselee replied, "The truth is that I have given up drinking but I still waste too much time." They talked about how his irresponsible behavior had allowed his business to deteriorate. Then Anderson asked the counselee about his marriage. Bill began to verbalize his irritation toward his wife.

Anderson: But what are *you* doing, not what is your wife doing, about your marriage?
Bill: Funny you should ask that. I've been having an affair with another woman for about six months, and I'm sick of it.
Anderson: Bill, I'm not surprised that you aren't happy. You are living an irresponsible life that you are hiding from your wife and associates. You don't have any right to be happy.

Bill agreed. Counseling focused on Bill's responsibilities. His wife soon joined the counseling, the marriage came under scrutiny, and a reconciliation was achieved in that relationship. As Bill began to act more responsibly, he reported that he was beginning to be happy again.[9]

Anderson's approach is an example of the confrontational thrust in contemporary counseling (also represented by Glasser's reality therapy). It concentrates on current rather than past relationships and on responsible behavior rather than on feelings. Acting more responsible in the here and now, rather than waiting until new feelings produce constructive behavior, is the central emphasis.

Pastoral counseling should learn from the confrontational therapies and thereby be helped to recover our heritage of reconciliation. Many will activate their potential for responsible living if the counselor firmly points out behaviors that produce spiraling guilt, fear of discovery, and lack of self-honesty and honesty in relationships, noting that they are trapped in a vicious cycle. The guiltier they feel, the more they hide; and the more they hide, the greater the buildup of guilt and fear. A caring approach that directly confronts guilt and irresponsible behavior may help them break out of this self-perpetu-ating cycle. The tremendous sense of relief and release experienced by many AA members when they do their "moral inventory" fully and make constructive amends illustrates the healing power of this process.

AA's 12-step recovery program demonstrates the importance of honest ethical self-confrontation. The rigor of this process is suggested by the fact that seven of the twelve steps deal with the process of doing "a searching and fearless moral inventory," which includes admitting (confessing) "to God, to ourselves, and to another human being the exact nature of our wrongs," making "a list of all the persons we have harmed," and making "direct amends to such persons whenever possible, except when to do so would injure them or others."[10] It is no accident that such an inner cleansing often leads recovering addicted persons to a spiritual awakening. Ethically effective caregivers should help nonalcoholic counselees be just as rigorous in clearing their lives of accu-mulated moral debris from sinful, irresponsible living. To do so is often the price of inner peace, forgiveness, and restored relationships. Protestant equivalents of the sacra-ment of reconciliation, integrated with skilled counseling, are needed in our society where guilt proliferates and corporate ways of moving from guilt to reconciliation (in the anemic confessional phase of public worship, for example) lack healing power for many people.

Confrontation is most likely to result in self-confrontation when it includes two aspects. These are expressed well in New Testament language as "speaking the truth in love" (Eph. 4:15). Speaking the truth is most effective when it is done in the context of caring love. Honest confrontation, after some trust is established, usually strengthens counseling relationships rather than weakens them. The counselor who speaks the truth (without caring), as she or he sees it, produces only feelings of rejection and defensive-ness in the other. Conversely, the counselor who is loving, in the shallow sense of always being permissive and accepting, actually deprives the counselee of the tough love that cares enough to risk speaking the truth.

Most people do not begin to change until they experience the pain of their present behavior. Confrontation may help them become aware of this pain. The pain and the appropriate guilt, which is part of it, may provide motivation to accept help and even-tually change their behavior. Many guilt-laden people need help in working through their feelings of guilt and in learning to live more responsibly. Some guilt feelings are so deeply repressed that only skilled psychotherapy can enable persons to become aware of and resolve them. If guilt is flowing from unconscious neurotic conflicts, neither the five-step path to reconciliation nor action-oriented therapies will be effective. But in some cases, by the use of caring confrontation it is possible to help persons gain clearer access to guilt feelings of which they are vaguely aware. Bringing such just-below-the-surface guilt into the open makes it accessible to resolution in counseling.

Methods of therapeutic confrontation are valuable in a variety of counseling situations not focusing primarily on ethical or meaning issues. James A. Knight writes, "Confrontation as a counseling technique offers the teacher and pastor endless opportunities for creative encounter. When there is awareness, sensitivity, and knowledge, the face-to-face struggle opens new pathways to relatedness between persons and possibilities for growth."[11] Confrontation, he points out, can be particularly useful in helping older adolescents and young adults grow toward maturity:

> The young person is in need of face-to-face relationships with authorities who demonstrate their concern for the individual both by support and judgment. During the tumultuous periods of psychological growth, confrontation at appropriate times will serve to open pathways for growth and to set necessary limits to behavior.[12]

A pastor met a teenage parishioner (Sam) hanging out at a video store during school hours.

Pastor: I see you decided not to go back to school.
Sam: Yeah, I couldn't seem to make it there.
Pastor: What are your plans? Maybe there's something else you should be preparing for.
Sam: Don't really know what I want to do. I suppose something will come along.

They talked about the future. The pastor stressed the desirability of Sam's choosing a route now that would lead to some work he found satisfying. Later, as counseling continued in the pastor's study, the pastor contacted and involved the state employment agency counselor to help the youth make and implement realistic plans. Eventually Sam entered training to become a refrigeration technician. By exercising his pastoral initiative and using confrontational and educative counseling methods, the pastor helped Sam interrupt what could have become a chronic failure cycle.

Confrontational methods are often essential in life-threatening crises. A young man reported intense fear that he would harm his woman friend. Knowing of his poorly controlled rage and his previous impulsive behavior toward women, the pastor insisted that he commit himself for psychiatric treatment. He confronted the man firmly with the real danger that he might do something irreparably destructive. Rather than resent the pastor's firm stance, the man was relieved and willing to comply. The pastor had used the strength of his position and his personality to protect the woman and to protect the man from his own destructiveness. The same kind of strong, caring confrontation is often essential in preventing suicides.

When the counselor makes a major error or misses the counselee's wavelength completely, it is well to discuss it openly as soon as possible.

Pastor: As I thought about our last talk, I realized that I had probably missed what you were trying to tell me at the end. I noticed that you got very quiet. How did you feel when I said...?

The counselor's nonapologetic self-confrontation usually helps repair damaged rapport in such situations. By admitting his fallibility, he strengthens the relationships.

Neomoralism: The Danger in Confrontation

Confrontational methods are analogous to powerful medicine. Used properly, they can be a potent means of healing. Yet the dangers of misuse are increased by their potency. James A. Knight observes, "Pastors and teachers have not always understood the meaning of confrontation in counseling. It is often confused with a vertical type of authoritarianism, moralistic preachments, or hostile attacks indulged in under the guise of 'righteous indignation.'"[13]

These principles can provide some protection against the danger of falling into moralisms: (a) Confrontation should be used with care and restraint. (b) The emphasis should be on helping persons face reality (self-confrontation) as *they* come to understand it and discover their own responsibility within it. (c) Counselees should be given full opportunity to respond to confrontation, to discuss it thoroughly, and to disagree with the counselor. In the final analysis, the pastor's level of maturity will determine whether he or she misuses confrontational methods to manipulate the counselee or uses the methods constructively. The crucial variable in all counseling on ethical and value issues is the counselor's ethical integrity and wholeness.

Health-nurturing Morality as Holistic Vision[14]

To contribute to wholeness, individual and group ethical thinking must transcend narrow legalism focusing primarily on don'ts! This thinking must affirm robustly the positive, constructive attitudes, values, and behaviors that nurture the well-being of individuals, cultures, institutions, and the natural world. This understanding recognizes and affirms that love-centered, justice-grounded "life in all its fullness" is the highest ethical value, and as such, it should guide both individual and group ethical decision making and behavior. Jesus went beyond a legalistic understanding of ethics because he saw that love takes precedence over institutional rules (Matt. 22:37-40).[15] Ethical guidance flowing from a vision of a transformed future transcends the negative controls of legalistic prohibitions. Such transformational ethics are evident in the moral struggles of the early church as reflected in the Apostle Paul's moving beyond the legalism of his religious background to emphasizing living a good life in response to gratitude for experiencing the love and grace of God. Holistic ethics are also reflected in the wisdom of the Hebrew Scriptures that points to the well-being of all future generations: "Choose life so that you and your descendants may live, loving the LORD your God, obeying him, and holding fast to him; for that means life to you and length of days" (Deut. 30:19a).

A life-transforming ethic calls for a vastly expanded worldview. As several astronauts pointed out, the view of our planet rising over the horizon of the moon should transform radically the worldviews of humans. The often-shown photos of the earth from outer space make it clear that the ultimate well-being of all humans could depend on adopting a cosmic perspective leading to the recognition that we are all one, whether or not we like one another. Only a value system based on this perspective can help us learn to live together in the justice-based peace on which the ultimate survival of a healthy planet home depends.[16]

It is also crucial in today's world to encourage people to be future oriented and to develop awareness of their ethical responsibility for the well-being of children and for generations yet unborn. A striking example of a person who embodied this orientation was Jonas Salk. In public statements, he often invited reflection on the health of future generations by raising questions such as these: "Are we being good ancestors? Are we contributing to shaping the human beings for the future by what we do now? Are we doing what we should to provide for them the optimal opportunities for carrying human values into the future? Can we become organized as a species to avoid destructiveness and bring peace for all humanity? Can we cultivate the wisdom necessary to create a positive future?"[17]

Cultivating Wholeness by Enlarging Horizons of Ethical Caring

Counseling to cultivate ethical healing and growth, like all counseling, must begin wherever careseekers are when they come for help with their problems. This approach means beginning with the care receiver's ethical priorities and values, however limited. By respectful listening and questioning, caregivers begin to understand the ethical orientations, conflicts, and dilemmas of care receivers as these relate to the problems in living that motivated them to seek counseling. The initial goal is to guide them to deal constructively with these problems, including their ethical component. Caregivers should always be aware of serious limitations as well as strengths and resources in counselees' ethical values and behaviors. This awareness should include alertness to opportunities to strengthen and repair ethical flaws from a wellness perspective. An ultimate objective is to coach counselees to grow their values and priorities and to enlarge their ethical horizons to make them more inclusive and justice generating. For example, consider a problem such as obesity. For those with sensitive ethical awareness, obesity is seen in the context of more than one billion people on earth suffering from hunger and malnutrition. When this occurs, the goal is to help the obese become aware of their need for ethical growth, seeing the issue as an opportunity to gain wisdom, courage, and strength for living life more fully and with deeper spiritual fulfillment, not only just to lose weight for their personal health reasons.

The double aim is to bring healing to those who are wounded by social injustices and ecological sins and to prevent these injuries by prophetic action. In doing so, caregivers are implementing the prophetic tradition of Jesus' religious heritage. This is expressed clearly in the verse from Hebrew Scripture,

> He has told you . . . what is good;
>   and what does the LORD require of you
> but to do justice, and to love kindness,
>   and to walk humbly with your God? (Mic. 6:8)

An Ethic for the Health of the Planet and the Biosphere

"Then he showed me the river of the water of life, bright as crystal, flowing from the throne of God. . . . On either side of the river, the tree of life . . . and the leaves of the tree were for the healing of the nations" (Rev. 22: 1-2 RSV).
The health and well-being of the more than six billion people on the planet are increasingly interdependent. There is an urgent need for a shared ethical commitment to work together for universal wholeness that transcends and unites people in all nations, races, cultures, and religions. Consider these grim statistics about our world:

- One hundred million people on earth are homeless.
- One-third of all children under age five suffer malnutrition.
- Thirty thousand children die each day from preventable illnesses.
- One billion people in developing countries lack safe drinking water.
- In those countries 2.4 billion lack adequate sanitation.
- Two hundred fifty million children are laborers in developing countries.
- Eleven people on the planet are infected with the HIV virus each minute.[18]

The human family desperately needs a collective survival ethic. This would be an ethical system to which people of widely diverse cultures and beliefs would commit themselves in order to save humankind and the biosphere from escalating destructive conflict. To be most wholeness generating, ethical commitments must begin by thinking globally and acting locally at the grassroots of personal, family, and community relationships. But on this shrinking planet with increasing interconnections, such commitments must also be expressed by taking action in the wider quadrants of people's world—regional, national, and even global. Environmental issues like global warming and the population explosion, which will determine whether all children will inherit a healthy earth, cannot be resolved by courageous action on local or even national levels alone. The dust-polluted air I breathed at times while teaching in Puerto Rico resulted from particles blown across the Atlantic from deserts in North Africa. The radioactive fallout from the nuclear generator meltdown at Chernobyl arrived in Poland, where I was teaching, in a matter of a few hours, and it circled the globe in a few days following that tragic accident.

Consider the economic plight of the human family. The yawning canyons separating excessively rich and demeaningly poor individuals, families, and nations are produced by injustices in the economic systems of countries around the world. The lifestyle and economic changes in affluent and impoverished countries that are necessary to bridge these chasms and also heal our wounded earth must begin on individual and local levels. But they also involve educational, scientific, and social policy changes on national and global levels.

The theological assumptions and worldviews that can guide and motivate such moral thinking and action must be rooted in local faith and value systems. But they must go far beyond these origins. Humankind must develop beliefs and ethical values that transcend the countless differences characterizing world religions and cultures. Such beliefs must affirm the oneness of the human family with one God who is understood and worshiped in many ways. Such moral commitments must give high ethical priority to creating local and global settings where people of all ages and both sexes have full opportunity to enjoy all those things needed to live healthy lives and develop their potential.

There is an increasing consensus among international scholars that all the major global problems, including starvation and environmental degradation, are rooted in the runaway population explosion and that sustainable change can be accomplished only by an integrated approach. Therefore, holistic counseling on ethical issues affecting individual and family well-being must confront the key complex population issue. This means facing the ethical problems implicit in these facts: it required all of human history and prehistory, up to the early 1700s, for the world's population to reach one billion people and until 1960 to reach three billion. Fifty years later the global population has doubled to six billion and is adding one billion people every eleven years. Unless this process is slowed, the planet will be struggling to feed, clothe, and provide adequate housing, education, and health care for an expected ten to twelve billion people by 2050. This increase will cause international violence, starvation, and epidemics to flourish as more and more people compete for less and less space and basic resources. The birth rate is highest in the poorest countries, and the projected estimate is that the forty-nine least-developed countries will almost triple in size by 2050.

What is the key to interrupting the population explosion and improving the quality of life around the world? The connection between empowering women and population growth has been demonstrated repeatedly in studies by the United Nations. In short, empowering women with education, economic opportunities, and opportunities for them to use their God-given potentialities more fully is the most effective way to reduce population growth and improve the overall quality of family life and societies. Educated women choose to have smaller families, and they marry and begin their families later. And yet 60 percent of the one hundred million children with no access to education are girls, and 67 percent of the world's illiterate adults are women.[19]

Hiroshima makes it clear that a small nuclear bomb can reduce an entire city to rubble. In the first half century after that global tragedy, eight nations, led by two superpowers, produced some fifty thousand nuclear weapons. Nuclear scientists say that these are more than enough to destroy most life on planet Earth many times over.[20] Rational people who care about the future of the human family cannot ignore the fact that our planet is infected by a potentially fatal, collective ethical disease. Along with all other caring human beings, Christians have reasons, at the center of their ethical mission, for including passionate concern for potential victims of this nuclear global disease. What follows is an overview of the dynamics and methods of helping people with the major types of ethical problems.

Helping Persons with Guilt

Distinguishing Appropriate and Neurotic Guilt

How caregivers deal with guilt problems depends on whether the guilt is appropriate and rational or neurotic. Guilt feelings are appropriate when one intentionally damages or diminishes the wholeness of oneself, others, society, or God's creation. Appropriate guilt results when authentic and significant values are violated by the misuse of whatever degree of inner freedom people possess in particular situations. In contrast, neurotic guilt is not the result of the real harm one has done intentionally.

Psychologically, neurotic guilt is produced by the immature side of one's conscience—the internalized values, behavior, and feelings that were rewarded or punished in one's culture as these were screened through the values of one's parents and other mentors and authority figures in one's childhood. (The initial contents of everyone's conscience are formed in this way.) Fear of punishment, rejection, and hope for rewards motivate behavior rather than positive strivings for what one wholeheartedly affirms as good. Neurotic guilt makes people feel burdened by a chronic sense of their sinfulness. They suffer from punitive, self-punishing consciences (roughly what Freud meant by the superego).[21] Because neurotic guilt feelings result mainly from violating internalized parental prohibitions, they usually focus on minor or insignificant ethical issues or on angry, aggressive, or sexual feelings, fantasies, and impulses. Neurotic guilt feelings and the diminished sense of well-being they produce are compulsive and therefore lacking in the freedom that must be present in any genuine ethical choice.

Guilt feelings (the inner sense of having violated one's principles) and shame (the fear of being caught, exposed, and punished) intermingle in the inner torment that persons with severe neurotic consciences experience. In many counselees, appropriate and neurotic guilt and shame feelings are intertwined. The neurotic elements can be identified by the characteristics just described, especially the focus on fantasies and feelings or on relatively trivial ethical behavior. Furthermore, because they are rooted in the obsessive need to be one's own punishing inner parent, neurotic guilt feelings do not respond to the confession-forgiveness process. In addition, they seldom motivate constructive amendment or long-term changes in the guilt-producing behavior.

Helping People with Appropriate Guilt

Holistic caregivers should help persons suffering appropriate guilt to walk the time-tested, healing path of moving from guilt and alienation to forgiveness, reconciliation, and peace. Both the church's century-spanning experience and 12-step recovery programs like Alcoholic Anonymous demonstrate that appropriate guilt feelings can be resolved via a five-stage process: confrontation, confession, forgiveness, restitution (including changing destructive behavior), and reconciliation. This time-tested healing path incorporates the wisdom of the sacrament of reconciliation (formerly referred to as the sacrament of penance in the Roman Catholic Church). A comparable healing process is found in seven of the twelve steps. The steps are on the path of healing from alienation (from oneself, others, nature, and God) caused by guilt and shame to forgiveness and reconciliation.

Enabling guilt-ridden counselees to take the first step, *confrontation*, can be an indispensable skill in pastoral counseling. It involves the sensitive use of the twin authority of clergy—the authority of their role and what Erich Fromm calls the "rational authority" derived from their competence as ethical guides. The underlying purpose of confronting persons is to encourage *self-confrontation*. This means helping them face the behavior that hurts them and/or others and experience appropriate guilt. In some counselees, appropriate guilt feelings are like an open, infected wound. Confrontation by another person is obviously not needed, since they are already confronting themselves forcefully. But many people are not fully aware of their destructive behavior. If their behavior is to be interrupted and their latent guilt healed, it must be brought out into the open by constructive confrontation. Hidden or denied guilt can easily be overlooked. In vicious marital conflicts, for example, couples should feel guilty because they are damaging themselves and each other severely. But the appropriate guilt is often hidden behind the spiral of mutual attack and projection of blame onto the other. Unless counselors recognize the latent guilt and intervene with a confrontational statement, such as, "I would think it would make you feel very bad to be hurting each other and yourselves so much," their guilt may grind on, feeding their blind, spiraling mutual attack.

A middle-aged man discussed with his pastor the affair he was having with his younger secretary. The pastor learned that the man was motivated to seek help because the man's wife had learned about the affair and was threatening to divorce him. The pastor decided not to focus initially on the man's inner conflicts about his behavior or on his side of the toxic interpersonal relationship with his wife that was at the root of the infidelity. Instead, the pastor asked, "How do you think your two children are affected by what is going on?" The discussion that followed helped the man face the harmful consequences of his behavior on his children, whom he loved deeply. The self-confrontation triggered by the pastor's query thus mobilized the man's appropriate guilt. The pastor then supported the side of the man's ambivalence that wanted to break off the exotic but damaging relationship. He encouraged the man to do so immediately. He also arranged with the man and his wife to enter marriage therapy together to learn ways to correct the way their relationship had been neglected so that its protracted deterioration had contributed to the affair. Because skillful confrontation is often so crucial in holistic caregiving, it will be explored more fully below.

Experiencing self-confrontation often leads people who are suffering appropriate guilt to spontaneously take the second step on the path to forgiveness—*confession*. Spontaneous confession often occurs during the early catharsis stage of counseling. It is important to encourage counselees to examine their guilt wound and to pour out their guilt feelings. Experiencing and expressing one's painful guilt feelings are essential in the cleansing and healing process. Rather than attempt to make such people feel better, the counselor-confessor should help them stay with the guilt until it is thoroughly experienced and expressed in all its facets.

Clergy hear confessions and serve as imperfect channels of God's forgiveness as representatives of the church and its heritage. The healing involves both the pastoral and the priestly functions of clergy. (The value of the priestly dimension of confession is often overlooked.) After extended counseling (including depth confession) with a man disabled by appropriate guilt from the irreparable harm he had done to several people by his excessive drinking, the pastor suggested that they go together to the church sanctuary. Wearing her clerical robe to symbolize her representative, priestly role, the pastor invited the man to pray for acceptance of God's forgiveness as he knelt at the Communion railing. Then the pastor said a prayer of absolution, followed by a prayer of thanksgiving for the gift of God's forgiveness. After this, they joined in the Lord's Prayer. Such priestly actions would not be meaningful for many people; however, in this case, the actions were bearers of the reconciling symbols of the good news of the Christian way, by which guilt can be transformed into forgiveness and reconciliation. They were channels of grace by which cleansing and *forgiveness* came alive for that man. It should be emphasized that the effectiveness of these priestly acts was built on and integrated with a meaningful counseling experience.

If the experiences of confession, absolution, and forgiveness are to lead to ongoing responsible action, meaning changing destructive behavior, attitudes, or beliefs, they must be followed by the fourth step. This is *restitution* addressed to the persons harmed. After the session just described, the counseling continued in the pastor's study for several sessions. The dual focus of these sessions was on what the man would do to make constructive amends to the persons who had been harmed and on what he had learned from the whole experience that could help him avoid repeating his self- and other-hurting behavior. As the man implemented his plans, his sense of *reconciliation* gradually grew stronger. He experienced increasing healing of his relationship with God, with himself, and with some of the people from whom he had been alienated by his attitudes and actions. Toward the conclusion of his counseling, he reported feeling "a wonderful sense of lightness in my mind and even in my body—like a heavy weight has been lifted off my soul!"

Helping Persons with Neurotic Guilt Find Healing

Some counselees are disabled—psychologically and spiritually—by neurotic consciences. They feel chronic inappropriate guilt and low self-esteem mixed with shame derived from rigid, legalistic, authority-centered value systems. Their self-evaluation is devoid of self-affirmation and experiences of living grace. This causes them to squander their ethical and caring energies in compulsive self-castigation concerning trivial ethical issues or their "bad" feelings. Consequently there is little energy left for the important values such as compassion, forgiveness, and justice. The goal of counseling with such persons is to help them achieve more accepting, grace-full consciences guided by more mature ethical standards focusing on significant values.

Neurotic guilt feelings can be reduced temporarily by persons being "spanked" psychologically and thus punished by those they regard as moral-authority figures. This explains why guilt-ridden people are attracted to punishing preachers and judgmental counselors who punish them by moralistic words that reinforce their rigid ethical beliefs. In a vicious cycle, the authority figures who help create the problem of neurotic guilt offer a temporary "solution" that actually reinforces the problem. Regular verbal pummeling provides neurotic atonement, thus lessening painful but inappropriate guilt feelings. The persons may feel better temporarily, but this feeling does not last or motivate constructive changes in their behavior. When the authority-centered relief diminishes, they will seek another verbal spanking.

The underlying causes of neurotic guilt are conflicted feelings, thoughts, and impulses in the sufferer's mind. A deeper cause is the process of giving away his or her ethical power to moralistic authority figures by submitting to their misused authority. Persons suffering from relatively mild neurotic guilt can be helped by skillful pastoral counseling to learn how to resolve the conflicts at the roots of their guilt and shame. But those affected by severe neurotic guilt need longer-term pastoral psychotherapy. This can bring the genuine healing of their neurotic guilt, embodied in the wonderful blessing of liberating self-acceptance grounded in awareness of God's unconditional acceptance. A guilt-burdened client replied to his pastoral counselor's query, "After I had gone over and over how guilty I felt about my sexual thoughts and feelings, you shook me up when you said, 'I wonder why it's so difficult for you to forgive yourself and treat your feelings with more Christian forgiveness.'" The counselor's implied question opened dialogue in which the roots of his load of neurotic guilt were illuminated.

The familiar Parent-Adult-Child concepts of transactional analysis (TA) therapy shed light on the dynamics of and recovery from neurotic guilt and shame. These feelings are the product of the inner Parent's punishing the inner Child for breaking prohibitions programmed in the Child's ethical belief system by the Parent. Effective pastoral caregivers become new, more accepting parent figures with whom care receivers identify and from whom they learn something of what Alfred Adler called "the courage of one's own imperfections." By identifying with and thus internalizing aspects of their counselors' more positive, life-affirming consciences, the person's inner Parent becomes less punishing of the inner Child. The punitive inner Parent is reprogrammed (known as Re-Parented in TA). As a result, the person experiences increased self-acceptance and inner freedom from the compulsive moralism that had disabled ethical (choice-making) capacities. The reconciliation of conflicted aspects within care receivers enables them to become reconciled with themselves and others.

During this healing process, caregivers encourage persons suffering from neurotic guilt and shame to exercise their inner Adult's ability to examine competing values and affirm those that are consistent with their own understanding of the good life. In healthy moral development during adolescence, the process of critiquing the internalized values of one's parents and other childhood authority figures is a part of discovering one's own meanings and values, which usually include some of the parents' values. In TA terms, this process could be described as letting go of submission of the inner Child to the inner Parent, and putting one's Adult in the driver's seat of one's conscience. If this ethical maturing does not occur, neurotic guilt and shame flourish, and long-term counseling may be required to release the person to become an adult ethically.

Neurotic guilt feelings, particularly about ethical trivia, occasionally hide appropriate guilt about unlived life and wholeness-diminishing behavior. The neurotic guilt is superimposed on the deeper guilt as a camouflage. However, what appears to be appropriate guilt may hide deeper neurotic guilt-producing conflicts based on unresolved problems in psychosexual development, such as oedipal attachments.

In pastoral counseling with guilt-laden persons, it is wise to begin by dealing with the obvious guilt problem. This may prove to be only a surface manifestation of deeper guilt and conflict. If after extended confessional catharsis and serious efforts at reconstruction of alienated relationships, self-forgiveness does not gradually emerge, a deeper conflict requiring psychotherapy probably is present.

A teenage girl, disturbed about her steadily worsening relationship with her mother, sought her youth minister's help. Two sessions were devoted to exploring her ambivalent feelings toward her mother—anger but also warm, positive feelings. Because there was no improvement in their daughter-mother relationship, the minister recommended that she try putting her positive feelings into action during the following week. At the next counseling session, she reported, "I was just furious at you for suggesting that I do something to show that I love my mother. But I found myself setting the table without being asked and actually enjoying it. I have no idea why. It just happened. We're getting along fine—the best we have in five years."

If the girl's inner conflicts regarding her mother had been severe, it is unlikely that the minister's recommendation would have been followed or, if followed, would have produced lasting benefits. What apparently occurred was that the counselor's confronting "push" interrupted the momentum of long-standing negative interaction between the girl and her mother. By doing something helpful, the girl reduced her guilt load and reestablished communication with her mother. The minister's action had enabled her to reestablish a relationship, which could then be helped further by counseling. At the minister's suggestion, the mother and daughter came in for several joint counseling sessions aimed at helping them make their communication more effective and thereby strengthening their relationship.

Helping Persons with Immature or Disabled, Destructive Consciences

Erik Erikson has shown that virtues such as hope, purpose, competence, fidelity, love, care, and wisdom are vital elements in enhancing children's and adults' ethical health and well-being. Those who do not have these vital personality nutrients are seriously disabled in living lives that are ethically healthy. In its extreme form this problem is called a "character disorder" or "sociopathic personality." With what Erich Fromm called its manipulative "marketing orientation," our culture spawns such character problems in all degrees and with great frequency. Such persons have one or more of these characteristics: (a) lack of appropriate guilt, anxiety, and sense of responsibility; (b) ineffective self-control of antisocial impulses; (c) chronic lying and irresponsible behavior; (d) shallowness of feelings and relationships; and (e) a *modus operandi* centered on manipulating and exploiting others.

People with relatively healthy, mature consciences have caring concern for others, including those who are marginalized, discriminated against, and put down in society. Sigmund Freud once wrote to his longtime friend Pastor Oskar Pfister: "Ethics are a kind of highway code for traffic among mankind."[22] Many people in today's society have not learned to respect this mutually protective code. They have not internalized the culture's guiding values and therefore have not learned to control their asocial impulses. Such character problems seem to result from people's early backgrounds, including cold, loveless homes as well as those in which parents mistook overpermissiveness for love and did not maintain appropriate limits with fair, consistent discipline. Furthermore, the epidemic of violence and narcissism in our culture causes disadvantaged people to internalize these dynamics, thus breeding a plethora of character problems. In this social context, many parents are fighting an uphill battle, even when they do their best with and for their children.

Caregivers often struggle silently with the dilemma of how to respond when careseekers express prejudiced ethical views that clearly are unhealthy for society as well as for them. One counselee declared passionately to his pastor, "My job problems are caused mostly by the greedy Jews that control our economy and by [the N word] who get all kinds of job favors because they're colored!" What is a constructive response to such rabid racism and distorted prejudice? For caregivers who are properly committed to accepting people where they are emotionally and ethically, deciding how to respond can be very problematic. The goal is to accept people where they are but to understand this as their starting place from which to move toward more constructive and inclusive ethical responsibility.

Confrontational methods are essential in counseling with people having immature or distorted consciences. A permissive, insight-oriented counseling approach may be effective with guilt- and anxiety-loaded psychoneurotics, but it almost always fails with those who have character problems.[23]

Sociologist David Riesman suggests that permissive therapists are useful with counselees who have been victims of arbitrary displays of power in childhood and for whom a permissive, accepting situation is a new experience: "But many of the college-educated have been brought up permissively both at home and at school and find little that is liberating in a therapist who only accepts them."[24] A pastoral psychotherapist who works with many disturbed adolescents reports that problems of weak or distorted consciences predominate among his counselees and that insight-oriented and psychoanalytic methods have proved strikingly ineffective with most of them. *Learning-theory* or *cognitive-behavioral therapy* has provided the most successful method. The therapist's emphasis is on setting and enforcing limits on the deviant behavior so that constructive patterns may be learned and reinforced through the rewards and punishments of the structure. For example, instead of being lenient and permissive with patterns of school truancy or of bringing weapons to school, he recommends that the school authorities take immediate disciplinary action. It is essential to his therapy that the youth involved know that this is his recommendation to the authorities.[25]

Here are some principles of counseling with persons who have immature, weak, or antisocial consciences, based on the approach of reality therapy: (1) Establish a relationship of rapport. This is often a difficult step because persons with this problem tend to distrust and stay distant from authority figures. (2) Confront persons firmly with the self-defeating nature of their reality-denying behavior by rejecting it as unrealistic while continuing to accept them as persons. (3) Do whatever is feasible to discourage the irresponsible, acting-out behavior. (4) Reward responsible, realistic behavior by affirming it with approval. (5) Coach persons in learning to satisfy their needs in socially constructive, reality-oriented ways. (6) Explore their aspirations and help them make and implement a realistic and constructive plan for their future.

Psychiatrist Jerome D. Frank states that persons who have difficulty controlling their impulses need to feel that the therapist has concern for them based on their potentiality: "This concern is best conveyed by a strong attack on the deviant behavior as unworthy of the patient. This type of attack, paradoxically, heightens the patient's self-esteem rather than damages it, because it is obviously based on real concern and respect."[26] Permissiveness, however, makes such a person feel that the therapist is indifferent or does not expect much of him or her. This feeling further hurts already shaky self-esteem. Consistent firmness, called "tough love," is essential in helping such a person.

William Glasser's reality therapy assumes that it is impossible to maintain self-esteem if one is living irresponsibly. Glasser declares, "Morals, standards, values, or right and wrong behavior are all intimately related to the fulfillment of our need for self-worth."[27] His therapy aims at teaching persons to credit themselves when they are right and correct themselves when they are wrong. Self-respect comes through self-discipline and responsible behavior, bringing increased respect from others.

Persons with severe character disorders are exceedingly difficult to help, even by a highly trained psychotherapist. For this reason, clergy are wise not to get involved in attempting to counsel with them unless they have special training and experience in working with this type of counselee. But some people with less severe weaknesses of conscience can benefit from skilled pastoral counseling following confrontational, reality therapy principles. A future orientation is essential in much pastoral counseling, including confrontational counseling. A favorite question in reality therapy is, "What is your plan?" This stimulates constructive thinking about the future. Glasser writes, "We must open up his life, talk about new horizons, expand his range of interests, make him aware of life beyond his difficulties."[28]

Many troubled people do not feel there really is a meaningful future for them. Awakening realistic dreams and making and implementing workable plans to move toward a viable future can be decisive in helping persons break away from the unconstructive patterns of the past. In counseling with persons who have weak inner controls, it is essential to help them discover something about which they can really care. A chaplain who leads group therapy with young adults having a history of behavior problems reports, "I try to find one thing the individual gives a damn about and then build on that!"

Helping Persons with Immature or Undeveloped Consciences

Some adolescents who act out in antisocial ways are not suffering from severe character defects. Instead their difficulty is often simply a retardation of the process by which consciences mature. By identifying with the pastor's more mature conscience, they may be able to gradually unlearn destructive patterns and internalize more constructive ethical guidelines and inner controls. Often, such adolescents do not know how to act in any but an antisocial way. In this case, role-playing alternative scenarios in situations in which the adolescent has been antisocial or in similar situations she or he may encounter is frequently helpful.

An undeveloped conscience may be the outcome of a family atmosphere in which the members, realistically or not, perceive the world as universally hostile or in which members have adopted an attitude of entitlement. In this case it is important, where possible, to involve the family in counseling. Moreover, antisocial behavior may be an adolescent's reaction to abuse or bullying. The pastoral counselor should avoid psychological labeling and investigate the young person's experience of relationships with adults and peers. If there is evidence of any form of abuse, counseling must focus primarily on dealing with the abusive situation rather than on conscience formation.

Helping Persons with Self-righteous Consciences Find Healing

As indicated by Jesus' observations about people with self-righteous consciences, they usually do not seek pastoral help with their own problems.[29] They usually come to talk with a pastoral caregiver about the faults of other people, including family members and the church staff. They often try to persuade counselors to use their authority to make family members shape up, and they criticize the pastor or someone in the congregation for not measuring up to their perfectionistic standards. The real problems, as self-righteous people see the situation, are the other people with their inferior values. The pain and alienation that self-righteousness generates in marriages and other close relationships usually bring this issue to a pastor's attention. As reported in the Synoptic Gospels, Jesus used his strongest confrontation in relating to the self-righteous religious leaders of his day.

People with righteous self-images usually are rigid conformists to conventional morality. They are legalistic and judgmental toward others who disagree with their views of right and wrong. Within religious circles, self-righteous people often misuse the Bible, "proof-texting" to claim divine support for their narrow ethical perspectives.

The familiar line, "Some people don't *have* problems; they *are* problems!" describes many self-righteous people. Actually they also *have* problems. Their self-righteousness is a symptomatic defense, enabling them to avoid facing their own problems. Self-righteousness often is a way of trying to reinforce shaky self-esteem by a sense of moral superiority. Feeling one-up on those perceived as ethically and religiously inferior enables such persons to avoid experiencing their deep feelings of self-rejection and self-judgment. Self-righteousness can also be a way of maintaining a sense of power over others—a spouse or children—and of justifying one's attempts to control them. The need for such feelings of power is a defense against hidden feelings of powerlessness and fear of not being in control. Self-righteousness enables persons to avoid confronting their neurotic guilt and unconscious conflicts about their own sexual and aggressive impulses. In Carl Jung's terms, self-righteousness is a way of disowning their "shadow" side, the dark, rejected, "inferior" part of the personality.[30] Their idealized self-image, character-ized only by light and goodness, is impoverished and threatened by being cut off from the dark, earthy, potentially creative as well as destructive side of themselves.

Helping self-righteous people soften and humanize their defensive conscience and self-image is nearly impossible until they sense some need for help. If they can let them-selves become aware of the exorbitant price they are paying—in the distancing of oth-ers and in their own loneliness and lack of joy—self-righteous people sometimes become open to counseling help. We do well to remind ourselves that some degree of defensive superiority is in most of us. Pastors and church lay leaders are far from immune. In fact, the pietistic and moralistic thrusts in many church traditions tend to encourage persons to maintain an idealized self-image. This makes it difficult to accept their shadow side and integrate it with their "good" side so that the two can balance and enrich each other within their personalities.

Self-righteousness has produced enormous destructiveness in individual lives and in history. Humankind's many tragic wars through the centuries have been fought with self-righteous consciences on both sides, justifying and even honoring the killing of those labeled "the enemy." The murders of many nonconforming religious people labeled "heretics" were perpetrated by self-righteous church leaders for reasons they believed to be both ethical and praiseworthy. The same is true of countless single women who were labeled as "witches" because they were outspoken and refused to conform to the belief systems and demands of the power brokers of organized religious systems. The Nazi per-petrators of the Holocaust claimed at the Nuremburg trials of war criminals only to be obeying their consciences in purifying the Aryan race by systematically destroying mil-lions of Jews and other "inferior" persons, including homosexuals and clergy who refused to accept the Nazi doctrines of hate.

Helping Persons with Undeveloped or Destructive Social Consciences

In the realm of life-guiding values and moral standards, the destructiveness of narrow, hyperindividualistic, in-group-limited ethical belief systems is clear. Such belief systems, often linked with privatized understandings of salvation, usually have little or no beliefs in social issues related to the wider systems of society and the world. Consequently they do not offer effective ethical guidance for individuals or groups on constructive social, political, economic, and ecological behaviors, or constraints on destructive behavior in these crucial value issues. They function with two sets of limiting ethical assumptions. One emphasizes control of and care for those inside their group; the other regards the rest of humankind and the biosphere as outside their circle of concern and caring.

Consider the threats to the well-being of the whole human family inherent in behavior guided by these assumptions, starting with the proliferating national and global problems of poverty, ecojustice, and sustainability. They can be solved only by regional and international ethical constraints and legal controls. Remember that the innumerable ethnic wars raging since the end of the cold war are justified by both sides in these tragic events by in-group ethical assumptions. All these and many other ethical issues point to the dangerous consequences of exclusivist, pathogenic ethical beliefs and codes.

Counseling Persons with Underdeveloped Social Consciences

Many church people have well-developed consciences on personal and interpersonal issues but a flabby, underdeveloped sense of responsibility and caring on social issues. They have a healthy capacity for appropriate guilt in individual relationships but a serious hiatus in feeling appropriate guilt for the oppressiveness of the institutions where they have at least some small influence. They do not experience appropriate guilt concerning our individual and collective sins of omission and commission that contribute to the deadly injustices, the growing gap between the rich and poor nations, the squandering of our planet's limited resources on genocidal weapons, the destructive population explosion, the oppression of women and people of color, and the dehumanizing effects of world hunger and poverty. The privatized consciences of many "good church people" keep them from feeling caring and responsible for human beings beyond their small circles of concern.

Social problems often cause or complicate personal problems. Prophetic confrontation in teaching, preaching, and counseling are essential to help "good people" expand the horizons of their caring and consciences. Consciousness-raising, which helps make the growth-oppressive sins of our institutions and social structures matters of Christian conscience, is essential in counseling for ethical wholeness.

Awakening people in severe crisis to wider concerns is usually impossible until the acute phase of their crisis has passed. Then some can reflect on the social injustices and oppression that underlay the crisis. It is the counselor's responsibility to raise these wider contextual issues. Educative counseling and growth groups offer seldom-used opportunities for such awakening, expanding, and empowering of social consciences. Methods of mobilizing the social dimensions of ethical responsibility and caring will be described in the chapter on educative counseling.

Characteristics of Consciences Supporting Holistic Wellness

Geoff Peterson describes six characteristics of such consciences, as understood in the light of Christ's life and teachings, pointing out that this is an ideal that no one ever achieves fully:[31]

1. *A healthy conscience is a positive, liberated conscience*, liberated through the love of God from subservience to rules and the compulsion to conform to legalistic codes or group pressures. Such a conscience is set free for caring, responsible service.

2. *It is a conscience shaped by participating in Christian community*, particularly in small, conscience-nurturing groups.

3. *It is a continually growing conscience* awakened to renewal by the confrontation of crises that challenge ethical blind spots and let us discover new areas of human need.

4. *It is an integrated conscience*, a call toward the wholeness of one's full humanity.

5. *It is a caring conscience*, helping other persons grow and accepting help in one's own growth.

6. *It is a socially responsible conscience* with a global inclusiveness to its caring.

I would add three characteristics to Peterson's list:

7. *A healthy, maturing conscience is an androgynous conscience*, equally prizing the *human* capacities that women have had to overdevelop in our culture—nurturing, sensitivity to feelings, caring for relationships—and the *human* capacities that men have had to overdevelop—achievement, rationality, technical skills. Wholeness in one's conscience and one's lifestyle as a male or a female must include valuing and developing both sides of our common human capacities.

8. *A healthy conscience today must be oriented to give highest priority to survival values for humankind.*

9. *A healthy conscience includes affirmation and celebration of constructive play and playfulness.*

Helping Persons with Meaning and Value Vacuums

Many people in our society suffer from zestlessness and a lack of dynamic meaning or moving purpose in their lives. There is nothing that they value enough to give them a sense of expectation and excitement when they wake up to a new day. Such chronic existential depression stems from what Viktor Frankl describes as a "value vacuum," a frustration of their basic "will to meaning." His "logotherapy" defines the central task of helping persons as that of enabling them to find a sense of meaning. Frankl's basic thesis is that "life is transformed when a mission worth carrying out is uncovered."[32]

Pastoral counselors encounter many people whose root problem is profound emptiness in the area of meanings and values. Their other problems in living are symptoms of this underlying vacuum. Frankl seeks to help persons find a motivating meaning for their lives in one or more of three kinds of values: (1) *creative values*, which involve doing something worthwhile, such as coaching a student who needs academic help, devising games for children with disabilities, or organizing a youth music group; (2) *experiential values*, derived from experiencing something satisfying such as a sunset, a good marriage, the fragrance of a flower, a precious memory, or the smile of a friend or stranger; and (3) *attitudinal values*, taking a constructive attitude toward whatever situation one is in—even the worst. In exploring this third value, Frankl stresses the "defiant power of the human spirit," the ability to rise above even the diabolic dehumanization of a Nazi death camp by choosing to find some meaning in that situation. The religious person, in his view, is the "one who says 'yes' to life;... who, in spite of everything that life brings, still faces existence with a basic conviction of the worthwhileness of life."[33]

Meaning vacuums occur at the intersection of the theological and value issues in people's lives. An open, energizing relationship with God and a dynamic commitment to a cause that is larger than one's circle of self-centered concerns are complementary, interrelated answers to problems of meaninglessness. Helping counselees find a worthwhile cause that excites them is important because it gives them an integrating purpose and because it may help reduce the social sources of individual problems. As Peterson points out, "For members of the Christian community, their mission will be a part of the mission of the church, which is to cooperate with God's saving work in the world. All such healing work may be seen as a part of the creative transformation that Christ is continually effecting in human life."[34]

When life "goes flat," as one client put it, it probably is a signal that one needs to rethink and revise one's priorities and values, and the lifestyle they create. Here are some questions designed to help couples or individuals discuss and revise their guiding values:

1. Do my (our) values and priorities, and the lifestyle they produce, allow me (us) to maintain robust physical-emotional health?
2. Do my (our) values and lifestyle allow me (us) time to develop my (our) potential—intellectually and spiritually?
3. Do my (our) values and lifestyle allow me (us) time to enjoy the good things of life and to do the creative, worthwhile, and fulfilling things I (we) could do?
4. Do my (our) present values and lifestyle leave me (us) enough time with the person or persons I (we) care most about?
5. Does my (our) lifestyle reflect the most significant and life-giving values? Maslow calls these "B-Values" (B for Being)—truth, goodness, beauty, wholeness, aliveness, justice, order, simplicity, playfulness, and autonomy.
6. Do my (our) values and lifestyle allow me (us) time for a significant cause, a challenge beyond my (our) inner circle, that will help others and improve our community?
7. Are my (our) values and lifestyle consistent with sound survival values (such as conservation of natural resources) for the whole human family of which I (we) am a part?[35]

Professional Ethical Guidelines for Caregivers

The personal ethical integrity of clergy, like their personal spirituality, has an impact on every aspect of their ministry. This is especially true of their caregiving on ethical issues. For better or for worse, the ethical lessons that caregivers teach by their own ethical attitudes and behavior are more important than what they say in words about these ethical issues. Here are some guidelines for the ethics of care and counseling by pastors and other caregivers:

- Exercise unwavering respect for the confidentiality of whatever is communicated in counseling relationships.
- Ask and gain permission from care receivers, preferably in writing, before sharing anything about them with others, including family members and professionals.
- Report threats or acts of homicide, suicide, domestic violence, and child endangerment, as required by the laws governing them, after informing care receivers why this is necessary.
- Never engage in behavior that could be understood as being sexual or otherwise exploitative of care receivers.
- Keep in a locked file careful records of all counseling sessions, recording process notes, and the essential facts, but not confidential information, recognizing that such records sometimes are required by courts to be made available in contentious litigation.
- Take prompt action to correct and, if appropriate, request forgiveness from the care receivers involved for any ethical failures on the caregiver's part. A full discussion of laws regarding clergy ethical boundary violations, privileged communication by clergy, and reducing legal risks to caregivers through the type of records kept is available in Aaron Liberman and Michael Woodruff's book *Risk Management*.[36]

Reality Practice Skill Development Session

Parishioner's role options: (1) Become aware of an area of ethical conflict or puzzlement within your own thinking and feelings. Discuss this with the pastor. (2) You were a young soldier who killed several young enemy soldiers during a war some years ago. There was also "collateral damage" in which innocent children were killed. Come to the pastor for help with the agony of your guilt or shame. (3) You are a young adult. During your teens, you rebelled against the rigid moral code of your fundamentalist family. Seek help from the pastor with your feelings of intense guilt about your behavior, particularly in the areas of sex and drugs.

Pastor's role: Use the counseling approaches described in this chapter as you seek to help one of these persons.

Observer-coach's role: Include as one part of your coaching feedback your observations on how the pastor's values influenced the way she or he responded to the parishioner on value issues. (To increase awareness of the interaction during this session, audio-record it and then play back significant dialogue.)

Recommended Reading

Clements, William M., and Howard W. Stone. *Theological Context for Pastoral Caregiving: Word in Deed.* New York: Haworth Press, 1996.

Feddler, Kyle. *Exploring Christian Ethics: Biblical Foundations for Morality.* Louisville: Westminster John Knox Press, 2006.

Green, Thomas F. *Voices: The Educational Formation of Conscience.* South Bend, Ind.: University of Notre Dame Press, 2003.

Nouwen, Henri J. M. *The Wounded Healer: Ministry in Contemporary Society.* New York: Doubleday, 1979.

CHAPTER 12

CRISIS COUNSELING AND ENRICHMENT WITH COUPLES

God is love, and those who abide in love abide in God.
—1 John 4:16

A faithful friend is the medicine of life.
—Ecclesiasticus 6:16

A relationship hemmed in love is less likely to unravel.
—Thought of the Week at a YMCA

Relationship counseling and enrichment skills are crucially important for the effectiveness of pastoral caregivers. A reasonable degree of expertise in all types of care and counseling is essential, but skills in relationship enrichment and crisis counseling need to have especially high priority. Several interrelated factors combine to make this true.

The opportunities in this area tend to be frequent. Only requests for crisis and grief caregiving rival those of individuals seeking help for close relationships. Pastors, more than any other caregiving professionals, are in a strategic position to do couple care and counseling. The settings within which they function as leaders of faith communities provide frequent and natural entrées to many family systems. Their professional role gives them continuing contacts with couples in the successive stages and stress points of the entire family life cycle.

The role of pastors as educators enables them to teach relationship-nurturing insights and skills now available in the burgeoning communication and conflict-resolution field. Such teaching often can help prevent or lessen the length and severity of couple problems. It also plants seeds that may flower in counseling opportunities when family crises strike. In my experience, an insightful, caring sermon or talk on marriage and other relationship issues frequently produces counseling opportunities. The importance of marriage and family skills is underlined by the fact that more than half of those who seek pastoral counseling seek help for marriage crises, parent-child issues, or other relationship problems.

Another factor making it essential for pastors to develop competence in this area is that precious human values often are at stake. A healthy, growing marriage or deep friendship with moments of joy and ecstasy mingled with times of conflict and pain often is as close to heaven on earth as many of us finite human beings will come. Conversely, a fractured marriage with mutually destructive relationships can be a close approximation of hell on earth. The stakes indeed are often very high in relationship caregiving!

Radical Changes in Women's and Men's Identities and Relationships

Relationship healing and enhancement skills are so crucial because of the contemporary crisis in intimate relationships. Symptoms of the crisis include high rates of divorce; family desertion; spousal battering; emotional and sexual child abuse, including incest; and youth delinquency and suicide, as well as widespread marital boredom and unhappiness among couples who continue to live alone together.

Many of these problems are derived from the fact that the institution of marriage is in radical and unprecedented transition. Traditional models are being challenged and rejected today as never before. Profound changes are occurring at an accelerating pace in female-male roles, relationships, power dynamics, work options, and both personal and couple identities. More and more women are insisting appropriately that they have equal opportunity to discover, develop, and use their God-given potentiality in careers *and* homemaking. They are expecting to participate equally in the decision making of their families. These expectations are threatening many men's vulnerable sense of security. These changes shake and often shatter the foundations of increasing numbers of traditional marriages.

The prediction made some time ago by my spouse, Charlotte Ellen, a psychotherapist and marriage counselor, has proved to be true in subsequent years:

> It is likely that we have thus far seen only the tip of the iceberg in the upheaval in relationships between women and men. Marriage relationships are especially vulnerable and responsive to changing roles and identities. More and more marriages will feel the pain and the excitement of change. It may be that the divorce rate will rise even higher as many couples struggle unsuccessfully to develop more satisfying marriage styles. At the same time, many couples will succeed in discovering the gains in more egalitarian and companionable marriages. Counselors of all disciplines can have a positive role in helping redefine the institution of marriage and in helping couples to develop creative and growth-producing relationships.[1]

The complexities and pressures of two-career marriages are faced by more and more couples in Western societies today. Because of economic necessity and/or the desire to have a fulfilling career, the majority of women now work for pay outside the home. This trend is complicated by the lack of wide availability of reliable, safe child care. A marriage relationship becoming more egalitarian is potentially more fulfilling for both women and men. But such relationships also are considerably more complicated and conflict prone than traditional marriages. This is particularly true for the countless couples who lack role models in their parents from which they could learn how to make an egalitarian relationship work. The widespread search by couples for more flexible and creative ways to be married and the rejection of rigidly defined sex roles will increase both marital conflict and the need for marriage care and counseling in the twenty-first century.

Remarriage, stepparenting, and blended families have become major phenomena in Western industrialized societies in our times. Countless marriages involve at least one formerly married person. Furthermore, major changes have occurred in attitudes and practices regarding sexual freedom and cohabitation, with more than a million unmarried couples living together, often in committed relationships. Much more effective methods of birth control and family planning, and the demand for equality by women, have drastically reduced and eventually may eradicate the male-female double standard of sexual freedom. However, the epidemic of AIDS and other STDs (sexually transmitted diseases) has put needed restraints on the exercise of this freedom. In addition, there is a continuing decline in the support available to couples and nuclear families from their extended families, making them more vulnerable during crises.

On top of all these issues is the fact that a promising but more demanding marriage style has emerged. It might be described as *the mutually fulfilling marriage*. Many couples report that they chose marriage mainly because of the expectation that it would provide a deeply satisfying relationship, meaningful communication, and personal growth.[2] This bumper sticker reflects what probably will be a futile effort to bring the exaggerated expectations of such couples down to earth: "Men are from earth. Women are from earth. Deal with it!" When couples enter marriage with unrealistic expectations about marriage and without the relationship-building communication skills required to fulfill even modest expectations, disillusionment is inevitable. This disappointment, coupled with the increased willingness of couples to end unsatisfying marriages, feeds the rising incidence of marital separation, desertion, and divorce.

Furthermore, couple counseling to help couples adjust constructively to the different life-cycle stages is complicated by societal changes in the life cycle itself. Dramatic increases in expected longevity create new problems and new possibilities for couples and families. The advances in electronic communication and reproductive technologies, together with continuing transformations in gender roles and cross-cultural partnerships, and the wider acceptance of same-sex committed relationships, raise many new issues for caregivers.[3] All these factors emphasize the growing importance of relational caregiving skills.

The Objectives of Relationship Caregiving

The ultimate goal of holistic pastoral care and counseling is cultivating spiritually centered wholeness; that is, nurturing well-being in all the interdependent dimensions of people's lives, including their relationships with themselves, other people, social institutions, and God's creation. This model of care and counseling is essentially relationship oriented because both healing and growth in wholeness are always relational. Fulfillment pursued without concern for the well-being of the social and ecological contexts of individuals' lives becomes a psychological cul-de-sac. Such egocentric striving does not create genuine wholeness.

In light of this, wholeness-oriented relational counseling and enrichment have as their fundamental objective enabling people to learn how to grow wholeness-creating love in all their close relationships, including marriages and families. Healthy, healing love in any relationship can be defined simply as *mutual caring about and commitment to enabling each other's fullest possible becoming* by using more of their gifts and potentials. Stated in religious language, such love involves enabling each other to discover and develop life in all its fullness using as many as possible of the gifts and graces that God has given them. This is a valuable working definition that can be used by couples as well as by counselors to evaluate any relationship in terms of how mutually growth producing it is. In light of this definition, the bottom-line objective of wholeness-oriented couple counseling and enrichment (including premarital educative counseling) is to *help couples learn how to cultivate healthy mutual love in their relationships.* To do this, couples are coached in creating ways of relating by which each person discovers and develops more of the latent strengths, resources, and gifts as individuals and in their shared relationship.

The ideal objective of relationship caregiving is to enable people to create covenants of mutual wholeness in which they develop and implement mutual plans to support each other—the dream of wholeness that God has for them as unique individuals. In covenantal relationships, persons take responsibility for keeping their side of the relationship growing and also offering support and encouragement for the other.

The spiritual goal of relationship caregiving is illuminated by the insights of the relational philosopher Martin Buber, who once observed, "All real living is meeting."[4] He distinguished *I-Thou* from *I-It* relationships. The former is meeting and seeing others as being of inestimable value in their unique selves and not as means to any end. Genuine dialogue occurs when two people meet and communicate as two Thous. In such I-Thou moments we humans encounter God insofar as our souls are nourished by this quality of relating. I-It relationships, however, are meetings when the other is viewed as a means to an end, as an object to be used. Although both I-Thou and I-It relating are essential in human relationships, and although we humans move back and forth between them, in Buber's terms, the ultimate goal of relational caregiving is to enhance the ability of persons to increase the I-Thou moments in their most important relationships.

The Many Facets of Intimacy

Another way to describe the basic objective of holistic couple caregiving is to enable them to cultivate whole-person intimacy in relationships. In our society, many people think of intimacy between couples as limited to sexual closeness and sharing. This certainly can be a pleasurable arena of intimacy, but it is only one of several. Holistic intimacy is like a musical instrument with many strings. The music that couples make together is created by their playing on a variety and combination of strings. The following overview suggests the possibilities for creative closeness in marriages and other close committed relationships. Caregivers can use this as a checklist to encourage care receivers to deepen their relationships by developing more facets of intimacy, pointing out that this is the way to strengthen and deepen their love:

- Sexual intimacy = erotic sharing of mutual pleasure
- Emotional intimacy = being tuned with empathy to each other's wavelength
- Spiritual intimacy = shared spirituality that deepens other interests
- Intellectual intimacy = exploring the exciting world of ideas together
- Aesthetic intimacy = sharing experience of beauty in music and the arts
- Creative intimacy = collaborating in the adventure of creating
- Recreational intimacy = enjoying the fun of playing together
- Work intimacy = closeness in sharing common tasks and goals
- Crisis intimacy = closeness in coping with problems and losses
- Conflict intimacy = overcoming differences by no-lose compromises
- Commitment intimacy = mutuality from shared values and causes
- Communication intimacy = the prerequisite for enhancing all other types of intimacy

Strategies for Turbulent Times of Relational Transition

Silver linings often can be found hidden behind the storm clouds produced by the radical changes in family life today. More than ever before in history, behind the increased conflicts there are positive but frustrated strivings for more in-depth relationships. These unexpected benefits can be actualized when relationship crises are reframed by those involved so that they transform these crises into growth opportunities.

How can people be helped to learn how to develop such silver linings in relationships affected by the current crises in marriage and family life? Clergy and congregations need to develop innovative programs with three strategic dimensions: the first is a vigorous, *preventive education* program, consisting of a variety of attractive marriage enrichment and creative singlehood events. These may include classes, workshops, retreats, and camps. The second needed program dimension is *relationship crisis counseling*, consisting of short-term marriage and family counseling for those going through crises that bring severe stresses. The third programmatic dimension is making *effective referrals* of couples and families who need help to persons with the special training and time to do relational therapies, including those focusing on marriage, divorce, and remarriage, as well as family therapy. This chapter will explore the first two of these dimensions—preventive education and short-term crisis counseling for relationships caught in interpersonal storms.

Each of these three dimensions can be made to undergird, complement, and help make people aware of the other two. Marriage enrichment and educational counseling can increase the growthfulness of many reasonably adequate marriages. Marriage crisis counseling can help some couples face their problems and resolve them in growthful ways. In deeply disturbed marriages, marital therapy is essential. A marriage enrichment program will enable some couples needing marital counseling or therapy to seek this help sooner. It does this by making them more aware of the painful inadequacies of their current relationship and the possibility that their marriage can become less frustrating and more mutually satisfying. The long-term effects of marriage counseling can be enhanced significantly by referring couples who complete counseling to marriage support and growth groups or to regular enrichment events that will support their continuing growth.

For parish pastors, chaplains, and other generalists in ministry it is important to learn how to distinguish couples and families who can be helped by brief relational crisis counseling from those who require long-term marriage or family therapy. Many couples with reasonably functional relationships can be thrown off keel by a severe crisis—a serious illness, the loss of a job by the sole or primary breadwinner, or the death of a family member. The pain of continuing mutual need deprivation leads to verbal attacks, diminished communication, counterattacks, and spiraling resentments and distancing. But a few crisis counseling sessions are often adequate to enable such functional couples to pull out of their relational tailspin, to mobilize their coping resources, and to work together enough to learn how to handle their crises more constructively.

In contrast, couples with chronically dysfunctional relationships dominated by neurotic interaction usually require more than short-term crisis counseling. They need marriage and/or family therapy to enable them to renegotiate their basic contract and thus rebuild their relationships on a stronger foundation. In addition, some who seek marriage counseling are so disturbed in their personalities that they must have individual psychotherapy before or concurrently with relational therapy. The task of those in general ministries is to assist such persons in finding competent help from specialists trained in the particular therapies they need.

Referral to a clinical member of the American Association of Pastoral Counselors (9508a Lee Highway, Fairfax, Virginia 22031; 703-385-6967; aapc.org) or the American Association for Marriage and Family Therapy (1717 K Street, N.W., #407, Washington, D.C. 20006; 202-429-1825; www.aamft.org) is required in such cases.

Understanding the Dynamics of Couple Interaction

The effectiveness of relational caregiving depends to a considerable degree on understanding the dynamics of marriages and other committed interpersonal relationships. This means developing awareness of the dynamic forces in such relationships—including those that cause partners to be attracted to and to become bonded with each other—and forces that cause love, growth, and mutual satisfaction, or stagnation, conflict, and alienation, in those relationships.

Of course all marriages, even the healthiest, like all individuals, have problems and conflicts. The pioneer psychiatrist Harry Stack Sullivan,[5] who developed the interpersonal relationship understanding of that field, once expressed this with a touch of humor: "I have yet to find a marriage which has only satisfactions and only securities. . . . If a person tells me his home-life is perfect, I take off my glasses, which means I can't see him, and gaze at him, and say, 'Extra-ordinary!' I then pass on to some other topic but I return to this later."[6]

Here is an overview of relationship dynamics. Two persons meet, begin to relate, and may eventually move into a committed relationship such as marriage. Their interaction before and during the course of their marriage results in the creation of a new psychological entity, namely, *their relationship.* This new entity, called the "identity of the marital pair" by family therapy pioneer Nathan W. Ackerman, includes what each brought to the relationship, including genetic background, needs, problems, personality patterns and resources, expectations, and hopes; but these develop into much more through the persons' interaction in responding to what the other is and becomes in the process of interacting.[7] Out of the intricacies of their relating on many levels emerges a unique creation—their marriage relationship. Then when couples have a child, their marriage identity is changed radically. It is enlarged if other children are born. What evolves is a new creation—the family identity. The characteristics and dynamics of this family system influence everything about its members as they change and interact through the years. Its unique and implicit rules and definitions of attitudes and behaviors shape their development.

Marriage enrichment, counseling, and therapy focus on healing relationship broken-ness and enhancing relationship wholeness. They do not focus mainly, as in most indi-vidual psychotherapy, on resolving intrapsychic personality conflicts. In relationship counseling and therapy, the disturbed relationship per se becomes the object of treat-ment. It is the "client." As a relationship becomes more constructive, the individuals who compose it become freer to change. Two persons are attracted to each other because each hopes that the relationship will satisfy a variety of heart hungers—meaning physi-cal, mental, emotional, relational, and sexual needs. Each brings a unique pattern of per-sonality needs to the relationship. These needs must receive at least minimal satisfaction if the person is to be capable of satisfying the partner's and the children's needs. A happy marriage or other close, committed relationship is one where there is a relatively high degree of mutual need satisfaction. Conversely, an unhappy relationship has a high degree of mutual need deprivation. If a relationship produces chronic, unmet emotional hungers, it will diminish the self-esteem and general well-being of those involved, result-ing in rejection, anger, and aggression.

The particular need-pattern that one brings to marriage depends to a large degree on the personality-molding experiences with need-satisfying adults in one's early life. Relational conflict is fundamentally the conflict of two need systems: the needs of one person colliding with the needs of the other. For example, Joan and Larry have been married three years, and each has an incompatible need to "parentify" the other. Each wants the other to be the all-loving parent both lacked in childhood. Their needs to be the child in a child-parent dependency relationship are mutually contradictory.

The conflicts in many marriages are rooted in the unrealistic hopes and expectations that people project on each other from their need-depriving childhood experiences. Excessive expectations are also derived from cultural stereotypes.

How Childhood Wounds Affect Adult Relationships

Because of severe early life need deprivation, many people bring *neurotic needs* (as contrasted with normal needs) to their intimate relationships. A neurotic need has two characteristics: (1) it is an *exaggeration* of a normal need, so much so that no one could possibly satisfy it, and (2) it is *ambivalent* or conflicted. On a conscious level, the person desires one thing; on an unconscious level, just the opposite! This inner contradiction makes interpersonal conflict inevitable. The person is always frustrated because it's impossible to eat one's cake and have it too. The counselor's awareness of such self-contradictory need patterns may help couples understand and interrupt their painful marital battles.

Carl was raised by a cold, wounded mother and a judgmental, emotionally distant father, neither of whom could feed their children's personality hungers. As a result, Carl, now in his late twenties, has an insatiable craving for reassurance, warmth, and emotional feeding. To him, normal amounts of affection from his wife, Patricia, provide an inadequate emotional diet. Unfortunately Patricia finds it difficult to give Carl even moderate amounts of emotional food. In spite of a warm exterior, she is remarkably like his mother in her underlying personality. Why was Carl attracted to a person who could not meet his needs? Because he has other, conflicting needs. He needs to be dependent, but he also needs to feel supermanly. His powerful dependency needs make him feel weak and unmasculine. To protect himself from these intolerable feelings, he must deny his dependence and strive for an exaggerated self-made-man independence. His fear of his dependency prevented him from marrying someone who could give him generous nurturing. On an unconscious level, Patricia has a parallel conflicted need system that drew her to Carl.

Let's look more deeply at how early life need deprivation influences the relationship of adults. All children have the need to be loved unconditionally by their parents, to feel safe, secure, and respected. They also need to not fear being abandoned, to know that they can accomplish their goals successfully and that others are proud of them. But because all parents are imperfect human beings, everyone experiences some degree of deprivation of these needs in childhood. If this deprivation is severe, the leftover unmet needs persist in adults in greatly exaggerated form. Such wounded people keep struggling to get insatiable needs met in relationships, even though they are so exaggerated that no one could satisfy them. These ghostly needs from the past are a major reason that self-help and short-term crisis counseling don't work for some couples. Instead the skills of a therapist trained in both individual and relationship skills are needed to help them learn how to make their relationships more mutually constructive, fulfilling, and loving.

The philosopher Schopenhauer told an insightful fable about two porcupines who alternately huddled together to avoid freezing and were pushed away by the pain from each other's quills. Some couples suffer from what might be called "the freezing porcupines' dilemma." As one troubled couple put it, "We live alone together." Such persons usually have an intense need for closeness, yet cannot risk it. Their defensive distancing results in failure to develop, by practice, the interpersonal skills needed to make close relationships satisfying. If people suffer from such childhood blocks to intimacy, personal and/or couple therapy may be necessary to help them unlearn intimacy-blocking responses while learning relationship-building skills and practice them in a safe therapeutic relationship. Fortunately, overcoming blocks to emotional closeness can prevent wounded persons from adopting a distancing or loner stance as an ongoing but very impoverishing lifestyle. This equips them to develop the intimate reciprocal relationships that people— single and in relationship—need for their wholeness, happiness, and well-being.

Guidelines for Reducing Conflict and Keeping Love Growing in Relationships

Holistic pastoral caregivers should balance their relationship crisis counseling with innovative strategies aimed at positive prevention of destructive conflict and mutually damaging spirals of verbal or physical violence in close relationships. The primary means of implementing this preventive ministry is relationship enhancement education.

Here are some time-tested guidelines for strengthening marriages, families, deep friendships, and other committed relationships. The guidelines are worded here so as to address couples. As such, they can be used as a resource in enrichment events or by couples as a do-it-yourself checklist to guide them in intentionally cultivating mutual need satisfaction, happiness, and love in their relationships. This list can be used by couples during or between sessions of enrichment events to identify areas where they need to nurture their love by doing growth work together. It is important to invite couples to improve the list for themselves by adding other items that express their particular needs and dreams:

- Set aside regular time to communicate what really matters to each of you, remembering that open communication is to a relationship what oxygen is to your bodies.
- Balance responding mutually to each other's basic needs with regular self-care to maintain your own wellness and thus be able to respond to each other's needs.
- Recognize and affirm the strengths and assets in each other and in your relationship. Do this regularly with warmth and caring.
- Keep the wall of unresolved anger, hurt, and resentment from growing between you by discussing disagreements and negotiating fair, win-win compromises to resolve inevitable conflicts in just, egalitarian ways.
- Provide equal opportunities for each person to discover and develop her or his unused strengths and possibilities.
- Let your child sides play together regularly; learn to laugh *at* yourself and *with* each other. Give yourselves several minivacations each day by taking some time to enjoy brief renewing times of relaxation and fun together.
- Enrich your emotional, spiritual, and intellectual life by practices such as reading books and magazines, listening to music, viewing or participating in art, reading or writing poetry, and being nurtured by nature. Also enrich your

inner life by practicing the spiritual disciplines you find satisfying. In all these and other ways you will develop more to share and to give to each other in your most vital relationships.

- Develop your mutual-support groups. Do this as individuals and as a couple.
- Create healthy spaces in your togetherness. Do this by balancing your times together with times by yourself and times with others. Dietrich Bonhoeffer's insight about this balance applies to couple relationships: "Let him who cannot be alone beware of community.... Let him who is not in community beware of being alone."[8] "Blessed is he who is alone in the strength of the fellowship."
- Find a cause bigger than yourselves and your relationship to share—a way of responding to the needs of your community and your world.
- Regularly revise and update your relationship covenant or "working agreement" between you to keep it fair, current, and as mutually satisfying as possible. Do this before your working agreement is not working as well as each of you would like. (An instrument for use in accomplishing this is the Relationship Satisfaction-Justice Inventory found later in this chapter.)
- Develop and implement an intentional growth plan for your relationship; choose growth goals that will improve your relationship in the ways you both want, and commit yourselves to concrete action plans. In this way you take charge of creating a better future for your relationship.

If you don't have time to do things like some of the above, you may need to check and revise your priorities—or find a reliable babysitter. If do-it-yourself methods don't work, remember that it's a sign of your strength to seek the help of a counselor or therapist trained in relationship-strengthening methods.[9]

Making Relationship Enrichment and Counseling Liberating

The deepest intimacy, including the most satisfying sexual intimacy, is psychologically possible only in relationships of genuine equality. For this reason the increasing liberation of women and men from the growth-limiting bonds of traditional one-up/one-down roles opens new possibilities for deepening love. Close relationships in which women feel exploited and disempowered by dominating males produce distancing, hiding, and hot or cold anger in many women. This dynamic inhibits deep, honest communication, the kind that generates mutually growth-producing intimacy. Patriarchal values produce relationships in which many women feel exploited and diminished.

But we men also are exploited by the present male success system, and we're also depriving ourselves of much of our personhood by the male rat race. This situation points to a crucial prophetic issue in caregiving—*human* liberation including both women and men. The prophetic caregiving justice goal is to cultivate values, institutions, and relationships in which both women and men have the greatest possible opportunities and resources to use their full intelligence, creativity, and productive energies. We who do marriage enrichment and counseling should be proactive in modeling and overcoming sexism, a central cause of diminished and destructive marriages. We can do this by struggling to create, and help others create, equal and mutually empowering relationships.

Sexism is a central cause of both diminished and destructive marriages. The institutional male chauvinism inherent in our society and in most churches and theologies militates against such liberating marriage counseling and enrichment. Theologically we must take seriously the liberating insight of Paul that in Christ there is neither male nor female (Gal. 3:28). That is, understanding that one's humanity, not one's gender, is what really matters. To be instruments of human liberation, relationship counselors must have a raised consciousness in the area of both women's and men's full liberation.[10] A pro-feminist orientation is invaluable in understanding and enhancing the dynamics of marriages and family life today. Pro-feminism is based on an understanding illuminated by the insights of studies of gender relationships and human dynamics by feminist scholars and practitioners of family life education. These scholars are aware of the pervasive, wholeness-diminishing impact of sexism in the lives of both women and men.

An experienced marriage therapist with keen insights, Carmen Knudson-Martin, declared,

> There is growing evidence that institutionally based, stereotypic gender differences are detrimental to mental health and to couple relationships. Men have been encouraged to deny their dependency needs and the emotionality available to them has been restricted, leading to behavior that is both self-destructive and hurtful to others. On the other hand, living in a context that devalues their experiences and limits their voices has contributed to problems such as depression, anxiety addictions, and eating disorders among women. Stereotypic gender differences are common among distressed couples but virtually disappear among successful ones. And, equality appears to be crucial to the establishment of intimacy.

She highlights the role of religion in these dynamics: "Family and religion constitute major venues through which male and female roles are defined, maintained and changed, and within which women and men create themselves."[11]

Operational Goals of Short-term Couple Crisis Counseling

Short-term crisis counseling as well as longer-term relationship therapy with persons suffering from relational problems share a common overall objective. This is to enable couples to learn how to make their relationships more mutually need satisfying and thereby more loving and growth nurturing. To help them accomplish this objective, certain operational goals should be in the counselor's mind during the helping process. The counselor seeks to help couples do the following:

Reopen their blocked communication lines, and learn more effective communication skills that are essential for accomplishing all the other goals.

Interrupt the escalating, self-perpetuating cycle of mutual attack, retaliation, and violence fed by the pain and anger derived from couples' severe frustration of mutual need satisfaction. To accomplish this, they usually must become somewhat aware of the futility and self-sabotaging consequences of their own behavior, including their efforts to reform each other. They must also be helped to adopt more constructive communication patterns, including the one expressed in the biblical wisdom about conflict resolution: "A gentle answer turns away wrath, but a harsh word stirs up anger" (Prov. 15:1 NIV).

Become aware of what they still value in their relationship and thus awaken hope and enable them to identify the latent strengths and unused assets that they can learn to use to make constructive changes in themselves and their marriage.

Identify specific areas where constructive change and growth must occur in each person's behavior in order to interrupt their crisis and move toward making their marriage more mutually need fulfilling.

Negotiate and then implement fair and workable plans for change in which both persons take responsibility for altering their side of the interaction between them. This often involves renegotiating some clauses of their marriage covenant. In this process, couples are helped to mobilize their latent coping resources, learning new problem-solving skills, especially constructive conflict resolution, and thus raise the level of mutual satisfaction in the relationship.

In doing the above, couples are coached in learning how to negotiate fair compromises that enable them to recognize that in a close relationship when one person loses or wins repeatedly, both persons lose. Marriage and family relationships prosper when couples learn the communication skills of negotiating win-win compromises. In such agreements, people meet in the middle, satisfying some but not all of each person's hopes and desires. Coaching people in how to find win-win solutions is a crucial part of conflict-reducing relationship enrichment as well as crisis counseling.

Identify and then revise by renegotiation the aspects of the marital contract that either person regards as unjust, unsatisfying, or unworkable.

Reawaken the energy-for-change in the dawning of reality-based hope for constructive change. Realistic hope is generated in three ways in counseling. It is first caught empathetically from the counselor's expectation that the couple has the capacity to change and grow. Hope is next nourished by counselees' increased awareness of the strengths and assets with which they can rebuild malfunctioning aspects of their relationship. Hope then is strengthened and reinforced as they actually change self-hurting behavior patterns in and between themselves. Constructive change generates realistic hope, and hope generates further change.

Couple therapy shares the goals of crisis counseling just enumerated. But in addition, this therapy involves

- more extensive learning of relationship-building and conflict-reducing skills;
- more basic revising of the relationship covenant—because this working contract clearly is not working;
- dealing with relationship-diminishing fantasies, conflicts, fears, and anger left in adults from childhood wounds (individual psychotherapeutic sessions may be needed concurrently with joint couple sessions to facilitate this individual and relational healing and growth);
- discovering, and to some degree, correcting the unconscious roots of conflicted role images as well as exaggerated and conflicted wants and needs, rooted in their childhood need deprivation.

Because of these additional goals, this therapy usually is longer term.

The Process of Couple Crisis Counseling

What occurs during the first contact in counseling and therapy often determines whether the foundation is laid for a workable therapeutic relationship. During the first session of couple crisis counseling, the following should be done:

If only one member of the couple has come to the session, do everything possible to have a session with both parties in order to focus on the relationship and gain some understanding of how each of them sees their problem.

Communicate warmth, caring, and a willingness to help. Also affirm them for their courage in seeking counseling help.

Find out how each feels about being there: why each person decided to come now, and what each wants, fears, expects, and hopes for from counseling. This dialogue usually lets the counselor discover the motivation of each person for getting counseling and how much each wants to continue the marriage. What if one person seems to be on the verge of deciding to terminate the relationship? If so, ask whether that person is willing to continue counseling for at least a few sessions aimed at discovering if the marriage can be transformed enough to make it more satisfying and less frustrating for both parties.

Help motivate them, especially the less-motivated partner who may have been nagged or dragged to come for counseling. Do this by building rapport with them and seeking to awaken realistic hope for more satisfaction and less pain in the marriage.

Discover how long the crisis or problems have been going on. Is the alienation chronic and protracted, or do they have periods of warmth and closeness between crises? If they suffer with a chronic, long-term pattern of severe problems, it is unlikely that short-term crisis counseling will provide the help they need.

Provide balanced opportunities for each person to describe the problems, express feelings, and say what changes must occur (usually in the other) to make the marriage better for them.

After their anger and hurt have been expressed enough to reduce the pressure from these intense feelings, find out what, if anything, each person still values about the marriage and about each other. The counselor should then affirm whatever positive feelings are still present in their relationship. Explain that these can provide a foundation on which they can be helped during counseling to rebuild their caring love.

Make a tentative decision, based on what has been discovered, about whether to recommend short-term marriage crisis counseling or to refer the couple to a marital therapist. If after three or four sessions of crisis counseling, the couple have made no constructive movement, they probably need longer-term marital and/or individual therapy.

If short-term counseling seems likely to help, ask the couple to agree to come for three or four additional sessions with the expectation that at the end of that series, they and the counselor will decide what is needed. If in the initial session it is obvious that a referral is needed, explain why and assure the couple that the counselor will assist them in finding the specialized help needed.

If a joint decision is made to continue counseling, give the couple some small, constructive action to do between sessions, explaining that it may help them move toward making their relating more mutually satisfying.

Near the close of the first session (and also other sessions), ask them how they feel about what has occurred. Drawing out and accepting any negative feelings they may have tend to reduce premature terminations by couples.

Use prayer or other religious resources only if these clearly are appropriate with a particular couple. Shape such resources to relate to their issues.

After each interview, counselors should reflect on what was learned and make tentative plans for next steps in helping the couple. If the situation is confusing, pastors should seek clarification by checking with a professional consultant or a more experienced colleague who is qualified to serve as a peer consultant.

IRM—A Relationship Self-help Tool

Here is a simple, highly useful communication exercise called the "Intentional Relationship Method" (IRM). It is designed to help couples and others increase mutual satisfaction and thus reduce mutually hurtful conflicts. Since it was first developed several decades ago,[12] it has proved repeatedly to have invaluable uses in a variety of settings. This IRM is really a communication paradigm that can be used productively in any close relationship; for example, by couples in marriage enrichment events, in prewedding educative counseling sessions, or in couple and family counseling sessions. It has also been adapted effectively for use in nonfamily events such as staff meetings, congregational leader planning retreats, and other working relationships, as well as church membership training classes. Usually those who learn to use it effectively value it greatly. Some decide to repeat it regularly on their own; for example, around their wedding anniversaries. It enables counselees and participants in educational counseling events to learn a paradigm for communicating constructively to prevent or resolve conflicts and increase their appreciation of the strengths in themselves, each other, and their relationships. In their evaluations of relationship enrichment events, couples rated this communication exercise as "most helpful" of the various relationship enhancement tools they had learned. The exercise is most productive when done with a relationship partner—friend-friend, wife-husband, lover-lover, colleague-colleague, parent-adult child, and so on. But using it alone, persons gain insight about how to develop more loving and mutually enriching intimate relationships.

Instructions: This do-it-yourselves communication tool has four steps that can evolve into a continuing process. The instructions are presented here as they might be described to participants in a couples' enrichment workshop, retreat, or seminar. (They would have been asked beforehand to bring a small notebook for use to facilitate relational enhancement during and following the event.) Here then are the instructions. (Bear in mind that the slash mark [/] means pause for a short time while you complete what has been asked.)

Step One: Begin by Identifying, Affirming, and Enjoying the Strengths and Assets in Your Relationship—The Things You Have Going for You

Find a comfortable place to sit facing each other, on the floor if you like. / To get ready for this step, you may find it helpful to jot down in your notebook the major things you like and are thankful for in the other person and your relationship. / Now, one of you complete the sentence, "I appreciate in you..." as many times as you can. (Put aside the things you wish were different, focusing only on what you appreciate.) The recipient should listen without responding verbally. Just listen carefully and enjoy the warm glow of being affirmed by your partner. / Now reverse roles as the recipient shares the things he or she appreciates. / When both persons have completed step one, take a few minutes to share your feelings. / You'll probably discover that this step enhances your helpful awareness of what you have going for you. These are the strengths and assets in your relationship on which you can build as you decide on positive changes that make your good relationship even better.

I trust that you discovered, as you took this step on your growth journey, the pleasure and the healing power of caring appreciation. If you enjoyed this mutual affirmation, you can nurture your love and heal hurts by doing this regularly. Starting on this positive note, rather than focusing on the wounds in your relationship, provides a firm foundation for constructive changes, including mutual forgiveness. In contrast, focusing first on nursing a grudge or clinging to a hurt tends to continue the process of mutually hurting.

Step Two: Identify the Growing Edge Issues in Your Relationship

This step enables you to state explicitly and reflect on your needs and wants that are areas of potential growth as well as conflict in your relationship. There is room for improvement, of course, in even healthy, basically happy relationships. The second step enables you to zero in on issues that will cause you to grow together intentionally if you choose. To develop a relational growth plan carefully, become aware of the things you wish were changed in the other person or your relationship. / Now one of you complete the sentence, "I want or need from you . . ." as many times as you can. State your unmet or partially met needs or wants in terms of the behavior you would like from the other. / After one person has completed this, the other should repeat what she or he has heard, to make sure the other's needs or wants have been understood accurately. (Try to avoid responding defensively, even though this may be difficult. Instead, concentrate on making sure you understand what that person wants or needs to make things better for him or her and therefore your relationship.) / Now, reverse roles as the other person verbalizes his or her wants and needs. / Take a few minutes to jot down each person's growth needs for future use.

In using this step in enrichment and counseling, it may be essential to do some consciousness-raising regarding needs that seem unjust or exaggerated and therefore are sources of strife. For example, Pete wants and expects his wife, Jane, to do most of the child care and housework in addition to her full-time job as a teacher. Attempting to meet this desire, rather than negotiating a fairer division of labor at home, would diminish Jane's well-being and undercut the overall health of their family. (The Relational Satisfaction-Justice Inventory that follows is a practical tool for you to use to deal with such issues.) In using this step, it is also important to point out that it is impossible for anyone to meet all of another's wants and needs. Expecting one's partner to do this is a source of unproductive conflict in intimate relationships. The purpose of this step is to state unmet needs and thus make them available for negotiation in step three.

It may be helpful to know that there are four types of needs in relationships:

1. *Shared needs* are those that both persons would like to have met. For example, many couples share the need to schedule more time in their busy lives to talk and play. These needs are the easiest to satisfy intentionally.

2. *Conflicted needs* are those that, if met, would make it impossible to meet an important need of the other person. For example, frequency of sex play is a common point of conflict in marriages. Such needs are the most difficult to meet for obvious reasons. But the conflicts can be resolved by negotiating a plan to compromise by meeting in the middle between differing desires. The key is to learn how to dialogue so as to develop win-win compromises.

3. *Parallel needs* are those that do not conflict with the other's major needs and are therefore easier to meet by alternating between responding to each person's need. For example, couples who have different favorite foods or recreational preferences, but who also like each other's favorites, can negotiate a plan to take turns enjoying each other's favorites.

4. *Exaggerated leftover needs* are from severe deprivation of normal needs in childhood, as discussed above.

Step Three: Intentionally Increase the Mutual Satisfaction of Your Relationship, and Thus Nurture Your Love, by Choosing a Shared Need that You Both Want to Meet

Work out a realistic, workable plan with a time schedule to meet this need. / Write down your plan to help you remember and implement it. This record should include what each person agrees to do and when. / In this step, you are beginning to intentionally revise or add a clause to your relationship's working agreement (contract or covenant) through discussion, negotiation, and justice-based compromise.

Step Four: Implement Your Change Plan

This step is the rewarding payoff of this love-nurturing tool. As you move ahead, the process of intentional relationship enhancement becomes self-reinforcing as the positive satisfactions increase for both partners. Congratulate each other for moving ahead intentionally on this path of continuing to cultivate love and caring in your most important relationship! / Then choose another pair of shared needs, devising and implementing a plan to intentionally fulfill these needs. / Continue this four-step process. When you run out of shared needs, focus on parallel needs that also are easier to meet than conflicted needs for obvious reasons. It is well to repeat step one, the "I appreciate in you..." step, regularly to remind yourselves of the things you have going for you as you work together to make your relationship more mutually loving and caregiving. Keep a written record of your progress. / Particular change plans may not work, especially conflicted needs. If this happens to you, don't invest more than a little energy on postmortems. Instead devise a better plan or shift to another set of needs.[13]

Enabling Couples to Revise Unjust or Unsatisfying Relational Covenants

Every committed, continuing relationship is based on an understanding that is usually implicit of what each person's privileges and rights, obligations, and duties are within that relationship. In marriage, this is called the "marital contract" or, to use the religious term, "covenant." Often there are major differences in the two partners' implicit understanding of their working contract. This discrepancy is a hidden source of conflict between them. Some marriage enrichment and counseling enable couples merely to adjust to their existing contracts more comfortably without evaluating and changing the unfair and unjust dimensions of them. But such approaches are inherently unliberating and will prevent them from maximizing their love in a mutually empowering way.

What are the characteristics of liberated and liberating relationships like marriages? These include

- regular open, honest, and caring communication;
- genuine fairness and equality;
- commitment to each other's growth;
- responsiveness to meeting each other's needs: physical, intellectual, emotional, recreational, and spiritual;
- deepening friendship and creative closeness balanced by respect for individual differences and needs for privacy and autonomy;
- the ability to resolve differences by negotiating rather than deadlocking and distancing, thus using conflict to deepen caring;
- positive fidelity based primarily on valuing each other as a person and valuing the relationship and therefore not wanting to risk damaging it;
- continued change and growth through the years;
- skill in using crises and losses as opportunities for mutual support, learning, and growth;
- playfulness and laughter and, when appropriate, deepening sexual pleasure integrated with mutual love and respect; and
- increased sharing in development of meaning and faith.[14]

To help couples avoid the problem of excessive expectations that could be called "relational perfectionism," counselors should make clear that attributes such as those just listed are ideal goals. They are achieved only to a degree even by those who are quite happy and satisfied with their relationship. When working with couples suffering in conflict, I sometimes toy with the thought that a "happy marriage" is one in which there are even a little more satisfactions than frustrations. In any case, the ideal toward which couples should be helped to grow is two autonomous, growing individuals with differing as well as complementary needs who choose to develop loving *interdependency* rather than the symbiotic dependency of two half-persons.

To be genuinely liberating and growth producing (rather than merely sugarcoating unjust relationships), marriage counseling and enrichment programs often should include consciousness-raising about justice issues. This means increasing couples' awareness of the ways in which the unequal allocation of power, decision making, and opportunities for growth are root causes of marital anger, unhappiness, and conflict. Consciousness-raising should increase a couple's understanding of how their sexist social programming as women and men diminishes mutual growth in marriage. Marriage counseling and enrichment should challenge and teach couples how to revise their contracts to make their relationships as just and equal as possible. The principle that the *only firm foundation for love is justice* should be implemented in marriage counseling and enrichment, particularly when injustices are obvious. The following communication exercise is a tool for doing this.

Relationship Satisfaction-Justice Inventory

As pointed out above, mutual love, respect, and wholeness flower most readily in relationships characterized by fairness and equality. For this reason it can be helpful to have a do-it-yourselves instrument to guide individuals and couples who want to strengthen their relationships by making them more just, as well as satisfying. The Relationship Satisfaction-Justice Inventory (RSJI) is such an instrument. It is designed to incorporate prophetic caregiving in relationships. As such, it complements and goes beyond the IRM by providing couples with a concrete self-evaluation and information concerning the strengths and the areas that need strengthening in their relationships. It is designed to guide couples in evaluating and revising their relationship covenants (contracts or working agreements) to make them explicit and to keep them updated and more fair and satisfying. This exercise can be used by individuals, couples, families, or anyone in intimate relationships. The instructions are stated as directed to couples:

Instructions: Pick a time when the two of you are feeling connected and communicating reasonably well. Each person should have a copy of the inventory. (Feel free to photocopy it from this book.) Set aside twenty or so minutes to take the inventory individually without talking with each other. Then set aside at least thirty minutes to begin the process of gaining the most benefits from the inventory.

Step 1: To prepare yourselves for using the RSJI most effectively, repeat the first step of the IRM by telling each other what you appreciate and perhaps love in each other and in your relationship. This mutual affirmation will awaken warm (even erotic) feelings by reminding you of the strengths and resources in your relationship that you can use in enhancing it further.

Step 2: Now decide who will be partner A and partner B, then each of you complete your copy of the inventory on your own. Begin this by glancing down the list of "Areas of Our Relationship" on the left. These are significant dimensions of your lives together, paragraphs in your relationship covenant that you can make even more just and satisfying by using this inventory. / In the blanks below the list add other important areas of your relationship. / Go back to the first item on the list—the necessary "dirty work" that no one wants to do, such as cleaning the toilet or the garage, or getting your car repaired. If you believe that responsibility for this is fair and satisfying to both partners, put an F and S in the first blank to the right of this item. / If you believe that responsibility for the dirty work is unfair or unjust to Partner A, put UF and US in the middle blank. / Do the same in the blank on the right. / Now repeat the process for each item on the list. /

****

Areas of Our Relationship
Rank each responsibility: Fair and Satisfying (FS), Unfair (UF), or Unsatisfying (US).

	Person A	Person B
Dirty work		
Educational growth		
Opportunities		
Opportunities for fulfilling work		
Child rearing		
Self-care opportunities		
Recreational opportunities		
Sexual satisfaction		
Leadership in the relationship		
Self-esteem enhancement		
Decisions about money		
Decisions about moving		
Decisions about jobs		
Relationships with relatives		

Responsibility for spiritual life
Community responsibility
Other areas of our relationship

Step 3: Now compare your responses on agreement and differences in your perceptions of which areas are satisfying and fair and which are not, simply trying to understand each other's feelings. Avoid wasting creative energy arguing about areas that either of you feels are unfair or unsatisfying. / Pay special attention to the UFs and USs, the areas in which either of you believes fairness and satisfaction need to be increased. You will find that these are the areas where conflicts occur most often and also the places where positive change and growth are most needed and therefore most rewarding. / Affirm each other for having the courage to face these troubling areas in your relationship. You already have taken a crucial step toward making changes to correct these problems and thus enhance your love. / If your perceptions of these areas are somewhat similar, you can consider this a relationship strength on which you can build your self-other relationship enhancement plan. / Now, list in your journal the UF and US areas, leaving blank space on the right of each item for notes. /

Step 4: Go down the lists, item by item, discussing and jotting down your tentative ideas about what you can do, individually and together, to make your relationship more fair and satisfying by negotiating constructive changes in your relationship covenant. Bear in mind that as you do this, you'll be nurturing your love. /

Step 5: Choose one area in which you agree that changes are needed to make your relationship more satisfying or more just to one of you, and a second area where changes are needed for the other person. / Discuss what you will do to improve your relationship in these two areas. As you do this, negotiate a mutual change plan, spelling out what each of you will do and when. Be sure to balance the satisfactions for each of you that will probably result from implementing this plan. / Write down your agreed-upon plan so you'll both have a written record for future reference.

Step 6: Commit yourselves to implementing your plan, and begin doing so soon, following the plan's timetable. / After each step you take to make your relationship more satisfying, just, and loving, give each other an affirming, congratulatory hug, and do something together you both enjoy. Use your imagination playfully to give yourselves rewards to offset the frustrations from having to give up unfair but satisfying (for one of you) things in your relationship. Fortunately most of the changes should be rewarding in and of themselves, reinforcing positive change. Agree in advance what rewards will be delayed or withheld if either of you fails to do what you promised.

Step 7: After making changes in the first two areas, go back and pick two other areas in which you agree changes are needed and doable, and repeat steps 1, 4, and 5. If a particular change plan doesn't work for any reason, don't waste creative energy on mutual accusations and futile postmortems. Instead, set aside that plan and negotiate another one in areas where changes promise to be easier. If one or both of you drop the ball, the withheld rewards should provide enough motivation to do better the next time.

By continuing the RSJI self-change process, you make the love-enhancing plan of the IRM more concrete as well as more just. Be aware that both are complementary, intentional self-change tools. If you find yourself resisting such organized, step-by-step approaches, you can do what many couples have done. Use the self-enhancement model implicit in these instruments informally to fit your preferences.

Moving to Enlightened Self-interest and Beyond

The working principle of both the IRM and the RSJI is that increasing mutual justice and need satisfaction is the road for couples to follow to increase love and wellness in their relationship. Negotiating a more just and satisfying relationship is the best place to begin relational self-care, but it is not the place to stop in enabling people to enliven their love. Of course, when couples are in mutually hurting times, they usually feel hostility, alienation, and diminished self-worth. They therefore tend to attack each other in ways that actually deepen their alienation, conflict, and pain. Helping them move beyond this mutual damaging self-sabotage to more enlightened self-interest is the first, essential step on their journey of relationship healing. Then as they make changes that increase their mutual fairness and satisfaction, their love increases, and a remarkable positive transformation can occur. They begin to replace the negative, mutually hurting cycle, in which they had been trapped, with a positive cycle, in which the needs of the other person gradually become shared needs. They start to feel, "Because I love you, the satisfaction of your needs is important to me. In this way your needs are among my needs."

As their love matures, couples discover the "new math" of loving relationships. They are surprised to learn that unlike the win or lose of sports and the marketplace, radically different dynamics operate in close relationships. They find that growing their love by meeting some of each other's needs is the way they get some of their own needs met in that relationship. The dynamics of maturing love are expressed well by this image from the Talmud: "Many candles can be lighted from one candle without diminishing it."[15]

As effective parents know intuitively, children need a lot of love—*especially when they don't deserve it*. The same is true of the little girl or boy inside all adults. It is also true in adult relationships characterized by maturing love. Partners who have experienced the transforming new math of loving give each other caring love willingly when either of them is unable to return that love in dark days. This response relates to the New Testament principle of going the second mile and turning the other cheek. However, going the second mile in relationships can be unhealthy when there is no reciprocation for a long time. It is healthy when there are sufficient mutual esteeming and caring and when the overall give-and-take is fairly balanced and reciprocal.

It is important to help couples recall any times, however brief, when their lives were not disrupted or controlled by their presenting problem. The pastor may ask the couple: "Can you remember times when your problems did not cause you to respond in an attacking way? What do these times tell you about yourself, your partner, and your relationship?" Such questions may lead them to new stories about their self-identity; to new understanding of the possibilities for different outcomes and fresh solutions. These discoveries provide concrete examples of their ability not to be controlled by their old beliefs, obsolete stories, and unworkable behavior responses.

Caregiving for Creative Singlehood

In contemporary society increasing numbers of people are choosing to marry later or not at all, or to cohabit for a while. But in many social circles being married is the norm. This means that almost one-third of adults in the United States are by definition regarded as abnormal, if not subnormal. In such circles, those who are unmarried, by choice or by circumstances, often feel like fifth wheels in social situations where most people are coupled. Even church programs with robust and much-needed emphasis on marriages and family life may provide a poverty of parallel programs for singles. It is crucial that congregational programs of care and counseling be structured so as to also include ministry with persons who are separated, divorced, widowed, or never married. Some of these persons, like some married persons, are in pressing need of care and counseling. The challenge is to devise strategies to make churches family-like environments for persons from the whole broad spectrum of relationships—single and unsingle. Churches should be supportive, extended family for everyone who wishes to participate in them, including persons who live alone and persons who are married or live in other committed relationships. Everyone needs a support system to nurture wholeness. Many single people have to work hard to build and maintain a viable support system of need-satisfying relationships. Churches, through their pastoral care, education, and growth group programs, should be oases for singles, offering no exploitative alternatives to singles bars.

Without weakening family programs, churches should model positive attitudes and develop programs that help make singlehood a genuine option and a fully appropriate lifestyle. As people become freer to choose singlehood in churches and our society, they will also be freer to choose marriage if that is feasible and their preference. Fewer people will marry for the inadequate reasons of seeking to escape from loneliness or to conform to family or societal norms of being coupled.

Based on his experiences, pastoral counseling teacher John Landgraf declares,

> It is not only tolerable to be single . . . it can even be good! Singleness is a legitimate choice, for the long run as well as the short. It is not necessarily a better choice than being unsingle, or married; but neither is it necessarily worse. The married state can be wonderfully fulfilling; so can the non-married state. Spousehood can be hellish; so can singlehood.[16]

Church caregivers should work with their single members to develop a variety of sharing and growth groups for singles, such as single-parent groups, widow-to-widow sharing-support groups, grief-healing groups, and events such as creative singlehood retreats, classes, or workshops. It is important to avoid thinking of singles programs as match-making opportunities, though that is one legitimate function for some singles. Many single folk do not like to feel really welcome only in all-singles groups. So unmarried persons should be made to feel welcome in the whole range of sharing and learning groups in the life of a wholeness-oriented church.

Some older unmarried women have special needs for pastoral care and counseling. They suffer from the pressures of the "coupleness" norm in our society and also from the social prejudices and stereotyping of older unmarried women. Helping to make single-hood a genuine option and erasing the cruel stereotypes that make many older unmarrieds feel themselves to be social failures are dual challenges to be faced in pastoral care and education programs. Older unmarried men also encounter alienating social attitudes that assume they are gay or must have mother attachments or other deep neurotic problems. The support and growth work occurring in creative singlehood groups and events can help singles—young and old—repair the damage to self-esteem inflicted by our mainly coupled society and its institutions, including churches.

Using the growth-in-wholeness approach in pastoral care and counseling can help singles see the unique potentialities of being single and also of being without children. These include the opportunity to invest the enormous time and energy that persons with children invest in child rearing in other forms of satisfying, socially useful, and generative ways. Another is the freedom and the motivation to develop new, more creative models of relating. There's no logical or psychological reason that one lifestyle—marriage—should be regarded as superior to all others for everyone. Singles can develop a variety of other fulfilling options. A third positive option in singleness is inescapable motivation to keep growing as persons. Many married persons can avoid facing their emotional immaturity because it's protected by a neurotic marriage. This protection carries the high price of mutual stifling of personal growth. It's much harder for a single person to avoid the challenge to continue personal development

Learning to affirm and develop one's singleness is as essential for creative marriage as it is for creative singlehood. From his experience, pastoral counselor John Landgraf observes, "Individuals with mutually satisfying marriages ... have either carried a healthy singlehood into their marriage relationships, or have painstakingly developed their capacity for a high level of autonomy within their marriages."

Our culture's attitudes and values about sex are in a state of transition, conflict, and confusion. In this context, sexuality is complicated for many married persons. It is doubly so for some singles. Abstinence and sublimation are the only options recognized by traditional morality and most churches as not ethically off-limits for singles. However, there is something dehumanizing about a society that simultaneously glamorizes sex and seeks to deny it to more than forty million adults. The majority of singles ignore society's limits, but often they do so at a price of guilt and inner conflicts as well as the danger of STDs (sexually transmitted diseases, including AIDS). Probably more frequently than in marriage, single sex is often separated from relationships of trust, commitment, mutual respect, and caring—the context in which sexuality flowers. Many people (single and married) hurt themselves and others by rebelling against old straitjacket sexual morality rather than struggling to discover new sexual values that are liberating and respectful of others. Some singles feel pressured by the swinging singles image. They feel social pressure to perform sexually in casual relationships when they would prefer to reserve sexual involvement for committed relationships. Many people, single and coupled, are searching for sound guidance and direction in this area. Pastoral caregivers need to be prepared to help such persons work through their ethical conflicts, confusion, and pain about sex to discover what constitutes life-affirming and person-enhancing sexuality for them. This includes helping single parents welcome and care lovingly for their babies, both those born to single mothers and those adopted.[17]

An Illustrative Case of Marriage Crisis Counseling

To understand the process of couple crisis counseling, consider the following illustration. It describes how to use the IRM and the RSJI with families suffering severe conflicts. Taken together, these two communication tools provide a valuable approach to relational crisis counseling that is effective and efficient. (To protect confidentiality, this is a composite case based on several experiences of marriage crisis counseling.)

Joan Sheldon phoned the Reverend Sally Marks to ask if she would see her about a problem. Joan (age thirty-four) and Bill (age thirty-six) are members of Rev. Marks's church. They have been married eight years and have two children, ages five and just over one. Rev. Marks said, "Yes, Joan, I'll be glad to be of whatever help I can. Tell me a little about what's happening." (This question was aimed at finding out how acute the crisis was and enough about its nature to decide whether to begin with individual or couple counseling.) Joan briefly described their marital problem that she understood as centering on Bill's heavy drinking. Their conflict had skyrocketed since he had been terminated three months ago from his position as a designer with a software company.

Joan: He's become unbearable—I guess because he is so depressed about not finding another job. He often just sits in front of the TV and drinks beer during the day. He yells at me when I ask him why he isn't out looking for a job and says I should find a job myself. What's more, his unemployment compensation will run out soon. I'm afraid to leave the kids with him. He's often so upset and half drunk, and he shouts at them when they make any noise like children do.

Pastor: Sounds as though things are really rough and that you've about had it, Joan! How would Bill feel about the three of us getting together to talk? Since the problem is in your relationship, that might be helpful.

Joan: He's very upset about the mess we're in and what's going on between us, but he feels our main problem is his being out of work. Actually, I think his heavy drinking is one reason he was fired!

Pastor: It sounds like that is a problem. But from what you say, it seems that the pain you're both feeling is made worse by what this is doing to your relationship as a family. Do you suppose he would be willing to come at least once so that I could hear his views about the crisis you're in and what would make things better?

Joan said her husband probably would come to a session. So a tentative appointment was made for the next day, to be confirmed after Joan had talked with Bill and he had agreed to come.

When the couple arrived, the pastor greeted them warmly and asked them to have a seat in a small cluster of three chairs away from the desk in her office.

Pastor: I appreciate your accepting my invitation to come, Bill. I can understand that you might be feeling some resistance since it wasn't your idea to talk with me. As I explained to Joan when she phoned, I think I may be more helpful if I know how each of you sees your situation.

Bill: Things have been going downhill since I lost my job. I'm willing to talk if it might help us.

Pastor: Joan told me a little about the problems on the phone, but I suspect that you may have different views of what's going on between you. How do you see the problem, Bill?

Bill: Well, I lost my job, and with the economy being in the miserable shape it's in, I haven't been able to find a comparable position in my field. It's been damn discouraging, and I guess I've been a little hard to live with. But her nagging me about what I'm doing wrong hasn't exactly helped!

Pastor: The job problem must be very rough on you, Bill. I realize that finding another job is your top concern right now, and talking with me won't help that directly. But it sounds as if what's going on between the two of you is making being out of work even harder for you and Joan. Perhaps we can discover some ways that the two of you can make things better for both of you. What needs to change in your marriage to make it less frustrating and more satisfying for you? [The pastor later asked Joan the same question.]

This way of framing the questions is designed to begin the process of awakening reality-based hope. It tries to do so by planting the idea that constructive change is possible and inviting each person to verbalize the concrete changes each perceives as needed.

As often happens, the couple first responded defensively, speaking accusingly in terms of what the other needed to change. This response began the necessary healing process of draining off the pressure of anger and grief derived from painful mutual frustration of their wants and needs. In describing their escalating crisis, Joan and Bill poured out their feelings in heated disagreement, especially about the role of Bill's drinking in his firing. After a heated interchange, Bill's defensiveness declined enough to allow him to admit his drinking maybe had hurt his job rating and had contributed to his being cut soon after his company began to reduce its professional staff because of economic difficulties. He later also admitted that his doctor had recommended that he reduce his drinking.

Pastor: Have you tried to cut down on your drinking, Bill?

Bill: Yeah, I tried and even went to a few AA meetings about a year ago, but that didn't seem to be what I needed.

The pastor focused her attention back and forth between them, thus giving each person opportunities to express conflicted feelings and perceptions of the issues. She watched their pattern of communication carefully, noting that they talked to each other only through her. This suggested that their communication, except for the circular arguing, mutual attacks, and heated accusations stemming from their suffering, had become constricted and ineffective as a means of problem solving. Effective communication, including all the verbal and nonverbal ways people exchange ideas, attitudes, meanings, desires, hopes, anger, fears, warmth, and caring, nurtures relationships. It does so by feeding people's basic psychological hungers and thus satisfying the profound human will to relate. Thus the pathology in the Sheldons' communication system was both a cause and an effect of their increasing alienation.

During this initial session, the pastor gave somewhat more attention to Bill, drawing him out and responding with warm empathy to his expressions of distress. The counseling principle used here was the importance of focusing on the less motivated or resistant spouse in order to establish a bond of rapport and thus increase the motivation of that person to continue counseling. This must be done without neglecting the more strongly motivated person.

The couple is trapped by spiraling resentment, feelings of rejection, and progressive breakdown of problem-solving communication. The more each person's self-esteem and sense of identity are undermined, the faster the rejection-anger spiral tends to whirl. The stronger the momentum of this vicious cycle, the more difficult it is for the couple to interrupt it on their own unassisted. Basic to interrupting this vicious cycle is draining off the intense feelings of hurt, resentment, anger, and rejection that feed it. The pastor did this by encouraging emotional catharsis. The reduction of the explosive head of emotional steam in both persons had to be accomplished *before* healing communication could occur. If a couple's rage is particularly intense or the counselor suspects there may be something crucial, such as a secret affair, that will not be brought out in a joint session, one or more individual sessions with each party are needed.

The presence of the pastor as a respected professional person outside their marital system changed the Sheldons' marital dyad, making it a three-person group. This helped them gradually interrupt the escalating cycle of mutual attack and retaliation that was paralyzing their interaction. As the pastor took the dual roles of mediator and communication-facilitator, the couple gained the ability to talk effectively about the issues at the roots of their suffering and conflict. In this way their blocked lines of communication were gradually reopened.

As their emotions cooled, the issue of Bill's drinking was raised again by the pastor.

Pastor: Bill, you mentioned that you drink partly to cope with Joan's nagging you to cut down on your drinking. And, Joan, you nag because you're worried about the effect of Bill's drinking on the family finances and Bill's health. The nagging gives you more reason to drink, Bill, which gives you more reason to keep after him, Joan. Does this sound to you like it sounds to me, that there's some mutual sabotaging going on between you? [Both nodded in tentative agreement.] It's as though what each of you is doing is producing the opposite of what you really want from the other.

This confrontation led into a discussion of what they might do to interrupt this self-defeating cycle.

During the first session, Rev. Marks encouraged each partner to give a brief chronological overview of their relationship since they met. They agreed that although they had had their share of pain and conflict, their marriage had been relatively good before the last few years.

Pastor: It's hopeful that you both have some good memories. It tells me that you have the capacity to make things better between you. You might learn how to draw on this awareness to help you pull out of this low point of feeling overwhelmed by this crisis.

Toward the end of the session, the pastor summarized what she had heard from them, pausing occasionally for their response.

Pastor: It sounds like each of you is suffering a lot because of at least three factors in your situation. One is the cluster of financial worries and problems caused by the loss of your major income, having to dip into your savings more and more, plus the big disruption of your familiar routines, schedules, and satisfactions by having Bill out of work. You lost a job, but also a lot more. The anxieties and tensions are a lot worse because the prospects aren't good for finding another job very soon. You've both had a many-sided loss with a lot of grief.

Both Joan and Bill agreed, saying they hadn't thought of what they were confronting as grief.

Pastor: The second cause of pain you're both feeling is what's going on between you. Your anxieties and frustration about the job loss have triggered the self-defeating cycle of blaming each other and pushing each other away just when you need to pull together to handle all the practical difficulties you're facing. The third issue, your use of alcohol, Bill, seems to be complicating the other two. The big blow to your self-esteem from losing a job you liked and the discouragement of not being able to find another one yet have made it easy to drink more. And, Joan, you feel strongly that this is interfering with his job hunting. Joan, because of Bill's behavior when he's drinking, you're reluctant to return to the nursing job you had before your second child was born. Do these seem to be the major problems to which you need to find some solutions?

The couple agreed. Then the pastor shifted gears dramatically.

Pastor: It's clear that both of you are feeling a lot of anger and pain from the way you have been hurting each other and that there are a lot of things you find annoying and frustrating about each other. But I'm wondering, what, if anything, do you still like about each other or your marriage?

The couple looked astonished by the question. Joan responded first, surprising Bill by affirming a number of things that she still liked about being married to him. He looked pleased, and responded, mentioning several things he appreciated about her. The constructive energy of a degree of mutual caring was clearly evident to them and the pastor at this point in the session.

Pastor: It's obvious to me that you two still have some crucial caring between you in spite of your painful problems and the crisis you're experiencing now. From my perspective you two have more going for you than you thought when you came to my office. Perhaps together we can develop ways that you can build on these assets in your relationship.

Thus reality-based hope was beginning to be awakened.

After the couple's positive responses to the first step of the IRM, the pastor repeated the question asked earlier of each of them: "What are the important things that need to be changed in your marriage to make it less frustrating and more satisfying for you?" This adaptation of the second step of the IRM gave Bill and Joan an opportunity to clarify in their minds and tell each other the particular changes they needed and/or wanted in the other in order to deal with the various facets of their problem as they had defined them. This time they moved immediately into a nondefensive response to the question. After they had each mentioned several changes they would like the other to make, the pastor continued,

Pastor: It sounds to me as if you both want less conflict and more love to grow between you [a shared need]. If you make even a few of the changes you each want, it is likely that both these things will happen—conflicts will diminish and positive feelings will grow between you. [They agree.] Also, I noticed, Bill, that you want Joan to stop getting after you about your drinking, and you, Joan, want Bill to stop drinking so much. These seem to be complementary wants in that if you each make these changes, it will give each other what you want. Can you think of ways to respond to what the other is asking?

The dialogue that followed culminated with an agreement that Bill would not drink alcohol during the day when job hunting and Joan would make a conscious effort to avoid criticizing him.

Pastor: If you each fulfill your agreement, the odds are better that you may get something else you both want—you'll find a new job, Bill. If you're both interested, I would be open to working with you to help you develop workable plans to meet more of each other's needs. Of course, it isn't realistic to expect that anyone can meet *all* of anyone else's needs. But in my experience, couples who still care about each other as you do can learn to meet more of each other's needs and wants. If you do this, the satisfactions in your marriage will increase, and the frustrations and conflict will decrease. Bill, would you be willing to meet weekly for three or four sessions to see what the three of us can do to help you work with, rather than against, each other in handling the crisis you're in? [The less motivated person was intentionally asked first.]

Bill responded that although what he needed most was to find a job, he would like to improve things in their marriage. As expected, Joan accepted the pastor's offer.

Pastor: Good, then I'll look forward to working with the two of you. Among the things you each said that need to be changed to make things better, are there steps you can take before we get together again? As you work on improving your situation, it will help you feel better.

After agreeing that alleviating their financial and job worries must have priority, they worked out a plan with the pastor's help aimed at this goal. Joan would take a part-time nursing position at the local hospital where she knew there was an opening. Bill would follow up a job lead he had seen in a professional journal but had put aside because of his depression. He also agreed not to drink, except in the evenings, and to be responsible for child care and meals on the days she worked. The pastor affirmed their willingness to take concrete steps to cope with their crisis and suggested that they would debrief how their plans worked when they met for their appointment a week later.

The pastor closed the session.

Pastor: How do each of you feel about our discussion today?
Bill: I feel a lot better. Also a little surprised, I guess, since I expected to only come once.
Joan: I am more hopeful, like there's really a way out of the mess we're in.
Pastor: The way you used this session is a good sign from my perspective—a sign that you both have important resources you can use in straightening out the mess so that things will be better for you and your children. I hope things go well as you do the things you agreed on.

When they returned the next week, Bill and Joan reported a serious problem in implementing their plans. Both were very discouraged. Bill had discovered that the job announced in the journal was already taken. When Joan returned from her job the second day, he had been drinking heavily. Their dinner was not prepared, and the children were crying. A fight ensued. Bill drank until he passed out. The pastor helped them look carefully at this incident.

Pastor: If you have a fight and don't learn something from it, you've wasted a good opportunity.

In the discussion that followed, Bill admitted that he had taken a drink that morning in spite of his strong intentions not to drink, and that, as on many earlier occasions, one drink led to getting drunk. In an individual session with the pastor, following the second joint session, Bill faced the fact that his drinking had cost him his job and that his loss of control over alcohol was hurting his family and interfering with his recovery from his job crisis. He agreed with the pastor's recommendation that he attend AA again on a regular basis, to give it another try.

In her individual session, Joan explored the way her responses to Bill's problem drinking were unwittingly exacerbating his problem. She agreed to attend a local Al-Anon meeting regularly to seek help with her side of this problem. They accepted the pastor's offer to put them in touch with two seasoned members of AA and Al-Anon who were also members of their church and who could help them feel at home in those groups. In addition to her Al-Anon meetings, Joan began attending the open AA meeting with Bill, one of the two he attended each week. Bill had apparently hit bottom, facing the fact that he needed to stop drinking if he was to avoid more serious damage to his family and his vocational future.

During subsequent counseling conversations, the pastor helped Joan and Bill focus on other major unmet needs in their relationship. Thus, the IRM model was used as the basic approach to counseling. Later in the process the couple also decided to use the RSJI to identify and plan changes to make their relationship more just and satisfying to both of them. Using this, they negotiated and made plans to set aside some time regularly to share experiences, hopes, and frustrations. Eventually they also agreed on plans to make the division of the housework and child care fairer to Joan. She also agreed to have sex more often, which was what Bill wanted. In this way, they gradually modified their marriage contract in constructive directions.

By the end of a month, they all evaluated what they had done together. It was clear that the couple had used the pastor's help well. She affirmed them warmly for their constructive changes. Communication was more open, they were talking regularly, and their joint problem-solving skills were improving. There were numerous unresolved issues in their relationship, but they were learning skills to work on these more effectively as well as on new problems as they emerged. Except for another brief slip, Bill had not had a drink since he returned to AA. With his sobriety firmer, he had found a job in middle management related to his field. Joan was supporting him in his struggles to learn the ropes in his new position. The satisfaction she was getting from her work made her realize that she needed, for her own well-being, to continue her career in nursing. Both of their relationships with their children had improved as they tried to live what they were learning in their 12-step recovery programs.

As they left the fifth session, Bill and Joan expressed heartfelt thanks for all the help the pastor had given them. The three joined hands as they prayed the AA serenity prayer, followed by a prayer by the pastor celebrating their growth and the gift of new life they had received. By mutual agreement, the couple agreed to meet briefly every other week for two months and then on a monthly basis to check in by phone as they continued to struggle with unsolved issues and consolidated their newly learned ways of relating.

Many couples who seek counseling from pastors are much more difficult to help than were the Sheldons. As indicated earlier, the problems of many couples are so deep that short-term counseling is not enough. Some couples come to pastors after their relationship has disintegrated beyond repair. Seeing a pastor is a kind of last resort, a way of pacifying their consciences by going through the motions of having counseling. When things have moved to the point of beginning divorce proceedings, it is important to ask for a moratorium, a postponement of further legal action until serious marriage therapy can be tried. It is usually futile to attempt marriage counseling or therapy in the midst of legal maneuvering. Often one partner is resistant or closed to receiving help. When only one person seeks help with a marriage problem, the pastor should take whatever initiative is needed to involve the other in the helping process. In many cases, an invitation by phone will get the person to come for one or two more sessions aimed at establishing rapport and reducing that person's resistance to continuing counseling. If only one person will come for counseling, it is essential to focus on what that person can do to improve her or his side of the relationship, including how to release the other emotionally so as to interrupt the neurotic interaction.

The Relationship Crisis Counselor's Role

In marriage counseling and therapy it is not the counselor's function to save all marriages. Rather, it is to help couples discover whether they can reconstruct their dysfunctional relationships with a more just, satisfying, and growthful working agreement. Some marriages are so irreversibly destructive to the couple and their children that a divorce is the only hope of salvaging anything constructive. Divorce obviously represents the failure of a relationship, but there is no reason to compound the harm by staying together in mutually damaging interaction, which often is a marriage in name only, after serious marriage therapy has failed to heal the marriage pathology. To facilitate a merciful release from such mutually strangling marriages is a constructive and essential ministry.

There are various ways of describing a counselor's roles. As was evident in the preceding case illustration, the pastor took an active role in working with the Sheldons. I agree with the view that "if joint interviews are to be constructive, the counselor must assume responsibility for establishing limits, structure, balance, and focus during the interview." In her counseling with the Sheldons, Pastor Sally aimed at being

- what psychiatrist Harry Stack Sullivan called a "participant observer," but also an "observant participant";
- a *referee* who saw that both persons had a fair chance to express their views and participate equally in decisions affecting both of them;
- a *relationship coach* who helped them learn how to play the game of marriage more creatively;
- a *mentor* who suggested and recommended actions for them to try.
- a *communicator-facilitator* who helped them practice the art of getting clear messages through to each other effectively;
- a caring, accepting, honest *authority figure* with some expertise in relationships; as such, she was not shy about speaking the truth in love as she confronted them caringly with the hurtful consequences of their mutually sabotaging behavior and affirming them when they responded to each other more constructively;
- an *awareness stimulator* who shared her views about what was happening in their interaction;
- a *reality tester* for them, enabling them to check their perceptions of the realities of their relationship against hers;
- a *guide* who encouraged them to explore more constructive relationship paths, including some learnings from her marriage;
- a *role model*, particularly for Joan, of a strong, competent, caring woman;
- a *pastor* who symbolized and sought to be a channel for the healing love of God to flow into the lives and the marriage of this couple;
- a *warm human being* who reached out, not down, to help Joan and Bill.

Being a constructive counselor does not mean making decisions for counselees, doing for them what they could do for themselves, or pushing them toward solutions chosen by the counselor. If persons ask, "Should I get a divorce?" accept their desire (ambivalent in most cases) for authoritative advice. But then gently but firmly, make it plain that this is too complex and personal a decision for anyone else to make for them. The counselor's role is to help counselees examine alternatives, face the consequences of various choices, deal with inner resistances (for example, to leaving a destructive marriage or working hard to salvage it), and in this way gain a greater degree of freedom and objectivity so as to make a wise decision.

Counseling Sexual Problems and for Enrichment

Human sexuality is one of God's best gifts. It is a vital part of human life and well-being, whether or not people regard themselves as sexually active. As psychoanalytic pioneer Sigmund Freud made clear, this is true from the beginning to the end of life. Sexual wellness is about being healthy, safe, and comfortable with your body and its remarkable and potentially life-enhancing sensual capacities. An important dimension of both marriage enrichment and crisis counseling is helping couples deal constructively with sexual issues. This includes enhancing their ability to enjoy sex more fully and in healthy ways. Contemporary sex therapies offer insights and methods that often are useful for sexual enhancement in marriage enrichment events and for helping couples with sexual problems in marriage counseling and therapy. Much treatment in sex therapy is not therapy in the usual sense. Rather, it consists of helping couples learn more sex-affirmative attitudes and skills.

Performance anxiety and fear-of-failure anxiety are gradually diminished by practicing arousal exercises with no other goal than their own inherent pleasure. The effectiveness of sex therapy techniques is increased dramatically when they are integrated with marriage counseling and therapy insights. (See the books by Helen Singer Kaplan in this chapter's "Recommended Reading.")

It is possible for many couples with functional marriages to improve their sex life. The following do-it-yourself guidelines are worded to enable care receivers to enhance their sexual satisfaction and well-being:

Always practice safe sex and responsible sex. This includes protecting oneself and one's partner from STDs (sexually transmitted diseases) and using the most reliable family planning methods, thus making as sure as possible that if babies result, they will be wanted and cared for in wholeness-giving, loving ways.

Liberate your attitudes toward sex. We human beings are the most highly sexed of all the animal species. Contrary to old dual-standard stereotypes, women have at least as rich a potential for sexual responsiveness as men. Theologically speaking, God would not have equipped us with such capacities for sexual satisfaction without also intending that we enjoy this gift. Sexual responsiveness begins in our heads rather than our genitals, so that's the place to begin enhancing sex. Many couples find it freeing to read together a book that describes and shows illustrations of ways to introduce imagination and playfulness into sexual relationships. Religion has often contributed to sex-inhibiting attitudes. A child named Neil wrote a letter to God asking, "Dear God, I went to a wedding and they kissed right in church. Is that OK?"

Keep love in your total relationship growing, and sex will tend to improve. Sex for us humans is a powerful form of communication. Whatever enhances your communication, caring, and companionship in other aspects of your marriage will tend to make sex better. So feed each other's heart hungers for appreciation, touching, and affirmation regularly, and sexual responsiveness will usually increase. Pioneer sexual researcher Virginia Johnson declares, "Nothing good is going to happen in bed between a husband and a wife unless good things have been happening between them before they got into bed. There is no way for a good sexual technique to remedy a poor emotional relationship."[18]

Resolve accumulated hurts, resentments, and anger by talking them through before you try to make love. Unresolved negative feelings build up into a wall of either hot or frozen anger. Such walls gradually diminish the flow of the loving emotions and the sensuous feelings that trigger sexual arousal. Eliminating the injustices and inequalities in a marriage reduces the causes of much anger. Sex between two liberated, growing, equal individuals with a loving bond of mutual caring tends to be rich, whole-person sex.

Discover and enjoy the special romance of your present life and relationship stage. Studies show that lusty, full-bodied sexual enjoyment can usually continue well into the latter years—if a couple's general relationship has been nurtured. The popular fallacy that sexual pleasure is mainly for the young ignores the fact that sex can improve with experience, especially in relationships that grow richer with the struggles and satisfactions of passing years. As you grow older, it becomes increasingly important to keep love nurtured and to widen the range of enjoying your own and your partner's body beyond genital intercourse.

Use your imagination to create new ways to let your inner-child sides play together. Set aside time regularly for mutual pleasuring sessions. Introduce variety and adventure into the places, positions, and surroundings of lovemaking. Take the telephone off the hook, add a childproof flip-lock on your bedroom door, turn on your favorite music, light a few candles, and let your inner-child sides frolic together. Having dinner out, going to the beach, walking in the woods, taking a shower together, and spending a night at a motel—these are but a few ways to give yourself a minivacation to let yourselves forget your adult worries and responsibilities for a time and just play! Sex can be a revitalizing form of shared recreation.

Discover what each partner enjoys sensually, and then coach each other on how to maximize each other's pleasure. Pleasure preferences vary widely among individuals, so experiment to discover your own. Find out what scents, words, flowers, pictures, jokes, caresses, approaches, positions, music, and drinks help you have the most luxurious feelings of body arousal. Then coach your partner in how to include these in your loving sensual play.

Learn and enjoy leisurely, nondemand mutual pleasuring. Many couples have discovered that this is the key to increasing sexual zest in marriages when sex becomes dull or boring. Avoid the "we try harder" approach to sex. It's a dead-end street. Give each other a full-body massage using a warm body lotion with a sensuous aroma. Relax and enjoy receiving and giving mutual pleasure, with no other goal or agenda. Just flow with the natural pleasures of your bodies. Wherever the flow takes you will probably be very good. Let yourself enjoy whatever the two of you like.

Don't judge yourself if you have sexual arousal problems. In our culture, many men and women have hang-ups about sex. Women often take longer to be aroused than men. Many men occasionally experience episodes of temporary impotence. A relationship of mutual caring and patient, relaxed, and playful lovemaking can help old inhibiting attitudes to be unlearned and transformed. Shifting to nondemand mutual pleasuring for a while usually reduces anxiety about failure and reduces self-imposed feelings of pressure to succeed. This usually helps to restore the ability to have and enjoy intercourse.

Avoid the triple traps of hurry, fatigue, and too much alcohol or other drugs that depress your central nervous systems. These often interfere with fully satisfying sex, especially in the midyears and beyond. Loving takes time, but it's so worth it. Don't always postpone having sex until everything else is finished, at which time both of you are exhausted.

Keep a playful attitude toward the ups and downs in your sex life. Try to see the humor in many relationship problems, including those in sexuality. A counselor described a certain couple I know who were sabotaging themselves, sexually and otherwise, by responding to each other in attacking ways that got them exactly what they didn't want from each other. Does this ring any bells for you?

If do-it-yourself methods such as these don't improve your sex life as you want, get the help of a qualified sex therapist who is also trained in marriage counseling. This can be a valuable investment in your future happiness and relationship well-being.

Reality Practice Skill Development Session

Parishioner's roles, option 1 (requires two people who are friends or spouses): Do the steps of the Intentional Relationship Method (IRM) and the Relationship Satisfaction-

Justice Inventory (RSJI) as described in this chapter. This is the most effective way to learn how to use it with others as well as a means of enriching your relationships.

Parishioner's roles, option 2 (requires two people taking the roles of a married couple): You are experiencing painful conflict in your relationship. Seek your pastor's help.

Pastor's role: As you practice crisis counseling with this couple, try to incorporate what you have learned in this chapter, including using the IRM and RSJI as described above.

Observer-coach's role: Give candid but caring feedback to the pastor.

Recommended Reading

Anderson, Herbert. *The Family and Pastoral Care*. Philadelphia: Fortress Press, 1984.

———. *The Family Handbook*. Louisville: Westminster John Knox Press, 1998.

Brown, Norman M., and Ellen S. Amatea. *Love and Intimate Relationships*. Philadelphia: Brunner/Mazel, 2000.

Christensen, Andrew, and Neil S. Jacobson. *Reconcilable Differences*. New York: Guilford Publications, 2002.

Clinebell, Howard J., Jr., and Charlotte H. Clinebell. *The Intimate Marriage*. New York: Harper & Row, 1970.

Hudson, Frederic M. *The Handbook of Coaching: A Comprehensive Resource Guide for Managers, Executives, Consultants, and Human Resource Professionals*. San Francisco: Jossey-Bass, 1999.

Nelson, James B. "Religious and Moral Issues in Working with Homosexual Counselees." In *Between Two Gardens: Reflections on Sexuality and Religious Experience*. New York: Pilgrim Press, 1983.

———. "New Ways in Our Sexual Spirituality." In *The Intimate Connection: Male Sexuality, Masculine Spirituality*. Philadelphia: Westminster Press, 1988.

Neuger, Christie Cozad. *Counseling Women: A Narrative, Pastoral Approach*. Minneapolis: Fortress Press, 2001.

Olson, David H. "Prepare/Enrich Marriage and Premarital Counseling." www.prepare-enrich.com.

Papp, Peggy. *Couples on the Fault Line: New Directions for Therapists*. New York: Guilford Publications, 2001.

Poling, Jim. "Sexuality: A Crisis for the Church." In *Pastoral Care and Social Conflict*, ed. Pamela D. Couture and Rodney J. Hunter. Nashville: Abingdon Press, 1999.

Spong, John Shelby. "Homosexuality: A Part of Life, Not a Curse" and "The Bible and Homosexuality." In *Living in Sin? A Bishop Rethinks Human Sexuality*. San Francisco: Harper & Row, 1988.

CHAPTER 13

PASTORAL CARE, COUNSELING, AND ENRICHING FAMILIES

No man is an island, entire of itself; every man is a piece of the continent, a part of the main. If a clod be washed away by the sea, Europe is the less . . . because I am involved in mankind.
—John Donne (1572–1631)

We are born of other lives; we possess the capacities to bring still other lives into existence. . . . So nature compels us to recognize the fact of mutual dependence, each life necessarily helping the other lives which are linked to it.
—Albert Schweitzer, "The Ethics of Reverence for Life"

Changing Families in a Changing World

As used here, *family* means the social system of primary relationships from which individuals derive their major psychological, spiritual, and physical nurture. There are many types of families in contemporary society and in congregations. These include traditional two-parent families, single-parent families, couples without children (and with no intention or possibility of having children), three-generation families, and a variety of committed, intimate relationships that are the families of unmarried adults. Most people who live alone also have a support and nurturing system of friends who constitute their family. This chapter focuses on transformative, prophetic caregiving with all types of families. Obviously the goals of family care, enrichment, and counseling are extensions of the goals of couple caregiving. But because many families today have single parents, not couples, at their helm, goals designed to respond to the needs of these families must be included.

Families in industrialized countries, including the United States, were changing rapidly and radically in the closing decades of the twentieth century. These trends continue and are accelerating in the twenty-first century. The 2000 U.S. census revealed dramatic changes in the variety and shape of what constitutes families. Slightly more than half of Americans live in households as married couples, and, for the first time, slightly fewer than one-fourth (24 percent) of all households were married couples with children. This trend is caused by several factors, including the fact that many women and men are delaying marriage and putting off having children. In addition, the number of single-parent families is growing faster than the number of married couples. The former now account for 7 percent of all families. The number of households headed by single women with children grew five times faster during the 1990s than those with married couples with children. Some 5 percent of households are composed of unmarried couples, including many gay male and lesbian couples. The divorce rate is estimated to be above 40 percent. The number of blended families formed after the divorce or death of a spouse has also increased dramatically. The fact that in one in four households people are living alone creates enlarging opportunities for family-like ministries. To respond to these continuing changes, pastoral caregivers must enlarge their thinking about families and develop innovative strategies and programs.

One significant family change in recent years is that grandparents in increasing numbers are raising grandchildren or even great-grandchildren.[1] In many cases, the children's parents are incapacitated by drug or alcohol addictions, mental illnesses, or AIDS. The predicament faced by many of these grandparents is that they are widowed or divorced and living on limited, fixed incomes. The children often have serious health problems that put the grandparents under heavy financial stress. As a result, one-fourth of children being raised by their grandparents are living at or below the government level of poverty. Most government aid for children is designed to help foster parents and single mothers, and not grandparents raising children. In light of the pressing needs of parenting grandparents, church-related caregivers have a significant opportunity to give emotional support to grandparents and their grandchildren as well as to make appropriate referral to community health services that can assist them. Trained lay volunteer caregivers can give much of the emotional support needed by these grandparents.

The Crucial Importance of Healthy Families

Healthy families are society's greatest wholeness resource because, for better or for worse, human personality is "homegrown." Families are the primary settings where the seeds of healthy or unhealthy religious and ethical values and behavior are planted. The master gardeners are parents, supported by grandparents and other relatives as well as teachers, including pastors. Thus we parents, individually and collectively, have the future wholeness of the human family at our fingertips. This is an awesome, demanding, and exciting responsibility as well as a wonderful opportunity.

A measure of the quality of life in a community is the way it treats its most vulnerable and defenseless citizens. Children constitute by far the largest group among the most vulnerable in society. Their well-being is an accurate indicator of their parents' well-being and that of the wider social system of that society. For example, when families are trapped in the vicious cycle of poverty with inadequate nutrition, housing, education, and health care, their children have few opportunities to break out to a healthier, more liberated lifestyle.

Fortunately the leaders of many countries are beginning to understand that investing in their children's well-being is the best way to move their country and the world toward a society that is less violent, healthier, and more secure. Almost all countries have ratified the United Nations' Convention on the Rights of the Child that requires countries around the planet to ensure that children have adequate nutrition, education, health care, and living standards. Obviously most countries, including the United States, have much to do to meet their obligations to families and children.

Characteristics of Healthy Families

To cultivate wholeness effectively in people's lives, pastoral caregivers need to understand the characteristics of wholeness-generating families. An illuminating survey of 550 professionals who work in family education and counseling identified these traits of healthy families. Such families

- communicate and listen;
- affirm and support one another and teach respect for others;
- develop a sense of mutual trust;
- have a spirit of playfulness and humor;
- exhibit shared responsibility and teach values and a sense of right and wrong;
- have a religious core and a robust sense of family identity in which rituals and traditions abound;
- respect one another's privacy;
- value and practice service to others;
- foster family conversations and table time, and share leisure time;
- admit to and seek help for problems.

In a comparable vein, family therapy pioneer Virginia Satir identified the following attributes of healthy families:

- they support one another's self-esteem;
- they communicate in clear, direct, and honest ways;
- they accept one another's differences and tolerate one another's mistakes;
- they have implicit rules that are fair and flexible;

313

- they are open systems that interact in mutually supportive ways with other people and other families, and with institutions.[2]

Satir describes parents as "architects of families." As such, they are the key to creating family systems in which the wholeness of both adults and children flourishes and is not disabled by social evils such as racism, sexism, consumerism, and violence. Instead, family members are freed and empowered to grow toward life in all its fullness that, from a Christian perspective, is God's desire and dream for all human beings.

Because parents are the major influence in shaping the well-being of their children, wholeness-oriented pastoral caregivers have significant opportunities to coach them in cultivating healthy, justice-grounded faith, hope, and love in their families. They can also help parents uproot the weeds that our violent society often plants in families. Healthy parenting involves relating to children in ways that satisfy their deep heart hungers for essential psychological, social, and spiritual "soul foods." These needs include having security, food, shelter, and health care; having a sense of belonging; receiving and giving love; being esteemed by oneself and others; living with autonomy and freedom balanced by responsibility to others; claiming hope amid life's tragedies; experiencing sensual satisfactions and playfulness; and having a vital faith that gives life meaning and is nurtured by a growing relationship with the God of love and justice.

Deprivation of these soul foods is at the roots of a variety of psychological, psychosomatic, interpersonal, physiological, and spiritual problems. Severe deficits generate violent, destructive behavior patterns that frequently wound the persons and those around them in their family, their community, and the wider world. Families in which adults satisfy the essential personality hungers of children generate psychologically and emotionally healthy children with the precious gift of spiritual awareness. Rachael Carson, nature-loving author of *Silent Spring*, points to a major key to this growth process: "If a child is to keep alive his inborn sense of wonder, he needs the companionship of at least one adult who rediscovers with him the joy, excitement and mystery of the world we live in."[3]

A statement called the "Girls' Bill of Rights"[4] describes some crucial needs that, when satisfied, adequately lay the foundation for healthy development in girls. These rights are equally important for boys, but in our sexist society many girls have less family and societal support for having these rights fulfilled. Girls have the right

- to be themselves and to resist gender stereotyping;
- to express themselves with originality and enthusiasm;
- to prepare for interesting work and economic independence;

- to have confidence in themselves and to be safe in the world;
- to accept and appreciate their bodies;
- to take risks, to strive freely, and to take pride in success.

Families Are Evolving: Transgenerational Social Systems

One of the many ways that pastoral caregiving has grown more resourceful in recent decades is the increasing use of the research findings and insights of social psychology, sociology, and multicultural anthropology. In contemporary language, the family is a social system or organism. Family therapy pioneer Nathan Ackerman once suggested that the term *organism* connotes the biological core of the family; its qualities of living process and functional unity; and its natural life history, "a period of germination, a birth, a growth and development, a capacity to adapt to change and crisis, a slow decline, and finally, dissolution of the old family into the new."[5] Whatever affects one part of the family organism automatically affects all parts, just as an infected, injured, or well-functioning hand influences the entire body. The family is the strategic center for understanding emotional disturbances and also for intervention in order to promote health and heal illness. In other words, the family group can make or break holistic health. It has this power insofar as it influences every aspect of human development and of human relations.

A family system, like other social organisms, is composed of several interdependent subsystems. It is important for family counselors to be aware of the patterns of interaction within and among these subsystems: husband-wife, mother-children, father-children, child-child, grandparents-parents, grandparents-grandchildren, child-pet, and so on. As an organism, a family has its unique psychological identity. The marital dyad identity becomes the core for the expanding family as children are added. The interaction, merging, and redifferentiation of this marital pair mold the identity of the new family. Just as a child's personality internalizes something of each parent and also evolves into something new, so too the identity of a new family incorporates something of the self-image of each marital partner and the images of their respective families of origin but also develops into something unique and new. The psychological identity of the marital pair shapes the child, but the child also shapes the parental pair to his or her needs.[6]

The behavior, attitudes, values, and relationship patterns of individual family members are shaped to a considerable degree by the family system—that is, the family rules, expectations, values, taboos, beliefs, stories, patterns of communication, and distribution of power among its members. This dynamic family system can frustrate or facilitate the healing and growth toward wholeness of all its members.[7]

An individual's symptoms can be understood as the product of that person's interaction with a total family organism that is not meeting the personality needs of its members. As Virginia Satir observes, the pain of the "identified patient" (the one who is labeled "sick," "neurotic," or "delinquent") is an overt expression of the covert pain that the whole family is suffering in its relationships.[8]

The "negative complementarity" of a disturbed family organism has been observed by many therapists. Psychoanalyst Martin Grotjahn describes the complementary neuroses that often exist among members of a family, producing mutual reinforcement of neurotic behavior.[9] Apparently all members in a disturbed family derive some emotional gains from the identified patient's sickness. The interpersonal balance in such families appears to be based on this unconscious family contract that says, "We all agree that this one of us will be 'sick' ['delinquent,' 'alcoholic'] so that the rest of us can continue to function." Numerous families encountered in counseling point to the dynamics of family systems. For example, addicted persons' spouses who become disturbed when their addict achieves sobriety, the "good" family that has unconsciously chosen a deviant member to act out the family's forbidden impulses, and the schizophrenic's family where the relative adequacy of the other members' functioning is contingent on the sick member staying sick can all be viewed as negative family dynamics complementarily. Families usually seek outside help only when the member who bears their conflicts disturbs persons outside the family or disrupts the precarious functioning of the "well" family members.

Since families function as living organic systems, it makes sense to enhance healthy families and treat unhealthy families as units. This is precisely what family enrichment and therapy seek to do. Pastors who grasp the profound implications of the family systems' perspective find that it makes a dramatic difference in all dimensions of their work with marriages and families, and also with individuals. In all counseling, caregivers are actually dealing with interlocking networks of persons, whether or not they are present in person. These networks include the individual's current family and family of origin. In individual counseling, one has direct access to only one part of that individual's total interpersonal network. The limitations are roughly analogous to those that physicians would face if they attempted to help all ill persons by examining and treating only one part of their physical organism. In spite of the limitations of this analogy, it communicates a fundamental truth: the essential interdependence of all persons.

Family enrichment and counseling are methods that intervene directly in total family systems, aiming at enabling all those involved to experience healing and growth in spiritually empowered wholeness. They do so by helping whole family systems to improve their interdependent network of need-satisfying relationships so that all will be freer to change and grow toward increased wholeness. The basic methods of conjoint couple enrichment and counseling, described in the preceding chapter, are equally useful in doing counseling and enrichment with whole families.

Caregiving for the Wider Human Family

As pointed out earlier, interaction with the wider social systems in which they are immersed affects and continually shapes the health of family systems. These wider systems include extended family, congregation, community, ethnic group, economic and political systems, country, and so on, out to the wider world of which they are a small part. Awareness of the impact of the wider society on individuals and families is essential for caregiving that seeks to be prophetic as well as holistic and transformational. Because the well-being of individuals and families is continually influenced by the health of all the institutions in their social context, these cannot be ignored when families seek help with their problems in living.

The social context perspective enables caregivers to be aware of the important fact that many pressures not experienced by more affluent upper- and middle-class families have an impact on poor families. For this reason, many poor, marginalized, and minority families suffer family disruptions rooted in their social, economic, and educational deprivation. From their perspective, family life programs in affluent congregations often seem elitist and irrelevant to their struggles to survive: their need to find adequate food, housing, health care, and employment. To make them more relevant to the needs of both rich and poor families, family programs should acknowledge the reality of social and economic issues and make concrete recommendations for meeting them.

From this wider perspective, it is important to recognize that many families feel trapped and helpless as they confront the reality of globalization and urbanization. These forces have led to the breakdown of traditional cultural modes of social support and caregiving, including extended family controls. We live in an interconnected world with powerful interdependent forces of economic, cultural, and technological communication, globalization, and the knowledge explosion of the Internet. All these forces reinforce one another and make it imperative that pastoral caregivers learn to use their healing and wellness tools far beyond the counseling room. These forces are producing profound transformations on many levels of human life, including family life in the twenty-first century. Individual, family, ethnic, and national identities influence one another in subtle and pervasive ways. The communication revolution being produced by the Internet is making the reality of Marshall McLuhan's global village more and more obvious.

Developing Marriage and Family Caregiving Programs

How can congregations develop comprehensive and innovative family caregiving programs to meet the enormous needs of families in today's turbulent society? Here are four steps in a process that has proved useful in developing such programs in classes, growth groups, workshops, or retreat settings:

Step 1: *Decide on responsibilities.* Congregational leaders need to designate who within their organizational structure will be responsible for developing innovative programs aimed at strengthening the quality of life for those in various types of relationships. In small congregations this can be the pastor and a few members whose backgrounds and training as educators equip them to be involved. In churches of any size, strengthening family ministries can be done by an existing group such as the one responsible for education, family life, or congregational caregiving. In larger churches a special relationship wholeness task group can be set up to coordinate relational ministries. The responsible group partners with the pastor or religious education director to plan and develop programs to enhance marriage, family, and singles relationships or a program tailored to meet the special needs growing out of the demographics of a particular congregation and its wider community. It is wise to include persons who reflect the ages as well as the ethnic and educational backgrounds of the congregation in such groups. It is also good to include persons from related committees and boards; for example, the education, caregiving, or program planning committees. Such overlapping membership makes for better coordination in developing new programs.

Step 2: *Evaluate the present program to identify unmet or partially met clusters of needs of families.* The checklist below is an instrument to stimulate the thinking and enlarge the vision of planners about possible services and groups to meet needs in their congregations. The list is an overview illustrating the rich variety of possible marriage and family resources. Wholeness-oriented churches are developing such programs. Congregations do not need all or even most of these programs because several of the needs can be met effectively in the same workshop, class, retreat, or growth group. For example, relationship enrichment, parenting skills training, coping with changing roles, and sexual enhancement can be included in a couple enrichment event. The key point is that major leadership resources should be devoted to developing a smorgasbord of such family enhancement experiences tailored to respond to the particular needs of congregational members and the wider community.

Step 3: *Devise goals, strategies, and a workable plan to meet major clusters of inadequately met needs.* After evaluating the present family programs and identifying unmet needs (perhaps by using the checklist), decision makers should prioritize the unmet needs, arranging them in order of importance, urgency, and feasibility. Then the sequence and timing for developing new family events and groups can be planned. The relationship wholeness committee or other planning group can delegate responsibility to ad hoc task groups for particular family life projects. In devising plans, it is good to remember that creating new groups may not be the most effective way to meet some needs more fully. Existing couples clubs, adult church school couples classes, and men's and women's groups should be encouraged to include relationship enrichment events in their programs regularly.

Step 4: *Implement the plan and then evaluate it before deciding on next steps to meet other families' wholeness needs.* Everyone who attends growth-in-wholeness events should be provided a form to evaluate them in writing. In addition, some who were invited but did not attend should be contacted. One church sponsored a poorly attended retreat for young marrieds at a hotel away from the local community. Phone calls to several couples who had been interested but did not attend made it clear that the cost and child-care problems were major reasons for the sparse attendance. The planning group decided to have subsequent enrichment events at the church with child-care services available.

Overview of Congregational Relationship Caregiving Groups and Services

Directions: Go through the services and groups listed below, and use the blank in front of them to note those that are now adequately covered and those that should be added or strengthened to enhance the caregiving ministry of a congregation. Bear in mind that many of these resources can be made available in a variety of educative counseling groups, workshops, retreats, or classes. A number of these services and groups will be explored in more depth later.

_____ Readily available counseling, support, and grief-healing groups for families hit by painful crises, disabilities, addictions, and losses

_____ Referral of families in severe crises to competent professionals or agencies

_____ Relationship skill training for youth and young adults

_____ Long-range relationship training for adolescents to enable them to prepare for creative marriage or singlehood

_____ Healthy sexuality class for children, youth, and parents

_____ Group preparation for creative marriage followed by a minimum of three educative counseling sessions with individual couples

_____ Relationship enrichment programs to keep love growing so as to make good marriages and families even better

_____ Program to help couples prepare for the challenges of remarriage and constructive stepparenting

_____ Program for supporting couples in the early adjustment years of marriage

_____ Postwedding-growth counseling sessions with couples at six months and one year

_____ Parenting skills training for expectant and new parents

_____ Parents' class to prepare for meaningful infant baptism or dedication

_____ Parents and teens dialogue group

_____ Emptying-nest enrichment retreat for midyears couples

_____ Multigenerational family enrichment retreat or workshop

_____ A family enrichment camp or workshop/playshop

_____ A parents and teens caring communication workshop

_____ Annual all-church enrichment celebration for singles, couples, and families in all life stages

_____ Annual fun day for couples and singles to enjoy playing together

_____ Single-parent support and enrichment group or class

_____ Grief-healing and growth group for divorced and widowed persons

_____ Grief-healing group for parents whose children have died or developed major disabilities

_____ A spiritual discovery class or personal Bible study group for couples, singles, and families to enhance their spirituality and values

_____ "Enjoying Health-giving Spirituality"—a class or retreat for couples, families, and singles (also an emphasis in all such events)

_____ Healthy sexuality, a topic in all premarriage, marriage, and singlehood events

_____ Creative divorce workshop for separating individuals

_____ Relationship enhancement and skill training for gay men, lesbians, and bisexual persons and their families of origin

_____ Gay and lesbian nuclear family support and enrichment programs

_____ Workshop for couples, families, and singles on cultivating the seven dimensions of wellness

_____ Creative coping with changing gender roles and relationships

_____ A parents' training workshop on raising liberated, nonsexist children

_____ A training program for lay marriage and family enrichment facilitators preparing them to support and coach newlywed couples, especially teens

_____ A training program in facilitating family support and wholeness for carefully selected laypersons caregivers

_____ A supportive growth group for parents and grandparents of seriously disabled and terminally ill children

_____ A growth group for individuals and families who have recently moved to the community

_____ "Making a Creative Difference"—events to train individuals, couples, and families for community outreach in both social service and social justice work

_____ Training events to equip individuals and couples with caring skills to respond to the needs of friends, family, and neighbors

_____ Healthy family enrichment workshops, classes, or growth groups

_____ Playing-for-fun and wholeness events for children and parents

_____ Study-for-growth classes aimed at intellectual growth and focusing on a stimulating book such as one about spirituality and ethical justice issues

_____ Liberation groups for women, for men, and for couples desiring fresh approaches to changing female/male roles

_____ "Enjoying Creativity"—groups using drama, poetry, painting, pottery, body movement, creative dance, yoga, and so on to stimulate creative growth

_____ Sharing and caring groups for mutual help in coping constructively with common causes of stress; for example, aging parents, physical and mental disabilities, a child with disabilities, "adolescing" children

_____ Study-action-growth groups for personal development and training for significant tasks such as community service and social action

_____ Spiritual growth

_____ Caring for creation—ecology groups for tuning in on nature, experiencing God in nature, and healing the wounded environment

_____ Multiple-family learning groups composed of several couples, singles, and persons from different racial, ethnic, and religious backgrounds

_____ Creating and maintaining loving family relationships when your gay and/or lesbian child comes out

_____ "Choosing Your Path"—classes on career choices and life planning with coaching for those in vocational transition

_____ "Continuing Your Growth Journey"—groups for individuals and couples who have completed counseling or therapy successfully

Caregiving in Chronic and Acute Family Crises

At their heart all human crises are interpersonal events. This is true in the sense that both the causes and the resources for constructive coping are derived, to a considerable degree, from one's interpersonal support system. People who live alone and lack robust support systems, as well as nuclear families who do not have close relationships with their extended family (or its psychological equivalent in a network of close friends), are acutely vulnerable to crises of all types. It behooves the pastor, therefore, to use the family systems perspective in approaching all crisis counseling, especially family crises.

When individuals are hit by trauma, their entire family network is affected. For this reason, it is important to provide pastoral care and, when needed, counseling for the whole family. All members of the family are probably hurting, some more obviously than others. To help families use their problems as opportunities for growth, it is essential, whenever possible, to intervene pastorally with the entire family. Be aware that when family members seek the help of counselors, they usually have reached an impasse in their relationships, are not coping effectively with their family problems, and are floundering in unproductive conflicts. The goal of counselors is not to solve their problems but to open up blocked communication in the family system so that they can understand and change the causes of their mutual attacking. The goal is also to coach them in trying more constructive approaches to their problems—approaches that will produce more mutual satisfaction of all family members' basic needs.

When pastors are contacted about a family crisis, usually by a troubled parent, it is important to establish rapport with that person and then, if possible, involve the whole family in conjoint counseling sessions. In contacting other family members by phone, the pastor may say, "In my experience, when one member of a family is hurting, others usually are feeling some pain. It may be helpful to all of you if your whole family would come to discuss the situation you all face and decide what you can do about it. Each of you probably has some useful ideas that would help make things better for all of you." Such family counseling meetings may take place in their home (if interruptions such as phone calls and TV can be kept at a minimum) or in the pastor's study. Different aspects of a family's interaction probably will be evident in each setting.

The most difficult transition in moving into whole-family counseling is helping family members enlarge their definition of "the problem" from the person who is obviously disturbed to the whole family system; but only to the degree that this occurs will other family members accept the fact that they have some responsibility to change their behavior in the family. Unless this happens, family counseling will be less than fully effective.

Gay and Lesbian Families

Gay and lesbian families have strengths and weaknesses similar to those of other families. They have, however, additional challenges that may or may not bring them to their pastor for help. Initially when members come out, the systems and identity of families of origin of gay and lesbian people (children, adolescent, or adult) will be disrupted and challenged to change. The disruption and challenge are particularly acute in religiously conservative families who may believe that the gay/lesbian has chosen his or her sexual orientation and can, if he or she wishes, change. The situation is complicated further when the parents and/or other family members believe that homosexual behavior is sinful. Tragically, such families may believe that it is their religious duty to cut off their gay and lesbian members. Some parents may blame themselves for their children's orientation, assuming that there must have been something wrong in their children's upbringing. If such families do not seek pastoral help, the pastor should offer support and help with sensitivity to their need for privacy and with loving impartiality. The aim of all pastoral care with such families is to educate them about the nature of homosexuality, support the ongoing integrity of the family, and facilitate loving relationships within it.

In his book *Pastoral Care of Gays, Lesbians, and Their Families*, David K. Switzer offers an excellent discussion of the nature of homosexuality and ethical issues surrounding it as well as insights from his rich experience doing pastoral care with gay and lesbian persons and their families. His section on pastoral care with homosexual teens and their families is particularly important because of the danger of suicide among such teens struggling with their sexual orientation. According to a study reported in *Prevention and Interventions in Youth Suicide*, gay and lesbian youth are more liable to commit suicide than straight youth. Thirty percent of all completed youth suicides involve sexual identity.[10]

In addition to the families of origin, there are a growing number of gay and lesbian families with children. There were an estimated 300,000 to 500,000 gay and lesbian biological parents in 1976. In 1990, an estimated 6 to 14 million children had gay or lesbian parents. Census 2000 reported 601,209 same-sex unmarried partner households in the United States, a 314 percent increase from 1990 when the census reported only 145,130 same-sex unmarried partner households. According to the Child Welfare Information Gateway, between 8 and 10 million children are being raised by gay parents. It is also notable that gay and lesbian families are to be found not only in large cities but also in small towns and rural areas in both the Deep South and the Pacific Northwest.[11] It is therefore likely that several of these families will be in a church community regardless of its geographical location.

Gay and lesbian families not only deal with the usual relationship problems—money and sexual problems, division of labor issues, personality and child-rearing styles—they also have to cope with job and legal discrimination as well as social stereotyping, such as the assumption that their children are per se disadvantaged or that they will turn out to be gay or lesbian. The components of the gay and lesbian family system are quite different from those of the traditional heterosexual family. Its members have few models for guidance. Then there is the necessity of coming out to the children, who may have been adopted, may have begun life in a heterosexual family, or may have surrogate biological parents. It seems likely that children of gay and lesbian families are vulnerable to bullying when their family situation becomes known to peers. All of these conditions highlight their need for supportive pastoral care and occasionally for pastoral counseling or therapy. It is imperative that "straight" pastoral caregivers become informed regarding the personal and social problems that confront gay and lesbian persons and their families. Regardless of the caregivers' personal beliefs regarding the gay and lesbian lifestyle, they are obliged to treat such persons and their families with love and justice. Otherwise they should refer them to someone who can be empathetic and impartial.

Methods of Family Counseling

The good news is that most of the "how to" methods for enhancing couple wholeness described in the previous chapter can be adapted for use in pastoral caregiving with families. For example, many parents discover that the Intentional Relationship Method and the Relationship Satisfaction-Justice Inventory are valuable tools for achieving constructive conflict resolution and enhancing love-nurturing communication in their families.

The ABCDE (see chapter 6) approach to crisis counseling can be integrated with the Intentional Relationship Method and used to help families cope and grow from their crises. In the A and B steps it is important to establish a trustful relationship with each family member. Each should have an opportunity to articulate perceptions and feelings regarding the family problem and thoughts about constructive solutions. Boiling down a family's problem by identifying its separate parts is best done with each family member contributing perspectives. Using the second step of the IRM ("What I want or need from this family is...") can be a valuable part of the diagnostic, boiling-down, or refining process. When young children are involved in family counseling sessions, the second step of the IRM can be paraphrased, "If you had a magic wand and could use it to make things better in your family, I would make the following changes..." The steps of the IRM can often be done by a series of family go-rounds, beginning with the least assertive and least verbal member.

Before the end of the first session, but after their hurt and anger have been expressed and reduced, give each member an opportunity to tell the others what she or he appreciates about the family and the individuals within it (step one in the IRM). It can be remarkably healing for families bogged down in cycles of mutual hurting to hear the mutual affirmations in this exercise. I recall being deeply touched when a long-alienated father and adolescent son began to be reconciled during a conjoint family session as they stated what they still liked about each other.

When the major unmet needs and wants that have caused and/or resulted from the crisis are out on the table for family discussion, the counselor should help the family negotiate a change plan enabling them to meet some of each person's needs. In this step, family members identify the growth points at which they can enhance their relationships by responding more fully and intentionally to one another's needs. Helping the family develop and act on a workable change plan is the third step in both the ABCDE crisis approach and the IRM. Relatively functional families often can, with an understanding pastor's coaching, decide within a few sessions on ways of making constructive changes in their basic family contract. Mutual family affirmation should be repeated occasionally during the process of family counseling as a way of making them aware of positive changes they are accomplishing together and encouraging them to build on these.

In negotiating a workable family change plan, it is essential to have an agreement about precisely what each person will do, and what each will give and get as the plan is implemented. In this way, a family can revise the family contract to make it fairer and more effective in coping with the family's crisis.

Pastoral Uses of Conjoint Family Therapy

Family group therapy, the simultaneous treatment of an entire family, is one of the most widely used and productive developments among current methods of helping troubled persons. During recent years, there has been a surge of interest in this approach, broadening the focus of many counselors and therapists from individual intrapsychic therapies to include family-organism therapies. A variety of distinctive styles of family therapy have been developed.[12]

Family therapist Jay Haley declares,

> The family therapist would seem to be arguing thus: psychopathology in the individual is a product of the way he deals with intimate relations, the way they deal with him, and the way other family members involve him in their relations with each other. Further, the appearance of symptomatic behavior in an individual is necessary for the continued functioning of that particular family system. Therefore, changes in the individual can only occur if the family system changes, and resistance to change in an individual centers in the influence of the family as a group. Most techniques of family therapy center in shifting the focus from the identified patient to the family and then resolving the problems in family relationships. At that point the individuals in the family undergo change.[13]

The common assumption of the family therapies is that the most effective way to help a troubled family member is to help the whole family change ways of relating and communicating. All these therapies start with the systems perspective described above. Their shared goal is to enhance relationships within families so that they will become better environments of healing and growth for all their members.

Objectives of Family Systems Counseling

Here is a summary of the major goals of family systems counseling. Counselors meet with the entire family, and occasionally with a subsystem within the family, to help the family learn the following:

1. To communicate their feelings (both positive and negative), needs, desires, values, and hopes more openly, clearly, and congruently. In this process, the therapist is a coach of effective, relationship-strengthening communication skills.

2. To shift from focusing mainly on the "identified patient" and to deal with the often hidden pain, conflict, and blocked growth in all family members that are at the roots of the individual's problems. This may involve a number of marriage therapy sessions with the wife-husband subsystem.

3. To interrupt their mutually damaging hurt-anger-attack cycles sooner and to gradually substitute self-feeding cycles of mutual need satisfaction among family members.

4. To mutually nourish rather than starve self-esteem among family members.

5. To become aware of the family's contract—its implicit rules, roles, values, expectations, stories, and beliefs—and then to renegotiate a more growthful working agreement that fairly distributes satisfactions and responsibilities, power, and growth opportunities.

6. To see the positive but abortive growth strivings in much of the frustrating behavior of family members and to learn how to encourage the expression of these strivings in more self-actualizing ways.

7. To resolve more constructively the inevitable conflicts of living together, recognizing that growth often can be activated precisely at the points of conflict.

8. To develop a healthier balance between the need for togetherness and the need for autonomy, giving more room for the latter.

9. To experiment with new behaviors and ways of relating that are more responsive to the real needs of all family members. This often involves doing family "homework" assignments between sessions.

10. To make the interaction within and among the subsystem more growth engendering.

11. To open up the family system by developing more supportive relationships with other people, families, and institutions outside the family.

12. To create an interpersonal climate of high-level wellness within the family, thus making it a better growth environment for all its members.[14]

Virginia M. Satir's conjoint family therapy approach emphasizes the marital relationship as the axis around which all other family relationships are formed. The identified patient—for example, a disturbed child or adolescent—is the family member who is most obviously affected by the pained marital relationship. But there is a circular relationship among all the persons within the family system; the disturbed child's behavior disturbs the parents' relationship and vice versa. The distorted communication patterns of a family reveal the nature of its underlying problems. The dysfunctional persons did not learn in childhood to communicate effectively because of low self-esteem and their own distorted parent-child communication. Dysfunctional parenting produces dysfunctional families, which perpetuate distorted communication patterns.[15] To correct these problems, family therapists aim at helping families

- improve communication of their feelings and family problems;
- take the risk of looking at themselves and their interactions, often for the first time;
- rebuild their self-esteem;
- renegotiate their implicit family rules and contract to make these more fair and need satisfying for all family members;
- unscramble garbled and conflicted "double-bind" messages (e.g., "Move away closer!");
- complete gaps in messages;
- recognize the hurt behind anger and the control behind silence;
- make sure no one in the family continues to speak for others.

Family therapists are teachers of conflict-resolving and need-nurturing communication. They are coaches of constructive interpersonal relating.

Like individual psychotherapy, effective family therapy with troubled families requires considerable therapeutic skill and understanding of individual and interpersonal dynamics.[16] Most clergy in generalist ministries have not had and do not need the training, and neither do they have time to do family therapy with dysfunctional families. As indicated earlier, a pastor's crucial function with such families is to help them find a well-trained family therapist.

Fortunately many insights and methods of family therapy can be used in enrichment work with healthy families, as well as in short-term crisis counseling with dysfunctional families. The family systems perspective that is the conceptual foundation of family therapy can function like a valuable new set of glasses for pastors, enabling them to see and understand families in fresh, illuminating ways. It is invaluable, for example, to become aware of the interpersonal atmosphere or emotional climate of a family when making a pastoral call in their home or seeing them for counseling during a family crisis. Otherwise enigmatic behavior is clarified when understood in the light of the family's general pattern and implicit rules for relating and communicating. The family systems perspective affirms the fact that we are "members of each other," that our brokenness and our wholeness reflect the quality of our network of need-satisfying relationships. This perspective tends to reduce unproductive blaming, since everyone in the family is involved in helping to maintain the family pattern of which much individual behavior is a manifestation.

Healthy Family Enrichment Sessions, with individual families or with several families in a family camp or workshop, is an adaptation of family therapy aimed at helping functional families develop more of their potentials and thus discover the hidden, latent family in every actual family.[17] The wholeness of families can be enhanced significantly by their regular participation in a family growth booster.

The systemic perspective also offers a variety of resources for enhancing spiritual and value growth in wholeness. Family therapy and family crisis counseling are ways of helping families revise their guiding values and priorities when these are not functioning constructively. A family's basic philosophy and theology of life—values and spiritual orientation—are "caught" much more than they are "taught," as children absorb the meaning and value orientation of their families. Continuing spiritual development throughout adulthood is best nurtured in family-like caring groups in which spiritual values are experienced in relationships. A vital dimension of an open, growing family system is its openness to the wider spiritual reality called God. This openness provides a transpersonal context of meaning and spiritual support. The wholeness of family members can be nurtured by their awareness of their profound connection with other persons, with humankind, with the biosphere, and with the divine Spirit of the universe.[18]

Helping Parents Help Troubled Children and Youth

Family crises in which the guidance of pastors is sought often involve parent-child, parent-adolescent, child-parent-grandparent, in-law, and sibling relationships. Adults who seek help for a child usually do so because the child's behavior worries them or because it concerns someone outside the family, often the school authorities or law enforcement officers. Pastoral counselors need to be able to help parents recognize seriously hurting children and youth. Signs of serious behavior problems include frequent aggressive and destructive behavior, lying and stealing, and severe learning problems. But some children who are deeply disturbed do not act in such ways that upset adults. Quiet, shy children are sometimes simply that. Certainly there's nothing wrong with being quiet or shy. But if this quietness seems excessive, there may be serious underlying problems. Symptoms of such problems include withdrawal from peer relationships; exaggerated fears, phobias, and terrifying nightmares; serious speech problems; and bizarre behavior. Severe or multiple psychosomatic problems, including asthma, colitis, frequent stomachaches and headaches, rashes, and other physiological problems, may be rooted in emotional conflict within the child or interpersonal conflict in the family.

To assist parents in identifying serious problems with which the help of a trained child therapist is needed, raise questions such as these: "Is the behavior you're worried about appropriate for your child's age? How severe is the problem, and how long has it been occurring? Does the behavior represent a sharp change? Is the child's behavior related to major stresses and crises in the family or in the community or world?" Children often respond in disturbed or disturbing ways after major grief experiences such as an uprooting move, the hospitalization and/or death of a family member, or parents' divorce. They frequently respond more than adults do to crises in their community or in the larger society because they have not developed the inner defenses to violence and tragedies that keep adults from responding as much.

Unless it is clear that a child is seriously disturbed and referral to a family therapist is needed, it is appropriate for pastors with some clinical supervised training in family counseling to discover whether they can help the family. When young children are in family counseling or enhancement sessions, I usually provide them with simple play therapy materials such as crayons and paper. Using these materials during the session provides something expressive and satisfying for children to do. It often also involves them in the therapeutic interaction of the family on their own level. Several times the pictures that children have drawn have shed light on family issues when they share them during a whole-family session.

Parents' Use of Play Therapy

Pastoral counselors can help parents in families going through crises to adapt play therapy methods in order to help prevent or heal their children's disturbances. Such crises include natural disasters, a death or divorce in the family, an auto accident, a major move, a war or terrorist attack, or the fear of one of these crises. Clark Moustakas, an expert in play therapy, recommends that parents create a particular place or corner in the child's room for do-it-yourself play therapy.[19] This corner should be stocked with a variety of play materials such as paints and paper; puppets or doll families for fantasy play; clay for making and squashing things; and toys for encouraging constructive release of pent-up frustration, anger, and aggressiveness—for example, pounding boards, punching devices, and things for throwing without hurting. With this equipment parents can encourage children to play through and resolve disturbing feelings generated by family or community crises. When our two sons were preschoolers, they were in the car when my spouse had an accident. For several weeks afterward, they spontaneously created and played a therapeutic game crashing their toy cars.

The role of counselors or parents in such play therapy is to encourage free expression, to be available to relate as children reach out, and, if necessary, to enforce ground rules such as, "Here we can do anything we like except hurt ourselves or others or destroy property." Communication and expression by children should be spontaneous and free through play, fantasy, words, paintings, acting with dolls, and expressing anxieties and aggressiveness. The facilitator doesn't pressure the children to discuss what they are doing, but welcomes and encourages spontaneous communication by listening attentively and responding warmly.

Such do-it-yourself play therapy can be done with individual children or in small groups. It encourages children to play out disturbing feelings such as anger, rage, jealousy, fear, guilt, shame, and destructiveness so that these will not be expressed in self-hurting or other-hurting behavior; will not block positive feelings such as joy, love, pleasure, and self-esteem; and will not distort relationships. Play therapy activities provide an experience of relating to adults, including parents, teachers, or counselors, who really value feelings, imagination, and play in children as well as in themselves.[20] They can also help children grow in their self-esteem by enhancing their all-important "it's good to be me" feelings.

Recommendations for Constructive Parenting

Constructive discipline. Caregivers can help parents raise nonviolent children by encouraging them to use positive reinforcement, such as praise, to handle situations requiring discipline. Negative reinforcement like spanking imprints children with a destructive message—namely, that violence dispensed by bigger people with more power is the appropriate way to respond when children become adults.

The shaping power of example. As someone has said, "In many nonverbal ways a child makes this demanding request of each parent: 'Please be the kind of person you want me to become.'" The most effective parental teaching is by setting example.

Raising Liberated Children

One important goal in all family education and parent training should be to help parents raise children who are as free as possible from sexism, racism, ageism, and the burdens of families oppressed by poverty and ignorance. An experienced child therapist declares,

It's not easy to be a child of either sex. Children are hurt very early by many things. Some are crippled for life by poverty, ignorance, fear and emotional or physical pain. Our rigid expectations of what's okay for boys and what's okay for girls is crippling too. It shows in homes, classrooms, and on playgrounds as well as in play therapy rooms. An image that comes to me now is the tiny bound feet of a Chinese baby. That practice has disappeared, but most cultures still bind the spirits of children in many ways. Girls are bound tighter than boys, particularly when it comes to passivity and aggressiveness and life choices. Very early, girls know that they are to be compliant and submissive and to behave so as to please others.[21]

Children acquire their basic attitudes and feelings about racial differences and about men and women by observing their parents. As Charlotte Holt Clinebell (now Charlotte Ellen) points out, "Children raised by liberated parents in equalitarian marriages will be liberated themselves. Their inner freedom will make it possible for them to cope with the cultural [sex role] boxes which change so slowly."[22]

The Family Crisis of Separation and Divorce

Divorce is one of the most widespread occasions of crisis and grief in Western societies. In the United States more than one million couples terminate their marriages each year. This means that nearly three million adults and children are directly involved in the trauma of the disintegration and death of a marriage and the rupturing of a family system. More than 50 percent of all marriages will end in divorce. Yet in spite of this statistic, our society suffers a severe shortage of resources for helping divorcing women and men do their grief work and grow during these painful experiences.

This great need makes it crucial that more and more congregations take the initiative in reaching out in healing ways to these countless wounded people who have often felt judged or kept at a distance in religious circles. Churches have strategic opportunities to develop innovative caregiving programs aimed at enabling people to grow in the losses of divorce by transforming them into opportunities for emotional, spiritual, and interpersonal growth. But to be effective in a healing ministry with divorcing people, clergy who have not experienced divorce personally often must increase understanding of and empathy for the experience. Nonjudgmental, in-depth listening to persons in the process of divorce and recovery is the most effective path to this understanding and empathy.

Powerful and painful emotions frequently occur during divorces. Intense anger, rage, bitterness, resentment, loneliness, disappointment, self-doubt, guilt, and depression often swirl within divorcing persons. If not resolved, these feelings frequently produce infected grief wounds that heal slowly or not at all. Even if people want divorces because they need to be free from destructive relationships, pain and grief are usually mingled with their sense of relief, release, and liberation.

Divorce diminishes feelings of self-confidence, self-worth, and cope-ability for a while. Because many women in our society are programmed to feel a special responsibility for the success of interpersonal relationships, their sense of failure and guilt tends to be more intense than men's. Both men and women feel the wound of rejection if they did not want or initiate the divorce. Unfortunately feelings of failure and rejection are reinforced by the judgmental attitudes of some people, including some in congregations. A study that compared the experiences of divorced and widowed women revealed that the divorced women felt significantly less social support and more sense of restriction and isolation than did widows. They also suffered from more physical and mental health disturbances than the widows.

Pastoral caregivers need to be aware that the decision to end a violent, destructive, or loveless marriage can be a first essential step toward a new, more constructive lifestyle for the couple and their children. The possibilities that it will be so can be increased by a skilled pastoral counselor and/or an effective divorce growth group. In her book *The Divorce Culture*, Barbara Dafoe Whitehead observes that around 1990 and continuing today, a change has taken place. The social stigma about divorce has declined and been replaced with a more accepting and nonjudgmental attitude that recognizes that all human relationships have problems. This hopeful trend is evident among many members of mainline religious groups.

When one or both persons are considering divorce, counselors should first encourage them to try to rebuild their dysfunctional relationship on a stronger foundation using couple crisis counseling. If this fails, they should be urged to move immediately into individual divorce recovery counseling. Unfortunately, many people terminate counseling relationships at that point because they feel that counseling has failed and do not realize that they could be helped greatly by skilled divorce counseling. Of course, some people are not open to divorce counseling by clergy because they fear that they will be judged and put down for failing to fulfill their wedding vows. If pastors are judgmental or feel that "saving marriages" is the sole purpose of their relationship counseling, such fears are appropriate.

Divorce counseling is an example of educative caregiving or coaching, a process that blends counseling skills with sound guidance and helpful information. The primary aims are to help couples learn how to come apart as constructively as possible, thus avoiding more bitterness and pain for themselves and for their children if they have them. Persons in individual counseling sessions must talk through and thus reduce, if not resolve, their grief, anger, and other painful feelings. This will reduce the emotional cost of splitting up their dysfunctional family system.

Beyond the goal of healing divorce wounds, the transformational or growth objective of divorce counseling is to help persons learn how to grow as much as possible from the painful experience. Coaching can focus on helping people to do things that will enable them to transform the painful crisis into an opportunity to learn and grow. In this way they can use their divorce to open a new, more constructive chapter in their lives and relationships. Accomplishing this is the best preparation for either creative singlehood or remarriage. Since only one-fourth of divorced persons remain single longer than five years, divorce counseling often is also preparation for remarriage. (Five out of six divorced men and three out of four divorced women in the United States marry again. Many others begin intimate relationships but do not remarry.) Helping people move toward this growth-in-wholeness objective involves encouraging them to face and change what they contributed to the sickness and death of their previous marriage. In addition, it involves coaching them as they learn essential communication and conflict-resolution skills, the lack of which contributed to the weakness of their failed relationships. The plethora of complex, new decisions divorcing persons are forced by their circumstances to make is much more likely to be constructive if they have reality-oriented coaching as they deal with these issues.

Participating in a creative divorce group or retreat, or taking part in a growing-through-loss group, can be a major stimulus for such learning and growth. After the acute crisis has passed, it may be a constructive move to invest in personal psychotherapy to resolve the emotional problems and change the behavior patterns that contributed to the disintegration of the marriage. This will help free persons to function more constructively as parents. It will also enable them to learn from their divorce, thus lessening the danger that they will repeat dysfunctional relationship patterns in the future.

Diminishing the Trauma of Divorce for Children

For couples with children, a crucial objective of divorce counseling should be to help them help their children cope constructively with the multiple losses and thus reduce to a minimum the emotional damage their children suffer. The heart of the trauma for children comes from the splitting apart of the marital dyad around which the family system had been formed and in which their identity has been rooted and shaped. Because their children's emotional well-being is at stake, divorcing parents often are highly motivated to negotiate what is best for them. It is crucial for divorcing couples to be helped to communicate in rational, nonattacking ways as they struggle to negotiate an agreement that will be best for them and their children. But communicating in nonattacking ways often is possible only after the adults involved have drained off and reduced the pressure of their hurt, anger, and grief through individual, growth-oriented counseling.

Most divorcing parents worry about the emotionally destructive impact on their children. Educative divorce counseling with parents includes communicating what is known about minimizing the trauma for children. Pastoral caregivers can coach divorcing parents to follow guidelines such as these to reduce the painful impact on their children:

• Avoid senseless rancor that will expose children to added trauma.
• Help children avoid blaming themselves for their parents' problems.

- Be honest with children about what is happening, but delay informing young children about an impending divorce until definite plans for their future have been agreed upon.
- Resist the temptation to use children as counselors, confidants, or spies, or to use them as a battleground for attacking the ex-spouse.
- Place the child or children with whichever parent is able to provide a more secure, nurturing relationship and home. One household should be established as home for the child with the other as a place to visit. Don't ask children under twelve to make the choice concerning which parent they will live with. Don't separate siblings.
- Make joint efforts to help children retain whatever feelings of love and respect they have for both parents.
- Get play therapy and/or talk therapy for children to help them work through and resolve painful feelings of grief and irrational feelings such as feeling responsible for parents' breaking up or for getting them back together.

Because of intense anger and hurt feelings, many divorcing couples are unable to implement sound recommendations until they have had extensive counseling. It is important to offer supportive educative counseling to parents to enable them to talk through their emotional blocks, such as hurt and hostility, that otherwise may interfere with their taking constructive action.

However, persons weathering the grief crisis of separation and divorce may find hope in knowing that these painful breakups do not always spell long-term psychological disaster. The most comprehensive longitudinal study of the impact of divorce on both adults and children was conducted by E. Mavis Hetherington, a retired professor at the University of Virginia.[23] She followed some families for more than three decades, beginning in the 1970s. Summarizing her findings, she writes, "Divorce can and does ruin lives . . . but I also think much current writing on divorce—both popular and academic—has exaggerated its negative effects and ignored its sometimes considerable positive effects." She reports that the vast majority of parents and children rebound from the upheaval and pain of divorce with resiliency overshadowing pathology. She found that the first postdivorce year is usually brutally painful for both parents and children, but the second year usually brings positive adjustments, even though problems continue. It is not until six years after divorce that most family members are fully back on their feet, mentally and emotionally.

By the time the children were young adults considering their own marriages, the percentage of those with serious psychological problems was found to be almost twice that of those from intact families. But on the hopeful side, Hetherington found that 75 to 80 percent were coping with life "fairly well" and that some were coping "very well." Based on her study, she supports the view that a family with two supportive parents is by far the best way to raise children. But she also believes that having one caring, competent custodial parent is the most potent protection against deep wounding of children. She also concludes that many couples bail out of troubled marriages far too quickly. To this I would add that caregivers can encourage couples to wait long enough to discover if they can, with the help of professional marital therapists, heal and grow their relationships so that they provide a more supportive and loving environment for their children and also for themselves. In light of these research findings, caregivers can give young adult children of divorced parents reality-based hope that their lives are not irreparably damaged. They also can be guided in taking steps to resolve and move beyond any lingering problems from their past that may diminish their well-being in marriage.

Numerous churches are developing creative responses to help meet the needs of divorcing individuals for mutual support, caring, and encouragement to not waste the growth possibilities of their painful experiences. These educative growth programs often focus on issues participants choose that reflect the needs they confront. These include child rearing, jobs, sex, personal growth, finances, legal problems, and learning the difficult but essential skills of stepparenting and coparenting blended families. A pastor who started one such group reports, "This group has been *koinonia* for these people!" Among the books used for discussion starters are Mel Krantzler's *Creative Divorce* and Henri Nouwen's *Reaching Out*.

Preventing and Healing Family Violence

As experienced counselors know all too well, we live in a society where individual, family, and collective or systemic violence is pandemic. Among its many expressions on a domestic level are spousal homicide, spouse beating, child battering, sexual molestation, rape, incest and other sexual and emotional violation of children, elder abuse, and abuse of disabled persons. On the societal level there are gang violence, school shootings by children and youth, murder, suicide, genocide, terrorism, the war system, and the economic violence of extreme poverty. Pastoral caregivers must be prepared to respond effectively to prevent such violence and to help heal it whenever it strikes in their congregation or community. Churches should include all types of violence among the social problems about which they inform their congregations, and they should support both preventive and therapeutic programs in their communities.

The vast majority of domestic violence is directed at women, and the widespread physical, sexual, spiritual, and psychological violence against women is a direct result of the ways our society socializes males and females. Many men are trained to feel strong and successful only if they are in positions of power over others. But since power is defined hierarchically, only the few men at the top can feel powerful. As a result, many men live with some feelings of failure, powerlessness, and rage.

The targets at whom men are conditioned to vent this frustration and rage are those who are weaker (children) or who are socially defined as less significant and powerful (women). In other words, violence against women is a predictable consequence of unequal distribution of social status and of economic, political, and legal power between women and men. It also is the consequence of the learned powerlessness and passivity that many women feel when they relate to men.[24] In addition, it is the result of the fact that most men in patriarchal cultures learn to define women as "other" and to feel masculine only to the degree that they are different from women. Thus the long-range solution to violence against women is the full liberation of women from their one-down position in society and from their alienation from their real strengths. It is also the full liberation of men from the destructive self-image that equates masculinity with male aggression (in sports, hunting, the competitive marketplace, war, and relations with women and children) and from success defined as dominance. On a biological level there is some evidence that higher testosterone levels may play some role in explaining why males in general are more aggressive than females. But how this is expressed is determined by other factors both cultural and personal.

Although many people in our society are becoming more enlightened on this issue, the odds are still great that a chronic wife beater will never be arrested and taken to court. The odds are even greater that if tried, he will not be convicted. Many police are reluctant to interfere in family fights unless the neighbors complain or the violence becomes extreme. Women who desperately need to flee from violent relationships often have no safe place to go, have inadequate funds, and cannot qualify for welfare because of their violent husband's salary.

Here are some recommendations that often help women in violent relationships:

First, if the violence is chronic and the man is not motivated to change, as most batterers are not, it is crucial to encourage the woman and her children to move to a place where they will be safe—for example, with relatives or to a shelter for battered women—and to initiate legal proceedings. Remember, as long as a violent culture reinforces their pattern of violence and the police and courts do not intervene effectively, batterers have little reason to change their violent behavior.

Second, pastoral caregivers should put victims of male violence in touch with hot lines or counseling programs staffed by women volunteers trained in working with women who have survived battering or rape. This is crucially important if the pastor is male.

Third, couple counseling or individual psychotherapy for batterers may be helpful in relationships in which there are constructive dimensions and infrequent violent behavior, if both partners are motivated to interrupt the escalating spirals of frustration, rage, and attack.

Fourth, in order to empower women so that they will stop accepting violence from men, it is essential for them to unlearn their "learned helplessness" and thus take back the power they have been giving away to men. A mutual support and consciousness-raising group of women can be of invaluable help to them in achieving this empowerment.

Caregiving with Families of Victims of Sexual Violence

Imagine that your phone rings and when you answer you hear a panic-stricken father in your congregation say, "My daughter has been raped! I don't know what to do! Please help me!" What do you need to know and do to respond constructively? First, ask whether the daughter is now in a safe place and whether she has been injured in any way so that she needs immediate medical attention. Recommend that the parent and/or the daughter call the Rape Crisis Hotline[25] staffed by women who understand her terrible trauma, know the community resources she may need, and help protect her from the accusatory attitudes of some medical personnel and police. Listen to this distressed parent with empathy, encouraging him to express all of his feelings and concerns. Point out that the sexual violence is not the daughter's fault, no matter what the circumstances, and that it's important that he believe her and reassure her. Also let him know that his rape survivor daughter may be feeling ashamed, dirty, embarrassed, afraid, guilty, angry, powerless, and out of control. Or she may be numb with shock and feeling little on a conscious level. All of these responses are normal.

Recommend strongly that the daughter call the nearest Rape Crisis Center (RCC) to talk with someone who can help her sort out her feelings and decide what to do, including reporting the attack to the police. Immediately get the daughter to a doctor known to understand the trauma, or to the emergency room of a hospital, to receive whatever medical treatment she needs and gather the evidence that will be required to press legal charges. A woman from the rape survivors' program should accompany her when she goes for medical help. Because of the risk of becoming pregnant or getting a sexually transmitted disease (STD), including AIDS, fast action is essential. To help heal the severe psychological wounds that usually result from being the victim of sexual violence, get the daughter into individual therapy with a woman therapist or into a rape or battered women's group. If a woman has a spouse or partner, joint counseling may be needed to help the two of them deal with the effects of the trauma of rape on intimate relationships. Encourage the woman to press charges if her assailant is caught, and help her find a lawyer, preferably a woman, who is known to be competent in handling rape and domestic violence issues.

Whether or not the daughter is ready to talk to someone, parents should be helped to decide what to do and how to cope with their own strong feelings. Significant others (parents, spouse, friends, partner, or relatives) probably are also feeling helpless, angry, and afraid. Pastoral caregivers with requisite understanding and expertise may be able to talk with significant others while the survivor works with a Rape Crisis Center advocate. If not, the RCC can also help significant others. If there is no RCC in your area and you're a woman with the knowledge and understanding of what the survivor and her loved ones are experiencing, you may be able to counsel with her and her loved ones. An important pastoral expression of prophetic ministry is to support the nearest Rape Crisis Center and, if none exists nearby, to support steps to begin one in your community.

Whether or not there is an easily available rape crisis service, you should know women in your community who have extensive knowledge, understanding, and expertise about sexual assault. It is also important to know about the laws concerning rape and sexual assault in your state, including whether you are mandated to report such crimes. You also should be informed about the general attitudes of local law enforcement and judges toward these crimes. Above all, understanding the nature of the rape crisis syndrome is essential for caregivers.

When child battering or sexual abuse occurs in families, it may be necessary for the courts to intervene, either to remove the abusive or molesting parent or other relative from the home or to place the child in a healthy foster home. Wife battering and child abuse often occur in the same families. Battered children who do not receive effective therapeutic help often grow up to be spouse and/or child batterers. An insightful poet-philosopher, in words written for his children, expresses the continuing captivity in the past of the countless people who are among the walking wounded in our society: "Remember that grownups with childhood wounds that haven't healed frame themselves as victims and often frame those who love them now as those who disappointed them once upon a time."[26] Also know your legal obligations about reporting abuse and suspected abuse to the authorities.

Families Face Aging, Dying, and Death

Demographic trends that point to increasing longevity carry huge challenges to caregivers. More and more older people need care from family members as well as from all our social institutions, including churches. Caregivers today are often called to consult with midyears adults facing difficult decisions concerning aging parents. Their dilemmas frequently involve perplexing issues around the last few years or months, or even the last few days and hours, of their parents' lives. It is often heartrending to try to find meaningful answers to questions such as these: What constitutes a quality of life worth living? How do I and my loved ones really want to die? Whose responsibility is it to decide when the technology that is keeping aging loved ones alive goes against their ultimate well-being? How can I do what I think I should for my parents without being submerged in guilt and remorse?

Equally perplexing is knowing how to minister with family members in hospital corridors and lonely nursing homes' waiting rooms late into the night. As nearly everyone eventually discovers, grief is a family affair. They also find that love, not time, heals wounds of the heart and spirit. All this makes insightful caregiving increasingly crucial.

Congregational Enrichment Programs

Congregations today confront exciting challenges to become healing and wholeness centers for both single and married people in their closest and most important relationships. To accomplish this, a church needs to create a smorgasbord of enrichment and growth opportunities designed to respond to the relationship needs of couples, families, and singles at all the stages of their life journeys. Marriage and family enrichment programs are designed to help couples and families make good relationships even better, meaning more mutually fulfilling and wholeness nurturing. Enrichment opportunities for singles seek to enable unmarried persons to do the same in their close relationships. In this growth process participants are encouraged to establish their own unique growth goals and then implement workable plans for moving toward these objectives.

The publicity for marriage, family, and singles enrichment events, like other growth-in-wholeness opportunities, should spell out their nature, purposes, and goals in a positive way. It should describe what is expected of participants and give a brief theological rationale for the event. This rationale keeps such programs rooted in a congregation's spiritual heritage. Here is a sample announcement for recruiting couples:

An Invitation to Couples

Our church is sponsoring a couples' enrichment group on the theme Spiritual Paths to Making Good Marriages Better. The group will meet in the church lounge on Tuesday evenings from 7:00 p.m. to 9:00 p.m. for five weeks, beginning October 7. (The second meeting will be an extended session beginning at 6:00 p.m. with a potluck supper and ending at 10:00 p.m.) The Christian life aims at nurturing love—for ourselves, each other, God, and God's world. This group will aim at increasing love in these four vital relationships by helping couples develop the unused strengths in their relationship. It will also provide methods of deepening communication, resolving conflicts more constructively, and keeping love growing. All couples—newly married, longer-married, and those planning marriage—are welcome. The group will be co-led by our pastor and her husband. Contact the pastor if you would like more information about this spiritually centered event or want to register for it.

****

Five types of activities have proved to be growth producing in enrichment events for couples, singles, and families: (1) *brief whole-group input sessions* in which the facilitator-couple, resource people, or group members share practical ideas that have worked for them (for example, about conflict resolution, spiritual sharing, or sex); (2) *whole-group awareness, communication,* and *love-strengthening exercises* led by the facilitator-couple and then used by individual couples; (3) *relationship-strengthening exercises done as couples*—the Intentional Relationship Method being one of the most helpful; (4) *small, usually leaderless sharing groups* of three of four couples, into which a larger group or workshop periodically divides to give everyone an opportunity to share concerns; and (5) *recreational renewal times,* both structured and unstructured, to allow for fun and playfulness between partners and among couples or families.

Here are some themes that may be included in relationship enrichment events depending on the interests and needs of participants and the time available:

- *Getting Connected as Couples (or Families) and as a Group.* This includes discussion of the hopes, expectations, and interests of couples (or families) and the leaders. On the basis of this discussion, a group agreement (or contract) on the topics to be emphasized is evolved.
- *Strengthening Communication Skills.* This includes self-awareness and responsive listening exercises.
- *Experiencing the Intentional Relationship Method.*
- *Moving from Unproductive Anger and Conflict to Greater Intimacy.*
- *Considering New Possibilities of Changing Women's/Men's Roles and Relationships.* This shares the positive potentialities of equal and more mutually fulfilling ways of relating.
- *Evaluating Our Life Investment Plans.* This increases awareness of the values and priorities that guide couples' and family's lives and the changes that can increase the quality of their lives together.
- *Enhancing Our Love Life.* This helps couples communicate openly about what they enjoy and hels them learn pleasuring that is not demanding—that is, mutual pleasuring done for its own enjoyment and not for any other goal or expectation. In family events the focus is on learning healthy sexual attitudes.
- *Coping Constructively with Family Crises.*
- *Enriching Parent-Child and Parent-Youth Relationships.* This explores how parenting can diminish or enhance the quality of marriages.
- *Deepening Our Spiritual Intimacy.* This resolves religious conflicts in marriages, increases shared peak experiences, and deepens enjoyment of the divine Spirit of life and love in marriages.

- *The Growth Possibilities of Our Marriage Stage.* This copes with problems by developing new possibilities for couples' present stage of marriage.
- *Developing Intimacy through Shared Outreach.* Near the close of enrichment events, this challenges couples to plan ways of reaching out to others in the church or community to share the growth they have experienced.
- *Planning Our Continuing Growth.* Before the end of enrichment events, this gives couples, singles, and families an opportunity to work out their own growth covenants, consisting of concrete plans for taking successive steps on their growth journey. If they desire, the group as a whole should make plans for follow-up reunions to give mutual support to one another's growth.
- *Evaluating the Experience.* Midway and at the close, this gives everyone a chance to indicate what has been most helpful and least helpful about the experience. At the end, suggestions for future events should be offered.
- *Closing Celebration.* This is a worshipful time of thankful celebration for the growth that has occurred and the recommitment to one another's continuing wholeness. This helps people become aware of God's love that undergirds and feeds their human love. In Christian circles where Communion (or the Lord's Supper) is meaningful, this ritual may a part of the closing celebration. An option that may be preferable is what in some Christian traditions is called a "love feast," where partners or family members feed one another bread and affirm their new growth covenants.

Douglas Anderson describes a variety of family growth groups—an approach he defines as "a program involving three to five families who meet together regularly and frequently for mutual care and support and for the development of family potential."[27] He sees such programs as having these unique advantages as family-strengthening approaches: (1) The family growth group goes beyond most traditional family life education programs by involving the whole family together as a unit in the experience....[28] (2) The family growth group provides a supportive network of families to strengthen the family unit. In a society that fragments the family and that isolates families from extended kin and other families in the community, there is increasing need for programs that give families a sense of community and belonging.[29] (3) The family growth group facilitates family change and growth by focusing on the development of family potential. Family potential can be understood as those latent resources within every family for changing and growing, loving and caring, communicating, resolving conflicts, adventuring, and creating and experiencing joy. The family growth group, focusing more on growth than upon problems, provides opportunities for families to increase their awareness of their unique strengths and resources and then to actualize these dormant capacities in family living.

Ideally marriage, singles, and family enrichment events should have male and female coleaders, both of whom are aware of the negative influence of sexism in close relationships. Coleaders should have balanced and equal roles in leading, modeling an egalitarian way of relating, including disagreeing and still being friends. Such a leadership team models what is being taught and brings the differing perspectives of two individuals who know women's and men's experiences from the inside.

Families Use the Internet to Stay Connected

There is unimagined family life education and relationship-enhancement potential inherent in the fact that the vast majority of people in an industrialized place like North America have access to the Internet. This lets them communicate and connect with friends and family easily and quickly at a low cost without the cost of transporting their bodies to one place. The relationship-nurturing uses of this technology have proliferated in ways that could not have been imagined before the cybernetic revolution. Increasing numbers of older people are using the Internet and e-mail (often with help from computer-savvy children and grandchildren). E-mail and family chat rooms allow family members to communicate as frequently and as long as they choose in spite of being widely dispersed geographically. This helps mitigate the lonely separation that many older people feel. It also enables multigenerational enrichment as grandchildren and grandparents communicate more regularly.

Narrative Approaches in Marriage and Family Caregiving

Narrative therapy, a more recent form of individual and family therapy, is the brainchild of two Australians, Michael White and David Epston. Briefly it can be described as follows: "In essence, within a narrative therapy approach, the focus is not on 'experts' solving problems, . . . it is on people discovering through conversations, the hopeful, preferred, and previously unrecognized and hidden possibilities contained within themselves and unseen story-lines." Healing and growth come about through what White calls "reauthoring" the family's stories, incorporating what has been omitted through social bias.[30]

For more information on this right-brain, self-empowering therapy, see Flaskas, Morgan, and Neuger in the "Recommended Reading" at the end of this chapter.

Here are some approaches that can facilitate growth in marriage and family enrichment and counseling. Counselors might say the statements in describing alternative ways as they lead couples or families into these experiences. After couples have experienced these, they should be encouraged to share what they experienced with each other. Here are some things you can suggest to couples:

Centering: "Go inside yourself and become aware of the place where you feel most 'together' [integrated] or most loving now. Then enjoy staying centered in that place for a little while. Now talk with each other from that center."

Guided imaging: "Picture yourself and your relationship whole—the way you would like it to be. Imagine yourself inside each other's skin. Surround your partner with loving energy, seeing him or her in your mind enveloped by a warm, healing light."

Stories and parables: "I knew a couple once who...This happened in our marriage..." [Share vignettes of your own struggles, with your partner's permission.] Your relationship reminds me of this story from the Bible [or from a movie, a folktale, or a fiction book]...."

Both daydreams and night dreams: "Describe what happened in your dream as though it is happening now. In your imagination, be the various parts of your dream. [These approaches to dream work are from Gestalt therapy.] Retell a dream or daydream so that your conflict is healed in it."

Reframing a problem: "What positive message to you is in your spouse's nagging—like she values and wants more of your attention? What useful things have you learned from your painful family crisis?"

Reliving creative memories: "Go back in your memory and let yourself relive...the first time you met. Go back and relive a crisis like this that you survived and in which you even grew a little stronger. Go back and relive a time when you really felt close and loving, or relive a beautiful experience you shared. Then share your thoughts and feelings triggered by this exercise."

Paradoxes (this example of a paradoxical technique is used with couples suffering from sexual problems): "Instead of trying harder [to maintain an erection or have an orgasm], let yourself relax and enjoy the closeness. Just flow with the pleasure, wherever it takes you."

Free drawing and painting: "Draw a symbol or a picture of the way you feel now about your marriage [or family]. / Now draw the way you'd like to feel about it. / Use circles to indicate the power and distance from each person in your family. Now draw a picture of your childhood family. Now draw the way you'd like your family to be."

Jokes and play: "See if you can discover anything a little absurd or funny in your ways of relating; for example, the way you are hurting yourselves as you get back at each other. Reenact that argument you had last night so we can see and understand what happened. / As your at-home assignment between sessions, plan together a minivacation, meaning a short time when you do things each of your child sides really enjoys." As couples are feeling better about each other: "Do you both feel that it would be good to take that vacation you planned together before you hit this crisis?"

Action imperatives: "Plan and then do something to improve things in your marriage a little this week. If you do this, you'll probably feel more hopeful. To help interrupt the vicious cycle between you of responding to verbal attacks by attacking back repeatedly, I recommend that each of you do one small thing the other person will like this week, even if you don't feel much like it yet." [This should be followed by couples developing concrete planning of what each will do.]

Affirmations: "It takes strength to admit that you need help and then take steps to get it, like you have done! It requires a lot of guts to survive what you two have been through! Take turns now telling each other what you still like about each other or what you still appreciate about your relationship."

Mutual body pleasuring: "To help satisfy your need for physical touching, try giving each other at least three hugs a day this week [or a back or foot minimassage]."

Using Rituals, Humor, and Wise Sayings to Enrich Family Life

Rituals

Caregivers should help families find or create rituals to cope with tragedies and losses, and to celebrate family victories and passages. Families coping with painful losses of loved ones can be helped by a day to remember with love. On such an occasion they are invited to bring photos of their loved ones to a worship service and place them on the altar during prayers and song celebrating the lives of the ones they mourn. A valuable resource is *Celebrating Passages in the Church: Reflections and Resources*, edited by Hugh W. Sanborn. Eleven contributors from different backgrounds offer a variety of ways of affirming life's passages.

Humor

The healing energy of laughter and aphorisms is an invaluable resource for counselors to help families use in coping with the sunlight and shadows of their life together. Here are two examples of letters written to God in a religious setting, preceded by notes on the family issues for which they could be relevant. For parents coping with sibling rivalry: "Dear God, Thank you for the baby brother, but what I prayed for was a puppy—Bruce." To emphasize where children learn values: "Dear God, Is it true that my father won't get into heaven if he uses his bowling words in the house?—Anita."

Wise Sayings

A midyears person observed, "I've learned that the older I get, the smarter my parents become." A Jewish philosopher columnist in the city where I live made a wise observation about the difficult changes on the road of being a parent: "Parenting is a lesson in moving from management to consultant—if you're lucky."

Reality Practice Skill Development Session

Parishioner's role: If three or four people are available for this session, take the roles of a family with whose dynamics and problems one of you is familiar. That person should help the others get into their roles.

Pastor's role: Counsel with the whole family, helping them communicate more openly. Use the steps of the Intentional Relationship Method, discussed in this chapter, as the structure of your counseling approach.

Observer-coach's role: Help the pastor be more effective in giving each person an opportunity to be heard by the other family members and in helping the family become aware of their strengths as well as their problems. Be aware of the family's dynamics.

Recommended Reading

Bigner, Jerry, and Joseph L. Wetchler, eds. *Relationship Therapy with Same-Sex Couples*. Binghamton, N.Y.: Haworth Press, 2004.

Flaskas, Carmel, ed. *Hope and Despair in Narrative and Family Therapy: Adversity, Forgiveness and Reconciliation*. New York: Routledge, 2007.

Morgan, Alice. *What Is Narrative Therapy?* Adelaide, Australia: Dulwich Center Publications, 2000.

Neuger, Christie Cozad. *Counseling Women: A Narrative, Pastoral Approach*. Minneapolis: Augsburg Fortress, 2001.

Weaver, Andrew J. *Counseling Troubled Teens and Their Families: A Handbook for Clergy and Youth Workers*. Nashville: Abingdon Press, 1999.

Wilcoxon, Allen, et al. *Ethical, Legal, and Professional Issues in the Practice of Marriage and Family Therapy*. Upper Saddle River, N.J.: Merrill Publishers, 2007.

Wimberly, Edward P. *Counseling African American Marriages and Families*. Louisville: Westminster John Knox Press, 1997.

Worden, Mark, and Barbara D. Worden. *The Gender Dance in Couples Therapy*. Belmont, Calif.: Brooks/Cole, 1997.

CHAPTER 14

EDUCATIVE COUNSELING

Be transformed by the renewal of your mind.
—Romans 12:2 RSV

A high school youth talks with his pastor about an emotionally charged vocational decision. His parents and school guidance counselor are giving him conflicting guidance, neither of which is close to his dreams. A couple come for their premarital conferences and are obviously resistant to this requirement by the congregation's educational committee. A young man seeks help with a perplexing religious issue. His rigid, negative beliefs reinforce his self-esteem problems and spiritual emptiness. A midyears woman seeks guidance from her pastor about a painful decision to put her Alzheimer-afflicted mother in a nursing facility. A congregation's social concerns committee seeks the pastor's help in planning its approach to a complex, controversial issue of injustice in their community. What needs do these diverse careseekers have in common? To meet their needs adequately, their pastors must be able to function simultaneously as teachers, counselors, and coaches. This chapter focuses on how to integrate these roles in what I call "educative counseling."

A pioneer in pastoral care and counseling, Paul E. Johnson, once challenged church leaders in this way:

> [In our] race between education and catastrophe we need the ministry of creative education. Every local church and every hard-pressed family becomes a center for creative learning in the midst of the realities and concrete dilemmas we face. On the scale of urgency to survive we must grow or perish. Learning is the first and last business of every growing-dying, time-bound finite person.[1]

His words, written years ago, are even more true today. We live in a world faced with the spiritual and ethical problems and possibilities of the Internet and the high-tech knowledge explosion.

The Historical Heritage of Educative Caregiving

Educative counseling by pastoral caregivers is rooted in the rich heritage of the Wisdom literature in the Hebrew Scriptures:

For the LORD gives wisdom;
>from his mouth come knowledge and understanding;
he stores up sound wisdom for the upright. (Prov. 2:6-7)

Get wisdom; get insight;...
Do not forsake her, and she will keep you;
>love her and she will guard you. (Prov. 4:5-6)

The purposes in the human mind are like deep water,
>but the intelligent will draw them out. (Prov. 20:5)

Jesus Christ stood in this heritage. He was called "Rabboni" (Teacher) by his followers. His teachings reflected the deep respect for spiritual wisdom in his Jewish tradition: "He entered the synagogue and taught. And they were astonished at his teaching, for he taught them as one who had authority" (Mark 1:21-22). He declared, "Love...God with all your heart, and with all your soul, and with all your mind, and with all your strength" (Mark 12:30). The Apostle Paul also saw himself as being in this wisdom tradition.

Educative Counseling's Key Role in Congregations

Many of the pastoral caregivers' most empowering opportunities involve educative counseling. This type of caregiving requires sensitive blending of their skills in creative education and guidance counseling. It brings together the insights and methods of two pastoral functions for the single objective of fostering healing and wholeness. It involves the personalized communication of certain knowledge, beliefs, values, and coping skills as an essential part of the counseling process. But educative counseling goes far beyond merely imparting information. By using counseling skills and sensitivities, it helps persons understand, evaluate, and then decide if and how they will apply the relevant information to coping more constructively with their stressful life situations. Education and counseling become natural allies with a common goal of maximizing whole-person growth.

There are some educative ingredients in almost all types of pastoral care and counseling. But in certain types educative elements are so crucial that it is appropriate to label these types "educative pastoral counseling." These include referral, vocational, sexual, premarital, prebaptismal, divorce, and life-stage or developmental counseling. Clergy have natural aptitude for this form of counseling. Their professional roles are defined to include both counseling and education. They have a certain message and worldviews that they are committed to communicate. These are particularly useful in preventive group counseling—small-group experiences designed to prevent future problems by preparing people to meet constructively "developmental crises" such as getting married, having a child, going to college, retiring, or dying.

For clergy the concept of educative counseling helps to resolve the conflict between their role as counselors, on the one hand, and their role as teachers who communicate the good news of the Christian gospel, on the other hand. This conflict is often the result of clergy counselors' self-image as relatively passive and value free, and of the false dichotomy between knowledge and feelings in the Rogerian approach. It is significant that the essential place of relevant knowledge in the helping process is emphasized in the cognitive-behavioral therapies. They provide rich resources for both the theory and the methodology of educative pastoral counseling.[2] These approaches understand counseling and therapy as different methods of reeducation with a common aim of helping persons replace faulty learning with creative learning regarding attitudes, ideas, relationship skills, and values.

A meaningful distinction should be drawn between high motivation and low motivation educative counseling. *High motivation* educative counseling occurs when persons are strongly impelled by the desire to reduce the pain caused by their problems. Divorcing couples who have children often are highly motivated to discover ways to diminish the emotional harm caused their children. Mandatory preparation for marriage sessions often begins with couples inhibited by the *low motivation* of satisfying the requirement. Such a requirement constitutes a wise congregational policy, but it makes it essential for the counselor to know how to awaken motivation. Methods for awakening motivation will be presented later in the section on preparation for marriage.

Christie Neuger identifies an educational ingredient in caregiving with women. She sees it as preliminary to women's awakening to the oppressive value system in which they are embedded. It primes the pump of their own inner knowledge, and brings to light and verifies the meaning of what they have experienced:

> Many feminist counselors suggest that the most important first step in counseling is to see some of the value conflicts or injustices in their lives. This is in part an educative process. But it is also, more importantly, a tapping into the latent self story within most women.... Therefore, it is helpful not just for the counselor to do educational work, but to help this alternative narrative (with its strong ambivalence) to be voiced.[3]

Understanding Educative Counseling

Educative counseling shares the common elements of all pastoral counseling. It becomes educative as it moves toward three goals:

1. discovering what facts, concepts, values, beliefs, skills, guidance, or advice are needed by persons in coping with their problems;
2. communicating these directly or helping persons discover them; for example, through assigned reading;

3. helping persons use this information to understand their situation, make wise decisions, or handle problems constructively.

Discovering what may be relevant to persons' needs obviously requires careful listening to people and interacting with them. It requires becoming aware of their inner interpersonal reality. To give information and/or advice in counseling prior to understanding people's needs and feelings weakens their trust in and empathy with counselors. Ideally the teaching aspects of counseling should be focused as sharply on each person's particular needs as is the medicine that a competent physician gives to a particular person for a specific medical problem.

In their discussion of "guiding" as one of the historic dimensions of caregiving, William Clebsch and Charles Jaekle declare,

> Fundamentally, the guiding ministry assumes that useful wisdom, which edifies and illuminates the meaning and direction of a person's life, can be made available within the framework of the helping act.... The wisdom must be fashioned or shaped to the immediate circumstances of the troubled person in order that it may be appropriated and used in the context of the particular trouble at hand. Guiding as a pastoral function does not develop ethical principles for general application to the process of living, but rather forges decision-guiding wisdom in the heat of specific troubles and strives to facilitate its use in particular situations. [4]

In doing educative counseling, pastors should share the aspects of their experience, insights, and knowledge that they sense, from their awareness of counselees' problems, will be helpful to them as tools or building materials in constructing a workable approach to their dilemmas. Counselors should not try to sell counselees on certain approaches to their problems. Instead they should encourage persons to consider what has been communicated, use only what speaks to their condition, and ignore the rest. As in all counseling, the focus of educative counseling is on the person and not on the ideas per se, however valid these may be. The cognitive input of educative counseling provides resources for persons' thought processes by which they search for constructive approaches to current problems or demanding future experiences, such as marriage, parenthood, moving, surgery, retirement, or dying.

Guidance in educative counseling employs two identifiable modes. *Educative guidance*[5] tends to draw out the individual's experiences and values as criteria and resources for use in making decisions, while *inductive guidance* tends to lead the individual to adopt an a priori set of values and criteria by which to make his or her decisions. Educational pastoral counseling blends inductive and educative methods of guidance in varying proportions. The pastor communicates information in this spirit: "Here are some concepts (values or approaches) that, from my experience and understanding, are valid. I believe they may be useful to you in meeting your needs, so I share them for you to consider. If you wish, I will help you evaluate their relevance and apply them to your situation." This method is inductive; it draws on the counselor's store of knowledge and insight from her or his religious tradition, study, and experience. It is educative because it seeks to draw out the person's inner problems and wisdom and facilitate an encounter between these and the ideas presented.

Counseling methods are used to help persons diminish their emotional blind spots and inner conflicts that otherwise would prevent them from understanding, evaluating, selecting, and then using the ideas that are relevant. Counselors should not be timid about sharing whatever wisdom about life they have gained from counseling others and from their own personal growth struggles. The difficult but crucial goal is to balance real authority based on expert knowledge with the right of persons to work through their problems in their own way in an empathetic relationship that respects this right.

To illustrate, a devout and conservative Protestant woman consults her pastor for help with a difficult decision—whether to terminate a romantic relationship obviously moving toward marriage with a devout Catholic man. To make an informed decision, this woman needs accurate knowledge about the two traditions' basic views concerning the Bible, the church, religious authority, and freedom to practice reliable family planning. She needs to face realistically tensions and conflicts that characterize most mixed marriages, including those around the decision concerning in which religious tradition children will be raised. From her training and experience, the pastor has at least some of the knowledge the woman needs to make a constructive decision. Complete objectivity is impossible, of course, particularly in such emotionally laden decisions, but having reliable facts can increase the degree of objectivity.

Sharing accurate information is seldom enough. Almost always, powerful feelings, interpersonal dynamics, fears, and prejudices are present in the problems with which people struggle in counseling. These must be dealt with if people are to make wise decisions. Information becomes useful only as it is related to each person's inner world of meanings. Skilled counseling in the case just described involved meeting with both persons several times as they struggled to make a decision. The pastor aimed at integrating relevant knowledge with their feelings, attitudes, beliefs, values, and love for each other. Only such integrated knowledge is really useful in decision making and problem solving.

Enhancing Mental, Physical, and Spiritual Well-being with Educative Counseling

One way to describe the objectives of educative counseling is to enable counselees, parishioners, and students to follow the Great Commandment to love God with our minds. This is another way of empowering minds by helping people increase the basic ingredients in such empowerment—self-esteem, competence, self-responsibility, and inner strength. There is a wealth of knowledge available regarding maintaining physical health through a balanced diet and exercise. Effective pastoral care must include care of the body, something often forgotten because of the traditional association of counseling and therapy with the emotional and interpersonal realm. Creative self-learning and holistic counseling approaches can be used together to produce the positive changes enjoined by Paul of Tarsus to first-century Christians—to "be transformed by the renewing of your minds" (Rom. 12:2).

Educative counseling seeks to enable people to awaken reality-based hope for a better future and to help them do what is necessary to move themselves and others toward that future. As indicated earlier, such hope can help people make the difficult changes necessary to grow healthier and have more ability to cope. My experience confirms this observation attributed to a wise woman leader of the twentieth century, Eleanor Roosevelt: "The future belongs to those who believe in the beauty of their dreams."[6]

Using Educative Counseling to Enhance Creativity

Pastoral caregivers can use educative counseling perspectives to enable people to develop increased creativity in their lives. In this way care receivers can enrich their lives and become, in some small but significant ways, cocreators with the divine source of all creativity. Brain research has revealed that we have one brain but two interconnected minds centering in two hemispheres of the brain.[7] In most educational settings in technological cultures one side of the brain (the left hemisphere in most right-handed people) receives most of the attention, and there its functions become more highly developed. This side specializes in rational, analytical, cognitive, verbal, mathematical, and scientific functions. It gets the psychic energy of most people during most of their waking hours. The development of the right-hemisphere functions is neglected in most people. These are the intuitive, imaging, nonverbal, artistic, relational, and holistic functions that are needed to balance left-hemisphere functions in the development of our fuller mental potentialities.

Creativity flows from a playful but serious dance between the left-brain and right-brain functions. The history of science reveals that most major discoveries came as intuitive, right-brain hunches when creative scientists were relaxing between periods of intensive left-brain research and theory generating.[8] Albert Einstein, for example, mentions playing with visual images before he undertook the rigorous left-brain work that connected these intuitive images with words, theoretical concepts, and mathematical theories that confirmed them. From this process came one of the most exciting breakthroughs in physics that revolutionized our understanding of the amazing universe in which we live.

Whole-brain creativity for most people involves cultivating our latent right-brain capacities so as to dance with our left-brain functions. Nurturing personality wholeness in our left-brain culture requires investing more time in right-brain activities such as storytelling, listening to music, contemplative praying, and playing and clowning around.

Research studies of how people use their minds to create innovative approaches to problems show that often there are four steps.[9] Here is how educative counselors can use this approach, stated as they might be described in guiding people through this process of creative problem solving:

Step 1: *Preparation.* Focus on a challenging project you need to accomplish, a complex decision you need to make, or a problem you are trying to resolve. In this step work intensively using your logical, analytical left-brain abilities to define the issue clearly, identify the parts of the problem, and then brainstorm freely (alone or with other interested people) to generate a wide variety of possible solutions. Keep notes on all these possibilities, including those that may seem way out. Keep working until the intertwined parts of the issue and the obstacles to easy solutions become evident. Jotting down notes on all this left-brain work will help you organize and analyze your information and options.

Step 2: *Incubation.* After finishing this disciplined preparation as fully as you can, put the whole issue on the shelf for a time. If you are able, let go of the pressure to solve the problem right away and allow the problem to stew on the back burner of your mind. Be aware that if you release the problem from your left-brain preoccupation for a while, something remarkable may occur. A different, perhaps a wiser part of your mind is working on the problem now in your nonconscious right-brain mind. Perhaps you can just turn the problem over to God as you understand him or her.

Step 3: *Illumination.* Light often comes spontaneously with either sudden or gradual dawning of an image, a hunch, or an insight that you sense may be the innovative solution to the issue. It may help the light to come on to do diagramming, doodling, or other free unplanned drawing of whatever images or thoughts come bubbling up from your nonconscious mind. Just jot down your free associations—words, images, stories, daydreams, ideas, or pictures. (In my experience as a left-brain dominant person, illumination sometimes comes while I sleep or when I relax after a second or third period of intense left-brain wrestling with a problem.)

Step 4: *Verification and implementation.* Now, take whatever has come to you intuitively and check its validity with tough-minded critical thought. Then organize whatever has been confirmed as valid into a workable plan with a practical strategy that includes the steps you'll take and a timeline for moving ahead on the plan.

Enhancing EQ by Educative Counseling

Educative counseling can help care receivers increase what is called "emotional intelligence" (EQ) in themselves and their children. Research has discovered that among the multiple types of human intelligence, EQ has crucial applications to caregiving in both religious education and educative counseling. Psychologist Daniel Goleman has illuminated the vital intellectual resources of this nonanalytic, right-brain function of the human mind. He gives convincing evidence demonstrating that EQ is more important for successful living, including constructive relationships, vocational success, life satisfactions, and mental well-being, than the left-brain cognitive, verbal, reasoning, and mathematical abilities measured by IQ tests. EQ includes the basic human strengths and abilities needed for individuals and societies to grow in wholeness. These vital EQ strengths include self-awareness, management of one's emotions, self-motivation, empathy for the feelings of others, relationship skills, impulse control, zest in living, robust character, self-discipline, altruism, and compassion.[10]

The good news is that EQ, in contrast to IQ, can be significantly increased. This occurs by experiences that produce whole-person learning, such as constructive parenting, creative mentoring, healthy relationships, reaching out to others, educative counseling, and psychotherapy. Faith communities should celebrate and use the breakthrough psychological evidence that nurturing and thus increasing EQ capacities are precisely what whole-person ministries are designed to do well. In fact, increasing EQ is the major goal of wholeness-enhancing counseling. All people have a mix of various degrees of IQ and EQ, and there is not a high degree of correlation between the two. Deficiencies in EQ produce countless counseling problems.

Following the Socratic injunction "know thyself," EQ research has shown that awareness of one's inner world is basic to all the other positive attributes. It enables people to pilot their lives and make sound decisions about many things, including who to marry and what job to take. Pastoral caregivers and educators can teach parents and other lifestyle mentors how to enable children and teens to grow their EQ. Caregiving methods described earlier increase self-awareness and with it empathy, enabling people to grow in "attunement" to themselves and others. This enhances relationship skills (also known as social or interpersonal intelligence), altruism, and outreach to others. Educative counseling or coaching for increasing EQ teaches people how to motivate themselves constructively; exercise emotional self-control; shake off or handle disturbing feelings such as anger, anxiety, and depression more constructively; and postpone immediate gratifications in order to achieve important goals. As Daniel Goleman puts it, EQ adds far more of the qualities that make people more whole and more fully human than does IQ. This insight is invaluable for caregiving with people of all IQs, especially those with lesser IQ.

The Dynamics of Educative Counseling

The fundamental question that must be answered to understand the possibilities and limitations of educative counseling is this: what is the function of knowledge in causing and curing human problems? Carl Rogers states, "Most maladjustments are not failures in knowing" but are rooted in emotional blocks.[11] It does not follow from this that the communication of information is unimportant in much counseling and therapy. Misconceptions, distorted beliefs, and unconstructive values often are significant, even crucial, dimensions of troubled people's problems in coping. Seldom are they the only factors, but they can be the crucial factor. Lack of accurate knowledge is sometimes a cause and frequently an aggravator of interpersonal problems. For example, Mrs. E.'s realistic fear of an unwanted pregnancy formed a vicious cycle with her conflicting sexual attitudes. This fear produced diminishing returns in the couple's sex life, which strained their interpersonal relationship. Their pastor referred Mrs. E. to a competent gynecologist who recommended a more effective contraceptive method for her. This diminished the fear of pregnancy and, together with the pastor's couple-counseling on their sexual and communication problems, improved their relationship. The extent to which persons are actually able to use knowledge depends on their degree of wholeness. No amount of information about reality will, in itself, transform a psychotic's deep distortions in perceiving reality. And yet as remotivation therapy has shown, even regressed schizophrenics have some conflict-free areas of their psyches. By starting in these areas and providing cognitive resources and reality-oriented coping skills, the therapist may help the healthy parts of the person's psyche grow stronger as they are exercised.

Six assumptions constitute the theoretical foundation of educative counseling:

1. Intellectual knowledge is an important resource for handling reality constructively.

2. Most counselees have sufficient conflict-free personality areas to allow them to make some use of information derived from educative counseling sessions and reading assignments between sessions.

3. Constructive coping strengthens their sense of identity, confidence, and worth.

4. Most pastoral caregivers possess knowledge, values, and skills that can be useful to many counselees.

5. Counseling skills can help persons use relevant information and cope more effectively with challenges.

6. Some of the most effective teaching that a pastor does in counseling and elsewhere is modeling constructive attitudes, beliefs, values, and behavior.

Pastoral Caregivers as Spiritual Coaches

A crucial form of educative counseling is the practice that is usually called "spiritual direction." I prefer "spiritual guidance" because the term *director* tends to have hierarchical connotations in our culture. It suggests that the person being directed is a passive recipient from a benevolent authority figure. It is true that the role of spiritual director arose within authority-centered cultures and undoubtedly has been misused on occasion in ways that did not empower recipients.

Many traditions and cultures regard the role of the personal guide of the inner life as crucially important. The shamans in preindustrial cultures, the gurus in Hinduism, the sage-teachers in classical Greek philosophy, and the spiritual guides in Native American spirituality and in ancient Judaism (prophets, priests, wise men and women) are examples. Within Christianity, the tradition of *spiritual direction* was flourishing by the fourth century as suggested by the writings of the desert fathers in the Eastern Orthodox tradition. It was also widely practiced in the Christian Celtic tradition through the custom of using a soul friend (*ánam cára*) as a spiritual confidant. The tradition continued in the medieval Roman Catholic Church and subsequently in the Anglican communion. Although the Protestant tradition has not used the term *spiritual direction* until relatively recently (because of suspicion of anything that seemed to undermine the place of Christ as mediator between persons and God), Martin Luther practiced a ministry of personal direction; John Calvin was concerned about the guidance of conscience; and Richard Baxter, in his classic book *The Reformed Pastor* (1656), recommended that pastors should not "slightly slubber over" the work of personal counsel, but "do it vigorously." In the Wesleyan tradition, bands and class meetings were settings organized by John Wesley for intensive spiritual direction and training in Christian living. Clearly the Christian tradition has regarded spiritual direction as a central dimension of pastoral care, and there are important resources within the tradition that need to be recovered and integrated with pastoral counseling to balance the valuable but often lopsided impact of psychological insights and psychotherapeutic techniques.

This thrust in spiritual direction has important implications for pastoral care and counseling. In our culture, where privatized salvation seeking (via religious and secular routes) is epidemic, it is well to remember that the health of our relationship with God is always interrelated with the health of all other facets of our lives—physical, psychological, interpersonal, ecological, and institutional. Spiritual growth is nurtured best in human relationships and groups committed to *mutual* spiritual searching and discovery. Our individual spiritual wholeness is deeply influenced by the quality of the institutional structures of our society and by our relationship with the biosphere. Living in ways that enhance the wholeness of the so-called nonspiritual dimensions of our lives helps to enrich the quality of our spiritual lives. The creative Spirit moves in all dimensions of our existence.

As Ruth Tiffany Barnhouse points out, there are significant similarities and differences between spiritual direction and secular psychotherapy. They are similar in that both involve inner motivation to change. Both involve a more objective person (therapist or director) to help one identify blind spots in one's awareness, both deal with specific and unique issues in people's lives, and both involve training in the technique of choice. They are different in the criteria by which the outcome is evaluated—psychotherapy focuses on the changes in the person's inner being and relationships; spiritual direction focuses on the person's relationship with God and how all other relationships interrelate with that primal relationship. Spiritual direction focuses explicitly on issues of ultimate meaning, raising such questions as: "What gives meaning to your life? What makes life worthwhile? How do you deal with the experience of being finite?" For those who have explicit religious beliefs, ask such questions as: "How do you experience God acting or present in your life? How do you deal with suffering in your life or in the lives of others?" These questions, of course, would be raised in a context in which they are relevant to the person's concerns. They are asked by one who is also engaged in pondering them, not so much with a view to getting answers as to facilitating the person's reflection on her or his experience of the existential mystery in which both are involved. Effective guides must have expertise and experience, but they must also walk *with* persons as colleagues and companions on their journeys.[12]

All of us who share the view that pastoral caregiving, to be truly pastoral, must include the perspectives and concerns of spiritual direction's ancient heritage can find a treasure in a book by Jean Stairs, *Listening for the Soul: Pastoral Care and Spiritual Direction*.[13] In these times of intense and unprecedented spiritual hunger and searching, Jean Stairs offers caregivers and other searchers a nourishing and comprehensive exploration of spiritual direction, focusing primarily on the Protestant context. The author illuminates and illustrates a challenging vision of "soulful pastoral care" in faith communities. She uses "soul listening" (meaning listening for the holy in the ordinary) and contemplative living as primary pathways to nurturing deeper relationships with God. Her feminist vision of caregiving is refreshingly contextual and holistic, going far beyond sharing God's care for individuals to also share God's care for the wholeness and justice of the world that God loves so deeply. Soulful spiritual direction is seen as one discrete, spiritually enriching channel for God-centered pastoral care.

Avoiding the Pitfalls of Educative Counseling

In educative counseling, the pastor faces several serious pitfalls. The most ominous is subtly manipulating the counselee. It requires considerable emotional maturity to present ideas for which one feels conviction (in theology, for example) without subtle pressure on the counselee to conform. Such pressure communicates disrespect for the person's precious right to choose her or his meaningful philosophy of life.

A closely related danger is that of slipping from rational authority, the healthy authority of competence (Erich Fromm), into authoritarianism, the authority of using power coercively in ways that diminish personality growth. Another pitfall is that of regarding information per se as adequate in helping troubled persons. This leads to an ineffective, advice-giving approach to counseling. It is important to listen for the hidden cries for help that often come disguised in innocuous-appearing requests for information. As noted in discussing supportive counseling, giving advice and sharing information are useful ways of nurturing persons under stress by gratifying dependency needs. The danger is that with markedly dependent people such approaches may foster even greater dependency. When a pastor senses that this is happening, her or his task is to wean the person by being gradually less advising and guiding. Doing this is often difficult because the dependent person's emptiness makes her or him long to be led and fed.

A final danger is that the pastor will equate transmitting information with genuine learning on the counselee's part. Nathaniel Cantor makes clear: "Significant learning stems from the self-directed motivation of the learner who wants something positive and creative for an unexpressed or unfulfilled need."[14] Genuine learning will occur only when a person's sense of need and certain ideas come together. In educative counseling, the person's sense of need is always the place to begin. Through the process of counseling, that person's understanding of what she or he needs often expands. Authoritarian educative counseling can stifle the desire for learning and growth. Cantor declares,

> Most of us learn how not to learn. That is, we learn very early how to avoid tangling with the authority of adults who are significant in our lives.... We learn to curb self-expression a good deal of the time. We learn how to submit, run away, cut corners, rationalize, defend ourselves, and to distort.... In brief, we are driven "to adjust" to threats, anxieties, and fears.[15]

Behavior that lessens anxiety is adjustive, not integrative. The essence of integrative behavior is the capacity to exercise one's curiosity, to derive positive satisfaction from the spontaneous expression of one's skills and powers. Motivation that leads to the spontaneous expression of one's self is different from the kind of learning that seeks to lessen anxiety and avoid threat. Educative counseling should aim at stimulating integrative learning—the kind that enables persons to discover and develop their God-given gifts and capacities.

Educative Counseling in Marriage Preparation

To illustrate the basic methods of educative counseling, here is how these methods are used in helping prepare couples for matrimony. This is one of clergypersons' most frequent opportunities to use their complementary skills as both counselors and teachers. Because premarital guidance is the parish pastor's most frequent educative counseling opportunity, I will use it to illustrate the methodology. There are two categories of educative counseling: (1) situations in which people come at the pastor's request; for example, premarital, prebaptismal, or church membership preparation, and (2) situations in which the counselee takes the initiative, seeking guidance on vocational, theological, or other problems. The rule of thumb is that pastor-initiated types of educative counseling often require a greater proportion of direct instruction than do counselee-initiated types. Most premarital sessions are actually individualized education or personalized training sessions. They usually are not counseling because the couples are generally not motivated by a desire for help with particular problems. But most couples are open to training and coaching (in relationship-building skills) that affirm their basic strength and respond to their desire to develop the best possible marriage relationship. Personalized education can be helpful to many couples if counseling skills and sensitivities are integral to the process.

The pastor who learns to do counseling-oriented education will find increasing opportunities to do actual counseling with some premarital couples. Here are useful methods:

As in other forms of counseling, relate warmly, empathetically, and openly so that a sturdy relationship with the couple will grow. Establishing a trustful and (if possible) ongoing relationship with the couple is the overarching goal of prewedding sessions. Such a bridge helps make the pastor emotionally accessible to them if they need and want help with a problem, now or in the future. Also establish a clear contract for how the session will be used.

Pastor: I'm sure you both want to keep your love growing as fully as possible through your years together. Building a good marriage takes the loving skills of two people who are willing to work and play at it—to keep growing. As your pastor, I'd like to help you in this exciting and demanding process. [Response by the couple.] I hope that these sessions will prove helpful to you in discovering more of the hidden strengths that you want to develop in your relationship. What would each of you like to get out of these sessions?

After the couple have described their interests and needs, the pastor may mention other topics or skills on which it may be helpful to focus; for example, tension areas in their relationship; family backgrounds; their understanding of marriage and of men-women roles; spiritual issues and growth in their marriage; sexual pleasuring skills; birth control methods; relating to relatives; love-nurturing communication skills; negotiating a mutually fair marriage covenant; conflict resolution skills; handling money issues; balancing autonomy and togetherness; conflicting values in their marriages; children—

whether or not to have children and dividing responsibility for their rearing; developing a support group; mutual need satisfaction; outreach to their community; making first-year adjustments; and the meaning of the wedding as a celebration of their committed and growing relationship. On the basis of what the couple and the pastor want and hope for from these sessions, a flexible schedule of topics can be set up. This collaborative structuring helps to reduce the initial anxiety that many couples bring to the first sessions.

Allow rapport to develop by asking nonthreatening, open-ended questions, beginning with informational queries about positive aspects of their relationship.

****

Pastor: Since I'm going to have the privilege of sharing in this important experience in your lives, it seems right that we should get better acquainted. Tell me, how did you meet?

Continuing to gently ask low-threat leading questions helps the couple talk about how their relationship began and developed. In the process, a tentative picture emerges of their current interaction and of their parental families that shaped it. This modification of Virginia M. Satir's method of taking a "family life chronology" can be useful in premarital sessions.[16] Threatening questions should be avoided until considerable trust has grown between the couple and the pastor.

Pastor: One reason we're meeting is to help you launch your marriage in the most creative direction possible. As you've been thinking about the kind of marriage you want, what thoughts have come to your minds?

If a couple does not respond by opening up issues that interest them, the pastor may ask a leading question or mention common issues related to one of the topics on the tentative agenda:

Pastor: As we meet for these three sessions, I'll have some suggestions to share about the issues we agreed on, but I'll save as much time as you want for any questions that come to your minds. We'll go through the ceremony step-by-step to discuss its meaning as well as the mechanics. At some point, I'd like to share some thoughts from my experience about how couples can keep their love growing over the years. How does all this sound to you?

What about the use of psychological inventories in premarital sessions? Psychological tests or inventories of any type tend to raise the anxiety level in counseling relationships. Their potential for usefulness must be weighed against this limitation. Inventories such as the Taylor-Johnson Temperament Analysis Inventory and PREPARE (Premarital Personal and Relationship Evaluation) can be useful in increasing a couple's awareness and opening up discussion of factors in each partner's personality that may influence their relationship.[17] To use such inventories meaningfully, pastors should read carefully the manual that accompanies particular instruments and also do background reading to acquire general understanding of personality inventories. Pastors can also use background information forms to generate discussion of significant issues with couples. Joan and Richard Hunt's *Growing Love in Christian Marriage* includes several useful checklists.[18] Such instruments are easily used, are less threatening than personality inventories, and provide an abundance of information quickly. A pastor's perceptive eye may pick up clues that point to fruitful topics of discussion and areas where a couple needs accurate information.

The Sex Knowledge Inventory (SKI) can be a helpful resource, particularly with couples who are inhibited in discussing this area openly. Their responses to eighty multiple choice questions identify gaps or inaccuracies in their knowledge about sexual relationships and suggest emotional areas that need to be discussed in prewedding sessions.[19]

Do everything possible to reduce any sense of threat so that a couple will feel free to reveal their real needs and worries. In addition to building rapport and providing structure, threat reduction involves communicating to the couple that they are not on trial. At the outset, the pastor may say, "I consider it a privilege to share in the launching of your marriage." This initial reassurance cannot be given, of course, until the pastor is certain that there are no insurmountable obstacles to the marriage or to her or his participation.[20]

Reducing the threat to open communication is often difficult on two frequently encountered issues: living together and pregnancy. In most areas of North America, it is safe to assume that the majority of couples in premarriage sessions have had intercourse and that many are living together. In a high percentage of teenage couples, the woman is pregnant before marriage. It is important to create a climate of acceptance (transcending differences in sexual standards) that will free couples to talk openly rather than remain defensive as they try to hide the fact that they are sexually active, living together, and/or the woman is pregnant. The fact that many young people talk so freely about sex today does not necessarily mean that they have accurate knowledge, constructive attitudes, or skills in full-body, mutual pleasuring. Premarital sessions with couples living together in committed relationships have many similarities to marriage counseling. They tend to be very different from sessions with couples who have not had such experiences.

A pastor who suspects that a couple is expecting a child should check this out by asking a simple question (when the issue of children is discussed): "When do you expect to have your first child?" If the woman is pregnant, the pastor should explore their feelings—for example, guilt, anxiety, blame, or joy—about this fact and determine whether they're being pressured to marry. Helping them evaluate their readiness for marriage is important so that they can consider alternatives, such as adoption, if they are clearly not yet capable of establishing a constructive marriage. The most important thing is to surprise couples with loving acceptance, rather than with a pastor's judgment, and an opportunity to learn how to cope healthily with the enormous challenges they face.

Become aware of the couple's learning readiness and their awareness of problems related to their relationship. This is done by responding to their feelings as they emerge, and by gradually asking more feeling-centered and relationship-probing questions; for example, "How do you respond when she [he] is very late for a date?"

Couples who answer in clichés, revealing only positive or surface-level feelings, either are unaware of deeper dimensions of their relationship or feel they must put their best foot forward with the pastor. The latter type of couple will bring less socially acceptable feelings and real problems out of hiding only when both feel safer in that relationship. A useful method of surfacing conflicted areas in a relationship (adapted from marriage counseling) is to scrutinize specific vignettes of interaction involving conflict.

Pastor (after rapport is well established): What happens when you disagree over something you both feel strongly about? Could you think of an example we could look at together?

Learning readiness varies greatly in different areas. It is helpful, therefore, to open up various key topics, watching for increased-energy responses that indicate awareness of need. Obviously this should not be done in lectures but briefly, informally, and in a personalized way.

Pastor: Most of us have some trouble with open communication. Let's look at a fairly typical scenario in a marriage. Larry and Sue, our hypothetical couple, have been married about a year. Larry is quite successful in his business and likes to talk frequently about deals that are in the offing or have been successfully completed. Sue gets her feelings hurt when Larry is preoccupied with business and seems uninterested in her work in the medical field. She has trouble letting him know what is really bothering her. Does this sound familiar to you?

When the signs of interest appear in a couple's responses, concentrate discussion on that area for a while, encouraging them to examine it and seeking to communicate constructive attitudes and relevant information. Begin with what they are interested in and build on that, sharing ideas, experiences (including personal experiences in one's own marriage), and relationship-building and communication skills that seem relevant to the couple's needs. Dialogue is invited around the axis of their needs. After brief, informal sharing, encourage feedback by asking, "How does this relate to your experience?" or "How do you feel about this?" Focus on a given topic long enough to give the couple ample opportunity to understand and discuss it. If a topic proves fruitless, move on to another. As one sows seeds in this way, some seeds will fall on the fertile soil of the couple's emerging interests and perceived needs. As Nathaniel Cantor observes, "Learning probably takes place in small increments which accumulate into insights."[21]

Some topics are so vital from the pastor's viewpoint that a general orientation should be given, even if the couple show little or no sense of need in those areas. Such presentations, done in moderation, will not diminish the quality of the relationship with the couple. One of my "must" topics is the importance of their working out (and writing down) a fair working agreement, a marriage covenant, providing equal opportunities for both persons to develop their potentialities and share in the satisfactions and responsibilities of the marriage. Other important topics include communication and conflict-resolution skills, sexual attitudes and techniques, and changing female-male roles.

Discussion should focus on present feelings and current issues more than on anticipated future problems. In Peace Corps training, "anticipatory guidance" was found to be most effective when it dealt with the current experiences of trainees in handling the minor crises of the training program; for example, their feelings of deprivation resulting from leaving their families, and their resentments arising from constantly being tested and observed during training. These feelings were similar to those that they would have overseas. Concentrating on these issues allowed the small training groups to work with live feelings.[22] A similar approach to premarital guidance gives attention to how the couple cope with tensions, feelings, and problems arising during the prewedding period, including the anxieties of the premarital sessions.

A couple's worries about the future are, of course, present feelings and should be examined thoroughly. When a couple chooses to reveal their problems or worries, premarital sessions become counseling in the full sense of the word. It is usually unproductive to dwell on possible future conflict areas of which they have no awareness. To do so usually seems, from their view, to be irrelevant or an inaccurate prophecy of gloom. It is much better to concentrate on learning how to cope growthfully with current issues and problems, and on developing their assets, strengths, and hopes for their marriage.

Take time to teach couples useful communication skills, letting them practice these during, as well as between, sessions. Coach a couple as they actually practice a communication tool during a session, and then talk briefly about how they can use such a tool on their own to enrich their relationship.

Assign carefully selected book chapters and articles as homework to be read and discussed together between sessions. This exposes the couple to awareness-stimulating material and increases their communication time with each other. During the next session after such an assignment, the pastor can ask, "How did the ideas in that chapter you read tie in with what you have experienced in your relationship?" A book such as *Equal Marriage* by Jean Stapleton and Richard Bright provides excellent homework assignments.[23]

A primary goal of the prewedding sessions is to inform the couple about the ongoing program of marriage enrichment in the congregation.

Pastor: Following the wedding, I would like to invite you to meet with me after six months and one year to chat about how things are going. Most couples find these sessions worthwhile.

A date should be made for the first such healthy-marriage checkup. Couples should also be encouraged to participate in a church-sponsored marriage enrichment class, workshop, or retreat at least once a year for a refresher course to help keep their marriage growing.

A line-by-line discussion of the wedding ceremony helps lessen a couple's anxieties about the mechanics of the service and provides a natural entrée to a discussion of its deeper meanings, including the spiritual dimension of their relationship. They might also be asked to consider the meaning of some traditional ceremonial customs, such as the bride being "given away" by her father. Many people are unaware that the implications of this custom are that the woman is being passed from one male guardianship (the father's) to that of another (the husband's). With this information the couple may wish to initiate or use a substitute custom that symbolizes better the adult status of both partners as well as their transition from their families of origin to begin a new family system. Another way to raise consciousness about outmoded parts of the ceremony would be to ask a question like, "Have you thought about what various elements of the marriage liturgy signify; for example, the vow to honor and obey?" Such a question would get the couple thinking about the significance of the ceremony and whether they wish to make appropriate changes that would reflect their relationship better.

Ideally a minimum of three sessions should be spent with each couple. The number of sessions a pastor needs to spend with each couple may be reduced dramatically if couples have been a part of a premarriage class, workshop, or retreat. Much of the premarital training and instruction can be done more effectively and efficiently in small groups than in individual sessions with couples. Those who have been through a weekend pre-marriage/marriage enrichment retreat or a four- to six-session enrichment class co-led by the pastor often do not need more than one individual session before the wedding.

Throughout premarital counseling, the pastor should bear these goals of the process in mind: (a) instructing the couple in the mechanics of the wedding; (b) giving them practical guidelines for the early adjustment stages of marriage; (c) communicating some awareness of the complexities, conflicts, and struggles of marriage while strengthening their sense of adventure; (d) strengthening their interpersonal competence based on effective communication skills; (e) giving them a taste of a deeper level of communication than they have hitherto experienced; (f) setting an example for them of communication openness on topics that are still taboo issues for some couples, such as sex and anger; (g) introducing them to the "language of relationships" (Reuel Howe); (h) supplying them with sound information and guidance to help them develop a satisfying, growing relationship; (i) helping them experience the wonder of the real presence of the love of God in their love; (j) helping them understand the differences between holy matrimony and just getting married; (k) making oneself emotionally available so that, if they choose, they may use the relationship with the pastor for more extended counseling, before or after the ceremony; and (l) seeking to involve them in the caring community of the congregation and in its ongoing program, including marriage and family enrichment events. The pastor should hold to these goals with a very light grip, remembering that if only the master goal is achieved—the establishment of a warm, caring, trustful relationship with the couple—the premarital sessions have been eminently worthwhile.

Educative Growth Counseling through Life Stages

Ideally a church should develop a ladder of growth to help people at each life stage cope constructively with the new problems and develop the new possibilities of their emerging stage. This should offer individual coaching conversations and small educative counseling groups. The ladder is the ideal way to help people prepare for handling constructively the high-stress transitions in their life journeys. Gerald Caplan calls the work of such groups "anticipatory guidance" or "emotional inoculation":

> In small groups, the specialist draws their attention to the details of the impending hazard and attempts to evoke ahead of time a vivid anticipation of the experience, with its associated feelings. . . . He then helps them begin to envisage possible ways of solving the problems, including mastery of their negative feelings. When the experience itself arrives, the hazards will be

attenuated because they have been made familiar by being anticipated, and the individuals will already have been set on the path of healthy coping responses.[24]

To show the usefulness of this approach to a life-cycle caring ministry, here are examples of congregational educative counseling programs designed to respond to the needs of persons during each of the eight stages outlined by Erik Erikson. It is noteworthy that the same class or group can serve the needs of parents in several life stages. Fortunately, smaller churches that don't have the space or the staff for such programs can use one of the numerous co-op preschools in churches and community colleges that offer parent education programs.

Stage 1: *Infancy (birth to 15 months)*. A preparation for parenthood class offered periodically can enable expecting couples and persons planning on adopting a child to increase their readiness for the rewarding but very demanding role of parenting. A new parents sharing and support group can help single parents and couples learn how to nurture in their children the foundational feeling of basic trust, the growth goal of stage 1. Such groups can respond to the needs of parents with children in all of the first three stages. They provide valuable peer support while parents learn from one another and benefit from guidance by professionals with useful insights about preschool children. A marriage enrichment component should be included in all preparation for parenthood and new parents programs to help couples cope creatively with the heavy pressures on their relationships of struggling to meet the enormous needs of babies. Also important are educative growth groups to train church school nurseries and each of the subsequent levels of the church school.

Stage 2: *Early childhood (toddlers, 15 months to 2 1/2 years)*. A parents' study, sharing, and support group can help parents learn how to respond to needs of children in this stage, and particularly how to nurture children's need for growing autonomy, the growth goal of this stage. In one church, a young couples' church school class choose to follow a child study theme for several years, using a child psychologist in the community as a resource person. The sharing in this class became very meaningful and helpful to many of these parents.

Stage 3: *Play age (preschool, 3 to 6 years)*. A sharing and growth program for parents of children at this stage can help parents learn how to nurture a child's sense of initiative, the central growth goal of this life stage. A church where one of my grandchildren attended preschool sponsors an outstanding family life education program in which parents are encouraged to get involved while receiving parenting information. It is reported to be "rewarding" for participants. This group illustrates the potential value of a growth group for parents of children in all three preschool stages.

The most exciting experience with parent educative caregiving during my parish ministry was a child-study nursery group in a congregation I served as a young pastor. As a pastor-participant, I experienced firsthand the value that many of us parents received. That group also demonstrated how a church with limited resources can provide growth group experiences for children. The social skills the children acquired through playing together and all they learned through the use of art, storytelling, and music made this a significant growth experience for the children. That group focused on mothers and their children, with occasional evening meetings for dads. In retrospect and with a raised consciousness I now realize that this program would have been strengthened significantly if we had devised a strategy for involving dads and whole families more regularly in learning experiences.

Psychotherapists and developmental psychologists have given us convincing evidence that the preschool years are the foundation-laying years for the wholeness of children. For better or for worse, their psychological development and well-being are deeply influenced by the quality of family relationships during this crucial period. Churches have a unique entrée to many family systems with children in these formative stages. This gives congregations strategic opportunities to develop educative caregiving programs to strengthen, inform, and energize fathers and mothers of children in these stages. Whatever a church does to respond to this opportunity through its education program and growth groups will pay psychological and spiritual dividends far into the future.[25]

Stage 4: *School age (6 to 12 years).* Growth programs for parents and for children at this stage should focus on enabling movement toward the children's primary growth goals—learning to relate to one's age group and acquiring the basic tools and relational skills for living productively in their culture. One pastor frequently encountered a sense of need among parents of preadolescents. So he invited a cluster of six to eight couples to meet for eight sessions to discuss matters of mutual concern. He began each session with a brief statement on some aspect of the psychology of preadolescents or of parent-child relationships. This precipitated spirited discussion of the parents' feelings and problems. This simple approach can be applied to a variety of parent enrichment classes. During the preadolescent stage and beyond, growth experiences for children with their peers become even more important than in the preschool years.[26]

Stage 5: *Adolescence (onset of puberty to age 18).* There is no life stage when small sharing groups can be more growth-producing than adolescence. Educative counseling approaches can be used productively with membership training groups and confirmation classes for youth. Growth groups can be used to help teens strengthen their sense of identity (their key growth goal); develop new relationship skills with persons of the other sex; enhance their feelings of self-worth; keep the adult side of their personality in the driver's seat of their lives; affirm and guide their blossoming sexuality; and develop their own viable faith and responsible ethical value. Credible evidence does not exist that teens who attend schools with abstinence-only programs wait longer to have sex. In contrast, those who attend schools with sex education that is comprehensive, medically accurate, and age appropriate delay sexual activity and make safer decisions when they do become sexually active.[27]

Stage 6: *Young adulthood (18 to 35 years).* Growth groups that are relevant to this stage include creative singlehood groups, preparation for marriage workshops, preparation for parenting classes, new parent growth groups, and creative marriage and sexuality enrichment groups.

Growing Together, a marital enrichment group for young adults in the first few years of marriage, was offered by a West Coast church where I was minister of counseling. Role-playing of typical adjustment problems of new marriages was used to help the group focus on their real growth issues. With one exception, the couples came to the group not because their marriages were in deep trouble, but because they desired to make good marriages better. This was an example of preventive pastoral care.

To become more responsive to the needs of persons who have never been married, divorced, or widowed, churches should devise singlehood enrichment classes and workshops, including growth groups. Such groups are effective ways of providing mutual care and growth for the young adults who in increasing numbers are choosing to delay getting married or are choosing singleness as a lifestyle. Groups can strengthen the communication and relationship-building skills that can make either singlehood or being coupled truly creative.

Stage 7: *Middle adulthood (midyears 1 and midyears 2).* Midyears 1 includes the years with adolescents in the home. A sharing group for parents can help them constructively handle the challenges of those relationships.[28] Transgenerational teen-parents communication events are also useful.

Midyears 2 (empty-nest years) confronts couples with new issues, needs, and possibilities. Growth groups should have a different orientation during this stage. A midyears pastor in Southern California sensed that one group needed to meet the needs of his people was an empty-nest marriage enrichment group.[29] He and his wife served as cofacilitators for a group of five couples, which met for six weekly two-and-a-half-hour sessions, plus an all-day Saturday retreat. The contract developed by the group included these purposes for the group:

To enable couples "to understand the dynamics of the empty nest stage of marriage, both as a crisis period and as highly creative, productive years; to help couples increase their communication skills and their experiences of the many facets of intimacy; to increase the spiritual quality of their relationships, including Christian values; to develop a network of support and trust among them and a sense of outreach to other couples." This group illustrates some of the rich possibilities of marriage enrichment groups during midyears 2, when many of us need to revitalize our marriages to enhance growth and generativity during the latter midyears and beyond. Spiritual growth around value and meaning-of-life issues is often center stage in the needs of persons in midyears 1 and 2. Preparation for creative retirement groups also serve an important function in midyears 2. Generativity groups can help later midyear adults develop the creative outreach dimension of their lives by sharing the knowledge and wisdom accrued through years of child rearing with younger parents. It is also a time when people are freer to devote themselves to social issues outside the home.

Stage 8: *Mature years.* The pastor of a New York church drew a retirement group together informally by simply inviting ten men on the verge of retirement or recently retired to meet with him six times to share ideas on making the most of retirement. The interaction was vigorous and helpful. Retirement growth groups should be available to both men and women and also to couples since the retiring of one or both partners usually introduces marriages to new stresses and possibilities.

Educative counseling methods have proved effective with many small groups of seniors. There is no life stage when the growth perspective on one's life is more difficult or crucial. Groups for spouses and other relatives of terminally ill persons can be very helpful. One minister in the Seattle area has formed several living-with-dying groups to help members of her congregation face the fact that all of us are living dying creatures. Elisabeth Kübler-Ross's *On Death and Dying* is used as a resource, with group members agreeing to read certain chapters between each session. The pastor who facilitated these groups divided the two-hour sessions equally between discussions of particular topics and experiential exercises designed to help people get in touch with their feelings and attitudes about death. These exercises included writing one's own epitaph and imagining that one has only a few months to live.

For younger caregivers, relating with older people can be challenging. This letter to Ann Landers, published shortly after her death in June 2002, illustrates a problem of some young adults:

> You recently printed a letter about visiting people in the hospital, and it reminded me of my mother. Mother is 97 years-old. She fell and hit her head, and was hospitalized for several days. A handsome young doctor came to check on her every day, and he would ask her if she knew the date and who the president was. After a couple of these visits, Mom looked at me and whispered, "What's the matter with that young man that he can't remember the president's name or what day it is?" I sure hope I have her genes.

Ann responded, "Your mother sounds like a sharp cookie. Thanks for my laugh for the day."[30] Ageist stereotypes of "how older adults are mentally," like most stereotypes, can blind caregivers to particular seniors really are.

Which particular life stage growth groups are most needed in a particular church can be determined by analyzing the age distribution of the congregation and community. In addition to life stage growth experiences, a church has a unique opportunity to offer a variety of growth group experiences that transcend age categories. I recall a marriage enrichment retreat where the oldest couple had been married nearly forty-five years and the youngest only four months, with the other couples sprinkled unevenly between. At first the wide age and marriage experience gaps seemed to present an unbridgeable communication chasm. It was a beautiful moment of mutual discovery when the longest married couple talked openly about an issue they were currently working on, and the newlyweds reported in astonishment that they were confronting a similar issue.

Making Educative Counseling More Holistic

Educative counseling is inherently holistic in that including cognitive insights in the counseling process is an essential part of caregiving in each of the seven dimensions of people's problems. By understanding the role of this personalized teaching, caregivers can strengthen the holistic emphasis. Here are some examples of how this may be done in each of the seven dimensions:

- Physical self-care and counseling
- Mental self-care and counseling
- Work and play self-care and counseling
- Ecotherapeutic concepts and methods
- Spiritual care and growth
- Social justice issues and counseling
- Educative counseling to prepare for developmental transitions

In all of these areas information can be helpful when it is needed and when it is linked to actual concerns. Churches can often draw on resources within the church membership or from ecumenical resources. For example, many church communities have, among their members, medical doctors who might be willing to provide information on medical issues and health care, especially for persons midyears and up who are interested in such information either for themselves or for older people in their care. There are also persons well informed about social justice issues, such as human trafficking, or ecological issues, such as the reality of global warming and ways we can conserve resources. Spiritual directors from the Roman Catholic or Anglican communities might be enlisted to provide short courses on spiritual growth, ways of praying, spiritual retreats, and so on.

Educative counseling also is holistic in another sense. All caregiving for wholeness uses both the left-brain and the right-brain problem-solving capacities of the human mind in the playful interaction between the functions of the two brain hemispheres, but in educational counseling the role of left-brain cognitive functions is especially crucial. In the dawning decades of modern pastoral counseling theory, it tended to be primarily left-brain oriented, emphasizing talking, analysis, and insight-oriented problem solving. More recent psychological research has found that ongoing changes are more likely to occur when these crucial functions are integrated with the intuitive, metaphoric, integrating, nonanalytic problem-solving capacities of the brain's right hemisphere. In short, human empowerment is nurtured best when the whole brains of caregivers and teachers and recipients of these life-changing activities interact creatively. This points to the importance of integrating imaginative, artistic, and narrative methods with left-brain methods. Whole-brain pastoral work can draw on a wealth of right-brain resources in the rituals and sacred stories of religious traditions balanced by, or even illustrating, the rich left-brain resources of theological and ethical belief systems that guide problem solving.

Educative Action Counseling on Social Problems

Educative counseling skills are useful tools in the prophetic caregiving ministry. They are useful for dealing constructively with community problems and issues of institutional injustice. The methodology of effective social action must use and also go beyond the educative counseling model to include political methods designed to influence the power structures of one's community. There are, of course, no easy ways to transform prejudicial attitudes, effect reconciliation between estranged groups, or stop the exploitative use of institutional power. But precisely because of the psychological-socio-logical complexities involved, it is imperative that insights and methods from the fields of group dynamics, social psychology, group counseling, and organizational development be applied to these societal problems.

The CR (consciousness-raising) group model can be applied productively in a congregation's educative and prophetic ministry. Such a group is an instrument of both personal and social liberation. The CR group approach has been developed and used extensively in the feminist liberation movement. Let me summarize the six steps of effective social action, showing how educative counseling methods are integral to this process. I will use the feminist CR group to illustrate how this approach helps bridge the gap between personal growth and social change.

Step 1: *Recruiting and training a growth-action task force.* To change institutional structures (the essential goal of social action) usually requires a team effort. The most effective instrument for this is a well-prepared task force with a focused change target. There are substeps within this first step:

(a) Awakening awareness. Awareness of the need for change and growth-action task forces in churches offer an ideal setting within which consciousness-raising regarding community problems and injustices can occur. As task force members encounter first-hand the victims of racism, sexism, classism, ageism, militarism, economic injustice, and other forms of growth oppression in their community, their awareness of the need for change increases.

The feminist CR group is a personal growth and empowerment group—not a task force for social action. But its ways of increasing its members' awareness of the destructive impact of the pervasive sexism of our society on their lives offers methods of consciousness-raising in growth-action groups generally. Such a group is one within which an awareness develops of the societal context and causes of the damaged self-esteem suffered by most women. The "click experience" in such a group occurs when an individual becomes aware of a powerful and transforming fact that many of her painful experiences and feelings are shared by the other women in the group and that these problems result to a considerable degree from their socialization as women in a society that treats them as second-class persons. The awareness that her personal problems are also social and political problems helps increase a woman's sense of worth and her sense of inner power. In growth-action groups generally, the awareness of group members that their lives are somehow diminished (directly or indirectly) by particular social evils seems to be the heart of the kind of consciousness-raising that motivates continuing commitment to social action.

For example, not until men sense that they, too, are oppressed, that their own development is diminished by their social programming as men in our male-dominated society, are they motivated to work for self-liberation and for the full liberation of women. Conscientization of those in power (such as men) is much more difficult than is the case of those who are obvious victims of social oppression. When men have the experience, they discover that they are the oppressed oppressors! Discovering this awakens their awareness of the need for liberating their personal relationships with women and changing society's institutions in which they participate (including marriage) so that they will nurture the full becoming of men and women.

(b) Team building. To work together effectively, a social action group must develop a sturdy sense of mutual trust and belonging. One ecumenical project designed to train laypersons as agents of social change in their communities discovered that unless a sense of belonging developed within a training group, many members did not finish the training, and there was little chance that those who did would move into social action. In an effective feminist CR group, a sense of group bonding and sisterhood deepens rapidly, and with this come empowerment and a sense of identifying with the struggles for liberation of women generally.

(c) Learning change agent skills. Social action groups frequently stumble over their own communication and relationship problems. It is crucial, therefore, that conflict-resolution and communication skills be taught in the training. In addition, training should include learning effectively the assertiveness skills needed in working with others to change power structures. Feminist CR groups have developed effective ways to reverse the learned helplessness and passivity of women. They do this by enabling them to get in touch with their justified, constructive anger (at their oppression) and by helping them mobilize their sense of inner competence and power.

Step 2: *Deepening understanding of the problem.* The first and second steps involve major cognitive as well as experiential elements. An understanding of the social issue on which a group has chosen to focus can be enhanced by disciplined study, input by those with expertise on the problem, and firsthand encounters with the victims. In a feminist CR group, information about the social, historical, and political roots of women's problems helps awaken awareness of the need for action and increases understanding of the complex issues involved. The political power dynamics that sustain our oppressive male-dominated institutions must be understood. Feminist CR groups may include discussion of the historical and sociological roots of current sexist attitudes and practices. Increased understanding of the ways patriarchal institutions both developed and continue to constrict the growth options of women is a force for self-liberation.

Step 3: *Deciding on action goals.* As understanding of problems deepens, various action goals are considered. Most social problems have many facets demanding action. Through group decision making, one or two of these facets should be selected and realistic change goals developed by the group. It is important to select "workable problems"—smaller parts of the larger social issue about which something concrete can be done, and on which the task force members are motivated to tackle.[31]

In feminist CR groups, action goals frequently emerge spontaneously as consciousness-raising increases and group support grows stronger. These goals have to do mainly with two areas: personal-relational issues (for example, how to relate to a man without giving one's power away) and wider institutional-societal issues (for example, how to get involved in the struggle to eliminate de facto discrimination against women in one's place of employment). At this point, CR groups occasionally decide to work together to accomplish one or more social change objectives. More often, certain members of a CR group get involved in existing feminist action projects. They do so with the motivation, understanding, and interpersonal skills acquired in their CR group experiences.

Step 4: *Developing an action plan.* When goals are agreed upon, a growth-action group needs to devise a plan for achieving them. A workable plan (1) identifies a measurable result, (2) names the action to be taken to accomplish it, (3) sets a date by which it will be completed, and (4) says who will do what. All key decisions in growth-action groups—for example, regarding goals and how to mobilize available resources, acquire allies, and divide responsibilities— should be made by group process. Each person needs to know that her or his views are heard and valued by the group and taken into consideration in developing the action plan. Group ownership of an action strategy depends on the use of this person-respecting, often time-consuming process.

Step 5: *Taking action.* The group's esprit de corps and sense of mutual support become crucial when action begins to have an impact on a community's customs, laws, or institutions in even a small way. When the "flak begins to fly" from defenders of the status quo, strong mutual support is essential. Social change of almost any kind is an uphill struggle. Open communication and mutual support within the group are, therefore, vital.

Experience in social action has demonstrated that the very act of working with others to change growth-constricting community problems tends to strengthen the participant's self-esteem and sense of competency. Personal healing and growth of the kind one would hope for in effective counseling often occur as a result of being involved in the struggles and successes, large or small, of a social change team.[32]

Step 6: *Evaluating and restrategizing.* Midway through an action project, it is important for a team to do critical evaluation, particularly if things are not going well. On the basis of this evaluation, a midcourse correction of strategy can be made. At the conclusion of an action project or a major phase of a project, in-depth evaluation allows a group to learn from its mistakes and achievements. This provides a basis for revising strategy and for choosing the next action goal and planning strategy. It may be necessary to go back to the second step to acquire more facts about the part of the larger problem that has been chosen as the new change target. The growth-action group may need to be reconstituted from persons with a dynamic interest in working for change in relation to the new action goal.

The effectiveness of the prophetic ministry of a congregation can be enhanced significantly if the personal growth–social change group model is used. Pastoral leadership that combines the skills of the creative educator, the effective group facilitator, and the political activist can help a church become a more significant influence for social change.

Because it integrates personal growth and social-political change, the CR group is a valuable innovation for the whole field of therapy and growth work. The CR group model can be used for therapeutic-growth–liberation work with any oppressed group. It may be the key to creating indigenous sociotherapies among those in pockets of poverty in affluent countries and among economically and politically oppressed people in developing countries.

Using Bibliotherapy and the Internet for Educative Caregiving

Educative counseling can well include encouraging people to read selected material, including books, that may provide resources for them to use in increasing their options, developing more of their gifts, coping constructively with their problems in living, and becoming better informed on social issues. An example of the latter is the book on human trafficking and contemporary slavery listed below: *The Slave Next Door*. Fifty-five scholars and practitioners in the field of religion and aging offer a wealth of resources on pastoral care, congregational ministry, community outreach, and theological and social scientific perspectives on aging persons in an aging society.

Asking counselees to read relevant material as homework between sessions can enhance the impact of the sessions by stimulating productive reflections. An ancient Chinese proverb declared, "A book is like a garden carried in the pocket." In this cybernetic information age, relevant reading material often can be found on the Internet. Assignments can be made and reinforced by e-mail messages.

Recommended Reading

Bales, Kevin, and Ron Soodalter. *The Slave Next Door*. Berkeley: University of California Press, 2002.

Hudson, Frederic M. *The Handbook of Coaching: A Comprehensive Resource Guide for Managers, Executives, Consultants, and Human Resource Professionals*. San Francisco: Jossey-Bass, 1999.

Kimble, Melvin A., Susan H. McFadden, James W. Ellor, and James J. Seeber, eds. *Aging, Spirituality, and Religion: A Handbook*. Minneapolis: Fortress Press, 1995.

Pue, Carson. Mentoring Leaders: *Wisdom for Developing Character, Calling, and Competency*. Grand Rapids: Baker Publishing Group, 2005.

CHAPTER 15

GROUP PASTORAL CARE AND COUNSELING

For where two or three are gathered in my name, there am I in the midst of them.
—Matthew 18:20 RSV

*That their hearts may be encouraged as they are knit together in love, to have all the riches of
assured understanding and the knowledge of God's mystery.*
—Colossians 2:2 RSV

Group caring and counseling methods constitute the single most useful resource for broadening and deepening a church's ministry of healing and growth. Group approaches applied to a wide spectrum of crises and issues in living can allow a church to become an increasing force for preventing personality problems by stimulating growth toward wholeness. Exciting developments are occurring in the use of small groups in some congregations, but most churches have only scratched the surface of the rich possibilities for small group ministries.

The Key Role of Groups in Caring and Counseling

Small groups are a natural and time-tested methodology in the church. Church historians have noted that the use of small groups has been a dynamic factor in every major surge of new spiritual vitality in the church. Christianity grew through the spread of its "network of new and tough groups."[1] In his doctoral dissertation, "Group Therapy as a Method for Church Work," Robert Leslie identifies these significant points at which small groups played a vital role in church history: Christ and his disciples, the apostolic church, Montanism, monasticism, the Waldenses, the Franciscans, the Friends of God, the Brethren of the Common Life, German Pietism, the Anabaptists, the Society of Friends, the Wesleyan Revival, the Great Awakening, the Iona Community, the Emmanuel Movement, and the Oxford Movement.[2]

The contemporary renaissance of small groups in churches follows a familiar path. In places where the church has been persecuted in recent history, Christians have rediscovered the power of small (forbidden) group meetings in homes. This time-tested Christian strategy for personal empowerment and transformation has also been discovered in recent years by secular psychotherapists and by the human potential movement.

Many church groups provide rich opportunities for developing interpersonal skills, leadership abilities, spiritual depth, and intellectual discipline. The existence of a variety of sizes and types of groups in a local church is an invaluable asset in fulfilling its ministry of growth, healing, service, reconciliation, training for service, and proclamation of the good news. The spiritual vitality of a local church is directly correlated with the health of its groups—particularly its small groups where a sense of Christian community can flourish.[3]

As pointed out earlier, a pastor is the leader of a social organism or system composed of a network of subsystems and small groups. For pastors, small groups are a natural form of caring ministry. Whatever pastors or seminarians can do to increase their knowledge of group dynamics and their skills in facilitating groups will strengthen their ministry to persons at many points. Such knowledge and skills will be assets both in enhancing the growth of existing groups and in helping to create new ones. Effective growth groups and regular growth events (such as marriage enrichment) can produce a creative leavening effect on the interpersonal climate of a whole congregation.

If a church is to be a creative cell in our mass society, it must offer people abundant opportunities to experience Christian community. Large groups have a vital function in achieving the instructional and inspirational objectives of a church. Think, for example, of the spiritual lift that comes from being a part of a congregation singing the mighty Easter hymns of resurrection. But a church's smaller groups are the settings in which lonely people can best experience the reality of religion as creative relationships—with self, others, God, and creation. In house churches, retreat centers, denominational and local church camps, youth assemblies, parent education, and Bible study groups, thousands of persons are discovering the excitement of life-to-life communication. There is no doubt that the small group is a powerful factor in the recovery of the power of personal growth and social transformation in the church.

George Webber holds that any congregation that is really in mission "will make basic provision for its members to meet in small groups (as well as corporate worship), not as a sideline or option for those who like it, but as a normative part of its life."[4] I agree. A church of any size can meet many of its members' pastoral care needs by a variety of small sharing groups. Each member of a church should have such opportunities to experience a warm, nurturing sense of belonging. In larger churches, a network of small groups is essential to an effective teaching and caring ministry. Some larger churches develop a geographical network of neighborhood sharing and caring groups. Others offer a smorgasbord of interest, study, growth, and action groups designed to respond to the varied needs and interests of their members. In Korea, many Methodist churches seek to relate each member to a small "class meeting," a contemporary version of the small groups created by John and Charles Wesley as the Methodist Church was being born in eighteenth-century England. These groups engage in Bible study, prayer, mutual caring, and service to the community.

> Small groups are particularly important in our period of history. It is psychologically true, as in John Donne's familiar line, that "No [one] is an island, entire of itself." But the fact is that millions of persons experience themselves as islands, cut off from the continent of humanity. Many are not aware of the depth of their loneliness. They live in what Tennessee Williams describes as "a lonely condition, so terrifying to think of that we usually don't." Cut off from real communication with others, they feel like grains of sand, washed back and forth by the waves of impersonal forces, having friction with others but no organic relatedness. In this kind of society, small, lively groups in a church offer sorely needed opportunities for persons to drink deeply from the fresh springs of relationship, discovering the reality of the New Testament experience of being "members one of another."[5]

A key weakness of many churches today is identified by Robert Leslie: "It is rather ironical that the church is often the last place where people talk freedom and openness about the concerns that touch them deepest."[6] Small sharing and growth groups are the most effective way of restoring and transforming power to a church.

Five types of groups can serve important functions in a church's ministry of healing and growth: (1) task, service, and action groups; (2) study groups; (3) supportive-inspirational groups (including corporate worship); (4) growth groups; and (5) crisis counseling and therapy groups. Many ongoing church groups combine the functions of service, study, mutual support, and inspiration in varying proportions. For reasons that will become clear, therapy groups are (and should be) relatively rare in churches. The most exciting frontiers in the church's group program are in the areas of crisis support and grief-healing groups and growth groups (educative counseling groups).

This chapter will focus on two issues: How can existing organizations and groups become more wholeness enabling? And how can new groups, with healing and growth as their central purpose, be created to broaden and deepen the caring ministry of a congregation?

The Advantages of Group Caring and Counseling

Group caring and counseling have several significant advantages over individual methods. First, much of the counseling and even more of the caring now done individually can be done more effectively in small groups. Most methods described in this book can be used in groups, often with more effectiveness than when used individually. As psychiatrist Jerome D. Franks says, "Intimate sharing of feelings, ideas and experiences in an atmosphere of mutual respect and understanding enhances self-respect, deepens self-understanding, and helps a person live with others. Such an experience can be helpful to persons at any level of illness or health."[7]

A second advantage is that it is obviously better stewardship of a pastor's or lay leader's time to help five or ten people simultaneously than to spend the same time helping one individual. This is crucial in light of the heavy demand on most pastors' time. The growth group approach is one key to broadening a church's general caring ministry. Pastors who learn how to organize and facilitate growth groups have an efficient method for providing mutual support, challenge, and help to scores of people hungering for the nourishing food of a small community of mutual caring!

A third advantage is that groups allow helpers to help themselves by helping one another. The unique element in group counseling and therapy is the presence of mutually "giving" relationships as distinguished from the largely "taking" role of clients in individual counseling and therapy. Counseling or growth group participants are often helper and helped in the same session. The group climate of interdependency facilitates the growth that comes when one becomes an agent of healing in the lives of others, even while one's healing is being nurtured by them. Group caring and counseling are closer to the reciprocity of everyday life. As a way of releasing the potentialities that are dormant in most people, caring and sharing groups are contemporary ways of implementing the ancient injunction, "Bear one another's burdens" (Gal. 6:2). In effective counseling or growth groups, the group as a whole becomes an instrument of healing and growth. This tends to distribute the dependency of needy individuals onto group members rather than concentrate it on an individual pastor.

A fourth advantage is that a small group is the most productive milieu for short-term educative counseling. Three sessions of prebaptismal counseling with a group of four to six couples often stimulate learning that exceeds that of a couple-by-couple approach because the participants learn from one another and are nourished by the group's esprit de corps. By modeling openness, the less inhibited couples encourage the others to open up about their real problems.

A fifth advantage is that small groups can be used to help many who will not attend formal counseling. A man who describes himself as "not the type who would go to a minister for counseling" reports that two years of participation in a "depth Bible study" group (which incorporates growth group methods) has helped him in profound ways.

Creating Growth and Healing Groups

In the psychological sense, a group is not just a collection of individuals in geographical proximity.[8] Fifty people packed like sardines in a subway train do not constitute a true group. A group comes into existence when, through interaction, there is a partial overlapping of the "psychological field" or "life space" of the individuals. The significant world of each is to some extent involved in the other. There are definite, predictable stages through which an aggregate of people go in the process of becoming a true group. When this process is well advanced, there is a strong sense of group identity, group boundaries, and cohesiveness, interdependency, and belonging.

Although the process of becoming a group is a natural one, certain factors in our society tend to block it; for example, competitiveness, fear of intimacy, and general reluctance to relax our defensive masks. Consequently many so-called groups meet in churches for years without achieving more than superficial interaction. Unfortunately, glib talk about Christian fellowship will not produce it. Only as a group satisfies the conditions under which vital interpersonal relationship can grow will genuine fellowship be experienced.

A group tends to develop a distinctive personality, a persistent emotional climate and style of relating that distinguishes it from other groups. Many groups have "personality problems." Since groups can be robust or sickly, energetic or anemic, it behooves church leaders who work constantly with groups to be able to diagnose and treat the factors that limit group health.

For any group to come into existence there must be "physical, social, and interactional proximity."[9] Physical proximity must be combined with continuity of meeting. It takes time together to develop a sense of group identity. Social proximity refers to the common goals or interests that bring certain individuals together. The sense of group identity grows as mutual need satisfaction develops and psychological fields overlap through interaction. Emotional involvement in the group flowers as its members communicate and share meaningful experiences. The more intense the experience in which they participate, the more powerful the bond—witness the rapport among men who have been through a battle together.

In the growth of a healthy group, openness and honesty of communication are essential. Speaking of small groups in churches, John Casteel declares, "The vitality of the group's life together depends upon the freedom, honesty, and depth with which members come to share their questions, problems, insights and faith with one another."[10] The kind of participation that produces emotional involvement is based on the awareness that one's feelings and opinions are recognized, valued, and taken into account in group decisions.

A unique aspect that contributes to a church group's health is its vertical as well as horizontal reference. The growth of individual group members is seen in relationship to God and the needs of the world. This helps balance the necessary introspective aspects of a sharing group. In her description of the spiritual pioneering of the Church of Our

Savior in Washington, D.C., Elizabeth O'Connor put the issue squarely: "The group does meet for the nurture of its own members, but it also meets in order that God may have an instrument through which His life may break in new ways for the world."[11]

Growth-nurturing Leadership

Although few, if any, church groups should be therapy groups, all church groups should have a therapeutic effect on the lives of their members. The most crucial factor in determining the healing and growth effects of a group is the nature and quality of its leadership. In an authority-centered group, open communication tends to be inhibited. Members hide their real feelings and withhold themselves from wholehearted participation. The more leaders assume responsibility for what happens in groups, the more the group lets them carry the ball. In a leader-centered group, members give only enough of themselves to get by. Uncreative conformity and passive resistance or foot-dragging flourishes. Coercive devices such as penalties and rewards become increasingly necessary to keep the wheels turning.

Various studies have shown that authority-centered patterns of leadership produce negative effects on personality health. The morale of workers and the emotional stability of children have been found to be enhanced by job situations and homes, respectively, in which they participated in some decisions affecting them.[12] The distribution of leadership in the therapeutic community approach in mental hospitals (including patient self-government) has produced impressive therapeutic results.

The leadership model that maximizes the growth-stimulating effects of groups is described by Thomas Gordon in *Group-Centered Leadership: A Way of Releasing the Creative Power of Groups*. Here are some functions of a growth-enabling leader:

1. Seeks the maximum distribution of leadership among the group members.
2. Sees that all members of the group have an opportunity to participate in group decisions.
3. Encourages freedom of communication.
4. Seeks to increase opportunities for participation.
5. Attempts to create a nonthreatening group climate in which feelings and ideas are accepted.
6. Conveys feelings of warmth and empathy, thus encouraging others to do likewise.
7. Sets the tone by paying attention to the contributions of others, perhaps reflecting what they are saying with, "Let's see if I understand what you mean...."

8. Helps build group-centered (as contrasted with self-centered) contributions by a linking function in which he or she points to the relationships among various individuals' contributions to the discussion.[13]

Such a leader is a catalyst and facilitator of the group process. As group-centeredness grows, dependence on the leader decreases, and the functions of the leader are gradually taken over by the group. The degree to which members give of their abilities to the group's thought and work is determined by their emotional ownership, elicited through the distribution of leadership and meaningful participation.

Group-centered leadership is not the same as laissez-faire leadership or leadership passivity. Group-centered leaders actively help the group release its own potentialities. They know that the only way this can happen is by not doing the things for group members that they can learn to do for themselves. Their respect for persons and for the group process assures them that they can depend on the group's discovering its identity and power. As midwives, they help in a "natural childbirth" process by which a creative group is born. Their job is to help the group achieve an emotional climate and a level of communication that will facilitate the growth of all group members.

The spirit rather than the mechanics of leadership is as the heart of this matter. An authority-centered person can misuse knowledge of group dynamics (or even the methods of group-centered leadership) to manipulate a group in subtle ways. In contrast, the leader who believes that the group-centered approach releases human potentialities will carry this spirit even into those situations requiring more directive approaches. Church groups require a variety of leadership styles, including the constructive use of authority. Like counseling, leadership calls for different facets of a leader's personality in different situations. On the same day, a pastor may function with a family temporarily paralyzed by a tragic loss, a ministerial association involving numerous routine administrative matters, and a planning retreat for church leaders. The use of any one leadership style in all these situations would miss the needs of the other two. The first calls for a firm, warm, supportive approach. The second requires efficient leadership in order to conserve the group's time for important matters. In the third situation, the planning retreat, group-centered methods are essential in order to reduce leader dependency and allow each person the freedom and incentive to contribute her or his creativity to the planning.

Leadership Training and Growth

A major challenge facing pastors and lay leaders is how to help existing church groups become more healing and growth nurturing. The most effective way of accomplishing this is a leadership training program combining growth group methods and experiential learning of leadership skills; for example, guiding a training group through a process of role-playing effective decision making on a knotty problem. Such training can be done in a variety of ways, for example, an intensive weekend leader effectiveness retreat; a Friday evening and an all-day Saturday mini-retreat for group leaders or teachers (church and/or public school teachers); or a four- to six-session, weekly training enrichment group for group leaders and/or teachers. To make a church's overall group program more growthful, a pastor needs to involve leaders and teachers in regular leadership training events and other growth groups.[14]

Several churches with which I am familiar have added spiritual growth and relationship-strengthening exercises to their church board's annual program-planning workshop and to their monthly meetings.[15] In one church, lay officers took turns at their meetings giving a brief description of their work and how they were seeking to express their faith through it. At the beginning of a planning retreat at another church, leaders were invited to share on the themes "My most painful and most joyful experiences last year" and "My most meaningful spiritual experience last year." Rich, relationship-building communication followed this sharing. Leaders of an inner-city church facing difficult problems in a changing neighborhood agreed to devote the opening session of a weekend planning retreat to communication exercises designed to deepen relationships among them. Those who wanted to "get on with our business" were reluctant to spend time in this way. But the group discovered that the struggles to solve the problems facing the congregation were unusually productive after this opening session.

Another strategy to enliven the caring and growth ministry of existing groups is to focus on this concern at an evaluation and planning session of the groups' officers. In one West Coast church, each group within the congregation was asked to do a self-study of its effectiveness as a caring community. A group vitality checklist was made available to leaders to assist them in the process. It contained items such as the group's growth in size; attention to newcomers, absentees, and members experiencing illness and other stresses; rotation and distribution of leadership and decision making; depth of sharing feelings and significant life experiences; and the degree of warmth and caring experienced within the group. One result of these group self-evaluations was a request from several group leaders for a leadership training course, which was held subsequently.

Groups with low levels of mutual support can often develop new warmth and caring through a renewal retreat spent in a remote spot. Such retreats aim at rethinking the group's purposes and guiding vision, including the caring and growth dimensions of this vision. During the fun times as well as the serious discussions, interpersonal barriers are lowered and relationship bridges are strengthened.

Creating New Groups

A church should develop new sharing and caring groups to meet the changing needs of persons in our contemporary society. In evaluating its present group structure, a church's leaders need to ask themselves questions such as these:

What are the gaps in group structure when viewed against the need for healing and growth of our particular congregation and community? Is it possible for persons of every age, with a wide range of interests and needs, to find nurturing group experiences in our church? What new groups should we create to respond to unmet needs? Who will take responsibility for developing these new groups?

Among the growth experiences that should be available in every congregation are classes, workshops, retreats, or groups devoted to (a) leadership training and growth; (b) teacher training and growth; (c) marriage/premarriage enrichment; (d) healing of bereavement (from losses of all kinds); (e) spiritual growth; and (f) outreach involving social issues. If such group opportunities do not exist, their development should be given high priority.

Group Counseling and Therapy

Paralleling its conventional, ongoing groups, every church ought to have several groups with explicit healing goals. These should include groups that (a) give support and spiritual healing during personal crises; (b) seek solutions to common problems in living (for example, being a single, two-in-one parent; relating constructively with a rebellious teenager; and so on); and (c) increase interpersonal effectiveness. Objectives such as these are often realized as by-products in other groups, but these goals are the primary raison d'être in some church groups.

Group therapy describes a cluster of varied group approaches to psychotherapy. Being a client in an effective therapy group can be an invaluable training and growth experience for seminarians and pastors. But doing therapy with a group (like doing individual psychotherapy) requires a high level of therapeutic awareness and skills that come from advanced training. In some ways, group psychotherapy is more complex than individual psychotherapy. Powerful positive and negative transference reactions may occur, and there is sometimes an acting out of these transference feelings among group members. It takes a skilled therapist to handle such incidents constructively. Pastors with limited counseling and group training should not attempt to lead group psychotherapy. If a church has a pastor of counseling or a mental health professional with group therapy training, it may be appropriate to provide this form of intensive help to people with deeper psychological problems. If such leadership is not available, a church should concentrate on the vital ministry of growth groups and group crisis counseling. The latter consists of relatively short-term counseling in groups aimed at helping people handle losses or crises constructively.

Varieties of Growth Groups

The mainstream of any church's group caring should be directed not at those who need group therapy but at the host of people who can profit from growth groups. In any church there are many persons in this broad category—those who have garden-variety problems and unhappiness, and those who wish to grow spiritually, improve their relationships, develop their creativity, and discover what life in all its fullness can mean in their life stage and situation.

A growth group is any group, whatever its name or other purposes, that has these characteristics:

1. The dominant (though not exclusive) purpose is the personal growth of participants—emotionally, interpersonally, intellectually, spiritually, and physically.
2. A group-centered, growth-facilitating style of leadership is used, first by the designated leader and gradually by the entire group so that the group itself becomes an instrument and environment of growth.
3. The growth orientation is the guiding perspective; the emphasis is more on unused potentialities, here-and-now effectiveness in living, and future growth than on past failures or present hang-ups and problems, though these are not excluded from consideration. Growth groups are primarily mutual care groups, not counseling or therapy groups.
4. The group is composed of relatively functional people so that its aim is making well people better.
5. It is small enough to allow group trust and depth relationships to develop.
6. There is back-and-forth movement from sharing of personal growth issues to considering content (ideas or relational skills) that is relevant to the growth needs of participants.

Group educative counseling blends personalized education with group counseling methods. Constructive changes in both attitudes and feelings, on the one hand, and in behavior and relationships, on the other, are encouraged in growth groups. Concerns for spiritual growth, understood as the heart of all human growth, should be a central thrust in all church-related groups. Empowerment to enable the growth of others should be one expression of the growth that individuals achieve in such a group.[16]

The versatility of the growth group approach can be suggested by listing some of the types of groups that have proved to be feasible and growth producing in various churches:

- Youth groups to work through unfinished personal identity issues
- Preparation for marriage groups
- Keeping our marriage growing groups (recently married)
- Marriage enrichment groups for parents of young children, for parents of adolescents, and for empty-nest marriages
- Creative singlehood groups
- Play-for-growth groups for children and parents
- Parent-child and parent-youth dialogue groups
- Preparation for childbirth, leaving home, retirement, and other developmental crises groups
- Study-growth groups with a focus on intellectual growth (often centering on a book)
- Liberation groups for women, for men, and for couples desiring fresh approaches to changing female/male roles
- Creativity groups using drama, poetry, painting, pottery, body movement, creative dance, yoga, and so on as a stimulus to growth
- Sharing groups for mutual help in coping constructively with common causes of stress; for example, aging parents, physical disabilities, a child with a disability, and adolescent children
- Action-growth groups with a dual focus on personal development and training for some significant task such as community service and social action
- Spiritual growth groups and Bible study aimed primarily at growth in the area of meaning, values, beliefs, and one's relationship with God
- Ecology groups for tuning in on nature and saving the environment
- Multiple-family growth networks
- Bereavement recovery groups
- Youth groups searching for nondrug ways of turning on
- Career choices, planning, and transition groups
- Follow-up groups for persons who have completed counseling or therapy[17]

This list is only suggestive. The possible applications of the growth group approach are limited only by one's imagination and leadership resources available.

A complementary relationship should exist in a church between pastoral counseling and growth groups. Each should strengthen the other. Growth groups often facilitate referral for counseling or therapy. Confronting personal and relationship issues openly in growth groups makes some people aware of their need for deeper help. By increasing awareness of these needs, growth groups may enable people to enter therapy considerably sooner than they otherwise would. Conversely, referral to a growth group is an ideal follow-up experience for persons who have completed counseling or therapy (individual or group). The healing and growth that occurred as a result of therapeutic experiences can best be consolidated and continued in the nurturing environment of a growth group. Participation in a growth group often accelerates the growth that occurs in individual or couple counseling. The long-range growth effects of pastoral counseling can be multiplied significantly if linked with growth groups.

Leadership for Growth Groups

Providing adequate leadership is one problem that prevents some churches from developing the sharing and growth groups their people need. Most pastors did not have formal training in group dynamics and group counseling in seminary. Some therefore feel inadequate to launch growth group programs in their congregations. Fortunately pastors with good interpersonal awareness and individual counseling skills can equip themselves to lead growth groups by following this process:

Step 1: *Experiencing several growth groups.* This aspect of training has a dual purpose: to maximize one's personal growth and to learn various growth-enabling styles and techniques by experiencing these as a group member.

Step 2: *Learning the basic working concepts of interpersonal and group dynamics, group methods, and facilitator skills, by reading several books in the field.* Learning the theory of small groups illuminates what one experiences in such groups. Thus one acquires the cognitive maps needed by a group facilitator.

Step 3: *Coleading one or more groups with an experienced facilitator.* This enables one to learn from observing the other facilitator and from getting supervisory feedback (after each session) on one's own facilitating.

In many communities, a pastoral counseling specialist or a mental health professional with training in group methods can be recruited by a pastor to colead a growth group. If it is not possible to involve an experienced coleader, solo leading of a group should be begun under the supervision of a competent group counselor. Recording group sessions (with the group's permission, of course) and playing segments of these in supervisory sessions increase the value of the supervision.

The full range of growth groups that a congregation should have to meet the varied needs of its people cannot possibly by led by any pastor. Fortunately much of the leadership for sharing and growth groups can be provided by carefully selected and trained laypersons. One reason it behooves pastors to learn group facilitator and supervisory skills is that they will be equipped to train and give backup support to lay facilitators. Thus pastors become facilitators of facilitators, enabling the impact of their caring skills to be multiplied through the ministries of these growth group leaders. Persons selected to receive training for this important work should be warm, congruent, and growing. One of the best ways to identify potential lay facilitators is to be aware of how people respond as members of existing growth groups. As the facilitating function begins to be shared by group members, it will become apparent who has natural facilitator aptitudes and therefore will be the most trainable.

The process of training lay group facilitators follows the three steps described above. But a fourth step should be added: ongoing supervision by a pastor or other professional with group expertise should be built into any growth group program using lay facilitators. (For criteria used for selecting trainable persons, see chapter 18.)

Growth Groups through the Life Stages

Ideally a church should develop a ladder of growth groups to help people at each major life stage cope constructively with the new problems and develop the new possibilities of their current stage. Small educative counseling groups can help people prepare for and handle constructively the stress periods in their life journeys. Gerald Caplan calls the work of such groups "anticipatory guidance" or "emotional inoculation[18]

Classes and groups focusing on common interests and needs tend to attract participants from various life stages. As Bob Leslie astutely observes:

> The most natural way to introduce the note of sharing into small groups is through study. Church people are used to the idea that study is done best in a class and hence have little resistance to coming together in a group. Almost every successful attempt at meaningful group life has involved study. Indeed, as groups grow in intimacy and in appreciation of each other there tends to develop a felt need for material really to grapple with in order to keep growing in depth.[19]

Principles of Effective Growth Groups

1. These factors seem to be involved in attracting members to growth groups:

(a) The group's goals are designed to respond to the felt needs of a particular group of persons in the congregation.

(b) A nonthreatening name and growth-oriented publicity are used.

(c) A personal invitation is extended by the pastor or a trusted lay leader to selected individuals.

(d) The group's purposes are stated clearly (psychologically, theologically) in all publicity and recruiting.

2. An effective growth group must be small enough to permit frequent participation and face-to-face communication among all its members.

3. At the outset, the leader should ask members to say what they hope to get from the experience. This gives the facilitator a tentative impression of the group's needs and learning readiness. Initial input by the leader should be brief and immediately relevant to the felt needs of the group. It is important to develop a group contract and agenda of

topics and issues, reflecting the needs and interests of the group. Long lectures are ver-boten because they kill dialogue. After six to ten minutes of seed-planting input, the leader should invite feedback and continue to raise pertinent questions until the group members become involved. The leader may increase feeling-level involvement on the part of the group members by personalizing an issue with a hypothetical but true-to-life case or by sharing her or his personal experience. The bulk of growth group sessions should be spent in the group's wrestling with the issues related to each person's situation and growth goals.

4. Having a resource book, a topic, or a flexible outline of how the sessions will be used tends to reduce group (and leader) anxiety as well as provide a flowchart of the group's plan and topics. The less structure a group has, the higher the anxiety level tends to be. Yet too much structure curtails group spontaneity and reduces personal involve-ment. An excess of instruction tends to trap a group in leader-centered dependence, which defeats the purpose of a growth group. Group centeredness is generated by throw-ing the group on its own resources, gently refusing to carry group members, and involv-ing the maximum number in decisions, goal setting, program planning, participation, evaluation, and recontracting.

5. Leaders should function in the group-centered manner described earlier in this chapter. They should attempt to create a warm, accepting climate; listen closely and responsively to what each person says; encourage openness of communication; draw less assertive members into the interaction by asking, "How do you feel about this matter, Carl?"; and build group centeredness by linking what various people say and by pointing to the connections or contrasts between their positions. Leaders may occasionally sum-marize what has been said, giving the group an overview of its process and content. Leaders should encourage feeling-level communication by sharing their own feelings and responding to feelings of others as they emerge. When someone opens a door to a deeper level of interaction by mentioning a personal issue, the leader helps the group walk through that door by focusing on that person's issue.

6. The leaders may suggest tools that the group can use to enhance interaction. For example, persons can be asked to "draw your childhood family," using different-sized circles to represent the relative influence of each and the distance between persons. Each group member then shares and comments on what he or she has drawn. The same can be done with current family constellations. Both stimulate rapid involve-ment. Another useful tool is role-playing. For example, a young man who consistently failed to get jobs for which he was interviewed brought up this problem during a young adult group. The pastor-leader suggested that the man reenact the interview of the day before, with a group member taking the company personnel director's part. It was

immediately apparent to the group that the young man was unwittingly sabotaging his chances by his behavior during the interview. Another group member then played the young man's role, allowing him to stand off and see himself making a negative impression. In this case, the person did not need to discover the underlying causes of his self-defeating behavior in order to change his approach enough to obtain the next job for which he applied. Thus, he interrupted his failure cycle.

7. Leaders should attempt to be aware of the group as a whole as well as of each individual. They may suggest that an observer-feedback person be selected to help the group become aware of its process and interaction. This is rewarding, but threatening at first, and it should be suggested only after a group gains some sense of mutual trust. The contemporary rediscovery of the power of small groups is an exciting development in the church. The imaginative use of such groups is one of the major frontiers in pastoral care and counseling.

Reality Practice Skill Development Session

Parishioner's role (three to five persons needed): Imagine yourselves (how do you constitute yourself) as members of a sharing and caring group whose goal is to communicate on a level that is mutually helpful and group building.

Pastor's role: Facilitate this group using the growth-enabling style of leadership described in this chapter.

Observer-coach's role: Give feedback concerning how the facilitator deepens the communication within the group.

Recommended Reading

Comiskey, Joel T. *Groups of 12: A New Way to Mobilize Leaders and Multiply Groups in Your Church.* New York: Merit Publishers, 1965.

Corey, Gerald. *Groups in Action: Evolution and Challenges.* Farmington, Utah: Wadsworth, 2006.

Donahue, Bill, and Russ Robinson. *Building a Church of Small Groups: A Place Where Nobody Stands Alone.* Grand Rapids: Zondervan, 2005.

Forsyth, Donelson R. *Group Dynamics.* Belmont, Calif.: Wadsworth, 2010.

Levi, Daniel. *Group Dynamics for Teams.* Thousand Oaks, Calif.: Sage Publications, 2010.

CHAPTER 16

THE ART OF REFERRAL IN PASTORAL CAREGIVING

Referral is not a pastoral failure. It is a subtle and important helping art. . . . I propose that we think about it as illustrative of the more generally useful skill of helping people to focus their needs and clarify their feelings.
—Thomas W. Klink[1]

Skill in the art of referral is an indispensable part of basic caring and counseling ministry. As Wayne Oates once declared, "One of the reasons that pastors do not have time to do their pastoral ministry is that they insist on doing it all themselves. . . . They have failed to build a detailed knowledge of their community as to the agencies, professional and private practitioners, etc., who could help them in their task."[2] By default, pastors who see themselves as a one-person band rather than the conductor of an orchestra often deprive troubled people of needed specialized help that is readily available in their communities. C. W. Brister touches the heart of the matter: "The minister calls upon community resources, not in order to pass the buck, but because he wishes the best for all persons concerned."[3]

Because many people trust the judgment of clergy and turn to them spontaneously when trouble strikes, pastors are in strategic positions to assist them in finding competent, specialized help. A review of the empirical research on counseling by clergy came to this significant conclusion: "Clergy bridge the gap between informal social support systems and more specialized formal helping professionals. Clergy have day to day contact with their parishioners and are highly visible in their communities when compared to agency or private therapists."[4]

A wise referral is one of the most significant caregiving services a pastor can offer suffering persons and their families. Families who, in the midst of traumatic and baffling problems, are guided by their pastors to effective help are usually eternally grateful to them. Pastors can multiply their help to troubled persons by using all the caregiving resources in their community to the hilt.

To make informed decisions regarding referrals, clergy in congregations and other "general practitioners" need to be informed and updated about the specialized health agencies and professionals in their geographic areas. They also need to learn enough about the goals of psychotherapy and other mental health interventions to make wise decisions.

Overcoming Resistances to Making Appropriate Referrals

Unfortunately some pastors feel that to refer is to admit inadequacy or failure. A nationwide study of where people take their problems revealed that "the helping process seems to stop with the minister and physician in the majority of cases, and far more so with the minister than with the physician."[5] In fact, physicians referred eight times as many persons to mental health facilities and practitioners as did pastors.[6] Obviously some pastors have much to learn about the importance of "pastoral care by referral," as Tom Klink has phrased it.

At the other extreme, there are a few pastors for whom referral is as automatic and as mechanical as the salivation of Pavlov's dogs. Because of this too-rapid referral reflex, their unique helping potentialities as pastors are not used fully. They miss some of the deeper satisfactions of their profession by not attempting to establish healing relationships with persons who may need precisely what they have to give. Troubled parishioners get the feeling that pastors are passing the buck (because they are)!

A significant discovery of one survey was that clergy's resistance to making referrals to other mental health professionals correlated with low levels of self-esteem in clergy. It was also discovered that more theologically conservative pastors refer less.

It may help to overcome such resistances if pastors see that making an effective referral is a means of using a team effort to help a troubled person. It is a broadening and sharing, not a total transfer, of responsibility. It employs the division-of-labor principle that is the basis of interprofessional cooperation. Only by drawing on the specialized helping skills of others can pastors have the time and energy to fulfill their unique pastoral function as leaders and wholeness enablers for entire congregations.

Deciding between Crisis Counseling, Getting Consultation, or Making a Referral

Clergy must respect the real limits posed by their time, training, and competence in counseling. But making automatic referrals to outside professionals is not necessarily appropriate only because of the time limitations and multiple roles of congregation-based clergy and other generalists in ministry. If these clergy have had basic clinical and academic education in short-term counseling, they can help many help seekers on their own using the variety of supportive caregiving people and programs in many congregations. Clergy can counsel safely and productively with many people they otherwise should refer if they have regular access to competent consultants. There is growing awareness among pastoral counseling specialists and mental health professionals that providing consultation to the "care-giving professions," including pastors, is essential if the yawning gap between the supply of and the need for trained therapists is to be even partially bridged.[7]

Regular or even occasional case conferences with a specialist in pastoral counseling or other competent psychotherapist can extend the range of pastors' helping abilities; give them expert assistance in handling counseling crises; and alert them to subtle dangers, such as transference and countertransference, in certain counseling relationships. Because they understand the ministry from the inside, pastoral counseling therapy specialists usually make excellent consultants for persons in general ministries. Because of their medical training, psychiatrists also are valuable as consultants, provided they are also well trained in psychodynamic theory and psychotherapy. Clinical social workers often bring extensive knowledge of community resources to consultations, and clinical psychologists offer expertise in psychological testing and evaluation.

Who Should Be Referred?

With what persons should a pastor use referral to broaden the base of help?

1. Those who can be helped more effectively by someone else
2. Those with problems for which effective specialized agencies are available in the community
3. Those who do not begin to find pastoral help useful in four or five sessions
4. Those whose needs obviously surpass the pastor's time and/or training
5. Those with severe chronic financial needs (Public welfare agencies with trained social workers are appropriate referrals.)
6. Those who need medical care and/or institutionalization
7. Those who need intensive psychotherapy
8. Those about the nature of whose problem one is in doubt
9. Those who are severely depressed and/or suicidal
10. Those toward whom the pastor has a strong negative reaction or intense sexual attraction

The anxiety that often underlies strong antipathy will tend to vitiate one's counseling effectiveness with such a person. If the pastor can discover what is causing this reaction and work through the negative countertransference feelings, she or he may do effective counseling and grow as a result of the experience. It is very difficult for any counselor to maintain the healthy objectivity needed in a counseling relationship if he or she is experiencing intense sexual attraction to a counselee.

It is important for pastors to build working relationships with one or more physicians in their community. A counselee who has not had a physical checkup recently should be strongly encouraged to do so if the pastor has any suspicion that the person may need medical attention. If there is the slightest suspicion that neurological, endocrine, or other medical problems may be lurking behind or complicating psychological or interpersonal conflicts, the pastor should insist that the person consult a doctor. A close collaborative relationship with a physician is also vital in counseling with persons who have psychosomatic problems, severe depression, suicidal tendencies, alcoholism, other addictions (including food addiction), menopausal problems, physical disabilities, chronic or terminal illness, severe sexual problems, geriatric problems, pronounced mood swings, or severe anxiety. In my experience, many physicians will welcome collaborative relationships with competent counseling pastors. In such mutually helpful relationships, referral becomes a two-way street, as it should be. The counselee's written permission to consult with the doctor (or therapist) should always be obtained before doing so.

Here are some signs of severe mental disturbances indicating a need for referral to a mental health facility or a psychotherapist:

- Persons believe (without any basis in reality) that others are attempting to harm them, assault them sexually, or influence them in strange ways.
- They have delusions of grandeur about themselves.
- They show abrupt changes in their typical patterns of behavior.
- They hallucinate, hearing nonexistent sounds or voices, or seeing nonexistent persons or things.
- They have rigid, bizarre ideas and fears, which cannot be influenced by logic.
- They engage in repetitive patterns of compulsive actions or obsessive thoughts.
- They are disoriented (unaware of time, place, or personal identity).
- They are depressed to the point of near stupor or are strangely elated and/or aggressive.
- They withdraw into their inner world, losing interest in normal activities.

When these signs appear, the pastor should help such persons' families get them mental health treatment as soon as possible. The recovery rate from severe mental disturbance is higher if intensive treatment is instituted at an early stage. Family physicians are the pastor's and family's logical allies in such situations. They can administer sedation or psychic energizers or other emergency medical care and can also make arrangements for hospitalization. Often they are an effective link with a psychiatric facility or individual psychiatrist.

Recognizing Psychological Problems Pointing to Referrals

What are some signals pointing to the need for referral for pastoral psychotherapy or other type of specialized helping agency? The presenting problems that people bring frequently are only the current manifestations of ongoing dysfunction. It is important, therefore, to watch for patterns of continuing problems in living that may be behind the initial problems that careseekers describe. Certain types of problems and lifestyle patterns of behavior signal high probability that careseekers would be best served by being referred to specialized therapists or healing agencies. There are patterns of behavior that usually are symptoms of a degree of general dysfunction that makes finding specialized help the appropriate pastoral response. Recognizing these problems and patterns can save pastoral caregivers from the frustration of trying to help people in ways that fall short of what they need. More important, it can also accelerate the process of enabling dysfunctional people to make the transition to the particular specialized help they most need.

What are some lifestyle behavioral patterns of careseekers, and what types of problems accompanying them as symptoms strongly suggest that the aim of pastoral caregivers should be to make effective referrals? A large cluster of such problems indicates that individuals are suffering from a degree of general dysfunction that far outweighs their present strengths and resources. If this is the case, short-term crisis intervention will probably not be enough to enable them to mobilize their inner strengths and coping resources and thus grow beyond their dysfunction by learning how to reduce the problems that are symptoms of their general dysfunction. Instead they need some type of investigative psychotherapy and/or help from a mutual-help group, such as AA, that has special experience, expertise, and resources in providing such help. In traditional psychiatric literature, elevated degrees of general dysfunction are usually described as resulting from what are called "deficiencies of ego strength."

Here is an overview of some chronic behavior patterns that frequently signal degrees of dysfunction that make referral the wisest pastoral response:

Changes in ego strength. Everyone's ego strength changes continually, to some degree, depending on shifting inner pressures and outer circumstances. As people reach their advanced years chronologically, they usually retain ego strength but may become somewhat less flexible in coping with change, particularly if they do not continue to learn new things. But in general, persons with relatively weaker, more rigid, or dysfunctional ego development tend not to respond to reconstructive, insight-oriented methods. Reality-oriented crisis approaches or supportive methods constitute the approach of choice. The ego is the executive branch of personality. Its functions are the integration of one's inner life in ways that enable one to cope with the external world. The ego's many skills include reasoning, problem solving, reflection, imagination, and motor activities such as walking and speaking. People's sense of personal identity and worth are at the center of their egos. Those with sturdy, functional egos have clear, empowering answers to three basic identity questions: "Who am I?" "What am I worth?" and "What can I do that matters?" People with relatively robust egos are able to handle their problems and responsibilities effectively. In TA terms, their Adult is able to guide and direct their inner Child and Parent. One or more of these characteristics usually indicate deficient ego strength:

Inability to handle ordinary adult responsibilities and everyday relationships constructively. The fact that a person has been chronically unable to hold a job or maintain ongoing relationships often indicates ego weakness. Conversely, the fact that a person has held a job or remained married to the same person for a considerable time may indicate inner strengths upon which counseling can build. Societal factors such as de facto discrimination against women and minorities must be taken into account in evaluating chronic unemployment and other factors as indicators of ego strength or weakness.

Inability to tolerate frustration and control impulses. Persons with weak egos tend to be pushed about by their impulses. Their frustration tolerance and willingness to postpone gratification in the interest of long-range goals are limited.

A low degree of ability to organize one's life, plan ahead realistically, or learn from experience. Persons with dysfunctional egos often suffer from chronic economic chaos, repetitive mistakes, and general disorganization. Their "executive department" is no match for the complex demands of economic reality, interpersonal relations, and everyday pressures. They suffer from what has been called "copelessness."

Pronounced, chronic dependency. Such persons tend to form parasitic relationships with others who give out signals that they will take care of them and perhaps give them a vicarious sense of importance, recognition, or strength.

Perceptual distortion. Since perception is an ego function, the degree to which people distort or reflect reality in their perceptions is an indication of their ego's relative strength. Distortions result from inner pressures and conflicts. The accuracy with which counselees see the counselor is one reliable index of their ego strength. Are their perceptions grounded in reality? Or do they see the pastor as a stern judge or magical protector when, in fact, she or he is neither? Individuals who suffer from major ego dysfunction also show significant perceptual distortions.

Personality rigidity. A lack of resiliency in the ways persons relate can often be sensed by caregivers. Rigid theological or political views, held with a kind of drowning-person-clutching-straw tenacity, are frequently present. Persons who hold obsessively to a cult or peace-of-mind ideology may be using this repressive mechanism to hold off inner chaos. Efforts to alter the views of such persons by rational, logical means are usually futile. The only humane approach is to respect persons' needs for such magical beliefs until they are able to relinquish them and grow beyond them. Magical, manipulative belief systems often are disturbed persons' only source of certainty and safety in a chaotic inner world of frightening fantasies and impulses, and an outer world that often is chaotic and oppressive.

Chronic use of rigid, regressive ego defenses. People have ego defenses such as denial, rationalization, and projection because they need them to maintain an essential minimal sense of safety and worth.[8] However, there often is a lag time during which people continue to use past defenses for a while as their wounded esteem and security sense gradually recover. Defenses are valuable because they operate automatically to protect people's minds from unbearable threats to their self-image and self-esteem stemming from societal, interpersonal, or intrapsychic sources. In a relatively healthy person, defenses operate with some flexibility. For example, students who fail exams often defend their sense of self-worth by the use of *rationalization*: "I flunked because I'm a well-rounded person and not a bookworm or a nerd." Or they may use *projection*: "It was the teacher's fault for giving an impossibly tough exam." *Denial* is also a commonly used ego defense: "Passing exams isn't all that important." But if their self-esteem gradually recovers, they let go of such defenses. They become aware of what they contributed to their failure and take appropriate action to better their situation.

In contrast, the defenses of those with less-functional egos tend to operate inflexibly, limiting their capacity for constructive change, insight, or problem solving as their situation changes. The goal of caring and counseling with such persons is to give them support and little successes (esteem-enhancing experiences) to lessen their need for heavy defenses such as projection and denial of reality.

Inability to benefit from insight and uncovering counseling approaches. Limited ego strength is characterized by diminished ability to engage in the prolonged self-scrutiny leading to self-understanding and the modification of basic attitudes. It may also lessen the capacity to order life, control impulses, and learn from or reflect on experiences. These factors tend to truncate the effectiveness of insight and uncovering methods. When counselees do not respond to insight-oriented approaches, it is wise to shift to more supportive or action-oriented approaches after a few sessions.

Insight-oriented talk therapy was created in the ethos of middle-class values, ways of thinking, communicating, and problem solving. The limited effectiveness of these approaches with nonmiddle-class persons, therefore, may be a result of class differences and should not be taken as necessarily a sign of ego weakness.

Insight-uncovering pastoral counseling or therapy is more likely to benefit persons who use neurotic, rather than acting out or psychotic, ways of attempting to handle their inner problems in living.[9] In contrast to acting out, persons who suffer from sociopathic or character disorders differ from neurotic people, who experience painful degrees of guilt and anxiety. Neurotic individuals have considerable ego strength, but their defenses are very heavy, inefficient, and costly, producing a variety of disturbing symptoms. Because they are motivated to search for reduction of their guilt and anxiety, and they have some ego strength, neurotic people often are helped by insight-oriented talk therapy.

In most cases, caregivers are dealing with a significant degree of ego weakness when counseling with chronic alcoholics; drug addicts; the overtly or borderline psychotic; the chronically depressed, delinquent, or dependent; and those suffering from chronic multiple psychosomatic problems. In working with such persons, a supportive approach is more likely to be helpful. (However, the dysfunction often diminishes greatly in drinking and/or drug-using addicted persons if they enter recovery and interrupt their addiction.)

The problems and crises of deeply dysfunctional persons usually are repetitive and chronic. Referrals to short-term or longer-term specialized individual or relationship therapy, or to an ongoing peer support group such as that available in 12-step recovery programs, are among the appropriate options. Often it becomes evident that persons who seek help have reasonably adequate coping skills but have been thrown into a temporary tailspin by a severe crisis or series of crises. If so, short-term crisis counseling may be all that is needed.

Where to Refer

Pastors should begin to prepare for making effective referrals soon after arriving in a new parish. This involves doing two things: (1) assembling a growing referral file of community resources and (2) building relationships with social agencies and helping professionals. An organized referral file becomes increasingly useful as the pastor accumulates information about social agencies: directories of pastoral counseling specialists, psychiatrists, clinical psychologists, marriage counselors, AA groups, and so on; and phone numbers of pastoral counseling centers, emergency psychiatric facilities, mental health clinics, suicide prevention centers, and so on.

A pastor should check to see whether the community has a welfare planning council or other community agency that provides a directory, Internet listings, and perhaps phone information assistance for community resources. Copies of such directories should be in the pastor's study and in the church library.

What are the major helping areas in which pastors (as well as pastoral counseling specialists) need to draw on outside helping resources? Pastors should keep a file of information on all the community, state, and national helping resources that are available for them to use in making future referrals. Here is a list of types of such resources: adoption and child placement, AIDS, alcohol and other drug problems, business problems, child guidance, child welfare, child abuse, crisis intervention, day care, correctional institutions, deafness, crime and delinquency, dental services, disabilities, disaster relief, education, employment, family life, family planning, financial assistance, health problems, homeless persons and transients, emergency housing, industrial problems, legal assistance, mental health facilities, minority groups, older persons, problem pregnancies and infertility, retirement, single parents, STDs (sexually transmitted diseases), sex therapies, speech problems, veterans, vocational guidance, and youth services. This file should also include a directory of national resources—church related, governmental, and voluntary—and a section where pastors may enter their own working list of local phone numbers and addresses. Parish pastors would do well to keep such a file at their fingertips.

Evaluating Referral Resources and Cultivating Teamwork

Accurate evaluations of the competence of the various counselors, psychotherapists, and agencies in one's community often are difficult to acquire. The reputation that therapists or agencies have among physicians, counselors, and pastors provides a reasonably reliable guide. Beyond this, it is helpful for pastors to become personally acquainted with as many as possible of their community's therapists and social agency personnel. In my experience, the most trustworthy evaluations of therapists' personal authenticity and professional competency come from direct contact with them and from observing the outcome of referrals to them. By having coffee or lunch with such persons, visiting the local child guidance or mental health clinic, and attending the open meetings of AA and Al-Anon, pastors build relationship bridges that can prove immensely useful when they need to make a referral. As they work with these persons in helping troubled parishioners, the relationship grows stronger. A collaborative interprofessional relationship may not be easy to maintain, but such a relationship is often in the best interests of the person being helped.

Pastors should refer people to health-care professionals who

- appreciate the importance of spiritual and ethical components in the causes and treatment of physical illnesses;
- are open to collaborating with pastoral caregivers as professional peers;
- integrate preventive wellness education with healing methods;
- use complementary, as well as mainstream, medical healing resources.

It is good to be aware that not all health-care professionals who are "Christians" in their personal beliefs demonstrate the openness, interprofessional cooperative spirit, and eclectic approach to healing implied in these criteria. Furthermore, many who hold to other faith traditions measure up well when evaluated by the criteria.[10]

A cooperative team spirit among a community's helping professionals does not happen by accident. Someone must take the initiative. In order to do pastoral work optimally, pastors need such a team spirit. What is more, pastors are in an ideal position to take the initiative, perhaps starting with a monthly breakfast meeting of a small group of helping professionals in their congregations and the wider community. Such meetings enhance communication of mutual concern and build working relationships. Participants may begin to ask the pastor for assistance in helping their clients or patients deal with value and meaning problems as well as overtly religious issues. Thus collaboration between clergy and other professionals becomes a two-way street, as it should be. To work effectively with physicians and mental health professionals, pastors may need to resolve self-esteem and authority problems that cause them to give their power away to other professionals.

Reciprocity of referrals between mental health professionals and clergy depends on mutual respect and perception of equality of roles in counseling. Clergy perceive their roles as being of major assistance to persons needing counseling, whereas mental health professionals often see clergy as having only a gatekeeping role as a source of referrals to them as mental health professionals.

Guidelines for Making Effective Referrals

John L. Mixon, an experienced social worker, once declared, "The two most important aspects of a good referral are: (1) a knowledge of the resource, its program, functions, intake policy, etc., and (2) the use of sound counseling procedures in interpreting the resources and the possible help the individual might expect to receive."[11]

The pastor of a rural church who was approached by a man who came to him "for help to defend myself against a conspiracy" suspected that the man was suffering from paranoid delusions. A psychiatric referral, though obviously essential, was difficult since this particular illness, by its very nature, made the man unaware of his need for help. Only by counseling with his family and collaborating with their physician over a period of weeks were an appointment with a psychiatrist and subsequent involuntary hospitalization accomplished. In the interim, the pastor maintained a supportive role with the man. He listened and did not attempt to dissuade him from his delusions, although he did raise gentle questions concerning whether the man felt that all the threatening aspects of his situation were objectively real or partly within his feelings. He did not challenge the man's paranoid defenses, but only tickled them. He stayed close to the burdened family while they were arranging, with the doctor's help, for hospitalization.

This is an example of stopgap supportive counseling, the valuable help a pastor gives until more basic help becomes available. Because of frequent resistance to psychiatric help, and the length of some agencies' or a therapist's waiting lists, the gap that must be "stopped" often extends over weeks or longer.

Here are some guidelines for effective referral counseling:

1. Create the expectation that referral might be helpful. The function of assisting persons in finding specialized help should always be mentioned when the pastor's availability for counseling is described in the church bulletin or newsletter.

2. When it is likely to occur, mention the possibility of referral early in counseling relationships, explaining why specialized help may be needed. Persons who have mustered their courage to come to their pastor expecting help usually feel some degree of rejection if it becomes necessary to refer them. This is true even if they understand intellectually why the referral is necessary. The longer the pastor waits to plant the seed of the possibility of referral, and the greater the dependence that has developed, the more likely referral will arouse feelings of rejection.

3. Start where persons are in their perception of their problems and the kind of help needed. Until pastors understand these perceptions and expectations, they are in no position to make a referral. Counselees' inner pictures of their problems and their solutions are often very different from the counselor's perception of the nature of the problems and the type of help needed.

4. Work to bring counselees' perception of their problems and solutions close enough to the counselor's perception to permit referrals to be effective. This may require several sessions of counseling. Referral efforts often fail because counselees' perception of their situation is fundamentally different from that of the referring pastor. Such persons naturally resist referral by not going to the helping resource or by not continuing long enough to receive benefit.

5. Help counselees resolve their emotional resistance to the particular helping person or agency recommended. Tom Klink emphasizes the linking of two vital helping processes—acceptance of feelings and support of reality testing—in enabling persons to accept referral. The pastor should ask about persons' feelings regarding a particular referral while helping them move toward accepting the reality of the need for specialized help. Attempts to refer persons, without clarifying and accepting their feelings and enabling them to become more realistic about their need for other help, usually fail.

Before suggesting that persons with drinking problems go to AA, it is important to find out how they view their problems. Do they feel that drinking is a cause or only an effect of (or even a solution to) their other problems? Do they have any desire for help in stopping their drinking? If so, AA is appropriate. In suggesting AA, ask persons what they have heard and how they feel about that group. This query, about any agency to which one is making a referral, is a valuable means of discovering the fears, misinformation, and emotional resistance that otherwise may sabotage the referral. Dealing with these inner blocks often takes time, but it is an essential part of motivating persons to accept the recommended help.

6. Interpret the general nature of the help that persons may expect to receive, relating it to their sense of need. Do this without making the mistake of overselling the potential help—a mistake that makes the therapist's or agency's work more difficult—or committing the agency or therapist to a specific treatment approach.

7. Establish strong enough rapport with persons to develop a bridge over which they may walk into another helping relationship. The use of this trust bridge is facilitated if counselees know that their pastor is personally acquainted with the persons or agency to whom they are being referred. The pastor is fortunate if she or he can say, "The therapist I want you to see is a person I know and trust." In any case, the pastor should say, "If you would like, I'll talk with the therapist about your situation so that she [or he] will know something about it before you go." This is a way of smoothing the transition.

Here is how the bridge principle was used in referring an alcoholic to AA. The pastor said, "Mac, if I understand what you're saying, you are beginning to suspect that you have a problem with drinking. I'd like you to chat with a friend of mine who struggled with this problem. He's found an answer that works for him in AA. Let's see if he's free to drink a cup of coffee with us, OK?" At the three-corner coffee klatch that followed, the AA member (who was also in the pastor's church) offered to take Mac to an AA meeting.

In making referrals to therapists and social agencies, it is generally wise to let persons make their own appointment. This keeps the initiative with them and, in addition, allows the relationship with the new helping person to begin on the phone. Talking with a therapist or an intake worker on the phone may help allay a person's anxiety about going for help. If possible, the pastor should check with a therapist or agency before suggesting that referral to make sure that the person referred can be seen and to explain that the person may be calling. It is also wise to ask persons who are referred to phone the referring pastor after making an appointment and after being seen for the first time. If a person does not call, the pastor should phone to see how things went. This procedure expresses continuing concern and allows the pastor to follow through with persons who resist obtaining the specialized help they seem to need.

8. Encourage referred persons to really try a given therapist or agency, even if they are

only mildly willing. A skilled psychotherapist may be able to reduce resistances to help that have not yet yielded to previous efforts. With alcoholics, I first do all I can to reduce their resistance to AA. Next, I urge them to attend an AA group regularly for at least a month, whether or not they particularly like it. In some cases, this exposure allows the warmth and the informal group therapy of AA to make an end run around their defenses. Their resistances gradually dissolve as they experience the satisfaction of sobriety and the warm acceptance of the AA group. If one waits until addicted persons are completely ready for help, they may be in mental hospitals, prisons, or cemeteries first. The same applies to many other problems. Of course, it is not wise to push persons beyond a certain point—the point at which the backlash phenomenon makes them more resistant to help.

9. Let persons know that one's pastoral care and concern will continue after the referral. A unique strength of referral by a pastor is that a pastoral care relationship can and should continue following a referral. This helps lessen the sense of rejection.

In communicating with anyone outside a counseling relationship, including those whom counselors wish to explore or to make a referral, it is both ethically and legally essential that counselees give their permission to counselors. The usual procedure is to ask clients to sign a brief permission to communicate statement such as this:

> I hereby waive my right of confidentiality and give permission for _____ to discuss my
> situation with _____.
> Signature_____ Date_____

Pastoral Care Involvement after Referrals

A "Pastor's Guide to Community Services" makes this wise recommendation:

> After you refer continue to show Christian concern and friendliness. Keep in touch with the agency...so that you can work together effectively to help the client. No community agency can take the place of a pastor or the fellowship of the church. In a healthy, collaborative working relationship, both the agency and the church should feel free to express any question or criticism of the other so that there can be better mutual understanding and appreciation.[12]

In making a referral for psychotherapy, the pastor may need to gradually diminish her or his supportive counseling in order to motivate the person to move into another relationship. A person who is in psychotherapy should not be allowed to defer bonding with the new psychotherapist by continuing to counsel with the pastor. The relationship should be one of pastoral care, not pastoral counseling. Otherwise, the person may attempt to use one parent figure against the other in a self-defeating manner. It is usually appropriate for the pastor to ask occasionally how things are going in therapy. If that relationship is unproductive, another therapist can be recommended.

What to Do When Referrals Fail

Not all referrals are successful. Some people may seem to accept referral to avoid offending the pastor but fail to make an appointment with the person to whom they were referred; others may simply refuse to see anyone other than the pastor; yet others may go for a few sessions and then terminate prematurely. Regarding the first category, the person who says he or she will go but does not, it is helpful to anticipate this reaction by exploring with the person the possibility of not following through and the reason he or she might be tempted to renege while seeking a commitment from her or him to go for at least three sessions. When the three sessions are over, the pastor might ask the person to evaluate how helpful they have been and to share what might be added or omitted in order to make the meetings more helpful. Regarding those who, even after the pastor has done everything recommended above in making the referral, refuse to see anyone except the pastor, it is important to respect their right to refuse the referral. It is also important for the pastor to refuse to counsel with them on an ongoing basis. Instead, she or he might check in with them from time to time to see how they are doing and whether they have had a change of mind. Often, when the pain of a problem outweighs the pain of facing the need for in-depth therapy, suffering people undergo a change of heart. Premature termination may be prevented by the ongoing support of the referring person. If it occurs, the referring pastor is in a position to encourage the person to make at least one more appointment with the therapist in order to terminate formally and to evaluate the experience. In the long run, everyone has the right to refuse a referral, but with that right goes the responsibility of accepting the consequence.

Making Referrals to Pastoral and Secular Psychotherapists

Most clergy in general ministries do not have the time or the necessary training to do longer-term, reconstructive pastoral psychotherapy. This type of healing ministry is primarily the function of those in specialized ministries of counseling and psychotherapy who have academic and clinical education in psychotherapy in addition to their basic seminary education. But for two reasons it is helpful for parish clergy to know something about contemporary psychotherapies and about pastoral psychotherapy in particular. The first reason is that such knowledge can equip them to make informed referrals to both secular and pastoral psychotherapists, knowing when the referral of choice is to one or the other. The second reason is that contemporary psychotherapeutic theories and practice are significant sources of useful concepts and methods that can be adapted to the types of counseling that parish pastors do most often.

The History of Pastoral Psychotherapy

How did pastoral psychotherapy develop as a specialty within the ministry? During the second half of the twentieth century, this new mental health specialty emerged within the ministry as a growing number of clergy chose to have the postseminary academic and clinical training necessary to become pastoral psychotherapists. Soon after the Second World War, the movement that could be called "the pastoral psychology/ pastoral theology revolution" developed in varied forms in North America, Great Britain, and several Western European countries. Over the next five decades this movement was gradually extended to numerous countries in Asia, Africa, Latin America, Australia, New Zealand, and the South Pacific region. This occurred as clergy from those countries received advanced clinical and academic training in Western countries and then returned to their homelands to serve countless burdened human beings. These multicultural pastoral counseling specialists often established both counseling programs and training centers reflecting their indigenous cultures.

As a participant in some of these innovative developments in the pastoral counseling field in the United States and, to a limited degree, in several other countries, I have only gradually realized its significance. It is that the influence of the evolving, growing pastoral counseling movement transcends the much-needed contribution of providing a widening network of theological-based counseling services. The writing, mentoring, and consultations of creative leaders in this movement have produced several significant changes in religious groups and the network of providers of mental health services. These influences have gradually raised the level of seminary and postseminary teaching of the arts of pastoral care and counseling. This continues to raise the levels of counseling competence of countless clergy in general ministries of caregiving. In addition, clergy with graduate education in caregiving skills have brought new needed skills to recipients of mental health services whose problems in living include serious spiritual and ethical issues.

Referring to Pastoral Psychotherapists

For parish-based caregivers and others in generalist ministries, referrals to pastoral psychotherapists should be given high priority. Referral to pastoral therapists is done only if they are considered as competent, caring, and ethical as secular therapists are appropriately expected to be. Because of their training in theological and ethical disciplines and their experience as clergy, such pastoral psychotherapists are particularly equipped to help some burdened people. They include anyone struggling with one or more of the expressions of unhealthy (pathogenic) consciences or personal belief systems.

Pastoral therapists with substantial clinical and academic training usually have much more expertise in helping people with complex spiritual or ethical problems than do most competent secular therapists. To locate such competent pastoral psychotherapists near enough for you to make referrals feasible, contact the AAPC at its website, aapc.org/.

Gaining Insights and Methods from Key Psychotherapies

Ours is a time of amazing fecundity in the fields of innovative health-care treatments and psychotherapies. In the latter field there is a flowering of effective, shorter-term approaches and methodologies. These include cognitive-behavioral, feminist-radical, solution-focused and goal-directed, and narrative therapies. Pastoral counselors, of course, should be critically aware of the implicit theological assumptions in whatever therapies they use.

Although clergy in generalist ministries should not attempt to do long-term psychotherapy, for reasons described earlier, it is to their advantage to learn all they can from different types of psychotherapy. Knowledge of the theory and practice of these psychotherapies can bring illuminating insights about the complex and often baffling dynamics of human thoughts, emotions, beliefs, and behaviors, including religious expressions. In addition, knowledge of certain psychotherapeutic methods may enable generalist clergy to adapt some of the methods to the short-term counseling they do.

In my experience, the many different psychotherapies offer helpful insights and/or useful methods that can be adapted to the generalist settings of ministry. The more pastors understand of these therapies, the more resources they will acquire for their ministry. Fuller exploration of the spiritual and growth resources in these psychotherapies is available elsewhere in my writings.[13]

It is illuminating to keep in mind that critiquing personality and psychotherapeutic theories as well as their implicit underlying assumptions is a responsibility of pastoral caregivers. Christie Neuger points to basic flaws in most personality and psychotherapeutic theories. She urges pastors to remember that the dominant culture of men's experiences has been used to create most theologies, psychologies, theories of personality, and psychotherapeutic schools, and that women's experiences and thinking have been largely ignored whereas men's experiences and thinking have been regarded as normative.[14]

Here is a brief description of various kinds of therapies:

Feminist therapies, along with feminist psychologies, provide invaluable understanding of women's development and life experiences and also provide knowledge of consciousness raising. Both are important resources in caregiving with women.

Cognitive-behavioral therapies highlight the ways in which cognitive concepts, values, and beliefs trigger emotional responses that call for caregiving. Rational-Emotive Therapy also provides methods for helping persons with wholeness-diminishing theological beliefs to change them if they desire to do so.

Narrative therapies highlight the key role of images and stories in influencing wholeness-enhancing or diminishing feelings and behaviors. They also provide methods for enabling people to rewrite and retell their life stories to give them a more constructive and hopeful outcome.

Short-term and solution-focused therapies undergird the approaches to caregiving described for pastors in this volume. They do so by elaborating on the goals and methods of these approaches.

Psychodynamic therapies based on the work of depth psychologists, including Freud and Jung, shed light on the depth, power, and creativity of the unconscious mind. They offer some understanding of otherwise enigmatic thoughts, emotions, beliefs, and behaviors encountered by pastoral caregivers. They illuminate the wholeness-diminishing religious beliefs and practices that are so abundant today. For pastoral psychotherapists, they offer methods of helping people get acquainted with and befriend the "stranger within" who is still powerfully present from their painful past. In spite of their sexist biases they can, if used in an enlightened manner, be helpful with persons whose unhealed childhood wounds are blocking their wholeness.

Jungian therapy offers caregivers numerous resources, including appreciation of the positive, creative energies of the unconscious mind and the collective unconscious, a concept that illuminates our deep human connectedness with the whole web of life—a web that shows the oneness of the human family. The complementarity of opposites and the archetypal images and myths spanning diverse human cultures, and Jung's concepts on spiritualities, are also potentially useful to pastoral caregivers.

Object relations therapies, a creative expression of psychoanalytic thought, offer valuable understanding of the interaction of intrapsychic and interpersonal dynamics in shaping human development and relationships. They also offer methods for bridging inner and relational factors in doing counseling with couples and families as well as individuals.

Psychosynthesis, based on the work of Roberto Assagioli, is a wellspring of valuable concepts and methods. It is both spiritually centered, with the concept of the Higher Self, and growth oriented.

Gestalt therapy offers a variety of insights and methods for enabling healthful changes in nonanalytic, often short-term counseling. These methods include focusing on coming alive in the present moment and looking at the past only when it seems to be preventing people from embracing more wholeness in the here and now.

Transactional analysis offers caregivers who do educative counseling ways of describing and making understandable what is called the Parent, Child, and Adult sides of everyone's personality. Its methods help people move toward more wholeness by learning to keep their rational, reality-coping Adult side in the driver's seat of their personalities so that their playful, creative Child side and the nurturing Parent side can assume their appropriate roles in everyday life.

Alfred Adler's approach to therapy views humans as possessing remarkable positive potentials and the ability to shape their heredity and environments creatively. He offers a positive, growth-oriented understanding of inferiority feelings. He saw that the basic human strivings for worth and power are to compensate for the natural childhood feelings of being weak and powerless, surrounded by powerful adults on whom these people were very dependent. He also saw that all individuals learn a particular lifestyle early in life, a pattern of behaving by which they seek to maintain at least the minimal self-esteem and power that everyone needs to cope with life. He recognized that humans have the capacity for continuing change during the latter years of their lives. Adler worked tirelessly for social justice by changing institutional practices and structures. He focused particularly on children's well-being, creating child guidance clinics and seeking to improve education. In addition, he had keen insights about the role of authoritarian, pathogenic religion in disabling self-esteem.

Otto Rank's approach to therapy made him a pioneer in the growth trends in counseling and health care that eventually resulted in Carl Roger's client-centered therapy and William Glasser's reality therapy, and influenced the wholeness orientation of this book. Like Adler, he focused mainly on the present, and correctly believed that people in general have what he called the "will-to-health" and that even the most dysfunctional persons have a strong, healthy side that can be built on in remedial therapy. He critiqued the ways that various forms of religion are used to escape responsibility. He saw the crucial role of mother-child relationships and of the trauma of birth. His concept of separation anxiety from that experience is illuminating in understanding grief. He emphasized the process of rebirth as dying to the old and being reborn to the new. Rank was far ahead of his time in his understanding of sexism's impact on women as well as the equality and psychological differences between women and men. In an insight close to the view of this book, he declared that real equality is "the equal right of each individual to become and to be himself, which actually means to accept his own difference and have it accepted by others."[15]

Self-other help groups, including 12-step recovery groups, demonstrate the life-changing power of such small groups and show that congregations can learn from, cooperate with, and adapt this group model for use in that setting.

When Referral Resources Are in Short Supply

Lack of essential community referral resources is a common dilemma for pastors, particularly those serving in small-town and rural areas. This problem should do more than frustrate pastors. It should touch our prophetic nerve and motivate us to help create the needed resources. If enough people of goodwill are informed of the unmet needs, and if some individual or group takes the initiative, referral resources can be created. A pastor or dedicated layperson in a helping profession is in a strategic position to spark and lead such a community project.

Pastors in rural and small, remote communities often find that making referrals and creating new resources is difficult, if not impossible. Having knowledge of the closest helping facility or professional is crucial in such situations. Correspondence with state mental health departments or with the national voluntary organization focusing on a particular problem usually brings reliable information concerning the most accessible help. A pastor working collaboratively with other pastors and community leaders may help a state health agency recognize the need for a mobile clinic or therapeutic service in their area on a regular basis.

The lack of mental health referral resources on an ability-to-pay basis constitutes an acute need in many communities for middle- and lower-income groups. A study of five socioeconomic classes in New Haven revealed that the bottom group, the most disadvantaged group, the poor, had a rate of psychiatric illness almost three times that of any other class.[16] Poor people are more likely to be diagnosed psychotic and sent to mental hospitals than are middle-class people with similar symptoms. The latter are given less stigmatized diagnoses and offered private psychotherapy more often. But the high cost of private therapy makes it unavailable, on any extended basis, to many middle-income people. A needed expression of pastoral care through prophetic ministry is challenging and working to change the medical and mental health delivery system so that all persons will have the preventive and therapeutic help they need. Establishing a church-related counseling service where skilled pastoral counseling and therapy are available on an ability-to-pay basis is one way of helping meet this need.

Reality Practice Skill Development Session

Parishioner's role: (Two persons volunteer to role-play counselees in a pastoral setting.) You are Ed and Sally Wright, the parents of seventeen-year-old Jim, who has taken money from the cash register at the store where he worked after school. You have two teenage daughters younger than Jim. You are deeply disturbed by what appears to be Jim's "delinquency" and are willing to do whatever is necessary to obtain help for him.

Pastor's role: Sally and Ed come to your office and tell you of Jim's problem. You sense that Jim's behavior may be a symptom of hidden pain in the family and that the parents (and perhaps the whole family) should be referred with Jim to the local pastoral counseling center of a family service agency. Attempt to make this referral after inviting Jim and his parents in for a talk, following the guidelines in this chapter.

Observer-coach's role: Help the pastor be more effective in enabling the couple to clarify their feelings and to understand their need for specialized help from a particular counseling agency.

In another session, practice referring an alcoholic to AA and the spouse of an alcoholic to Al-Anon.

Recommended Reading

Charry, Dana. *Mental Health Skills for Clergy: Evaluation, Intervention, Referral.* Valley Forge, Pa: Judson Press, 1981.

Jacobson-Wolf, Joan E. *When to Counsel, When to Refer: A Diagnostic Manual for Clergy on Mental Health Referral.* Lima, Ohio: CSS Publishing, 1989.

Oglesby, William B., and Dana Charry. *Referral in Pastoral Counseling.* Nashville: Abingdon Press, 1978.

Switzer, David K. *Pastoral Care Emergencies.* Minneapolis: Augsburg Fortress, 2000.

INCLUSIVE CAREGIVING: BRIDGING CULTURAL, RACIAL, ETHNIC, CLASS, AND GENDER DIVERSITY

God who made the world and everything in it. . . . From one ancestor he made all nations to inhabit the whole earth.
—Paul speaking in Athens (Acts 17:24, 26)

God has a dream—a dream that we will realize that we are members of one family. That's the one lesson God is hoping we will learn.
—Archbishop Desmond Tutu[1]

All humans see and understand their world through an invisible screen of cultural conditioning—a veil filled with assumptions, beliefs, and values that operate mainly outside conscious awareness. People's perceptions are shaped by a variety of cultures in which they are embedded. Western caregivers and care receivers see their world through a number of cultural lenses. These may include Western philosophies, religions, values, and worldviews as well as the cultures of their age group, vocation, and social class. Cultural assumptions become problematic when there is a sharp disparity between caregivers' cultural conditioning and that of clients, and caregivers are not aware of the disparity.

Caregivers Build Bridges over Cultural Chasms

In these times of increasing global Internet communication, jet travel, and multinational immigration, clergy often are confronted by people from other than their own cultures who need pastoral care. Caregiving issues stemming from the conflicts, tensions, and mutual misunderstandings abound among persons of diverse backgrounds. In the United States, clergy probably give care to more people from other cultures and religions than anywhere else on the planet. In some communities, pastoral care is needed by various people who celebrate Christmas, Hanukkah, Ramadan, Kwanzaa, or Winter Solstice. Caregivers using any monocultural approach cannot respond effectively to the needs of an increasingly multicultural society and world.

Pastoral care and counseling in today's increasingly pluralistic church and society involve multicultural, gender, and social-class issues much more frequently than in the early decades of the modern pastoral counseling movement. Depending on the demographic makeup of a congregation and its community, such issues are encountered in some, if not many, caregiving situations. In addition to care receivers, a fortunate fact is that an increasing number of women and ethnically diverse persons are entering Christian ministry today. This means that pastoral caregivers bring a wider variety of cultural, gender, and social-class attitudes and gifts to the caregiving dimension of ministry than in the past. All this makes awareness of diverse caregiving patterns and expectations in major ethnic, gender, and social-class groups increasingly important for effectiveness in this ministry.

Christie Neuger states a crucial challenge to caregivers in our society:

> It is the responsibility of counselors to have a complex enough understanding of the cultural dynamics around sexism, racism, classism, and heterosexism that they can place the particular stories of counselees in the context of those dynamics. In doing pastoral counseling, the pastoral counselor must know enough about the cultural realities for women and men, of all races and classes, that, if unknown, distort the counselees' stories in harmful ways.[2]

Inclusive caregiving has major implications and applications for those who give care and for those who receive it from them. Holistic caregivers must learn to reach out to lower the innumerable barriers and bridge the many canyons that divide the human family, and become increasingly multicultural in their understanding and practice with people from a variety of backgrounds and cultures. They must become citizens of the divided, often violent planet. In addition, holistic caregivers must seek to enable care receivers to enlarge their horizons of caring as far as possible beyond their comfortable clan and culture.

Based on in-depth research in a wide variety of cultures, pastoral counseling teacher David W. Augsburger puts forcefully the challenge that caregivers faced in the twentieth century. The challenge is equally relevant in the twenty-first.

> The time has come for the pastoral counseling movement to function from an expanded, intercultural perspective. The counseling theories and therapies that have emerged as modes of healing and grown in each culture, useful and effective as they are in their respective locales, are too limited, too partial to serve human needs in a world community where people of many cultures meet, compete, and relate.[3]

Understanding the dynamic impact of cultures on all human problems is increasingly crucial today. As Archie Smith Jr. observes,

> Those of us who have been trained to think primarily in terms of the individual and of the impor-
> tance of subjective experience often find ourselves in circumstances in which the interconnected-
> ness of the self and the social order must of necessity be largely invisible to us. The critical point
> is to recognize how personal life and social structure intersect in society and to heighten awareness
> of the role the individual can play as a passive subject or an active agent in social transformation
> and change.[4]

From any enlightened perspective, it is essential for human well-being and even survival that we transform our destructive responses to cultural and religious differences.
We must do this by learning to live in community with diverse people and cultures and
also with the interdependent network of all living things on the earth. As emphasized
earlier, all the profound differences that are now sources of tragic conflict and killing
must be transcended to make possible the survival of healthful social and natural environments that will enable future generations of our species and all species to live healthy
lives together. Because so much of the tragic violence around the planet has major religious dynamics, it is essential for clergy and other religious leaders to take responsibility
for discovering ways to resolve these conflicts nonviolently. Remember the words of
Jesus spoken in his sermon on the mountainside: "Blessed are the peacemakers, for they
will be called children of God" (Matt. 5:9). The fact that the other major faith traditions
in the world also honor peacemaking in their belief systems provides a theological foundation for religious people and their leaders to practice what they preach for spiritual
reasons. There is no doubt that this ministry is crucially and urgently needed today.

Pastoral caregivers must have key roles in responding as peacemakers to this challenge. Their dual training in the continuing revelations of the human sciences and the
riches of many spiritual traditions, together with their ability to integrate these streams
of insight in caregiving ministries, gives them resources for helping to heal the conflict-
causing distortions of religions. But to use their resources well in peacemaking, they must
be open and growing in their inclusive attitudes toward persons in widely diverse religious and cultural contexts.

Empowering Holistic Caregiving by a Whole, Inclusive Theology

Through the centuries, the Bible, traditional theology, ethical systems, and creedal
formulations have been derived mainly from the thought and experiences of middle-
class male church leaders. The power holders in our Judeo-Christian heritage have
largely ignored as unimportant the rich contributions of women, the poor, and the powerless. The insights and ways of understanding as well as facilitating Spirit-centered
wholeness, derived from the oppression of these ignored voices, can complement and
enrich theologically rooted caregiving.

Speaking personally, I often have difficulty hearing with understanding what spiritual thinkers in one-down groups, including feminists, are saying. But to the degree that I can "get" their messages, my spirituality is enriched. I receive gifts of insights and images that complement and correct the spiritual heritage shaped mainly by male spiritual searchers. Continuing the recovery of the spiritual and theological riches of these ignored and silenced voices is essential if churches are to become more spiritual places of healing and wholeness in this new century. Pastoral caregiving cannot realize its full potentiality for healing, liberation, and growth if its theological-biblical foundations are half-foundations built mainly by middle-class, male, Caucasian, Western theological thinkers. The foundation must be extended and strengthened by integrating the theological experiences and wisdom of poor, oppressed, and socially rejected persons of both genders from many cultures and religious traditions.

Theologian Rosemary R. Ruether declares, "Traditional theological images of God as Father have been the sanctification of sexism and hierarchicalism...allowing ruling class males to identify themselves with this divine fatherhood in such a way as to establish themselves in the same kind of hierarchical relationship to women and lower classes."[5] As we saw earlier, there are many examples of the ways theological system builders, including pastoral theologians, have misused biblical images in ways that justify oppression and spawn brokenness not only in women but also in marginalized men.

What are the theological and biblical bases for multicultural, inclusive caregiving? Strong inclusivistic religious and ethical motifs are present in both biblical testaments, as evident in the theme that all humans are part of one human family with one divine Creator. These motifs provide sturdy theological foundations for holistic pastoral caregiving. Although these perspectives are in tension with exclusivistic religious and ethical perspectives, Jesus' mind and message clearly reflect the inclusive tradition. Evidence is his dramatic story of the great feast to which social rejects—people who were poor, disabled, or blind—were invited (Matt. 22:1-14; Luke 14:16-24). His countercultural rejection of religious exclusivism is also implicit in his choosing a Samaritan, a member of a group despised by his people, as the hero of his story, answering the query, "Who is my neighbor?" Jesus' behavior was often strikingly inclusive; for example, eating with despised tax collectors and persons regarded as "sinners" by religious leaders, and also talking about serious issues and asking for a drink of water from the Samaritan woman by Jacob's well.

In the third chapter of Galatians, an illustration of how biblical resources can be used by pastoral caregivers in inclusiveness-generating ways is the ringing affirmation of human equality and oneness as children of God. Here Paul declares that in the Christian perspective, all persons are precious children of God through faith. There is "no longer male and female" (v. 28) or any other one-up/one-down grouping. Our humanity, not our gender, class, language, or cultural or ethnic background, really matters before God.

To be more wholeness nurturing, pastoral theology for caregiving must become increasingly whole in terms of gender, race, class, culture, ethnicity, sexual orientation, and limitations of psychological or physical abilities. Toward this objective, the caregiving model and methods in these pages emphasize cultivating healing and wholeness by enabling persons to develop their unique resources, and also those of their social, cultural, racial, ethnic, and religious roots, while also being willing to appreciate and learn from persons in other cultures. Issues such as gender, race, religious background, sexual orientation, ethnicity, and cultural traditions are all potential grist for the mill of healing and wholeness.

In this spirit, it is important to see that the new world opens doors to far more than new problems. It also creates challenging and often exciting new possibilities for enhancing wholeness by inclusive caregiving. One possibility meriting high priority is for caregivers to discover how to learn from care receivers and other caregivers who are "very different" from them. Every culture has unique ways of understanding and seeking to help troubled people. Learning from people in diverse cultural traditions can broaden and strengthen caregivers' multicultural insights and skills. Another crucial possibility for caregivers is to discover how best to use these enhanced caregiving resources to help transform age-old intercultural barriers into sturdy relationship bridges.

By so doing, pastoral caregivers can help realize the passionate hope expressed in this contemporary extension of Martin Luther King Jr.'s powerful "I have a dream" speech: we will speed up the day when all of God's children—of both genders and all races, religions, nations, ethnic groups, languages, cultures, lifestyles, and sexual orientations—will be able to join hands and sing in the words of the old Negro spiritual, "Free at last! Free at last! Thank God Almighty, we are free at last!" This chapter explores ways to participate in this sorely needed bridge-building and thus enable some members of the human family to discover and affirm our profound but often denied human oneness.[6]

Dr. Joseph C. Hough Jr., a former president of Union Theological Seminary in New York, called for Christians to adopt a new theological approach to other faiths, one that goes considerably beyond simple tolerance, as a response to Americans' growing awareness of religious diversity in the United States and the world. Certainly tolerance was important in a time when the justification of terrorism was based on the perpetrators' own twisted religious fundamentalism. Yet many Christians seem unaware that toleration, while desirable, is not sufficient in a world of religious pluralism. The fear that openness to other religious traditions will destabilize our Christian faith has led many to resist full recognition of the adequacy of other religions to transform human beings with hope and promise. What is essential for Christian faith is that we know we have seen the face of God in the face of Jesus Christ. It is not essential to believe that no one else has seen God and experienced redemption in another place or time.

> I am a Christian who strongly believes that God has always been and now is working everywhere in every human culture to redeem the world. I believe that there is ample evidence in the best of the world's religions, including our own, that God's work is effective. Muslims, Jews, Hindus, Buddhists, and others have been and are being transformed by a powerful vision of God that redeems them with hope and infuses their religious practice with compassion, justice, and peace. Wherever there are peace and movement toward peace, where there are justice and movement toward justice, God is present and working.[7]

The bridge-building spirit that enables caregivers to be effective when they reach out to persons in other cultures, races, genders, religious, and ethnic groups is highlighted in the following quotation: "Our task in approaching another people, another culture, another religion, is to take off our shoes, for the place we are approaching is holy, else we find ourselves treading on another's dream. More serious still, we may forget that God was present before our arrival."[8]

Challenges of Becoming a Multicultural Caregiver

A wise Southeast Asian axiom declares, "Persons who understand only their own culture are like frogs under coconut shells."[9] In our global village of economic and communication interdependence, on a speedily shrinking planet, we somehow must enlarge our circles of consciousness, conscience, and caring. How can we pastoral caregivers liberate ourselves to wider perspectives and become more inclusive and multicultural in our working attitudes, assumptions, theories, and practical methods? To do so is difficult because in profound but often recognized ways, we all are comfortable captives of our cultures to some degree. Lifting our cultural coconut shells is threatening because it threatens the feelings of comfort and security within them. Unfortunately the view inside anyone's shell is far too constricted to allow caregiving in healing ways to persons in other and often radically different cultural shells. African Americans, Asian Americans, Latinos, Native Americans, Womanist theology, and pastoral care understandings—each emerging from its own cultural context—have enriched the overall field of pastoral caregiving immensely in recent years.

In *Cultural Psychotherapy: Working with Culture in the Clinical Encounter*, Karen Seeley reminds psychotherapists and counselors of the widespread tendency to universalize Western understandings of human development and the psyche when dealing with ethnic and foreign clients and to dismiss their culturally shaped perceptions of their problems and their solutions.[10]

What occurs when pastoral caregivers are blind to the culturally specific meanings and cosmologies of troubled persons from other cultures? The caregivers assume that their own meanings and cosmologies are normative and therefore project these onto careseekers, making the latter experience rejection and shame rather than accepting empathy. Persons in so-called minority groups assume every day that they must conform to the dominant culture's language and norms and denigrate their own indigenous perceptions if they are to survive and prosper in it. All this damages their self-esteem with shame about who they are. To counteract this tendency, culturally competent pastoral caregivers must develop methods aimed at drawing out and learning from careseekers' culturally specific life experiences. For example, ask foreign and ethnic clients to describe stories about everyday relationships and crisis experiences they had in their families of origin and their current family constellations. This encourages them to lift up the assumptions, expectations, relationship patterns, and self-understandings that shaped their identities. Caregivers cannot assume that they understand the dynamics that produced their crises. Rather, the culturally specific dynamics must be discovered as something new and unique in each care recipient. To admit to oneself that one does not understand another's inner world is to make oneself vulnerable. But it is also to embark on a voyage of discovery in a strange sea. Don't interpret the spiritual experiences and religious beliefs of such clients in terms of your own theology.

Guidelines for Becoming More Inclusive, Bridge-building Caregivers

American church historian Martin Marty points out that all individuals have their own "horizons" born out of the particular backgrounds of their family, culture, ethnic group, worldview, religious practices, ethnic rules, burdens, hopes, experiences, language, and geographic, economic, and political (and, I would add, natural) environments. When two people interact, they struggle to develop some fusion of their horizons.[11] This occurs in new marriages. In a highly pluralistic society like the United States[12] where people hold to dozens of religions, belief systems, and practices, conflicts among horizons are pervasive. In relatively homogeneous societies the majority group seeks to maintain its power position by silencing minority voices or excluding those who are "other," meaning anyone who is different, strange, or alien.[13]

A highly pluralistic society like the United States struggles to develop what Marty calls "civil pluralism." This means getting along in nonviolent, legal, ethical, and just ways. For this to happen, ways must be found for clashing cultures to cope constructively with the fact that differentness threatens the sense of security found in believing that one's own way is the right, enlightened, and ethically superior way. The goal is to enable pluralism to enrich the society by letting people form multiple "webs of affiliation" in which they can meet the "others" in some depth. This lets people question their own horizons as they broaden them. Civic pluralism moves far beyond merely tolerating the others with the attitude expressed in the statement, "You do your thing your way and I'll do things God's way!" Marty observed that the leaders who helped bridge communities in the last century—people like Gandhi, Dorothy Day, Desmond Tutu, and Martin Luther King Jr.—were people who held to their own horizons but were open to learn from other horizons. He went on to point out that studying the Bible and the Koran side by side can awaken new insights in people in both religions.

An essential step in broadening our perspectives is becoming aware of our coconut shells and then taking action intentionally to raise them enough to see far beyond them. Challenging the in-group, collective narcissism and defensive grandiosities that exist to some degree in all cultures is also necessary. Letting go of any such dysfunctional parochialism involves a difficult surrender of feelings that one's culture is superior to and normative for other cultures. The liberation process is facilitated by being actively receptive to learning from both colleagues and care receivers whose gender, class, educational, linguistic, religious, and ethnic backgrounds are radically different from one's own. Those of us in socially dominant groups have special problems in lifting our shells. It behooves us to learn from women, from the poor and powerless, from ethnic minorities, and from those of non-Western cultures and other faith traditions around us. This involves increasing our respect for persons who have been one-down and largely voiceless in the first six decades of modern pastoral care's formative development.[14]

In an increasingly diverse world, caregivers must bring their methods into continuing dialogue with the uniqueness of care receivers' ethnic backgrounds, cultural heritages, spiritual traditions, and, very important, their power position in their society. Caregivers must see people and their experiences as deeply embedded in family and interacting social systems that provide keys to understanding their problems, healing issues and resources, and growth needs. Avoiding the cul-de-sac of making normative any one type of experience is enabled by seeing each person's experiences, problems, and resources as unique. Certainly a more inclusive view of empathy is needed: seeing it as an effort to understand the worldview and frame of reference of each unique person who is by definition different from the caregiver.

It is tempting to think of people's problems as idiosyncratic, internal, and individual and to forget that everyone's life is affected by the weaknesses and pathologies as well as the strengths and resources available in their social context. For many people in oppressed groups, including women and African Americans, personal problems are rooted in social problems and the inequalities in the distribution of power among different groups. To treat their problems exclusively or even primarily as intrapsychic difficulties harms them with a superficial diagnosis leading to misdirected therapies. The severity of their problems is increased in the futile efforts to help them cope. If they accept this shallow understanding, they deprive themselves of a key resource they need—solidarity with others who are resisting cultural oppressions, and a group in which identity-strengthening counterstories for motivating resistance and transformation are generated mutually.

With people who seek help, a caregiver must be able to shift gears by using methods appropriate to their unique problems and resources, limitations and strengths. Applying this principle to cross-cultural caregiving involves learning to use the culturally appropriate approaches required to nurture wholeness, taking into account the attitudes, beliefs, and resources of particular cultural contexts.

Guidelines for Making Caregiving More Inclusive and Multicultural

Here are some guidelines for being more inclusive and multicultural in pastoral caregiving. Implicit in them are the characteristics of caregivers who are inclusive and multicultural in their attitude and skills:

1. *Awareness of the influence of the cultural orientation of one's background and its subtle influences on one's approach to caregiving* is important when caregiving with persons within that culture and with persons from other cultures.

In ministering with persons from different ethnic, cultural, or religious backgrounds, it is important to be aware of the universal tendency to feel, often with little or no awareness, that one's background and culture are normative for all human beings. Depending on the degree to which this tendency operates in us, we will judge the differences of those in other groups as inferior, if not in error. To the degree that we are unliberated from cultural narcissism and myopia, we will not be able to see the many subtle but significant differences in the ways care receivers from other backgrounds perceive, conceptualize, feel, solve problems, and create their own worldview.

2. *To be relevant to persons whose identity has been shaped by different gender, ethnic, and cultural backgrounds, pastoral caregiving must be holistic in its awarenesses and responses.* Mainstream, middle-class, dualistic European American pastoral care has tended to focus primarily on only three of the seven dimensions of life—mind, spirit, and relationships. These remain important when working with persons from other cultural, racial, and social-class backgrounds, which tend to be more holistic in their orientation. But being holistic in caregiving, healing, and wholeness, though increasingly important in all cultures, is especially so in these contexts. For example, among individuals and families in the "culture of poverty," the pressures of concern for physical necessities and

social justice are immediate and pressing. Moreover, non-Western cultures, which often are less urban and industrialized, have unique strengths and resources that can be mobilized in caregiving.

3. *Multicultural pastoral caregiving must be more aware of power and cultural control issues when working with people in one-down cultures.* Doing whatever one can to lessen the massive wellness-damaging injustices that result from cultural power inequalities is increasingly important for holistic pastoral caregiving with middle-class persons and those in the "culture of poverty." Pastoral theology teacher James Poling reflects on the deleterious impact on the counselors in dominant cultural groups: "Cultural dominance is dangerous because it make the full identity and needs of careseeking persons invisible to pastoral counselors."[15] He goes on to say that they must abandon the assumption that the dominant theories and methods of modern pastoral counseling, rooted in the dominant middle-class, Caucasian, male culture, are necessarily valid and normative for caregiving with one-down persons. We must remember that the voices of those in underside cultural groups in Western society—for example, women, ethnic minorities, immigrants, and poor, disabled, or non-English-speaking persons—too often have been silenced by the dominant culture and therefore unheard. Unless we learn to hear these voices, our caregiving with persons on the other side of culture chasms will be irrelevant at best and damaging at worst.

We who are in the dominant culture and benefit from it must struggle to become more aware of how the wholeness of individuals and families in nondominant cultures has been diminished by dominant cultures. We must resist tenaciously the temptation to seek to fit everyone into the procrustean bed of our cultural counseling norms. And most difficult of all, we must develop enough humility to recognize that we can understand only in partial ways the countless attitudes, images, rituals, behaviors, spiritual beliefs, and ethical practices in the dominated cultures around us. Because they have learned to survive in one-down power positions, we whose professional training and identity are rooted in the dominant culture probably understand considerably less about them than they understand about us.

4. *Awareness of the influences on caregiving of the dominant subculture or the subcultures of one's congregation if it is multicultural.*

5. *With impoverished people and those from ethnic minorities, short-term, solution-based counseling often is most effective.* It encourages clients to focus mainly on solvable problems in the present and move intentionally into a better future by coping with these more creatively, dealing with the past only if it haunts and limits constructive change. This approach concentrates on helping people find what is most effective to do to make their lifestyles more constructive, without ignoring their feelings if these are blocking

their healing and growth. It also is hope oriented, seeking to awaken reality-based hope by seeing people's promising strengths and possibilities and enabling them to discover what they can do to make their own hopes turn into reality.

6. *In caregiving with many persons of ethnic minorities who tend to honor biblical images and narratives,* it is important to use biblical images in the process because these are familiar and loved images in their lives.

7. *Applying the EISPUA model in caregiving* with persons from cultures that view clergy as strong, good-father or good-mother authority figures requires cross-cultural adaptations. In particular, they probably will expect more A (advice-giving), S (supportive), and E (evaluative) responses than is true of most middle-class care receivers. Numerous I (interpretive) and even U (understanding) responses probably will seem frustratingly irrelevant to their pressing need to get practical help quickly for urgent problems. Without abandoning the foundational responsive listening methods (see chapter 4), effective caregivers should meet care receivers halfway in such situations. Give them whatever A, S, and E responses that seem potentially useful in their unique healing journey.

For more information regarding cultures represented by groups within the United States, see titles in the "Recommended Reading" section at the end of this chapter. However, regardless of how much general information a pastoral caregiver may acquire from reading, remember that each member of a racial or ethnic group represents that culture in a unique way. She or he is best equipped to recount the experience of belonging to a minority culture. Pastors have an advantage in doing pastoral cross-cultural caregiving because they are in a position to know persons of different cultures within their church. Personal knowledge may prevent them from applying generic cultural characteristics stereotypically to individuals.

Bridging Economic and Social Chasms between the Poor and the Rich

The need for pastoral caregivers to become more inclusive in their understanding often is as close as their doorstep, even though the need may stretch to the far reaches of the global community. The far and the near merge whenever care receivers from different cultures immigrate to one's hometown. To be effective, caregivers must find ways to bridge the yawning chasms—economic, social, cultural, religious, educational, and class—between affluent people who have the power in both rich and poor countries, and impoverished, oppressed people concentrated in poor countries but also present in more affluent ones.

Robert D. Kaplan uses a striking image in a confronting analysis of worldwide chasms that deeply fragment the human family:

> Think of a stretch limo in the potholed streets of New York City, where homeless beggars live. Inside the limo are the air-conditioned post-industrial regions of North America, Europe, the emerging Pacific Rim, and a few other isolated places.... Outside is the rest of mankind, going in a completely different direction.[16]

The middle-class counseling concerns that usually are central for those inside the stretch limo are remote, even alien, issues for the vast majority of people struggling to survive. Poor people consider many of the healing and wholeness benefits sought by middle-class care receivers to be irrelevant luxuries in light of their survival needs.

This holistic model gives attention to counseling with persons in minority ethnic groups and the social "ecosystem of the poor."[17] These persons often do not respond to counseling approaches designed to fit the lifestyles, values, and assumptions of people of middle-class, Caucasian, European backgrounds. To have empathy with them, caregivers must take into account the interdependence of all aspects of their lives. These include the strong impact of their extended family, community, congregation, and culture, and their often polluted natural environments, as well as the racism, classism, and antipoverty prejudices that infect the dominant society. It is crucial to address these wider systemic issues whenever they are relevant to resolving clients' pressing problems in living and also to draw on the unique caring and healing resources in their cultures.

Addressing pastoral counseling specialists, pastoral counselor and social worker Richard W. Voss illuminates counseling with poor persons:

> Therapists are inextricably a part of the value system of the larger society, and inadvertently conduct "business as usual" with patients, who in turn become more isolated and alienated. Usual therapeutic rules reenact and reinforce the socially sanctioned values of competitiveness, individualism, and dominance in the therapeutic relationship.... To be true to the reality of the patient's human situation, the therapist's intervention will go against the grain of the dominant methods of psychotherapeutic treatment.

Voss goes on to share from his experiences "in the trenches" that middle-class therapists feel shame when working with impoverished, powerless, dependent clients. The shame is derived from the insensitivity of society, whose values reject these clients, and from counselors' awareness of their own dependence and powerlessness, as well as from having internalized the dominant culture's values. He concludes,

> Effective psychotherapy with the poor requires the therapist accept his or her own existential pain, powerlessness, and shame, and enter into a mutually vulnerable relationship with the patient. When the "doctor-patient" of the therapist is in touch with the "patient-doctor" of the patient, the therapist and patient are engaged in a mutually transforming human encounter.[18]

It is clear that pastoral counselors, to be effective with poor persons who are not esteemed or empowered in our culture, must become aware of our own cultural boxes and become vulnerable enough to learn from the impoverished and socially rejected. For Christians who seek to follow the example of Jesus, his accepting attitudes toward the poor and socially rejected in his society should provide guideposts.

Pastors who serve inner-city or blue-collar congregations soon discover that the goals and the methods of pastoral counseling, as traditionally conceived, are relatively ineffective with many persons from nonmiddle-class backgrounds. Goals borrowed from insight psychotherapy—growth through resolving inner conflicts—are alien to the world of many of these persons. The same is true of the usual psychotherapeutic model—a series of formal, scheduled, one-to-one interviews where persons are expected to talk at deeper and deeper levels about their feelings. A perceptive student of this problem observes that many poor persons do not express themselves well. They do not see how just talking can resolve their problems. For them, their concerns are immediate, concrete, and pressing. They need to see fast, even if limited, improvement. Introspective methods of counseling seem like a waste of time to many persons whose culture, unlike the middle-class ethos, does not condition them to look within to find help. This is particularly true if they feel overwhelmed by practical problems. When such persons are seen by pastors who have not transcended their middle-class backgrounds, they often do not return after the first session. It is tempting to believe that such persons are unmotivated. Actually most are powerfully motivated to seek help. They leave counseling because the kind of help they want and probably need first is utterly different from the counselor's. Disadvantaged persons, as well as those from authority-centered ethnic and cultural groups, tend to expect that help will include advice-giving and will be focused on solving, alleviating, or helping them bear their practical problems. Therefore, effective approaches with nonmiddle-class people, and those from authority-centered ethnic and cultural groups, focus on the concrete crisis they face. Often the primary goal is to help them discover practical ways of resolving their economic, employment, relationship, and health crises. Improvements need not be dramatic or total, but they need to occur fairly soon in the helping process.

Nonmiddle-class people tend to view clergy primarily as religious authority figures. To start with this perception and use it constructively, pastoral caregivers often need to take the initiative in giving them useful information (for example, where to find a job or medical care), suggestions concerning constructive steps to take, and practical support. The willingness to use the pastoral authority one has—the authority of one's social role, pastoral identity, and competence—in growth-enabling rather than authoritarian, growth-stifling ways is important in all pastoral counseling. It is essential in working with persons from authority-centered backgrounds. Unconstructive uses of authority involve manipulating counselees by coercive advice or taking action and making decisions for them that they could do for themselves with the counselor's guidance and support. The growthful use of the counselor's authority aims at gradually diminishing the dependence of persons on this authority. It seeks to help counselees mobilize their own power by the exercise of their latent coping capacities. This will enable them to handle their problems more constructively, improve their life situation, and do whatever possible to overcome the economic discrimination where their problems often originate.

Because coming to an office for "counseling" is foreign to the lifestyle of many non-middle-class persons, much of the helping must be done in informal settings without the formal label of counseling. A study of mental health treatment approaches for low-income groups revealed that

> therapists who play a pastoral type of role are most successful. Those who will leave their offices and relate to their patients informally in their place of work, in the family setting, in informal street visits, etc., soon become trusted members of the patients' community. The poor person welcomes direct intervention during his time of crisis.[19]

This study found that informal group counseling was effective with blue-collar workers. Group members, drawn from similar ethnic and language backgrounds, visit and help one another between sessions. Persons who have recovered from problems such as delinquency or drug addiction make excellent role models and group leaders. (The similarity of this approach to AA is striking.) Of special relevance to pastoral counseling is the study's finding that "the psychological difficulties of many low-income patients diminish as they become involved in some meaningful commitment, whether it be religious activity, a hobby, a labor union, or participation in a block committee."[20] It is obvious that pastoral counseling is of the greatest help to the poor when it is most *pastoral* in its methods. The vast majority of caregiving opportunities with disadvantaged people occur during crisis situations. Charles Kemp's *Pastoral Care of the Poor* is a valuable resource for those who minister to nonmiddle-class persons.[21]

If prophetic pastoral caregiving is to reach out effectively beyond the affluent middle class to poor people in both rich and poor nations, it must face the global need for economic justice. Of the world's 6 billion people, 1.3 billion live on less than one dollar a day. An additional 3 billion live on less than two dollars a day. As the Archbishop of Canterbury said in a lecture at Al-Azhar University, Cairo, "The human misery reflected in those figures alone testifies to the 'absolute poverty' in which 2/3 of our world is sunk. This is a moral and an economic problem and it must be in the forefront of our [religious] agenda."[22]

Caregiving with Women and Men to Bridge Gender Differences

Radical changes in gender identity have a significant impact and represent a huge social transformation because they involve the ways 51 percent of the world's population (women) relate to the other 49 percent (men). Gender biases are so pervasive and dominant in our culture that they shape each of us in damaging, wholeness-diminishing ways. But although change is much too slow,[23] unprecedented improvements in the self-esteem and empowerment of countless women are occurring, enabling millions of women to use more of their God-given gifts. These changes also have produced radical changes in female-male relationships and necessitate profound changes for many men in the ways they understand genuine male strength and how to relate to women as equals. Men often resist making changes until they discover that letting go of "macho" male stereotypes releases them to become more whole persons. Gender issues will continue to affect many, if not most, of the relationship problems that bring troubled couples to counseling.

Holistic caregivers, both male and female, must practice their art in nonsexist, gender-liberating ways. This requires rejecting any gender-role stereotypes that limit the healing and growth potentials of care receivers of either gender. This must have high priority for all caregivers. Only then will they be equipped to enable care receivers to grow in their own unique directions unfettered by constricting gender-role stereotypes of what it is to be a "healthy" or "strong" woman or man. Only such liberated caregivers can be effective in nurturing new, more empowered identities in both women and men.

Understanding brokenness, healing, and wholeness in the context of gender influences is an essential perspective for working in liberating ways with both sexes. In what often is identified as a Jungian understanding of the bisexual nature of the human psyche, wholeness comes by balancing the development of the receptive, nurturing, vulnerable, feelingful, intuitive human capacities (often called, in error, the "feminine" capacities), on the one side, with their lineal-thinking, rational, assertive, leadership capacities (often erroneously called the "masculine" capacities), on the other. Unfortunately, traditional cultural pressures push many girls and women to overdevelop the so-called feminine side and underdevelop the so-called masculine side, whereas many males do the opposite. Caregivers increase their ability to cultivate wholeness when they recognize that these clusters of capacities are available and valuable in men and women, and their balanced development is the path to fuller, healthier humanity for both sexes.

There are significant cross-cultural dynamics in counseling of women by male pastors, and vice versa. The fact that the majority of pastors are men and the majority of persons they counsel are women poses serious problems. A study by Inge K. Broverman and others reveals that many counselors and therapists (both male and female) function with unconscious sex-role stereotypes that constrict their effectiveness, as growth enablers, with women clients.[24] It is imperative that all counselors understand their own sexism and the oppressive impact of our society's sexism on problems of women and men.

Male ministers need to recognize that there are inherent limitations to their ability to be facilitators of psychological and spiritual growth in counseling with women. Many women counselees, having been socially programmed to be dependent on males, form strong dependency ties with them and try to please them. Unless this pattern is challenged by the male counselor, it will work against the woman's developing her full strengths and pursuing her autonomous spiritual search. A male counselor cannot give her the special help she may find in relating to a liberated woman pastoral counselor, who knows a woman's experience from the inside.

In her book *Counseling for Liberation*, Charlotte Holt Clinebell (who changed her name to Charlotte Ellen in 1978) gives this description of the characteristics of a liberated and liberating counselor:

> Such a counselor:
> 1. values being female equally with being male. A woman counselee cannot learn to value herself from a counselor who devalues women.
> 2. believes in complete equality between women and men at all levels and in all areas of public and private life, on the job, and at home.
> 3. is aware of the fact that deeply imbedded cultural stereotypes are likely to have their influence on him or her at an unconscious level, even though intellectually he or she rejects such stereotypes.
> 4. is non-defensive, unpretentious, and nonjudgmental.
> 5. holds the basic philosophy that it is his or her job to help the client find out who she or he is and wants to be. This may mean raising the issue of other choices and options for persons who are not raising that issue for themselves.
> 6. is constantly aware of his or her limitations in working with persons of the other sex.
> 7. is in the process of becoming (and encouraging counselee and client to become) a more fully androgynous person.[25]

Until our society is fully liberated from sexism, women counselors will have special advantages in facilitating the liberation and growth of women, just as men counselors have advantages in the liberation and growth of men. The same principle applies in counseling with persons from different racial and ethnic backgrounds.

Those of us who do counseling from a one-up position of greater power in a culture, as white males do, have a special problem in this regard. It is probably impossible for those in a one-down position to fully trust those in a one-up power position or to experience their fullest possible liberation and empowerment in a counseling relationship with them. To meet the need for growth enablers for women and ethnic minorities, many more persons from those groups must be trained as pastoral counselors.

Issues of Gender and Sexual Orientation in Pastoral Counseling

We live in a world in which gender is a central organizing category, which carries with it a set of rules, structures through which those rules are enforced, and consequences for following the rules and/or breaking them. In our culture, a powerful narrative strand suggests that certain people are more valuable than others. Gender is one such strand.

In pastoral care and counseling, gender awareness and analysis are necessary in every pastoral encounter. It is important to recognize that the way girls and boys, women and men are socialized and the way power relationships are maintained in our culture have a significant impact on the lives of women and men and on the issues they bring for pastoral care and counseling. For example, every pastoral caregiver should know that

- approximately one out of two women is beaten in intimate relationships;
- one-third of all women homicide victims are killed by their husbands;
- approximately 49 percent of all girls are sexually molested/abused by the age of eighteen—either inside or outside their families;[26]
- the group of women most at risk for depression are married women who do not work outside the home;[27]
- men's death rate from lung cancer is nearly six times that of women and twice as high from cirrhosis of the liver—both probably related to limited masculine coping styles;[28]
- men's sense of isolation, their preoccupation with prestige and success, and their sense of spiritual emptiness have been clearly demonstrated and linked to gender training;
- men generally are denied access to their own emotional systems even to the point of not being able to identify emotions other than those of anger and sexuality.

These cultural realities are part of the stories of men's and women's lives that we have to carry into the counseling room. We must be aware that these realities shape the particular story of each counselee. We also have to be aware of our gender training and the impact of our experiences of power and powerlessness, entitlement and victimization, in order to best identify the assumptions and biases we may bring to our care and counseling work.

Because of their gender training (although these dimensions of gender training are particular to other elements of our social location such as race, sexual orientation, and class), women and men pastoral counselors have a tendency to play out their gendered patterns of behavior with their care receivers. For example, women may have the tendency to give up their own authority and voice in their counseling work, to be intimidated by male anger, or to place a high value on harmony and adjustment. When women work with women, they may have higher expectations for them, projecting their self-critical tendencies and low self-esteem onto other women. When women work with men, they may have the tendency to work very hard to understand them, working harder than a male care receiver, in their assumption that they are responsible for articulating the emotional dynamics. When male caregivers work with men, they may have a tendency, for example, to avoid tender emotions as they seek to have credibility within a traditional male value system. When men engage in pastoral counseling with women, they may feel responsible for solving women's problems or shouldering their concerns, or they may use their women counselees' emotional lives to gain access to their own.

Whatever the particulars, it's important to know that the gender dynamics of our culture, which include power arrangements, value assignments, and socialized roles, follow pastoral caregivers into care and counseling ministries. Without careful attentiveness to these dynamics in our own lives and without significant work that challenges the cultural assumptions about gender in a sexist world, we are very likely to do harm in our care and counseling work with men and women.

Every pastoral caregiver has the responsibility to educate herself or himself, therapeutically and academically, about the issues of gender and their impact on the lives of real people who come to pastors for care.

Counseling with Lesbians, Gay Men, and Bisexual Persons

A powerful cultural dynamic related to gender is that of sexual orientation, identity, and behavior. It has an impact on everyone, including counselors and clients. The emotional baggage in our culture, especially in religious denominations, around sexual orientation is intense and divisive. This significantly complicates effective caregiving with LGBT (lesbian, gay, bisexual, and transgendered) persons and their families. It also complicates caregiving with religious people who have intense positive or negative emotions about nonheterosexual orientations and behaviors. Challenging counseling opportunities with LGBT persons focus on numerous issues. These include deciding whether to "come out" (reveal their sexual orientation) and, if so, how and with whom; handling rejection from family, heterosexual friends, and employers; experiencing depression and suicidal impulses (especially among LGB adolescents); and encountering domestic violence and other relationship problems with same-sex or other-sex partners (in cases of bisexuals or married homosexuals).

Our culture divides gender into two neat halves, and each half (male and female) has been defined as opposite to the other. Maleness and femaleness have been assigned traits, behaviors, roles, and goals as essential to each, with very little room for deviating from those assignments. Hence what is defined as normal and healthy is contextually defined. When we talk about the cultural context for working with gay, lesbian, bisexual, and transgendered folk, we are talking about a culture where homophobia is deeply linked to the rigid, binary gender roles of maleness and femaleness.

Most literature on men's studies, which attempts to talk about the problems with masculinity constructs, ends up talking about the essentially homophobic nature of masculinity programming. Men are deeply socialized to reject anything that doesn't fit male norms, and especially anything that could fit under the opposite to masculinity—in other words, anything feminine. Several studies that measured strain or conflicts generated by not feeling successful enough at being male show that men with the highest gender role conflict scores also demonstrated the highest levels of anger at and distrust of women and strong negative attitudes toward gay men. Much feminist literature suggests links between homophobia and sexism or patriarchy as well. Women who are lesbian are seen as exceptions to femaleness; women who can demonstrate the fallacy of patriarchy by living fully competent, fully satisfying, and fully sexual lives without intimate relationships with men create enormous anxiety for a society determined to rely on an intrinsic division of roles and beings according to gender. The strict division of gender in our dominant culture into male and female—masculine and feminine—with strict and complementary rules about what that means, does not allow for a sexual orientation that challenges any of those rules.

Thus, we have two primary issues. Men and women, regardless of their sexual orientations, are deeply socialized in this society into strict gender roles. And there is a deep homophobic anxiety in our culture toward persons whose sexual orientation demonstrates a denial of a strict binary, complementary gender division.[29] So, when we think about pastoral care with people whose sexual orientation is as gays, lesbians, bisexuals, or transgendered people, we do so in the context of their having to live in a culture full of anxiety about the ramifications of accepting nonheterosexual orientations on the culture's deepest order—gender complementarity and its implications.

There is probably no purpose served by trying to explore the roots of homosexuality. Debates run the whole gamut of possibilities about etiology. There are genetic arguments; there are other biological arguments (embryonic, developmental, and so on); there are biosocial arguments; there are behavioral arguments, family system dynamic arguments, decision-oriented arguments, and flexible/fluid sexual identity arguments. Some etiologic arguments have better credibility than others, of course, but probably the focus of a pastoral care discussion doesn't need to be on cause as much as it needs to be on how to best offer healthy and empowering pastoral care and counseling with those who identify as gay, lesbian, bisexual, or transgendered.

Despite the fact that we assume for the sake of this discussion that homosexuality is a normal variation of human sexual identity, the dominant cultural narrative has tended to identify homosexuality as sickness, sin, or deviance. Because of this, as men and women discover a nonheterosexual orientation in themselves, they also discover and internalize something that they have known at least unconsciously all along—that nonheterosexual (and nongender-conforming) folk are despised and punished in many dimensions of the culture.

Since it is often in adolescence that sexual identity becomes more evident and motivating, a time when much about life seems uncertain and unclear, this can be a very difficult time for gay boys and lesbian girls. In fact, girls and boys who have found a real home in the church may find that they have to pull away from it (and friendship groups and families) as they discover an identity disapproved by church and other important communities. No wonder that despair is a common response. Another dynamic of adolescence for gay youth is that gender training heats up during this time. There is a great deal of pressure on boys and girls to narrowly conform to the particular "proofs" of masculinity and femininity. The culture gives a great deal of permission and guidance for this process; youth are encouraged to experiment appropriately with their sexuality with the "opposite" sex. However, for the homosexual person, sexual development and practice often can't occur until he or she is able to identify as gay, and can identify a community of support and attraction. This may be developmentally out of sync for a person, especially since coming out to self and others occurs at very different times for different people.

Often gay men and lesbian women seek counseling during the coming-out process, particularly as it affects key relationships for them. Another time that gay or lesbian folks seek counseling is when family conflict occurs. Coming out to family or letting family know about an important sexual relationship may stimulate unexpected and/or intolerable conflict or abuse. Another time when a pastoral caregiver may work with gay, lesbian, or bisexual folk may have to do with relational challenges they face in an intimate relationship. There are few models for how to develop an intimate relationship that is not grounded in clear, complementary gender roles. Thus, although this allows for both creativity and justice, it also may result in confusion as models are tried and discarded and unknown assumptions come to the surface.

The situation for bisexual men and women is certainly reflected in the above comments, especially when they are in same-sex relationships. However, there are other cultural issues. Many people in the heterosexual and homosexual communities have doubted the reality of bisexuality. Many in the gay community have suggested that bisexuals are gay folk who just haven't come to terms with their sexual orientation. Many in the heterosexual community have suggested that bisexuality is proof that a gay orientation is a choice and a distortion. Gays fear that invalidation. Consequently the bisexual person may have more difficulty finding a supportive community. Other psychologists have suggested that all humans are bisexual and that a variety of factors, including context, determine sexual orientation.

There is a great deal of evidence that there are many more bisexual people in our society than are apparent. Considerable feminist literature suggests that female sexual orientation may be much more fluid than is male sexual orientation and that bisexual women may move from one dominant orientation to another over their life cycle, with both orientations being fully legitimate in their context rather than being part of a developmental process. Others talk about female bisexuality in more traditional, contextual ways. One thing to keep in mind is that bisexuality may create more anxiety in the culture than homosexuality because it suggests that gender does not have to be the deciding factor in determining with whom one will be in an intimate relationship. Gay relationships can be seen as some sort of "reversal" process, but bisexuality denies gender as an exclusive deciding factor for human relationships.

But maybe even more than bisexuality, transgendered identity seems to create cultural anxiety. Transgendered identity suggests that people's internal sense of themselves and their desires and identities don't fit with the physical reality of their bodies or with the cultural norms for those bodies. Some authors distinguish transgendered identity from transvestite identity, which means that a person feels more comfortable dressed in clothing that more typically is assigned to the biological sex that she or he isn't. Some folk suggest that transgendered identity involves a range of experiences, which include transvestitism and surgical reassignment, or a desire for it, because of feeling trapped in the wrong-sexed body. Most suggest that folks who are trying to decide about their transgendered dynamics seek an affirmative and specialized counselor who can help persons experiment with gender changes of various types and make appropriate decisions.

Larry Graham is very helpful in looking at the basic pastoral requirements for working with gay, lesbian, bisexual, and transgendered careseekers. He suggests that the caregiver must confront his or her attitudes about sexual orientation at psychological, theological, and moral levels. He says, "Without that deep self-awareness, harm may well be done. . . . Homosexuality may be identified with sin and brokenness or with the highest human capacities under God, depending upon which strain of religious training is appropriated."[30]

Caregivers must have a solid working knowledge of this highly complex subculture with all its diversity. The caregiver needs to have done his or her homework. If she or he is gay, the caregiver should not assume that personal experience is definitive.

Counselors must believe that being gay or lesbian is a healthy variant of human sexuality, fully compatible with Christian values and ethics. (Both the American Psychiatric Association and the American Psychological Association have removed gayness from being classified as pathological conditions.)

Counselors must be able to enter and work with the belief systems of gay and lesbian persons as well as discuss sexual behaviors and attitudes in concrete and specific terms. Many would say that specialized training in counseling with LGBT is necessary.

Graham also suggests that caregivers need to help counselees work through their own internalized homophobia, which is often the most debilitating at the time of coming out. In order to do this, he says, caregivers have to work on their own internalized homophobia, be good listeners, be affirming of homosexual orientations, be able to absorb anger at the church and culture, and be able to give care receivers space to work out their conflicts while offering adequate support for looking at difficult issues of deep meaning. Caregivers also need to be able to stand the pain of working with folk who have HIV/AIDS and may die. Cumulative grief becomes an issue for people who do a lot of this counseling.

Furthermore, Graham says that the caregiver needs to be able to make links and deep connections between spirituality and sexuality. He says that spirituality is integrated wholeness. Our sexuality as embodied beings is a key piece of our spirituality.[31]

Finally, caregivers need to know what different denominations have to say about homosexuality and their positions and policies so that they can make appropriate referrals for LGBT folk as they seek to care for their spiritualities.

Building Bridges with Persons in Nontraditional, Alternative Lifestyles

Many people, especially young adults, are experimenting with alternatives to traditional sexually exclusive marriages with lifetime commitments. These alternative lifestyles include cohabitation (living together), trial marriages, communes, gay marriages, open marriages, and swinging. People are drawn to alternative styles for a variety of reasons. The majority have some degree of commitment and continuity in their relationship contracts, although usually not of a till-death-do-us-part duration. Many cohabiting couples have what amounts to trial marriages, which can be more difficult than marriage because of the lack of legal or social recognition. They seek fresh ways to satisfy the universal human needs for closeness, mutual caring, and sex, but in relationships in which love and freedom can exist together more fully than they do in many marriages. Many young people are reacting against the hypocrisy, sterility, or emotional dishonesty of conventional marriages they have observed in their parents' generation.

All close relationships involve conflict and problems. It is not surprising that some persons in such alternative relationships have the same types of interpersonal conflicts and pain that traditional marriages have. For those in relationships that are still stigmatized by many in our society, such as gay couples, there is the added burden of hiding or of learning to live with social prejudice, homophobia, and discrimination.

Persons living in lifestyles radically different from mainstream lifestyles probably do not seek counseling help from clergy in as great proportion as traditionally married couples. This is because of their expectations, which are sometimes justified, that pastors will judge or otherwise reject them because of their lifestyles. But pastors who become known in their communities as being warm, open, accepting human beings have opportunities to counsel with such persons. If congregations are to become healing and wholeness centers for human brokenness in our world, they should seek to become so for persons in the variegated lifestyles of our society, not just for persons in traditional marriages.

Many couples who are living together without being married need the kinds of relationship enrichment, care, and counseling needed by couples in traditional marriages. Unfortunately it is a rare church where they feel accepted if they attend a marriage enrichment event.

Fortunately the basic principles of marriage enhancement and counseling are useful in working with any close, committed relationship. However, in counseling with gay couples and persons in radically different lifestyles, it is important to help them identify and deal with the dynamics of their interpersonal conflicts, as distinguished from the burden of hiding or the social rejection, prejudice, and discrimination that complicate their personal and relationship problems. In this sense, counseling persons with different sexual preferences or alternative lifestyles involves issues similar to those confronted in working with persons from any minority—religious, ethnic, national, or racial—who suffer from a one-down position in our society. In such counseling, pastors need to feel and create a climate of genuine respect for differentness. People who have been rejected by others quickly sense subtle condescension and disguised judgmentalism in a counselor. It is possible to accept the right of others to be different and to respect them as persons without necessarily agreeing with their choices.

Caregiving with Victims of Ableism

The issue of what has been called "ableism" is discrimination, prejudice, and stereotyping against people with disabilities. The old, unfortunate attitudes that fuel this social violence against the millions of us who have significant disabilities die very hard. Only in the last few decades, since the Americans with Disabilities Act was passed by Congress, has our society had to face this myopic perspective and the practices that flow from it that limit unfairly the abilities of disabled people to use their potential capacities more fully.

Pastoral caregivers often encounter people who have been constricted and hurt by this evil. Here are some guidelines for ministering to their woundedness:

- Provide supportive counseling and resources for their families.
- Treat the disability as something they have, not who they are.
- Help them grieve what they have lost because of the disability. (Even if people have had the disability since birth, it is possible to have grief because they lack what others have.)
- Inform them about helpful resources that are available.
- Advocate for help not yet available.
- Encourage them to develop their talents in spite of their disability.
- Provide them with stories of persons such as Helen Keller and Christy Brown, who have overcome severe disabilities.
- Introduce them and their families to existing support groups and/or create such groups.

Learning from the Wisdom of Other Cultures

All cultures are enriched by wisdom about spirituality, healing, and wholeness. Caregivers can have their lives and spirits made more inclusive and enriched through openness to learn from the wisdom of other caregivers, as well as care receivers, from different traditions than their own. Consider these insights from other cultures:

"Kujikwaa si kuanguka, bali ni kwenda mbele!"
[To stumble is not to fall down, but it is to go forward!]
—Swahili proverb used by the CPE supervisor in Tanzania with his students[32]

"It is my firm faith that we can conquer the world by truth and love."
—Mahatma Gandhi

"A donde el corazon se inclina, el pie camina."
["Where the heart leans, the foot follows," meaning the things one cares about rule one's actions.]
—Hispanic proverb

The traditions of the Lakota Sioux nations of Native Americans hold that the most sacred of their rituals, the Sundance, is not complete until they express gratitude for all the help they received, by saying, "Pilamaya'pelo!" (Thank you!) "Chan'te u'waste'a" (with a good heart).[33] Medical research on the immune system has discovered that feeling and expressing thankfulness activate the body-mind's marvelous health-enhancing biochemistry.

A group asked the Dalai Lama what he believed to be the five most important questions confronting humans in the dawning years of the new millennium. He responded, "How do we address the widening gap between the rich and the poor? How do we protect the earth? How do we educate children? How do we help Tibet and other oppressed countries and peoples of the world? How do we bring spirituality (deep caring for one another) to all disciplines of life?" He said that all of these questions fall under the last one: "If we have true compassion in our hearts, our children will be educated wisely, we will care for the earth and those who 'have not' will be cared for." He then asked everyone in the group to share the following simple practice with as many people as they could, a practice that will increase love and compassion in the world:

> Spend five minutes at the beginning of each day remembering we all want the same things (to be happy and loved) and that we are all connected to one another.
> Spend five minutes breathing-in, cherishing yourself; and breathing-out cherishing each other. If you think about people you have difficulty cherishing, extend your cherishing to them anyway.
> During the day extend that attitude to everyone you meet. Practice cherishing the "simplest" person (clerks, attendants, etc.), as well as the important people in your life. Cherish the people you love and the people you dislike.
> Continue this practice no matter what happens or what anyone does to you.
> This practice, done wordlessly, enables you to feel the love and appreciation, for yourself and others and the world that already exist in your heart.[34]

If you decide to implement this exercise, you may discover that your well-being, including the awareness of your interconnection with the earth and the whole human family, will be deepened.

Reality Practice Skill Development Session

Parishioner's roles: You two are parents of Jerry, age seventeen, who has always been a good student, an obedient son, and a regular participant in your church's educational and youth programs. He has just "come out," revealing to you that he is gay. You are in great distress when you phone your pastor, Carla, asking to see her soon about a "family problem."

Pastor's role: Respond as seems appropriate to you in light of what you now know about pastoral caregiving with family systems in crisis and also both cultural and congregational attitudes toward homosexuals.

Observer-coach's role: Be aware of the quality, warmth, and accuracy of the pastor's U responses. Interrupt the flow of the counseling periodically (every five to ten minutes or so) to share your observations about the interaction between pastor and parishioners. Invite feedback, raise issues, and make suggestions for improving the pastor's responses. Call attention to responses that were not U but were E, I, S, P, or A responses. Discuss how the pastor's responses could have communicated more empathic understanding.

After twenty minutes or so of counseling, debrief fully and then switch roles so that each person has an opportunity to be pastor, parishioner, and observer-coach during the session.

Recommended Reading

Atkinson, Donald R. *Counseling American Minorities: A Cross-Cultural Perspective*. New York: McGraw Hill, 2004.

Bridges, Flora Wilson. *Resurrection Song: African-American Spirituality*. Maryknoll, N.Y.: Orbis Books, 2001.

Borhek, Mary V. *Coming Out to Parents: A Two-way Survival Guide for Lesbians and Gay Men and Their Parents*. Rev. ed. Cleveland: Pilgrim Press, 1993.

Butler, Lee H., Jr. *A Loving Home: Caring for African American Marriage and Families*. Cleveland: Pilgrim Press, 2000.

Chinula, Donald. *Building King's Beloved Community: Foundations for Pastoral Care and Counseling with the Oppressed*. Cleveland: United Church Press, 1997.

Dotterweich, Kass P. *Grieving as a Woman: Moving through Life's Many Losses*. St. Meinrad, Ind.: Abbey Press, 1998.

Friedman, Rabbi Dayle. *Jewish Pastoral Care: A Practical Handbook from Traditional and Contemporary Sources*. Woodstock, Vt.: Jewish Lights Publishing, 2001.

Fukuyama, Mary, and Todd Sevig. *Integrating Spirituality into Multicultural Counseling*. Thousand Oaks, Calif.: SAGE, 1999.

Gorsuch, Nancy. *Introducing Feminist Pastoral Care and Counseling: Introductions in Feminist Theology*. Cleveland: Pilgrim Press, 2001.

Grossoehme, Daniel. *The Pastoral Care of Children*. Binghamton, N.Y.: Haworth Press, 1999.

Hwang, Philip O. *Other-Esteem: Meaningful Life in a Multicultural Society*. Philadelphia: Accelerated Development, 2000.

Lee, Wanda. *An Introduction to Multicultural Counseling*. Philadelphia: Accelerated Development, 1999.

Marsh, Charles. *The Beloved Community: How Faith Shapes Social Justice, from the Civil Rights Movement to Today*. New York: Basic Books, 2006.

Martin, Terry, and Kenneth Doka. *Men Don't Cry . . . Women Do: Transcending Gender Stereotypes of Grief*. Philadelphia: Brunner/Mazel, 2000.

Nader, Kathleen, et al. *Honoring Differences: Cultural Issues in the Treatment of Trauma and Loss*. Philadelphia: Brunner/Mazel, 1999.

Neuger, Christie Cozad, ed. *The Arts of Ministry: Feminist-Womanist Approaches*. Louisville: Westminster John Knox Press, 1996.

————. *Counseling Women: A Narrative, Pastoral Approach*. Minneapolis: Fortress Press, 2001.

Neuger, Christie Cozad, and James Newton Poling, eds. *The Care of Men*. Nashville: Abingdon Press, 1997.

Parks, Colin Murray, et al. *Death and Bereavement across Cultures*. New York: Routledge, 1998.

Solomon, Norman. *Judaism: A Very Short Introduction*. New York: Oxford University Press, 1996.

Somaya, Abdulla. "Islam and Counseling: Models of Practice in Muslim Communal Life." *Journal of Pastoral Counseling* (January 1, 2007).

Stevenson-Moessner, Jeanne, ed.. *In Her Own Time: Women and Developmental Issues in Pastoral Care*. Minneapolis: Fortress Press, 2000.

Stretch, John J., et al. *Raising Our Children Out of Poverty*. Binghamton, N.Y.: Haworth, 1999.

Switzer, David K. *Coming Out as Parents: You and Your Homosexual Child*. Louisville: Westminster John Knox Press, 1996.

Wimberly, Edward P. *African American Pastoral Care*. Nashville: Abingdon Press, 1991.

————. *Counseling African American Marriages and Families*. Louisville: Westminster John Knox Press, 1997.

CHAPTER 18

EQUIPPING LAYPERSONS FOR CAREGIVING MINISTRIES

Bear one another's burdens, and so fulfill the law of Christ.
—Galatians 6:2 RSV

Teach us his ways . . . that we may walk in [God's] paths.
—Isaiah 2:3

The Significance of the Lay Renaissance in Caregiving

The pastor of a downtown church in the Midwest discovered that ministering to the bereaved was requiring much more of his time than anything else. As he became aware of the many widows and widowers in his congregation, he realized that he had a rich potential caregiving resource at his fingertips. So, he invited these widowed people to meet with him to plan a lay ministry to the bereaved. Each year there was a training period of six weeks for new recruits to this ministry. When someone died, the pastor selected a grief caregiver from this trained group to be introduced to the bereaved individual or family. The caregivers committed themselves to minister to the bereaved people, making regular contacts that complemented the pastor's ministry. This lay ministry has continued for many years, helping that congregation become a healing community.

In recent decades there has been a dramatic rediscovery of a striking reality—all Christians are called to minister because they are Christians, whether or not they are ordained. People's individual missions are as unique as their fingerprints, reflecting the special interests, values, and gifts of each individual. Awareness that they have their own special religious vocation or calling gives laypersons new empowered self-images. They know that they are no longer second-class Christians who leave significant spiritual work to their clergy. They have a vital and unique ministry within congregations and in the wider community and world beyond their church—to their neighbors, their business associates, their union, their friends, their enemies, and especially the disadvantaged, rejected, and exploited people in their community. The vitality of the ministry of the laity may be reaching a level that has not existed since the early decades of the Christian movement. The potentiality of this development is almost unlimited. A growing group of laypersons of many ages and backgrounds is responding to the invitation of God's exciting call.

As early as 1955 the World Council of Churches affirmed this ministry with this statement:

> Any emphasis on the ministry of the laity means not only training but a special kind of pastoral care. Lay men and women should be encouraged to use the pastoral gifts that many of them possess. Mutual care of members by each other as well as by the clergy is needed in the Church. Christians have many natural opportunities for the pastoral care of neighbors, workmates, and others.[1]

Rewards of Lay Caregiving for Pastors, Participants, and Congregations

The general ministry of pastoral care is one of presence, listening, warmth, and practical support. Trained lay caregivers can carry a substantial share of what is often a heavy caregiving load in congregations. They can provide backup for their pastor, who can then add crisis intervention skills when these are needed. The hospice program illustrates the effectiveness of collaboration between medical professionals and trained volunteer caregivers working with people who are terminally ill.

Ordained pastors can put into practice a player-coach approach to ministry by equipping lay caregivers in congregations by training and coaching them well. A player-coach approach to ministry is an ideal way to empower a congregation for healing, wholeness, and outreach.

Implications of Lay Caregiving for Pastoral Care and Counseling

The implications of the lay caregiving movement are challenging as well as profound for pastoral care and counseling. Pastoral care, rightly understood, is a vital ministry of the entire congregation. A local church should strive to become a healing, growth-stimulating, redemptive organism. The aim of the church's pastoral care program should be to develop a dynamic climate of mutual, loving, enlightened concern, which gradually leavens the whole congregation. Church administration and small group programs should be oriented toward this objective. To the extent that *koinonia* exists in a congregation, mutual ministry occurs spontaneously as individual members seek to give themselves, in Luther's words, "as a Christ to [their] neighbor."[2] Every member has pastoral care opportunities that are uniquely hers or his. Only as increasing numbers of us accept this challenge can our churches fulfill their mission as training and empowering centers for healing, liberation, justice, and peacemaking.

Research on church growth and decline shows that a robust and comprehensive ministry of caring is a crucial variable in the health and growth of such faith communities. This ministry is not possible unless trained laypersons are deeply involved in caring within a congregation and its community. Lay training is an effective way of enlarging the circle of congregational caregiving by extending this vital ministry to more needy people more frequently.

The Nature of Lay Caregiving Ministry

The lay caregiving ministry is multileveled with different training and appropriate functions on each level. It is basically a ministry of caring presence and empathic listening to burdened people in their dark days. In addition, some lay caregivers with training in basic crisis intervention methods occasionally can help people by using problem solving, guidance, or advising as reflected in the ABCDE model.

Pioneer teacher Seward Hiltner aptly described the lay renaissance as the "pastorhood of all believers." As this pastorhood becomes a reality in congregations and laypersons begin to fulfill their personal ministries, their spiritual growth is stimulated by putting their faith to work in direct loving service. A church's caring ministry to persons in the community who are lonely, sick, older, bereaved, homebound, newly arrived, institutionalized, exploited, and socially and economically oppressed can be at least quadrupled by involving trained laypersons fully in caring work. When dedicated laypersons become informal pastors to their neighbors, associates, and fellow church members, they become the church—the body of Christ serving those needing care, support, and guidance.

Two persons who have developed a lay training program declare:

> Enabling lay people in the caring ministry of the church involves far more than getting a few people to help the ministry with calling. We believe lay pastoral care manifests the very nature and foundation of the church as a caring community with its common priesthood of all believers. It provides a place in the life and ministry of the church for those who hear and believe, and want to put their faith into practice in a visible, tangible way.[3]

Theological-Biblical Foundations of Lay Caregiving Ministry

This lay renaissance is based on the rediscovery of the New Testament understanding of the church as the people of God, the body of Christ, and the community of the Holy Spirit in which each member has her or his ministry. The New Testament word *laos*, from which "laity" is derived, refers to all Christians. The "ministry of reconciliation" (described in 2 Cor. 5:17) was entrusted to the whole church, not just to professional ministers.

The caring ministry of laypersons is essentially an outreach ministry to persons in need within the congregation but also in the wider community, including their family, friends, and work colleagues. The challenge of Jesus' parable of the man who was robbed and beaten beside the Jericho Road was directed to all of Christ's followers. The criteria in his description of the Last Judgment were all matters of loving service: "For I was hungry and you gave me food, I was thirsty and you gave me drink, I was a stranger and you welcomed me, I was naked and you clothed me, I was sick and you visited me, I was in prison and you came to me" (Matt. 25:35-36 RSV). John Patton points to the New Testament roots of this understanding of mutual ministry: "The ministry of pastoral care should be understood holistically rather than hierarchically, following the body image of Paul in I Corinthians 12 and Ephesians 4."[4]

In this context, what is the function of clergy? By virtue of training and ordination, clergy are equipped and designated to function as leaders, trainers, and specialists in what is the work of every Christian. Instead of being a one-person band who performs each Sunday for passive congregations, as some clergy do, they should function as conductors of orchestras who enable all those in a gathered community of faith to each make his or her unique contributions to the symphony of the good news. The key role of clergypersons, as described in Paul's letter to the early church in Ephesus, is "to equip God's people for work in his service" (Eph. 4:12 NEB). The job of clergy is to train, inspire, guide, coach, and work alongside lay ministers as "teachers of teachers," "pastors of pastors," and "counselors of counselors".[5]

Overview of Various Models of Lay Caregiving

To be most effective in various congregations, the approaches to lay caregiving should be designed to fit the needs and resources of each particular faith community. But fortunately we can learn much from examining various models that effective leaders have used through the years as well as those that they have described in their writings.

Many denominations have an existing group (often called deacons) that do pastoral care with hospitalized, homebound, or older members. Some denominational structures give special responsibility for care of the ill and others in special need to a particular committee or group, such as stewards. It is the pastor's role to help these groups maximize their effectiveness in fulfilling their responsibilities by means of an ongoing program of training and supervision such as the one described below. In situations where there is no such group, or a group exists but concentrates in only a limited area of caring (for example, hospital calling), the maximizing of caring action by the laity can best be enabled by recruiting and training a pastoral care team. Such a team can enrich and spearhead the general caring ministry of a congregation. They should work under the direction and with the coaching of their pastor (or another professional member of the church staff) as lay copastors.

Ministries of lay caring are blossoming in many places. In one midwestern city, a council of churches conducted a workshop to train laypersons to visit older persons. This led several congregations to "adopt" a nursing home. Laypersons visited residents regularly and provided caring services. A church in the San Francisco area sponsors a halfway house for young adults in outpatient mental health treatment and persons recently released from mental hospitals. Twenty-three laypersons completed a sixteen-week training course to prepare for their roles in this project. In Southern California, an ecumenical group of laywomen call regularly on the families of prisoners.

Churches in many countries have set up Lifeline Centers where trained volunteers give crisis help to persons who phone. This worldwide lay caring program was started in Sydney, Australia, by a minister, Alan Walker, and his staff.[6] The training in this program is extensive and rigorous; it involves careful supervision and consultation with mental health professionals and ministers who are trained in counseling.

Kenneth Haugk, a pastoral and clinical psychologist in Saint Louis, was troubled by parishioners' lack of ownership of his church's overall ministry. He began to wonder what would happen if phrases like "priesthood of all believers," "body of Christ," and "equipping God's people for work in his service" became not theological clichés but the basis around which to build a congregation's ministry. "What would the church look like if people really did minister to each other? If a congregation was really marked by 'rejoicing with those who rejoice, weeping with those who weep'? What if it didn't depend so heavily on one overworked pastor? What if we could develop a whole church full of pastors?"[7]

Seeking an answer, Haugk began to train a small group of his parishioners to do lay caregiving with others in that congregation. This was so effective that two persons who had been trained, believing that "this is too good to keep to ourselves," urged their pastor to share it with other congregations. Eventually the Stephen Series was developed (named after Stephen in the New Testament) to train interested pastors and laity to do lay training in their own churches. Numerous congregations in a variety of denominations have participated in this pastoral care team ministry training program. As in other effective lay training, this approach includes regular meetings of the caregivers (after the initial training) for group support, supervision (usually by the pastor), and ongoing training. Haugk observes that many lay caring programs fall flat after a year or less because continuing support and training aren't provided. He also has found that lay caregivers receive a good response from 90 percent or more of those to whom they reach out if the pastor prepares them for the call.

Howard Stone has developed an uncomplicated model for training lay caregivers, described in *The Caring Church: A Guide for Lay Pastoral Care*. The eight sessions focus on these topics and skills: What is lay pastoral care? Lay caregiving establishes a care relationship by listening effectively; responding in facilitative ways; making hospital and shut-in visits (calls in a nursing home are assigned during this session); caring in grief situations; discussing the visits the trainees have made; solving problems and referring; and presenting the method of crisis caregiving. Stone emphasizes that most pastors who develop lay caring programs do not reduce their pastoral care load. However, they have the satisfaction of knowing that their people's pastoral care needs are being served far more fully than they could possibly have done alone.

Diane Detwiler-Zapp and William Dixon have developed a multifaceted approach to lay training. They emphasize ways of using the pastoral care opportunities in already existing parish activities—evangelism and incorporating new members, hospital visitation and bereavement care, visiting older and homebound persons, canvassing for annual stewardship pledges, Sunday school classes, and women's groups. They offer suggestions for the structuring, content, and supervision of training.

From their broad experience in training caregivers, Detwiler-Zapp and Dixon declare,

> One of the most caring things you can do for a church and for yourself is to enable others in caregiving. Putting theology into practice in this way can change the whole life of a congregation. We believe that you will be awed and inspired by the gifts, talents, and commitments that lay people bring to this mutual ministry.[8]

In commenting on the positive reception of lay caregivers, Dick Watts, whose congregation uses the Stephen Series program, says, "I'm reminded of the comment by the actress Melina Mercouri: 'In Greece we are too poor to have psychiatrists. And so we have friends instead.'"[9]

Here is how a lay caregiving program developed spontaneously in one congregation led by an experienced pastor, Robert A. Raines. He reports that lay pastoring developed as a result of the spiritual deepening of a network of spiritual growth groups engaged in depth Bible study. A depressed, convalescing woman was helped so much by a visit from a friend in her group that, quite informally, she took up a lay ministry to sick and hospitalized people.

The pastor reports,

> One morning in a sermon I mentioned what this woman was doing and asked any persons who were interested in this kind of ministry to speak to me. The response was amazing. I discovered that a veritable well of compassion existed which had only been waiting to be tapped. Approximately twenty-five persons said they wanted to take up this ministry. I am now working with them, informing them when people are hospitalized, sending them to visit the sick, shut-ins, those in hospitals, new mothers, and in some instances bereaved families.[10]

Starting Lay Caregiving Simply and Informally

In congregations in which the laity have had little experience in practicing the "pastorhood of all believers," pastors are wise to begin small and informally without a formal training program. Gradually as participation in an emerging program of lay caregiving develops, a more formal, structured, and comprehensive program can be implemented. An informal method of involving more laypersons in caregiving ministries is the practice of "linking" described in the chapter on grief. This involves simply asking those struggling to cope with current crises or losses if they would like to talk with someone who has weathered and learned from similar difficult situations. If so, inviting that person to meet with the one who has been through a similar experience can be fruitful for both.

Guidelines for Developing a Lay Caring Ministry

Here are some guidelines for developing a lay caring ministry in your congregation. It is important to recognize that there are different kinds and levels of lay training for caregiving, all of which are needed in the life of a church. "Throughout their lives, most people encounter problems, unexpected crises, or troublesome transitions. The majority of individuals depend on their social network of family, friends, and neighbors as a major source of help."[11] Every member of a congregation is a part of some type of informal social support network. Therefore, everyone should be offered an opportunity to enhance caring skills by learning, for example, how to listen in more depth. Pastors and mental health professionals in congregations can help raise the general level of caring within their congregation and within the supportive networks of individual members by an ongoing education-for-caring emphasis. This can use sermons as well as lectures and training sessions with church school classes, youth groups, women's and men's groups, family events, and so on.

A second and deeper level of training for caring should be focused on all the laypersons who call on others as a part of the church's program. Some churches involved with the Stephen Ministry provide training in caring for those who do home evangelism, calling on newcomers and the unchurched to invite them to join the church. On one occasion in my church, I gave instruction in caring methods to the stewardship team, those persons visiting church members to ask them to pledge financial support. They were given this training before they made their calls, for three reasons: to help them heal the wounds of members who were angry and alienated from the church; to recognize and respond helpfully to the needs of persons going through crises; and to be alert to and aware of situations where counseling by the pastor was needed. Training provided to persons doing home visitation creates a double benefit from their calls. The task of recruiting new members or underwriting the budget is accomplished more effectively, creating a vital pastoral care ministry.

In-depth training of a pastoral care team is a third essential level of a caring congregation's program. Although pastoral care is the function of the whole congregation, some group or groups need to be selected and trained to spearhead this ministry. Every church member should be challenged to become a part of the caring network of supportive, growth-nurturing relationships that is the church at its best. But within a church, there should be one or more task forces (depending on the size of a church) of persons committed to pastoral care as their primary lay ministry. Pastors do not need to wait until they can launch a formal training program in their churches. Many parishioners are already engaged in informal, spontaneous caring with persons in crises. When a pastor learns about this, she or he can give such persons encouragement, make suggestions aimed at improving their helping, and suggest a relevant book or article to help them make their caring more effective.

Whenever the pastor encounters an individual or family in crisis, it can be very helpful to link them with someone in the congregation who has weathered a similar situation and grown as a result of this struggle.[12] From personal experience, I have learned that a person whose diabetes has just been diagnosed can be helped tremendously by talking with someone who has learned to live effectively with this frustrating metabolic problem. The two persons usually establish instant rapport. The more experienced one knows many of the other's feelings from the inside and therefore can give both empathetic support and practical suggestions for coping with the many new demands imposed by the problem. The linking of persons with similar losses, crises, and life situations in informal dyads or clusters of mutual support is one of the simplest and most helpful strategies a pastor can use to enable lay caring. A layperson who is sensitive, caring, and informed about the issues other parishioners are facing can be used to coordinate such a mutual ministry in partnership with the pastor.

Individuals and couples who have graduated from pastoral counseling or therapy and have grown as a result of coping with the crisis that brought them to help can be used as informal resources to befriend others going through similar problems. In such cases, the pastor should do the linking, clearing the way first to see if both persons would be open to such a relationship. The name of the other person should not be mentioned until the pastor has that person's permission, since to do so would violate the professional confidentiality essential in all caring and counseling. Using persons who have had counseling and therapy in this way, often facilitates their continuing growth as well as gives peer support to other persons wrestling with similar dilemmas.

An Effective Lay Training Program

Let me describe the steps by which effective pastoral caregiving teams can be developed in congregations. This approach was derived primarily from experiences I have had in coaching the development and ongoing services of congregational lay caregiving programs, one in a United Church of Christ congregation, and the other in a United Methodist congregation. The model can be adapted for training lay volunteers in hospitals and counseling programs of both church-related and secular organizations.

Step 1: *Selection and recruitment.* In most situations it is necessary to recruit team members actively. Doing so has the clear advantage of allowing one to invite persons with natural caring aptitudes. These are the special people in congregations to whom wounded friends gravitate spontaneously—those like the woman in the congregation described above. They have "gifts of healing," as Paul described them (1 Cor. 12:28 NEB). In recruiting potential trainees, such persons are identified and invited, if not urged, to participate. In every congregation, there are persons with a high degree of the personal qualities that nurture creative change in close relationships—self-respect and caring for others, and the capacity for empathetic understanding and authenticity or congruence. Such individuals are growing persons who possess personal warmth, a love of people, sturdy self-esteem, contagious aliveness, a dynamic faith and trust in the universe, and a demonstrated capacity to grow from their own losses and painful experiences.

Other people feel more whole in their presence. They are natural caregivers. The pastor or a committee recruiting potential caring team members can identify these persons simply by recognizing those to whom others turn spontaneously for help. Those who should not be recruited for a caring team (and who should be gently but firmly channeled into other service if they volunteer) are so-called do-gooders. Such persons are strongly motivated by a self-aggrandizing need to be of service, and they usually lack the openness required to be teachable. Equally important to avoid are persons who do not keep confidences. It is crucial that all team members be able to keep privileged communication absolutely confidential.

Among those recruited for a caring team, include persons of both sexes, from different racial and ethnic backgrounds and of varied ages and life experiences. In addition, it is helpful to have AA members of each sex with stable sobriety; an experienced member of Al-Anon; a physician; an experienced businessperson; and a member of one or more of the counseling-therapy professions, including a social worker or staff member of a community agency who knows the referral resources of the community. It is also important to recruit persons who have grown from the losses and tragedies in their own lives; for example, persons who have lost a child, experienced divorce or the death of a spouse, survived a major accident or surgery, and so on. Such people often have a hidden asset of which they are unaware. They can relate as "wounded healers" to others going through crises.

At the time trainees are recruited, ask them to commit themselves to complete the basic training. But make clear that the decisions concerning their ongoing participation will be made by them (in consultation with the trainers) at the end of the initial training. Fortunately, experienced training itself is an excellent natural screening process. Some people discover during the training that they are not particularly effective in caring work. They should be encouraged to serve in areas of the life of their congregation that do not require a high degree of interpersonal skills. Persons who choose not to continue after training should be able to leave the training group without a sense of guilt or failure. Whatever caring skills they learned will be used productively in their relationships.

The effectiveness of lay caring programs is directly correlated with the selection of teachable trainees and the rigor of the training program. Even persons with strong natural caring aptitudes need to develop them by continuing in-service training. Since effective lay caring teams usually work closely with pastors, it is important that they be involved in the selection and training. If the responsibility for selecting and training is given to a lay task group, they should function in close consultation with the pastor. If the pastor has a strong background in pastoral psychology and counseling, he or she can well be the primary trainer of the team. In any case, the pastor should provide theological-biblical input and help define the role of the team in that congregation's total pastoral care program. There are few, if any, ways that pastors can invest their professional expertise that pay richer dividends than helping to equip lay carers. The sense of colleagueship and mutual ministry that develops within a caring team can nurture and energize the pastor as well as team members.

Step 2: *Basic training.* Most of the varied formats used in training programs begin with a period of intensive team-building and training in fundamental skills. The basic training of the United Church of Christ (UCC) group mentioned above consisted of two weekend training retreats at a church camp in the mountains, one month apart. To give a picture of the flow and content of one approach to lay training, I will describe the process used with this group. After supper on Friday evening of the first weekend, we did a get-acquainted exercise, and the cotrainers dialogued briefly on our hopes and expectations for the training, emphasizing the following points:

> The purpose of these training events is to increase our abilities to relate in ways that help and strengthen others. In order to do this, we need to become as aware as possible of our relationships, including blocks, feelings others stir in us (and vice versa), to better ways of communicating. Another purpose is to understand the ways in which helping relationships are established and to be aware of the theology of such relationships. The training also will aim at the acquisition of certain helping skills which are useful in relationships. These skills will be the main thrust of our second weekend. However, since the essence of any helpful relationship is a rich, full, mutual experience of relating, we'll keep working on that throughout our training.[13]

Trainees were then invited to say what they hoped to get from the training. A tentative group contract was developed, spelling out the aims of the weekend and how the time would be used, reflecting the hopes and goals of both the trainees and the trainers. Two hours were spent on Friday evening in communication exercises designed to increase self-other awareness and to build trust within the group.

On Saturday morning, after a period of tuning in spiritually through prayer, meditation, and guided imaging, there was a dialogue "lecturette" by the coleaders on "the process of growth in sharing groups." Three hours were then spent in two subgroups where the trainees worked on their own feelings and relationships. These persons had been chosen for their aptitudes as helpers, but the opportunity to share honestly brought their human pain and loneliness to the surface quickly. The debriefing of the morning showed that the depth of the communication had been powerful and trust-building for many.

The grief experience, as a universal crisis, provides an ideal context for the teaching of helping skills. After lunch and volleyball, the cotrainers talked candidly about some of their own recent experiences of loss. Then in growth groups of six, centering on the biblical words "Blessed are those who mourn, for they will be comforted" (Matt. 5:4), each person was given an opportunity to share something that caused him or her grief or pain. It was suggested that comforting by group members should be done nonverbally to allow the use of a wider range of ways of communicating strong feelings. These powerful sharing groups elected to meet again on Saturday evening; one continued until 2:00 a.m.

On Sunday, the training focus shifted to explicit skill practice. After a few comments on the centrality of listening skills in all caring, the cotrainers demonstrated responsive listening by taking turns responding with empathy to each other's current feelings. Then the trainees divided into triads for reality practice, taking turns expressing their feelings and being listener-responder and observer-coach. The trainers circulated among these small groups to provide coaching. This was followed by a session on "the theology of helping relationships" where group members shared the biblical insights that had come alive for them during the weekend. A lively discussion then ensued on "what our church and community need from a Samaritan group."[14] Tentative action goals were drawn up by the group as it discussed the possible uses of the training in caring work. Then came a group evaluation of the weekend and discussion of homework to be done before the next training retreat, which was, to practice responsive listening daily, to reflect further on the caring needs of their church and community, and to read one of the books suggested. After lunch, the group closed the event with an outdoor workshop celebration, planned by a small group of trainees, to pick up the main learning from the weekend.

Never in my experience have I seen a group more turned on and sensitized to caring relationships after so brief a time together.

The meaningfulness of the first weekend was indicated by the fact that only one person missed the second weekend a month later. In the opening reconnecting session on Friday night, there was sharing of significant happenings in trainees' lives resulting from the first training event; for example, two women reported that they had been able to listen in new ways to their teenagers. The remainder of Friday evening was spent in a meeting of the two growth groups, followed by a creative-movement-to-music session. Most of Saturday morning was spent introducing the group to the ABCDE method of crisis help. Here is how this approach was presented:

First, the coleaders presented the ABCDE model as the "basic caring and helping tool that can be adapted to help people cope constructively with many types of crises." Then the trainees did an overview of the steps, concluding with "you have already learned the first step. Responsive listening is the main way a relationship of trust is established and strengthened."

Second, as a live demonstration of how to use the ABCDE method, my cotrainer counseled with me to help me deal with a crisis I was facing at that time.

Third, most of the remaining time on Saturday morning was spent in the two groups, doing reality practice. Trainees had an opportunity to use the ABCDE method as they worked with one another's actual struggles and pain. The cotrainers coached the reality practice groups. After an early afternoon hike, the trainers helped the whole group apply the ABCDE model to three common types of human crises: being a newcomer in a community, being hospitalized, and experiencing bereavement.

On Saturday evening, the whole group brainstormed the question, "What action should our group take to respond to the unmet needs for caring in our church and community?" Ideas were pooled and a committee was chosen to set priorities and recommend next steps. This was followed by a time of singing and very lighthearted socializing. When the committee reported on Sunday morning, discussion was intense. The group agreed on an action plan, and the basic training was then concluded with a worship celebration of the growth we had experienced and the commitment the group had developed to the ministry of wholeness and caring.

The approach to basic training used in the United Methodist church employed many of the methods and exercises described above. But the training format consisted of two, seven-hour miniretreats (Sunday afternoon and evening) held at the church two weeks apart.[15] There was a stronger emphasis on the explicit task of developing a caring program for the congregation than in the UCC training. Some intensive time was used for group-building near the beginning of that training project.

Step 3: *Supervised training calls*. After completing the basic training, trainees should exercise their option of deciding whether to continue in the ongoing caring program. Those who elect to do so should be asked to begin making calls on persons in need of caring and to participate in a regular bimonthly supervisory group focused on learning about caregiving from their calls. To maximize learning, team members should be encouraged to write brief verbatim accounts of significant interchanges between them and the persons being visited. These are used in supervisory sessions.

It is wise to assign newly trained people to situations that are likely to be low threat; for example, newcomers, homebound persons, or older persons, rather than persons known to be in major crisis. As lay caregivers grow in confidence and competence, they can be assigned calls requiring more sophisticated crisis-helping skills; for example, the bereaved, the sick, families of terminally ill persons, those going through separation and divorce, or parents with a child who has a severe disability. Special instruction on caring with particular problems should be provided by the pastor or other trainer(s) before and after calls are made on those suffering from those kinds of problems. Persons with special expertise should be invited to be resource persons during supervisory sessions dealing with particular issues; for example, an AA member and an Al-Anon member can brief the team on working effectively with alcoholics and their families.

The initial anxiety of lay caregivers is usually painfully high, even if the types of calls they are asked to make seem unthreatening from inside the pastor's role. To help them keep their anxiety from interfering with their effectiveness, suggest that they make their calls in pairs to give each other support. This also tends to increase significant learnings by allowing the two persons to debrief the call immediately, giving each other feedback concerning the strengths and weaknesses of what each said and did. Writing verbatim accounts of important segments of calls, to use in coaching sessions, is initially threatening but very valuable to most trainees.

When using a verbatim in training, robust affirmation of its strengths and only gentle criticism of its weaknesses should be given. After examining crucial interchanges of a verbatim report (written or oral), the person who presented the verbatim should be invited to role-play the person needing help while others try various approaches to caring.

It is essential that the pastor stand both beside and behind laypersons who get involved in lay caring, especially during the early stages of their calling. In many cases, they find it much more difficult than they had imagined. The pastor should let lay caregivers know that he or she is glad to be contacted whenever the caregiver feels uncertain about what to do or whenever a helpee seems to be in need of assistance from the pastor or some other trained professional. The lines of communication should always be open for consultation and referral with the pastor and other backup professionals.

The ongoing training design that the United Methodists found most helpful was built around meeting for three hours once a month (on a Sunday afternoon). Information from the pastor about persons needing calls was shared at the outset. Team members then chose two names; calls were made during the next hour and fifteen minutes. Then the whole team reassembled at the church to receive supervision of their calls and share their personal feelings and issues. Although this format precluded the opportunity to write verbatims, the two team members who had made a call sometimes role-played perplexing or effective segments of the call they had just completed. At the end of each supervisory session, the members chose a particular problem that had emerged during one of the calls, on which to focus the next time.

Step 4: *Annual refresher event and recontracting.* At least once a year a caring team should hold a Friday night–Saturday or a whole weekend retreat to evaluate their service to others, strengthen their resources for caring, renew their commitment to the program (if they elect to continue for another year) or do their leave-taking (if they decide not to continue), and integrate additional persons into the caring team. Both the UCC and the UM groups became small caring communities for their members, including the trainers. A strong bond grew among us, strengthened by sharing the ministry to others and by the mutual caring that had developed. During the first year of the UM group, two members experienced the loss of parents, and one discovered that her long bout with cancer had taken a turn for the worse. We discovered that only as we responded caringly to one another's needs were we able to reach out effectively to persons outside the group. Outreach to others and personal support and growth within the group need to be kept in balance.

If lay caring team members are to function well, their satisfaction must outweigh the anxiety and frustration of the experience. The satisfactions that people can derive include

- enjoying the openness, honesty, and life-affirming atmosphere of mutuality that comes to characterize the group;
- being involved in a team that is learning and doing significant things;
- experiencing the satisfaction of growth in interpersonal competence;
- discovering that one can relate more helpfully;
- being part of a support group that helps trainees and leaders cope constructively with their personal pain and loneliness.

Here are significant learnings from these two training experiences:

1. It is important to have the contract between the leaders and the group members clear and mutually acceptable from the beginning. This requires an explicit statement by

the leader-trainer regarding the goals of the group; for example, that it is primarily for training for helping others and for the personal growth needed to make helping effective.

2. It is important to blend and balance, from the beginning, the three basic ingredients in effective lay training—input of functional concepts; personal growth and relationship-building experiences; and skill practice and coaching.

3. Inductive teaching of helping skills is the most effective approach. This means beginning with a learning experience of some kind (for example, a role-play, live demonstrations, or a verbatim of a call) and then, through group reflection, deriving the principles of caring that are operative in the experience.

4. It is good to use only simple operational models—for example, the ABCDE method of crisis help—in the input and skill practice sessions.

5. Teaching understanding of human dynamics can best be accomplished by focusing on a few common problems that the trainees have experienced—for example, bereavement, sickness, aging, and moving.

6. Try to use the ability and ideas of all trainees from the beginning by involving them in planning their own learning goals and experiences.

7. Frequent evaluative group discussion during the training is important. The trainer must be open to renegotiating the original group contract to keep it related to emerging needs—the group's, her or his own, and those of the congregation and community.

8. Theological resourcing should occur throughout the training. Leaders need to be open about what is theologically meaningful to trainees with respect to the *why* of their caring, the need to incarnate theological truths in caring relationships, and the need to live in pro-life partnership with the creative Spirit of the universe in caring work. Theological reflection by the group can help them capture the learnings that are potentially available in those precious moments when the theological truths implicit in all close relationships become most transparent—moments when time stands still and one knows that one stands on holy ground! Those involved in personal caring ministries encounter such moments frequently; for example, when they are with persons who are standing in the valley of the shadow of death; or persons on some mountaintop, celebrating a milestone in their lives.

Overcoming Resistance to Lay Caregiving

The resistance in the feelings of many pastors to involving laypersons in this way must be reduced, if not resolved, before an effective program of lay caring can be fully implemented. Some pastors feel guilty when they ask others to do pastoral care tasks. The "indispensability complex" makes sharing this ministry with the laity threatening. Some pastors allow themselves to be so overloaded by the demands and needs of their people that the time to train lay caregivers seems like an impossible additional burden. One pastor said after a workshop, "I am already running to stand still. I don't have any extra time to spend coaching laypersons in giving care." Furthermore, most pastors in seminary were not shown the crucial importance of training lay caregivers, nor did they have opportunities to learn the coaching skills required. Consequently many pastors feel, and some are, inadequate in this area of ministry. Pastors' self-images must be rethought and their supervisory skills increased so that enabling lay ministry can be a central and satisfying part of their tasks.

Resistance in pastors is reinforced by certain attitudes prevalent in typical congregations. When the idea of training lay caregivers is presented, the initial response of some church members is, "We hired our pastor to give us pastoral care, not to teach someone else to do it." Some parishioners feel that when a layperson calls on them, they are getting second-class help from amateurs. Both pastors and congregations need to learn that training lay caregivers is not a pastor's way of passing the buck, but a powerful way of deepening, broadening, and sharing the ministry of caring with the whole congregation. It does not replace pastoral care by a pastor, but rather complements and greatly augments it.

An appropriate concern of pastors is with the quality of lay caring and helping programs. Is it really possible for laypersons to give effective help to burdened, hurting people? Fortunately studies have confirmed the effectiveness of lay and paraprofessional helping persons. Robert R. Carkhuff, a pioneer in the field of training lay helpers, makes this striking (and disturbing to some professionals) statement about the research literature comparing the effectiveness of lay and professional training and treatment: "Briefly, the available evidence indicates that lay training programs have been more effective in demonstrating change on indexes that measure constructive helpee change."[16] Experience with lay caring programs in churches has shown that inadequately trained and unsupervised laypersons can do harm, particularly if they try to work with individuals or families who need counseling or therapy. (The same could be said of inadequately trained and unsupervised pastors and other professionals, of course.) But the clear evidence is that in doing pastoral care, well-trained laypersons can make a constructive and unique contribution to the total caring ministry of a church, hospital, or other institution!

Multileveled Lay Caregivers Training Programs

Comprehensive caregiving training in congregations should be available on at least three levels. (1) To increase the informal mutual caregiving in the entire faith community, training should be offered in elective workshops in which anyone can enhance skills in listening and responding with effective care. (2) More extensive training followed by coaching can enhance the caregiving effectiveness of church school teachers, group leaders, and those who do any types of home visits to members and potential members, as well as those who support a congregation financially. (3) In-depth training with continuing follow-up coaching should be given to a carefully selected caregiving team whose function is to work with the pastor in providing the most effective care possible for people going through grief and other severe stress periods in their lives.

Lay Mutual Help Groups

The flowering of self-help groups is an exciting development in the contemporary caring and counseling scene. It shows that the lay renaissance is a lively reality, not just in the churches, but in the whole field of healing and health. The power of mutual healing available from nonprofessional persons and groups is increasingly evident in the self-help groups of many types that are flourishing in most communities. Think for a moment of the tremendous implications of what has happened in Alcoholics Anonymous, the grandparent and model for many other self-help groups. In 1980, the more than one million recovered alcoholics in AA, in some 110 countries, were living miracles, demonstrating the healing power of spiritually centered self-help groups. The effectiveness of self-help groups is a dramatic confirmation of the wisdom of making mutual ministry of, by, and for the laity a dominant thrust in the caring program of a church. There is a largely undiscovered gold mine of caring and helping that can be developed by increasing the lay, self-help groups in any church. The self-help group model can be applied in a variety of forms to strengthen a congregation's caring program.

Persons who have grown as a result of having weathered painful life problems should be linked with others who are encountering similar problems to give support and an insider's understanding and practical guidance in constructive coping. A natural extension of the practice of linking individuals for mutual care is to create informal clusters of three or more persons struggling with similar problems, disabilities, losses, and crises. When such clusters become mutually helpful, they draw others with similar needs to them. The potential lay leadership for such caring clusters is already available in most congregations. With minimal coaching and ongoing backup and support from the pastor, many people who have used their problems as growth opportunities can learn the skills of leading a mutual help group. Whenever a pastor discovers two or more individuals or families with a common problem, he or she can invite them to meet informally to share what they have learned. Such persons usually discover that they can help one another in different ways and, in some cases, more than professionals who have not experienced their problems.

The variety of human situations where the self-help group model can be applied productively is almost limitless. Every church should have caring clusters for persons going through the stress of divorce or unemployment, raising a child who is disabled, retiring, moving, or living with an alcoholic or emotionally disturbed person. Caring clusters should also be developed for persons whose growth potentials are constricted by oppressive economic, institutional, or social prejudices and practices, in order to combine support with consciousness-raising.

In small- and medium-sized congregations, a single sharing group for persons experiencing any type of crisis or loss can be formed. Large congregations may find it feasible and helpful to have separate caring clusters for those going through such common losses as divorce. A church should be bold and imaginative in experimenting with a variety of self-help groups in its caring program as well as in opening the use of its facilities to self-help groups in the community.

What should the role of pastors and other helping professionals be in relation to self-help groups in the church? First of all, they should recognize that they cannot be the ongoing leader of such a group unless they have experienced the type of problem that has drawn the group members together. However, a pastor can serve these functions: (1) inviting persons with a common personal issue together to form the nucleus from which a self-help group can grow; (2) giving continuing moral support to the group and its leaders; (3) referring other persons to the group; (4) being available as a consultant when invited by the group, for example on spiritual growth issues; and (5) asking for the guidance of group members when counseling with persons facing the problem on which a particular group focuses.

Among the mutual help groups with which churches should consider experimenting is a group where the 12-step recovery and growth program of AA is applied to other problems of living with which church members are struggling. The AA steps represent a systematizing of some basic thrusts of our religious tradition—awareness of need, repentance (surrender of narcissism), openness and dependence on God, self-examination, honest confession, restitution and renewal, deepening one's contract with God, and sharing with others in need the new life one has found. It may well be that these steps provide a path by which a distinctively religious-oriented approach to group counseling eventually will be evolved.

As groups like Al-Anon, Gamblers Anonymous, Overeaters Anonymous, and Neurotics Anonymous have discovered, the AA steps are readily adaptable to nonalcoholic problems. The difficulty in developing such groups for people with better-hidden problems is that many of them are unaware of how much their lives are diminished by their problems. To be effective, a group should be composed of persons who are hurting in some area of their lives and who are aware of their pain. The leadership of such a group should rotate. Leaders should have a lay perspective—that is, they should make their own needs clear and be full participants in the group's search for healing and help. They cannot stand apart as leaders or therapists without damaging the basic therapeutic dynamic of a self-help group. Professional persons who have experienced and found workable solutions to problems similar to those shared by most of the group make ideal leaders, provided they have genuine humility and are aware of their own need for continuing growth. Without these qualities they will alienate others by an unrealistic I've-got-it-made attitude. Leaders should serve as models of openness in discussing their continuing struggles as well as sharing what has worked for them. Such openness is contagious. Preparation for leading an AA-patterned self-help group should include study of the AA principles and attendance at a number of open meetings of that fellowship.

The entire lay caring program of a church should be an outreach ministry to persons in need in the wider community and the world as well as within the congregation. The outreach targets of lay caregivers must include lonely, marginalized, and oppressed persons. As the "pastorhood of all believers" is implemented and celebrated in more and more congregations and other church-related institutions, a new energy is being released into the hurting, violent society.

Reality Practice Skill Development Session

Parishioner's role: You are a layperson receiving training in methods of lay caring (a small group of two to five people is ideal).

Pastor's role: Instruct the layperson(s) in the training session on how to use the ABCDE method of crisis intervention.

Observer-coach's role: Give feedback on the training methods that the pastor uses, particularly the blending of cognitive instruction and experiential practice of methods.

Recommended Reading

Benner, D. G. *Strategic Pastoral Counseling: A Short-term Structured Model.* Grand Rapids: Baker Books, 2006.

Culbertson, Philip L. *Caring for God's People.* Minneapolis: Fortress Press, 2000.

Egan, Gerard. *The Skilled Helper: A Problem Management and Opportunity Development Approach to Helping.* Florence, Ky.: Thompson, 2006.

Farabaugh, Tim. *Lay Pastoral Caregiving.* Nashville: Discipleship Resources, 2008.

Patton, John. *Pastoral Care in Context: An Introduction to Pastoral Care.* Louisville: Westminster John Knox Press, 2005.

Stone, Howard. *The Caring Church: A Guide for Lay Pastoral Care.* Minneapolis: Augsburg Fortress Press, 1983.

CHAPTER 19

SELF-CARE FOR CAREGIVERS

Keeping Your Vision Alive and Well

Over the years I have counseled numerous clergy who have suffered from burnout. They had lost zest, excitement, and motivation in their professional lives. The root cause of their depression and distress usually was their long neglect of basic self-care in overloaded schedules. Prominently absent were sufficient pleasure and fun. When they explored deeper levels of their problems, they often discovered that their distress also flowed from vision vacuums—the guiding, energizing visions that had enlivened their early ministry had grown boringly dull and even lifeless.

Donald Smith attributes burnout to overwork, dealing with too many and conflicting expectations, working constantly with needy people, confusing the masks they wear with the persons they are, not knowing if they have really accomplished anything, groping for a relevant faith, and living with pressing personal or family needs.[1]

Highly dependent people are often attracted to churches where they attach themselves to available parent figures, including warm, caring clergy. How can clergy and lay caregivers avoid caregiver burnout and protect their mental health, creative energies, self-care, and family relationships from the exorbitant demands of the dependent people they encounter in their ministry? Caregivers can become less vulnerable to this hazard by taking the following precautions:

- Become aware of and resistant to any neurotic tendency they may have to "collect" dependent relationships.
- Learn how to say no clearly and firmly whenever this is necessary and appropriate for them to honor the important things to which they need to say yes, including their self-care.
- Distribute and thus share overdependent people's consuming needs for support with trained lay caring team members and also church groups, whenever feasible. Clergy who train and continue coaching carefully selected laypersons in caring skills have a vital supportive network of de facto copastors who can carry a substantial portion of the load of needy, dependent people.

461

• Resist letting the needs of dependent people deplete the essential renewal of emotional and spiritual energy for this demanding ministry, energy that comes from attending to regular self-care and opening to the divine Spirit.

Setting Boundaries to Protect Your Well-being

Clergy caregivers must learn how to set firm internal and external boundaries on their time and availability. Only by doing so can they protect their own well-being and avoid caregiving burnout. Needy people are everywhere, and human need is a bottomless pit. Caregivers set internal limits on their availability by making a decision that they will keep a firm but flexible balance among their professional duties, including caregiving, care for their families, and self-care to sustain their mental, spiritual, and physical well-being. Unless they do this in their own minds, it is not likely that they will set external boundaries by letting their congregations know when they will be and will not be available to respond to parishioners' needs. Flexible firmness means that clergy recognize and let people in their congregations know that there are some circumstances when they will be available, even though these happen outside the usual times of their availability. Major crises such as death and serious accidents are examples of such times.

What types of careseekers make the keeping of firm but flexible boundaries so crucial for clergy's health, well-being, and even survival in effective ministry? Every congregation and community includes people for whom chronic crises seem to be a way of life. In addition there are some who overuse caregivers in their family and congregation because they derive satisfaction from being sick or helpless. Because the symptoms bring satisfaction and control over others, they change little, if anything at all, and become increasingly adept at getting others to play the transactional analysis game of "ain't it awful" with them. Then there are some troubled people for whom manipulation of others is a way of maintaining some feelings of being in control in their chaotic inner world. Driven by this insatiable need, they have little concern for the needs, schedules, or well-being of caregivers or others. Those who follow a pattern of doing what appears to be "seeking help" from a continuing series of counselors, clergy, and health professionals are often motivated by unconscious hungers for attention, control, or simply being listened to by nearly everyone, especially those they perceive as authority figures.

What they receive, even from competent caregivers and healers, is almost never satisfactory to them, and they seldom implement the recommendations of caregivers. They complain to each of their successive caregivers about the inadequacy and failure of those they consulted earlier. Some people with severe personality disorders are intentional in their deception and manipulation of others. Clergy who counsel are often fooled and manipulated by such persons, and they need to develop ways to spot and not be manipulated by them. But many troubled and troubling people who seek help are not consciously aware or intentional about why they follow compulsive behavior patterns that exhaust one caregiver after another.

Self-care and Training

Some clergy feel and, in fact, *are* inadequate in their counseling role because they have limited academic education and clinical supervision that are needed for competent counseling with persons suffering from complex problems. The findings in several studies consistently point to the inadequacy of much seminary education.[2] Many feel "caught between a rock and a hard place," as one minister said, meaning between recognizing the need for advanced training and making what often are considerable career and family sacrifices necessary to obtain this training. If such training, though desired, is unavailable or unaffordable, other options are available to them. They can enhance their short-term skills significantly by continuing education workshops and/or supervision sessions that they arrange to have with pastoral counseling specialists or other mental health professionals. These experiences can increase pastoral skills in brief crisis counseling, referral counseling, and other short-term counseling that should be the focus of their counseling ministry.

Self-care to Avoid Professional Burnout

An overburdened pastor, clearly at his wit's end, phoned a pastoral counselor and asked, "What should I do with a depressed woman in my parish who is driving me up the wall? She keeps phoning and whining about her situation. She makes thinly veiled suicide threats at the same time she gives endless reasons why she can't or won't do what either her doctor or I recommend. I think she's got me trapped in her codependency web." In today's chaotic church and world it is not surprising that ministry burnout and burnup are epidemic. Working with numerous troubled people, some of whom not only have problems but also *are* problems, is stressful at best. Learning how to avoid burnout by regular self-care that nurtures wellness is essential.

A congregation's innovative program of mutually caring and enlivening can bring much-needed health nurture and renewal to caregivers, clergy and lay, as well as to many in a faith community and in its wider community. Such renewal often comes like refreshing rain to a parched land. To be effective growth nurturers, we caregivers must continue to grow. To be spiritual enliveners, we must stay alive spiritually. To enable healing, we must be vulnerable enough to face and accept our continuing need for healing. By so doing, our limitations become bridges and not barriers to helping other wounded persons. In my experience, this is the most challenging and difficult but also the most exciting part of being in mutual ministry.

Pastoral psychologist Donald B. Cozzens speaks from his long experience as a mentor and therapist for his fellow Catholic priests: "Never has the interior life of today's priest been so important to his spiritual and personal health and to his effectiveness as pastor and shepherd during this time of seeking and waiting."[3] It is clear that his statement is relevant to clergy of all denominations in this troubled transition time, which is also a time of hopeful birthing. This time of hope includes self-care of the interior life to empower deepening care for others.

Chronic Sleep Deprivation

Chronic sleep deprivation, or sleep debt, has become increasingly widespread among persons suffering from frantic, high-stress lifestyles and work addiction. Because pushing the limits is seen as normal behavior that is often rewarded in our society, the problem often goes unrecognized by victims and undiagnosed as well as untreated by healing professionals, including pastoral counselors.

William C. Dement is a leading pioneer in sleep medicine who chaired a National Commission on Sleep Disorders Research. He has conducted in-depth research and reported on the interrelated issues of persistent insomnia, snoring and sleep apnea, chronic fatigue syndrome, narcolepsy, circadian rhythms, dreaming and creativity, and sleep's crucial function in cell repair, vitality, longevity, and immune system protection from viruses, germs, and carcinogens. He points out that severe sleep deprivation has effects similar to alcohol intoxication in many ways and that very few health care providers are aware that we are a sleep-sick society: "For nearly half a century, a huge reservoir of knowledge about sleep, sleep deprivation, and sleep disorders has been building up behind a dam of pervasive lack of awareness. . . . We don't know how many preventable tragedies are occurring right now, today, this very instant. It is time to blow up the dam."[4]

Dement cites an extreme example of a huge, preventable sleep debt tragedy by pointing to the National Transportation Safety Board's final report on the Exxon *Valdez* disaster. It held that the direct cause of one of the nation's worst oil spills was the sleep deprivation of the third mate, who was at the helm and made deadly mistakes after only six hours of sleep in the previous forty-eight hours. Several studies show that several widely publicized airline disasters and countless fatal auto accidents were caused by sleep debt on the parts of pilots and drivers. He calls this warning a simple lifesaving principle: "If you become drowsy at any time during the day, you have a sizable sleep debt and you should resolve to be cautious in hazardous situations."

Adopting a sleep-smart lifestyle that recognizes the importance of healthy sleep often includes adopting strategies such as these:[5]

- Find out how much sleep you need in each twenty-four hours, and measure your sleep debt. Inventories for measuring this are available from sleep experts.[6] But you can simply use the basic question on which they are constructed: where are you on the daytime continuum from usually feeling vital, alert, and wide awake versus feeling drowsy, foggy, and let down?
- If you frequently feel drowsy or nod off unemotionally during the day, pay back your debt intentionally by going to bed earlier than usual and getting up later than usual, until you feel wide awake when you are awake. Taking naps is by far the most effective tool for coping with a temporary sleep crisis such as that caused by jet lag.
- Make sure that your usual sleeping place is dark and quiet and that you have a comfortable bed, bedclothes, covers, and temperature.
- Avoid caffeinated drinks in the evening. Also avoid chronic use of alcohol and sleeping pills to get to sleep—a practice that usually produces "drug tolerance," meaning needing to keep taking more to get the desired effect. Also avoid watching stimulating TV after 9:00 p.m.
- Have a regular bedtime, at least three hours after your evening meal, and get up at a regular time, both with only rare exceptions.
- Follow relaxing evening rituals such as taking a hot bath, listening to soothing music, or reading a few comforting or boring pages, letting drowsiness sneak up on you.
- Take regular refreshing, relatively brief siestas, a beneficial practice confirmed by research comparing the health of men in southern and northern Europe.
- Avoid upsetting arguments just before bedtime.
- Hold a peaceful mental image in your mind, like a quiet scene in nature.
- Let go of the day's cares by letting the divine Spirit take the night shift.

Like adopting a health-enhancing diet and exercising, becoming more sleep smart requires self-discipline and self-knowledge of one's organism's needs, including sleep needs. Sufferers from severe sleep debt resulting from chronic insomnia should be urged to try these strategies. If self-help does not suffice, referral to one of many accredited sleep disorder treatment centers is indicated.[7]

The Pastor's Personality

Empirical studies have identified three crucial counselor characteristics—often called the "therapeutic triad." When they are present in a helper and are perceived by the recipient, the relationship tends to be used by that person for healing and growth. They are congruence, nonpossessive warmth (caring and respect), and empathic understanding.

Congruence, in this context, means inner genuineness, integration, and openness. Carl Rogers observes, "The most basic learning for anyone who hopes to establish any kind of helping relationship is that it is safe to be transparently real." The opposite of congruence is "being a phony" or "putting on an act." In such persons, there is incongruence between their words and their real feelings.[8]

Persons who have had to hide their real feelings from others for extended periods in order to feel accepted eventually become unaware of many of their feelings. These repressed feelings produce emotional blind spots, frequently in the areas of hostility, aggressiveness, sexuality, and tenderness. A counselor's emotional blind spots prevent him or her from being inwardly congruent in those areas—from being the self he or she truly is. This keeps the person from relating therapeutically to others in these blocked-off areas.

To experience *unconditional positive regard* (Rogers's term for nonpossessive warmth)[9] is to experience the human equivalent of grace in a relationship. Grace is the love one does not have to earn because it is already there in a relationship. Actually it is only through the experience of a relationship in which one is loved (something very close, I believe, to what theologians call *agape*) that the individual can begin to feel a dawning respect for, an acceptance of, and finally even a fondness for oneself. One can thus begin to sense oneself as lovable and worthwhile, in spite of one's mistakes, and begin to feel love and tenderness for others.[10]

Unconditional positive regard is a blend of warmth, liking, caring, acceptance, interest, and respect for the person. A significant study by Julius Seeman "found that success in psychotherapy is closely associated with a strong and growing mutual liking and respect between client and therapist."[11] The counselor becomes a companion-guide in a warm, human relationship that helps clients find courage to face their situation, bear their load, or go on the often frightening journey into the unexplored areas of their personhood. Unconditional positive regard, in Martin Buber's terms, is the counselor's ability to establish I-Thou relationships.

Empathic understanding means entering the person's inner world of meanings and deep feelings through listening with caring awareness. The counseling pastor's continuing prayer might well be the hymn line, "Take the dimness of my soul away." Fortunately for most of us, even a "bumbling and faulty attempt to catch the confused complexities of the client's meanings" often is helpful to her or him.[12]

One barrier to empathic understanding is our defensive narcissism. To the extent that we are overly invested in ourselves, we find it impossible to enter another's inner world. Self-absorption and depth self-awareness are opposite psychological conditions. Self-centered persons are mainly aware of their own painful insecurity, inferiority feelings, and demanding need for affirmation and attention. Their consuming question, "Will I get my needs for approval satisfied?" blocks awareness of their deeper feelings and limits their capacity for empathy.

In addition to the three qualities of a good counselor just described, I would add a sturdy sense of one's identity as a person. A theological student, reflecting on a reality practice session where she was the "parishioner," said of the counselor: "I felt his compassion, but not the hope that his strength and know-how would help me pull myself together and set me up for a working-together relationship. I felt I had pulled him down in the hole with me." To avoid this, pastors need the firm sense of their identity and personal worth that are at the nucleus of ego strength. Counselors are able to be sensitive and responsive to the needs of others to the degree that they possess this centered awareness of their own value and personhood. Persons who are not centered are out of touch with the only secure locus for stable self-esteem and identity. They "give their power away" (as Gestalt therapists put it) by allowing others to define their worth by external evaluations.

A fifth essential quality in a counselor is the therapeutic attitude described by Henri Nouwen as that of the "wounded healer." This results from a vivid awareness of one's affinity with the sickness and sin, loneliness, alienation, and despair of the troubled person. This attitude begins to dawn as we pastors sense, in the presence of the person with alcoholism, psychosis, or suicidal impulses, that "there but for the grace of God go I!" It emerges more fully when we move beyond this to the deflating awareness, "There go I!" This feeling somehow lowers the walls that block the flow of healing forces in relationships.

Retaining this acceptance of our only partially healed brokenness is often difficult when one is "the helper." To identify with the essential humanness of despairing persons threatens our fragile defenses against our despair. To recognize that the regressed catatonic in a mental hospital is more like than different from oneself shakes the very foundations of our defensive self-image.[13] To accept this truth at a deep level requires an inward surrender of subtle feelings of self-idolatry and spiritual superiority. One of my students referred to this as "getting off the omnipotence kick." A potential advantage of growing older is that the accumulating blows of life may shatter to some degree our defensive facade of pseudo-omnipotence, which was easier to maintain in our youthful years. Even a partial surrender of one's defensive superiority feelings helps to open the door to mutually healing relationships. Somehow it melts a hole in the icy barrier of pride that keeps people—especially disturbed people—at a distance from us.

A sixth essential quality in counselors is personal aliveness. If pastoral counselors are enliveners—enablers of life in all its fullness in others—our most important task is to learn how to stay as fully alive as possible. Aliveness is contagious! So is deadness! Think for a moment of how weighed down you feel after spending even a short time with certain people. Compare this with the zestful aliveness that fills you after the same amount of time with others.

Imaging Exercise for Liberating and Playfulness

This valuable awareness exercise has two objectives. It is designed as a tool for encouraging self-liberation from oppressive belief systems, self-images, and circumstances. It also can enhance people's ability to enjoy the healing power of laughter and playfulness.

Instructions: Do whatever is needed to enable your mind-body-spirit organism to become more relaxed and more alert. / Form a clear picture in your mind of a box large and strong enough for a person to be inside. / Reflect on the meaning of the type of box you have chosen to create in your imagination. / Now, see yourself moving toward the box and getting inside. / Be inside the box for the next few minutes. If you are doing the exercise for self-care and learning as a caregiver, imagine that the box has been closed and locked from the outside. / Inside your box, push on its walls and ceiling, becoming aware that you are in a no-exit situation unless someone you ask for help chooses to help you get out. / Be aware that this is how many folk feel when they trust caregivers to hear, without judgment, their stories of their agonizing crises and problems in living. / As you experience being boxed in, ask yourself if there is something in your everyday life that feels like a box limiting your options and blocking your release. / Now, do whatever is necessary to get out of your box. If you have to ask for help, be aware of how you feel about being dependent on someone else for release.

As soon as you're outside the box, imagine being in a beautiful spring meadow. Create it as a safe, free place, perhaps with flowers, birds, fresh air, and a small stream. / Open your mind-body-spirit to be nurtured by nature in all seven dimensions of your life. / If you have trouble letting go to enjoy, let your inner child coach you to enhance your joy in being playful together without restraint there in the freedom of the meadow, enjoying the wonderful freedom and openness of the place. / Be aware of how you feel as your playful side enjoys this free place, compared with your experience inside the box. / Now, if you're playing alone, invite someone you love to play with you in the meadow to discover how your experience of playing is changed by sharing it with a special friend or family member. / If you want to find out how integrated your spirituality is with your playfulness, imagine that Jesus or a leading female spiritual figure is joining you to play in the meadow. /

Now, leave the meadow and return to where you left your box. / As you see the box again, how do you feel about it now, having enjoyed the freedom of the beautiful meadow? / If there is something you want to do to or with the box, go ahead. After all, it is your box. / Finish the exercise in whatever way you choose to give it a sense of closure for you. / Reflect on what you taught yourself by using this exercise as you did. If you are like me, you need to spend more time playing in your meadow and less time sitting in the boxes created by circumstances or the ones you unwittingly create for yourself. / If you enjoyed playing in the meadow, affirm your inner child for continuing to enjoy celebrating living. /

Depth Training in Creative Counseling

What kinds of learnings enable pastors to use the many facets of their complex personalities more creatively? Which experiences will enhance their inner congruence, warm caring, and empathic understanding; their sense of identity and worth; their capacity to use their brokenness as a healing resource; and their sense of aliveness? Carroll A. Wise puts his finger on the key: "The pastor needs to know himself [or herself] as well as to understand the dynamic processes of personality as they find expression in the counselee."[14] Being able to form a helping relationship with another is dependent on forming a "helping relationship to myself."[15] Our self-awareness catalyzes the process of increasing self-awareness in others. Our inner freedom helps awaken the freedom of the spirit in others. Rogers summarizes, "The degree to which I can create relationships which facilitate the growth of others as separate persons is a measure of the growth I have achieved in myself."[16] Grace communicators must be growing persons. Renewal agents must know firsthand the struggles, discipline, and joy of ongoing personal renewal. Staying alive requires continuing to grow through all of our lives, in our awareness of here-and-now experience, particularly of our inner depths. As Dag Hammarskjöld observes, "The longest journey is the journey inwards."[17] We can establish deep, transforming relationships with others only to the degree that we are in touch with our depths and are open to continuing transformation within ourselves.

What experiences available to pastors stimulate personal growth most effectively? Academic courses, seminars, and books per se usually have limited effects on this level, although they may be valuable on a cognitive and skill-building level. Six types of experiences provide, in varying degrees, the deeper self-encounter that accelerates the counselor's personal growth: psychotherapy, clinical pastoral education, supervision of one's counseling, growth groups, reality practice, and spiritual disciplines. The learning accruing from these experiences, to quote a choice Shakespearean line, "adds a precious seeing to the eye."[18] It increases the capacity for "thou-ness" in relationships.

Optimally, personal psychotherapy should be an integral part of the training of every pastor. Anyone's ministry can be deepened and enriched by it. Psychotherapy tends to sharpen one's interpersonal awareness and makes previously unused facets of one's personality available for more person-enhancing relationships. A pastor's personality is her or his only instrument for communicating the good news (through relationships). Psychotherapy is a means of removing the inner blocks that diminish the ability of one's personality to be the fine, effective instrument it can be. Psychotherapy cannot and need not eradicate all inner blocks and conflicts. It can make one aware enough of those that remain to drastically reduce their interference with growthful relationships. Without personal therapy, some pastors distort their counseling by projecting their inner conflicts and repressed impulses onto relationships without realizing it.

For many pastors, group therapy is more effective than individual psychotherapy because it offers wider opportunities to become aware of interpersonal distortions and transference problems, to be confronted with one's unconstructive attitudes and behavior, and to experiment with creative relating in the group. Individual therapy is indicated where distortions in relating stem mainly from need deprivation in the preschool years. Group therapy is ideal for rectifying distortions derived primarily from later inadequacies in peer relationships. Ideally a seminarian's or pastor's training therapy should include both.

It is imperative that psychotherapy, individual or group, be done by a highly trained professional person—a specialist in pastoral counseling, a psychiatrist, a social worker, or a clinical psychologist. Because of the extensive training required and the relative scarcity of qualified therapists, the cost is usually high. Ordinarily group therapy is less expensive than individual. But whatever the cost, personal psychotherapy is a valuable investment in one's future and in one's ability to relate more growthfully in all dimensions of ministry. Pastors often have to make financial sacrifices to obtain therapy. But those who do so usually discover that it is the most valuable learning experience of their entire education, paying rich dividends in subsequent years—both personally and professionally.

To help pastors experience healing and growth, therapists should be thoroughly trained in depth psychotherapy. This should include their own personal therapy. They should be skilled in dealing with unconscious material—dreams, fantasies, free associations, and transference feelings. Based on my experiences through the years with several therapists who had a variety of orientations, I would recommend an eclectic therapist who understands psychodynamics theory from the depth psychologists (particularly Freud and Jung) but who uses the more active methods of the contemporary therapies, especially Gestalt, psychosynthesis, and the body therapies. These methods tend to facilitate more rapid healing and growth than do unmodified psychoanalytic methods. To the pastor contemplating therapy, I would pass along the words that Fritz Kunkel inscribed on the flyleaf of my copy of one of his books: "Good luck on the journey down and up!" (I didn't understand his words until years later.)

Clinical pastoral education (CPE) also provides a depth encounter with oneself. In some four hundred accredited centers in North America, mainly in general and psychiatric hospitals and in correctional institutions (but also in a few parishes), theological students and pastors spend eleven weeks or longer working under supervision (by a chaplain supervisor) with people in crises.

Clinical training has many values. It forces the student to ask searching and sometimes disturbing questions concerning the dynamic meaning of religion in troubled people's lives. It raises the confronting question of relevancy: How is my understanding of religion relevant to the real needs of this mental patient (or delinquent, drug addict, or cancer patient)? CPE helps reveal the strengths and weaknesses of one's pattern of relating in all aspects of one's ministry. It provides opportunities to learn to work with the other helping professions and to define one's unique professional function and pastoral identity in relation to them and in the light of one's tradition. CPE also involves participation in a personal growth group that usually is very valuable.

Parish ministers who take a three-month sabbatical from their churches for CPE (as I did after nearly a decade in the parish ministry) usually find it to be one of the richest learning experiences of their lives. Some accredited centers offer extended quarters on a two-days-per-week basis for those who cannot arrange to take full-time CPE. Clinical training, both full- and part-time, offers unique opportunities to strengthen not just one's counseling, but one's total ministry to persons.

One of the finest resources for enhancing interpersonal skills is at the fingertips of most pastors: the opportunity to obtain supervision of one's pastoral relationships—including one's counseling. Competent supervision is the most direct and efficient way of upgrading interpersonal skills. To help seminarians and pastors shape and strengthen their professional identity, at least a part of one's supervision should be done by trained and experienced clergy supervisors who understand and appreciate the church context, the faith perspective, and the pastoral role in the faith community. Any pastor who lives within reasonable driving distance of a well-trained pastoral psychotherapist or chaplain supervisor may obtain this valuable training by a modest investment of time and money. The procedure is simply to arrange with that person to have weekly or biweekly supervision sessions of one's caring, counseling, growth group leadership and other pastoral relationships.

Most pastoral counseling specialists and mental health professionals welcome the opportunity to do supervision and consultation with pastors. Small groups of pastors (two to eight) can make arrangements for group supervision, dividing the cost among them. Significant new resources for enabling parish pastors to increase their counseling skills have emerged in recent years in the training programs developed by a growing number of church-related counseling centers. Ideally, church-related counseling programs should devote at least one-fourth of their staff time to providing continuing education and training for pastors!

A West Coast pastoral counseling center sponsors pastoral case conferences following this pattern: the group, limited to ten parish pastors, meets once a week for two hours. The leader is the center's director, a pastor with advanced training in counseling. At each session, one pastor makes a detailed presentation of one of his or her counseling experiences. Emergency counseling problems are discussed as they are raised by group members. Occasionally the leader highlights a new development in pastoral counseling. Audio- and videotapes of actual counseling sessions are used in the supervision, as are reality practice techniques. For this service, each pastor pays a modest sum per session to the center.

Supervision is potentially more widely and readily available than any other form of counselor training. In many situations, all that is required is for the pastor to take the initiative in arranging with a therapist for such an experience. In ongoing supervisory groups, the interaction often approaches the group therapy level. Depth understanding of any counseling relationship throws as much light on the counselor as on the counselee. Like CPE, supervision can sharpen a pastor's self-awareness as it strengthens her or his ability to help troubled persons. Supervision groups often become peer support groups, thus helping to meet one of the most pressing needs of many pastors.

Growth groups offer another valuable learning experience for pastors, though they are not a substitute for personal therapy, clinical training, and in-depth supervision. Such groups are widely used in workshops and human relations labs to enhance the participants' skills in relating. For more than a decade, the seminary where I taught required a group experience called "Personal Growth through Group Interaction" for all first-year theological students. The aim of these sharing groups was to enhance students' abilities to communicate and relate in healing, growthful ways. A research project that studied these groups, and comparable groups at two other seminaries, demonstrated the value of even two semesters in growth groups as part of preparation for person-centered ministry.

The ministry can be a lonely and depleting profession because of the multiplicity of contacts with needy people. One way to refuel one's energies is to establish a peer support nurture group. To be effective, pastoral support groups must learn how to interrupt the "games that pastors play" and relate to the real hopes and hurts, the real needs, of persons in our demanding profession. Pastors and their spouses should do whatever is necessary to find or cocreate (with other individuals and couples) a support group in which they are not the leaders. One's spouse can give valuable support, but it is also important to have a support group in which both spouses receive as well as give nurturing care. A support system is especially helpful in one's early ministry and when one is going through a crisis in one's personal life or ministry.

Practicing the spiritual disciplines of prayer and meditation is vital to pastors. By keeping open to our true spiritual center—the Higher Self within us—we are in touch with God's spirit, the Source of aliveness. Learning a simple method of meditation can enrich experiences of prayer and help one open the sluice gate on the inner channel through which flows the renewing energy of God's love—within us and through our relationship to others.

Here are some suggestions for self-nurture for the pastoral care of pastors:

1. Make some time in your daily schedule for yourself, to do something you find satisfying and renewing. Let your inner Child (in transactional analysis terms) play regularly. Give yourself several minivacations each day—a few minutes to do something really fun. (This will feel frivolous to your inner Parent.) No one can be a nurturing Parent and/or Adult all the time.

2. Give yourself a gift each day—something you find satisfying and nurturing.

3. Take a full day off each week, the equivalent of a long weekend off each month with no professional duties, and a study leave in addition to a vacation each year. You may have to get away from your home base, the telephone, fax, and pager to have these renewal breaks.

4. Try to be realistic in the goals for your ministry and your life. Stop trying to be the "bionic minister."[19]

5. Jog and/or do yoga each day (or some other form of enjoyable exercise) to reduce tension and tune up your cardiovascular system.

6. Develop various techniques of stress reduction and inner quieting that work for you, and practice at least one of them every day.

7. Find a person or small group with whom you can let down your hair, relax and ventilate the frustrations that have built up, discuss personal as well as professional issues, and get affirmation and objective feedback.

8. Let yourself laugh regularly—with others and at yourself. Someone has called laughing "internal jogging." Its therapeutic, stress-reducing effects are well documented.

9. Risk letting your vulnerability show more, but in safe contexts. Sitting on a ministerial pedestal is not only lonely but also keeps one from receiving the mutual nurture of close relationships.

10. Treat yourself to regular experiences of intellectual stimulation such as a workshop or continuing education course, time to immerse yourself in an exciting book, or a long, refreshing conversation with a close friend.
11. When your inner flow of creative energy gets blocked, treat yourself to a "therapeutic retreat," some reenergizing sessions with a competent therapist.

Understanding Basic Concepts

I have discussed clinical learning and personal growth first to emphasize their foundational importance in any sound approach to counselor training and renewal. The deepening of one's ability to relate is essential if conceptual tools are to be useful. Otherwise the mastery of concepts can make one a clever technician but not a growth enabler. But as pastors grow as whole persons, their conceptual grasp of psychodynamics and counseling theories becomes increasingly valuable in ministering to troubled persons. Through disciplined reading and study, including continuing education courses, a pastor or theological student should acquire a workable understanding of the following:

1. Normal personality growth and development (including child, adolescent, and adult psychology). Erik Erikson's stages and more recent studies of the special aspects of adult life stages and the unique development of women are useful tools for understanding the life cycle.[20]
2. Marriage and family dynamics, enrichment, and counseling, including changing women's-men's identities, relationships, and roles.
3. Group dynamics.
4. Psychopathology (abnormal psychology).
5. Methods of individual counseling.
6. Growth groups and group counseling methods.
7. Community referral resources.
8. Personality and cultures (socioeconomic-political forces as they influence personality health and growth in one's own culture and others).
9. History and theory of pastoral care.
10. Theology and counseling (including the theology of counseling and the dynamic role of religion in human wholeness and brokenness).

This list may arouse the response expressed by Chaucer's line: "The lyf so short, the craft so long to lerne."[21] But these are fundamental subject areas that should be mastered at some point during a pastor's education—in college, seminary, or continuing education—if she or he is to be equipped for growthful work with people in all dimensions of ministry.

A major study of theological education stated,

> When one considers the revitalization of much in the theological curriculum today through new emphases in psychology and pastoral counseling, it must be concluded that a significant new turn in the education of the ministry has been taken. Powerful new resources are available throughout the curriculum because of work in this field.[22]

Much has happened in seminaries and in continuing education during the last few decades to make these powerful resources more available to seminarians and pastors. However, much more needs to be done, particularly in supervised education, before seminary graduates in general will enter parishes with the basic psychological understanding and competence in counseling that they sorely need. Theological students should be urged to take at least one quarter of CPE during their seminary career, preferably after the first year. Pastors who are aware of needing more counseling skills should explore, with nearby seminaries, CPE supervisors, or pastoral counseling centers with training programs, the possibility of setting up the continuing education opportunities they need. Most DMin (Doctor of Ministry) programs offer pastors the option of focusing on pastoral psychology or counseling. Seminary PhD/ThD programs in pastoral counseling are designed to equip specialists to staff pastoral counseling centers (and other specialized ministries).

Denominational leaders have a key role in helping enhance the quality of the interpersonal ministry by their clergy. Increasingly pastors sense that intentional career planning and lifelong continuing education must include personal and professional growth experiences that enable them to learn the new concepts and methods that are emerging continually in the counseling field. Denominations should provide experiential learning events focusing on new approaches to this pastoral art. In addition, denominational decision makers should make personal therapy and marriage counseling readily available to clergy and their families when this kind of help is needed. Such pastoral counseling specialists know the frustrations, problems, and rewards of the ministry from the inside. They have this distinct advantage over secular therapists in helping clergy and their spouses deal with the common issues of role identity and conflict.

To keep abreast of new thinking and research in the field of pastoral psychology and counseling, pastors should read one or both of the two leading journals in the field: *Journal of Pastoral Care* (jpcp.org), published by several professional associations in the pastoral care field, including the Association for Clinical Pastoral Education and the American Association of Pastoral Counselors, and *Pastoral Psychology* (www.springer.com/psychology /journal/11089).

Pastors who emphasize counseling in their ministry should join the American Association of Pastoral Counselors as pastoral affiliates or as members, depending on the category for which their training in the field qualifies them. A primary goal of AAPC is to help raise the general level of training and practice of pastoral counseling in all settings in which it occurs. Participating in the national convention and regional meetings, and reading the newsletter of this professional association, can help a counseling pastor keep in touch with innovative developments in this field. A growing network of AAPC-accredited training programs and centers offers opportunities to keep one's caring and counseling tools sharp through individual and/or group supervision, workshops, and other training experiences.

Some Final Perspectives

In the practice of the counseling art, it is helpful to remember these perspective-giving facts:

1. The pastor's focus on the acute needs of individuals who seek counseling should always be balanced by developing a broad ministry of pastoral care by lay caregivers as well as the pastor.

2. One can help many troubled people without becoming a specialist in pastoral counseling and therapy. At every level of growth in caring skills—professional and lay—there are countless opportunities to be of genuine help.

3. Every pastoral counselor, however skilled, fails to help some people. It is good to remember the human limitations of all of us counselors and of all helping relationships. Jesus' lack of success with Judas, in spite of their close association, is a case in point. As in Jesus' parable of the sower, the seeds in counseling do not always fall on receptive soil. The counselor's job is to keep sowing, trusting the God-given growth forces in people and relationships, and remembering that, at best, he or she is an imperfect instrument for communicating healing resources beyond himself or herself.

4. Increasing one's caring and counseling skills is a continuing, lifelong challenge. One never "arrives." The heart of the counseling art can be learned only by experience. However, this learning is accelerated immensely if one's experiences are exposed to systematic reflection and evaluation. This is why supervision, consultation, and reality practice can be so fruitful.

5. Having examined a variety of theories and methods of counseling, it is important to reemphasize the heart of the matter. Without minimizing the importance of theories and methods of counseling, it is important to remember Jung's advice.: "Learn your theories as well as you can, but put them aside when you touch the miracle of the living soul. Not theories but your own creative individuality alone must decide."[23] Engraved in every pastor's mind should be these words: *Caring relationships—the instruments of help!*

Without a warm, accepting relationship, the methods of counseling described in these pages become mere techniques—sterile, manipulative, and ineffective. But when skill-fully employed within an accepting, energized, caring relationship, they become the means by which that relationship's healing power is released.

6. It is liberating to remember that all healing and all growth are gifts of the creative Spirit of life whom we call God. Healing and growth occur in counseling relationships because persons have become more open in their minds and bodies and relationships to the re-creating energies of Spirit. As I am often aware in my counseling, healing and growth may occur in spite of, not because of, what a counselor says or does. This aware-ness is no excuse for doing poor counseling. It is a reminder that at best a counselor is a finite and often fractured channel for the healing power of the universe! Paul Tillich once declared,

> The power which makes acceptance possible is the resource in all pastoral care. It must be effec-tive in him who helps, and it must become effective in him who is helped. . . . This means that both the pastor and the counselee . . . are under the power of something which transcends both of them. One can call this power the new creature or the New Being. The pastoral counselor can be of help only if he himself is grasped by this power.[24]

With all the encouraging developments in the field, the helping potential of the min-istry of caring and counseling has only begun to be released. As more and more of us strengthen our competence as counselors, this potential wellspring of healing and growth will become more available to the millions who desperately need what it can give. The challenge that confronts each of us is to help release this potential by becom-ing incarnation counselors, persons whose imperfect relationships somehow enable the liberating word to become flesh and to dwell in and among us with healing power—heal-ing us as well as those with whom we minister.

Our heritage from the past is rich indeed! Current developments show that the field is alive and growing. The future is pregnant with exciting possibilities for new ministries to people. The continuing rebirth of this art of ministry depends on the willingness of people like you and me to dream and to do, to use our imaginations and invest our ener-gies in developing innovative ministries of caring and counseling. The living Spirit calls us to participate joyfully in cocreating a future in which the church's tremendous unde-veloped potentialities for healing and wholeness can be actualized.

Whether you are a beginner or a veteran in the ministry of caregiving, I wish you courage and challenge, fulfillment, joy, and *shalom* on your continuing journey as a grow-ing participant in the lighthouse rescue team of your church and community, and as a growing gardener who cultivates healing and wholeness, both in yourself and in those whose lives are touched by your spiritually empowered ministry.

Recommended Reading

Doehring, Carrie. *Taking Care: Monitoring Power Dynamics and Relational Boundaries in Pastoral Care and Counseling*. Nashville: Abingdon Press, 1995.

Harbaugh, Gary L. *Pastor as Person: Maintaining Personal Integrity*. Minneapolis: Augsburg Fortress, 1984.

Koenig, Harold G., and Daniel L. Langford. *The Pastor's Family: The Challenges of Family*. Binghamton, N.Y.: Haworth Press, 1998.

Kornfield, Margaret. *Cultivating Wholeness: A Guide to Care and Counseling in Faith Communities*. New York: Continuum International Publishing Company, 1998.

Lehr, Fred. *Clergy Burnout: Recovering from the 70 Hour Week . . . and Other Self-Defeating Practices*. Minneapolis: Augsburg Fortress, 2006.

Melander, Rochelle, and Harold Eppley. *The Spiritual Leader's Guide to Self-Care*. Washington, D.C.: Alban Institute, 2002.

Oswald, Roy M. *Clergy Self-Care: Finding a Balance for Effective Ministry*. Washington, D.C.: Alban Institute, 1991.

NOTES

1. Pastoral Care and Counseling: Challenges and Opportunities

1. This parable originally appeared in an article by Theodore O. Wedel, "Evangelism—the Mission of the Church to Those Outside Her Life," in *The Ecumenical Review* (October 1953): 24. The above paraphrases the original by Richard Wheatcroft which appeared in Letters to Laymen, May-June 1962.

2. Margaret Zipse Kornfeld, *Cultivating Wholeness: A Guide to Care and Counseling in Faith Communities* (New York: Continuum International Publishing Group, 1998), 167.

3. Wayne E. Oates, *An Introduction to Pastoral Counseling* (Nashville: Broadman Press, 1959), vi.

4. The Gallup survey on trust was conducted in 1990. A 1985 Gallup poll found that religious counseling was given a "helpful" rating by 87 percent compared with 71 percent for physicians and professional counselors.

5. This survey, funded by AAPC and the Samaritan Institute, was completed in November 2000 by Greenberg Quinlan Research, Inc., of Washington, D.C. It had a margin of error of +/- 3.2. Although it focused on pastoral counseling specialists, as in AAPC, most of its findings are also relevant to counseling by parish clergy. C. Roy Woodruff, "New National Survey Powerfully Affirms Desire for Pastoral Counseling!" in *Currents; A Newsletter for Members of AAPC* 39, no. 2 (Spring 2001): 1–2.

6. In terms of the financial cost of providing caregiving training and counseling services, two-thirds of all contributions to nonprofit organizations in this country go to religious groups.

7. John Patton, *Pastoral Care in Context: An Introduction to Pastoral Care* (Louisville: Westminster John Knox Press, 1993), 56.

8. Many pastoral counseling specialists mainly do psychotherapy, even though the term *counselors* is retained in their primary professional guild—the American Association of Pastoral Counselors.

9. Because inclusiveness is absolutely crucial in pastoral caregiving today, it will be explored in detail (see chapter 17).

10. William A. Clebsch and Charles R. Jaekle, *Pastoral Care in Historical Perspective* (Englewood Cliffs, N.J.: Prentice-Hall, 1964), 79.

11. *Letters and Papers from Prison* (New York: Macmillan, 1972), 124.

12. See Wayne Oates, *Pastoral Counseling* (Philadelphia: Westminster Press, 1974), 11–12.

13. Tillich made this statement in his address at the National Conference on Clinical Pastoral Education, Atlantic City, New Jersey, November 1956.

14. Clergy are the only counseling professionals whose usual training includes disciplined study of philosophy, systematic and pastoral theology, individual and social ethics, biblical studies, church history, world religions, and—very important for skilled counseling—psychology and sociology of religion, meaning the psychosocial understanding of religious behaviors.

15. The development of crisis hot lines and walk-in crisis clinics to which troubled people can go without an appointment shows that some mental health professionals are aware of the practical value of what has been clergy's availability through the centuries.

16. Knowing that their jobs may be in jeopardy if they alienate powerful lay leaders gives clergy an appropriate reason not to offend them by being totally frank.

17. For this apt image, I am indebted to Daniel Yankelovich's *New Rules: Searching for Self-Fulfillment in a World Turned Upside Down* (New York: Random House, 1981). He describes changes in the closing decades of the last century that were radical but not nearly as profound as those occurring in this new century.

18. "The Therapeutic Tradition's Theological and Ethical Commitment Viewed through Its Pedagogical Practices: A Tradition in Transition," in Rodney Hunter and Pamela Couture, eds., *Pastoral Care and Social Conflict* (Nashville: Abingdon Press, 1995), 32, 43.

19. For more on this issue see Nicholas Negroponte, *Being Digital* (New York: Vantage Press, 1995), and John M. Grohol, *The Insider's Guide to Mental Health Resources Online* (New York: Guilford Press, 1996).

20. Christie Cozad Neuger, "Reclaiming Pastoral Counseling as a Ministry of the Church: An Opinion and an Invitation," *Journeys* (Winter–Spring 2001): 16.

2. A Model for Spiritually Centered Holistic Pastoral Caregiving

1. *Holistic* is used in these pages as a rough synonym for wholeness, well-being, wellness, and positive health.

2. Even pastoral counseling specialists with postseminary training in psychological and psychotherapeutic theory and methods were first trained as generalists in their profession.

3. Tom Munnecke and Heather Wood Ian, "Jonas Salk's Questions," *A Transformational Notion of Health*, November 8, 2000, http://www.munnecke.com/papers/D20.doc.

4. I am indebted to Gary Gunderson for introducing me to the transformational model of health and the pivotal thought of Tom Munnecke. (See Munnecke, "Assumptions of the Transactional Model of Health," www.Munnecke.com/papers/D19.doc, September 2000.)

5. Ursula K. Le Guin, *A Fisherman of the Inland Sea: Science Fiction Stories* (New York: HarperCollins, 1994), 147.

6. For a discussion of cognitive-behavioral and other short-term methods in pastoral caregiving, see Howard Stone, *Brief Pastoral Counseling: Short-term Approaches and Strategies* (Minneapolis: Augsburg Fortress Press, 1994), and *Strategies for Brief Pastoral Counseling* (Minneapolis: Augsburg Fortress Press, 2001).

7. Jill Freedman and Gene Coombs, *Narrative Therapy* (New York: W. W. Norton and Company, 1996), 69.

8. Ibid.

9. For more information about postmodernism in pastoral care and counseling, see Nancy Ramsay, ed., *Pastoral Care and Counseling: Redefining the Paradigm* (Nashville: Abingdon Press, 2004). For more information about narrative counseling theory in pastoral care, see Christie Cozad Neuger's *Counseling Women: A Narrative, Pastoral Approach* (Minneapolis: Fortress Press, 2001), Edward Wimberly's *Claiming God: Reclaiming Dignity* (Nashville: Abingdon Press, 2004), and Andrew Lester's *Hope in Pastoral Care and Counseling* (Louisville: Westminster John Knox Press, 1995).

10. One resource for the kind of coaching being discussed here from a pastoral perspective is Neuger's *Counseling Women*. A secular approach to counseling is Laura Whitworth, Henry Kimsey-House, and Phil Sandahl, *Co-Active Coaching: New Skills for Coaching People toward Success in Work and Life* (Palo Alto, Calif.: Davies-Black Publishing, 1998).

11. Neuger, *Counseling Women*, 60. I also identify in this chapter that the image of a God who destroys the entire Egyptian army is a problematic drawback in the exodus story.

12. Ibid., 13, 16.

13. For an in-depth analysis and pastoral care proposals regarding interculturality, see Emmanuel Lartey, *In Living Color,* 2nd ed. (London: Jessica Kingsley Publishers, 2003).

14. "Doing Well by Doing Good," *Wellness Letter* (School of Public Health, University of California, Berkeley) 18 (January 2002): 1.

15. For a variety of insights and methods for ministry in all the dimensions of life, see Howard Clinebell, *Well Being: A Personal Plan for Exploring and Enriching the Seven Dimensions of Life* (San Francisco: HarperSanFrancisco, 1997).

16. Personal communication with Howard Clinebell, December 1981.

17. E-mail from Cecilia O. Lioanag, Director of Services, Well-Being Foundation, Inc., Quezon City, Philippines, April 24, 2002. In her gracious spirit, Cecilia was writing to say, "Thank you for introducing the framework to me and to all those who have found it helpful in their work with themselves and in helping others." I remember getting to know Cecilia during a workshop I was leading in the Philippines on the seven-dimensions model, soon after my book *Well Being* was first published. With no previous knowledge of my writings, she had launched the People's Well-Being Center in Manila some years before that time. Both of us were pleased to discover our shared interest in wholeness. When the original publisher of *Well Being,* HarperSanFrancisco, informed her that another printing was not planned, she arranged to keep the book available by having it published in the Philippines.

18. Daniel Goleman, *Emotional Intelligence* (New York: Bantam Books, 1995).

19. Kennith Paul Kramer, *Martin Buber's* I and Thou: *Practicing Living Dialogue* (New York: Paulist Press, 2003), 43.

20. Neuger, *Counseling Women,* 1.

21. Richard W. Voss, "Pastoral Social Ministry in the Ecosystem of the Poor: Breaking through the Illusions," *Journal of Pastoral Care* 47, no. 2 (Summer 1993): 105–6.

22. I (HC) remember with gratitude the times I met with Tai-Young Lee and her staff at her center in Seoul that provides sorely needed legal aid to women who are poor, victims of sexism, and often trapped in marriages disabled by domestic violence. For more about her, see the "Window of Wholeness" devoted to her in *Well Being,* 271–72.

23. I (HC) discovered this statement at Chapman University in Orange, California, where it is a part of its Albert Schweitzer Exhibit.

24. K. Lauren de Boer coined this term in "Inhabiting the Living Present," *EarthLight: The Magazine of Spiritual Ecology* (Winter 2001): 5.

25. "Twentieth Century: Striking Developments and Policy Lessons," chapter 5 of *World Economic Outlook: Asset Prices and the Business Cycle: A Survey by the Staff of the International Monetary Fund* (May 2000); online at the International Monetary Fund's website: www.imf.org/external/pubs/ft/weo/2000/01/pdf/chapter5.pdf.

26. Numerous studies confirm that well-being is enhanced through a healthy relationship with nature. For example, one study of children in schools in three states revealed that children learn faster and score higher on standardized tests in classrooms with windows than in rooms with no windows. Their teachers were also more awake and enlivening. See "Students Learn Faster in Rooms with Sunlight, Study Shows," *Santa Barbara News-Press,* July 1, 1999, A14. Another study found that children who moved to high-rise apartments with a lot of trees showed significant improvement in cognitive functioning within a year after the move, compared to their functioning when living in high-rise apartments without trees in the environment. See Nancy M. Wells,

"At Home with Nature: Effects of 'Greenness' on Children's Cognitive Functioning," *Environment and Behavior* vol. 32, no. 6 (November 2000): 775–95.

27. William A. Clebsch and Charles R. Jaekle, *Pastoral Care in Historical Perspective* (Englewood Cliffs, N.J.: Prentice-Hall, 1964), 33. The authors acknowledge their indebtedness to Seward Hiltner for his delineation of the first three functions, ibid., 9.

3. The History, Mission, and Theological-Biblical Foundations of Pastoral Caregiving

1. Columnist Maureen Dowd attributes this image to historian Daniel Boorstin in her essay "The Search for Authenticity," *Santa Barbara News-Press*, December 21, 1999, A13.

2. For an insightful overview of today's pastoral care field, from the perspective of a female pastoral care specialist, see Bonnie Miller-McLemore's first chapter in Jeanne Stevenson Moessner, *Through the Eyes of Women* (Minneapolis: Augsburg Fortress, 1996).

3. See Anton Boisen, *The Explanation of the Inner World* (New York: Willet, Clark & Co., 1936). Russel Dicks was my first teacher of pastoral care and counseling.

4. From his wide experience of leadership in the American and international pastoral care movement, John Patton identifies three paradigms in pastoral care's history, each still having values worth retaining and reinterpreting. The protracted *classical paradigm*, with an emphasis on the caring elements in Christian theology and tradition, spanned the centuries from the church's beginnings to the advent of modern psychology and psychotherapy. This launched the half century of the CPE *paradigm* that emphasized the person giving and receiving pastoral care. He labels the contemporary model as the *communal context paradigm*. It brings together the "biblical tradition's presentation of a God who cares and who forms those who have been claimed as God's own into a community celebrating that care and extending it to others" with contemporary understandings of caring social systems, the caregiving of the laity, and the many settings in which pastoral care occurs. *Pastoral Care in Context: An Introduction to Pastoral Care* (Louisville: Westminster John Knox Press, 1993), 5.

5. Christie Cozad Neuger, *Counseling Women: A Narrative, Pastoral Approach* (Minneapolis: Fortress, 2001), 56–63.

6. Some critics of my holistic approach have described it as "New Age." The guiding model in this book affirms certain neglected emphases in traditional theology that have parallels with New Age beliefs. These include recognizing the wealth of human gifts, affirming persons' strengths, aiming at enabling them to develop more of their God-given assets, and being open to learn from other religious worldviews, not just those of the West. But the biblically grounded model differs profoundly from many New Age beliefs in four respects. First, in contrast to New Age hyperindividualism, it understands full individual well-being as possible only in health-nurturing interpersonal and community relations. Second, it recognizes the reality of human sin, evil, and brokenness, in contrast to the superficial optimism of New Age thinking. Third, in contrast to the amorphous New Age spirituality, it emphasizes the crucial importance for wholeness of relationship with God. Fourth, it understands justice as an essential part of healing and wholeness, not just love and peace, as in much New Age thought.

7. Daniel Day Williams, *The Minister and the Cure of Souls* (New York: Harper & Row, 1977), 15.

8. Ibid, 13.

9. Neuger, *Counseling Women*, 59.

10. Rollo May, *The Courage to Create* (New York: Bantam Books, 1975), 134.

11. Paraphrased from Tillich's *Systematic Theology*, vol. 2 (Chicago: University of Chicago Press, 1957), 60.

12. Elisabeth Schüssler Fiorenza attributes the word to Ada Maria Isasi Diaz. In a presentation to the Women's Ordination Conference, July 2003, Fiorenza said, " We have come from near and far to be church—a kindom of priests—to use a term coined by *mujerista* theologian Ada Maria Isasi Diaz." See Elisabeth Schüssler Fiorenza, "We Are Church—A Kindom of Priests," *WOW* (July 22, 2005).

13. Don Chinula, *Building King's Beloved Community: Foundations for Pastoral Care and Counseling with the Oppressed* (Cleveland: United Church Press, 1997), 54.

14. From the URI brochure. For more information on this movement, go to its website, www.uri.org.

15. For more on partnering with nature in ministry, see Mary Elizabeth Moore, *Ministering with the Earth* (St. Louis: Chalice Press, 1998). For an in-depth exploration of the theological issues in ecology, see "Spiritual, Ethical, Cosmological, and Meaning-of-Life Issues in Ecotherapy and Ecoeducation," in *Ecotherapy*, chapter 4.

16. In a classic statement, pioneer existentialist psychiatrist Ludwig Binswanger made this point forcefully. See Ulrich Sonnemann, *Existence and Therapy* (New York: Grune & Stratton, 1954), 343.

4. *Foundational Skills for Most Types of Caring and Counseling*

1. See Robert R. Carkhuff and William A. Anthony, *The Skills of Helping* (Amherst, Mass.: Human Resource Development Press, 1979).

2. I have added three other responses to the five (EISPU) described by Porter in *An Introduction to Therapeutic Counseling* (Boston: Houghton Mifflin, 1950), 201. Because Porter was writing about counseling from a Rogerian client-centered orientation, he emphasizes strongly the value of Understanding responses and underplays the value of other types of response.

3. Adapted in part from Porter, *An Introduction to Therapeutic Counseling*, 12. Here is the key to this exercise: (1) PF=Probing for Feelings; (2) I=Interpretive; (3) PI=Probing for Information; (4) E=Evaluative; (5) S=intended to be Supportive but actually not effective as such; (6) U=Understanding; (7) S=genuinely Supportive; (8) C=Clarifying; (9) A=Advising.

4. See the fifth edition (Pacific Grove, Calif.: Brooks/Cole, 1995). Also see Egan's companion training manual, *Exercises in Helping Skills* (Monterey, Calif.: Brooks/Cole, 1975). Allen E. Ivey offers another systematic method of learning basic counselor skills. He calls it "microtraining." The approach uses video feedback to teach the skills in sequence. See Allen E. Ivey and Jerry Authier, *Microtraining*, 2nd ed. (Springfield, Ill.: Charles C. Thomas, 1978).

5. From the Greek word *maieutikos*, "midwife."

6. R. D. Quinn, *Psychotherapist's Expression as an Index of the Quality of Early Therapeutic Relationships*, (PhD dissertation, University of Chicago, 1950), cited by Carl Rodgers in *On Becoming a Person* (Boston: Houghton Mifflin, 1961), 44.

7. *Learning to Live in the World: Earth Poems* by William Stafford, selected by Jerry Watson and Laura Apol Obbink (San Diego: Harcourt Brace, 1994), 65.

8. Nelle Morton, *The Journey Is Home* (Boston: Beacon Press, 1985), 127–28.

9. Dietrich Bonhoeffer, *Life Together* (San Francisco: Harper & Bros., 1954), 97–98.

10. William Shakespeare, *Henry IV*, part 2, act 1, scene 2, lines 138–40.

11 For more on how problems can be totally defining of people, see Michael White and David Epston, *Narrative Means to Therapeutic Ends* (New York: Norton, 1990).

12. Christie Cozad Neuger, *Counseling Women: A Narrative, Pastoral Approach* (Minneapolis: Fortress Press, 2001), ix.

13. See Maxine Glaz, "Reconstructing the Pastoral Care of Women," *Second Opinion* 17, no. 2 (October 1991): 95–107. She gives an example of a pastor encouraging catharsis of many details of a woman incest survivor's traumatic memories. The woman became agitated, depressed, and suicidal as a result.

14. In deciding which type of caregiving particular persons may find most helpful, bear in mind the differences as well as the overlap among pastoral care, pastoral counseling, and pastoral psychotherapy. These distinctions were described in the definitional section of chapter 1.

15. (Minneapolis: Augsburg Fortress Press, 1998), 3.

16. See Neuger, *Counseling Women*, 37–38. She points out that the diagnostic symptoms of so-called borderline personality—rage, confusion, low self-esteem, emotional swings, feelings of emptiness—are very similar to the adaptive responses of many women when they become aware of their oppression in our sexist society.

17. A similar approach should be used if one wishes to tape-record sessions in longer-term counseling: "I'd like to tape our conversations in order to reflect between sessions on what was said. We may decide to listen together to a playback of part of a session occasionally. OK?"

18. I recall hearing founder Alan Walker use this slogan at the launching of the telephone crisis help Lifeline movement in Sydney, Australia, many years ago.

19. Many of the insights about nonverbal communication are adapted from an insightful presentation by marriage counselor Deborah A. de Camaret, the Psychiatric Ground Rounds at Cottage Hospital, Santa Barbara, California, January 12, 2000.

20. Before sessions are recorded with actual care receivers, the value for them of taping should be explained. If they agree to taping, they should be asked to sign a taping consent form that includes assurances about protecting confidentiality and the limits on who will hear the tapes.

5. Methods of Holistic Supportive Caregiving

1. William A. Clebsch and Charles R. Jaekle, *Pastoral Care in Historical Perspective* (Englewoods Cliffs, N.J.:Prentice Hall, 1964), 80.

2. Franz Alexander, *Psychoanalysis and Psychotherapy* (New York: Norton, 1956), 55–56.

3. Carl Rogers, *Client-Centered Therapy* (Boston: Houghton Mifflin, 1951).

4. See Michael White and David Epston, *Narrative Means to Therapeutic Ends* (New York: Norton, 1990).

5. Sandra Spence, "Elite Controller Research," AIDS Research Institute at the University of California, San Francisco, 2010; http://ari.ucsf.edu/programs/elite.aspx (accessed June 3, 2011).

6. Short-term Pastoral Counseling in Crises

1. Herman Melville, *Moby Dick* (Oxford: Oxford University Press, 2008), 1.

2. Short-term pastoral counseling means four sessions or less. As pointed out earlier, it is radi-

cally different from what is meant by *short-term psychotherapy*. This usually means less than twenty or so sessions.

3. Howard Stone, *Brief Pastoral Counseling: Short-term Approaches and Strategies* (Minneapolis: Augsburg Fortress Press, 1994), 18. One research project showed that counseling is more likely to be reported by clients to have been helpful when their counselors expected it to be helpful.

4. *Single-Session Therapy: Maximizing the Effect of the First (and Often Only) Therapeutic Encounter* (San Francisco: Jossey-Bass, 1990).

5. Ibid., 17. Even psychoanalysts report: "Both the theoretical survey of the psychodynamics of therapy and the impressive evidence gained from actual observation require us to abandon the old belief that permanent changes of the ego cannot be accomplished through shorter and more intensive methods." Franz Alexander and Thomas Morton French et al., *Psychoanalytic Therapy* (New York: Ronald Press, 1946), 164.

6. Seward Hiltner, *Pastoral Counseling* (Nashville: Abingdon Press, 1949), 83.

7. A guide is *Co-Active Coaching: New Skills for Coaching People toward Success in Work and Life* by Laura Whitworth, Henry Kimsey-House, and Phil Sandahl (Palo Alto, Calif: Davies-Black, 1998).

8. See Gerald Caplan, *Principles of Preventive Psychiatry* (New York: Basic Books, 1964), 25–55.

9. Ibid., 40–41.

10. Stone, *Brief Pastoral Counseling*, 1.

11. The Social Readjustment Rating Scale

Life Event	Mean Stress Value
1. Death of spouse	100
2. Divorce	73
3. Marital separation from mate	65
4. Detention in jail or other institution	63
5. Death of a close family member	63
6. Major personal injury or illness	53
7. Marriage	50
8. Being fired at work	47
9. Marital reconciliation with mate	45
10. Retirement from work	45
11. Major change in the health or behavior of a family member	44
12. Pregnancy	40
13. Sexual difficulties	39
14. Gaining a new family member (through birth, adoption, older family member moving in, etc.)	39
15. Major business readjustment (merger, reorganization, bankruptcy, etc.)	39
16. Major change in financial state (a lot worse off or a lot better off than usual)	38
17. Death of a close friend	37
18. Changing to a different line of work	36

19. Major change in the number of arguments with
    spouse (either a lot more or a lot less than usual
    regarding child rearing, personal habits, etc.)   35
20. Taking out a mortgage or loan for a major
    purchase   31
21. Foreclosure on a mortgage or loan   30
22. Major change in responsibilities at work
    (promotion, demotion, lateral transfer)   29
23. Son or daughter leaving home (marriage,
    attending college, etc.)   29
24. Trouble with in-laws   29
25. Outstanding personal achievement   28
26. Wife beginning or ceasing work outside the home   26
27. Beginning or ceasing formal schooling   26
28. Major change in living conditions (building a
    new home, remodeling, deterioration of home or
    neighborhood)   25
29. Revision of personal habits (dress, manners,
    association, etc.)   24
30. Troubles with the boss   23
31. Major change in working hours or conditions   20
32. Change in residence   20
33. Changing to a new school   20
34. Major change in usual type and/or amount
    of recreation   19
35. Major change in church activities (a lot more
    or a lot less than usual)   19
36. Major change in social activities (clubs, dancing,
    movies, visiting, etc.)   18
37. Taking out a mortgage or loan for a lesser
    purchase (for a car, TV, freezer, etc.)   17
38. Major change in sleeping habits (a lot more or a
    lot less sleep, or change in part of day when asleep) 16
39. Major change in number of family get-togethers   15
40. Major change in eating habits (a lot more or a
    lot less food intake, or very different meal hours or
    surroundings)   15
41. Vacation   13
42. Christmas   12
43. Minor violations of the law (e.g., traffic tickets)   11

All the stressful life events on the scale produce some stress and grief. Holmes and Rahe discovered that approximately 50 percent of persons with a cumulative stress score (within one year) between 150 and 299 became sick—physically, psychologically, or psychosomatically. Some 80 percent of those with stress levels over 300 got sick. This scale can alert pastoral counselors and lay crisis caregivers to the importance of searching for clusters of life changes from which people are suffering cumulative stress overloads. Other major life stresses are not included in this scale: changing female/male roles; spouse and child battering (abuse); rape; the loss of one's dreams, faith, idealism, and values; hunger; poverty; discrimination; environmental pollution; sexism; racism; and the threat of nuclear holocaust. Factors such as these add significantly to the cumulative stress in many people's lives.

12. Viktor Frankl, *Man's Search for Meaning* (New York: Washington Square Press, 1963), 121.

13. Margaret Zipse Kornfeld, *Cultivating Wholeness: A Guide to Care and Counseling in Faith* (New York: Continuum International Publishing Group, 1998), 231.

14. "About Jonas Salk," Salk Institute for Biological Studies, La Jolla, Calif., www.salk.edu/news/publications.html (accessed June 3, 2011).

15. These guidelines include recommendations by Howard Stone in *Brief Pastoral Counseling*, 19–30.

16. Prescribing more activity may not be helpful when people respond to trauma by hyperactivity in a vain attempt to avoid facing the pain by running.

17. Wayne Oates, *An Introduction to Pastoral Counseling* (Nashville: Broadman Press, 1959), 111.

18. See Gerald Corey, *Theory and Practice of Counseling and Psychotherapy*, 6th ed. (Stamford, Conn.: Brooks/Cole, 2001), 433.

19. The "A-B-C Method of Crisis Helping" was developed by Warren Jones, a psychiatrist of my acquaintance years ago. He designed it for training the lay staff of a community crisis center in Pasadena, California, incorporating the essence of crisis intervention theory current at that time. The ABCDE model incorporates numerous additions to and interpretations of his original approach that I have made during the years since I began using it in many teaching contexts.

7. Holistic Caregiving in Challenging Crises

1. I have paraphrased and added ideas to Margaret Kornfeld's succinct list of such resources in *Cultivating Wholeness: A Guide to Care and Counseling in Faith Communities* (New York: Continuum International Publishing Group, 1998), 232–33.

2. See more about the Interim Pastors Training Network at www.imnedu.org.

3. Walter Brueggemann, "Truth-Telling Comfort," Columbia Theological Seminary, September 12, 2001, 1–7.

4. Personal letter from Brueggemann, October 23, 2001.

5. He discusses systemic grief briefly in his book *The Message of the Psalms*, Augsburg Old Testament Studies (Minneapolis: Augsburg, 1984).

6. Leah K. Glasheen, "Becoming a Mature Nation" (an interview with Haynes Johnson), *AARP Bulletin*, November 2001, 2–3.

7. See Kornfeld, *Cultivating Wholeness*, 232.

8. A letter from Tipper Gore, Honorary Chair, National Mental Health Awareness Campaign, appearing in one of the last of Ann Landers's columns, *Santa Barbara News-Press*, June 26, 2002), D8.

9. Karl A. Menninger, *The Human Mind* (New York: Knopf, 1947), 122.

10. These signs of high suicidal risk are adapted from Kornfeld, *Cultivating Wholeness*, Appendix E, 325–27. They include recent major losses; serious depression as indicated by feeling worthless, hopeless, overwhelmed by guilt, shame, or self-hatred; loss of religious faith; and loss of

usual interest in friends, sex, or activities previously enjoyed.

11. I learned this approach from Eric Berne, who created the theory of transactional analysis. He described and recommended it in a workshop.

12. Los Angeles Suicide Prevention Center manual for handling telephone calls.

13. This psychiatrist was interviewed in a report on terrorist suicidal attackers on PBS's *NewsHour*, March 19, 2002.

14. 2002 update, *Elder Abuse Guidelines and Resources for Identification, Reporting, Prevention*, produced by the Elder and Dependent Adult Abuse Council of Santa Barbara, California.

15. In 2007, there were 248,300 victims of sexual assault (Rape, Abuse and Incest National Network Statistics).

8. Caregiving in Chronic and Long-term Illness

1. See Morton Kelsey, *Healing and Christianity* (New York: Harper & Row, 1973).

2. This information was cited by a knowledgeable pharmacist, Bruce Reed, PhD, Psychiatric Grand Rounds, Santa Barbara Cottage Hospital, November 14, 2001. In 2000, the estimate of pharmaceutical advertising was $5 billion, and the deaths from prescription drug misuse totaled 218,000 in the United States.

3. John Swinton (lecturer in practical theology at the University of Aberdeen, Scotland), *Resurrecting the Person* (Nashville: Abingdon Press, 2001), 17.

4. See "The Schizophrenic Mind," *Newsweek* (March 11, 2002): 44–52.

5. NIMH, "The Numbers Count: Mental Illness in America," *Science on Our Minds Fact Sheet Series*, January 15, 2005.

6. Andy Behrman, "Types of Depression," About.com (About.com Health's Disease and Condition content is reviewed by the Medical Review Board).

7. Mayo Clinic staff, "Cognitive Therapy for Depression," Psychology Information Online, www.psychologyinfo.com/depression/cognitive.htm.

8. David D. Burns, *Feeling Good* (New York: William Morrow, 1980).

9. Mary H. Sarafolean, "Depression in School-Age Children and Adolescents: Characteristics, Assessment and Prevention," www.healthyplace.com, January 2, 2009.

10. Ibid.

11. Vincent Ianelli MD, "Symptoms of Depression in Children and Teens," About.com, Health's Disease and Condition, March 29, 2009.

12. Glenn Stimmel, PharmD, professor of clinical pharmacology, University of Southern California, Psychiatric Grand Rounds, Santa Barbara Cottage Hospital, October 23, 2002.

13. Rashmi Nemade, PhD, and Mark Dombeck, PhD, "Schizophrenia Symptoms, Patterns and Statistics and Patterns," Mentalhelp.net, August 7, 2009.

14. Howard Brody with Daralyn Brody, *The Placebo Response: How You Can Release the Body's Inner Pharmacy for Better Health* (New York: Cliff Street Books, 2000).

15. Ibid. Howard Brody, a physician with expertise in the mysteries of mind-body healing, is a professor of family practice and philosophy at the Center for Ethics and Humanities in the Life Sciences at Michigan State University.

16. Brody, "Tapping the Power of the Placebo," *Newsweek* (August 14, 2000): 66.

17. Brody, *The Placebo Response*.

18. For elaboration and clinical examples of this process, see ibid., 176–88.

19. Ibid.

20. In counseling with persons addicted to alcohol and other drugs, caregivers do well to be aware that after the initial period of painful withdrawal when craving is acute, the craving usually diminishes dramatically for a while. But around three months after drinking and using has terminated, what is called "latent withdrawal" may produce another period of severe craving that lasts several months.

21. "Clinton Speaks at FDR Statue Unveiling," usinfo.org/wfarchive/2001/010110/epf305.htm (accessed October 26, 2010).

9. Bereavement Caregiving: Before, During, and After Losses

1. His initial findings were presented in Erich Lindemann, "Symptomology and Management of Acute Grief," *American Journal of Psychiatry* (September 1944): 141–48.

2. Erich Lindemann, "Grief and Grief Management: Some Reflections," *Journal of Pastoral Care* 30, no. 3 (September 1976): 198.

3. For a comprehensive discussion of current knowledge of chemical and behavioral addictions, see Howard Clinebell, *Understanding and Counseling Persons with Alcohol, Drug, and Behavioral Addictions* (Nashville: Abingdon Press, 1982).

4. This was the Pomona Valley Pastoral Counseling and Growth Center in Claremont, California.

5. For example, in the mid-eighteenth century, an innovative Anglican priest named John Wesley was keenly aware of this connection. He authored a remarkable self-care manual for preventing and healing illnesses that was published in London on June 11, 1747. In the preface, Wesley stated, "The flow and lasting passions [feelings] such as grief and hopeless love, bring on chronical diseases. Till the passion which caused the disease is calmed, medicine is applied in vain." John Wesley, *Primitive Physic, or, An Easy and Natural Method of Curing Most Diseases*, 24th ed. (London: G. Paramore, 1792), xiv.

6. I shall always be grateful for what Lois shared with me from her experience of being terminally ill with cancer.

7. (New York: Scribner, 1997).

8. Kübler-Ross's belief that acceptance was the optimal goal for all terminally ill patients has been widely challenged by subsequent empirical studies. If people have been fighters, for example, they tend to fight to the end of their lives.

9. Alice Miller, *For Your Own Good: Hidden Cruelty in Child-Rearing and the Roots of Violence* (New York: Farrar, Straus and Giroux, 1990), 279.

10. "Homage to an Exile," *Actuelles III* (1958): 50–58.

11. I have recommended journaling in workshops and caregiving for years, but I am indebted to Ken Reed for his sharpening the focus on grief-healing issues such those suggested here.

12. To illustrate, whenever I hear the sad sound made by mourning doves, fleeting memories of my father return in a wave of gentle, nostalgic sadness. Now, several decades after his death, I am reminded of how much I still miss the father who loved me but with whom I never felt as close as I wanted to be. These wistful birdcalls also remind me of how much I value the earthy heritage my father and mother gave me from their roots in the soil of Midwest farms, their affinity with growing plants, and their love of the natural world.

13. Gerald Caplan, *Principles of Preventive Psychiatry* (New York: Basic Books, 1964), 45–46.

14. She died from the complication of whooping cough before effective treatments were available.

15. I decided to share some vignettes about my agonizing encounter with death in my childhood family to highlight why skilled grief caregiving is so vital. I do not believe my experiences are normative for others. I share these personal stories to offer one person's insider perspective on key points in pastoral grief-healing ministry.

16. Mitch Albom, *Tuesdays with Morrie* (New York: Doubleday, 1997), 133.

17. See Kübler-Ross, *On Death and Dying*, or *Death: The Final Stage of Growth* (New York: Simon & Schuster, 1986).

18. From a presentation by Gail M. Rink, MSW: "Helping Loved Ones Before You Say Goodbye: The Legacy of Meaning," Psychiatric Grand Rounds, Cottage Hospital Health Care System, Santa Barbara, California, March 27, 2002. I found her approach very illuminating. Many of her insights parallel experiences with dying persons.

19. Warren Nyberg, personal communication, August 2001.

20. As this is being written, the average cost is between $5,000 and $8,000, and rising.

21. Carol Krohn, "The Comfort of Food," *Food and Home* (Fall–Winter 2001–2002).

22. Cicely Sanders's foreword in Jack M. Zimmerman, *Hospice: Complete Care for the Terminally Ill* (Baltimore: Urban & Schwarzenberg, 1981), ix.

23. *Walden* (Boston: Beacon Press, 2004), 85.

24. Rev. Joyce Bueker, whose ministry is with a large hospice program in Phoenix, Arizona, has pioneered in playing harp music in vigils with terminally ill patients and their families.

25. I am indebted to Ruth Bright, a music registered therapist and member of the Order of Australian Grief Counselors, for information on music therapy in grief healing. See Bright, "Music Therapy in Grief Resolution," *Bulletin of the Menninger Clinic* 63, no. 4 (Fall 1999): 481–89.

26. Through the years, I have asked numerous seminary students at what age they first became aware of death. What was most striking was the considerable number who reported that they had lost a parent, sibling, or other close relative at an early age. It seems likely that these early encounters with death may have influenced their interest in a religious vocation.

10. *Healing Spiritual Brokenness and Cultivating Spiritual Wholeness in Pastoral Care and Counseling*

1. Edward Zerin, "Paradigm Shifts and Bible Perspectives: How New Views of Nature Impact Culture," *Skeptic*. 8, no. 2 (2000): 73.

2. Christie Cozad Neuger, *Journeys* (magazine of the AAPC) (Winter–Spring 2001): 16.

3. Augustine of Hippo, *Confessions*, trans. R. S. Pine-Coffin, (New York, Penguin Books, 1961), 21.

4. Gabriele Uhlein, *Meditations with Hildegard of Bingen* (Santa Fe: Bear and Co., 1983), 92, 106.

5. Quoted by Margaretta K. Bowers et al., in *Counseling the Dying* (New York: Thomas Nelson & Sons, 1964), 21, from Heidegger's *Being and Time* (New York: Harper & Row, 1962).

6. Paul Tillich explored this in *The Courage to Be* (New Haven: Yale University Press, 1952), chapter 2, and also in his *Systematic Theology*, vol. 1 (Chicago: University of Chicago Press, 1951), 193.

7. See Tillich, *The Courage to Be*, 67, 151.

8. Existentialist psychologist J. F. T. Bugental set forth this view. See Bugental, *The Search for Authenticity* (New York: Holt, Rinehart & Winston), 15.

9. Mary Daly, *Beyond God the Father* (Boston: Beacon Press, 1973), 23.

10. Jung, *Modern Man in Search of a Soul* (Orlando: Harcourt Brace, 1933), 264.

11. Kierkegaard, *The Concept of Dread* (Princeton, N.J.: Princeton University Press, 1944), 104.

12. The view that many sicknesses, including mental health problems, are rooted in spiritual dynamics has a long history. In biblical times and through much of church history, this was expressed in ways that reduced the causes of most illnesses to sin on the part of suffering people. But in his remarkable eighteenth-century self-care manual, Anglican priest John Wesley, the founder of the Methodist denominations, anticipated a view that was confirmed by twentieth-century research in psychosomatic medicine. He expressed his passionate belief in a spiritually grounded understanding of sickness and health: "The love of God, as it is the sovereign remedy of all miseries, so in particular it effectually prevents all the bodily disorders the passions [feelings] introduce, by keeping the passions within due bounds. And by the unspeakable joy and perfect calm, serenity, and tranquility it gives the mind, it becomes the most powerful of the means of health and long life"(*Primitive Physick: An Easy and Natural Method of Curing Most Diseases* [Nashville: Abingdon Press, 1992], 3).

13. Seward Hiltner, *Pastoral Counseling* (Nashville: Abingdon Press, 1949), 17.

14. Reported in "The Case for Health and Faith: An Open Letter," *Newsletter from the Interfaith Health Program of Emory University*, Fall 2001, Gary Gunderson, director.

15. Reported by David Briggs of the Religious News Service, *The United Methodist Review* (February 5, 1999): 1–3.

16. This was according to a national survey of health care between 1990 and 1997.

17. William James, *Varieties of Religious Experience* (New York: Routledge, 2002), 66–164.

18. G. W. Allport and J. M. Ross, "Personal Religious Orientation and Prejudice," *Journal of Personality and Social Psychology* 5 (1967): 432–43. See also G.W. Allport, *The Individual and His Religion* (New York: McMillan, 1950).

19. The vesper service was sponsored by Orthodox Bishops in the Americas, October 9, 2001.

20. I shall always be grateful and inspired by the memories of Erma Pixley. Sadly, she died unexpectedly a few months before the launching of the Institute for Religion and Wholeness that we had envisioned collaboratively.

21. As this is being written, thirty wars (defined as "significant conflicts") are raging around the planet in the Middle East, Asia, Africa, Europe, and Latin America. Of these, sixteen had religious conflict as a primary cause, often mixed with ethnic conflict and the drug trade. Twelve other wars had ethnic conflict or ideology as primary causes. The motivation for this violence is religious when the cultures and ideologies involved are elevated to worshipful status by fanatic devotees. Of the over thirty wars, only four had freedom and independence as a primary cause. Based on in-depth research by Center for Defense Information and reporter Daniel Smith, "The World at War," *The Defense Monitor* 31, no. 1 (January 2002): 1–5.

22. William A. Beardslee, "Incarnation, Part III," *Creative Transformation* 7, no. 3 (Spring 1998): 20.

23. Albert Einstein, *Ideas and Opinions*, Carl Seelig and Sonja Bargmann, eds. (New York: Crown, 1954), 143.

24. Adapted from "Creating Sacred Space with Clients" by clinical social worker Jolene Benedict, *Society for Spirituality and Social Work Newsletter* (Spring 1995): 3.

25. You will find information about why and how to create sacred spaces in these books: Philip Sheldrake, *Spaces for the Sacred: Place, Memory and Identity* (Baltimore: Johns Hopkins University Press, 2001); Peg Streep, *Altars Made Easy: A Complete Guide to Creating Your Own Sacred Space* (San Francisco: HarperSanFrancisco, 1997); Denise Linn, *Altars: Bringing Sacred Shrines into Your Everyday Life* (New York: Ballantine Books, 1999).

24. Christie Cozad Neuger, *Counseling Women: A Narrative, Pastoral Approach* (Minneapolis: Fortress Press, 2001), 61–63.

27. (Bethesda, Md.: The Alban Institute, 2000).

28. Richard Foster, *Streams of Water: Celebrating the Great Traditions of Christian Faith* (San Francisco: HarperSanFrancisco, 1998), 49.

29. Nouwen, *Reaching Out* (Garden City, N.Y.: Doubleday, 1975), 55–56.

30. William E. Hulme, *Pastoral Care and Counseling* (Minneapolis: Augsburg Press, 1981), 11–12.

31. See Herbert Anderson and Ed Foley, *Mighty Stories and Dangerous Rituals*, (San Francisco: Jossey-Bass, 1997).

32. John B. Cobb Jr., *Theology and Pastoral Care* (Philadelphia: Fortress Press, 1977), 61.

33. See *The Minister as Diagnostician* (Philadelphia: Westminster Press, 1976).

34. David K. Switzer, *Pastor, Preacher, Person* (Nashville: Abingdon Press, 1979), 133.

35. Walter Wink's *The Bible in Human Transformation* (Minneapolis: Fortress Press, 2010; originally published, Philadelphia: Fortress Press, 1972) describes ways to use the Bible for spiritual growth.

36. See Jay Adams, *Competent to Counsel* (Grand Rapids: Baker Book House, 1970).

37. See Thomas R. Blakeslee, *The Right Brain* (New York: Anchor Press/Doubleday, 1980), for a description of the findings of split brain research and their applications to education and creativity.

38. See Carol P. Christ and Judith Plaskow, eds., *Womanspirit Rising: A Feminist Reader in Religion* (New York: Harper & Row, 1979), 273–87.

11. *Ethical, Meaning, and Value Issues in Pastoral Care and Counseling*

1. Larry Chang, *Wisdom for the Soul: Five Millennia of Prescriptions for Spiritual Healing* (Washington, D.C.: Gnosophia Publishers, 2006), 659.

2. See Mary Potter Engel's chapter "Evil, Sin, and Violation of the Vulnerable," in *Lift Every Voice*, Engel and Susan B. Thistlethwaite, eds. (Maryknoll, N.Y.: Orbis Books, 1998).

3. Christie Cozad Neuger, *Counseling Women: A Narrative, Pastoral Approach* (Minneapolis: Fortress Press, 2001), 12–13.

4. Don S. Browning, *The Moral Context of Pastoral Care* (Philadelphia: Westminster Press, 1976), 109.

5. William A. Clebsch and Charles R. Jaekle, *Pastoral Care in Historical Perspective* (Englewood Cliffs, N.J.: Prentice Hall, 1994), 63, 66.

6. I am indebted to Geoffrey Peterson's delineation and discussion of several of these types of conscience problems in *Conscience and Caring* (Philadelphia: Fortress Press, 1982).

7. Ibid., 21.

8. William Glasser, *Reality Therapy* (New York: Harper & Row, 1965), 60.

9. Philip Anderson, "A Ministry to Troubled People," *Chicago Theological Seminary Register* (February 1965): 5.

10. For a discussion of the twelve steps, see *Alcoholics Anonymous*, 3rd ed. (New York: AA Publishing Co., 1976), 58–71, and *Twelve Steps and Twelve Traditions* by a cofounder of AA (New York: Harper & Bros., 1952).

11. James A. Knight, "Confrontation in Counseling with Special Emphasis on the Student Setting," *Pastoral Psychology* (December 1965): 48.

12. Ibid., 49.

13. Ibid.

14. I am indebted in this discussion of morality as vision to chapter 4, "Morality and Drugs," in Bucky Dann's *Addiction: Pastoral Responses* (Nashville: Abingdon Press, 2002), 99–130.

15. This is in sharp contrast to the thought of social psychologists and sociologists who (following the lead of Emile Durkheim) understand morality as not reflecting any external reality. Instead they view it reductionistically as only a disciplinary tool that humans create to control individual behavior and provide the social order necessary for civilization. In actuality, healthy morality is a means of social control that reflects the relationship principles of the spiritual universe.

16. This perspective was suggested by William Edelen in a column titled "Earthrise," *Santa Barbara News-Press*, August 4, 2002.

17. See "Planning Your Estate," Salk Institute for Biological Studies, www.plan.gs/Home.do?orgId=5888; "Interview: Jonas Salk" (May 16, 1991), Academy of Achievement, www.achievement.org/autodoc/printmember/sal0int-1 (accessed November 4, 2010).

18. These statistics are from the United Nations Human Development Report 2000, cited in the *Direct Relief International Bulletin* (Spring 2001).

19. These facts and statistics are mainly from "Population…Women, Environment… Family…Connecting the Dots" by researcher Radhika Sarin in *The Population Connection Reporter* 34, no. 2 (Spring–Summer 2002): 4–7.

20. Newsletter, *PeacePac: For the Prevention of Nuclear War* (April 2002): 1.

21. For Freud the superego was primarily the unconscious, internalized prohibitions of one's parents. He used the term *ego ideal* to describe the internalized positive values of the parents.

22. "Letter from Sigmund Freud to Oskar Pfister" (February 24, 1928), The International Psycho-Analytical Library, www.pep-web.org/document.php?id=ipl.059.0122a (accessed July 5, 2011).

23. Howard Clinebell, *Mental Health through Christian Community* (Nashville: Abingdon Press, 1965), 232–33. This approach represents a form of supportive counseling in that the counselee draws on the inner controls of the pastor to support her inadequate controls. Thomas Klink says, "The modern pastor must represent transcendent values to persons who live in settings untouched by traditional controls" (*Depth Perspectives in Pastoral Work* [Englewood Cliffs, N.J.: Prentice Hall, 1965], 65).

24. Stanley W. Standal and Raymond J. Corsini, *Critical Incidents in Psychotherapy* (Englewood Cliffs, N.J.: Prentice Hall, 1959), 84.

24. From a communication from Billy Sharp; Robert A. Blees describes his method of limit setting in counseling with people in their middle teens in *Counseling with Teen-Agers* (Englewood Cliffs, N.J.: Prentice Hall, 1965), 65–80.

26. Standal and Corsini, *Critical Incidents in Psychotherapy*, 249.

27. William Glasser, *Reality Therapy*, 11.

28. Ibid., 31.

29. Peterson, *Conscience and Caring*. Peterson's discussion of the dynamics of the self-righteous conscience is illuminating.

30. Ibid., 62–63.

31. Ibid., 67–73.

32. Robert C. Leslie, *Jesus and Logotherapy* (Nashville: Abingdon Press, 1965), 75.

33. Ibid., 14.

34. Peterson, *Conscience and Caring*, 40.

35. Adapted from Clinebell, *Growth Counseling for Mid-Years Couples* (Minneapolis: Fortress Press, 1977), 36–38.

36. Liberman and Woodruff, *Risk Management* (Minneapolis: Fortress Press, 1993). Clergy ethical boundary violations are discussed in depth by Marie Fortune.

12. Crisis Counseling and Enrichment with Couples

1. Charlotte Holt Clinebell, *Counseling for Liberation* (Philadelphia: Fortress Press, 1976), 34.

2. Jean Stapleton and Richard Bright, *Equal Marriage* (Nashville: Abingdon Press, 1976), 19.

3. See Peggy Papp, *Couples on the Fault Line: New Directions for Therapists* (New York: Guilford Publications, 2001).

4. *I and Thou*, 2nd ed., trans. R. G. Smith (New York: Charles Scribner's Sons, 1958), 11.

5. Sullivan was still lecturing at the William Alanson White Institute of Psychiatry when I did graduate studies there.

6. Henry Stack Sullivan, *The Psychiatric Interview* (New York: Norton, 1954), 171.

7. Nathan W. Ackerman, *The Psychodynamics of Family Life* (New York: Basic Books, 1958), 22.

8. Dietrich Bonhoeffer, *Life Together* (New York: Harper & Row, 1954), 77.

9. The names and addresses of qualified marriage therapists can be found on the AAPC and the AAMFT websites.

10. Adapted from Howard Clinebell, *Growth Counseling for Marriage Enrichment: Pre-Marriage and the Early Years* (Philadelphia: Fortress Press, 1975), 24.

11. Carmen Knudson-Martin, "Spirituality and Gender in Clinical Practice," *Family Therapy News* (August-September 2001): 4–5.

12. My spouse and I created it for use in marriage enrichment workshops, classes, and retreats.

13. A detailed description of how to use this communication tool with couples is found in Clinebell, *Growth Counseling for Marriage Enrichment*, chapter 2, and with families in *Contemporary Growth Therapies* (Nashville: Abingdon Press, 1981), 233–34.

14. Clinebell, *Growth Counseling for Marriage Enrichment*, 25.

15. Elliot Beier, ed., *Wit and Wisdom of Israel* (Mount Vernon, N.Y.: 1968), 32.

16. John Landgraf, *Creative Singlehood and Pastoral Care* (Philadelphia: Fortress Press, 1982), 22, 58.

17. For an enlightening discussion of ministry to singles by religious communities, see "Caring for and Celebrating the Lives of Single Adults," in Margaret Zipse Kornfeld, *Cultivating Wholeness: A Guide to Care and Counseling in Faith Communities* (New York: Continuum International Publishing Group, 1998), 174–78.

18. William H. Masters and Virginia A. Johnson, *The Pleasure Bond: A New Look at Sexuality and Commitment* (Boston: Little, Brown, 1974), 107–8.

13. Pastoral Care, Counseling, and Enriching Families

1. See www.censusscope.org/2koo.xls for 2000 census data.

2. See Virginia M. .Satir, *Peoplemaking* (Palo Alto, Calif.: Science and Behavior Books, 1972), 26–27.

3. Rachel Carson, *A Sense of Wonder* (New York: Harper & Row, 1956), 55.

4. Girls Inc., "Girls' Bill of Rights," www.girlsinc.org/about/girls-bill-of-rights/ (accessed November 6, 2010).

5. Nathan W. Ackerman, "Emergence of Family Psychotherapy on the Present Scene," in *Contemporary Psychotherapies*, ed. Morris I. Stein (Glencoe, Ill.: Free Press, 1961), 231.

6. Nathan W. Ackerman, *The Psychodynamics of Family Life* (New York: Basic Books, 1958), 21–22.

7. Ibid., 218.

8. See chapter 1 in Satir, *Conjoint Family Therapy* (Palo Alto, Calif.: Science and Behavior Books, 1963).

9. Martin Grotjahn, *Psychoanalysis and Family Neurosis* (New York: Norton, 1960).

10. Paul Gibson, "Gay Male and Lesbian Youth Suicide," in M. R. Feinleib, ed., *Report of the Secretary's Task Force on Youth Suicide*, vol. 3, *Prevention and Interventions in Youth Suicide* (Washington, D.C.: U.S. Department of Health and Human Services, 1989), 110–12.

11. Douglas A. Anderson, "The Family Growth Group: Guidelines for an Emerging Means of Strengthening Families," *The Family Coordinator* (January 1974): 7.

12. See Susan L. Jones, *Family Therapy: A Comparison of Approaches* (Bowie, Md.: Robert J. Brady Co., 1980).

13. Jay Haley, "Whither Family Therapy?" *Family Process* (March 1962): 70.

14. Howard Clinebell, *Contemporary Growth Therapies: Resources for Actualizing Human Wholeness* (Nashville: Abingdon Press, 1981), 222–23.

15. See chapter 6 in Satir, *Conjoint Family Therapy*.

16. Couple counseling involves three interactional axes (pastor-husband, pastor-wife, husband-wife) of which the counselor must have awareness. Family counseling with a couple plus one child doubles the interactional axes (to six). A couple plus two of their children in a session increases the axes to ten, and a couple plus three children raises it to fifteen interactional axes.

17. I have described Healthy Family Enrichment Sessions and illustrated them with segments from an interview with a family in audiocassette course IIIB in *Growth Counseling: New Tools for Clergy and Laity*, Part I (Nashville: Abingdon Press, 1973).

18. Adapted from Clinebell, *Contemporary Growth Therapies*, 226.

19. For a full description of how to do parental play therapy, see chapter 8 in Clark E. Moustakas, *Psychotherapy with Children: The Living Relationship* (New York: Harper & Bros., 1959).

20. The IRM is described more fully as an experiential exercise in Clinebell, *Contemporary Growth Therapies*, 233–34.

21. Charlotte Holt Clinebell, *Meet Me in the Middle: On Becoming Human Together* (New York: Harper & Row, 1973), 80.

22. Ibid., 88.

23. E. Mavis Hetherington, *For Better or for Worse, Divorce Reconsidered* (New York: W. W. Norton, 2002).

24. This understanding of the sociological causes of violence against women and children is documented in Del Martin's *Battered Wives* (San Francisco: Volcano Press, 1981).

25. You can reach your local crisis center at any time by calling the National Sexual Assault Hotline at 1-800-656-HOPE (4673).

26. Noah benShea, "Loss and Losing Pain," Noah's Blog, Soul GPS, noahbenshea.com/2010/02/09/loss-and-losing-pain/ (accessed June 8, 2011).

27. Anderson, "The Family Growth Group, " 7.

28. Ackerman, *The Psychodynamics of Family Life*, 17.

29. Ackerman, "Emergence of Family Psychotherapy on the Present Scene," 231.

30. See Michael White, *NTC Newsletter*, Narrative Therapy Centre, Ajax, Ontario, Canada; Michael White with Alice Morgan, *Narrative Therapy with Children and their Families* (Adelaide, South Australia: Dulwich Centre Publication, 2006).

14. Educative Counseling

1. Paul E. Johnson, "Where We Are Now in Pastoral Care," *Christian Advocate* (September 26, 1965): 8.

2. Educative counseling could also be called "counseling-oriented education." Counseling-oriented education and education-oriented counseling actually form a continuum. Awareness of this allows the pastor to move freely toward a greater emphasis on the educative or the counseling dimensions as the needs of a particular person, couple, or family require. A synonym for educative counseling is *pastoral guidance*.

3. Christie Cozad Neuger, *Counseling Women: A Narrative Pastoral Approach* (Minneapolis: Fortress Press, 2001), 30.

4. William A. Clebsch and Charles R. Jaekle, *Pastoral Care in Historical Perspective* (Englewood Cliffs, N.J.: Prentice-Hall, 1964), 50.

5. From the Latin *educare*, meaning "to lead forth." The client-centered therapy of Carl Rogers was a relatively pure educative approach. Traditional churches' guidance practices have used moral theology, codes of ethics, and advice giving.

6. Eleanor Roosevelt, as quoted in Leonard C. Schlup and Donald W. Whisenhunt, *It Seems to Me: Selected Letters of Eleanor Roosevelt* (Lexington: University Press of Kentucky, 2001), 2.

7. Brain research has shown that communication between the two hemispheres is instant and continual and that the emphasis on the distinctive functions of the two is simply a convenient way to describe these.

8. See Thomas R. Blakeslee, *The Right Brain* (Garden City, N.Y.: Anchor Press/Doubleday, 1980), 45–46.

9. Blakeslee points out that these stages were actually described in 1926 in a book by Graham Wallas, *The Art of Thought*. I have adapted much of this section from my book *Anchoring Your Well Being: Christian Wholeness in a Fractured World* (Nashville: Upper Room Books, 1997), 57–59.

10. See Daniel Goleman, *Emotional Intelligence* (New York: Bantam Books, 1995).

11. Carl R. Rogers, *Counseling and Psychotherapy* (Boston: Houghton Mifflin, 1942), 29. Rogers was reacting to an older approach to counseling, consisting of exhorting, advising, and persuading. He retained the either/or, feeling/knowing dichotomy of that approach but opted for feeling instead of knowing. Educative counseling seeks to move beyond the either/or to a both/and position.

12. Ruth Tiffany Barnhouse, "Spiritual Direction and Psychotherapy," *Journal of Pastoral Care* 33, no. 3 (September 1979): 149–63.

13. Jean Stairs, *Listening for the Soul: Pastoral Care in Spiritual Direction* (Minneapolis: Augsburg Fortress, 2000).

14. Nathaniel Cantor, *Dynamics of Learning* (East Aurora, N.Y.: Henry Steward, 1946), xiv–xv.

15. Ibid., xiii–xiv.

16. See Virginia M. Satir, *Conjoint Family Therapy* (Palo Alto, Calif.: Science and Behavior Books, 1963), 112–35.

17. The Taylor-Johnson is available from Psychological Publications, 5300 Hollywood Blvd., Los Angeles, CA 90027. PREPARE is available from PREPARE, Inc., P.O. Box 190, Minneapolis, MN 55440.

18. A *Pastor's Manual* by Antoinette and Leon Smith, designed to be used with Joan and Richard Hunt's *Growing Love in Christian Marriage* (Nashville: Abingdon Press, 1981), provides excellent suggestions on group preparation for marriage, the theology of marriage, and the content of the five sessions they recommend.

19. The SKI (revised, 1979) is available with a manual for its use by Gelolo McHugh, from Thomas McHugh, Family Life Publications, P.O. Box 427, Saluda, NC 28773.

20. I am thinking of severe emotional disturbance on the part of one or both, and of the ecclesiastical strictures in some denominations against remarriage of divorced persons.

21. Cantor, *Dynamics of Learning*, 281.

22. Gerald Caplan, *Principles of Preventive Psychiatry* (New York: Basic Books, 1964), 84–85.

23. See Jean Stapleton and Richard Bright, *Equal Marriage* (Nashville: Abingdon Press, 1976).

24. Caplan, *Principles of Preventive Psychiatry*, 84.

25. Ibid., 255.

26. These steps are explored in more depth in Howard Clinebell, *Growth Groups* (Nashville: Abingdon Press, 1977), 150–58.

27. Reported by the U.S. Surgeon General in 2001.

28. See Speed Leas and Paul Kittlaus, *The Pastoral Counselor in Social Action* (Philadelphia: Fortress Press, 1981), 57.

29. See Peggy Way, "Community Organization and Pastoral Care: Drum Beat for Dialogue," *Pastoral Psychology* (March 1968): 25–36, 66.

30. *Santa Barbara News-Press*, July 1, 2002, D2.

31. Lea and Kittlaus, *The Pastoral Counselor in Social Action*, 40–58.

32. Way, "Community Organization and Pastoral Care: Drum Beat for Dialogue," 25–36, 66.

15. Group Pastoral Care and Counseling

1. George Homans, *The Human Group* (New York: Harcourt, Brace, 1956), 658.

2. Robert Leslie, PhD dissertation, Boston University, 1948.

3. Robert Leslie, *Sharing Groups in the Church* (Nashville: Abingdon Press 1971), 19.

4. George Webber, *The Congregation in Mission*, (Nashville: Abingdon Press, 1964), 116–17.

5. Howard Clinebell, *The Mental Health Ministry of the Local Church*, (Nashville: Abingdon Press, 1972), 153–54; Tennneesee Williams, *Cat on a Hot Tin Roof* (New York: New Dimensions, 1955), vi.

6. Leslie, *Sharing Groups in the Church*, 14.

7. Jerome D. Franks, *Group Methods in Therapy*, Public Affairs Pamphlet, 284, 3, 4.

8 . This section and the next are adapted from Clinebell, *The Mental Health Ministry of the Local Church*, 154–57.

9. Quoted from Eugene Jennings of Michigan State University in *You Can't Be Humans Alone* (New York: HarperCollins, 2009), 6.

10. John Casteel, ed., *Spiritual Renewal through Personal Groups* (New York: Association Press, 1957), 201.

11. Elizabeth O'Connor, *Call to Commitment* (New York: Harper & Row, 1965), 37.

12. Thomas Gordon, *Group-Centered Leadership: A Way of Releasing the Creative Power of Groups* (Boston: Houghton Mifflin, 1955), 8–9.

13. Paraphrased from Thomas Gordon, "Group-Centered Leadership and Administration," in Carl R. Rogers, *Client-Centered Therapy* (Boston: Houghton Mifflin, 1959), chapter 8.

14. The pastor of a church where Charlotte and I co-led a couple enrichment retreat focused his recruitment efforts on his key lay leaders and church school teachers. This was a strategy to strengthen support for an ongoing marriage enrichment and growth group program in his congregation and also a way of enriching the leaders and teachers of his church.

15. See Howard Clinebell, *Growth Groups* (Nashville: Abingdon Press, 1972), 48–52, for a description of such exercises.

16. Adapted from ibid., 11–12.

17. Ibid., 167–68.

18. See chapter 14.

19. Leslie, *Sharing Groups in the Church*, 32.

16. The Art of Referral in Pastoral Caregiving

1. Thomas W. Klink, "The Referral: Helping People Focus Their Needs," *Pastoral Psychology* (December 1962): 11.

2. Wayne E. Oates, *Protestant Pastoral Counseling* (Philadelphia: Westminster Press, 1974), 112–13.

3. C. W. Brister, *Pastoral Care in the Church* (New York: Harper & Row, 1977), 162.

4. J. David Arnold and Connie Schick, "Counseling by Clergy: A Review of Empirical Research," *Journal of Pastoral Counseling* 14, no. 2 (Fall–Winter 1979): 96.

5. Gerald N. Grob, ed., *Action for Mental Health* (New York: Basic Books, 1961), 104.

6. Quoted by Klink, "The Referral," 10.

7. See Gerald Caplan, *Principles of Preventive Psychiatry* (New York: Basic Books, 1964), 212–65, for an excellent discussion of types and methods of mental health consultation.

8. Sigmund Freud used the term *ego defenses* to describe the unconscious mechanisms that children's egos adopt early in life to protect them from overwhelming impulses and conflicts within themselves and in their families. These defenses operate automatically outside conscious control. They include repression, regression, projection, rationalization, fixation, denial (of reality), introjection, dissociation, and reaction formations. Freud's daughter Anna explored ego defenses in depth and wrote an illuminating book on them, *The Ego and the Mechanisms of Defense* (New York: International Universities Press, 1946).

9. I am using the three traditional categories of personality disorders as found in traditional psychiatric nomenclature—psychoneurotic (or simply neurotic), psychotic, and character problems (also called "psychopathic or sociopathic disorders"). Neurotic persons internalize conflicts, whereas those with character problems externalize them, acting out their conflicts in relationships. In contrast to both, persons suffering from psychoses have fragile ego defenses that have ruptured to some degree, allowing portions of their egos to be overwhelmed by powerful impulses from their unconscious minds.

10. Linda Webster, "Clergy-Social Work Interface in the Provision of Mental Health Care" (PhD diss., Graduate School of Social Work, University of Utah, June 1997), 41–42.

11. Personal communication: John L. Mixon suggests these principles for making good referrals to social agencies: "(a) Secure basic information regarding the agency. This should include an understanding of the purpose, functions, and intake policy. To guess at possible services to be rendered by an agency resulting in indiscriminative referrals is a waste of everybody's time and frustrating to the person to be served. (b) Do not commit an agency to a specific service or solution. The agency must be free to assist within the limit of its resources and its relation to the real needs of the applicant. (c) Provide such information as you may have to the agency called upon, either by letter or by phone. (d) Follow up all referrals. This will enable you to evaluate the services for the future. Your understanding of what took place will assist you to further consultation if the person returns to you."

12. Produced by Protestant Community Services of the Los Angeles Council of Churches, 1965. The paragraph quoted is from the introduction.

13. See Howard Clinebell, *Contemporary Growth Therapies: Resources for Actualizing Human Wholeness* (Nashville: Abingdon Press, 1981). The full text of this book is available and can be downloaded from the Internet at Religion on Line, www.religion-online.org.

14. Christie Cozad Neuger, *Counseling Women: A Narrative Pastoral Approach* (Minneapolis: Fortress Press, 2001), 36.

15. Ibid., 61n18.

16. A. B. Hollingshead and F. C. Redlich, *Social Class and Mental Illness: A Community Study* (New York: John Wiley & Sons, 1958).

17. Inclusive Caregiving: Bridging Cultural, Racial, Ethnic, Class, and Gender Diversity

1. From Nobel Prize laureate Tutu's address at the New Year's 2000 program at the Washington Cathedral, Washington, D.C. President Bill Clinton emphasized a parallel insight in his remarks at the National Congressional Prayer Breakfast, February 3, 2000: "Modern science has taught us what we always learned from ancient faiths, the most important fact of life on this Earth is our common humanity."

2. Christie Cozad Neuger, *Counseling Women: A Narrative, Pastoral Approach* (Minneapolis: Fortress Press, 2001), 15.

3. David W. Augsburger, *Pastoral Counseling across Cultures* (Philadelphia: Westminster Press, 1986), 13.

4. Archie Smith, *The Relational Self: Ethics and Therapy from a Black Church Perspective* (Nashville: Abingdon Press, 1982), 38.

5. Rosemary R. Ruether, *New Woman–New Earth: Sexist Ideologies and Human Liberation* (New York: Seabury Press, 1973), 65.

6. The human genome research has revealed that all humans, across racial and ethnic lines, are 99.9 percent the same genetically. It has also discovered that genetic differences within racial and ethnic groups are greater than differences from group to group.

7. Gus Niebuhr, *New York Times*, national ed., January 12, 2002, section A.

8. Author unknown.

9. I learned of this axiom from Jean Masamba Ma Mpolo who taught in the Protestant Theological faculty in the Republic of the Congo.

10. Karen M. Seeley, *Cultural Psychotherapy: Working with Culture in the Clinical Encounter* (New Jersey: Jason Aronson, 2000).

11. Lecture at the University of California, Santa Barbara, November 27, 2001.

12. A striking indication of this, cited by Marty, is that the Baptists in this country included Harvey Cox and Jesse Jackson, on the one hand, and Jerry Falwell and Jesse Helms, on the other.

13. Of the original thirteen colonies, nine established religions and were formed to exclude other religions.

14. To understand the urgency of making pastoral caregiving increasingly multicultural, consider the rainbow transformation occurring demographically in American culture. Because of immigration and high birth rates among immigrants, it is projected that people of other than Caucasian and European backgrounds will constitute a majority of the population by the middle decades of this twenty-first century. Parallel changes are occurring in other Western industrialized countries, producing acute social and interpersonal challenges that often cry out for caregiving.

15. James Poling, paper presented at the conference of the International Pastoral Care Network for Social Responsibility, Accra, Ghana, August 1999. I am indebted to his insights on this issue.

16. Kaplan cites this image, which he got from Tad Homer-Dixon, in an article, "The Coming Anarchy," *Atlantic Monthly* (February 1994): 72. Kaplan describes the miserable megacities in developing countries that are cauldrons of collective chaos with exploding populations, hunger, ethnic turmoil, epidemic violence, drug cartels, rampant disease, and environmental disaster.

17. See Richard W. Voss, "Pastoral Social Ministry in the Ecosystem of the Poor: Breaking through the Illusions," *Journal of Pastoral Care* 47, no. 2 (Summer 1993): 100–108.

18. Ibid., 107–8.

19. Dale White, "Mental Health and the Poor," *Concern* (October 15, 1964): 6–7. The study was done by Frank Riessman of Columbia University.

20. Ibid., 7.

21. See Charles Kemp, *Pastoral Care of the Poor* (Nashville: Abingdon Press, 1972).

22. "Perspective, Archbishop of Canterbury's View: Another Way," *Sequoia: News of Religion and Society* 20, no. 4 (Winter 2000): 8.

23. A study by the United Nations revealed that at the present rate of change in the status of women around the world, it will require approximately four hundred years for them to achieve full equality of opportunity economically and educationally.

24. Inge K. Broverman et al., "Sex-Role Stereotypes and Clinical Judgments of Mental Health," *Journal of Consulting and Clinical Psychology* 34, no.1 (February 1970): 4–7.

25. Charlotte Holt Clinebell, *Counseling for Liberation* (Philadelphia: Fortress Press, 1976), 22–23.

26. See the Domestic Violence Statistics website at http://domesticviolencestatistics.org.

27. "Depression Statistics, Depression Statistics United States," *Depression, Treatment for Depression, Symptoms of Depression*, Dec. 15, 2010, http://www.indepression.com/depression-statistics.html (accessed July 14, 2011).

28. "Why Do Women Live Longer than Men?" National Center for Biotechnology Information, www.ncbi.nlm.nih.gov/pubmed/1018115 (accessed July 14, 2011).

29. J. Pleck, "Men's Power," in *Men's Lives*, ed. Michael A. Messner and Michael S. Kimmel (Needham Heights, Mass.: Allyn & Bacon, 1995), 8–9.

30. Larry Graham, "Caregiving and Spiritual Direction with Lesbian and Gay Persons: Common Themes and Sharp Divergencies," *Journal of Pastoral Care* 50, no. 1 (Spring 1996): 97–104.

31. Ibid.

32. John Eybel supervises CPE at Bugando Medical Centre in Mwanza, Tanzania.

33. I am indebted to Professor Richard W. Voss, whose practice of pastoral psychotherapy and social work has been enhanced by learning from the healing wisdom and practices of the Lakota Sioux.

34. This spiritual practice was described in "Cross-Cultural Thoughts," *A New Communion, Justice, Ecology, Spirit, Community* 8, no. 2 (June 2000): 11.

18. Equipping Laypersons for Caregiving Ministries

1. Report of the Second Assembly of the World Council of Churches, The Evanston Report (New York: Harper & Bros., 1955), 170.

2. John Dillenberger, ed., *Martin Luther: Selections from His Writings* (New York: Doubleday, 1961), 75.

3. Diane Detwiler-Zapp and William Caveness Dixon, *Lay Caregiving* (Philadelphia: Fortress Press, 1982), 5.

4. John Patton, *Pastoral Care in Context: An Introduction to Pastoral Care* (Louisville: Westminster John Knox Press, 2005), 3–4.

5. See H. Richard Niebuhr et al., *The Purpose of the Church and Its Ministry* (New York: Harper & Bros., 1956), 83.

6. See Alan Walker, *Help Is as Near as Your Telephone* (Nashville: Abingdon Press, 1967) for a description of this program.

7. This quotation and the description of this program are taken from *The Pastor's Letter*, April 1980, by Dick Watts of Lakewood, Ohio, a pastor trained in the program.

8. Detwiler-Zapp and Dixon, *Lay Caregiving*, 80.

9. Watts, *The Pastor's Letter*.

10. Robert A. Raines, *New Life in the Church*, rev. ed. (New York: Harper & Row, 1980), 126–27.

11. E. Litwak and I. Szelenyi, "Primary Group Structures and Their Functions: Kin, Neighbors, and Friends," *American Sociological Review* 34 (1969): 465–81.

12. I am indebted to Diane Detwiler-Zapp and Will Dixon for these suggestions.

13. Howard Clinebell, "Experiments in Training for Laity for Ministry," *Pastoral Psychology* 22, no. 6 (June 1971): 36.

14. This name was drawn from the Samaritan movement, a crisis program that began in England under the leadership of Chad Varah.

15. Charlotte Ellen and I were the cotrainers of the United Methodist church group; in contrast to the UCC group, the UM trainees had been recruited with the explicit understanding that a lay caring team would be the outcome of the training.

16. Robert R. Carkhuff, *Helping and Human Relations: A Primer for Lay and Professional Helpers*, vol. 1. (New York: Holt, Rinehart and Winston, 1969), 1.

19. Self-care for Caregivers

1. From Donald Smith, *Empowering Ministry: Ways to Grow in Effectiveness* (Louisville: Westminster John Knox Press, 1996), 141.

2. Charles R. DeGroat, *Expectation versus Reality among Male Graduates of Seminary Who*

Entered Ministry: A Phenomenological Study, PhD dissertation, Capella University, February 2008.

3. Donald B. Cozzens, ed., *The Spiritual Life of the Diocesan Priest* (Collegeville, Minn.: Liturgical Press, 1977), vii.

4. From Dr. Dement's revealing book, *The Promise of Sleep* (New York: Delacorte Press, 1999), 2, 10, 50.

5. Ibid., 423; adapted with additions from my personal and counseling experience.

6. See ibid., chapter 15.

7. See ibid., 449–506. Frederic M. Hudson, *The Handbook of Coaching: A Comprehensive Resource Guide for Managers, Executives, Consultants, and Human Resource Professionals* (San Francisco: Jossey-Bass, 1999).

8. Carl Rogers, *On Becoming a Person* (New York: Houghton Mifflin, 1961), 21.

9. Ibid.

10. Review of Reinhold Niebuhr's "The Self and the Dramas of History," *Chicago Theological Seminary Review* (January 1956): 14. It is not possible, of course, for acceptance and positive regard to be totally unconditioned in any of us. As human beings, we embody agape or grace in only very partial ways.

11. Rogers, *On Becoming a Person*, 44.

12. Ibid., 53.

13. One of my mentors, the late Frieda Fromm-Reichmann, once declared that effectiveness in dealing with psychotics is contingent on the therapist's awareness of this fact (lecture, William A. White Institute of Psychiatry, 1948).

14. Caroll A. Wise, *Pastoral Counseling: Its Theory and Practice* (New York: Harper & Bros., 1956), 11.

15. Rogers, *On Becoming a Person*, 51.

16. Ibid., 56.

17. Dag Hammarskjöld, *Markings*, trans. Leif Sjöberg and W. H. Auden (New York: Knopf, 1964), 24.

18. William Shakespeare, *Love's Labour's Lost*, act 4, scene 3, line 333.

19. William Rabior, "Ministerial Burnout," *Ministry* (March 1979): 25. Several of my suggestions are from this article.

20. See Carol Gilligan, *In a Different Voice: Psychological Theory and Women's Development* (Cambridge, Mass.: Harvard University Press, 1982).

21. Geoffrey Chaucer, *The Parliament of Fowles*, line 1.

22. H. Richard Niebuhr, Daniel Day Williams, and James M. Gustafson, *The Advancement of Theological Education* (New York: Harper & Bros., 1957), 128.

23. Carl Jung, *Psychological Reflections* (New York: Pantheon Books, 1953), 73.

24. Paul Tillich, "The Theology of Pastoral Care," 4.

INDEX

CPSIA information can be obtained at www.ICGtesting.com
Printed in the USA
LVOW06s1557290114

371495LV00005B/756/P